CCNP Building Scalable Internetworks
(BSCI 642-901) Lab Portfolio

David Kotfila

Joshua Moorhouse

Ross G. Wolfson, CCIE No. 16696

Cisco Press

800 East 96th Street

Indianapolis, Indiana 46240 USA

CCNP Building Scalable Internetworks
(BSCI 642-901) Lab Portfolio

David Kotfila · Joshua Moorhouse · Ross Wolfson

Copyright© 2008 Cisco Systems, Inc.

Published by:
Cisco Press
800 East 96th Street
Indianapolis, IN 46240 USA

Printed in the United States of America

First Printing   December 2007

Library of Congress Cataloging-in-Publication Data:

                 Library of Congress Cataloging-in-Publication Data
Kotfila, David A.
  CCNP building scalable internetworks (BSCI 642-901) lab portfolio / David Kotfila, Joshua Moorhouse, Ross G. Wolfson.
       p. cm.
   ISBN 978-1-58713-213-1 (pbk.)
  1. Internetworking (Telecommunication)--Examinations--Study guides. 2. Telecommunications engineers--Certification--Study guides. I. Moorhouse, Joshua D. II. Wolfson, Ross G. III. Title.

   TK5105.5.K68 2007
   004.6--dc22

2007043824

ISBN-13: 978-1-58713-213-1

ISBN-10: 1-58713-213-3

Publisher
Paul Boger

Associate Publisher
Dave Dusthimer

Cisco Representative
Anthony Wolfenden

Cisco Press Program Manager
Jeff Brady

Executive Editor
Mary Beth Ray

Managing Editor
Patrick Kanouse

Senior Development Editor
Christopher Cleveland

Senior Project Editor
San Dee Phillips

Copy Editors
Keith Cline and Language Logistics, LLC

Technical Editors
Tommy Crawford

Geovany González

Editorial Assistant
Vanessa Evans

Book and Cover Designer
Louisa Adair

Composition
Bronkella Publishing LLC

Proofreader
Kathy Ruiz

cisco

Warning and Disclaimer

This book provides labs consistent with the Cisco Networking Academy CCNP Building Scalable Internetworks (BSCI 642-901) curriculum. Every effort has been made to make this book as complete and as accurate as possible, but no warranty or fitness is implied.

The information is provided on an "as is" basis. The authors, Cisco Press, and Cisco Systems, Inc. shall have neither liability nor responsibility to any person or entity with respect to any loss or damages arising from the information contained in this book or from the use of the discs or programs that may accompany it.

The opinions expressed in this book belong to the authors and are not necessarily those of Cisco Systems, Inc.

Trademark Acknowledgments

All terms mentioned in this book that are known to be trademarks or service marks have been appropriately capitalized. Cisco Press or Cisco Systems, Inc., cannot attest to the accuracy of this information. Use of a term in this book should not be regarded as affecting the validity of any trademark or service mark.

Corporate and Government Sales

The publisher offers excellent discounts on this book when ordered in quantity for bulk purchases or special sales, which may include electronic versions and/or custom covers and content particular to your business, training goals, marketing focus, and branding interests. For more information, please contact: **U.S. Corporate and Government Sales** 1-800-382-3419 corpsales@pearsontechgroup.com

For sales outside the United States please contact: **International Sales** international@pearsoned.com

Feedback Information

At Cisco Press, our goal is to create in-depth technical books of the highest quality and value. Each book is crafted with care and precision, undergoing rigorous development that involves the unique expertise of members from the professional technical community.

Readers' feedback is a natural continuation of this process. If you have any comments regarding how we could improve the quality of this book, or otherwise alter it to better suit your needs, you can contact us through email at feedback@ciscopress.com. Please make sure to include the book title and ISBN in your message.

We greatly appreciate your assistance.

Americas Headquarters	Asia Pacific Headquarters	Europe Headquarters
Cisco Systems, Inc.	Cisco Systems, Inc.	Cisco Systems International BV
170 West Tasman Drive	168 Robinson Road	Haarlerbergpark
San Jose, CA 95134-1706	#28-01 Capital Tower	Haarlerbergweg 13-19
USA	Singapore 068912	1101 CH Amsterdam
www.cisco.com	www.cisco.com	The Netherlands
Tel: 408 526-4000	Tel: +65 6317 7777	www-europe.cisco.com
800 553-NETS (6387)	Fax: +65 6317 7799	Tel: +31 0 800 020 0791
Fax: 408 527-0883		Fax: +31 0 20 357 1100

Cisco has more than 200 offices worldwide. Addresses, phone numbers, and fax numbers are listed on the Cisco Website at **www.cisco.com/go/offices.**

About the Authors

David Kotfila, CCNP, CCAI, is the Director of the Cisco Academy at Rensselaer Polytechnic Institute (RPI), Troy, New York. Under his direction, 350 students have received their CCNA, 150 students have received their CCNP, and 8 students have obtained their CCIE. David is a consultant for Cisco, working as a member of the CCNP assessment group. His team at RPI has authored the four new CCNP lab books for the Academy program. David has served on the National Advisory Council for the Academy program for four years. Previously he was the Senior Training Manager at PSINet, a Tier 1 global Internet service provider. When David is not staring at his beautiful wife, Kate, or talking with his two wonderful children, Chris and Charis, he likes to kayak, hike in the mountains, and lift weights.

Joshua Moorhouse, CCNP, recently graduated from Rensselaer Polytechnic Institute (RPI) with a B.S. in Computer Science, where he also worked as a teaching assistant in the Cisco Networking Academy. He currently works as a network engineer at Factset Research Systems in Norwalk, Connecticut. Josh enjoys spending time with his wife, Laura, his family, and friends.

Ross Wolfson, CCIE No. 16696, recently graduated from Rensselaer Polytechnic Institute (RPI) with a B.S. in Computer Science. He currently works as a network engineer at Factset Research Systems. Ross enjoys spending time with his friends, running, and biking.

About the Technical Reviewers

Tommy J. Crawford is the manager of network engineering and architecture for a publicly traded company within the entertainment industry. Prior to his current position, Tommy consulted as a lead network engineer designing, implementing, and troubleshooting complex IP network infrastructures for many Fortune 500 companies and Internet service providers. Tommy holds his Cisco Certified Academy Instructor (CCAI) certification and has developed course work and taught CCNA, CCNP, and Network Security courses for Westwood College, Denver North Campus, in Denver, Colorado.

Geovany González is an electrical engineer with a B.S. degree from the National University of Colombia in Medellín, Colombia. He has obtained networking certifications in different areas, such as quality of service, routing and switching, LAN and WAN design, network security, operational systems such as Linux and Windows, and voice and telephony over IP (a field in which Geovany is a Cisco IP telephony specialist). He is also the author of a technical course used for several service providers to train their engineers. Geovany's professional experience has focused on education and consulting, including working as an instructor at the National University in Colombia and as an Academic Manager at Cisco Networking Academy Program for Colombia and Ecuador, South America. Geovany has also worked as an international Cisco Systems instructor working for a Cisco Learning Solution Partner. Currently, he is the Latin American Representative for the Network Development Group. His enthusiasm for education and technical expertise have enabled him to play a key role in the promotion of NETLAB+, a remote lab appliance for information technology training, in Latin America and throughout the world.

Acknowledgments

David A. Kotfila: Every teacher lives for highly motivated students who love a challenge. It has been both a privilege and *fun* to work with Josh Moorhouse and Ross Wolfson, my co-authors. Their tireless efforts to produce these labs deserve high praise.

Many, many thanks to Mary Beth Ray and Chris Cleveland of Cisco Press. I had both some health issues and some overcommitment issues that made me a difficult author to work with. Both Mary Beth and Chris deserve sainthood status for their patience.

Jeremy Creech was the manager of the lab authoring process. Jeremy brought years of classroom experience and an encyclopedic knowledge of the technology to this project. Jeremy's hands-on approach is the model for what a technical manager should be.

Many thanks to Geovany González of NDG, NetLabs. Geovany was tireless in his efforts to make these labs technically more accurate. Thanks also to Tommy Crawford for his careful reading and editing of the text.

Joshua D. Moorhouse: David Kotfila and Chris Price deserve high praise for their tireless work in pushing our Cisco Networking Academy to reach for the stars. Ross Wolfson has been fantastic to work with in developing practical ways to teach networking concepts.

It was a pleasure to work with the production teams at Cisco Press and with the teams in the Networking Academy Program on this project. Finally, many thanks to the folks at NDG for helping us to make these labs accessible to the broader Cisco Academy audience.

Ross G. Wolfson: I would like to thank David and Josh for being a great team to work with and write these labs. I especially want to thank David because without him, this book would have never happened.

Dedications

To my daughter, Charis, whose laugher, honesty, courage in the face of adversity, love of literature, and love of life are a constant inspiration to me. Care Bear—I love you more than you will ever know. To my favorite "slacker." —Dad

—David A. Kotfila

To my parents, who taught me focus and dedication and showed me faith, hope, and love.

To my siblings, Sandra and Peter, with whom I have found camaraderie, fun, and laughter for many years.

—Joshua D. Moorhouse

I would like to dedicate this book to my mom, Joanne, my dad, George, and my brother, Todd.

—Ross G. Wolfson

Contents at a Glance

Contents

Icons Used in This Book

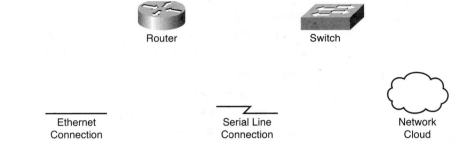

Router

Switch

Ethernet
Connection

Serial Line
Connection

Network
Cloud

Command Syntax Conventions

The conventions used to present command syntax in this book are the same conventions used in the Cisco IOS Command Reference. The Command Reference describes these conventions as follows:

- **Boldface** indicates commands and keywords that are entered literally as shown. In actual configuration examples and output (not general command syntax), boldface indicates commands that are manually input by the user (such as a **show** command).

- *Italics* indicate arguments for which you supply actual values.

- Vertical bars (|) separate alternative, mutually exclusive elements.

- Square brackets [ ] indicate optional elements.

- Braces { } indicate a required choice.

- Braces within brackets [{ }] indicate a required choice within an optional element.

NETLAB+® Compatibility

NDG has worked closely with the Cisco CCNP lab team to develop BSCI labs that are compatible with the installed base of NETLAB AE router pods. For current information on labs compatible with NETLAB+® go to http://www.netdevgroup.com/ae/labs.htm.

Introduction

My first motivation for writing this book was to serve the needs of CCNP instructors and students in the Cisco Academy Program. For the past four years, I (David) have had the privilege of serving on the National Advisory Council for the Cisco Academy Program representing four-year colleges and universities. Also on that council are a number of two-year community colleges. Inevitably, at council meetings we would discuss both CCNP curriculum and labs. As I spoke with a number of my CCNP instructor peers, a common theme emerged. Instructors felt that the labs needed to be rewritten to be more comprehensive. Labs in the past have lacked complexity. When I realized that I was rewriting the Academy CCNP labs, and that my peers were rewriting the same labs, the thought occurred to me that perhaps an engineering school such as RPI was up to the task of writing these labs in a way which would better serve the needs of the community. It is not that the previous labs were inappropriate. Rather, I think it is that the Academy Program has grown up. Having just celebrated its tenth birthday, folks in the Academy are ready for bigger challenges. I hope that these labs will fill that role.

My second motivation for writing these labs was to help network professionals who are trying to upgrade their skill set to the CCNP level. As a former hiring manager at a Tier 1 ISP, I have a strong sense of what industry is looking for when they hire someone with CCNP credentials. A number of hiring managers from Fortune 500 companies contact me each year about hiring my students. I know the level of expertise they expect from a CCNP. These labs reflect the convictions those managers have shared with me.

My third motivation for writing these labs was to see how much of a challenge a university undergraduate could rise to if they were asked to do a big job. My co-authors, Josh Moorhouse and Ross Wolfson, were both undergraduates when they authored these labs. I gave them a huge task, and they responded with skill and grace. I firmly believe that we frequently do not ask enough of our students. If we ask for greatness, sometimes we will get it. If we settle for the normal, we are more assured of success, but we may miss the opportunity to see our students soar to heights undreamed of. Whether an instructor or student, I hope that your technical knowledge will soar to new heights with these labs.

Goals and Methods

The most important goal of this book is to help you master the technologies necessary to configure advanced routing on a production network. After all, what is the point of getting certified and getting that dream job or promotion, if you cannot perform once you are there. While it is impossible to simulate a network of 300 routers, we have added loopback interfaces to simulate additional networks and to increase complexity.

A secondary goal of this book is to help people pass the BSCI certification exam. For two years I was on the CCNP Assessment authoring team. After all those years of complaining, "What were they thinking when they put *that* question on the exam?" suddenly the questions I was writing were the subject of someone else's complaint. I know how important it is both to students and network professionals to pass certifications. Frequently, prestige, promotion, and money are all at stake. While all the core configurations on the certification exam are covered in this book, no static document like a book can keep up with the dynamic way in which the certification exam is constantly being upgraded.

Who Should Read This Book?

Cisco Academy instructors and students who want a written copy of the electronic labs will find this book of great use. In addition to all the official labs that are part of the Academy curriculum, Challenge and Troubleshooting labs have been added to test your mastery.

Network professionals, either in formal classes or studying alone, will also find great value in this book. Knowing how expensive it can be to purchase your own lab equipment, as many labs as possible were written with only three routers. To adequately cover some topics, four routers were necessary. For those seeking in-depth understanding, there are *optional* case studies that use either five or six routers.

What You Need to Configure the Labs

These labs were written on four Cisco 2811 routers using the following Cisco IOS Software image: c2800nm-advipservicesk9-mz.124-10.bin.

You should be able to configure the labs on any Cisco router that is using a 12.4 advanced IP services image of the Cisco IOS.

Classes and individuals using older Cisco devices, or less-robust versions of IOS will not be able to do the Toolkit Command Language (TCL) scripting lab in Chapter 1 (and at the end of every other lab in the book) or IPv6 in Chapter 8.

For example, it is not possible to run the 12.4 release of the advanced IP services IOS image on a Cisco 2600 series router. It is possible to run this image on a Cisco 2600XM router if you upgrade the flash and RAM and can obtain the new IOS image.

In addition, for any labs where you are instructed to copy and paste the configurations, you can find the configurations in .txt files, downloadable as a .zip file located under the More Information section at the website for this book at www.ciscopress.com/title/1587132133.

How This Book Is Organized

Those preparing for the BSCI certification exam should work through this book cover to cover. Network professionals needing help or a refresher on a particular topic can skip right to the area in which they need assistance.

The chapters cover the following topics:

- **Chapter 1, Designing Scalable Networks**: The actual design of large networks is covered in the curriculum. The concern of this chapter is to verify that every subnet in those scalable networks is reachable from every other subnet. When working in a lab environment with four routers, it is easy to use the **ping** command to verify that all networks are reachable. When working in a large network with hundreds of routers and thousands of subnets, it becomes burdensome to manually ping each network to verify reachability.

  Fortunately, the advanced IP services image that is used for these labs (c2800nm-advipservicesk9-mz.124-10.bin) supports the use of the scripting language TCL. You do not need to know how to program in TCL to use this powerful tool. The instructions in this lab show you how to use a TCL script to verify the reachability of all the subnets in the networks that you build.

The authors are continually amazed how verifying connectivity using this TCL script in even a small network of six routers reveals configuration errors that were not immediately apparent. Use of this tool to verify reachability is definitely a best practice.

- **Chapter 2, EIGRP:** This chapter provides the steps to configure the Cisco-proprietary routing protocol Enhanced Interior Gateway Routing Protocol. EIGRP adjacencies, load balancing, summarization, and default network advertisement are all covered. Routing EIGRP over Frame Relay is shown using either a router or an Adtran unit as a Frame Relay switch. The Challenge Lab will help you to determine your level of mastery of the topics. The Troubleshooting Lab will highlight your ability to spot problems with routing EIGRP.

- **Chapter 3, OSPF**: This chapter provides the steps to configure the Open Shortest Path First Protocol. OSPF is one of the most commonly used IP routing protocols in both enterprise and service provider networks. It is an open-standard protocol based primarily on RFC 2328. Configuration topics include link costs, interface priorities, stub areas, virtual links, area summarization, and authentication. Routing OSPF over Frame Relay will be configured using either a router or an Adtran unit as a Frame Relay switch. The Challenge Lab will help you determine your level of mastery of the topics. The Troubleshooting Lab will help you spot problems with faulty OSPF configurations.

- **Chapter 4, IS-IS**: The Intermediate System-to-Intermediate System routing protocol has very fast convergence and is very scalable. Configuration topics include basic integrated IS-IS, multi-area Integrated IS-IS, and IS-IS over Frame Relay using either a router or an Adtran unit as a Frame Relay switch.

- **Chapter 5, Route Optimization**: Anyone who has had to call the Cisco TAC (Technical Assistance Center) to receive help with a routing problem knows that one of the first questions you will be asked are these: "Are you using route redistribution in your network? If you are, can you eliminate it?" In a perfect world, each network would only use one routing protocol and there would not be the need to redistribute routes between different routing protocols. However, with corporate mergers and legacy networks, it is almost inevitable that you will need to know how to distribute routes between different routing protocols. This chapter shows you how.

- **Chapter 6, BGP**: Border Gateway Protocol is the routing protocol that makes the backbone of the Internet work. BGP configuration topics include BGP with default routing, the AS_PATH attribute, Interior BGP (IBGP) and Exterior BGP (EBGP), local preference, MED, route reflectors, and route filters.

- **Chapter 7, Multicast**. Multicast as it is currently deployed in production networks almost universally uses PIM Sparse-Dense mode. Why then even bother to cover PIM Sparse mode and PIM Dense mode separately? If you just need to quickly configure a multicast network, skip right to Lab 4 in this chapter. If you are seeking to understand multicast, work through these labs systematically from start to finish.

- **Chapter 8, IPv6**: This chapter provides the steps to configure IPv6. Configuration topics include OSPFv3 for IPv6 and both manual and 6to4 IPv6 tunnels. Challenge and Troubleshooting Labs are provided to test your mastery.

- **Chapter 9, Case Studies**: Using a four-router topology, there is a case study for both EIGRP and OSPF. For schools or individuals who may have more equipment to play with, there are some optional five- and six-router topologies. Even if you do not have the actual equipment to configure these more complex topologies, it is worth thinking through these labs to expand your thinking into more complex networking solutions.

CHAPTER 1

Scalable Network Design

 ## Lab 1-1: BSCI Lab Configuration Guide (1.5.1)

Figure 1-1 and Figure 1-2 describe Ethernet and serial connectivity between the routers of your pod. These 13 connections, 8 Ethernet and 5 serial, will be used as the master template for most labs in the Building Scalable Cisco Internetworks (BSCI), Implementing Secure Converged Wide Area Networks (ISCW), Optimizing Converged Cisco Networks (ONT) curricula. In fact, almost all scenarios in the BSCI lab curriculum use only R1, R2, and R3, excluding the connections to R4.

Figure 1-1   Ethernet Connectivity Diagram

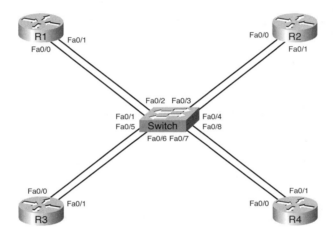

Figure 1-2   Serial Connectivity Diagram

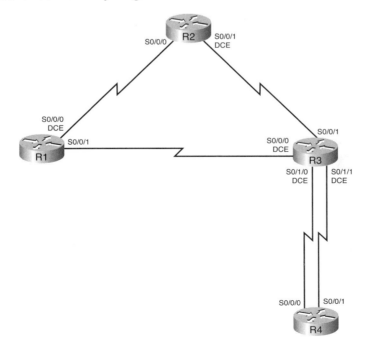

Notable exceptions to the diagrams do occur because of content covered in some of the courses, namely:

- BSCI Case Study 3: OSPF Five Routers
- BSCI Case Study 4: BGP
- ISCW Lab 4-2: Implementing MPLS VPNs, Challenge Lab
- ONT Lab 6-1: Configuring a WLAN Controller
- ONT Lab 6-2: Configuring a WLAN Controller via the Web Interface
- ONT Lab 6-3: Configuring a Wireless Client
- ONT Lab 6-4: Configuring WPA Security with Preshared Keys
- ONT Lab 6-5: Configuring LEAP

You should also have no trouble using the diagrams in Figure 1-1 and Figure 1-2 as the Frame Relay topology in the following labs:

- BSCI Lab 2-5: EIGRP Frame Relay Hub and Spoke
- BSCI Lab 3-4: OSPF over Frame Relay
- BSCI Lab 4-4: Configuring IS-IS over Frame Relay
- BSCI Case Study 2: OSPF with Four Routers

All labs assume that you have complete control over each of the devices in your pod, including access to the switch to configure VLANs and assign switchports as access ports on a VLAN or as trunk ports.

Although most labs do not make use of every single link, you should cable your pod according to the diagrams in order to avoid re-cabling your pod for each lab.

Lab 1-2: TCL Script Reference and Demonstration (1.5.1)

The objectives of this lab are as follows:

- Learn to use TCL scripts to verify full connectivity

- Identify causes of failures

Figure 1-3 illustrates the topology that will be used for this lab.

Figure 1-3   Network Topology for Lab 1-2

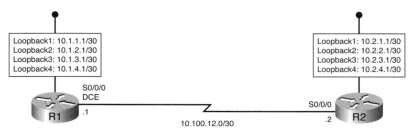

Quick TCL Reference

Refer back to this tutorial whenever needed as you progress through the labs in this book. You can download the TCL Script at www.ciscopress.com/title/1587132133 under the More Information section on the page.

```
tclsh
```

```
foreach address {
  10.1.1.1
  10.1.2.1
  10.1.3.1
  10.1.4.1
  10.100.12.1
  10.2.1.1
  10.2.2.1
  10.2.3.1
  10.2.4.1
  10.100.12.2
} {
  ping $address
}

tclquit
```

Step 1: Initial Configuration

Paste in the initial configurations that follow (you can download the configurations at www.ciscopress.com/title/1587132133 under the More Information section on the page):

```
R1:
!
hostname R1
!
interface loopback 1
 ip address 10.1.1.1 255.255.255.252
!
interface loopback 2
 ip address 10.1.2.1 255.255.255.252
!
interface loopback 3
 ip address 10.1.3.1 255.255.255.252
!
interface loopback 4
 ip address 10.1.4.1 255.255.255.252
!
interface serial 0/0/0
 ip address 10.100.12.1 255.255.255.252
 clock rate 64000
 no shutdown
!
router rip
 version 2
 network 10.0.0.0
 no auto-summary
!
end

R2:
!
hostname R2
!
interface loopback 1
 ip address 10.2.1.1 255.255.255.252
!
interface loopback 2
 ip address 10.2.2.1 255.255.255.252
!
interface loopback 3
 ip address 10.2.3.1 255.255.255.252
!
```

```
interface loopback 4
 ip address 10.2.4.1 255.255.255.252
!
interface serial 0/0/0
 no shutdown
!
router rip
 version 2
 network 10.0.0.0
 no auto-summary
!
end
```

Do you think that these configurations will achieve full connectivity between R1 and R2? Explain.

_____

_____

_____

_____

Step 2: Verify Connectivity

The simplest way to verify OSI Layer 3 connectivity between two routers is to use the Internet Control Message Protocol (ICMP). ICMP defines a number of message types in RFC 792 for IPv4 and RFC 4443 for IPv6. (For copies, go to www.ietf.org.)

ICMP defines procedures for echo (ping), traceroute, and source notification of unreachable networks. Pinging an IP address can result in a variety of ICMP messages, but the only message indicating that a ping is successful is the ICMP echo reply message indicated by an exclamation point (!) in the output of the **ping** command.

```
R1# ping 10.1.1.1
```

```
!!!!!
```

In Step 1, you may have noticed that R2's configuration omits an IP address on Serial0/0/0. R2 does not exchange updates with R1 because the IP protocol is not running on R2's serial interface until the IP address has been configured.

Without this IP address, for which addresses in the topology diagram do you expect the ping to fail?

_____

_____

_____

_____

Cisco IOS Software Release 12.3(2)T and later supports TCL scripting in the Cisco IOS.

To construct a simple connectivity verification script, do the following:

1. Open a text editor and create a new document. Using a text file saves time, especially if you are pasting the TCL script into multiple devices.

2. On the first line, enter the **tclsh** command and then press **Enter** four times to leave a pause while the TCL shell starts. The **tclsh** command, when entered on a supported switch or router, enters TCL shell mode, in which you can use native TCL instructions like **foreach** or issue EXEC-mode commands. You can also access configuration mode from within the TCL shell and issue configuration commands from their respective menus, although these features are not explored in this lab.

    ```
    tclsh
    ```

3. Begin a loop using the **foreach** instruction. The loop iterates over a sequence of values, executing a defined sequence of instructions once *for each* value. Think of it as "for each *value* in *Values*, do each *instruction* in *Instructions*." For each iteration of the loop, *$identifier* reflects the current *value* in *Values*. The **foreach** instruction follows the model given here:

    ```
    foreach identifier {
    value1
    value2
    .
    .
    .
    valueX
    } {
    instruction1
    instruction2
    .
    .
    .
    instructionY
    }
    ```

4. To create a TCL script that pings each IP address in the topology, enter each of the IP addresses in the value list. Issue the **ping $address** command as the only instruction in the instruction list:

    ```
    foreach address {
     10.1.1.1
     10.1.2.1
     10.1.3.1
     10.1.4.1
     10.100.12.1
     10.2.1.1
    ```

```
    10.2.2.1
    10.2.3.1
    10.2.4.1
    10.100.12.2
} {
ping $address
}
```

5. Copy the TCL script from the text file and paste it into each device.

```
R1# tclsh
R1(tcl)#
R1(tcl)#
R1(tcl)#
R1(tcl)# foreach address {
+>(tcl)# 10.1.1.1
+>(tcl)# 10.1.2.1
+>(tcl)# 10.1.3.1
+>(tcl)# 10.1.4.1
+>(tcl)# 10.100.12.1
+>(tcl)# 10.2.1.1
+>(tcl)# 10.2.2.1
+>(tcl)# 10.2.3.1
+>(tcl)# 10.2.4.1
+>(tcl)# 10.100.12.2
+>(tcl)# } {
+>(tcl)# ping $address
+>(tcl)# }

Type escape sequence to abort.
Sending 5, 100-byte ICMP Echos to 10.1.1.1, timeout is 2 seconds:
!!!!!
Success rate is 100 percent (5/5), round-trip min/avg/max = 1/1/4 ms
Type escape sequence to abort.
Sending 5, 100-byte ICMP Echos to 10.1.2.1, timeout is 2 seconds:
!!!!!
Success rate is 100 percent (5/5), round-trip min/avg/max = 1/1/4 ms
Type escape sequence to abort.
Sending 5, 100-byte ICMP Echos to 10.1.3.1, timeout is 2 seconds:
!!!!!
Success rate is 100 percent (5/5), round-trip min/avg/max = 1/1/4 ms
Type escape sequence to abort.
Sending 5, 100-byte ICMP Echos to 10.1.4.1, timeout is 2 seconds:
!!!!!
Success rate is 100 percent (5/5), round-trip min/avg/max = 1/1/4 ms
```

```
Type escape sequence to abort.
Sending 5, 100-byte ICMP Echos to 10.100.12.1, timeout is 2 seconds:
.....
Success rate is 0 percent (0/5)
Type escape sequence to abort.
Sending 5, 100-byte ICMP Echos to 10.2.1.1, timeout is 2 seconds:
.....
Success rate is 0 percent (0/5)
Type escape sequence to abort.
Sending 5, 100-byte ICMP Echos to 10.2.2.1, timeout is 2 seconds:
.....
Success rate is 0 percent (0/5)
Type escape sequence to abort.
Sending 5, 100-byte ICMP Echos to 10.2.3.1, timeout is 2 seconds:
.....
Success rate is 0 percent (0/5)
Type escape sequence to abort.
Sending 5, 100-byte ICMP Echos to 10.2.4.1, timeout is 2 seconds:
.....
Success rate is 0 percent (0/5)
Type escape sequence to abort.
Sending 5, 100-byte ICMP Echos to 10.100.12.2, timeout is 2 seconds:
.....
Success rate is 0 percent (0/5)


R2# tclsh
R2(tcl)#
R2(tcl)#
R2(tcl)#
R2(tcl)# foreach address {
+>(tcl)# 10.1.1.1
+>(tcl)# 10.1.2.1
+>(tcl)# 10.1.3.1
+>(tcl)# 10.1.4.1
+>(tcl)# 10.100.12.1
+>(tcl)# 10.2.1.1
+>(tcl)# 10.2.2.1
+>(tcl)# 10.2.3.1
+>(tcl)# 10.2.4.1
+>(tcl)# 10.100.12.2
+>(tcl)# } {
```

```
+>(tcl)# ping $address
+>(tcl)# }

Type escape sequence to abort.
Sending 5, 100-byte ICMP Echos to 10.1.1.1, timeout is 2 seconds:
.....
Success rate is 0 percent (0/5)
Type escape sequence to abort.
Sending 5, 100-byte ICMP Echos to 10.1.2.1, timeout is 2 seconds:
.....
Success rate is 0 percent (0/5)
Type escape sequence to abort.
Sending 5, 100-byte ICMP Echos to 10.1.3.1, timeout is 2 seconds:
.....
Success rate is 0 percent (0/5)
Type escape sequence to abort.
Sending 5, 100-byte ICMP Echos to 10.1.4.1, timeout is 2 seconds:
.....
Success rate is 0 percent (0/5)
Type escape sequence to abort.
Sending 5, 100-byte ICMP Echos to 10.100.12.1, timeout is 2 seconds:
.....
Success rate is 0 percent (0/5)
Type escape sequence to abort.
Sending 5, 100-byte ICMP Echos to 10.2.1.1, timeout is 2 seconds:
!!!!!
Success rate is 100 percent (5/5), round-trip min/avg/max = 1/1/4 ms
Type escape sequence to abort.
Sending 5, 100-byte ICMP Echos to 10.2.2.1, timeout is 2 seconds:
!!!!!
Success rate is 100 percent (5/5), round-trip min/avg/max = 1/1/4 ms
Type escape sequence to abort.
Sending 5, 100-byte ICMP Echos to 10.2.3.1, timeout is 2 seconds:
!!!!!
Success rate is 100 percent (5/5), round-trip min/avg/max = 1/1/1 ms
Type escape sequence to abort.
Sending 5, 100-byte ICMP Echos to 10.2.4.1, timeout is 2 seconds:
!!!!!
Success rate is 100 percent (5/5), round-trip min/avg/max = 1/1/1 ms
Type escape sequence to abort.
Sending 5, 100-byte ICMP Echos to 10.100.12.2, timeout is 2 seconds:
!!!!!
Success rate is 0 percent (0/5)
```

6. Exit the TCL script using the **tclquit** command on each device.

```
R1(tcl)# tclquit


R2(tcl)# tclquit
```

Notice that in the previous output, R1 and R2 could not route pings to the remote loopback networks for which they did not have routes installed in their routing tables.

You might have also noticed that R1 could not ping its local address on Serial0/0/0. In HDLC, Frame Relay, and ATM serial technologies, all packets, including pings to the local interface, must be forwarded across the link.

For instance, R1 attempts to ping 10.100.12.1 and routes the packet out Serial0/0/0, even though the address is a local interface. Assume that there are working configurations with an IP address of 10.100.12.2/30 assigned to the Serial0/0/0 interface on R2. Once a ping from R1 to 10.100.12.1 reaches R2, R2 evaluates that this is not its address on the 10.100.12.0/30 subnet and routes the packet back to R1 on its Serial0/0/0 interface. R1 receives the packet and evaluates that 10.100.12.1 is the address of the local interface. R1 opens this packet using ICMP and responds to the ICMP echo request (ping) with an echo reply destined for 10.100.12.1. R1 encapsulates the echo reply at Serial0/0/0 and routes the packet to R2. R2 receives the packet and routes it back to R1, the originator of the ICMP echo. The ICMP protocol on R1 receives the echo reply, associates it with the ICMP echo it sent, and prints the output in the form of an exclamation point.

To understand this behavior, observe the output of the **debug ip icmp** and **debug ip packet** commands on R1 and R2 while pinging with the configurations given in Step 3.

Step 3: Resolve Connectivity Issues

On R2, assign the IP address 10.100.12.2/30 to Serial0/0/0:

```
R2# configure terminal
R2(config)# interface serial 0/0/0
R2(config-if)# ip address 10.100.12.2 255.255.255.0
```

On each router, verify the receipt of RIPv2 routing information with the **show ip protocols** command:

```
R1# show ip protocols
Routing Protocol is "rip"
  Outgoing update filter list for all interfaces is not set
  Incoming update filter list for all interfaces is not set
  Sending updates every 30 seconds, next due in 28 seconds
  Invalid after 180 seconds, hold down 180, flushed after 240
  Redistributing: rip
  Default version control: send version 2, receive version 2
    Interface          Send  Recv  Triggered RIP  Key-chain
    Serial0/0/0         2     2
    Loopback1           2     2
    Loopback2           2     2
    Loopback3           2     2
    Loopback4           2     2
```

```
Automatic network summarization is not in effect
Maximum path: 4
Routing for Networks:
   10.0.0.0
Routing Information Sources:
   Gateway          Distance      Last Update
   10.100.12.2          120       00:00:13
Distance: (default is 120)
```

```
R2# show ip protocols
Routing Protocol is "rip"
  Outgoing update filter list for all interfaces is not set
  Incoming update filter list for all interfaces is not set
  Sending updates every 30 seconds, next due in 26 seconds
  Invalid after 180 seconds, hold down 180, flushed after 240
  Redistributing: rip
  Default version control: send version 2, receive version 2
     Interface           Send  Recv  Triggered RIP  Key-chain
     Serial0/0/0          2     2
     Serial0/0/1          2     2
     Loopback1            2     2
     Loopback2            2     2
     Loopback3            2     2
     Loopback4            2     2
  Automatic network summarization is not in effect
  Maximum path: 4
  Routing for Networks:
     10.0.0.0
  Routing Information Sources:
     Gateway          Distance      Last Update
     10.100.12.1          120       00:00:14
  Distance: (default is 120)
```

On each router, verify full connectivity to all subnets in the diagram by pasting the TCL script on the command line in privileged EXEC mode:

```
R1# tclsh
R1(tcl)#
R1(tcl)#
R1(tcl)#
R1(tcl)# foreach address {
+>(tcl)# 10.1.1.1
+>(tcl)# 10.1.2.1
+>(tcl)# 10.1.3.1
+>(tcl)# 10.1.4.1
```

```
+>(tcl)# 10.100.12.1
+>(tcl)# 10.2.1.1
+>(tcl)# 10.2.2.1
+>(tcl)# 10.2.3.1
+>(tcl)# 10.2.4.1
+>(tcl)# 10.100.12.2
+>(tcl)# } {
+>(tcl)# ping $address
+>(tcl)# }


Type escape sequence to abort.
Sending 5, 100-byte ICMP Echos to 10.1.1.1, timeout is 2 seconds:
!!!!!
Success rate is 100 percent (5/5), round-trip min/avg/max = 1/1/4 ms
Type escape sequence to abort.
Sending 5, 100-byte ICMP Echos to 10.1.2.1, timeout is 2 seconds:
!!!!!
Success rate is 100 percent (5/5), round-trip min/avg/max = 1/1/4 ms
Type escape sequence to abort.
Sending 5, 100-byte ICMP Echos to 10.1.3.1, timeout is 2 seconds:
!!!!!
Success rate is 100 percent (5/5), round-trip min/avg/max = 1/1/1 ms
Type escape sequence to abort.
Sending 5, 100-byte ICMP Echos to 10.1.4.1, timeout is 2 seconds:
!!!!!
Success rate is 100 percent (5/5), round-trip min/avg/max = 1/1/4 ms
Type escape sequence to abort.
Sending 5, 100-byte ICMP Echos to 10.100.12.1, timeout is 2 seconds:
!!!!!
Success rate is 100 percent (5/5), round-trip min/avg/max = 56/57/64 ms
Type escape sequence to abort.
Sending 5, 100-byte ICMP Echos to 10.2.1.1, timeout is 2 seconds:
!!!!!
Success rate is 100 percent (5/5), round-trip min/avg/max = 28/28/32 ms
Type escape sequence to abort.
Sending 5, 100-byte ICMP Echos to 10.2.2.1, timeout is 2 seconds:
!!!!!
Success rate is 100 percent (5/5), round-trip min/avg/max = 28/28/28 ms
Type escape sequence to abort.
Sending 5, 100-byte ICMP Echos to 10.2.3.1, timeout is 2 seconds:
!!!!!
Success rate is 100 percent (5/5), round-trip min/avg/max = 28/28/32 ms
Type escape sequence to abort.
Sending 5, 100-byte ICMP Echos to 10.2.4.1, timeout is 2 seconds:
```

```
!!!!!
Success rate is 100 percent (5/5), round-trip min/avg/max = 28/28/28 ms
Type escape sequence to abort.
Sending 5, 100-byte ICMP Echos to 10.100.12.2, timeout is 2 seconds:
!!!!!
Success rate is 100 percent (5/5), round-trip min/avg/max = 28/28/32 ms
R1(tcl)# tclquit


R2# tclsh
R2(tcl)#
R2(tcl)#
R2(tcl)#
R2(tcl)# foreach address {
+>(tcl)# 10.1.1.1
+>(tcl)# 10.1.2.1
+>(tcl)# 10.1.3.1
+>(tcl)# 10.1.4.1
+>(tcl)# 10.100.12.1
+>(tcl)# 10.2.1.1
+>(tcl)# 10.2.2.1
+>(tcl)# 10.2.3.1
+>(tcl)# 10.2.4.1
+>(tcl)# 10.100.12.2
+>(tcl)# } {
+>(tcl)# ping $address
+>(tcl)# }

Type escape sequence to abort.
Sending 5, 100-byte ICMP Echos to 10.1.1.1, timeout is 2 seconds:
!!!!!
Success rate is 100 percent (5/5), round-trip min/avg/max = 28/28/32 ms
Type escape sequence to abort.
Sending 5, 100-byte ICMP Echos to 10.1.2.1, timeout is 2 seconds:
!!!!!
Success rate is 100 percent (5/5), round-trip min/avg/max = 28/28/32 ms
Type escape sequence to abort.
Sending 5, 100-byte ICMP Echos to 10.1.3.1, timeout is 2 seconds:
!!!!!
Success rate is 100 percent (5/5), round-trip min/avg/max = 28/28/32 ms
Type escape sequence to abort.
Sending 5, 100-byte ICMP Echos to 10.1.4.1, timeout is 2 seconds:
!!!!!
```

```
Success rate is 100 percent (5/5), round-trip min/avg/max = 28/28/32 ms
Type escape sequence to abort.
Sending 5, 100-byte ICMP Echos to 10.100.12.1, timeout is 2 seconds:
!!!!!
Success rate is 100 percent (5/5), round-trip min/avg/max = 28/28/28 ms
Type escape sequence to abort.
Sending 5, 100-byte ICMP Echos to 10.2.1.1, timeout is 2 seconds:
!!!!!
Success rate is 100 percent (5/5), round-trip min/avg/max = 1/1/4 ms
Type escape sequence to abort.
Sending 5, 100-byte ICMP Echos to 10.2.2.1, timeout is 2 seconds:
!!!!!
Success rate is 100 percent (5/5), round-trip min/avg/max = 1/1/1 ms
Type escape sequence to abort.
Sending 5, 100-byte ICMP Echos to 10.2.3.1, timeout is 2 seconds:
!!!!!
Success rate is 100 percent (5/5), round-trip min/avg/max = 1/1/4 ms
Type escape sequence to abort.
Sending 5, 100-byte ICMP Echos to 10.2.4.1, timeout is 2 seconds:
!!!!!
Success rate is 100 percent (5/5), round-trip min/avg/max = 1/1/4 ms
Type escape sequence to abort.
Sending 5, 100-byte ICMP Echos to 10.100.12.2, timeout is 2 seconds:
!!!!!
Success rate is 100 percent (5/5), round-trip min/avg/max = 56/58/68 ms
R2(tcl)# tclquit
```

Notice that the average round-trip time for an ICMP packet from R1 to 10.100.12.1 is approximately twice that of a ping from R1 to Loopback1 on R2. This verifies the conclusion reached in Step 2 that the ICMP echo request to 10.100.12.1 and the ICMP echo reply from 10.100.12.1 each traverse the link *twice* to verify full connectivity across the link.

Conclusion

Use TCL scripts to verify all your configurations in this course and observe the output. If you verify your work, both academically and in production networks, you will gain knowledge and save time in troubleshooting.

Lab 2-1: EIGRP Configuration, Bandwidth, and Adjacencies (2.7.1)

The objectives of this lab are as follows:

- Configure EIGRP on an interface

- Configure the bandwidth command to limit EIGRP bandwidth

- Verify EIGRP adjacencies

- Verify EIGRP routing information exchange

- Utilize debugging commands for troubleshooting EIGRP

- Challenge: Test convergence for EIGRP when a topology change occurs

Figure 2-1 illustrates the topology that will be used for this lab.

Figure 2-1   Topology Diagram

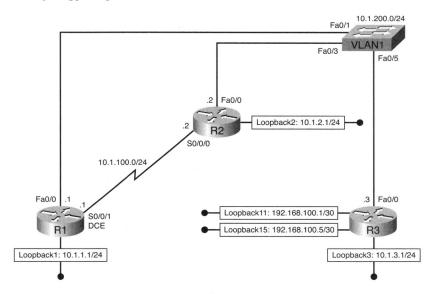

Scenario

You are responsible for configuring the new network to connect your company's Engineering, Marketing, and Accounting departments, represented by the loopback interfaces on each of the three routers. The physical devices have just been installed and are connected by Fast Ethernet and serial cables. Your task is to configure Enhanced Interior Gateway Routing Protocol (EIGRP) to enable full connectivity between all departments.

Step 1: Addressing

Using the addressing scheme in the diagram, apply IP addresses to the Fast Ethernet interfaces on R1, R2, and R3. Then create Loopback 1 on R1, Loopback 2 on R2, and Loopback 3 on R3, and address them according to the diagram in Figure 2-1:

```
R1# configure terminal
R1(config)# interface Loopback1
R1(config-if)# description Engineering Department
R1(config-if)# ip address 10.1.1.1 255.255.255.0
R1(config-if)# exit
R1(config)# interface FastEthernet0/0
R1(config-if)# ip address 10.1.100.1 255.255.255.0
```

```
R2# configure terminal
R2(config)# interface Loopback2
R2(config-if)# description Marketing Department
R2(config-if)# ip address 10.1.2.1 255.255.255.0
R2(config-if)# exit
R2(config)# interface FastEthernet0/0
R2(config-if)# ip address 10.1.100.2 255.255.255.0
```

```
R3# configure terminal
R3(config)# interface Loopback3
R3(config-if)# description Accounting Department
R3(config-if)# ip address 10.1.3.1 255.255.255.0
R3(config-if)# exit
R3(config)# interface FastEthernet0/0
R3(config-if)# ip address 10.1.100.3 255.255.255.0
```

Leave the switch in its default (blank) configuration. By default, all switch ports are in VLAN1 and are not administratively down.

For now, also leave the serial interfaces in their default configuration. You configure the serial link between R1 and R2 in Step 4.

Verify that the line protocol of each interface is up and that you can successfully ping across each link. You should see similar output on each router:

```
R1# show ip interface brief
```

Interface	IP-Address	OK? Method Status	Protocol
FastEthernet0/0	10.1.100.1	YES manual up	up
FastEthernet0/1	unassigned	YES unset administratively down	down
Serial0/0/0	unassigned	YES manual up	up
Serial0/0/1	unassigned	YES unset administratively down	down
Loopback1	10.1.1.1	YES manual up	up

Step 2: Configuring EIGRP Across VLAN1

After you have implemented your addressing scheme, create an EIGRP autonomous system (AS) on R1 using the following commands in global configuration mode:

```
R1(config)# router eigrp 1
R1(config-router)# network 10.0.0.0
```

Using **network** statements with major networks causes EIGRP to begin sending EIGRP hello packets out all interfaces in that network (that is, subnets of the major network 10.0.0.0/8). In this case, EIGRP should start sending hello packets out of its Fast Ethernet and loopback interfaces. To check whether this is occurring, use the **debug eigrp packets** in privileged EXEC mode:

```
R1# debug eigrp packets
*Sep 25 21:27:09.547: EIGRP: Sending HELLO on Loopback1
*Sep 25 21:27:09.547:   AS 1, Flags 0x0, Seq 0/0 idbQ 0/0 iidbQ un/rely 0/0
*Sep 25 21:27:09.547: EIGRP: Received HELLO on Loopback1 nbr 10.1.1.1
*Sep 25 21:27:09.547:   AS 1, Flags 0x0, Seq 0/0 idbQ 0/0
*Sep 25 21:27:09.547: EIGRP: Packet from ourselves ignored
*Sep 25 21:27:10.203: EIGRP: Sending HELLO on FastEthernet0/0
*Sep 25 21:27:10.203:   AS 1, Flags 0x0, Seq 0/0 idbQ 0/0 iidbQ un/rely 0/0
R1# undebug all
```

These hello packets are unanswered by the other routers because EIGRP is not yet running on R2 or R3. R1 ignores the hello packets from itself on Loopback 1. Use the **undebug all** command to stop the debug output.

Which interfaces are involved in EIGRP's routing process on this router? Use **show ip eigrp interfaces** to show which interfaces are participating in EIGRP. You should see output similar to the following:

```
R1# show ip eigrp interfaces
IP-EIGRP interfaces for process 1

                  Xmit Queue   Mean   Pacing Time  Multicast    Pending
Interface  Peers  Un/Reliable  SRTT   Un/Reliable  Flow Timer   Routes
Fa0/0        0      0/0         0        0/1           0            0
Lo1          0      0/0         0        0/1           0            0
```

You are interested in seeing the adjacency initiate on R1 and R2, so you issue **debug eigrp packets** on R1 and R2 to monitor the adjacency taking place in real time while you configure R2.

Now, in global configuration mode on R2, issue the same set of commands you issued on R1 to create EIGRP AS 1 and advertise the 10.0.0.0/8 network. You should see debug output similar to the following:

```
R2# debug eigrp packets
EIGRP Packets debugging is on
    (UPDATE, REQUEST, QUERY, REPLY, HELLO, IPXSAP, PROBE, ACK, STUB, SIAQUERY,
SIAREPLY)
```

```
R2#configure terminal
Enter configuration commands, one per line.  End with CNTL/Z.
R2(config)#router eigrp 1
R2(config-router)#network 10.0.0.0
R2(config-router)#
*Sep 25 20:32:28.427: EIGRP: Sending HELLO on FastEthernet0/0
*Sep 25 20:32:28.427:   AS 1, Flags 0x0, Seq 0/0 idbQ 0/0 iidbQ un/rely 0/0
*Sep 25 20:32:28.431: EIGRP: Received HELLO on FastEthernet0/0 nbr 10.1.100.1
*Sep 25 20:32:28.431:   AS 1, Flags 0x0, Seq 0/0 idbQ 0/0
*Sep 25 20:32:28.431: %DUAL-5-NBRCHANGE: IP-EIGRP(0) 1: Neighbor 10.1.100.1
(FastEthernet0/0) is up: new adjacency
*Sep 25 20:32:28.431: EIGRP: Enqueueing UPDATE on FastEthernet0/0 nbr 10.1.100.1
iidbQ un/rely 0/1 peerQ un/rely 0/0
*Sep 25 20:32:28.435: EIGRP: Received UPDATE on FastEthernet0/0 nbr 10.1.100.1
*Sep 25 20:32:28.435:   AS 1, Flags 0x1, Seq 1/0 idbQ 0/0 iidbQ un/rely 0/1 peerQ
un/rely 0/0
*Sep 25 20:32:28.435: EIGRP: Requeued unicast on FastEthernet0/0
*Sep 25 20:32:28.435: EIGRP: Sending HELLO on FastEthernet0/0
*Sep 25 20:32:28.435:   AS 1, Flags 0x0, Seq 0/0 idbQ 0/0 iidbQ un/rely 0/0
*Sep 25 20:32:28.439: EIGRP: Sending UPDATE on FastEthernet0/0 nbr 10.1.100.1
*Sep 25 20:32:28.439:   AS 1, Flags 0x1, Seq 1/1 idbQ 0/0 iidbQ un/rely 0/0 peerQ
un/rely 0/1
*Sep 25 20:32:28.443: EIGRP: Received UPDATE on FastEthernet0/0 nbr 10.1.100.1
*Sep 25 20:32:28.443:   AS 1, Flags 0x8, Seq 2/0 idbQ 0/0 iidbQ un/rely 0/0 peerQ
un/rely 0/1
*Sep 25 20:32:28.447: EIGRP: Received ACK on FastEthernet0/0 nbr 10.1.100.1
*Sep 25 20:32:28.447:   AS 1, Flags 0x0, Seq 0/1 idbQ 0/0 iidbQ un/rely 0/0 un/rely
0/1
*Sep 25 20:32:28.447: EIGRP: Enqueueing UPDATE on FastEthernet0/0 nbr 10.1.100.1
iidbQ un/rely 0/1 peerQ un/rely 0/0 serno 1-2
*Sep 25 20:32:28.451: EIGRP: Requeued unicast on FastEthernet0/0
*Sep 25 20:32:28.455: EIGRP: Sending UPDATE on FastEthernet0/0 nbr 10.1.100.1
*Sep 25 20:32:28.455:   AS 1, Flags 0x8, Seq 2/2 idbQ 0/0 iidbQ un/rely 0/0 peerQ
un/rely 0/1 serno 1-2
*Sep 25 20:32:28.455: EIGRP: Enqueueing UPDATE on FastEthernet0/0 iidbQ un/rely 0/1
serno 3-3
*Sep 25 20:32:28.455: EIGRP: Received UPDATE on FastEthernet0/0 nbr 10.1.100.1
*Sep 25 20:32:28.455:   AS 1, Flags 0x8, Seq 3/1 idbQ 0/0 iidbQ un/rely 0/1 peerQ
un/rely 0/1
*Sep 25 20:32:28.455: EIGRP: Enqueueing ACK on FastEthernet0/0 nbr 10.1.100.1
*Sep 25 20:32:28.455:   Ack seq 3 iidbQ un/rely 0/1 peerQ un/rely 1/1
*Sep 25 20:32:28.459: EIGRP: Received ACK on FastEthernet0/0 nbr 10.1.100.1
*Sep 25 20:32:28.459:   AS 1, Flags 0x0, Seq 0/2 idbQ 0/0 iidbQ un/rely 0/1 peerQ
un/rely 1/1
*Sep 25 20:32:28.467: EIGRP: Forcing multicast xmit on FastEthernet0/0
*Sep 25 20:32:28.467: EIGRP: Sending UPDATE on FastEthernet0/0
*Sep 25 20:32:28.467:   AS 1, Flags 0x0, Seq 3/0 idbQ 0/0 iidbQ un/rely 0/0 serno 3-
3
```

```
*Sep 25 20:32:28.471: EIGRP: Received ACK on FastEthernet0/0 nbr 10.1.100.1
*Sep 25 20:32:28.471:    AS 1, Flags 0x0, Seq 0/3 idbQ 0/0 iidbQ un/rely 0/0 peerQ
un/rely 1/1
*Sep 25 20:32:28.471: EIGRP: FastEthernet0/0 multicast flow blocking cleared
*Sep 25 20:32:28.479: EIGRP: Sending ACK on FastEthernet0/0 nbr 10.1.100.1
*Sep 25 20:32:28.479:    AS 1, Flags 0x0, Seq 0/3 idbQ 0/0 iidbQ un/rely 0/0 peerQ
un/rely 1/0
```

The **debug** output displays the EIGRP Hello, Update, and ACK packets. Because EIGRP uses Reliable Transport Protocol (RTP) for Update packets, you see routers replying to Update packets with the ACK packet. You can turn off debugging with **undebug all**.

Configure EIGRP on R3 using the same commands:

```
R3(config)# router eigrp 1
R3(config-router)# network 10.0.0.0
```

Step 3: Verifying the EIGRP Configuration

When R3 is configured, issue **show ip eigrp neighbors** on each router. If you have configured each router successfully, there are two adjacencies on each router:

```
R1# show ip eigrp neighbors
IP-EIGRP neighbors for process 1
```

H	Address	Interface	Hold Uptime	SRTT	RTO	Q	Seq
			(sec)	(ms)		Cnt	Num
1	10.1.100.3	Fa0/0	10 00:00:17	1	200	0	7
0	10.1.100.2	Fa0/0	11 00:02:01	5	200	0	6
!							

```
R2# show ip eigrp neighbors
IP-EIGRP neighbors for process 1
```

H	Address	Interface	Hold Uptime	SRTT	RTO	Q	Seq
			(sec)	(ms)		Cnt	Num
1	10.1.100.3	Fa0/0	13 00:00:56	1	200	0	7
0	10.1.100.1	Fa0/0	12 00:02:40	1	200	0	47
!							

```
R3# show ip eigrp neighbors
IP-EIGRP neighbors for process 1
```

H	Address	Interface	Hold Uptime	SRTT	RTO	Q	Seq
			(sec)	(ms)		Cnt	Num
1	10.1.100.2	Fa0/0	11 00:01:21	819	4914	0	6
0	10.1.100.1	Fa0/0	11 00:01:21	2	200	0	47

Now check whether the EIGRP routes are being exchanged between the routers using **show ip eigrp topology**:

```
R1# show ip eigrp topology
IP-EIGRP Topology Table for AS(1)/ID(10.1.1.1)
```

```
Codes: P - Passive, A - Active, U - Update, Q - Query, R - Reply,
       r - reply Status, s - sia Status


P 10.1.3.0/24, 1 successors, FD is 156160
        via 10.1.100.3 (156160/128256), FastEthernet0/0
P 10.1.2.0/24, 1 successors, FD is 156160
        via 10.1.100.2 (156160/128256), FastEthernet0/0
P 10.1.1.0/24, 1 successors, FD is 128256
        via Connected, Loopback1
P 10.1.100.0/24, 1 successors, FD is 28160
        via Connected, FastEthernet0/0
```

You should see all the networks currently advertised by EIGRP on every router. Lab 2-2 explores the output of this command in more detail. For now, verify that each of the loopback networks exist in the EIGRP topology table. Because EIGRP is the only routing protocol running and currently has routes to these networks, issuing **show ip route eigrp** displays the best route to the destination network:

```
R1# show ip route eigrp
     10.0.0.0/24 is subnetted, 4 subnets
D       10.1.3.0 [90/156160] via 10.1.100.3, 00:00:53, FastEthernet0/0
D       10.1.2.0 [90/156160] via 10.1.100.2, 00:00:53, FastEthernet0/0
```

To check whether you have full connectivity, ping the remote loopbacks from each router. If you have successfully pinged all the remote loopbacks, congratulations! You have configured EIGRP to route between these three remote networks.

Step 4: Configuring EIGRP on the Serial Interfaces

Your serial interfaces are still in their default configuration. Address the interface according to the diagram in Figure 2-1, and set the clock rate to 64 Kbps:

```
R1(config)# interface serial 0/0/0
R1(config-if)# ip address 10.1.200.1 255.255.255.0
R1(config-if)# clock rate 64000
R1(config-if)# no shut
!
```

```
R2(config)# interface serial 0/0/0
R2(config-if)# ip address 10.1.200.2 255.255.255.0
R2(config-if)# no shut
```

Notice that even though you have clocked the interface at 64 Kbps, issuing **show interface Serial0/0/0** reveals that the interface still is a full T1 bandwidth of 1544 Kbps:

```
R1# show interfaces serial 0/0/0
Serial0/0/0 is up, line protocol is up
  Hardware is GT96K Serial
  Internet address is 10.1.200.1/24
```

```
     MTU 1500 bytes, BW 1544 Kbit, DLY 20000 usec,
         reliability 255/255, txload 1/255, rxload 1/255
...
```

By default, EIGRP uses up to 50 percent of the bandwidth that your interface reports to the Cisco IOS Software. Suppose there was a significant routing instability in some other part of our EIGRP AS. If EIGRP were to use 50 percent of 1544 Kbps for its own routing information traffic, EIGRP traffic would fully saturate our measly 64-Kbps serial link!

Also, recall that EIGRP makes bandwidth computations using a composite metric in which one of the variables is the bandwidth of the interface. For EIGRP to make an accurate computation, it needs correct information about the bandwidth of your serial link. Therefore, you need to manually configure the bandwidth variable to 64 Kbps. Apply the **bandwidth 64** command to the R1 and R2 serial interfaces as follows:

```
R1:
!
interface Serial0/0/0
 bandwidth 64
!
```

```
R2:
!
interface Serial0/0/0
 bandwidth 64
!
```

Verify that your bandwidth configuration is reflected in the **show interface Serial0/0/0** output:

```
R1# show interfaces serial 0/0/0
Serial0/0/0 is up, line protocol is up
  Hardware is GT96K Serial
  Internet address is 10.1.200.1/24
  MTU 1500 bytes, BW 64 Kbit, DLY 20000 usec,
      reliability 255/255, txload 1/255, rxload 1/255
...
```

```
R2# show interfaces serial 0/0/0
Serial0/0/0 is up, line protocol is up
  Hardware is GT96K Serial
  Internet address is 10.1.200.2/24
  MTU 1500 bytes, BW 64 Kbit, DLY 20000 usec,
      reliability 255/255, txload 1/255, rxload 1/255
...
```

Now, issue the **show ip eigrp neighbors command**, which displays the following neighbor relationship between R1 and R2:

```
R1# show ip eigrp neighbors
IP-EIGRP neighbors for process 1
H   Address                 Interface       Hold Uptime   SRTT   RTO   Q   Seq
                                            (sec)         (ms)         Cnt Num
```

2	10.1.200.2	Se0/0/0	10 00:03:03	24	200	0	53
1	10.1.100.2	Fa0/0	14 09:22:42	269	1614	0	54
0	10.1.100.3	Fa0/0	11 09:22:42	212	1272	0	59

Step 5: Configuring Network Statement Wildcard Masks

On R3, create Loopback 11 with IP address 192.168.100.1/30, and Loopback 15 with IP address 192.168.100.5/30:

```
R3(config)# interface Loopback11
R3(config-if)# ip address 192.168.100.1 255.255.255.252
R3(config-if)# exit
R3(config)# interface Loopback15
R3(config-if)# ip address 192.168.100.5 255.255.255.252
R3(config-if)# exit
```

How can you add the 192.168.100.0/30 network to EIGRP without involving the 192.168.100.4/30 network as well?

_____

_____

_____

In Step 2, you looked at how **network** statements select networks for routing using major network boundaries. EIGRP also provides a way to select networks using wildcard masks. In a wildcard mask, bits that might vary are denoted by 1s in the binary bit values. If you want to route both Loopback 11 and Loopback 15 with EIGRP, you could use a wildcard mask that includes both of their network addresses, such as **network 192.168.100.0 0.0.0.7** or **network 192.168.100.0 0.0.0.255.** However, in this scenario, you only want to select Loopback 11's IP network.

On R3, issue the following commands:

```
R3(config)# router eigrp 1
R3(config-router)# network 192.168.100.0 0.0.0.3
```

Did this solution work? Check it with the **show ip eigrp interfaces** command. Notice that Loopback 11 is involved in EIGRP, and Loopback 15 is not:

```
R3# show ip eigrp interfaces
IP-EIGRP interfaces for process 1
```

Interface	Peers	Xmit Queue Un/Reliable	Mean SRTT	Pacing Time Un/Reliable	Multicast Flow Timer	Pending Routes
Fa0/0	2	0/0	5	0/1	50	0
Lo3	0	0/0	0	0/1	0	0
Lo11	0	0/0	0	0/1	0	0

Which of these two IP networks can you see in the routing table on R1 after EIGRP converges with the new network? Look at the output of **show ip route eigrp** on R1:

```
R1# show ip route eigrp
     10.0.0.0/24 is subnetted, 5 subnets
D       10.1.3.0 [90/156160] via 10.1.100.3, 00:05:59, FastEthernet0/0
D       10.1.2.0 [90/156160] via 10.1.100.2, 00:12:16, FastEthernet0/0
D     192.168.100.0/24 [90/156160] via 10.1.100.3, 00:03:05, FastEthernet0/0
```

Notice that the subnet mask for the 192.168.100.0 network advertised by R3 is 24 bits. This will be examined in much further depth in the next lab. Do you remember the command to allow R3 to advertise the proper subnet mask to its adjacent routers? If so, record it below:

_____

Challenge: Topology Change

You have been reading up about the advantages of different routing protocols in your spare time. You noticed statements claiming that EIGRP converges significantly faster than other routing protocols in a topology where there are multiple paths to the destination network. You are interested in testing this before you bring the network that you are designing online.

Verify that all the neighbor relationships are active and that the routing tables of each router have the original three loopback interfaces of the other routers as described in the initial diagram. Make sure you issue the **debug ip eigrp 1 command** on all routers. You are not going to want to miss this!

You have observed the following output:

```
R2# show ip route eigrp
     10.0.0.0/24 is subnetted, 5 subnets
D       10.1.3.0 [90/156160] via 10.1.100.3, 00:05:22, FastEthernet0/0
D       10.1.1.0 [90/156160] via 10.1.100.1, 00:05:22, FastEthernet0/0
!
```

```
R3# show ip route eigrp
     10.0.0.0/24 is subnetted, 5 subnets
D       10.1.2.0 [90/156160] via 10.1.100.2, 09:25:37, FastEthernet0/0
D       10.1.1.0 [90/156160] via 10.1.100.1, 09:25:37, FastEthernet0/0
D       10.1.200.0 [90/40514560] via 10.1.100.2, 00:03:01, FastEthernet0/0
                   [90/40514560] via 10.1.100.1, 00:03:01, FastEthernet0/0
!
R3# traceroute 10.1.1.1

Type escape sequence to abort.
Tracing the route to 10.1.1.1

  1 10.1.100.1 4 msec *  0 msec
R3#
```

R3 is using R1 as the next hop to get to destination network 10.1.1.0/24 per R3's routing table. However, R3 could potentially get to R1 through R2 via the serial link if the Fast Ethernet port on R1 were shut down.

From R3, issue a **ping** with a high repeat count to destination address 10.1.1.1:

ping 10.1.1.1 repeat 100000

Issued with output for the following steps:

```
R3# ping 10.1.1.1 repeat 100000

Type escape sequence to abort.
Sending 100000, 100-byte ICMP Echos to 10.1.1.1, timeout is 2 seconds:
!!!!!!!!!!!!!!!!!!!!!!!!!!!!!!!!!!!!!!!!!!!!!!!!!!!!!!!!!!!!!!!!!!!!!!!!
!!!!!!!!!!!!!!!!!!!!!!!!!!!!!!!!!!!!!!!!!!!!!!!!!!!!!!!!!!!!!!!!!!!!!!!!
!!!!!!!!!!!!!!!!!!!!!!!!!!!!!!!!!!!!!!!!!!!!!!!!!!!!!!!!!!!!!!!!!!!!!!!!
!!!!!!!!!!!!!!!!!!!!!!!!!!!!!!!!!!!!!!!!!!!!!!!!!!!!!!!!!!!!!!!!!!!!!!!!
!!!!!!!!!!!!!!!!!!!!!!!!!!!!!!!!!!!!!!!!!!!!!!!!!!!!!!!!!!!!!!!!!!!!!!!!
!!!!!!!!!!!!!!!!!!!!!!!!!!!!!!!!!!!!!!!!!!!!!!!!!!!!!!!!!!!!!!!!!!!!!!!!
!!!!!!!!!!!!!!!!!!!!!!!!!!!!!!!!!!!!!!!!!!!!!!!!!!!!!!!!!!!!!!!!!!!!!!!!
!!!!!!!!!!!!!!!!!!!!!!!!!!!!!!!!!!!!!!!!!!!!!!!!!!!!!!!!!!!!!!!!!!!!!!!!
!!!!!!!!!!!!!!!!!!!!!!!!!!!!!!!!!!!!!!!!!!!!!!!!!!!!!!!!!!!!!!!!!!!!!!!!
!!!!!!!!!!!!!!!!!!!!!!!!!!!!!!!!!!!!!!!!!!!!!!!!!!!!!!!!!!!!!!!!!!!!!!!!
!!!!!!!!!!!!!!!!!!!!!!!!!!!!!!!!!!!!!!!!!!!!!!!!!!!!!!!!!!!!!!!!!!!!!!!!
!!!!!!!!!!!!!!!!!!!!!!!!!!!!!!!!!!!!!!!!!!!!!!!!!!!!!!!!!!!!!!!!!!!!!!!!
!!!!!!!!!!!!!!!!!!!!!!!!!!!!!!!!!!!!!!!!!!!!!!!!!!!!!!!!!!!!!!!!!!!!!!!!
!!!!!!!!!!!!!!!!!!!!!!!!!!!!!!!!!!!!!!!!......!!!!!!!!!!!!!!!!!!!!!!!!!!!!

*Nov  5 23:11:28.311: %DUAL-5-NBRCHANGE: IP-EIGRP(0) 1: Neighbor 10.1.100.1
(FastEthernet0/0) is down: holding time
expired!!!!!!!!!!!!!!!!!!!!!!!!!!!!!!!!!!!!!!!!!!!!!!!!!!!!!!!!!!!!!!!!!!!!!!!!!!!!
!!!!!!!!!!!!!!!!!!!!!!!!!!!!!!!!!!!!!!!!!!!!!!!!!!!!!!!!!!!!!!!!!!!!!!!!
!!!!!!!!!!!!!!!!!!!!!!!!!!!!!!!!!!!!!!!!!!!!!!!!!!!!!!!!!!!!!!!!!!!!!!!!
!!!!!!!!!!!!!!!!!!!!!!!!!!!!!!!!!!!!!!!!!!!!!!!!!!!!!!!!!!!!!!!!!!!!!!!!
!!!!!!!!!!!!!!!!!!!!!!!!!!!!!!!!!!!!!!!!!!!!!!!!!!!!!!!!!!!!!!!!!!!!!!!!
!!!!!!!!!!!!!!!!!!!!!!!!!!!!!!!!!!!!!!!!!!!!!!!!!!!!!!!!!!!!!!!!!!!!!!!!
!!!!!!!!!!!!!!!!!!!!!!!!!!!!!!!!!!!!!!!!!!!!!!!!!!!!!!!!!!!!!............!
!!!!!!!!!!!!!!!!!!!!!!!!!!!!!!!!!!!!!!!!!!!!!!!!!!!!!!!!!!!!!!!!!!!!!!!!
!!!!!!!!!!!!!!!!!!!!!!!!!!!!!!!!!!!!!!!!!!!!!!!!!!!!!!!!!!!!!!!!!!!!!!!!
!!!!!!!!!!!!!!!!!!!!!!!!!!!!!!!!!!!!!!!!!!!!!!!!!!!!!!!!!!!!!!!!!!!!!!!!
!!!!!!!!!!!!!!!!!!!!!!!!!!!!!!!!!!!!!!!!!!!!!!!!!!!!!!!!!!!!!!!!!!!!!!!!
!!!!!!!!!!!!!!!!!!!!!!!!!!!!!!!!!!!!!!!!!!!!!!!!!!!!!!!!!!!!!!!!!!!!!!!!
!!!!!!!!!!!!!!!!!!!!!!!!!!!!!!!!!!!!!!!!!!

*Nov  5 23:12:10.147: %DUAL-5-NBRCHANGE: IP-EIGRP(0) 1: Neighbor 10.1.100.1
(FastEthernet0/0) is up: new adjacency!!!!!!!!!!!!!!!!!!!!!!!!!!!!!!!!!!!!!
!!!!!!!!!!!!!!!!!!!!!!!!!!!!!!!!!!!!!!!!!!!!!!!!!!!!!!!!!!!!!!!!!!!!!!!!

(etc)
```

You should see multiple exclamation points flooding the console output from R3. On R1, shut down the FastEthernet0/0 interface:

```
R1(config)# interface FastEthernet0/0
R1(config-if)# shutdown
```

From R3's perspective, how many packets were dropped? Which of the EIGRP timers causes this delay in the route recalculation?

_____

_____

_____

Use the **traceroute** tool to find the new route from R3 to R1:

```
R3# traceroute 10.1.1.1

Type escape sequence to abort.
Tracing the route to 10.1.1.1

  1 10.1.100.2 0 msec 4 msec 0 msec
  2 10.1.200.1 12 msec *  12 msec
```

Start your repeated ping again from R3 and administratively open the FastEthernet0/0 interface on R1 again.

How many packets were dropped when the FastEthernet0/0 interface went up?

_____

If you were using Routing Information Protocol Version 2 (RIPv2) as your routing protocol instead of EIGRP, would fewer packets or more packets be dropped?

_____

_____

_____

_____

Lab 2-2: EIGRP Load Balancing (2.7.2)

The objectives of this lab are as follows:

- Review basic EIGRP configuration

- Explore the EIGRP topology table

- Learn to identify successors, feasible successors, and feasible distances

- Learn to use **debug** commands for EIGRP's topology table

- Configure and verify equal-cost load balancing with EIGRP

- Configure and verify unequal-cost load balancing with EIGRP

Figure 2-2 illustrates the topology that will be used for this lab.

Figure 2-2   Topology Diagram

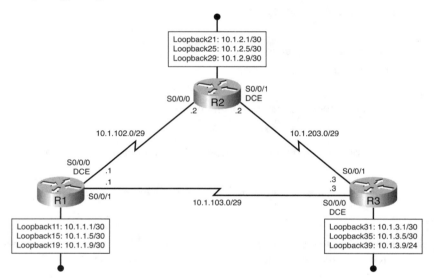

Scenario

As a senior network engineer, you are considering deploying EIGRP in your corporation and want to evaluate its ability to converge quickly in a changing environment. You are also interested in equal-cost and unequal-cost load balancing, because your network is filled with redundant links. These links are not often used by other link-state routing protocols because of high metrics. Because you are interested in testing the EIGRP claims that you have read about, you decide to implement and test on a set of three lab routers before deploying EIGRP throughout your corporate network.

Step 1: Addressing and Serial Configuration

Create three loopback interfaces on each router and address them 10.1.*X*.1/30, 10.1.*X*.5/30, and 10.1.*X*.9/30, where *X* is the number of the router. Use the formation in Table 2-1 or the configurations listed in the section "Initial Configurations" for this lab to complete this step.

Table 2-1   Interface IP Addresses

Router	Interface	IP Address/Mask
R1	Loopback 11	10.1.1.1/30
R1	Loopback 15	10.1.1.5/30
R1	Loopback 19	10.1.1.9/30
R2	Loopback 21	10.1.2.1/30
R2	Loopback 25	10.1.2.5/30
R2	Loopback 29	10.1.2.9/30
R3	Loopback 31	10.1.3.1/30
R3	Loopback 35	10.1.3.5/30
R3	Loopback 39	10.1.3.9/30

```
R1(config)# interface Loopback 11
R1(config-if)# ip address 10.1.1.1 255.255.255.252
R1(config-if)# exit
R1(config)# interface Loopback 15
R1(config-if)# ip address 10.1.1.5 255.255.255.252
R1(config-if)# exit
R1(config)# interface Loopback 19
R1(config-if)# ip address 10.1.1.9 255.255.255.252
R1(config-if)# exit
!
R2(config)# interface Loopback 21
R2(config-if)# ip address 10.1.2.1 255.255.255.252
R2(config-if)# exit
R2(config)# interface Loopback 25
R2(config-if)# ip address 10.1.2.5 255.255.255.252
R2(config-if)# exit
R2(config)# interface Loopback 29
R2(config-if)# ip address 10.1.2.9 255.255.255.252
R2(config-if)# exit
!
R3(config)# interface Loopback 31
R3(config-if)# ip address 10.1.3.1 255.255.255.252
R3(config-if)# exit
R3(config)# interface Loopback 35
R3(config-if)# ip address 10.1.3.5 255.255.255.252
R3(config-if)# exit
R3(config)# interface Loopback 39
R3(config-if)# ip address 10.1.3.9 255.255.255.252
R3(config-if)# exit
```

Address the serial interfaces with the addressing shown in the Figure 2-2. Set the clock rate to 64 Kbps, and manually configure the interface bandwidth to 64 Kbps:

```
R1(config)# interface Serial 0/0/0
R1(config-if)# description R1-->R2
R1(config-if)# clock rate 64000
R1(config-if)# bandwidth 64
R1(config-if)# ip address 10.1.102.1 255.255.255.248
R1(config-if)# no shutdown
R1(config-if)# exit
R1(config)# interface Serial 0/0/1
R1(config-if)# description R1 ->R3
R1(config-if)# bandwidth 64
R1(config-if)# ip address 10.1.103.1 255.255.255.248
R1(config-if)# no shutdown
R1(config-if)# exit
```
```
R2(config)# interface Serial 0/0/0
R2(config-if)# description R2 ->R1
R2(config-if)# bandwidth 64
R2(config-if)# ip address 10.1.102.2 255.255.255.248
R2(config-if)# no shutdown
R2(config-if)# exit
R2(config)# interface Serial 0/0/1
R2(config-if)# description R2 ->R3
R2(config-if)# clock rate 64000
R2(config-if)# bandwidth 64
R2(config-if)# ip address 10.1.203.2 255.255.255.248
R2(config-if)# no shutdown
R2(config-if)# exit
```
```
R3(config)# interface Serial 0/0/0
R3(config-if)# description R3 ->R1
R3(config-if)# clock rate 64000
R3(config-if)# bandwidth 64
R3(config-if)# ip address 10.1.103.3 255.255.255.248
R3(config-if)# no shutdown
R3(config-if)# exit
R3(config)# interface Serial 0/0/1
R3(config-if)# description R3 ->R2
R3(config-if)# bandwidth 64
R3(config-if)# ip address 10.1.203.3 255.255.255.248
R3(config-if)# no shutdown
R3(config-if)# exit
```

Verify connectivity by pinging across each of the local networks connected to each router.

Step 2: EIGRP Configuration

Now set up EIGRP AS 100 using the same commands you used in the first EIGRP lab.

Use the **debug ip eigrp 100** command to watch EIGRP install the routes in the routing table when your routers become adjacent. Step 3 examines what is occurring behind the scenes in greater detail.

For your reference, these are the commands:

```
R1(config)# router eigrp 100
R1(config-router)# network 10.0.0.0
!
```

```
R2(config)# router eigrp 100
R2(config-router)# network 10.0.0.0
!
```

```
R3(config)# router eigrp 100
R3(config-router)# network 10.0.0.0
```

You get **debug** output similar to the following:

```
R1# debug ip eigrp 100

R1# configure terminal

R1(config)# router eigrp 100

R1(config-router)# network 10.0.0.0

R1(config-router)#

*Sep 26 16:16:23.740: %DUAL-5-NBRCHANGE: IP-EIGRP(0) 100: Neighbor 10.1.102.2
(Serial0/0/0) is up: new adjacency

*Sep 26 16:16:23.748: IP-EIGRP(Default-IP-Routing-Table:100): Processing incoming
UPDATE packet

*Sep 26 16:16:25.748: IP-EIGRP(Default-IP-Routing-Table:100): 10.1.102.0/24 - do
advertise out Serial0/0/0

*Sep 26 16:16:25.748: IP-EIGRP(Default-IP-Routing-Table:100): 10.1.103.0/29 - do
advertise out Serial0/0/0

*Sep 26 16:16:25.748: IP-EIGRP(Default-IP-Routing-Table:100): Int 10.1.103.0/29
metric 40512000 - 40000000 512000

*Sep 26 16:16:25.748: IP-EIGRP(Default-IP-Routing-Table:100): 10.1.1.0/30 - do
advertise out Serial0/0/0

*Sep 26 16:16:25.748: IP-EIGRP(Default-IP-Routing-Table:100): Int 10.1.1.0/30 metric
128256 - 256 128000

*Sep 26 16:16:25.748: IP-EIGRP(Default-IP-Routing-Table:100): 10.1.1.4/30 - do
advertise out Serial0/0/0

*Sep 26 16:16:25.748: IP-EIGRP(Default-IP-Routing-Table:100): Int 10.1.1.4/30 metric
128256 - 256 128000

*Sep 26 16:16:25.748: IP-EIGRP(Default-IP-Routing-Table:100): 10.1.1.8/30 - do
advertise out Serial0/0/0

*Sep 26 16:16:25.748: IP-EIGRP(Default-IP-Routing-Table:100): Int 10.1.1.8/30 metric
128256 - 256 128000

*Sep 26 16:16:25.800: IP-EIGRP(Default-IP-Routing-Table:100): Processing incoming
UPDATE packet

*Sep 26 16:16:25.800: IP-EIGRP(Default-IP-Routing-Table:100): Int 10.1.103.0/29 M
41024000 - 40000000 1024000 SM 40512000 - 40000000 512000

*Sep 26 16:16:25.800: IP-EIGRP(Default-IP-Routing-Table:100): 10.1.103.0/29 routing
table not updated thru 10.1.102.2
```

```
*Sep 26 16:16:25.800: IP-EIGRP(Default-IP-Routing-Table:100): Int 10.1.2.0/30 M
40640000 - 40000000 640000 SM 128256 - 256 128000

*Sep 26 16:16:25.800: IP-EIGRP(Default-IP-Routing-Table:100): route installed for
10.1.2.0  ()

*Sep 26 16:16:25.800: IP-EIGRP(Default-IP-Routing-Table:100): Int 10.1.2.4/30 M
40640000 - 40000000 640000 SM 128256 - 256 128000

*Sep 26 16:16:25.800: IP-EIGRP(Default-IP-Routing-Table:100): route installed for
10.1.2.4  ()

*Sep 26 16:16:25.800: IP-EIGRP(Default-IP-Routing-Table:100): Int 10.1.2.8/30 M
40640000 - 40000000 640000 SM 128256 - 256 128000

*Sep 26 16:16:25.800: IP-EIGRP(Default-IP-Routing-Table:100): route installed for
10.1.2.8  ()

*Sep 26 16:16:25.804: IP-EIGRP(Default-IP-Routing-Table:100): 10.1.102.0/24 - do
advertise out Serial0/0/0

*Sep 26 16:16:25.804: IP-EIGRP(Default-IP-Routing-Table:100): 10.1.103.0/29 - do
advertise out Serial0/0/0

*Sep 26 16:16:25.804: IP-EIGRP(Default-IP-Routing-Table:100): Int 10.1.103.0/29 met-
ric 40512000 - 40000000 512000

*Sep 26 16:16:25.804: IP-EIGRP(Default-IP-Routing-Table:100): 10.1.1.0/30 - do adver-
tise out Serial0/0/0

*Sep 26 16:16:25.804: IP-EIGRP(Default-IP-Routing-Table:100): Int 10.1.1.0/30 metric
128256 - 256 128000

*Sep 26 16:16:25.804: IP-EIGRP(Default-IP-Routing-Table:100): 10.1.1.4/30 - do adver-
tise out Serial0/0/0

*Sep 26 16:16:25.804: IP-EIGRP(Default-IP-Routing-Table:100): Int 10.1.1.4/30 metric
128256 - 256 128000

*Sep 26 16:16:25.804: IP-EIGRP(Default-IP-Routing-Table:100): 10.1.1.8/30 - do adver-
tise out Serial0/0/0

*Sep 26 16:16:25.804: IP-EIGRP(Default-IP-Routing-Table:100): Int 10.1.1.8/30 metric
128256 - 256 128000

*Sep 26 16:16:25.848: IP-EIGRP(Default-IP-Routing-Table:100): Processing incoming
UPDATE packet

*Sep 26 16:16:25.848: IP-EIGRP(Default-IP-Routing-Table:100): Int 10.1.1.0/30 M
4294967295 - 40000000 4294967295 SM 4294967295 - 40000000 4294967295

*Sep 26 16:16:25.848: IP-EIGRP(Default-IP-Routing-Table:100): Int 10.1.1.4/30 M
4294967295 - 40000000 4294967295 SM 4294967295 - 40000000 4294967295

*Sep 26 16:16:25.848: IP-EIGRP(Default-IP-Routing-Table:100): Int 10.1.1.8/30 M
4294967295 - 40000000 4294967295 SM 4294967295 - 40000000 4294967295
```

Essentially, EIGRP's DUAL state machine has just computed the topology table for these routes and installed them in the routing table. Leave the **debug** command on for the duration of the lab, because it is used in Step 5.

Check to see that these routes exist in the routing table with the **show ip route** command:

```
R1#show ip route
Codes: C - connected, S - static, R - RIP, M - mobile, B - BGP
       D - EIGRP, EX - EIGRP external, O - OSPF, IA - OSPF inter area
       N1 - OSPF NSSA external type 1, N2 - OSPF NSSA external type 2
       E1 - OSPF external type 1, E2 - OSPF external type 2
       i - IS-IS, su - IS-IS summary, L1 - IS-IS level-1, L2 - IS-IS level-2
       ia - IS-IS inter area, * - candidate default, U - per-user static route
```

```
        o - ODR, P - periodic downloaded static route

Gateway of last resort is not set

     10.0.0.0/8 is variably subnetted, 12 subnets, 2 masks
D        10.1.3.8/30 [90/40640000] via 10.1.103.3, 00:00:16, Serial0/0/1
D        10.1.2.8/30 [90/40640000] via 10.1.102.2, 00:00:16, Serial0/0/0
C        10.1.1.8/30 is directly connected, Loopback19
D        10.1.3.0/30 [90/40640000] via 10.1.103.3, 00:00:16, Serial0/0/1
D        10.1.2.0/30 [90/40640000] via 10.1.102.2, 00:00:16, Serial0/0/0
C        10.1.1.0/30 is directly connected, Loopback11
D        10.1.3.4/30 [90/40640000] via 10.1.103.3, 00:00:18, Serial0/0/1
D        10.1.2.4/30 [90/40640000] via 10.1.102.2, 00:00:18, Serial0/0/0
C        10.1.1.4/30 is directly connected, Loopback15
C        10.1.103.0/29 is directly connected, Serial0/0/1
C        10.1.102.0/29 is directly connected, Serial0/0/0
D        10.1.203.0/29 [90/41024000] via 10.1.103.3, 00:00:18, Serial0/0/1
                      [90/41024000] via 10.1.102.2, 00:00:18, Serial0/0/0
```

Once you have full adjacency between the routers, ping all the remote loopbacks to ensure full connectivity, or use the following Toolkit Command Language (TCL) script. If you have never used TCL scripts before or need a refresher, see the TCL lab in the routing module. (You can download the TCL Script at www.ciscopress.com/title/1587132133 under the More Information section on the page):

```
foreach address {
10.1.1.1
10.1.1.5
10.1.1.9
10.1.2.1
10.1.2.5
10.1.2.9
10.1.3.1
10.1.3.5
10.1.3.9
10.1.102.1
10.1.102.2
10.1.103.1
10.1.103.3
10.1.203.2
10.1.203.3
} { ping $address }
```

You get Internet Control Message Protocol (ICMP) echo replies for every address pinged. Check the TCL script output against the output in the section "Initial Configurations" for this lab. Make sure you run the TCL script on each router and get the output listed in the section "TCL Script Output" for this lab before continuing with the lab.

Note   While unlikely, it is possible to ping all the loopback interfaces without having full EIGRP adjacency between all routers. Verify that all the EIGRP neighbor relationships are active with the **show ip eigrp neighbors** command:

R1# `show ip eigrp neighbors`

IP-EIGRP neighbors for process 100

H	Address	Interface	Hold Uptime (sec)	SRTT (ms)	RTO	Q Cnt	Seq Num
0	10.1.102.2	Se0/0/0	10 00:00:22	1	5000	2	0
1	10.1.103.3	Se0/0/1	13 00:04:36	24	2280	0	14

R2# `show ip eigrp neighbors`

IP-EIGRP neighbors for process 100

H	Address	Interface	Hold Uptime (sec)	SRTT (ms)	RTO	Q Cnt	Seq Num
0	10.1.102.1	Se0/0/0	14 00:00:37	1	5000	1	22
1	10.1.203.3	Se0/0/1	11 00:03:29	143	2280	0	15

R3# `show ip eigrp neighbors`

IP-EIGRP neighbors for process 100

H	Address	Interface	Hold Uptime (sec)	SRTT (ms)	RTO	Q Cnt	Seq Num
1	10.1.203.2	Se0/0/1	14 00:03:43	241	2280	0	18
0	10.1.103.1	Se0/0/0	14 00:05:05	38	2280	0	17

Step 3: EIGRP Topology Table

EIGRP builds a topology table where it keeps all successor routes.

The course reading covered the vocabulary for EIGRP routes in the topology table. Can you identify the feasible distance of route 10.1.1.0/30 in R3's topology table in the following output?

R3# `show ip eigrp topology`

```
IP-EIGRP Topology Table for AS(100)/ID(10.1.3.9)


Codes: P - Passive, A - Active, U - Update, Q - Query, R - Reply,
       r - reply Status, s - sia Status


P 10.1.3.8/30, 1 successors, FD is 128256
        via Connected, Loopback31
P 10.1.2.8/30, 1 successors, FD is 40640000
        via 10.1.203.2 (40640000/128256), Serial0/0/1
P 10.1.1.8/30, 1 successors, FD is 40640000
        via 10.1.103.1 (40640000/128256), Serial0/0/0
P 10.1.2.0/30, 1 successors, FD is 40640000
        via 10.1.203.2 (40640000/128256), Serial0/0/1
P 10.1.1.0/30, 1 successors, FD is 40640000
```

```
              via 10.1.103.1 (40640000/128256), Serial0/0/0
P 10.1.2.4/30, 1 successors, FD is 40640000
              via 10.1.203.2 (40640000/128256), Serial0/0/1
P 10.1.1.4/30, 1 successors, FD is 40640000
              via 10.1.103.1 (40640000/128256), Serial0/0/0
P 10.1.103.0/29, 1 successors, FD is 40512000
          via Connected, Serial0/0/0
P 10.1.102.0/29, 2 successors, FD is 41024000
          via 10.1.103.1 (41024000/40512000), Serial0/0/0
          via 10.1.203.2 (41024000/40512000), Serial0/0/1
P 10.1.203.0/29, 1 successors, FD is 40512000
          via Connected, Serial0/0/1
```

The most important thing is the two successor routes in the passive state on R3. R1 and R2 are both advertising their connected subnet of 10.1.102.0/30. Since both routes have the same reported distance of 40512000, both are installed in the topology table.

This distance of 40512000 reflects the composite metric of more granular properties about the path to the destination network. Can you see the metrics before the composite metric is computed?

Use the **show ip eigrp topology 10.1.102.0/29** command to view the information EIGRP has received about the route from R1 and R2:

```
R3# show ip eigrp topology 10.1.102.0/29
IP-EIGRP (AS 100): Topology entry for 10.1.102.0/29
  State is Passive, Query origin flag is 1, 2 Successor(s), FD is 41024000
  Routing Descriptor Blocks:
  10.1.103.1 (Serial0/0/0), from 10.1.103.1, Send flag is 0x0
      Composite metric is (41024000/40512000), Route is Internal
      Vector metric:
        Minimum bandwidth is 64 Kbit
        Total delay is 40000 microseconds
        Reliability is 255/255
        Load is 1/255
        Minimum MTU is 1500
        Hop count is 1
  10.1.203.2 (Serial0/0/1), from 10.1.203.2, Send flag is 0x0
      Composite metric is (41024000/40512000), Route is Internal
      Vector metric:
        Minimum bandwidth is 64 Kbit
        Total delay is 40000 microseconds
        Reliability is 255/255
```

```
        Load is 1/255
        Minimum MTU is 1500
        Hop count is 1
```

Several things to remember about the output of this command regarding EIGRP are as follows:

- Bandwidth metric represents minimum bandwidth over the path to the destination network.

- Delay metric represents total delay over the path.

- MTU represents the minimum maximum transmission unit over the path.

- The hop count to a destination network is visible, which may prove useful. If you do not have full knowledge of your network, you can still check how many Layer 3 devices are between your router and the destination network.

Step 4: Equal-Cost Load Balancing

EIGRP produces equal-cost load balancing to the destination network 10.1.102.0/29 from R1. Two equal-cost paths are available to this destination per the topology table output above.

Recent Cisco IOS releases have Cisco Express Forwarding (CEF) enabled by default. CEF allows fast switching of packets based on a per-destination switching architecture. The first packet in a flow is routed, and the rest are switched. This is the preferred behavior in most circumstances, because it allows load balancing in fast-switching architectures. However, if we were to ping the destination network, we would not see load balancing occurring on a packet level because CEF treats the entire series of pings as one flow.

CEF on R3 overrides the per-packet balancing behavior of process switching with per-destination load balancing. To see the full effect of EIGRP equal-cost load balancing, disable CEF so that all IP packets are processed individually and not fast-switched by CEF:

```
R3(config)# no ip cef
```

Note Typically, you would not disable CEF in a production network. It is done here only to illustrate load balancing.

Now, verify load balancing with the **debug ip packet** command, and then ping 10.1.102.1. You see output similar to the following:

```
R3# debug ip packet
IP packet debugging is on
R3# ping 10.1.102.1

Type escape sequence to abort.
Sending 5, 100-byte ICMP Echos to 10.1.102.1, timeout is 2 seconds:
!!!!!
Success rate is 100 percent (5/5), round-trip min/avg/max = 1/3/4 ms
R3#
RIB
*Sep 26 22:07:41.943: IP: s=10.1.103.3 (local), d=10.1.102.1 (Serial0/0/0), len 100,
sending
*Sep 26 22:07:41.947: IP: tableid=0, s=10.1.102.1 (Serial0/0/0), d=10.1.103.3
(Serial0/0/0), routed via RIB
```

```
*Sep 26 22:07:41.947: IP: s=10.1.102.1 (Serial0/0/0), d=10.1.103.3 (Serial0/0/0), len
100, rcvd 3

*Sep 26 22:07:41.947: IP: tableid=0, s=10.1.203.3 (local), d=10.1.102.1
(Serial0/0/1), routed via RIB

*Sep 26 22:07:41.947: IP: s=10.1.203.3 (local), d=10.1.102.1 (Serial0/0/1), len 100,
sending

*Sep 26 22:07:41.947: IP: tableid=0, s=10.1.102.1 (Serial0/0/1), d=10.1.203.3
(Serial0/0/1), routed via RIB

*Sep 26 22:07:41.951: IP: s=10.1.102.1 (Serial0/0/1), d=10.1.203.3 (Serial0/0/1), len
100, rcvd 3

*Sep 26 22:07:41.951: IP: tableid=0, s=10.1.103.3 (local), d=10.1.102.1
(Serial0/0/0), routed via RIB

*Sep 26 22:07:41.951: IP: s=10.1.103.3 (local), d=10.1.102.1 (Serial0/0/0), len 100,
sending

*Sep 26 22:07:41.951: IP: tableid=0, s=10.1.102.1 (Serial0/0/0), d=10.1.103.3
(Serial0/0/0), routed via RIB

*Sep 26 22:07:41.951: IP: s=10.1.102.1 (Serial0/0/0), d=10.1.103.3 (Serial0/0/0), len
100, rcvd 3

*Sep 26 22:07:41.951: IP: tableid=0, s=10.1.203.3 (local), d=10.1.102.1
(Serial0/0/1), routed via RIB

*Sep 26 22:07:41.951: IP: s=10.1.203.3 (local), d=10.1.102.1 (Serial0/0/1), len 100,
sending

*Sep 26 22:07:41.955: IP: tableid=0, s=10.1.102.1 (Serial0/0/1), d=10.1.203.3
(Serial0/0/1), routed via RIB

*Sep 26 22:07:41.955: IP: s=10.1.102.1 (Serial0/0/1), d=10.1.203.3 (Serial0/0/1), len
100, rcvd 3

*Sep 26 22:07:41.955: IP: tableid=0, s=10.1.103.3 (local), d=10.1.102.1
(Serial0/0/0), routed via RIB

*Sep 26 22:07:41.955: IP: s=10.1.103.3 (local), d=10.1.102.1 (Serial0/0/0), len 100,
sending

*Sep 26 22:07:41.959: IP: tableid=0, s=10.1.102.1 (Serial0/0/0), d=10.1.103.3
(Serial0/0/0), routed via RIB

*Sep 26 22:07:41.959: IP: s=10.1.102.1 (Serial0/0/0), d=10.1.103.3 (Serial0/0/0), len
100, rcvd 3
```

In the preceding output, notice that EIGRP load balances between Serial0/0/0 and Serial0/0/1. This behavior is part of EIGRP. It can help utilize underused links in a network, especially during periods of congestion.

Step 5: Alternate EIGRP Paths Not in the Topology Table

Perhaps you expected to see more paths to the R1 and R2 loopback networks on in R3's topology table.

Why aren't these routes shown in the topology table?

_____

_____

_____

_____

_____

_____

What is the advertised distance of those routes from R1 and R2?

_____

_____

_____

_____

_____

Issue the **show ip eigrp topology all-links** command to see all routes that R3 has learned through EIGRP. This command shows you all entries EIGRP holds on this router for networks in the topology, including the serial number of each destination network, which uniquely identifies a destination network in EIGRP:

```
R3# show ip eigrp topology all-links
IP-EIGRP Topology Table for AS(100)/ID(10.1.3.9)


Codes: P - Passive, A - Active, U - Update, Q - Query, R - Reply,
       r - reply Status, s - sia Status


P 10.1.3.8/30, 1 successors, FD is 128256, serno 3
        via Connected, Loopback31
P 10.1.2.8/30, 1 successors, FD is 40640000, serno 24
        via 10.1.203.2 (40640000/128256), Serial0/0/1
        via 10.1.103.1 (41152000/40640000), Serial0/0/0
P 10.1.1.8/30, 1 successors, FD is 40640000, serno 17
        via 10.1.103.1 (40640000/128256), Serial0/0/0
        via 10.1.203.2 (41152000/40640000), Serial0/0/1
P 10.1.2.0/30, 1 successors, FD is 40640000, serno 22
        via 10.1.203.2 (40640000/128256), Serial0/0/1
        via 10.1.103.1 (41152000/40640000), Serial0/0/0
P 10.1.1.0/30, 1 successors, FD is 40640000, serno 15
        via 10.1.103.1 (40640000/128256), Serial0/0/0
        via 10.1.203.2 (41152000/40640000), Serial0/0/1
P 10.1.2.4/30, 1 successors, FD is 40640000, serno 23
        via 10.1.203.2 (40640000/128256), Serial0/0/1
        via 10.1.103.1 (41152000/40640000), Serial0/0/0
P 10.1.1.4/30, 1 successors, FD is 40640000, serno 16
        via 10.1.103.1 (40640000/128256), Serial0/0/0
        via 10.1.203.2 (41152000/40640000), Serial0/0/1
P 10.1.103.0/29, 1 successors, FD is 40512000, serno 13
        via Connected, Serial0/0/0
P 10.1.102.0/29, 2 successors, FD is 41024000, serno 42
        via 10.1.103.1 (41024000/40512000), Serial0/0/0
        via 10.1.203.2 (41024000/40512000), Serial0/0/1
P 10.1.203.0/29, 1 successors, FD is 40512000, serno 12
        via Connected, Serial0/0/1
```

Use the **show ip eigrp topology 10.1.2.0/30** command to see the granular view of the alternate paths to 10.1.2.0, including ones with a higher reported distance than the feasible distance:

```
R3# show ip eigrp topology 10.1.2.0/30
IP-EIGRP (AS 100): Topology entry for 10.1.2.0/30
  State is Passive, Query origin flag is 1, 1 Successor(s), FD is 40640000
  Routing Descriptor Blocks:
  10.1.203.2 (Serial0/0/1), from 10.1.203.2, Send flag is 0x0
      Composite metric is (40640000/128256), Route is Internal
      Vector metric:
        Minimum bandwidth is 64 Kbit
        Total delay is 25000 microseconds
        Reliability is 255/255
        Load is 1/255
        Minimum MTU is 1500
        Hop count is 1
  10.1.103.1 (Serial0/0/0), from 10.1.103.1, Send flag is 0x0
      Composite metric is (41152000/40640000), Route is Internal
      Vector metric:
        Minimum bandwidth is 64 Kbit
        Total delay is 45000 microseconds
        Reliability is 255/255
        Load is 1/255
        Minimum MTU is 1500
        Hop count is 2
```

Why is the route through R1 not in the topology table?

_____

_____

_____

_____

What is its advertised distance?

_____

What is its feasible distance?

_____

If R2's Serial0/0/1 interface were shut down, would EIGRP route through R1 to get to 10.1.2.0/30? Would the switch be immediate?

_____

_____

_____

_____

_____

Record your answer, then experiment with the following method.

Start a ping with a high repeat count on R3 to 10.1.102.1:

R3# **ping 10.1.1.1 repeat 100000**

Then enter interface configuration mode on R1 and shut down port Serial0/0/1, which is the direct link from R1 to R3:

R1(config)# **interface serial 0/0/1**

R1(config-if)# **shutdown**

After the adjacency has gone done between R1 and R3, you can stop the ping using Ctrl+ ⌘.

What output did you observe?

_____

_____

_____

How many packets were dropped? Does this match your answer from before we tested this?

_____

Issue the **no shutdown** command on R1's Serial0/0/1 interface before continuing to the next section.

Step 6: Unequal-Cost Load Balancing

Look again at the composite metrics advertised by EIGRP with **show ip eigrp topology 10.1.2.0/30** as shown in Step 4:

R3# **show ip eigrp topology 10.1.2.0/30**

IP-EIGRP (AS 100): Topology entry for 10.1.2.0/30

  State is Passive, Query origin flag is 1, 1 Successor(s), FD is 40640000

  Routing Descriptor Blocks:

  10.1.203.2 (Serial0/0/1), from 10.1.203.2, Send flag is 0x0

     Composite metric is (40640000/128256), Route is Internal

    Vector metric:

      Minimum bandwidth is 64 Kbit

      Total delay is 25000 microseconds

      Reliability is 255/255

      Load is 1/255

```
        Minimum MTU is 1500
        Hop count is 1
    10.1.103.1 (Serial0/0/0), from 10.1.103.1, Send flag is 0x0
        Composite metric is (41152000/40640000), Route is Internal
        Vector metric:
          Minimum bandwidth is 64 Kbit
          Total delay is 45000 microseconds
          Reliability is 255/255
          Load is 1/255
          Minimum MTU is 1500
          Hop count is 2
```

The reported distance for a loopback network is higher than the feasible distance, so DUAL does not consider it a successor route.

To show unequal-cost load balancing in your internetwork, you need to upgrade the path to the destination network through R1 to have a higher bandwidth. Change the **clock rate** on both of the serial interfaces connected to R1 to 128 Kbps and use the **bandwidth** command to reflect the same:

```
R1(config)# interface serial 0/0/0
R1(config-if)# bandwidth 128
R1(config-if)# clock rate 128000
R1(config-if)# interface serial 0/0/1
R1(config-if)# bandwidth 128
!
```
```
R2(config)# interface serial 0/0/0
R2(config-if)# bandwidth 128
!
```
```
R3(config)# interface serial 0/0/0
R3(config-if)# clock rate 128000
R3(config-if)# bandwidth 128
```

Issue the **show ip eigrp topology 10.1.2.0/30** command again on R3 to see what has changed:

```
R3# show ip eigrp topology 10.1.2.0/30
IP-EIGRP (AS 1): Topology entry for 10.1.2.0/30
  State is Passive, Query origin flag is 1, 1 Successor(s), FD is 2297856
  Routing Descriptor Blocks:
  10.1.103.1 (Serial0/0/0), from 10.1.103.1, Send flag is 0x0
      Composite metric is (20642560/156160), Route is Internal
      Vector metric:
        Minimum bandwidth is 128 Kbit
        Total delay is 25100 microseconds
```

```
        Reliability is 255/255
        Load is 1/255
        Minimum MTU is 1500
        Hop count is 2
  10.1.203.2 (Serial0/0/1), from 10.1.203.2, Send flag is 0x0
      Composite metric is (40640000/128256), Route is Internal
      Vector metric:
        Minimum bandwidth is 64 Kbit
        Total delay is 25000 microseconds
        Reliability is 255/255
        Load is 1/255
        Minimum MTU is 1500
        Hop count is 1
```

After manipulating the bandwidth parameter, R3's preferred path to R2's loopback interfaces is now through R1! However, your objective is accomplished in that the paths are now significantly nearer in terms of composite metric.

For a before-and-after look of the load-balancing, use the **show ip route** command:

```
R3# show ip route eigrp
     10.0.0.0/8 is variably subnetted, 13 subnets, 2 masks
D       10.1.2.8/30 [90/20642560] via 10.1.103.1, 00:01:26, Serial0/0/0
D       10.1.1.8/30 [90/20640000] via 10.1.103.1, 00:01:26, Serial0/0/0
D       10.1.2.0/30 [90/20642560] via 10.1.103.1, 00:01:26, Serial0/0/0
D       10.1.1.0/30 [90/20640000] via 10.1.103.1, 00:01:26, Serial0/0/0
D       10.1.2.4/30 [90/20642560] via 10.1.103.1, 00:01:26, Serial0/0/0
D       10.1.1.4/30 [90/20640000] via 10.1.103.1, 00:01:26, Serial0/0/0
D       10.1.102.0/29 [90/21024000] via 10.1.103.1, 00:01:26, Serial0/0/0
D       10.1.200.0/29 [90/20514560] via 10.1.103.1, 00:01:26, Serial0/0/0
```

First, issue the **debug ip eigrp 100** command on R3 to show route events changing in real time. Then, under EIGRP's router configuration on R3, issue the **variance 2** command, which allows unequal-cost load balancing bounded by a maximum distance of $(2) \times$ (FD), where FD represents the feasible distance for each route in the routing table:

```
R3# debug ip eigrp 100
IP-EIGRP Route Events debugging is on
R3# configure terminal
Enter configuration commands, one per line.  End with CNTL/Z.
R3(config)# router eigrp 100
R3(config-router)# variance 2
R3(config-router)#

*Sep 26 23:52:35.875: IP-EIGRP(Default-IP-Routing-Table:100): 10.1.3.8/30 routing
table not updated thru 10.1.203.2

*Sep 26 23:52:35.875: IP-EIGRP(Default-IP-Routing-Table:100): route installed for
10.1.2.8  ()
```

```
*Sep 26 23:52:35.875: IP-EIGRP(Default-IP-Routing-Table:100): route installed for
10.1.2.8  ()

*Sep 26 23:52:35.875: IP-EIGRP(Default-IP-Routing-Table:100): route installed for
10.1.1.8  ()

*Sep 26 23:52:35.875: IP-EIGRP(Default-IP-Routing-Table:100): route installed for
10.1.1.8  ()

*Sep 26 23:52:35.875: IP-EIGRP(Default-IP-Routing-Table:100): 10.1.3.0/30 routing
table not updated thru 10.1.203.2

*Sep 26 23:52:35.875: IP-EIGRP(Default-IP-Routing-Table:100): route installed for
10.1.2.0  ()

*Sep 26 23:52:35.879: IP-EIGRP(Default-IP-Routing-Table:100): route installed for
10.1.2.0  ()

*Sep 26 23:52:35.879: IP-EIGRP(Default-IP-Routing-Table:100): route installed for
10.1.1.0  ()

*Sep 26 23:52:35.879: IP-EIGRP(Default-IP-Routing-Table:100): route installed for
10.1.1.0  ()

*Sep 26 23:52:35.879: IP-EIGRP(Default-IP-Routing-Table:100): 10.1.3.4/30 routing
table not updated thru 10.1.203.2

*Sep 26 23:52:35.879: IP-EIGRP(Default-IP-Routing-Table:100): route installed for
10.1.2.4  ()

*Sep 26 23:52:35.879: IP-EIGRP(Default-IP-Routing-Table:100): route installed for
10.1.2.4  ()

*Sep 26 23:52:35.879: IP-EIGRP(Default-IP-Routing-Table:100): route installed for
10.1.1.4  ()

*Sep 26 23:52:35.879: IP-EIGRP(Default-IP-Routing-Table:100): route installed for
10.1.1.4  ()

*Sep 26 23:52:35.879: IP-EIGRP(Default-IP-Routing-Table:100): 10.1.103.0/29 routing
table not updated thru 10.1.203.2

*Sep 26 23:52:35.879: IP-EIGRP(Default-IP-Routing-Table:100): route installed for
10.1.102.0  ()

*Sep 26 23:52:35.879: IP-EIGRP(Default-IP-Routing-Table:100): route installed for
10.1.102.0  ()

*Sep 26 23:52:35.879: IP-EIGRP(Default-IP-Routing-Table:100): 10.1.203.0/29 routing
table not updated thru 10.1.103.1

*Sep 26 23:52:35.879: IP-EIGRP(Default-IP-Routing-Table:100): route installed for
10.1.200.0  ()

*Sep 26 23:52:35.879: IP-EIGRP(Default-IP-Routing-Table:100): route installed for
10.1.200.0  ()
```

Now, look at the routing table to see how things have changed:

```
R3# show ip route
Codes: C - connected, S - static, R - RIP, M - mobile, B - BGP
       D - EIGRP, EX - EIGRP external, O - OSPF, IA - OSPF inter area
       N1 - OSPF NSSA external type 1, N2 - OSPF NSSA external type 2
       E1 - OSPF external type 1, E2 - OSPF external type 2
       i - IS-IS, su - IS-IS summary, L1 - IS-IS level-1, L2 - IS-IS level-2
       ia - IS-IS inter area, * - candidate default, U - per-user static route
       o - ODR, P - periodic downloaded static route


Gateway of last resort is not set
```

```
        10.0.0.0/8 is variably subnetted, 13 subnets, 2 masks
C       10.1.3.8/30 is directly connected, Loopback39
D       10.1.2.8/30 [90/40640000] via 10.1.203.2, 00:00:12, Serial0/0/1
                    [90/20642560] via 10.1.103.1, 00:00:12, Serial0/0/0
D       10.1.1.8/30 [90/40642560] via 10.1.203.2, 00:00:12, Serial0/0/1
                    [90/20640000] via 10.1.103.1, 00:00:12, Serial0/0/0
C       10.1.3.0/30 is directly connected, Loopback31
D       10.1.2.0/30 [90/40640000] via 10.1.203.2, 00:00:13, Serial0/0/1
                    [90/20642560] via 10.1.103.1, 00:00:13, Serial0/0/0
D       10.1.1.0/30 [90/40642560] via 10.1.203.2, 00:00:13, Serial0/0/1
                    [90/20640000] via 10.1.103.1, 00:00:13, Serial0/0/0
C       10.1.3.4/30 is directly connected, Loopback35
D       10.1.2.4/30 [90/40640000] via 10.1.203.2, 00:00:13, Serial0/0/1
                    [90/20642560] via 10.1.103.1, 00:00:13, Serial0/0/0
D       10.1.1.4/30 [90/40642560] via 10.1.203.2, 00:00:14, Serial0/0/1
                    [90/20640000] via 10.1.103.1, 00:00:14, Serial0/0/0
C       10.1.103.0/29 is directly connected, Serial0/0/0
D       10.1.102.0/29 [90/41024000] via 10.1.203.2, 00:00:14, Serial0/0/1
                      [90/21024000] via 10.1.103.1, 00:00:14, Serial0/0/0
C       10.1.203.0/29 is directly connected, Serial0/0/1
D       10.1.200.0/29 [90/40514560] via 10.1.203.2, 00:00:14, Serial0/0/1
                      [90/20514560] via 10.1.103.1, 00:00:14, Serial0/0/0
```

These unequal-cost routes also show up in the EIGRP topology table, even though they are not considered successor routes (their reported distance is not less than the feasible distance). Check this with the output of the **show ip eigrp topology** command:

```
R3# show ip eigrp topology
IP-EIGRP Topology Table for AS(100)/ID(10.1.3.9)

Codes: P - Passive, A - Active, U - Update, Q - Query, R - Reply,
       r - reply Status, s - sia Status

P 10.1.3.8/30, 1 successors, FD is 128256
        via Connected, Loopback39
P 10.1.2.8/30, 1 successors, FD is 20642560
        via 10.1.103.1 (20642560/156160), Serial0/0/0
        via 10.1.203.2 (40640000/128256), Serial0/0/1
P 10.1.1.8/30, 1 successors, FD is 20640000
        via 10.1.103.1 (20640000/128256), Serial0/0/0
        via 10.1.203.2 (40642560/156160), Serial0/0/1
P 10.1.3.0/30, 1 successors, FD is 128256
        via Connected, Loopback31
```

```
P 10.1.2.0/30, 1 successors, FD is 20642560
         via 10.1.103.1 (20642560/156160), Serial0/0/0
         via 10.1.203.2 (40640000/128256), Serial0/0/1
P 10.1.1.0/30, 1 successors, FD is 20640000
         via 10.1.103.1 (20640000/128256), Serial0/0/0
         via 10.1.203.2 (40642560/156160), Serial0/0/1
P 10.1.3.4/30, 1 successors, FD is 128256
         via Connected, Loopback35
P 10.1.2.4/30, 1 successors, FD is 20642560
         via 10.1.103.1 (20642560/156160), Serial0/0/0
         via 10.1.203.2 (40640000/128256), Serial0/0/1
P 10.1.1.4/30, 1 successors, FD is 20640000
         via 10.1.103.1 (20640000/128256), Serial0/0/0
         via 10.1.203.2 (40642560/156160), Serial0/0/1
P 10.1.103.0/29, 1 successors, FD is 20512000
         via Connected, Serial0/0/0
P 10.1.102.0/29, 1 successors, FD is 21024000
         via 10.1.103.1 (21024000/20512000), Serial0/0/0
         via 10.1.203.2 (41024000/20512000), Serial0/0/1
P 10.1.203.0/29, 1 successors, FD is 40512000
         via Connected, Serial0/0/1
P 10.1.200.0/29, 1 successors, FD is 20514560
         via 10.1.103.1 (20514560/28160), Serial0/0/0
         via 10.1.203.2 (40514560/28160), Serial0/0/1
R3#
```

Load balancing over serial links occurs in blocks of packets, the number of which are recorded in the routing table's detailed routing information. Use the **show ip route 10.1.2.0** command to get a detailed view of how traffic sharing occurs:

```
R3# show ip route 10.1.2.0
Routing entry for 10.1.2.0/30
  Known via "eigrp 100", distance 90, metric 20642560, type internal
  Redistributing via eigrp 100
  Last update from 10.1.203.2 on Serial0/0/1, 00:14:23 ago
  Routing Descriptor Blocks:
    10.1.203.2, from 10.1.203.2, 00:14:23 ago, via Serial0/0/1
      Route metric is 40640000, traffic share count is 61
      Total delay is 25000 microseconds, minimum bandwidth is 64 Kbit
      Reliability 255/255, minimum MTU 1500 bytes
      Loading 1/255, Hops 1
  * 10.1.103.1, from 10.1.103.1, 00:14:23 ago, via Serial0/0/0
      Route metric is 20642560, traffic share count is 120
      Total delay is 25100 microseconds, minimum bandwidth is 128 Kbit
      Reliability 255/255, minimum MTU 1500 bytes
      Loading 1/255, Hops 2
```

Finally, check the actual load balancing using the **debug ip packet** command. Ping from R3 to 10.1.2.1 with a high enough repeat count to view the load balancing over both paths. In the case of the preceding **show ip route 10.1.2.0** output on R3, the traffic share is 61 packets routed to R2 to every 120 packets routed to R1. To filter the **debug** output to make it more useful, use the following extended access list:

```
R3(config)# access-list 100 permit icmp any any echo

R3(config)# end

R3# debug ip packet 100

IP packet debugging is on for access list 100

R3# ping 10.1.2.1 repeat 250


Type escape sequence to abort.

Sending 250, 100-byte ICMP Echos to 10.1.2.1, timeout is 2 seconds:

!!!!!!!!!!!!!!!!!!!!!!!!!!!!!!!!!!!!!!!!!!!!!!!!!!!

*Sep 27 00:50:54.215: IP: tableid=0, s=10.1.103.3 (local), d=10.1.2.1 (Serial0/0/0),
routed via RIB

*Sep 27 00:50:54.215: IP: s=10.1.103.3 (local), d=10.1.2.1 (Serial0/0/0), len 100,
sending

*Sep 27 00:50:54.231: IP: tableid=0, s=10.1.103.3 (local), d=10.1.2.1 (Serial0/0/0),
routed via RIB

*Sep 27 00:50:54.231: IP: s=10.1.103.3 (local), d=10.1.2.1 (Serial0/0/0), len 100,
sending

*Sep 27 00:50:54.247: IP: tableid=0, s=10.1.103.3 (local), d=10.1.2.1 (Serial0/0/0),
routed via RIB

*Sep 27 00:50:54.247: IP: s=10.1.103.3 (local), d=10.1.2.1 (Serial0/0/0), len 100,
sending

*Sep 27 00:50:54.263: IP: tableid=0, s=10.1.103.3 (local), d=10.1.2.1 (Serial0/0/0),
routed via RIB

*Sep 27 00:50:54.263: IP: s=10.1.103.3 (local), d=10.1.2.1 (Serial0/0/0), len 100,
sending

*Sep 27 00:50:54.279: IP: tableid=0, s=10.1.103.3 (local), d=10.1.2.1 (Serial0/0/0),
routed via RIB

*Sep 27 00:50:54.279: IP: s=10.1.103.3 (local), d=10.1.2.1 (Serial0/0/0), len 100,
sending

*Sep 27 00:50:54.295: IP: tableid=0, s=10.1.103.3 (local), d=10.1.2.1 (Serial0/0/0),
routed via RIB

!!!!!!!!!!!!!!!!!!!!!!!!!!!!!!!!!!!!!!!!!!!!!!!!!!!

*Sep 27 00:50:54.295: IP: s=10.1.103.3 (local), d=10.1.2.1 (Serial0/0/0), len 100,
sending

*Sep 27 00:50:54.311: IP: tableid=0, s=10.1.103.3 (local), d=10.1.2.1 (Serial0/0/0),
routed via RIB

*Sep 27 00:50:54.311: IP: s=10.1.103.3 (local), d=10.1.2.1 (Serial0/0/0), len 100,
sending

!

<output omitted until the switch to the other path takes place>

!

*Sep 27 00:50:55.395: IP: tableid=0, s=10.1.203.3 (local), d=10.1.2.1 (Serial0/0/1),
routed via RIB

!

! R3 just switched to load-share the outbound ICMP packets to Serial0/0/1!!
```

```
!
*Sep 27 00:50:55.395: IP: s=10.1.203.3 (local), d=10.1.2.1 (Serial0/0/1), len 100,
sending
*Sep 27 00:50:55.423: IP: tableid=0, s=10.1.203.3 (local), d=10.1.2.1 (Serial0/0/1),
routed via RIB
*Sep 27 00:50:55.423: IP: s=10.1.203.3 (local), d=10.1.2.1 (Serial0/0/1), len 100,
sending
*Sep 27 00:50:55.451: IP: tableid=0, s=10.1.203.3 (local), d=10.1.2.1 (Serial0/0/1),
routed via RIB
*Sep 27 00:50:55.451: IP: s=10.1.203.3 (local), d=10.1.2.1 (Serial0/0/1), len 100,
sending
*Sep 27 00:50:55.483: IP: tableid=0, s=10.1.203.3 (local), d=10.1.2.1 (Serial0/0/1),
routed via RIB
*Sep 27 00:50:55.483: IP: s=10.1.203.3 (local), d=10.1.2.1 (Serial0/0/1), len 100,
sending
*Sep 27 00:50:55.511: IP: tableid=0, s=10.1.203.3 (local), d=10.1.2.1 (Serial0/0/1),
routed via RIB
*Sep 27 00:50:55.511: IP: s=10.1.203.3 (local), d=10.1.2.1 (Serial0/0/1), len 100,
sending
*Sep 27 00:50:55.539: IP: tableid=0, s=10.1.203.3 (local), d=10.1.2.1 (Serial0/0/1),
routed via RIB
*Sep 27 00:50:55.539: IP: s=10.1.203.3 (local), d=10.1.2.1 (Serial0/0/1), len 100,
sending
*Sep 27 00:50:55.567: IP: tableid=0, s=10.1.203.3 (local), d=10.1.2.1 (Serial0/0/1),
routed via RIB
```

Initial Configurations

You can download these router configurations at www.ciscopress.com/title/1587132133 under the More Information section on the page.

```
R1:
!
interface Loopback11
 ip address 10.1.1.1 255.255.255.252
!
interface Loopback15
 ip address 10.1.1.5 255.255.255.252
!
interface Loopback19
 ip address 10.1.1.9 255.255.255.252
!
interface Serial0/0/0
 bandwidth 64
 ip address 10.1.102.1 255.255.255.248
 clock rate 64000
!
interface Serial0/0/1
 bandwidth 64
 ip address 10.1.103.1 255.255.255.248
```

```
!
end
```

R2:

```
!
interface Loopback21
 ip address 10.1.2.1 255.255.255.252
!
interface Loopback25
 ip address 10.1.2.5 255.255.255.252
!
interface Loopback29
 ip address 10.1.2.9 255.255.255.252
!
interface Serial0/0/0
 bandwidth 64
 ip address 10.1.102.2 255.255.255.248
interface Serial0/0/1
 bandwidth 64
 ip address 10.1.203.2 255.255.255.248
 clock rate 64000
!
end
```

R3:

```
!
hostname R3
!
interface Loopback31
 ip address 10.1.3.1 255.255.255.252
!
interface Loopback35
 ip address 10.1.3.5 255.255.255.252
!
interface Loopback39
 ip address 10.1.3.9 255.255.255.252
!
interface Serial0/0/0
 bandwidth 64
 ip address 10.1.103.3 255.255.255.248
clock rate 64000
!
interface Serial0/0/1
 bandwidth 64
 ip address 10.1.203.3 255.255.255.248
!
end
```

TCL Script Output

```
R1# tclsh
R1(tcl)# foreach address {
+>(tcl)# 10.1.1.1
+>(tcl)# 10.1.1.5
+>(tcl)# 10.1.1.9
+>(tcl)# 10.1.2.1
+>(tcl)# 10.1.2.5
+>(tcl)# 10.1.2.9
+>(tcl)# 10.1.3.1
+>(tcl)# 10.1.3.5
+>(tcl)# 10.1.3.9
+>(tcl)# 10.1.102.1
+>(tcl)# 10.1.102.2
+>(tcl)# 10.1.103.1
+>(tcl)# 10.1.103.3
+>(tcl)# 10.1.203.2
+>(tcl)# 10.1.203.3
+>(tcl)# } { ping $address }

Type escape sequence to abort.
Sending 5, 100-byte ICMP Echos to 10.1.1.1, timeout is 2 seconds:
!!!!!
Success rate is 100 percent (5/5), round-trip min/avg/max = 1/1/4 ms
Type escape sequence to abort.
Sending 5, 100-byte ICMP Echos to 10.1.1.5, timeout is 2 seconds:
!!!!!
Success rate is 100 percent (5/5), round-trip min/avg/max = 1/1/4 ms
Type escape sequence to abort.
Sending 5, 100-byte ICMP Echos to 10.1.1.9, timeout is 2 seconds:
!!!!!
Success rate is 100 percent (5/5), round-trip min/avg/max = 1/1/1 ms
Type escape sequence to abort.
Sending 5, 100-byte ICMP Echos to 10.1.2.1, timeout is 2 seconds:
!!!!!
Success rate is 100 percent (5/5), round-trip min/avg/max = 1/2/4 ms
Type escape sequence to abort.
Sending 5, 100-byte ICMP Echos to 10.1.2.5, timeout is 2 seconds:
!!!!!
Success rate is 100 percent (5/5), round-trip min/avg/max = 1/2/4 ms
Type escape sequence to abort.
Sending 5, 100-byte ICMP Echos to 10.1.2.9, timeout is 2 seconds:
!!!!!
```

```
Success rate is 100 percent (5/5), round-trip min/avg/max = 1/2/4 ms
Type escape sequence to abort.
Sending 5, 100-byte ICMP Echos to 10.1.3.1, timeout is 2 seconds:
!!!!!
Success rate is 100 percent (5/5), round-trip min/avg/max = 1/2/4 ms
Type escape sequence to abort.
Sending 5, 100-byte ICMP Echos to 10.1.3.5, timeout is 2 seconds:
!!!!!
Success rate is 100 percent (5/5), round-trip min/avg/max = 1/2/4 ms
Type escape sequence to abort.
Sending 5, 100-byte ICMP Echos to 10.1.3.9, timeout is 2 seconds:
!!!!!
Success rate is 100 percent (5/5), round-trip min/avg/max = 1/2/4 ms
Type escape sequence to abort.
Sending 5, 100-byte ICMP Echos to 10.1.102.1, timeout is 2 seconds:
!!!!!
Success rate is 100 percent (5/5), round-trip min/avg/max = 1/2/4 ms
Type escape sequence to abort.
Sending 5, 100-byte ICMP Echos to 10.1.102.2, timeout is 2 seconds:
!!!!!
Success rate is 100 percent (5/5), round-trip min/avg/max = 1/2/4 ms
Type escape sequence to abort.
Sending 5, 100-byte ICMP Echos to 10.1.103.1, timeout is 2 seconds:
!!!!!
Success rate is 100 percent (5/5), round-trip min/avg/max = 1/3/4 ms
Type escape sequence to abort.
Sending 5, 100-byte ICMP Echos to 10.1.103.3, timeout is 2 seconds:
!!!!!
Success rate is 100 percent (5/5), round-trip min/avg/max = 1/2/4 ms
Type escape sequence to abort.
Sending 5, 100-byte ICMP Echos to 10.1.203.2, timeout is 2 seconds:
!!!!!
Success rate is 100 percent (5/5), round-trip min/avg/max = 1/1/4 ms
Type escape sequence to abort.
Sending 5, 100-byte ICMP Echos to 10.1.203.3, timeout is 2 seconds:
!!!!!
Success rate is 100 percent (5/5), round-trip min/avg/max = 1/1/4 ms
R1(tcl)# tclquit
R1#
```

```
R2# tclsh
R2(tcl)# foreach address {
+>(tcl)# 10.1.1.1
+>(tcl)# 10.1.1.5
```

```
+>(tcl)# 10.1.1.9
+>(tcl)# 10.1.2.1
+>(tcl)# 10.1.2.5
+>(tcl)# 10.1.2.9
+>(tcl)# 10.1.3.1
+>(tcl)# 10.1.3.5
+>(tcl)# 10.1.3.9
+>(tcl)# 10.1.102.1
+>(tcl)# 10.1.102.2
+>(tcl)# 10.1.103.1
+>(tcl)# 10.1.103.3
+>(tcl)# 10.1.203.2
+>(tcl)# 10.1.203.3
+>(tcl)# } { ping $address }

Type escape sequence to abort.
Sending 5, 100-byte ICMP Echos to 10.1.1.1, timeout is 2 seconds:
!!!!!
Success rate is 100 percent (5/5), round-trip min/avg/max = 1/2/4 ms
Type escape sequence to abort.
Sending 5, 100-byte ICMP Echos to 10.1.1.5, timeout is 2 seconds:
!!!!!
Success rate is 100 percent (5/5), round-trip min/avg/max = 1/2/4 ms
Type escape sequence to abort.
Sending 5, 100-byte ICMP Echos to 10.1.1.9, timeout is 2 seconds:
!!!!!
Success rate is 100 percent (5/5), round-trip min/avg/max = 1/2/4 ms
Type escape sequence to abort.
Sending 5, 100-byte ICMP Echos to 10.1.2.1, timeout is 2 seconds:
!!!!!
Success rate is 100 percent (5/5), round-trip min/avg/max = 1/1/4 ms
Type escape sequence to abort.
Sending 5, 100-byte ICMP Echos to 10.1.2.5, timeout is 2 seconds:
!!!!!
Success rate is 100 percent (5/5), round-trip min/avg/max = 1/1/4 ms
Type escape sequence to abort.
Sending 5, 100-byte ICMP Echos to 10.1.2.9, timeout is 2 seconds:
!!!!!
Success rate is 100 percent (5/5), round-trip min/avg/max = 1/1/4 ms
Type escape sequence to abort.
Sending 5, 100-byte ICMP Echos to 10.1.3.1, timeout is 2 seconds:
!!!!!
Success rate is 100 percent (5/5), round-trip min/avg/max = 1/2/4 ms
Type escape sequence to abort.
```

```
Sending 5, 100-byte ICMP Echos to 10.1.3.5, timeout is 2 seconds:
!!!!!
Success rate is 100 percent (5/5), round-trip min/avg/max = 1/2/4 ms
Type escape sequence to abort.
Sending 5, 100-byte ICMP Echos to 10.1.3.9, timeout is 2 seconds:
!!!!!
Success rate is 100 percent (5/5), round-trip min/avg/max = 1/2/4 ms
Type escape sequence to abort.
Sending 5, 100-byte ICMP Echos to 10.1.102.1, timeout is 2 seconds:
!!!!!
Success rate is 100 percent (5/5), round-trip min/avg/max = 1/2/4 ms
Type escape sequence to abort.
Sending 5, 100-byte ICMP Echos to 10.1.102.2, timeout is 2 seconds:
!!!!!
Success rate is 100 percent (5/5), round-trip min/avg/max = 1/2/4 ms
Type escape sequence to abort.
Sending 5, 100-byte ICMP Echos to 10.1.103.1, timeout is 2 seconds:
!!!!!
Success rate is 100 percent (5/5), round-trip min/avg/max = 1/1/4 ms
Type escape sequence to abort.
Sending 5, 100-byte ICMP Echos to 10.1.103.3, timeout is 2 seconds:
!!!!!
Success rate is 100 percent (5/5), round-trip min/avg/max = 1/2/4 ms
Type escape sequence to abort.
Sending 5, 100-byte ICMP Echos to 10.1.203.2, timeout is 2 seconds:
!!!!!
Success rate is 100 percent (5/5), round-trip min/avg/max = 1/3/4 ms
Type escape sequence to abort.
Sending 5, 100-byte ICMP Echos to 10.1.203.3, timeout is 2 seconds:
!!!!!
Success rate is 100 percent (5/5), round-trip min/avg/max = 1/2/4 ms
R2(tcl)# tclquit
R2#
```

```
R3# tclsh
R3(tcl)# foreach address {
+>(tcl)# 10.1.1.1
+>(tcl)# 10.1.1.5
+>(tcl)# 10.1.1.9
+>(tcl)# 10.1.2.1
+>(tcl)# 10.1.2.5
+>(tcl)# 10.1.2.9
+>(tcl)# 10.1.3.1
+>(tcl)# 10.1.3.5
```

```
+>(tcl)# 10.1.3.9
+>(tcl)# 10.1.102.1
+>(tcl)# 10.1.102.2
+>(tcl)# 10.1.103.1
+>(tcl)# 10.1.103.3
+>(tcl)# 10.1.203.2
+>(tcl)# 10.1.203.3
+>(tcl)# } { ping $address }

Type escape sequence to abort.
Sending 5, 100-byte ICMP Echos to 10.1.1.1, timeout is 2 seconds:
!!!!!
Success rate is 100 percent (5/5), round-trip min/avg/max = 1/2/4 ms
Type escape sequence to abort.
Sending 5, 100-byte ICMP Echos to 10.1.1.5, timeout is 2 seconds:
!!!!!
Success rate is 100 percent (5/5), round-trip min/avg/max = 1/2/4 ms
Type escape sequence to abort.
Sending 5, 100-byte ICMP Echos to 10.1.1.9, timeout is 2 seconds:
!!!!!
Success rate is 100 percent (5/5), round-trip min/avg/max = 1/2/4 ms
Type escape sequence to abort.
Sending 5, 100-byte ICMP Echos to 10.1.2.1, timeout is 2 seconds:
!!!!!
Success rate is 100 percent (5/5), round-trip min/avg/max = 1/2/4 ms
Type escape sequence to abort.
Sending 5, 100-byte ICMP Echos to 10.1.2.5, timeout is 2 seconds:
!!!!!
Success rate is 100 percent (5/5), round-trip min/avg/max = 1/2/4 ms
Type escape sequence to abort.
Sending 5, 100-byte ICMP Echos to 10.1.2.9, timeout is 2 seconds:
!!!!!
Success rate is 100 percent (5/5), round-trip min/avg/max = 1/2/4 ms
Type escape sequence to abort.
Sending 5, 100-byte ICMP Echos to 10.1.3.1, timeout is 2 seconds:
!!!!!
Success rate is 100 percent (5/5), round-trip min/avg/max = 1/1/1 ms
Type escape sequence to abort.
Sending 5, 100-byte ICMP Echos to 10.1.3.5, timeout is 2 seconds:
!!!!!
Success rate is 100 percent (5/5), round-trip min/avg/max = 1/1/4 ms
Type escape sequence to abort.
Sending 5, 100-byte ICMP Echos to 10.1.3.9, timeout is 2 seconds:
!!!!!
```

```
Success rate is 100 percent (5/5), round-trip min/avg/max = 1/1/1 ms
Type escape sequence to abort.
Sending 5, 100-byte ICMP Echos to 10.1.102.1, timeout is 2 seconds:
!!!!!
Success rate is 100 percent (5/5), round-trip min/avg/max = 1/2/4 ms
Type escape sequence to abort.
Sending 5, 100-byte ICMP Echos to 10.1.102.2, timeout is 2 seconds:
!!!!!
Success rate is 100 percent (5/5), round-trip min/avg/max = 1/2/4 ms
Type escape sequence to abort.
Sending 5, 100-byte ICMP Echos to 10.1.103.1, timeout is 2 seconds:
!!!!!
Success rate is 100 percent (5/5), round-trip min/avg/max = 1/1/1 ms
Type escape sequence to abort.
Sending 5, 100-byte ICMP Echos to 10.1.103.3, timeout is 2 seconds:
!!!!!
Success rate is 100 percent (5/5), round-trip min/avg/max = 1/3/4 ms
Type escape sequence to abort.
Sending 5, 100-byte ICMP Echos to 10.1.203.2, timeout is 2 seconds:
!!!!!
Success rate is 100 percent (5/5), round-trip min/avg/max = 1/1/4 ms
Type escape sequence to abort.
Sending 5, 100-byte ICMP Echos to 10.1.203.3, timeout is 2 seconds:
!!!!!
Success rate is 100 percent (5/5), round-trip min/avg/max = 1/3/4 ms
R3(tcl)# tclquit
R3#
```

Lab 2-3: Summarization and Default Network Advertisement (2.7.3)

The objectives of this lab are as follows:

- Review basic EIGRP configuration
- Configure and verify EIGRP auto-summarization
- Configure and verify EIGRP manual summarization
- Learn to use **debug** commands for EIGRP summarization
- Configure **ip default-network** advertisement with EIGRP
- Consider the effects of summarization and default routes in a large internetwork

Figure 2-3 illustrates the topology that will be used for this lab.

Figure 2-3   Topology Diagram

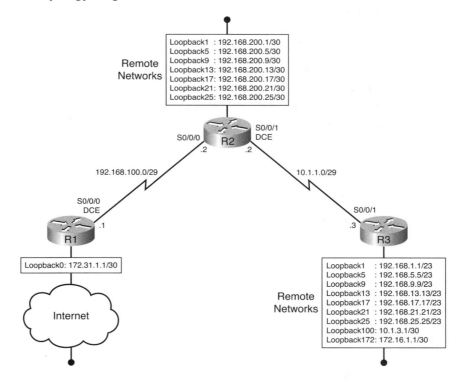

Scenario

A network engineer has been having trouble with high memory, bandwidth, and CPU utilization on her routers that are running EIGRP. Over lunch, she mentions to you that she has flapping routes in remote parts of the EIGRP autonomous system and suspects that these are the cause of the performance impediment. The engineer's network has only one path out to the Internet and her Internet service provider (ISP) has mandated that she use 172.31.1.1/30 on the end of the backbone connection.

After asking if you could take a look at her network, you discover that the routing tables are filled with 29-bit and 30-bit IP network prefixes, some of which are unstable and flapping. You observe that summarization would prompt a dramatic improvement in network performance and volunteer to implement it.

She asks you to show her proof-of-concept in the lab first, so you copy the configuration files to paste into your lab routers.

Step 1: Initial Configuration

Paste the following configurations into each of your routers to simulate this network (you can download these router configurations at www.ciscopress.com/title/1587132133 under the More Information section on the page):

```
:
R1:
!
hostname R1
!
interface Loopback0
 ip address 172.31.1.1 255.255.255.0
!
interface Serial0/0/0
 bandwidth 64
 ip address 192.168.100.1 255.255.255.248
 clock rate 64000
 no shutdown
!
router eigrp 100
 network 172.31.0.0
 network 192.168.100.0
 no auto-summary
!
end
```

```
R2:
!
hostname R2
!
interface Loopback1
 ip address 192.168.200.1 255.255.255.252
!
interface Loopback5
 ip address 192.168.200.5 255.255.255.252
!
interface Loopback9
 ip address 192.168.200.9 255.255.255.252
!
interface Loopback13
 ip address 192.168.200.13 255.255.255.252
```

```
!
interface Loopback17
 ip address 192.168.200.17 255.255.255.252
!
interface Loopback21
 ip address 192.168.200.21 255.255.255.252
!
interface Loopback25
 ip address 192.168.200.25 255.255.255.252
!
interface Serial0/0/0
 bandwidth 64
 ip address 192.168.100.2 255.255.255.248
 no shutdown
!
interface Serial0/0/1
 bandwidth 64
 ip address 10.1.1.2 255.255.255.248
 clock rate 64000
 no shutdown
!
router eigrp 100
 network 10.0.0.0
 network 192.168.100.0
 network 192.168.200.0
 no auto-summary
!
end
```

R3:
```
!
hostname R3
!
interface Loopback1
 ip address 192.168.1.1 255.255.254.0
!
interface Loopback5
 ip address 192.168.5.5 255.255.254.0
!
interface Loopback9
 ip address 192.168.9.9 255.255.254.0
!
interface Loopback13
 ip address 192.168.13.13 255.255.254.0
!
interface Loopback17
```

```
 ip address 192.168.17.17 255.255.254.0
!
interface Loopback21
 ip address 192.168.21.21 255.255.254.0
!
interface Loopback25
 ip address 192.168.25.25 255.255.254.0
!
interface Loopback100
 ip address 10.1.3.1 255.255.255.252
!
interface Loopback172
 ip address 172.16.1.1 255.255.255.0
!
interface Serial0/0/1
 bandwidth 64
 ip address 10.1.1.3 255.255.255.248
 no shutdown
!
router eigrp 100
 network 10.0.0.0
 network 172.16.0.0
 network 192.168.0.0 0.0.31.255
 no auto-summary
!
end
```

Now you have full EIGRP adjacency between R1 and R2 and between R2 and R3. Verify this with the **show ip eigrp neighbors** command:

```
R1# show ip eigrp neighbors
IP-EIGRP neighbors for process 100
H   Address             Interface       Hold Uptime   SRTT   RTO   Q   Seq
                                        (sec)         (ms)        Cnt Num
0   192.168.100.2       Se0/0/0          10 00:00:13   40   2280   0   38
```

```
R2# show ip eigrp neighbors
IP-EIGRP neighbors for process 100
H   Address             Interface       Hold Uptime   SRTT   RTO   Q   Seq
                                        (sec)         (ms)        Cnt Num
1   10.1.1.3            Se0/0/1          14 00:00:33    6   2280   0   28
0   192.168.100.1       Se0/0/0          10 00:00:40   21   2280   0   21
```

```
R3# show ip eigrp neighbors
IP-EIGRP neighbors for process 100
H   Address             Interface       Hold Uptime   SRTT   RTO   Q   Seq
                                        (sec)         (ms)        Cnt Num
0   10.1.1.2            Se0/0/1          13 00:00:52   13   2280   0   37
```

Ping all the IP addresses to ensure full connectivity, or use the following TCL script. If you have never used TCL scripts, or need a refresher, see "Lab 1-2: TCL Script Reference and Demonstration (1.5.1)," in Chapter 1, " Scalable Network Design." (You can download this TCL script at www.ciscopress.com/title/1587132133 under the More Information section on the page):

```
foreach address {
10.1.1.2
10.1.1.3
10.1.3.1
172.16.1.1
172.31.1.1
192.168.1.1
192.168.5.5
192.168.9.9
192.168.13.13
192.168.17.17
192.168.21.21
192.168.25.25
192.168.100.1
192.168.200.1
192.168.200.5
192.168.200.9
192.168.200.13
192.168.200.17
192.168.200.21
192.168.200.25
192.168.100.2
} { ping $address }
```

You will get ICMP echo replies for every address pinged. Check the TCL script output against the section, "All Pings Successful." Make sure you run the TCL script on each router.

Step 2: Summarization Analysis

Currently, the engineer has the networks documented in Table 2-2 configured within her network.

Table 2-2   Interface IP Addresses

Router	Interface	IP Address/Mask
R1	Loopback 0	172.31.1.1/30
R1	Serial0/0/0	192.168.100.1/29
R2	Loopback 1	192.168.200.1/30
R2	Loopback 5	192.168.200.5/30
R2	Loopback 9	192.168.200.9/30
R2	Loopback 13	192.168.200.13/30

continues

Table 2-2   Interface IP Addresses *continued*

Router	Interface	IP Address/Mask
R2	Loopback 17	192.168.200.17/30
R2	Loopback 21	192.168.200.21/30
R2	Loopback 25	192.168.200.25/30
R2	Serial0/0/0	192.168.100.2/29
R2	Serial0/0/1	10.1.1.2/29
R3	Loopback1	192.168.1.1/23
R3	Loopback 5	192.168.5.5/23
R3	Loopback 9	192.168.9.9/23
R3	Loopback 13	192.168.13.13/23
R3	Loopback 17	192.168.17.17/23
R3	Loopback 21	192.168.21.21/23
R3	Loopback 25	192.168.25.25/23
R3	Loopback 100	10.1.3.1/30
R3	Loopback 172	172.16.1.1/30
R3	Serial0/0/1	10.1.1.3/29

Given this addressing scheme, how many major networks are involved in this simulation? What are they?

_____

_____

_____

_____

_____

_____

_____

_____

_____

_____

_____

_____

_____

_____

———————————————

———————————————

———————————————

———————————————

———————————————

———————————————

———————————————

Note If you are unsure, use the **show ip route** command on R1 and look at the analysis of the output in the section "TCL Script Output" for this lab.

The engineer has not configured any automatic or manual EIGRP summarization in her topology. How would summarization benefit her network, especially in light of the fact that she has outlying flapping routes? List at least two reasons.

1. _____

_____

_____

2. _____

_____

_____

For the following networks, which router should you summarize to minimize the size of the routing table for all the involved routers? What summary should you use?

10.0.0.0/8 – _____

172.16.0.0/16 – _____

172.31.0.0/16 – _____

192.168.100.0/24 – _____

192.168.200.0/24 – _____

192.168.0.0/23 through 192.168.24.0/23 – _____

If EIGRP auto-summarization is turned on in this topology, will 192.168.0.0/23 through 192.168.24.0/23 be summarized?

_____

Because all routes involved in this lab, including later summary routes, will be installed in the routing table by EIGRP, observe the routing table on each router with the **show ip route eigrp** command. We will periodically observe the routing table with the output of this command throughout the duration of the lab:

```
R1# show ip route eigrp
     172.16.0.0/24 is subnetted, 1 subnets
D       172.16.1.0 [90/41152000] via 192.168.100.2, 00:01:14, Serial0/0/0
     192.168.200.0/30 is subnetted, 7 subnets
```

```
D         192.168.200.0 [90/40640000] via 192.168.100.2, 00:03:09, Serial0/0/0
D         192.168.200.4 [90/40640000] via 192.168.100.2, 00:03:09, Serial0/0/0
D         192.168.200.8 [90/40640000] via 192.168.100.2, 00:03:09, Serial0/0/0
D         192.168.200.12 [90/40640000] via 192.168.100.2, 00:03:09, Serial0/0/0
D         192.168.200.16 [90/40640000] via 192.168.100.2, 00:03:09, Serial0/0/0
D         192.168.200.20 [90/40640000] via 192.168.100.2, 00:03:09, Serial0/0/0
D         192.168.200.24 [90/40640000] via 192.168.100.2, 00:03:09, Serial0/0/0
      10.0.0.0/8 is variably subnetted, 2 subnets, 2 masks
D         10.1.3.0/30 [90/41152000] via 192.168.100.2, 00:03:09, Serial0/0/0
D         10.1.1.0/29 [90/41024000] via 192.168.100.2, 00:03:09, Serial0/0/0
D     192.168.12.0/23 [90/41152000] via 192.168.100.2, 00:03:09, Serial0/0/0
D     192.168.8.0/23 [90/41152000] via 192.168.100.2, 00:03:11, Serial0/0/0
D     192.168.24.0/23 [90/41152000] via 192.168.100.2, 00:03:11, Serial0/0/0
D     192.168.4.0/23 [90/41152000] via 192.168.100.2, 00:03:11, Serial0/0/0
D     192.168.20.0/23 [90/41152000] via 192.168.100.2, 00:03:11, Serial0/0/0
D     192.168.0.0/23 [90/41152000] via 192.168.100.2, 00:03:11, Serial0/0/0
D     192.168.16.0/23 [90/41152000] via 192.168.100.2, 00:03:11, Serial0/0/0
R2# show ip route eigrp
      172.16.0.0/24 is subnetted, 1 subnets
D         172.16.1.0 [90/40640000] via 10.1.1.3, 00:01:40, Serial0/0/1
      172.31.0.0/24 is subnetted, 1 subnets
D         172.31.1.0 [90/40640000] via 192.168.100.1, 00:03:35, Serial0/0/0
      10.0.0.0/8 is variably subnetted, 2 subnets, 2 masks
D         10.1.3.0/30 [90/40640000] via 10.1.1.3, 00:06:21, Serial0/0/1
D     192.168.12.0/23 [90/40640000] via 10.1.1.3, 00:04:04, Serial0/0/1
D     192.168.8.0/23 [90/40640000] via 10.1.1.3, 00:04:04, Serial0/0/1
D     192.168.24.0/23 [90/40640000] via 10.1.1.3, 00:04:04, Serial0/0/1
D     192.168.4.0/23 [90/40640000] via 10.1.1.3, 00:04:05, Serial0/0/1
D     192.168.20.0/23 [90/40640000] via 10.1.1.3, 00:04:04, Serial0/0/1
D     192.168.0.0/23 [90/40640000] via 10.1.1.3, 00:04:05, Serial0/0/1
D     192.168.16.0/23 [90/40640000] via 10.1.1.3, 00:04:04, Serial0/0/1
R3# show ip route eigrp
      172.31.0.0/24 is subnetted, 1 subnets
D         172.31.1.0 [90/41152000] via 10.1.1.2, 00:04:12, Serial0/0/1
      192.168.200.0/30 is subnetted, 7 subnets
D         192.168.200.0 [90/40640000] via 10.1.1.2, 00:06:58, Serial0/0/1
D         192.168.200.4 [90/40640000] via 10.1.1.2, 00:06:58, Serial0/0/1
D         192.168.200.8 [90/40640000] via 10.1.1.2, 00:06:58, Serial0/0/1
D         192.168.200.12 [90/40640000] via 10.1.1.2, 00:06:58, Serial0/0/1
D         192.168.200.16 [90/40640000] via 10.1.1.2, 00:06:58, Serial0/0/1
D         192.168.200.20 [90/40640000] via 10.1.1.2, 00:06:58, Serial0/0/1
D         192.168.200.24 [90/40640000] via 10.1.1.2, 00:06:58, Serial0/0/1
      192.168.100.0/29 is subnetted, 1 subnets
D         192.168.100.0 [90/41024000] via 10.1.1.2, 00:06:58, Serial0/0/1
```

How do you expect the output of this command to change if you implement the summarization you described above? Record your answer, and compare it with the results you observe later.

_____

_____

_____

You can also look at the size of each router's routing table with the **show ip route summary** command:

```
R1# show ip route summary
IP routing table name is Default-IP-Routing-Table(0)
IP routing table maximum-paths is 16
```

Route Source	Networks	Subnets	Overhead	Memory (bytes)
connected	0	2	144	272
static	0	0	0	0
eigrp 100	7	10	1224	2312
internal	5			5780
Total	12	12	1368	8364

```
R2# show ip route summary
IP routing table name is Default-IP-Routing-Table(0)
IP routing table maximum-paths is 16
```

Route Source	Networks	Subnets	Overhead	Memory (bytes)
connected	0	9	648	1224
static	0	0	0	0
eigrp 100	7	3	720	1360
internal	5			5780
Total	12	12	1368	8364

```
R3# show ip route summary
IP routing table name is Default-IP-Routing-Table(0)
IP routing table maximum-paths is 16
```

Route Source	Networks	Subnets	Overhead	Memory (bytes)
connected	14	3	1224	2312
static	0	0	0	0
eigrp 100	0	9	648	1224
internal	5			5780
Total	19	12	1872	9316

Step 3: EIGRP Auto-Summarization

The network engineer reminds you that EIGRP auto-summarization is turned on by default, but that she turned it off because she had discontiguous networks that she later removed. It is now safe to begin using auto-summarization again.

Verify that EIGRP AS 100 is not using auto-summarization on R1 with the **show ip protocols** command:

```
R1# show ip protocols
Routing Protocol is "eigrp 100"
  Outgoing update filter list for all interfaces is not set
  Incoming update filter list for all interfaces is not set
  Default networks flagged in outgoing updates
  Default networks accepted from incoming updates
  EIGRP metric weight K1=1, K2=0, K3=1, K4=0, K5=0
  EIGRP maximum hopcount 100
  EIGRP maximum metric variance 1
  Redistributing: eigrp 100
  EIGRP NSF-aware route hold timer is 240s
  Automatic network summarization is not in effect
  Maximum path: 4
  Routing for Networks:
    172.31.0.0
    192.168.100.0
  Routing Information Sources:
    Gateway         Distance      Last Update
    192.168.100.2         90      00:04:31
  Distance: internal 90 external 170
```

This command displays detailed information about EIGRP's status that we will use later in the lab, including whether

- EIGRP will flag default networks sent to other routers
- EIGRP will accept default networks advertised to this router
- Auto-summarization is turned on

You can enable EIGRP route and summary route debugging on each router, which allows you to observe when summary routes are advertised from the router with the **debug ip eigrp 100** and **debug ip eigrp summary** commands:

```
R1# debug ip eigrp 100
R1# debug ip eigrp summary
```
```
R2# debug ip eigrp 100
R2# debug ip eigrp summary
```
```
R3# debug ip eigrp 100
R3# debug ip eigrp summary
```

On R3, execute the **auto-summary** command in EIGRP's configuration menu. This produces system logging messages on both routers and **debug** output on R3:

```
R3(config)# router eigrp 100
R3(config-router)# auto-summary
```

You get the following types of log messages:

On R3:

```
*Sep 27 16:55:03.035: %DUAL-5-NBRCHANGE: IP-EIGRP(0) 100: Neighbor 10.1.203.2
(Serial0/0/1) is resync: summary configured
```

On R2:

```
*Sep 27 16:56:54.539: %DUAL-5-NBRCHANGE: IP-EIGRP(0) 100: Neighbor 10.1.203.2
(Serial0/0/1) is resync: peer graceful-restart
```

Your router issues a notification similar to the former message when you either configure or disable auto-summary on the local router. You receive a notification similar to the latter message when you configure auto-summary on an adjacent router. The adjacency must be resynchronized so that EIGRP update packets advertising the new summary routing information are sent.

Following the log messages, you get a flood of **debug** output on R3 as it searches its topology table for routes that can be summarized. EIGRP attempts to automatically summarize both 172.16.0.0/16 and 10.0.0.0/8 on R3, because R3 hosts the classful boundary between those networks. However, the output has been boiled down to only the debug messages concerning the 172.16.0.0/16 network. You should receive the same messages for 10.0.0.0/8, with the exception of the addition of the Serial0/0/1 interface. The reason for this exception is explained later:

```
<output regarding network 10.0.0.0/8 omitted>

*Sep 28 19:23:37.811: IP-EIGRP: add_auto_summary: Serial0/0/1 172.16.0.0/16 5

*Sep 28 19:23:37.811: IP-EIGRP: find_summary: add new sum: 172.16.0.0/16 5

*Sep 28 19:23:37.811: IP-EIGRP: find_summary: add new if: Serial0/0/1 to
172.16.0.0/16 5

*Sep 28 19:23:37.811: IP-EIGRP(Default-IP-Routing-Table:100): process_summary:
172.16.0.0/16 1

*Sep 28 19:23:37.811: IP-EIGRP: add_auto_summary: Loopback100 172.16.0.0/16 5

*Sep 28 19:23:37.811: IP-EIGRP: find_summary: add new if: Loopback100 to
172.16.0.0/16 5

*Sep 28 19:23:37.811: IP-EIGRP(Default-IP-Routing-Table:100): process_summary:
172.16.0.0/16 1

*Sep 28 19:23:37.811: IP-EIGRP: add_auto_summary: Loopback1 172.16.0.0/16 5

*Sep 28 19:23:37.811: IP-EIGRP: find_summary: add new if: Loopback1 to 172.16.0.0/16
5

*Sep 28 19:23:37.811: IP-EIGRP(Default-IP-Routing-Table:100): process_summary:
172.16.0.0/16 1

*Sep 28 19:23:37.811: IP-EIGRP: add_auto_summary: Loopback5 172.16.0.0/16 5

*Sep 28 19:23:37.811: IP-EIGRP: find_summary: add new if: Loopback5 to 172.16.0.0/16
5

*Sep 28 19:23:37.811: IP-EIGRP(Default-IP-Routing-Table:100): process_summary:
172.16.0.0/16 1

*Sep 28 19:23:37.811: IP-EIGRP: add_auto_summary: Loopback9 172.16.0.0/16 5

*Sep 28 19:23:37.811: IP-EIGRP: find_summary: add new if: Loopback9 to 172.16.0.0/16
5

*Sep 28 19:23:37.811: IP-EIGRP(Default-IP-Routing-Table:100): process_summary:
172.16.0.0/16 1

*Sep 28 19:23:37.811: IP-EIGRP: add_auto_summary: Loopback13 172.16.0.0/16 5

*Sep 28 19:23:37.815: IP-EIGRP: find_summary: add new if: Loopback13 to
172.16.0.0/16 5
```

```
*Sep 28 19:23:37.815: IP-EIGRP(Default-IP-Routing-Table:100): process_summary:
172.16.0.0/16 1

*Sep 28 19:23:37.815: IP-EIGRP: add_auto_summary: Loopback17 172.16.0.0/16 5

*Sep 28 19:23:37.815: IP-EIGRP: find_summary: add new if: Loopback17 to
172.16.0.0/16 5

*Sep 28 19:23:37.815: IP-EIGRP(Default-IP-Routing-Table:100): process_summary:
172.16.0.0/16 1

*Sep 28 19:23:37.815: IP-EIGRP: add_auto_summary: Loopback21 172.16.0.0/16 5

*Sep 28 19:23:37.815: IP-EIGRP: find_summary: add new if: Loopback21 to
172.16.0.0/16 5

*Sep 28 19:23:37.815: IP-EIGRP(Default-IP-Routing-Table:100): process_summary:
172.16.0.0/16 1

*Sep 28 19:23:37.815: IP-EIGRP: add_auto_summary: Loopback25 172.16.0.0/16 5

*Sep 28 19:23:37.815: IP-EIGRP: find_summary: add new if: Loopback25 to
172.16.0.0/16 5

*Sep 28 19:23:37.815: IP-EIGRP(Default-IP-Routing-Table:100): process_summary:
172.16.0.0/16 1

*Sep 28 19:23:37.815: %DUAL-5-NBRCHANGE: IP-EIGRP(0) 100: Neighbor 10.1.1.2
(Serial0/0/1) is resync: summary configured

*Sep 28 19:23:37.815: IP-EIGRP(Default-IP-Routing-Table:100): get_summary_metric:
172.16.0.0/16

*Sep 28 19:23:37.819: IP-EIGRP(Default-IP-Routing-Table:100): get_summary_metric:
172.16.0.0/16

*Sep 28 19:23:37.819: IP-EIGRP(Default-IP-Routing-Table:100): get_summary_metric:
172.16.0.0/16

*Sep 28 19:23:37.823: IP-EIGRP(Default-IP-Routing-Table:100): get_summary_metric:
172.16.0.0/16

*Sep 28 19:23:37.823: IP-EIGRP(Default-IP-Routing-Table:100): get_summary_metric:
172.16.0.0/16

*Sep 28 19:23:37.823: IP-EIGRP(Default-IP-Routing-Table:100): get_summary_metric:
172.16.0.0/16

*Sep 28 19:23:37.827: IP-EIGRP(Default-IP-Routing-Table:100): get_summary_metric:
172.16.0.0/16

*Sep 28 19:23:37.827: IP-EIGRP(Default-IP-Routing-Table:100): get_summary_metric:
172.16.0.0/16

*Sep 28 19:23:37.831: IP-EIGRP(Default-IP-Routing-Table:100): get_summary_metric:
172.16.0.0/16
```

Each get_summary_metric message at the end represents a function call to create a composite metric for the summary route for each outbound interface.

Imagine that you have EIGRP neighbors out each loopback interface connected to R3. How many interfaces will receive the 172.16.0.0/16 summary route?

_____

_____

_____

Which summary routes are sent to R2?

_____

Check with the **show ip route eigrp** command:

```
R2# show ip route eigrp
<output omitted>
D    172.16.0.0/16 [90/40640000] via 10.1.1.3, 00:38:38, Serial0/0/1
     172.31.0.0/24 is subnetted, 1 subnets
D       172.31.1.0 [90/40640000] via 192.168.100.1, 00:47:51, Serial0/0/0
     10.0.0.0/8 is variably subnetted, 2 subnets, 2 masks
D       10.1.3.0/30 [90/40640000] via 10.1.1.3, 00:50:36, Serial0/0/1
D    192.168.12.0/23 [90/40640000] via 10.1.1.3, 00:48:20, Serial0/0/1
D    192.168.8.0/23 [90/40640000] via 10.1.1.3, 00:48:20, Serial0/0/1
D    192.168.24.0/23 [90/40640000] via 10.1.1.3, 00:48:19, Serial0/0/1
D    192.168.4.0/23 [90/40640000] via 10.1.1.3, 00:48:20, Serial0/0/1
D    192.168.20.0/23 [90/40640000] via 10.1.1.3, 00:48:19, Serial0/0/1
D    192.168.0.0/23 [90/40640000] via 10.1.1.3, 00:48:20, Serial0/0/1
D    192.168.16.0/23 [90/40640000] via 10.1.1.3, 00:48:20, Serial0/0/1
```

Notice that the summary route has the same composite metric as the previous single route to 172.16.1.0/30.

When the summary route is generated, what happens in R3's routing table?

Issue the **show ip route eigrp** command to check:

```
R3# show ip route eigrp
<output omitted>
     172.16.0.0/16 is variably subnetted, 2 subnets, 2 masks
D       172.16.0.0/16 is a summary, 00:46:00, Null0
     10.0.0.0/8 is variably subnetted, 3 subnets, 3 masks
D       10.0.0.0/8 is a summary, 00:46:00, Null0
```

In the output of the **debug ip eigrp summary** command, there were also messages pertaining to 10.0.0.0/8. Although R3 has a summary route for 10.0.0.0/8 installed in its routing table to Null0, why did R3 not send the summary route for 10.0.0.0/8 to R2? The 10.0.0.0/8 summary will not be sent out to a connected subnet within that major network. Automatic summarization takes place at the classful boundary by sending a classful network summary to all local EIGRP interfaces not in the summarized network. Because Serial0/0/1 has an IP address that is part of the 10.0.0.0/8 network, R3 does not send that summary to R2 through the Serial0/0/1 interface. Notice that it is not in the EIGRP topology table on R2:

```
R2# show ip eigrp topology
IP-EIGRP Topology Table for AS(100)/ID(192.168.200.25)

Codes: P - Passive, A - Active, U - Update, Q - Query, R - Reply,
       r - reply Status, s - sia Status

P 10.1.3.0/30, 1 successors, FD is 40640000
```

```
         via 10.1.1.3 (40640000/128256), Serial0/0/1
P 10.1.1.0/29, 1 successors, FD is 40512000
         via Connected, Serial0/0/1
!
!  Note the lack of the summary route to 10.0.0.0/8
!
P 192.168.100.0/29, 1 successors, FD is 40512000
         via Connected, Serial0/0/0
P 192.168.8.0/23, 1 successors, FD is 40640000
         via 10.1.1.3 (40640000/128256), Serial0/0/1
P 192.168.12.0/23, 1 successors, FD is 40640000
         via 10.1.1.3 (40640000/128256), Serial0/0/1
P 192.168.0.0/23, 1 successors, FD is 40640000
         via 10.1.1.3 (40640000/128256), Serial0/0/1
P 192.168.4.0/23, 1 successors, FD is 40640000
         via 10.1.1.3 (40640000/128256), Serial0/0/1
P 192.168.24.0/23, 1 successors, FD is 40640000
         via 10.1.1.3 (40640000/128256), Serial0/0/1
P 192.168.16.0/23, 1 successors, FD is 40640000
         via 10.1.1.3 (40640000/128256), Serial0/0/1
P 192.168.20.0/23, 1 successors, FD is 40640000
         via 10.1.1.3 (40640000/128256), Serial0/0/1
P 192.168.200.0/30, 1 successors, FD is 128256
         via Connected, Loopback1
P 192.168.200.4/30, 1 successors, FD is 128256
         via Connected, Loopback5
P 192.168.200.8/30, 1 successors, FD is 128256
         via Connected, Loopback9
P 192.168.200.12/30, 1 successors, FD is 128256
         via Connected, Loopback13
P 192.168.200.16/30, 1 successors, FD is 128256
         via Connected, Loopback17
P 172.31.1.0/24, 1 successors, FD is 40640000
         via 192.168.100.1 (40640000/128256), Serial0/0/0
P 192.168.200.20/30, 1 successors, FD is 128256
         via Connected, Loopback21
P 192.168.200.24/30, 1 successors, FD is 128256
         via Connected, Loopback25
P 172.16.0.0/16, 1 successors, FD is 40640000
         via 10.1.1.3 (40640000/128256), Serial0/0/1
```

Finally, which of R3's connected networks are not being summarized?

_____

_____

_____

Review your answers to the questions at the end of Step 2. Why is this summarization not occurring?

_____

_____

_____

Because the engineer has no discontiguous networks in her internetwork, you decide to enable EIGRP auto-summary on all routers:

```
R1(config)# router eigrp 100
R1(config-router)# auto-summary
R2(config)# router eigrp 100
R2(config-router)# auto-summary
```

Verify that the summaries are shown by issuing the **show ip eigrp topology** command on each router. You should see summary routes on each router for each major network that is not part of the /23 supernets. Supernets are not included in auto-summary routes because EIGRP automatically summarizes only to the classful boundary and no further. Compare your output with the following output:

```
R1# show ip eigrp topology
IP-EIGRP Topology Table for AS(100)/ID(172.31.1.1)

Codes: P - Passive, A - Active, U - Update, Q - Query, R - Reply,
       r - reply Status, s - sia Status


P 10.0.0.0/8, 1 successors, FD is 41024000
        via 192.168.100.2 (41024000/40512000), Serial0/0/0
P 192.168.100.0/24, 1 successors, FD is 40512000
        via Summary (40512000/0), Null0
P 192.168.100.0/29, 1 successors, FD is 40512000
        via Connected, Serial0/0/0
P 192.168.8.0/23, 1 successors, FD is 41152000
        via 192.168.100.2 (41152000/40640000), Serial0/0/0
P 192.168.12.0/23, 1 successors, FD is 41152000
        via 192.168.100.2 (41152000/40640000), Serial0/0/0
P 192.168.0.0/23, 1 successors, FD is 41152000
        via 192.168.100.2 (41152000/40640000), Serial0/0/0
P 192.168.4.0/23, 1 successors, FD is 41152000
        via 192.168.100.2 (41152000/40640000), Serial0/0/0
P 192.168.24.0/23, 1 successors, FD is 41152000
        via 192.168.100.2 (41152000/40640000), Serial0/0/0
```

```
P 192.168.16.0/23, 1 successors, FD is 41152000
        via 192.168.100.2 (41152000/40640000), Serial0/0/0
P 192.168.20.0/23, 1 successors, FD is 41152000
        via 192.168.100.2 (41152000/40640000), Serial0/0/0
P 192.168.200.0/24, 1 successors, FD is 40640000
        via 192.168.100.2 (40640000/128256), Serial0/0/0
P 172.31.1.0/24, 1 successors, FD is 128256
        via Connected, Loopback0
P 172.31.0.0/16, 1 successors, FD is 128256
        via Summary (128256/0), Null0
P 172.16.0.0/16, 1 successors, FD is 41152000
        via 192.168.100.2 (41152000/40640000), Serial0/0/0
```

```
R2# show ip eigrp topology
IP-EIGRP Topology Table for AS(100)/ID(192.168.200.25)

Codes: P - Passive, A - Active, U - Update, Q - Query, R - Reply,
       r - reply Status, s - sia Status


P 10.1.3.0/30, 1 successors, FD is 40640000
        via 10.1.1.3 (40640000/128256), Serial0/0/1
P 10.0.0.0/8, 1 successors, FD is 40512000
        via Summary (40512000/0), Null0
P 10.1.1.0/29, 1 successors, FD is 40512000
        via Connected, Serial0/0/1
P 192.168.100.0/24, 1 successors, FD is 40512000
        via Summary (40512000/0), Null0
P 192.168.100.0/29, 1 successors, FD is 40512000
        via Connected, Serial0/0/0
P 192.168.8.0/23, 1 successors, FD is 40640000
        via 10.1.1.3 (40640000/128256), Serial0/0/1
P 192.168.12.0/23, 1 successors, FD is 40640000
        via 10.1.1.3 (40640000/128256), Serial0/0/1
P 192.168.0.0/23, 1 successors, FD is 40640000
        via 10.1.1.3 (40640000/128256), Serial0/0/1
P 192.168.4.0/23, 1 successors, FD is 40640000
        via 10.1.1.3 (40640000/128256), Serial0/0/1
P 192.168.24.0/23, 1 successors, FD is 40640000
        via 10.1.1.3 (40640000/128256), Serial0/0/1
P 192.168.16.0/23, 1 successors, FD is 40640000
        via 10.1.1.3 (40640000/128256), Serial0/0/1
P 192.168.20.0/23, 1 successors, FD is 40640000
        via 10.1.1.3 (40640000/128256), Serial0/0/1
P 192.168.200.0/24, 1 successors, FD is 128256
        via Summary (128256/0), Null0
```

```
P 192.168.200.0/30, 1 successors, FD is 128256
        via Connected, Loopback1
P 192.168.200.4/30, 1 successors, FD is 128256
        via Connected, Loopback5
P 192.168.200.8/30, 1 successors, FD is 128256
        via Connected, Loopback9
P 192.168.200.12/30, 1 successors, FD is 128256
        via Connected, Loopback13
P 192.168.200.16/30, 1 successors, FD is 128256
        via Connected, Loopback17
P 172.31.0.0/16, 1 successors, FD is 40640000
        via 192.168.100.1 (40640000/128256), Serial0/0/0
P 192.168.200.20/30, 1 successors, FD is 128256
        via Connected, Loopback21
P 192.168.200.24/30, 1 successors, FD is 128256
        via Connected, Loopback25
P 172.16.0.0/16, 1 successors, FD is 40640000
        via 10.1.1.3 (40640000/128256), Serial0/0/1
R3# show ip eigrp topology
IP-EIGRP Topology Table for AS(100)/ID(192.168.25.25)

Codes: P - Passive, A - Active, U - Update, Q - Query, R - Reply,
       r - reply Status, s - sia Status

P 10.1.3.0/30, 1 successors, FD is 128256
        via Connected, Loopback100
P 10.0.0.0/8, 1 successors, FD is 128256
        via Summary (128256/0), Null0
P 10.1.1.0/29, 1 successors, FD is 40512000
        via Connected, Serial0/0/1
P 192.168.100.0/24, 1 successors, FD is 41024000
        via 10.1.1.2 (41024000/40512000), Serial0/0/1
P 192.168.8.0/23, 1 successors, FD is 128256
        via Connected, Loopback9
P 192.168.12.0/23, 1 successors, FD is 128256
        via Connected, Loopback13
P 192.168.0.0/23, 1 successors, FD is 128256
        via Connected, Loopback1
P 192.168.4.0/23, 1 successors, FD is 128256
        via Connected, Loopback5
P 192.168.24.0/23, 1 successors, FD is 128256
        via Connected, Loopback25
P 192.168.16.0/23, 1 successors, FD is 128256
        via Connected, Loopback17
```

```
P 192.168.20.0/23, 1 successors, FD is 128256
        via Connected, Loopback21
P 192.168.200.0/24, 1 successors, FD is 40640000
        via 10.1.1.2 (40640000/128256), Serial0/0/1
P 172.31.0.0/16, 1 successors, FD is 41152000
        via 10.1.1.2 (41152000/40640000), Serial0/0/1
P 172.16.0.0/16, 1 successors, FD is 128256
        via Summary (128256/0), Null0
P 172.16.1.0/24, 1 successors, FD is 128256
        via Connected, Loopback172
```

Step 4: EIGRP Manual Summarization

Recall that when you configured the auto-summary, **debug** output showed that EIGRP summary routes were generated on a per-interface basis. EIGRP calculates summaries, whether manually or automatically, on a per-interface basis. Although the EIGRP **auto-summary** command turns auto-summarization on globally on a router, you can configure summary routes manually as well with the interface-level command **ip summary-address eigrp as network mask**.

Normally, you need to leave EIGRP auto-summarization off in topologies with discontiguous networks and create manual summary routes instead. In this case, to show the engineer how summarization can further benefit her network, you enable manual summarization on R3's Serial0/0/1 interface. R3 should therefore advertise the /23 subnets to R2.

What is the most efficient mask to summarize these routes?

_____

Implement the summarization on R3 as follows:

```
R3(config)# interface Serial 0/0/1
R3(config-if)# ip summary-address eigrp 100 192.168.0.0 255.255.224.0
```

The 100 parameter instructs this to be sent out only to neighbors in EIGRP AS 100.

Use the inline IOS help system with the "?" if you are unfamiliar with the parameters of this command. Use this as a common practice to familiarize yourself with parameters when working through these labs.

The adjacency between R2 and R3 resynchronizes after the summary is configured. The routing tables should appear similar to the following:

```
R1# show ip route
<output omitted>


Gateway of last resort is not set

D    172.16.0.0/16 [90/41152000] via 192.168.100.2, 04:04:11, Serial0/0/0
        172.31.0.0/16 is variably subnetted, 2 subnets, 2 masks
C       172.31.1.0/24 is directly connected, Loopback0
D       172.31.0.0/16 is a summary, 02:47:43, Null0
```

```
D     192.168.200.0/24 [90/40640000] via 192.168.100.2, 02:47:34, Serial0/0/0
D     10.0.0.0/8 [90/41024000] via 192.168.100.2, 02:47:34, Serial0/0/0
      192.168.100.0/24 is variably subnetted, 2 subnets, 2 masks
C        192.168.100.0/29 is directly connected, Serial0/0/0
D        192.168.100.0/24 is a summary, 02:47:44, Null0
D     192.168.0.0/19 [90/41152000] via 192.168.100.2, 02:32:07, Serial0/0/0
R2# show ip route
<output omitted>


Gateway of last resort is not set


D     172.16.0.0/16 [90/40640000] via 10.1.1.3, 02:33:29, Serial0/0/1
D     172.31.0.0/16 [90/40640000] via 192.168.100.1, 02:48:58, Serial0/0/0
      192.168.200.0/24 is variably subnetted, 8 subnets, 2 masks
C        192.168.200.0/30 is directly connected, Loopback1
D        192.168.200.0/24 is a summary, 02:48:58, Null0
C        192.168.200.4/30 is directly connected, Loopback5
C        192.168.200.8/30 is directly connected, Loopback9
C        192.168.200.12/30 is directly connected, Loopback13
C        192.168.200.16/30 is directly connected, Loopback17
C        192.168.200.20/30 is directly connected, Loopback21
C        192.168.200.24/30 is directly connected, Loopback25
      10.0.0.0/8 is variably subnetted, 3 subnets, 3 masks
D        10.1.3.0/30 [90/40640000] via 10.1.1.3, 02:33:30, Serial0/0/1
C        10.1.1.0/29 is directly connected, Serial0/0/1
D        10.0.0.0/8 is a summary, 02:49:00, Null0
      192.168.100.0/24 is variably subnetted, 2 subnets, 2 masks
C        192.168.100.0/29 is directly connected, Serial0/0/0
D        192.168.100.0/24 is a summary, 02:49:00, Null0
D     192.168.0.0/19 [90/40640000] via 10.1.1.3, 02:33:31, Serial0/0/1
R3# show ip route
<output omitted>


Gateway of last resort is not set


      172.16.0.0/16 is variably subnetted, 2 subnets, 2 masks
D        172.16.0.0/16 is a summary, 04:07:05, Null0
C        172.16.1.0/24 is directly connected, Loopback172
      172.31.0.0/16 is subnetted, 1 subnets
D        172.31.0.0 [90/41152000] via 10.1.1.2, 02:35:00, Serial0/0/1
D     192.168.200.0/24 [90/40640000] via 10.1.1.2, 02:50:28, Serial0/0/1
      10.0.0.0/8 is variably subnetted, 3 subnets, 3 masks
C        10.1.3.0/30 is directly connected, Loopback100
```

```
C       10.1.1.0/29 is directly connected, Serial0/0/1
D       10.0.0.0/8 is a summary, 04:07:06, Null0
D       192.168.100.0/24 [90/41024000] via 10.1.1.2, 02:50:29, Serial0/0/1
C       192.168.12.0/23 is directly connected, Loopback13
C       192.168.12.0/22 is directly connected, Loopback13
C       192.168.8.0/23 is directly connected, Loopback9
C       192.168.8.0/22 is directly connected, Loopback9
C       192.168.24.0/23 is directly connected, Loopback25
C       192.168.24.0/22 is directly connected, Loopback25
C       192.168.4.0/23 is directly connected, Loopback5
C       192.168.4.0/22 is directly connected, Loopback5
C       192.168.20.0/23 is directly connected, Loopback21
C       192.168.20.0/22 is directly connected, Loopback21
C       192.168.0.0/23 is directly connected, Loopback1
C       192.168.0.0/22 is directly connected, Loopback1
D       192.168.0.0/19 is a summary, 02:35:02, Null0
C       192.168.16.0/23 is directly connected, Loopback17
C       192.168.16.0/22 is directly connected, Loopback17
```

Notice that on each router the only EIGRP routes (marked as D) are summary routes to locally connected networks (Null0) or summary routes to remote networks.

At this point, you have efficiently summarized the network. Based on your knowledge of routing protocols and techniques, are there any other ways to minimize the routing table even further for this topology without filtering routes?

_____

_____

Step 5: Default Network Advertisement

Suppose this engineer has another branch office of her core network that is also running EIGRP in a different autonomous system, AS 200, connected to the FastEthernet0/0 interface on R1. However, the branch you are modeling is completely independent of that topology and vice versa.

Based on this corporation's new routing policies, EIGRP AS 100 only needs to know that all traffic out of its network is forwarded to R1. The engineer queries you as to how she could still preserve connectivity to AS 200 networks, but also minimize her routing tables within AS 100.

What solutions would you propose?

_____

_____

You decide that this company's policies match the idea of using a default route out of the system. The default network you will configure is 172.31.0.0/16, because this is the path to the Internet.

The IP network 0.0.0.0/0 matches all unknown destination prefixes because the routing table acts in a classless manner. Classless routing tables use the first match based on the longest IP subnet mask for that destination network. If the routing table has no matches for a subnet mask greater than 0 bits for a given destination network, the shortest subnet mask (/0) matches any of the 32 bits of a destination network if the routing table is acting in a classless manner.

For instance, if the router does not have a route to 192.168.7.0/24, it tries to match against any routes it has to 192.168.6.0/23, 192.168.4.0/22, 192.168.0.0/21, and so on. If it does not find any routes to destinations within those networks, it eventually gets to the 0.0.0.0/0 network, which matches all destination IP addresses, and sends the packet to its "gateway of last resort."

The **ip default-network** command that you will configure on R1 propagates through the EIGRP system so that each router sees its candidate default network as the path with shortest feasible distance to the default network (172.31.0.0/16). Issue this command on R1:

```
R1(config)# ip default-network 172.31.0.0
```

This routes all traffic through R1 to destination networks not caught by any other networks or subnets in the routing table to the 172.31.0.0 network. EIGRP flags this route as the default route in advertisements to other routers. Verify that the flag is set on updates to R2 using the **show ip eigrp topology 172.31.0.0/16** command:

```
R2# show ip eigrp topology 172.31.0.0/16
IP-EIGRP (AS 100): Topology entry for 172.31.0.0/16
  State is Passive, Query origin flag is 1, 1 Successor(s), FD is 40640000
  Routing Descriptor Blocks:
  192.168.100.1 (Serial0/0/0), from 192.168.100.1, Send flag is 0x0
      Composite metric is (40640000/128256), Route is Internal
      Vector metric:
        Minimum bandwidth is 64 Kbit
        Total delay is 25000 microseconds
        Reliability is 255/255
        Load is 1/255
        Minimum MTU is 1500
        Hop count is 1
      Exterior flag is set
```

How has the routing table changed on each of your routers? Use the command **show ip route**:

```
R1# show ip route
Codes: C - connected, S - static, R - RIP, M - mobile, B - BGP
       D - EIGRP, EX - EIGRP external, O - OSPF, IA - OSPF inter area
       N1 - OSPF NSSA external type 1, N2 - OSPF NSSA external type 2
       E1 - OSPF external type 1, E2 - OSPF external type 2
       i - IS-IS, su - IS-IS summary, L1 - IS-IS level-1, L2 - IS-IS level-2
       ia - IS-IS inter area, * - candidate default, U - per-user static route
       o - ODR, P - periodic downloaded static route

Gateway of last resort is 0.0.0.0 to network 172.31.0.0

D    172.16.0.0/16 [90/41152000] via 192.168.100.2, 06:32:23, Serial0/0/0
```

```
*     172.31.0.0/16 is variably subnetted, 2 subnets, 2 masks
C          172.31.1.0/24 is directly connected, Loopback0
D*         172.31.0.0/16 is a summary, 00:02:04, Null0
D     192.168.200.0/24 [90/40640000] via 192.168.100.2, 05:15:46, Serial0/0/0
D     10.0.0.0/8 [90/41024000] via 192.168.100.2, 05:15:46, Serial0/0/0
      192.168.100.0/24 is variably subnetted, 2 subnets, 2 masks
C          192.168.100.0/29 is directly connected, Serial0/0/0
D          192.168.100.0/24 is a summary, 05:15:56, Null0
D     192.168.0.0/19 [90/41152000] via 192.168.100.2, 05:00:19, Serial0/0/0


R2# show ip route
Codes: C - connected, S - static, R - RIP, M - mobile, B - BGP
       D - EIGRP, EX - EIGRP external, O - OSPF, IA - OSPF inter area
       N1 - OSPF NSSA external type 1, N2 - OSPF NSSA external type 2
       E1 - OSPF external type 1, E2 - OSPF external type 2
       i - IS-IS, su - IS-IS summary, L1 - IS-IS level-1, L2 - IS-IS level-2
       ia - IS-IS inter area, * - candidate default, U - per-user static route
       o - ODR, P - periodic downloaded static route


Gateway of last resort is 192.168.100.1 to network 172.31.0.0


D     172.16.0.0/16 [90/40640000] via 10.1.1.3, 04:58:38, Serial0/0/1
D*    172.31.0.0/16 [90/40640000] via 192.168.100.1, 00:00:09, Serial0/0/0
      192.168.200.0/24 is variably subnetted, 8 subnets, 2 masks
C          192.168.200.0/30 is directly connected, Loopback1
D          192.168.200.0/24 is a summary, 05:14:07, Null0
C          192.168.200.4/30 is directly connected, Loopback5
C          192.168.200.8/30 is directly connected, Loopback9
C          192.168.200.12/30 is directly connected, Loopback13
C          192.168.200.16/30 is directly connected, Loopback17
C          192.168.200.20/30 is directly connected, Loopback21
C          192.168.200.24/30 is directly connected, Loopback25
      10.0.0.0/8 is variably subnetted, 3 subnets, 3 masks
D          10.1.3.0/30 [90/40640000] via 10.1.1.3, 04:58:39, Serial0/0/1
C          10.1.1.0/29 is directly connected, Serial0/0/1
D          10.0.0.0/8 is a summary, 05:14:09, Null0
      192.168.100.0/24 is variably subnetted, 2 subnets, 2 masks
C          192.168.100.0/29 is directly connected, Serial0/0/0
D          192.168.100.0/24 is a summary, 05:14:09, Null0
D     192.168.0.0/19 [90/40640000] via 10.1.1.3, 04:58:40, Serial0/0/1
R3# show ip route
Codes: C - connected, S - static, R - RIP, M - mobile, B - BGP
       D - EIGRP, EX - EIGRP external, O - OSPF, IA - OSPF inter area
```

```
       N1 - OSPF NSSA external type 1, N2 - OSPF NSSA external type 2
       E1 - OSPF external type 1, E2 - OSPF external type 2
       i - IS-IS, su - IS-IS summary, L1 - IS-IS level-1, L2 - IS-IS level-2
       ia - IS-IS inter area, * - candidate default, U - per-user static route
       o - ODR, P - periodic downloaded static route


Gateway of last resort is 10.1.1.2 to network 172.31.0.0


       172.16.0.0/16 is variably subnetted, 2 subnets, 2 masks
D          172.16.0.0/16 is a summary, 06:37:06, Null0
C          172.16.1.0/24 is directly connected, Loopback172
D*     172.31.0.0/16 [90/41152000] via 10.1.1.2, 00:06:32, Serial0/0/1
D      192.168.200.0/24 [90/40640000] via 10.1.1.2, 05:20:29, Serial0/0/1
       10.0.0.0/8 is variably subnetted, 3 subnets, 3 masks
C          10.1.3.0/30 is directly connected, Loopback100
C          10.1.1.0/29 is directly connected, Serial0/0/1
D          10.0.0.0/8 is a summary, 06:37:07, Null0
D      192.168.100.0/24 [90/41024000] via 10.1.1.2, 05:20:31, Serial0/0/1
C      192.168.12.0/23 is directly connected, Loopback13
C      192.168.12.0/22 is directly connected, Loopback13
C      192.168.8.0/23 is directly connected, Loopback9
C      192.168.8.0/22 is directly connected, Loopback9
C      192.168.24.0/23 is directly connected, Loopback25
C      192.168.24.0/22 is directly connected, Loopback25
C      192.168.4.0/23 is directly connected, Loopback5
C      192.168.4.0/22 is directly connected, Loopback5
C      192.168.20.0/23 is directly connected, Loopback21
C      192.168.20.0/22 is directly connected, Loopback21
C      192.168.0.0/23 is directly connected, Loopback1
C      192.168.0.0/22 is directly connected, Loopback1
D      192.168.0.0/19 is a summary, 05:05:22, Null0
C      192.168.16.0/23 is directly connected, Loopback17
C      192.168.16.0/22 is directly connected, Loopback17
```

On R1, the gateway of last resort is designated as 172.31.0.0. What routers correspond to the IP address of the gateway of last resort on R2 and R3?

_____

_____

What are the benefits of introducing the routing information of the other autonomous system into EIGRP AS 100?

_____

_____

_____

_____

_____

_____

What are the drawbacks of configuring the default network to propagate from R1?

_____

_____

_____

_____

_____

_____

If R3 were to ping a destination network that is not reachable from this internetwork, how far would the data travel?

_____

_____

Does this make the network more or less susceptible to denial-of-service (DoS) attacks from within?

_____

_____

Which routers in this scenario could be overloaded by such unreachable traffic?

_____

_____

Always consider the benefits and drawbacks in summarization and using default routing techniques before implementing them in an internetwork. These tools are useful in decreasing the size of a routing table, but may have drawbacks as well based on your topology. For instance, auto-summarization should not be used in topologies with discontiguous networks.

What would happen if the connection to the Internet on R1 were a subnet of the 172.16.0.0/16 network?

_____

_____

_____

_____

Conclusion

Issue the **show ip protocols** command again. How has the output changed?

```
R1# show ip protocols
Routing Protocol is "eigrp 100"
  Outgoing update filter list for all interfaces is not set
  Incoming update filter list for all interfaces is not set
  Default networks flagged in outgoing updates
  Default networks accepted from incoming updates
  EIGRP metric weight K1=1, K2=0, K3=1, K4=0, K5=0
  EIGRP maximum hopcount 100
  EIGRP maximum metric variance 1
  Redistributing: eigrp 100
  EIGRP NSF-aware route hold timer is 240s
  Automatic network summarization is in effect
  Automatic address summarization:
    192.168.100.0/24 for Loopback0
      Summarizing with metric 40512000
    172.31.0.0/16 for Serial0/0/0
      Summarizing with metric 128256
  Maximum path: 4
  Routing for Networks:
    172.31.0.0
    192.168.100.0
  Routing Information Sources:
    Gateway         Distance      Last Update
    (this router)         90      00:23:10
    Gateway         Distance      Last Update
    192.168.100.2         90      00:30:32
  Distance: internal 90 external 170
```

Run the TCL script from Step 1 again. Are all your pings successful? Verify your output against the section "TCL Script Output" for this lab.

When configuring a major network change such as summarization and default network, always test to see not only if you achieve the desired effect within your core paths but on the outlying branches as well.

The engineer still wants to know if all of these solutions decreased the size of the routing table as you claimed. Display the size of the routing table on R1, R2, and R3 with the **show ip route summary** command you used at the end of Step 1. By what amount has the total routing table size decreased on each router?

```
R1# show ip route summary
IP routing table name is Default-IP-Routing-Table(0)
IP routing table maximum-paths is 16
Route Source    Networks     Subnets      Overhead     Memory (bytes)
connected       0            2            144          272
static          0            0            0            0
eigrp 100       4            2            432          2856
internal        2                                      2312
Total           6            4            576          5440
```

```
R2# show ip route summary
IP routing table name is Default-IP-Routing-Table(0)
IP routing table maximum-paths is 16
Route Source    Networks     Subnets      Overhead     Memory (bytes)
connected       0            9            648          1224
static          0            0            0            0
eigrp 100       3            4            504          1972
internal        3                                      3468
Total           6            13           1152         6664
```

```
R3# show ip route summary
IP routing table name is Default-IP-Routing-Table(0)
IP routing table maximum-paths is 16
Route Source    Networks     Subnets      Overhead     Memory (bytes)
connected       14           3            1224         2312
static          0            0            0            0
eigrp 100       4            2            432          2856
internal        2                                      2312
Total           20           5            1656         7480
```

_____

_____

_____

_____

Although this may seem like a trivial amount in terms of bytes, you should understand the principles involved and the outcome of a much more converged, scalable routing table. Consider also that summaries cause less EIGRP Query, Reply, Update, and ACK packets to be sent to neighbors every time an EIGRP interface flaps. Queries can be propagated far beyond the local link and, by default, EIGRP may consume up to 50 percent of the bandwidth with its traffic. This could have severe repercussions on bandwidth consumption on a link.

Consider also the routing table of the Internet and how candidate default routing within an enterprise network can help minimize routing tables by routing traffic to a dynamically identified outbound path from a network. For enterprise-level networks, the amount of space and CPU utilization saved in storing topology and routing tables, and maintaining routing tables with constant changes, can be an important method for developing a faster and more converged network.

TCL Script Output

```
R1# tclsh
R1(tcl)# foreach address {
+>(tcl)# 10.1.1.2
+>(tcl)# 10.1.1.3
+>(tcl)# 10.1.3.1
+>(tcl)# 172.16.1.1
+>(tcl)# 172.31.1.1
+>(tcl)# 192.168.1.1
+>(tcl)# 192.168.5.5
+>(tcl)# 192.168.9.9
+>(tcl)# 192.168.13.13
+>(tcl)# 192.168.17.17
+>(tcl)# 192.168.21.21
+>(tcl)# 192.168.25.25
+>(tcl)# 192.168.100.1
+>(tcl)# 192.168.200.1
+>(tcl)# 192.168.200.5
+>(tcl)# 192.168.200.9
+>(tcl)# 192.168.200.13
+>(tcl)# 192.168.200.17
+>(tcl)# 192.168.200.21
+>(tcl)# 192.168.200.25
+>(tcl)# 192.168.100.2
+>(tcl)# } { ping $address }


Type escape sequence to abort.
Sending 5, 100-byte ICMP Echos to 10.1.1.2, timeout is 2 seconds:
!!!!!
Success rate is 100 percent (5/5), round-trip min/avg/max = 28/28/32 ms
Type escape sequence to abort.
Sending 5, 100-byte ICMP Echos to 10.1.1.3, timeout is 2 seconds:
!!!!!
Success rate is 100 percent (5/5), round-trip min/avg/max = 28/29/32 ms
Type escape sequence to abort.
Sending 5, 100-byte ICMP Echos to 10.1.3.1, timeout is 2 seconds:
!!!!!
Success rate is 100 percent (5/5), round-trip min/avg/max = 28/29/32 ms
Type escape sequence to abort.
Sending 5, 100-byte ICMP Echos to 172.16.1.1, timeout is 2 seconds:
```

```
!!!!!
Success rate is 100 percent (5/5), round-trip min/avg/max = 28/29/32 ms
Type escape sequence to abort.
Sending 5, 100-byte ICMP Echos to 172.31.1.1, timeout is 2 seconds:
!!!!!
Success rate is 100 percent (5/5), round-trip min/avg/max = 1/1/4 ms
Type escape sequence to abort.
Sending 5, 100-byte ICMP Echos to 192.168.1.1, timeout is 2 seconds:
!!!!!
Success rate is 100 percent (5/5), round-trip min/avg/max = 28/29/32 ms
Type escape sequence to abort.
Sending 5, 100-byte ICMP Echos to 192.168.5.5, timeout is 2 seconds:
!!!!!
Success rate is 100 percent (5/5), round-trip min/avg/max = 28/29/32 ms
Type escape sequence to abort.
Sending 5, 100-byte ICMP Echos to 192.168.9.9, timeout is 2 seconds:
!!!!!
Success rate is 100 percent (5/5), round-trip min/avg/max = 28/29/32 ms
Type escape sequence to abort.
Sending 5, 100-byte ICMP Echos to 192.168.13.13, timeout is 2 seconds:
!!!!!
Success rate is 100 percent (5/5), round-trip min/avg/max = 28/29/32 ms
Type escape sequence to abort.
Sending 5, 100-byte ICMP Echos to 192.168.17.17, timeout is 2 seconds:
!!!!!
Success rate is 100 percent (5/5), round-trip min/avg/max = 28/29/32 ms
Type escape sequence to abort.
Sending 5, 100-byte ICMP Echos to 192.168.21.21, timeout is 2 seconds:
!!!!!
Success rate is 100 percent (5/5), round-trip min/avg/max = 28/29/32 ms
Type escape sequence to abort.
Sending 5, 100-byte ICMP Echos to 192.168.25.25, timeout is 2 seconds:
!!!!!
Success rate is 100 percent (5/5), round-trip min/avg/max = 28/29/32 ms
Type escape sequence to abort.
Sending 5, 100-byte ICMP Echos to 192.168.100.1, timeout is 2 seconds:
!!!!!
Success rate is 100 percent (5/5), round-trip min/avg/max = 56/57/64 ms
Type escape sequence to abort.
Sending 5, 100-byte ICMP Echos to 192.168.200.1, timeout is 2 seconds:
!!!!!
Success rate is 100 percent (5/5), round-trip min/avg/max = 28/28/32 ms
Type escape sequence to abort.
Sending 5, 100-byte ICMP Echos to 192.168.200.5, timeout is 2 seconds:
```

```
!!!!!
Success rate is 100 percent (5/5), round-trip min/avg/max = 28/28/28 ms
Type escape sequence to abort.
Sending 5, 100-byte ICMP Echos to 192.168.200.9, timeout is 2 seconds:
!!!!!
Success rate is 100 percent (5/5), round-trip min/avg/max = 28/28/32 ms
Type escape sequence to abort.
Sending 5, 100-byte ICMP Echos to 192.168.200.13, timeout is 2 seconds:
!!!!!
Success rate is 100 percent (5/5), round-trip min/avg/max = 28/28/32 ms
Type escape sequence to abort.
Sending 5, 100-byte ICMP Echos to 192.168.200.17, timeout is 2 seconds:
!!!!!
Success rate is 100 percent (5/5), round-trip min/avg/max = 28/28/28 ms
Type escape sequence to abort.
Sending 5, 100-byte ICMP Echos to 192.168.200.21, timeout is 2 seconds:
!!!!!
Success rate is 100 percent (5/5), round-trip min/avg/max = 28/28/28 ms
Type escape sequence to abort.
Sending 5, 100-byte ICMP Echos to 192.168.200.25, timeout is 2 seconds:
!!!!!
Success rate is 100 percent (5/5), round-trip min/avg/max = 28/28/32 ms
Type escape sequence to abort.
Sending 5, 100-byte ICMP Echos to 192.168.100.2, timeout is 2 seconds:
!!!!!
Success rate is 100 percent (5/5), round-trip min/avg/max = 28/28/32 ms
R1(tcl)# tclquit
R1#
```

```
R2# tclsh
R2(tcl)# foreach address {
+>(tcl)# 10.1.1.2
+>(tcl)# 10.1.1.3
+>(tcl)# 10.1.3.1
+>(tcl)# 172.16.1.1
+>(tcl)# 172.31.1.1
+>(tcl)# 192.168.1.1
+>(tcl)# 192.168.5.5
+>(tcl)# 192.168.9.9
+>(tcl)# 192.168.13.13
+>(tcl)# 192.168.17.17
+>(tcl)# 192.168.21.21
+>(tcl)# 192.168.25.25
+>(tcl)# 192.168.100.1
+>(tcl)# 192.168.200.1
```

```
+>(tcl)# 192.168.200.5
+>(tcl)# 192.168.200.9
+>(tcl)# 192.168.200.13
+>(tcl)# 192.168.200.17
+>(tcl)# 192.168.200.21
+>(tcl)# 192.168.200.25
+>(tcl)# 192.168.100.2
+>(tcl)# } { ping $address }
```

```
Type escape sequence to abort.
Sending 5, 100-byte ICMP Echos to 10.1.1.2, timeout is 2 seconds:
!!!!!
Success rate is 100 percent (5/5), round-trip min/avg/max = 1/2/4 ms
Type escape sequence to abort.
Sending 5, 100-byte ICMP Echos to 10.1.1.3, timeout is 2 seconds:
!!!!!
Success rate is 100 percent (5/5), round-trip min/avg/max = 1/2/4 ms
Type escape sequence to abort.
Sending 5, 100-byte ICMP Echos to 10.1.3.1, timeout is 2 seconds:
!!!!!
Success rate is 100 percent (5/5), round-trip min/avg/max = 1/2/4 ms
Type escape sequence to abort.
Sending 5, 100-byte ICMP Echos to 172.16.1.1, timeout is 2 seconds:
!!!!!
Success rate is 100 percent (5/5), round-trip min/avg/max = 1/2/4 ms
Type escape sequence to abort.
Sending 5, 100-byte ICMP Echos to 172.31.1.1, timeout is 2 seconds:
!!!!!
Success rate is 100 percent (5/5), round-trip min/avg/max = 28/28/32 ms
Type escape sequence to abort.
Sending 5, 100-byte ICMP Echos to 192.168.1.1, timeout is 2 seconds:
!!!!!
Success rate is 100 percent (5/5), round-trip min/avg/max = 1/2/4 ms
Type escape sequence to abort.
Sending 5, 100-byte ICMP Echos to 192.168.5.5, timeout is 2 seconds:
!!!!!
Success rate is 100 percent (5/5), round-trip min/avg/max = 1/2/4 ms
Type escape sequence to abort.
Sending 5, 100-byte ICMP Echos to 192.168.9.9, timeout is 2 seconds:
!!!!!
Success rate is 100 percent (5/5), round-trip min/avg/max = 1/2/4 ms
Type escape sequence to abort.
Sending 5, 100-byte ICMP Echos to 192.168.13.13, timeout is 2 seconds:
!!!!!
```

```
Success rate is 100 percent (5/5), round-trip min/avg/max = 1/2/4 ms
Type escape sequence to abort.
Sending 5, 100-byte ICMP Echos to 192.168.17.17, timeout is 2 seconds:
!!!!!
Success rate is 100 percent (5/5), round-trip min/avg/max = 1/2/4 ms
Type escape sequence to abort.
Sending 5, 100-byte ICMP Echos to 192.168.21.21, timeout is 2 seconds:
!!!!!
Success rate is 100 percent (5/5), round-trip min/avg/max = 1/2/4 ms
Type escape sequence to abort.
Sending 5, 100-byte ICMP Echos to 192.168.25.25, timeout is 2 seconds:
!!!!!
Success rate is 100 percent (5/5), round-trip min/avg/max = 1/2/4 ms
Type escape sequence to abort.
Sending 5, 100-byte ICMP Echos to 192.168.100.1, timeout is 2 seconds:
!!!!!
Success rate is 100 percent (5/5), round-trip min/avg/max = 28/28/32 ms
Type escape sequence to abort.
Sending 5, 100-byte ICMP Echos to 192.168.200.1, timeout is 2 seconds:
!!!!!
Success rate is 100 percent (5/5), round-trip min/avg/max = 1/1/4 ms
Type escape sequence to abort.
Sending 5, 100-byte ICMP Echos to 192.168.200.5, timeout is 2 seconds:
!!!!!
Success rate is 100 percent (5/5), round-trip min/avg/max = 1/1/1 ms
Type escape sequence to abort.
Sending 5, 100-byte ICMP Echos to 192.168.200.9, timeout is 2 seconds:
!!!!!
Success rate is 100 percent (5/5), round-trip min/avg/max = 1/1/1 ms
Type escape sequence to abort.
Sending 5, 100-byte ICMP Echos to 192.168.200.13, timeout is 2 seconds:
!!!!!
Success rate is 100 percent (5/5), round-trip min/avg/max = 1/1/4 ms
Type escape sequence to abort.
Sending 5, 100-byte ICMP Echos to 192.168.200.17, timeout is 2 seconds:
!!!!!
Success rate is 100 percent (5/5), round-trip min/avg/max = 1/1/4 ms
Type escape sequence to abort.
Sending 5, 100-byte ICMP Echos to 192.168.200.21, timeout is 2 seconds:
!!!!!
Success rate is 100 percent (5/5), round-trip min/avg/max = 1/1/1 ms
Type escape sequence to abort.
Sending 5, 100-byte ICMP Echos to 192.168.200.25, timeout is 2 seconds:
!!!!!
```

```
Success rate is 100 percent (5/5), round-trip min/avg/max = 1/1/1 ms
Type escape sequence to abort.
Sending 5, 100-byte ICMP Echos to 192.168.100.2, timeout is 2 seconds:
!!!!!
Success rate is 100 percent (5/5), round-trip min/avg/max = 56/57/64 ms
R2(tcl)# tclquit
R2#
```
```
R3# tclsh
R3(tcl)# foreach address {
+>(tcl)# 10.1.1.2
+>(tcl)# 10.1.1.3
+>(tcl)# 10.1.3.1
+>(tcl)# 172.16.1.1
+>(tcl)# 172.31.1.1
+>(tcl)# 192.168.1.1
+>(tcl)# 192.168.5.5
+>(tcl)# 192.168.9.9
+>(tcl)# 192.168.13.13
+>(tcl)# 192.168.17.17
+>(tcl)# 192.168.21.21
+>(tcl)# 192.168.25.25
+>(tcl)# 192.168.100.1
+>(tcl)# 192.168.200.1
+>(tcl)# 192.168.200.5
+>(tcl)# 192.168.200.9
+>(tcl)# 192.168.200.13
+>(tcl)# 192.168.200.17
+>(tcl)# 192.168.200.21
+>(tcl)# 192.168.200.25
+>(tcl)# 192.168.100.2
+>(tcl)# } { ping $address }

Type escape sequence to abort.
Sending 5, 100-byte ICMP Echos to 10.1.1.2, timeout is 2 seconds:
!!!!!
Success rate is 100 percent (5/5), round-trip min/avg/max = 1/2/4 ms
Type escape sequence to abort.
Sending 5, 100-byte ICMP Echos to 10.1.1.3, timeout is 2 seconds:
!!!!!
Success rate is 100 percent (5/5), round-trip min/avg/max = 1/3/4 ms
Type escape sequence to abort.
Sending 5, 100-byte ICMP Echos to 10.1.3.1, timeout is 2 seconds:
!!!!!
Success rate is 100 percent (5/5), round-trip min/avg/max = 1/1/4 ms
```

```
Type escape sequence to abort.
Sending 5, 100-byte ICMP Echos to 172.16.1.1, timeout is 2 seconds:
!!!!!
Success rate is 100 percent (5/5), round-trip min/avg/max = 1/1/4 ms
Type escape sequence to abort.
Sending 5, 100-byte ICMP Echos to 172.31.1.1, timeout is 2 seconds:
!!!!!
Success rate is 100 percent (5/5), round-trip min/avg/max = 28/29/32 ms
Type escape sequence to abort.
Sending 5, 100-byte ICMP Echos to 192.168.1.1, timeout is 2 seconds:
!!!!!
Success rate is 100 percent (5/5), round-trip min/avg/max = 1/1/4 ms
Type escape sequence to abort.
Sending 5, 100-byte ICMP Echos to 192.168.5.5, timeout is 2 seconds:
!!!!!
Success rate is 100 percent (5/5), round-trip min/avg/max = 1/1/1 ms
Type escape sequence to abort.
Sending 5, 100-byte ICMP Echos to 192.168.9.9, timeout is 2 seconds:
!!!!!
Success rate is 100 percent (5/5), round-trip min/avg/max = 1/1/4 ms
Type escape sequence to abort.
Sending 5, 100-byte ICMP Echos to 192.168.13.13, timeout is 2 seconds:
!!!!!
Success rate is 100 percent (5/5), round-trip min/avg/max = 1/1/1 ms
Type escape sequence to abort.
Sending 5, 100-byte ICMP Echos to 192.168.17.17, timeout is 2 seconds:
!!!!!
Success rate is 100 percent (5/5), round-trip min/avg/max = 1/1/4 ms
Type escape sequence to abort.
Sending 5, 100-byte ICMP Echos to 192.168.21.21, timeout is 2 seconds:
!!!!!
Success rate is 100 percent (5/5), round-trip min/avg/max = 1/1/1 ms
Type escape sequence to abort.
Sending 5, 100-byte ICMP Echos to 192.168.25.25, timeout is 2 seconds:
!!!!!
Success rate is 100 percent (5/5), round-trip min/avg/max = 1/1/4 ms
Type escape sequence to abort.
Sending 5, 100-byte ICMP Echos to 192.168.100.1, timeout is 2 seconds:
!!!!!
Success rate is 100 percent (5/5), round-trip min/avg/max = 28/29/32 ms
Type escape sequence to abort.
Sending 5, 100-byte ICMP Echos to 192.168.200.1, timeout is 2 seconds:
!!!!!
Success rate is 100 percent (5/5), round-trip min/avg/max = 1/2/4 ms
```

```
Type escape sequence to abort.
Sending 5, 100-byte ICMP Echos to 192.168.200.5, timeout is 2 seconds:
!!!!!
Success rate is 100 percent (5/5), round-trip min/avg/max = 1/2/4 ms
Type escape sequence to abort.
Sending 5, 100-byte ICMP Echos to 192.168.200.9, timeout is 2 seconds:
!!!!!
Success rate is 100 percent (5/5), round-trip min/avg/max = 1/2/4 ms
Type escape sequence to abort.
Sending 5, 100-byte ICMP Echos to 192.168.200.13, timeout is 2 seconds:
!!!!!
Success rate is 100 percent (5/5), round-trip min/avg/max = 1/2/4 ms
Type escape sequence to abort.
Sending 5, 100-byte ICMP Echos to 192.168.200.17, timeout is 2 seconds:
!!!!!
Success rate is 100 percent (5/5), round-trip min/avg/max = 1/2/4 ms
Type escape sequence to abort.
Sending 5, 100-byte ICMP Echos to 192.168.200.21, timeout is 2 seconds:
!!!!!
Success rate is 100 percent (5/5), round-trip min/avg/max = 1/2/4 ms
Type escape sequence to abort.
Sending 5, 100-byte ICMP Echos to 192.168.200.25, timeout is 2 seconds:
!!!!!
Success rate is 100 percent (5/5), round-trip min/avg/max = 1/2/4 ms
Type escape sequence to abort.
Sending 5, 100-byte ICMP Echos to 192.168.100.2, timeout is 2 seconds:
!!!!!
Success rate is 100 percent (5/5), round-trip min/avg/max = 1/2/4 ms
R3(tcl)# tclquit
R3#
```

Analyzing Major Networks

The output of the **show ip route** command in this scenario is somewhat complicated, but useful for you to understand since you will see similar output in production networks. This output involves both subnets and supernets and the major networks themselves as group headings:

```
R1# show ip route
<output omitted>

Gateway of last resort is not set

     172.16.0.0/24 is subnetted, 1 subnets
D       172.16.1.0 [90/41152000] via 192.168.100.2, 00:10:31, Serial0/0/0
     172.31.0.0/24 is subnetted, 1 subnets
```

```
C        172.31.1.0 is directly connected, Loopback0
         192.168.200.0/30 is subnetted, 7 subnets
D        192.168.200.0 [90/40640000] via 192.168.100.2, 00:11:14, Serial0/0/0
D        192.168.200.4 [90/40640000] via 192.168.100.2, 00:11:14, Serial0/0/0
D        192.168.200.8 [90/40640000] via 192.168.100.2, 00:11:14, Serial0/0/0
D        192.168.200.12 [90/40640000] via 192.168.100.2, 00:11:15, Serial0/0/0
D        192.168.200.16 [90/40640000] via 192.168.100.2, 00:11:15, Serial0/0/0
D        192.168.200.20 [90/40640000] via 192.168.100.2, 00:11:15, Serial0/0/0
D        192.168.200.24 [90/40640000] via 192.168.100.2, 00:11:15, Serial0/0/0
         10.0.0.0/8 is variably subnetted, 2 subnets, 2 masks
D        10.1.3.0/30 [90/41152000] via 192.168.100.2, 00:10:32, Serial0/0/0
D        10.1.1.0/29 [90/41024000] via 192.168.100.2, 00:10:39, Serial0/0/0
         192.168.100.0/29 is subnetted, 1 subnets
C        192.168.100.0 is directly connected, Serial0/0/0
D     192.168.12.0/23 [90/41152000] via 192.168.100.2, 00:10:32, Serial0/0/0
D     192.168.8.0/23 [90/41152000] via 192.168.100.2, 00:10:32, Serial0/0/0
D     192.168.24.0/23 [90/41152000] via 192.168.100.2, 00:10:32, Serial0/0/0
D     192.168.4.0/23 [90/41152000] via 192.168.100.2, 00:10:32, Serial0/0/0
D     192.168.20.0/23 [90/41152000] via 192.168.100.2, 00:10:32, Serial0/0/0
D     192.168.0.0/23 [90/41152000] via 192.168.100.2, 00:10:33, Serial0/0/0
D     192.168.16.0/23 [90/41152000] via 192.168.100.2, 00:10:33, Serial0/0/0
R1#
```

Notice that the output of the **show ip route** command displays all subnets of a given major network grouped by major network:

- 10.0.0.0/8
- 172.16.0.0/16
- 172.31.0.0/16
- 192.168.100.0/24
- 192.168.200.0/24

Each /23 supernet consists of two major networks combined into one /23. For example, the 192.168.0.0/23 network covers the major network 192.168.0.0/24 and the major network 192.168.1.0/24.

You may wonder why do 172.16.0.0/24, 172.31.0.0/24, 192.168.100.0/30, and 192.168.200.0/29 appear as group headings with longer masks than the classful mask.

When you subnet a major network into subnets that all have the same mask and advertise those networks to a router, the routing table simply decides that it will do all lookups for that major network in a classless way using the mask provided. The routing table is not expecting any variable-length subnet masks (VLSM) for those major networks because it has not yet learned of any. Therefore, the headings listed above display as the headings in the routing table.

Analyze the output of the **show ip route** command as follows:

- The 172.16.0.0/24 indicates that the 172.16.0.0/16 major network is only divided into subnets of 24-bit masks.

- The 172.31.0.0/24 indicates that the 172.31.0.0/16 major network is only divided into subnets of 24-bit masks.

- The 192.168.100.0/30 indicates that the 192.168.100.0/24 major network is only divided into subnets of 24-bit masks.

- The 192.168.200.0/29 indicates that the 192.168.200.0/24 major network is only divided into subnets of 29-bit masks.

You should not observe this behavior with the 10.0.0.0/8 network because R1's routing table has had subnets installed with VLSMs within that major network. Because R1 cannot generalize its destination prefixes for the 10.0.0.0/8 network, it forces the subnet into VLSM mode and shows it as "variably subnetted."

Lab 2-4: EIGRP Frame Relay Hub and Spoke: Router Used as Frame Switch (2.7.4)

The objectives of this lab are as follows:

- Review basic configuration of EIGRP on a serial interface

- Configure the **bandwidth-percent** command

- Configure EIGRP over Frame Relay hub and spoke

- Use EIGRP in nonbroadcast mode

- Enable EIGRP manual summarization in topologies with discontiguous major networks

Figure 2-4 illustrates the topology that will be used for this lab.

Figure 2-4   Topology Diagram

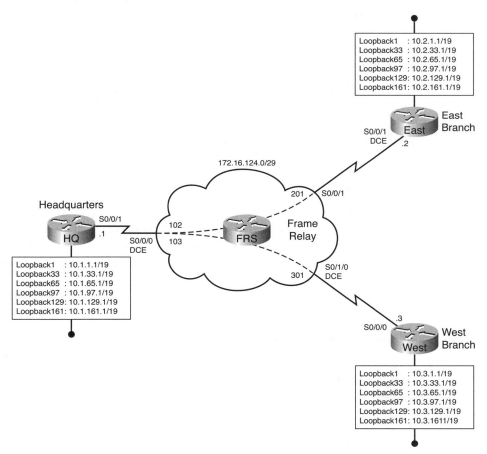

Note Given the diversity of router models and the differing naming conventions for serial interfaces (S0, S0/0, S0/0/0), the interface numbers on your devices will probably differ from those in the topology diagram. The same is true for which side of the link is DCE or DTE. You should always draw your network diagram to reflect your topology. If you are uncertain which side of the connection is DCE, use the **show controllers serial** *interface-number* command:

```
HQ# show controllers serial0/0/0
Interface Serial0/0/0
Hardware is GT96K
DCE V.35, clock rate 2000000
<output omitted>
```

Scenario

You are responsible for configuring and testing the new network that connects your company's headquarters and East and West branches. The three locations are connected over hub-and-spoke Frame Relay, using the company headquarters as the hub. Model each branch office's network with multiple loopback interfaces on each router, and configure EIGRP to allow full connectivity between all departments.

To simulate the Frame Relay WAN connections, use a router with three serial ports configured as a frame switch. The router configuration is described in Step 2.

Note If your site uses an Adtran Atlas to simulate Frame Relay, use Lab 2-5 to complete this exercise.

Step 1: Addressing

Using the addressing scheme in Figure 2-4, apply IP addresses to the loopback interfaces on HQ, East, and West. You may paste the following configurations into your routers to begin. You must be in configuration mode when you do this. You can download these router configurations at www.ciscopress.com/title/1587132133 under the More Information section on the page.

```
HQ:
!
interface Loopback1
 ip address 10.1.1.1 255.255.224.0
interface Loopback33
 ip address 10.1.33.1 255.255.224.0
interface Loopback65
 ip address 10.1.65.1 255.255.224.0
interface Loopback97
 ip address 10.1.97.1 255.255.224.0
interface Loopback129
 ip address 10.1.129.1 255.255.224.0
interface Loopback161
 ip address 10.1.161.1 255.255.224.0
!
end
```

East:

```
!
interface Loopback1
 ip address 10.2.1.1 255.255.224.0
interface Loopback33
 ip address 10.2.33.1 255.255.224.0
interface Loopback65
 ip address 10.2.65.1 255.255.224.0
interface Loopback97
 ip address 10.2.97.1 255.255.224.0
interface Loopback129
 ip address 10.2.129.1 255.255.224.0
interface Loopback161
 ip address 10.2.161.1 255.255.224.0
!
end
```

```
West:
!
interface Loopback1
 ip address 10.3.1.1 255.255.224.0
interface Loopback33
 ip address 10.3.33.1 255.255.224.0
interface Loopback65
 ip address 10.3.65.1 255.255.224.0
interface Loopback97
 ip address 10.3.97.1 255.255.224.0
interface Loopback129
 ip address 10.3.129.1 255.255.224.0
interface Loopback161
 ip address 10.3.161.1 255.255.224.0
!
end
```

For now, the IP address is the only configuration on the serial interfaces. Leave the serial interfaces with their default encapsulation (High-Level Data Link Control [HDLC]). This will change in Step 3.

Step 2: Configuring the Frame Relay Switch

To use a fourth Cisco router with three serial interfaces as a Frame Relay switch, cable the routers according to Figure 2-4. Paste the following configuration into the router (depending on which equipment you have, the interface numbers may be different). You can download these router configurations at www.ciscopress.com/title/1587132133 under the More Information section on the page.

```
!
hostname FRS
!
```

```
frame-relay switching
!
interface Serial0/0/0
 description FR to HQ
 encapsulation frame-relay
 clock rate 128000
 frame-relay lmi-type cisco
 frame-relay intf-type dce
 frame-relay route 102 interface Serial0/0/1 201
 frame-relay route 103 interface Serial0/1/0 301
 no shutdown
!
interface Serial0/0/1
 description FR to East
 no ip address
 encapsulation frame-relay
 clock rate 64000
 frame-relay lmi-type cisco
 frame-relay intf-type dce
 frame-relay route 201 interface Serial0/0/0 102
 no shutdown
!
interface Serial0/1/0
 description FR to West
 no ip address
 encapsulation frame-relay
 clock rate 64000
 frame-relay lmi-type cisco
 frame-relay intf-type dce
 frame-relay route 301 interface Serial0/0/0 103
 no shutdown
!
end
```

Step 3: Configuring the Frame Relay Endpoints

You will be configuring HQ to be the Frame Relay hub, with East and West as the spokes. Check the topology diagram for the data-link connection identifiers (DLCI) to use in the Frame Relay maps. Turn Frame Relay Inverse Address Resolution Protocol (InARP) off for all interfaces. Configure all Frame Relay interfaces as physical interfaces.

InARP allows a Frame Relay network to discover the IP address associated with the virtual circuit. This is sometimes a desirable trait in a production network. However, in the lab, we turn off InARP to limit the number of dynamic DLCIs that are created.

First, enter the configuration menu for that interface in global configuration mode and assign it an IP address using the **ip address** command. Assign the Frame Relay subnet to be 172.16.124.0 /29. The fourth octet of the IP address is the router number (HQ=1, East=2, West=3).

Next, enable Frame Relay encapsulation using the interface configuration command **encapsulation frame-relay**. Disable Frame Relay InARP with the **no frame-relay inverse-arp** command. Finally, map the other IPs in the subnet to DLCIs, using the **frame-relay map ip address dlci broadcast** command. The **broadcast** keyword is important because, without it, EIGRP hello packets are not sent through the Frame Relay cloud. Do not forget to bring up your interfaces with the **no shutdown** command:

```
HQ# configure terminal
HQ(config)# interface serial 0/0/1
HQ(config-if)# ip address 172.16.124.1 255.255.255.248
HQ(config-if)# encapsulation frame-relay
HQ(config-if)# no frame-relay inverse-arp
HQ(config-if)# frame-relay map ip 172.16.124.2 102 broadcast
HQ(config-if)# frame-relay map ip 172.16.124.3 103 broadcast
HQ(config-if)# no shutdown
```
```
East# configure terminal
East(config)# interface serial 0/0/1
East(config-if)# ip address 172.16.124.2 255.255.255.248
East(config-if)# encapsulation frame-relay
East(config-if)# no frame-relay inverse-arp
East(config-if)# frame-relay map ip 172.16.124.1 201 broadcast
East(config-if)# frame-relay map ip 172.16.124.3 201 broadcast
East(config-if)# no shutdown
```
```
West# configure terminal
West(config)# interface serial 0/0/0
West(config-if)# ip address 172.16.124.3 255.255.255.248
West(config-if)# no frame-relay inverse-arp
West(config-if)# encapsulation frame-relay
West(config-if)# frame-relay map ip 172.16.124.1 301 broadcast
West(config-if)# frame-relay map ip 172.16.124.2 301 broadcast
West(config-if)# clock rate 64000
West(config-if)# no shutdown
```

Note that you have not yet configured the bandwidth parameter on these serial links, as you did in Lab 2-2. This will be done in Step 4.

Verify that you have connectivity across the Frame Relay network by pinging the remote routers from each of the Frame Relay endpoints. Using the preceding configuration, you will find that you cannot ping your own local interface. For instance, ping 172.16.124.1 from HQ:

```
HQ# ping 172.16.124.1
Type escape sequence to abort.
Sending 5, 100-byte ICMP Echos to 172.16.124.1, timeout is 2 seconds:
.....
Success rate is 0 percent (0/5)
```

The only interface your Frame Relay interface is unable to communicate with is itself. This is not a significant problem in Frame Relay networks, but you could map the local IP address to be forwarded out a permanent virtual circuit (PVC). The remote router at the other end of the PVC can then forward it back based on its Frame Relay **map** statements. This solution is so that the TCL scripts we use for testing return successful echo replies under all circumstances. You do not need the **broadcast** keyword on this DLCI, because it is not important to forward broadcast and multicast packets (such as EIGRP hellos) to your own interface.

Implement the local mappings as follows:

```
HQ(config-if)# frame-relay map ip 172.16.124.1 102
```
```
East(config-if)# frame-relay map ip 172.16.124.2 201
```
```
West(config-if)# frame-relay map ip 172.16.124.3 301
```

HQ now forwards packets destined for 172.16.124.1 first to 172.16.124.2 and then back. In a production network in which a company is billed based on per-PVC usage, this is not a preferred configuration. However, in your lab network, this helps ensure full ICMP connectivity in your TCL scripts.

For more information about this behavior of Frame Relay, see the following FAQ page: http://www.cisco.com/warp/public/116/fr_faq.pdf

Step 4: Setting Interface-Level Bandwidth

On the three routers, set the Frame Relay serial interface bandwidth with the interface-level command **bandwidth** *bandwidth*, specifying the bandwidth in kilobits per second. For HQ, use 128 Kbps. On East and West, use 64 Kbps.

Recall from Lab 2-1 that, by default, EIGRP limits its bandwidth usage to 50 percent of the value specified by the bandwidth parameter. The default bandwidth for a serial interface is 1544 Kbps.

Over multipoint Frame Relay interfaces, EIGRP limits its EIGRP traffic to a total of 50 percent of the bandwidth value. This means that each neighbor for which this is an outbound interface has a traffic limit of a fraction of that 50 percent, represented by $1/N$, where N is the number of neighbors out that interface:

```
HQ(config)# interface serial 0/0/1
```
```
HQ(config-if)# bandwidth 128
```
```
East(config)# interface serial 0/0/1
```
```
East(config-if)# bandwidth 64
```
```
West(config)# interface serial 0/0/0
```
```
West(config-if)# bandwidth 64
```

HQ's serial interface divides its total EIGRP bandwidth into the fractional amounts according to the number of neighbors out that interface.

How much bandwidth on Serial0/0/1 on HQ is reserved for EIGRP traffic to East?

_____

_____

You can control both the bandwidth parameter and the EIGRP bandwidth percentage on a per-interface basis. On HQ, limit the bandwidth used by EIGRP to 40 percent without changing the bandwidth parameter on the interface. You can accomplish this with the interface-level command **ip bandwidth-percent eigrp** *as_number percent*:

```
HQ(config-if)# ip bandwidth-percent eigrp 1 40
```

Step 5: Configuring EIGRP

Configure EIGRP AS 1 on HQ, East, and West. First use the global configuration mode command **router eigrp** *as_number* to get the EIGRP configuration prompt.

The network represented in Figure 2-4 is a discontiguous network (10.0.0.0/8) configured on all three of the routers. If you turned on auto-summarization, HQ sends and receives summaries for 10.0.0.0/8 from both East and West. Auto-summarization provokes considerable routing disruptions in the network, because HQ does not know which of the two spokes is the correct destination for subnets of 10.0.0.0/8. For this reason, turn off auto-summarization on each router.

Add your **network** statements to EIGRP. The two major networks we are using here are **network 10.0.0.0** for the loopbacks, and **network 172.16.0.0** for the Frame Relay cloud. Perform this configuration on all three routers:

```
HQ(config)# router eigrp 1
HQ(config-router)# network 10.0.0.0
HQ(config-router)# network 172.16.0.0
HQ(config-router)# no auto-summary
```
```
East(config)# router eigrp 1
East(config-router)# network 10.0.0.0
East(config-router)# network 172.16.0.0
East(config-router)# no auto-summary
```
```
West(config)# router eigrp 1
West(config-router)# network 10.0.0.0
West(config-router)# network 172.16.0.0
West(config-router)# no auto-summary
```

Issue the **show ip eigrp topology** command on East:

```
East# show ip eigrp topology
IP-EIGRP Topology Table for AS(1)/ID(172.16.124.2)

Codes: P - Passive, A - Active, U - Update, Q - Query, R - Reply,
       r - reply Status, s - sia Status

P 10.2.0.0/19, 1 successors, FD is 128256
        via Connected, Loopback1
P 10.1.0.0/19, 1 successors, FD is 40640000
         via 172.16.124.1 (40640000/128256), Serial0/0/1
P 10.2.32.0/19, 1 successors, FD is 128256
        via Connected, Loopback33
P 10.1.32.0/19, 1 successors, FD is 40640000
        via 172.16.124.1 (40640000/128256), Serial0/0/1
```

```
P 10.2.64.0/19, 1 successors, FD is 128256
        via Connected, Loopback65
P 10.1.64.0/19, 1 successors, FD is 40640000
        via 172.16.124.1 (40640000/128256), Serial0/0/1
P 10.2.96.0/19, 1 successors, FD is 128256
        via Connected, Loopback97
P 10.1.96.0/19, 1 successors, FD is 40640000
        via 172.16.124.1 (40640000/128256), Serial0/0/1
P 10.2.128.0/19, 1 successors, FD is 128256
        via Connected, Loopback129
P 10.1.128.0/19, 1 successors, FD is 40640000
        via 172.16.124.1 (40640000/128256), Serial0/0/1
P 10.2.160.0/19, 1 successors, FD is 128256
        via Connected, Loopback161
P 10.1.160.0/19, 1 successors, FD is 40640000
        via 172.16.124.1 (40640000/128256), Serial0/0/1
P 172.16.124.0/29, 1 successors, FD is 40512000
        via Connected, Serial0/0/1
East#
```

Which networks are missing from the topology database?

_____

_____

What do you suspect as being responsible for this problem?

_____

_____

Router 1 needs the **no ip split-horizon eigrp** *as_number* command on its serial Frame Relay interface:

```
HQ(config)# interface serial 0/0/1
HQ(config-if)# no ip split-horizon eigrp 1
```

This command disables split horizon for an EIGRP autonomous system. If split horizon is enabled (the default), route advertisements from East to HQ do not travel to West and vice versa, as shown in the preceding output.

Verify that you see the correct EIGRP adjacencies with the **show ip eigrp neighbors** command:

```
HQ# show ip eigrp neighbors
IP-EIGRP neighbors for process 1
H   Address          Interface       Hold Uptime   SRTT   RTO  Q   Seq
                                     (sec)         (ms)       Cnt Num
1   172.16.124.2     Se0/0/1         176 00:00:05  1588   5000 0   6
0   172.16.124.3     Se0/0/1         176 00:00:05    23   1140 0   6
East# show ip eigrp neighbors
IP-EIGRP neighbors for process 1
```

H	Address	Interface	Hold Uptime (sec)	SRTT (ms)	RTO	Q Cnt	Seq Num
0	172.16.124.1	Se0/0/1	129 00:00:52	20	2280	0	20

West# **show ip eigrp neighbors**

IP-EIGRP neighbors for process 1

H	Address	Interface	Hold Uptime (sec)	SRTT (ms)	RTO	Q Cnt	Seq Num
0	172.16.124.1	Se0/0/0	176 00:00:55	20	2280	0	13

Verify that you have IP routes on all three routers for the entire topology with the **show ip route** command:

HQ# **show ip route**

```
<output omitted>

    172.16.0.0/29 is subnetted, 1 subnets
C      172.16.124.0 is directly connected, Serial0/0/1
    10.0.0.0/19 is subnetted, 18 subnets
D      10.2.0.0 [90/20640000] via 172.16.124.2, 00:04:36, Serial0/0/1
D      10.3.0.0 [90/20640000] via 172.16.124.3, 00:04:20, Serial0/0/1
C      10.1.0.0 is directly connected, Loopback1
D      10.2.32.0 [90/20640000] via 172.16.124.2, 00:04:36, Serial0/0/1
D      10.3.32.0 [90/20640000] via 172.16.124.3, 00:04:20, Serial0/0/1
C      10.1.32.0 is directly connected, Loopback33
D      10.2.64.0 [90/20640000] via 172.16.124.2, 00:04:37, Serial0/0/1
D      10.3.64.0 [90/20640000] via 172.16.124.3, 00:04:21, Serial0/0/1
C      10.1.64.0 is directly connected, Loopback65
D      10.2.96.0 [90/20640000] via 172.16.124.2, 00:04:37, Serial0/0/1
D      10.3.96.0 [90/20640000] via 172.16.124.3, 00:04:21, Serial0/0/1
C      10.1.96.0 is directly connected, Loopback97
D      10.2.128.0 [90/20640000] via 172.16.124.2, 00:04:37, Serial0/0/1
D      10.3.128.0 [90/20640000] via 172.16.124.3, 00:04:21, Serial0/0/1
C      10.1.128.0 is directly connected, Loopback129
D      10.2.160.0 [90/20640000] via 172.16.124.2, 00:04:37, Serial0/0/1
D      10.3.160.0 [90/20640000] via 172.16.124.3, 00:04:21, Serial0/0/1
C      10.1.160.0 is directly connected, Loopback161
```

East# **show ip route**

```
<output omitted>

    172.16.0.0/29 is subnetted, 1 subnets
C      172.16.124.0 is directly connected, Serial0/0/1
    10.0.0.0/19 is subnetted, 18 subnets
C      10.2.0.0 is directly connected, Loopback1
D      10.3.0.0 [90/41152000] via 172.16.124.1, 00:01:31, Serial0/0/1
D      10.1.0.0 [90/40640000] via 172.16.124.1, 00:07:12, Serial0/0/1
```

```
C       10.2.32.0 is directly connected, Loopback33
D       10.3.32.0 [90/41152000] via 172.16.124.1, 00:01:31, Serial0/0/1
D       10.1.32.0 [90/40640000] via 172.16.124.1, 00:07:13, Serial0/0/1
C       10.2.64.0 is directly connected, Loopback65
D       10.3.64.0 [90/41152000] via 172.16.124.1, 00:01:32, Serial0/0/1
D       10.1.64.0 [90/40640000] via 172.16.124.1, 00:07:13, Serial0/0/1
C       10.2.96.0 is directly connected, Loopback97
D       10.3.96.0 [90/41152000] via 172.16.124.1, 00:01:32, Serial0/0/1
D       10.1.96.0 [90/40640000] via 172.16.124.1, 00:07:13, Serial0/0/1
C       10.2.128.0 is directly connected, Loopback129
D       10.3.128.0 [90/41152000] via 172.16.124.1, 00:01:32, Serial0/0/1
D       10.1.128.0 [90/40640000] via 172.16.124.1, 00:07:13, Serial0/0/1
C       10.2.160.0 is directly connected, Loopback161
D       10.3.160.0 [90/41152000] via 172.16.124.1, 00:01:32, Serial0/0/1
D       10.1.160.0 [90/40640000] via 172.16.124.1, 00:07:13, Serial0/0/1
```

```
West# show ip route
<output omitted>

        172.16.0.0/29 is subnetted, 1 subnets
C       172.16.124.0 is directly connected, Serial0/0/0
        10.0.0.0/19 is subnetted, 18 subnets
D       10.2.0.0 [90/41152000] via 172.16.124.1, 00:02:00, Serial0/0/0
C       10.3.0.0 is directly connected, Loopback1
D       10.1.0.0 [90/40640000] via 172.16.124.1, 00:07:41, Serial0/0/0
D       10.2.32.0 [90/41152000] via 172.16.124.1, 00:02:00, Serial0/0/0
C       10.3.32.0 is directly connected, Loopback33
D       10.1.32.0 [90/40640000] via 172.16.124.1, 00:07:43, Serial0/0/0
D       10.2.64.0 [90/41152000] via 172.16.124.1, 00:02:01, Serial0/0/0
C       10.3.64.0 is directly connected, Loopback65
D       10.1.64.0 [90/40640000] via 172.16.124.1, 00:07:43, Serial0/0/0
D       10.2.96.0 [90/41152000] via 172.16.124.1, 00:02:01, Serial0/0/0
C       10.3.96.0 is directly connected, Loopback97
D       10.1.96.0 [90/40640000] via 172.16.124.1, 00:07:43, Serial0/0/0
D       10.2.128.0 [90/41152000] via 172.16.124.1, 00:02:01, Serial0/0/0
C       10.3.128.0 is directly connected, Loopback129
D       10.1.128.0 [90/40640000] via 172.16.124.1, 00:07:43, Serial0/0/0
D       10.2.160.0 [90/41152000] via 172.16.124.1, 00:02:01, Serial0/0/0
C       10.3.160.0 is directly connected, Loopback161
D       10.1.160.0 [90/40640000] via 172.16.124.1, 00:07:43, Serial0/0/0
```

Run the following TCL script on all routers to verify full connectivity. You can download this TCL Script at www.ciscopress.com/title/1587132133 under the More Information section on the page.

```
foreach address {
10.1.1.1
```

```
10.1.33.1
10.1.65.1
10.1.97.1
10.1.129.1
10.1.161.1
172.16.124.1
10.2.1.1
10.2.33.1
10.2.65.1
10.2.97.1
10.2.129.1
10.2.161.1
172.16.124.2
10.3.1.1
10.3.33.1
10.3.65.1
10.3.97.1
10.3.129.1
10.3.161.1
172.16.124.3
} { ping $address }
```

If you have never used TCL scripts or need a refresher, see "Lab 1-2: TCL Script Reference and Demonstration (1.5.1)" in Chapter 1.

You get ICMP echo replies for every address pinged. Make sure you run the TCL script on each router and get the same output as listed in the section "TCL Script Output" for this lab before continuing.

Step 6: Using Nonbroadcast EIGRP Mode

Currently, we are using EIGRP in its default mode, which multicasts packets to the link-local address 224.0.0.10. However, not all Frame Relay configurations support multicast. EIGRP supports unicasts to remote destinations using nonbroadcast mode on a per-interface basis. If you are familiar with RIPv2, this mode is analogous to configuring RIPv2 with a passive interface and statically configuring neighbors out that interface.

To implement this functionality, do the following:

```
HQ(config)# router eigrp 1
HQ(config-router)# neighbor 172.16.124.2 serial 0/0/1
HQ(config-router)# neighbor 172.16.124.3 serial 0/0/1
```
```
East(config)# router eigrp 1
East(config-router)# neighbor 172.16.124.1 serial 0/0/1
```
```
West(config)# router eigrp 1
West(config-router)# neighbor 172.16.124.1 serial 0/0/0
```

HQ now has two neighbor statements, and the other two routers have one. Once you configure neighbor statements for a given interface, EIGRP automatically stops multicasting packets out that interface and starts unicasting packets instead. You can verify that all your changes have worked with the **show ip eigrp neighbors** command:

```
HQ# show ip eigrp neighbors
IP-EIGRP neighbors for process 1
H    Address            Interface      Hold Uptime   SRTT   RTO  Q  Seq
                                       (sec)         (ms)        Cnt Num
1    172.16.124.2       Se0/0/1         153 00:00:28   65    390  0  9
0    172.16.124.3       Se0/0/1         158 00:00:28 1295   5000  0  9
```

```
East# show ip eigrp neighbors
IP-EIGRP neighbors for process 1
H    Address            Interface      Hold Uptime   SRTT   RTO  Q  Seq
                                       (sec)         (ms)        Cnt Num
0    172.16.124.1       Se0/0/1         146 00:02:19   93    558  0  15
```

```
West# show ip eigrp neighbors
IP-EIGRP neighbors for process 1
H    Address            Interface      Hold Uptime   SRTT   RTO  Q  Seq
                                       (sec)         (ms)        Cnt Num
0    172.16.124.1       Se0/0/0         160 00:03:00   59    354  0  15
```

Step 7: Implementing EIGRP Manual Summarization

Implement EIGRP manual summarization on each of the routers. Each router should advertise only one network summarizing all of its loopbacks. Using the commands you learned in Lab 2-3, configure the summary address on the serial interfaces.

What is the length of the network mask that is used to summarize all the loopbacks on each router?

Look at the simplified EIGRP topology table on each router using the **show ip eigrp topology** command:

```
HQ# show ip eigrp topology
IP-EIGRP Topology Table for AS(1)/ID(10.1.12.1)

Codes: P - Passive, A - Active, U - Update, Q - Query, R - Reply,
       r - reply Status, s - sia Status


P 10.2.0.0/16, 1 successors, FD is 2297856
         via 172.16.124.2 (2297856/128256), Serial0/0/1
P 10.3.0.0/16, 1 successors, FD is 2297856
         via 172.16.124.3 (2297856/128256), Serial0/0/1
P 10.1.0.0/16, 1 successors, FD is 128256
         via Summary (128256/0), Null0
P 10.1.0.0/19, 1 successors, FD is 128256
         via Connected, Loopback1
P 10.1.32.0/19, 1 successors, FD is 128256
         via Connected, Loopback33
```

```
P 10.1.64.0/19, 1 successors, FD is 128256
         via Connected, Loopback65
P 10.1.96.0/19, 1 successors, FD is 128256
         via Connected, Loopback97
P 10.1.128.0/19, 1 successors, FD is 128256
         via Connected, Loopback129
P 10.1.160.0/19, 1 successors, FD is 128256
         via Connected, Loopback161
P 172.16.124.0/29, 1 successors, FD is 2169856
         via Connected, Serial0/0/1
East# show ip eigrp topology
IP-EIGRP Topology Table for AS(1)/ID(10.2.161.1)

Codes: P - Passive, A - Active, U - Update, Q - Query, R - Reply,
       r - reply Status, s - sia Status


P 10.2.0.0/16, 1 successors, FD is 128256
         via Summary (128256/0), Null0
P 10.2.0.0/19, 1 successors, FD is 128256
         via Connected, Loopback1
P 10.3.0.0/16, 1 successors, FD is 2809856
         via 172.16.124.1 (2809856/2297856), Serial0/0/1
P 10.1.0.0/16, 1 successors, FD is 2297856
         via 172.16.124.1 (2297856/128256), Serial0/0/1
P 10.2.32.0/19, 1 successors, FD is 128256
         via Connected, Loopback33
P 10.2.64.0/19, 1 successors, FD is 128256
         via Connected, Loopback65
P 10.2.96.0/19, 1 successors, FD is 128256
         via Connected, Loopback97
P 10.2.128.0/19, 1 successors, FD is 128256
         via Connected, Loopback129
P 10.2.160.0/19, 1 successors, FD is 128256
         via Connected, Loopback161
P 172.16.124.0/29, 1 successors, FD is 2169856
         via Connected, Serial0/0/1
East#
West# show ip eigrp topology
IP-EIGRP Topology Table for AS(1)/ID(172.16.124.3)

Codes: P - Passive, A - Active, U - Update, Q - Query, R - Reply,
       r - reply Status, s - sia Status


P 10.2.0.0/16, 1 successors, FD is 2809856
```

```
          via 172.16.124.1 (2809856/2297856), Serial0/0/0
P 10.3.0.0/16, 1 successors, FD is 128256
          via Summary (128256/0), Null0
P 10.3.0.0/19, 1 successors, FD is 128256
          via Connected, Loopback1
P 10.1.0.0/16, 1 successors, FD is 2297856
          via 172.16.124.1 (2297856/128256), Serial0/0/0
P 10.3.32.0/19, 1 successors, FD is 128256
          via Connected, Loopback33
P 10.3.64.0/19, 1 successors, FD is 128256
          via Connected, Loopback65
P 10.3.96.0/19, 1 successors, FD is 128256
          via Connected, Loopback97
P 10.3.128.0/19, 1 successors, FD is 128256
          via Connected, Loopback129
P 10.3.160.0/19, 1 successors, FD is 128256
          via Connected, Loopback161
P 172.16.124.0/29, 1 successors, FD is 2169856
          via Connected, Serial0/0/0
```

TCL Script Output

```
HQ# tclsh
HQ(tcl)# foreach address {
+>(tcl)# 10.1.1.1
+>(tcl)# 10.1.33.1
+>(tcl)# 10.1.65.1
+>(tcl)# 10.1.97.1
+>(tcl)# 10.1.129.1
+>(tcl)# 10.1.161.1
+>(tcl)# 172.16.124.1
+>(tcl)# 10.2.1.1
+>(tcl)# 10.2.33.1
+>(tcl)# 10.2.65.1
+>(tcl)# 10.2.97.1
+>(tcl)# 10.2.129.1
+>(tcl)# 10.2.161.1
+>(tcl)# 172.16.124.2
+>(tcl)# 10.3.1.1
+>(tcl)# 10.3.33.1
+>(tcl)# 10.3.65.1
+>(tcl)# 10.3.97.1
+>(tcl)# 10.3.129.1
+>(tcl)# 10.3.161.1
+>(tcl)# 172.16.124.3
```

```
+>(tcl)# } { ping $address }

Type escape sequence to abort.
Sending 5, 100-byte ICMP Echos to 10.1.1.1, timeout is 2 seconds:
!!!!!
Success rate is 100 percent (5/5), round-trip min/avg/max = 1/1/1 ms
Type escape sequence to abort.
Sending 5, 100-byte ICMP Echos to 10.1.33.1, timeout is 2 seconds:
!!!!!
Success rate is 100 percent (5/5), round-trip min/avg/max = 1/1/4 ms
Type escape sequence to abort.
Sending 5, 100-byte ICMP Echos to 10.1.65.1, timeout is 2 seconds:
!!!!!
Success rate is 100 percent (5/5), round-trip min/avg/max = 1/1/4 ms
Type escape sequence to abort.
Sending 5, 100-byte ICMP Echos to 10.1.97.1, timeout is 2 seconds:
!!!!!
Success rate is 100 percent (5/5), round-trip min/avg/max = 1/1/4 ms
Type escape sequence to abort.
Sending 5, 100-byte ICMP Echos to 10.1.129.1, timeout is 2 seconds:
!!!!!
Success rate is 100 percent (5/5), round-trip min/avg/max = 1/1/4 ms
Type escape sequence to abort.
Sending 5, 100-byte ICMP Echos to 10.1.161.1, timeout is 2 seconds:
!!!!!
Success rate is 100 percent (5/5), round-trip min/avg/max = 1/1/1 ms
Type escape sequence to abort.
Sending 5, 100-byte ICMP Echos to 172.16.124.1, timeout is 2 seconds:
!!!!!
Success rate is 100 percent (5/5), round-trip min/avg/max = 84/85/92 ms
Type escape sequence to abort.
Sending 5, 100-byte ICMP Echos to 10.2.1.1, timeout is 2 seconds:
!!!!!
Success rate is 100 percent (5/5), round-trip min/avg/max = 40/42/44 ms
Type escape sequence to abort.
Sending 5, 100-byte ICMP Echos to 10.2.33.1, timeout is 2 seconds:
!!!!!
Success rate is 100 percent (5/5), round-trip min/avg/max = 40/42/44 ms
Type escape sequence to abort.
Sending 5, 100-byte ICMP Echos to 10.2.65.1, timeout is 2 seconds:
!!!!!
Success rate is 100 percent (5/5), round-trip min/avg/max = 40/43/44 ms
Type escape sequence to abort.
Sending 5, 100-byte ICMP Echos to 10.2.97.1, timeout is 2 seconds:
```

```
!!!!!
Success rate is 100 percent (5/5), round-trip min/avg/max = 40/43/44 ms
Type escape sequence to abort.
Sending 5, 100-byte ICMP Echos to 10.2.129.1, timeout is 2 seconds:
!!!!!
Success rate is 100 percent (5/5), round-trip min/avg/max = 40/42/44 ms
Type escape sequence to abort.
Sending 5, 100-byte ICMP Echos to 10.2.161.1, timeout is 2 seconds:
!!!!!
Success rate is 100 percent (5/5), round-trip min/avg/max = 40/42/44 ms
Type escape sequence to abort.
Sending 5, 100-byte ICMP Echos to 172.16.124.2, timeout is 2 seconds:
!!!!!
Success rate is 100 percent (5/5), round-trip min/avg/max = 40/42/44 ms
Type escape sequence to abort.
Sending 5, 100-byte ICMP Echos to 10.3.1.1, timeout is 2 seconds:
!!!!!
Success rate is 100 percent (5/5), round-trip min/avg/max = 40/43/44 ms
Type escape sequence to abort.
Sending 5, 100-byte ICMP Echos to 10.3.33.1, timeout is 2 seconds:
!!!!!
Success rate is 100 percent (5/5), round-trip min/avg/max = 40/43/44 ms
Type escape sequence to abort.
Sending 5, 100-byte ICMP Echos to 10.3.65.1, timeout is 2 seconds:
!!!!!
Success rate is 100 percent (5/5), round-trip min/avg/max = 40/42/44 ms
Type escape sequence to abort.
Sending 5, 100-byte ICMP Echos to 10.3.97.1, timeout is 2 seconds:
!!!!!
Success rate is 100 percent (5/5), round-trip min/avg/max = 40/41/44 ms
Type escape sequence to abort.
Sending 5, 100-byte ICMP Echos to 10.3.129.1, timeout is 2 seconds:
!!!!!
Success rate is 100 percent (5/5), round-trip min/avg/max = 40/42/44 ms
Type escape sequence to abort.
Sending 5, 100-byte ICMP Echos to 10.3.161.1, timeout is 2 seconds:
!!!!!
Success rate is 100 percent (5/5), round-trip min/avg/max = 40/43/44 ms
Type escape sequence to abort.
Sending 5, 100-byte ICMP Echos to 172.16.124.3, timeout is 2 seconds:
!!!!!
Success rate is 100 percent (5/5), round-trip min/avg/max = 40/42/44 ms
HQ(tcl)# tclquit
```

East# **tclsh**

```
East(tcl)# foreach address {
+>(tcl)# 10.1.1.1
+>(tcl)# 10.1.33.1
+>(tcl)# 10.1.65.1
+>(tcl)# 10.1.97.1
+>(tcl)# 10.1.129.1
+>(tcl)# 10.1.161.1
+>(tcl)# 172.16.124.1
+>(tcl)# 10.2.1.1
+>(tcl)# 10.2.33.1
+>(tcl)# 10.2.65.1
+>(tcl)# 10.2.97.1
+>(tcl)# 10.2.129.1
+>(tcl)# 10.2.161.1
+>(tcl)# 172.16.124.2
+>(tcl)# 10.3.1.1
+>(tcl)# 10.3.33.1
+>(tcl)# 10.3.65.1
+>(tcl)# 10.3.97.1
+>(tcl)# 10.3.129.1
+>(tcl)# 10.3.161.1
+>(tcl)# 172.16.124.3
+>(tcl)# } { ping $address }

Type escape sequence to abort.
Sending 5, 100-byte ICMP Echos to 10.1.1.1, timeout is 2 seconds:
!!!!!
Success rate is 100 percent (5/5), round-trip min/avg/max = 40/42/44 ms
Type escape sequence to abort.
Sending 5, 100-byte ICMP Echos to 10.1.33.1, timeout is 2 seconds:
!!!!!
Success rate is 100 percent (5/5), round-trip min/avg/max = 40/42/44 ms
Type escape sequence to abort.
Sending 5, 100-byte ICMP Echos to 10.1.65.1, timeout is 2 seconds:
!!!!!
Success rate is 100 percent (5/5), round-trip min/avg/max = 40/43/44 ms
Type escape sequence to abort.
Sending 5, 100-byte ICMP Echos to 10.1.97.1, timeout is 2 seconds:
!!!!!
Success rate is 100 percent (5/5), round-trip min/avg/max = 40/43/44 ms
Type escape sequence to abort.
Sending 5, 100-byte ICMP Echos to 10.1.129.1, timeout is 2 seconds:
!!!!!
Success rate is 100 percent (5/5), round-trip min/avg/max = 40/42/44 ms
```

```
Type escape sequence to abort.
Sending 5, 100-byte ICMP Echos to 10.1.161.1, timeout is 2 seconds:
!!!!!
Success rate is 100 percent (5/5), round-trip min/avg/max = 40/41/44 ms
Type escape sequence to abort.
Sending 5, 100-byte ICMP Echos to 172.16.124.1, timeout is 2 seconds:
!!!!!
Success rate is 100 percent (5/5), round-trip min/avg/max = 40/42/44 ms
Type escape sequence to abort.
Sending 5, 100-byte ICMP Echos to 10.2.1.1, timeout is 2 seconds:
!!!!!
Success rate is 100 percent (5/5), round-trip min/avg/max = 1/1/4 ms
Type escape sequence to abort.
Sending 5, 100-byte ICMP Echos to 10.2.33.1, timeout is 2 seconds:
!!!!!
Success rate is 100 percent (5/5), round-trip min/avg/max = 1/1/4 ms
Type escape sequence to abort.
Sending 5, 100-byte ICMP Echos to 10.2.65.1, timeout is 2 seconds:
!!!!!
Success rate is 100 percent (5/5), round-trip min/avg/max = 1/1/4 ms
Type escape sequence to abort.
Sending 5, 100-byte ICMP Echos to 10.2.97.1, timeout is 2 seconds:
!!!!!
Success rate is 100 percent (5/5), round-trip min/avg/max = 1/1/4 ms
Type escape sequence to abort.
Sending 5, 100-byte ICMP Echos to 10.2.129.1, timeout is 2 seconds:
!!!!!
Success rate is 100 percent (5/5), round-trip min/avg/max = 1/1/4 ms
Type escape sequence to abort.
Sending 5, 100-byte ICMP Echos to 10.2.161.1, timeout is 2 seconds:
!!!!!
Success rate is 100 percent (5/5), round-trip min/avg/max = 1/1/1 ms
Type escape sequence to abort.
Sending 5, 100-byte ICMP Echos to 172.16.124.2, timeout is 2 seconds:
!!!!!
Success rate is 100 percent (5/5), round-trip min/avg/max = 84/84/88 ms
Type escape sequence to abort.
Sending 5, 100-byte ICMP Echos to 10.3.1.1, timeout is 2 seconds:
!!!!!
Success rate is 100 percent (5/5), round-trip min/avg/max = 84/84/84 ms
Type escape sequence to abort.
Sending 5, 100-byte ICMP Echos to 10.3.33.1, timeout is 2 seconds:
!!!!!
Success rate is 100 percent (5/5), round-trip min/avg/max = 84/85/92 ms
```

```
Type escape sequence to abort.
Sending 5, 100-byte ICMP Echos to 10.3.65.1, timeout is 2 seconds:
!!!!!
Success rate is 100 percent (5/5), round-trip min/avg/max = 84/84/84 ms
Type escape sequence to abort.
Sending 5, 100-byte ICMP Echos to 10.3.97.1, timeout is 2 seconds:
!!!!!
Success rate is 100 percent (5/5), round-trip min/avg/max = 84/84/88 ms
Type escape sequence to abort.
Sending 5, 100-byte ICMP Echos to 10.3.129.1, timeout is 2 seconds:
!!!!!
Success rate is 100 percent (5/5), round-trip min/avg/max = 84/84/84 ms
Type escape sequence to abort.
Sending 5, 100-byte ICMP Echos to 10.3.161.1, timeout is 2 seconds:
!!!!!
Success rate is 100 percent (5/5), round-trip min/avg/max = 84/84/84 ms
Type escape sequence to abort.
Sending 5, 100-byte ICMP Echos to 172.16.124.3, timeout is 2 seconds:
!!!!!
Success rate is 100 percent (5/5), round-trip min/avg/max = 84/84/88 ms
East(tcl)# tclquit
```

```
West# tclsh
West(tcl)# foreach address {
+>(tcl)# 10.1.1.1
+>(tcl)# 10.1.33.1
+>(tcl)# 10.1.65.1
+>(tcl)# 10.1.97.1
+>(tcl)# 10.1.129.1
+>(tcl)# 10.1.161.1
+>(tcl)# 172.16.124.1
+>(tcl)# 10.2.1.1
+>(tcl)# 10.2.33.1
+>(tcl)# 10.2.65.1
+>(tcl)# 10.2.97.1
+>(tcl)# 10.2.129.1
+>(tcl)# 10.2.161.1
+>(tcl)# 172.16.124.2
+>(tcl)# 10.3.1.1
+>(tcl)# 10.3.33.1
+>(tcl)# 10.3.65.1
+>(tcl)# 10.3.97.1
+>(tcl)# 10.3.129.1
+>(tcl)# 10.3.161.1
+>(tcl)# 172.16.124.3
```

```
+>(tcl)# } { ping $address }


Type escape sequence to abort.
Sending 5, 100-byte ICMP Echos to 10.1.1.1, timeout is 2 seconds:
!!!!!
Success rate is 100 percent (5/5), round-trip min/avg/max = 40/42/44 ms
Type escape sequence to abort.
Sending 5, 100-byte ICMP Echos to 10.1.33.1, timeout is 2 seconds:
!!!!!
Success rate is 100 percent (5/5), round-trip min/avg/max = 40/42/44 ms
Type escape sequence to abort.
Sending 5, 100-byte ICMP Echos to 10.1.65.1, timeout is 2 seconds:
!!!!!
Success rate is 100 percent (5/5), round-trip min/avg/max = 40/42/44 ms
Type escape sequence to abort.
Sending 5, 100-byte ICMP Echos to 10.1.97.1, timeout is 2 seconds:
!!!!!
Success rate is 100 percent (5/5), round-trip min/avg/max = 40/43/44 ms
Type escape sequence to abort.
Sending 5, 100-byte ICMP Echos to 10.1.129.1, timeout is 2 seconds:
!!!!!
Success rate is 100 percent (5/5), round-trip min/avg/max = 40/43/44 ms
Type escape sequence to abort.
Sending 5, 100-byte ICMP Echos to 10.1.161.1, timeout is 2 seconds:
!!!!!
Success rate is 100 percent (5/5), round-trip min/avg/max = 40/43/44 ms
Type escape sequence to abort.
Sending 5, 100-byte ICMP Echos to 172.16.124.1, timeout is 2 seconds:
!!!!!
Success rate is 100 percent (5/5), round-trip min/avg/max = 40/42/44 ms
Type escape sequence to abort.
Sending 5, 100-byte ICMP Echos to 10.2.1.1, timeout is 2 seconds:
!!!!!
Success rate is 100 percent (5/5), round-trip min/avg/max = 84/84/88 ms
Type escape sequence to abort.
Sending 5, 100-byte ICMP Echos to 10.2.33.1, timeout is 2 seconds:
!!!!!
Success rate is 100 percent (5/5), round-trip min/avg/max = 84/84/84 ms
Type escape sequence to abort.
Sending 5, 100-byte ICMP Echos to 10.2.65.1, timeout is 2 seconds:
!!!!!
Success rate is 100 percent (5/5), round-trip min/avg/max = 84/85/92 ms
Type escape sequence to abort.
Sending 5, 100-byte ICMP Echos to 10.2.97.1, timeout is 2 seconds:
```

```
!!!!!
Success rate is 100 percent (5/5), round-trip min/avg/max = 84/84/84 ms
Type escape sequence to abort.
Sending 5, 100-byte ICMP Echos to 10.2.129.1, timeout is 2 seconds:
!!!!!
Success rate is 100 percent (5/5), round-trip min/avg/max = 84/84/88 ms
Type escape sequence to abort.
Sending 5, 100-byte ICMP Echos to 10.2.161.1, timeout is 2 seconds:
!!!!!
Success rate is 100 percent (5/5), round-trip min/avg/max = 80/83/84 ms
Type escape sequence to abort.
Sending 5, 100-byte ICMP Echos to 172.16.124.2, timeout is 2 seconds:
!!!!!
Success rate is 100 percent (5/5), round-trip min/avg/max = 84/84/84 ms
Type escape sequence to abort.
Sending 5, 100-byte ICMP Echos to 10.3.1.1, timeout is 2 seconds:
!!!!!
Success rate is 100 percent (5/5), round-trip min/avg/max = 1/1/4 ms
Type escape sequence to abort.
Sending 5, 100-byte ICMP Echos to 10.3.33.1, timeout is 2 seconds:
!!!!!
Success rate is 100 percent (5/5), round-trip min/avg/max = 1/1/4 ms
Type escape sequence to abort.
Sending 5, 100-byte ICMP Echos to 10.3.65.1, timeout is 2 seconds:
!!!!!
Success rate is 100 percent (5/5), round-trip min/avg/max = 1/1/1 ms
Type escape sequence to abort.
Sending 5, 100-byte ICMP Echos to 10.3.97.1, timeout is 2 seconds:
!!!!!
Success rate is 100 percent (5/5), round-trip min/avg/max = 1/1/4 ms
Type escape sequence to abort.
Sending 5, 100-byte ICMP Echos to 10.3.129.1, timeout is 2 seconds:
!!!!!
Success rate is 100 percent (5/5), round-trip min/avg/max = 1/1/1 ms
Type escape sequence to abort.
Sending 5, 100-byte ICMP Echos to 10.3.161.1, timeout is 2 seconds:
!!!!!
Success rate is 100 percent (5/5), round-trip min/avg/max = 1/1/1 ms
Type escape sequence to abort.
Sending 5, 100-byte ICMP Echos to 172.16.124.3, timeout is 2 seconds:
!!!!!
Success rate is 100 percent (5/5), round-trip min/avg/max = 84/84/84 ms
West(tcl)# tclquit
```

Lab 2-5: EIGRP Frame Relay Hub and Spoke: Adtran Used as Frame Switch (2.7.4)

The objectives of this lab are as follows:

■ Review basic configuration of EIGRP on a serial interface

■ Configure the bandwidth percentage

■ Configure EIGRP over Frame Relay hub and spoke

■ Use EIGRP in a nonbroadcast mode

■ Enable EIGRP manual summarization in topologies with discontiguous major networks

Figure 2-5 illustrates the topology that will be used for this lab.

Figure 2-5   Topology Diagram

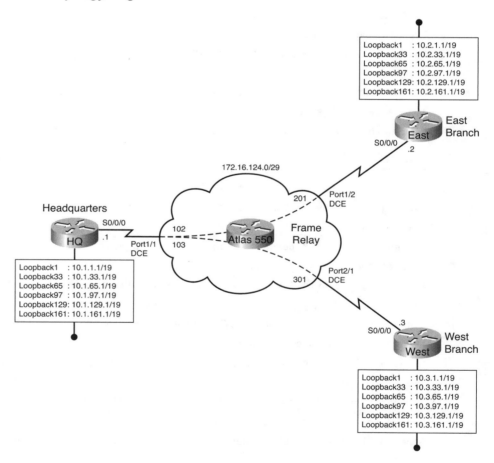

Note   Given the diversity of router models and the differing naming conventions for serial interfaces (S0, S0/0, S0/0/0), the interface numbers on your devices probably differ from those in the topology diagram. The same is true for which side of the link is DCE or DTE. You should always draw your network diagram to reflect your topology. If you are uncertain which side of the connection is DCE, use the **show controllers serial** *interface-number* command:

```
HQ# show controllers serial 0/0/0
Interface Serial0/0/0
Hardware is GT96K
DCE V.35, clock rate 2000000
<output omitted>
```

Scenario

You are responsible for configuring and testing the new network that connects your company's headquarters, and East and West branches. The three locations are connected over hub-and-spoke Frame Relay, using the company headquarters as the hub. Model each branch office's network with multiple loopback interfaces on each router, and configure EIGRP to allow full connectivity between all departments.

Step 1: Addressing

Using the addressing scheme in Figure 2-5, apply IP addresses to the loopback interfaces on HQ, East, and West. You may paste the following configurations into your routers to begin. You must be in configuration mode when you do this. You can download these router configurations at www.ciscopress.com/title/1587132133 under the More Information section on the page.

```
HQ:
!
interface Loopback1
 ip address 10.1.1.1 255.255.224.0
interface Loopback33
 ip address 10.1.33.1 255.255.224.0
interface Loopback65
 ip address 10.1.65.1 255.255.224.0
interface Loopback97
 ip address 10.1.97.1 255.255.224.0
interface Loopback129
 ip address 10.1.129.1 255.255.224.0
interface Loopback161
 ip address 10.1.161.1 255.255.224.0
!
end
```

```
East:
!
interface Loopback1
 ip address 10.2.1.1 255.255.224.0
```

```
interface Loopback33
 ip address 10.2.33.1 255.255.224.0
interface Loopback65
 ip address 10.2.65.1 255.255.224.0
interface Loopback97
 ip address 10.2.97.1 255.255.224.0
interface Loopback129
 ip address 10.2.129.1 255.255.224.0
interface Loopback161
 ip address 10.2.161.1 255.255.224.0
!
end
```

```
West:
!
interface Loopback1
 ip address 10.3.1.1 255.255.224.0
interface Loopback33
 ip address 10.3.33.1 255.255.224.0
interface Loopback65
 ip address 10.3.65.1 255.255.224.0
interface Loopback97
 ip address 10.3.97.1 255.255.224.0
interface Loopback129
 ip address 10.3.129.1 255.255.224.0
interface Loopback161
 ip address 10.3.161.1 255.255.224.0
!
end
```

For now, the IP address is the only configuration on the serial interfaces. Leave the serial interfaces with their default encapsulation (HDLC). This will change in Step 3.

Step 2: Frame Relay Network

An Adtran Atlas 550 is preconfigured to simulate a Frame Relay service that provides the PVCs documented in Table 2-3.

Table 2-3   Frame Relay Switching Configuration

Connected Router	Router Interface	Adtran Interface	Ingress DLCI	Egress DLCI	Egress Router
HQ	S0/0/0 DTE	port 1/1	102	201	East
HQ	S0/0/0 DTE	port 1/1	103	301	West
East	S0/0/0 DTE	port 1/2	201	102	HQ
West	S0/0/0 DTE	port 2/1	301	103	HQ

Step 3: Configuring the Frame Relay Endpoints

You will be configuring HQ to be the Frame Relay hub, with East and West as the spokes. Check Figure 2-5 for the data-link connection identifiers (DLCI) to use in the Frame Relay maps. Turn off Frame Relay InARP for all interfaces. Configure all Frame Relay interfaces as physical interfaces.

InARP allows a Frame Relay network to discover the IP address associated with the virtual circuit. This is frequently a desirable trait in a production network. However, in the lab, we off turn InARP to limit the number of dynamic DLCIs that are created.

First, enter the configuration menu for that interface in global configuration mode and assign it an IP address using the **ip address** command. Assign the Frame Relay subnet to be 172.16.124.0 /29. The fourth octet of the IP address is the router number (HQ=1, East=2, West=3).

Next, enable Frame Relay encapsulation using the interface configuration command **encapsulation frame-relay**. Disable Frame Relay InARP with the **no frame-relay inverse-arp** command. Finally, map the other IPs in the subnet to DLCIs, using the **frame-relay map ip address dlci broadcast** command. The **broadcast** keyword is important because, without it, EIGRP hello packets are not sent through the Frame Relay cloud. Do not forget to bring up your interfaces with the **no shutdown** command.

Note   The default Frame Relay encapsulation type on a Cisco router is **cisco**. Because you are connecting your routers to a non-Cisco device (the Adtran), you must use the nonproprietary Internet Engineering Task Force (IETF) standard, so use the **encapsulation frame-relay ietf** command.

```
HQ# configure terminal
HQ(config)# interface serial 0/0/0
HQ(config-if)# ip address 172.16.124.1 255.255.255.248
HQ(config-if)# encapsulation frame-relay ietf
HQ(config-if)# no frame-relay inverse-arp
HQ(config-if)# frame-relay map ip 172.16.124.2 102 broadcast
HQ(config-if)# frame-relay map ip 172.16.124.3 103 broadcast
HQ(config-if)# no shutdown
```
```
East# configure terminal
East(config)# interface serial 0/0/0
East(config-if)# ip address 172.16.124.2 255.255.255.248
East(config-if)# encapsulation frame-relay ietf
East(config-if)# no frame-relay inverse-arp
East(config-if)# frame-relay map ip 172.16.124.1 201 broadcast
East(config-if)# frame-relay map ip 172.16.124.3 201 broadcast
East(config-if)# no shutdown
```
```
West# configure terminal
West(config)# interface serial 0/0/0
West(config-if)# ip address 172.16.124.3 255.255.255.248
West(config-if)# no frame-relay inverse-arp
West(config-if)# encapsulation frame-relay ietf
West(config-if)# frame-relay map ip 172.16.124.1 301 broadcast
West(config-if)# frame-relay map ip 172.16.124.3 301 broadcast
West(config-if)# no shutdown
```

Note that you have not yet configured the bandwidth parameter on these serial links yet, as you did in Lab 2-2. This will be done in Step 4.

Verify that you have connectivity across the Frame Relay network by pinging the remote routers from each of the Frame Relay endpoints. Using the configuration above, you will find that you cannot ping your own local interface. For instance, ping 172.16.124.1 from HQ:

```
HQ# ping 172.16.124.1
Type escape sequence to abort.
Sending 5, 100-byte ICMP Echos to 172.16.124.1, timeout is 2 seconds:
.....
Success rate is 0 percent (0/5)
```

In essence, the only interface your Frame Relay interface is unable to communicate with is itself. This is not a significant problem in Frame Relay networks, but you could map the local IP address to be forwarded out a PVC. The remote router at the other end of the PVC can then forward it back based on its Frame Relay **map** statements. This solution is so that the TCL scripts we use for testing return successful echo replies under all circumstances. You do not need the **broadcast** keyword on this DLCI, because it is not important to forward broadcast and multicast packets (such as EIGRP hellos) to your own interface.

Implement the local mappings as follows:

```
HQ(config-if)# frame-relay map ip 172.16.124.1 102
```
```
East(config-if)# frame-relay map ip 172.16.124.2 201
```
```
West(config-if)# frame-relay map ip 172.16.124.3 301
```

HQ now forwards packets destined for 172.16.124.1 first to 172.16.124.2 and then back. In a production network in which a company is billed based on per-PVC usage, this is not a preferred configuration. However, in your lab network, this helps ensure full ICMP connectivity in your TCL scripts.

For more information about this behavior of Frame Relay, see the following FAQ page: http://www.cisco.com/warp/public/116/fr_faq.pdf

Step 4: Setting Interface-Level Bandwidth

On the three routers, set the Frame Relay serial interface bandwidth with the interface-level command **bandwidth** *bandwidth*, specifying the bandwidth in kilobits per second. For HQ, use 128 Kbps. On East and West, use 64 Kbps.

Recall from Lab 2-1 that, by default, EIGRP limits its bandwidth usage to 50 percent of the value specified by the bandwidth parameter. The default bandwidth for a serial interface is 1544 Kbps.

Over multipoint Frame Relay interfaces, EIGRP limits its EIGRP traffic to a total of 50 percent of the bandwidth value. This means that each neighbor for which this is an outbound interface has a traffic limit of a fraction of that 50 percent, represented by $1/N$, where N is the number of neighbors out that interface:

```
HQ(config)# interface serial 0/0/0
HQ(config-if)# bandwidth 128
```
```
East(config)# interface serial 0/0/0
East(config-if)# bandwidth 64
```
```
West(config)# interface serial 0/0/0
West(config-if)# bandwidth 64
```

HQ's serial interface divides its total EIGRP bandwidth into the fractional amounts according to the number of neighbors out that interface.

How much bandwidth on Serial0/0/0 on HQ is reserved for EIGRP traffic to East?

_____

_____

You can control both the bandwidth parameter and the EIGRP bandwidth percentage on a per-interface basis. On HQ, limit the bandwidth used by EIGRP to 40 percent without changing the bandwidth parameter on the interface. You can accomplish this with the interface-level command **ip bandwidth-percent eigrp** *as_number percent*:

```
HQ(config-if)# ip bandwidth-percent eigrp 1 40
```

Step 5: Configuring EIGRP

Configure EIGRP AS 1 on HQ, East, and West. First use the global configuration mode command **router eigrp** *as_number* to get the EIGRP configuration prompt.

The network represented in Figure 2-5 is a discontiguous network (10.0.0.0/8) configured on all three of the routers. If you turned on auto-summarization, HQ sends and receives summaries for 10.0.0.0/8 from both East and West. Auto-summarization provokes considerable routing disruptions in the network, because HQ does not know which of the two spokes is the correct destination for subnets of 10.0.0.0/8. For this reason, turn off auto-summarization on each router.

Add your **network** statements to EIGRP. The two major networks we are using here are **network 10.0.0.0** for the loopbacks, and **network 172.16.0.0** for the Frame Relay cloud. Perform this configuration on all three routers:

```
HQ(config)# router eigrp 1
HQ(config-router)# network 10.0.0.0
HQ(config-router)# network 172.16.0.0
HQ(config-router)# no auto-summary
```

```
East(config)# router eigrp 1
East(config-router)# network 10.0.0.0
East(config-router)# network 172.16.0.0
East(config-router)# no auto-summary
```

```
West(config)# router eigrp 1
West(config-router)# network 10.0.0.0
West(config-router)# network 172.16.0.0
West(config-router)# no auto-summary
```

Issue the **show ip eigrp topology** command on East:

```
East# show ip eigrp topology
IP-EIGRP Topology Table for AS(1)/ID(172.16.124.2)

Codes: P - Passive, A - Active, U - Update, Q - Query, R - Reply,
       r - reply Status, s - sia Status

P 10.2.0.0/19, 1 successors, FD is 128256
       via Connected, Loopback1
```

```
P 10.1.0.0/19, 1 successors, FD is 40640000
        via 172.16.124.1 (40640000/128256), Serial0/0/0
P 10.2.32.0/19, 1 successors, FD is 128256
        via Connected, Loopback33
P 10.1.32.0/19, 1 successors, FD is 40640000
        via 172.16.124.1 (40640000/128256), Serial0/0/0
P 10.2.64.0/19, 1 successors, FD is 128256
        via Connected, Loopback65
P 10.1.64.0/19, 1 successors, FD is 40640000
        via 172.16.124.1 (40640000/128256), Serial0/0/0
P 10.2.96.0/19, 1 successors, FD is 128256
        via Connected, Loopback97
P 10.1.96.0/19, 1 successors, FD is 40640000
        via 172.16.124.1 (40640000/128256), Serial0/0/0
P 10.2.128.0/19, 1 successors, FD is 128256
        via Connected, Loopback129
P 10.1.128.0/19, 1 successors, FD is 40640000
        via 172.16.124.1 (40640000/128256), Serial0/0/0
P 10.2.160.0/19, 1 successors, FD is 128256
        via Connected, Loopback161
P 10.1.160.0/19, 1 successors, FD is 40640000
        via 172.16.124.1 (40640000/128256), Serial0/0/0
P 172.16.124.0/29, 1 successors, FD is 40512000
        via Connected, Serial0/0/0
East#
```

Which networks are missing from the topology database?

_____

_____

What do you suspect is responsible for this problem?

_____

_____

HQ needs the **no ip split-horizon eigrp** *as_number* command on its serial Frame Relay interface:

```
HQ(config)# interface serial 0/0/0
HQ(config-if)# no ip split-horizon eigrp 1
```

This command disables split horizon for an EIGRP autonomous system. If split horizon is enabled (the default), route advertisements from East to HQ do not travel to West and vice versa, as shown in the preceding output.

Verify that you see the correct EIGRP adjacencies with the **show ip eigrp neighbors** command:

```
HQ# show ip eigrp neighbors
IP-EIGRP neighbors for process 1
```

```
H    Address           Interface      Hold Uptime    SRTT    RTO   Q   Seq
                                       (sec)          (ms)          Cnt Num
1    172.16.124.2      Se0/0/0        176 00:00:05   1588   5000   0   6
0    172.16.124.3      Se0/0/0        176 00:00:05     23   1140   0   6
```

```
East# show ip eigrp neighbors
IP-EIGRP neighbors for process 1
H    Address           Interface      Hold Uptime    SRTT    RTO   Q   Seq
                                       (sec)          (ms)          Cnt Num
0    172.16.124.1      Se0/0/0        129 00:00:52     20   2280   0   20
```

```
West# show ip eigrp neighbors
IP-EIGRP neighbors for process 1
H    Address           Interface      Hold Uptime    SRTT    RTO   Q   Seq
                                       (sec)          (ms)          Cnt Num
0    172.16.124.1      Se0/0/0        176 00:00:55     20   2280   0   13
```

Verify that you have IP routes on all three routers for the entire topology with the **show ip route** command:

```
HQ# show ip route
<output omitted>


      172.16.0.0/29 is subnetted, 1 subnets
C        172.16.124.0 is directly connected, Serial0/0/0
      10.0.0.0/19 is subnetted, 18 subnets
D        10.2.0.0 [90/20640000] via 172.16.124.2, 00:04:36, Serial0/0/0
D        10.3.0.0 [90/20640000] via 172.16.124.3, 00:04:20, Serial0/0/0
C        10.1.0.0 is directly connected, Loopback1
D        10.2.32.0 [90/20640000] via 172.16.124.2, 00:04:36, Serial0/0/0
D        10.3.32.0 [90/20640000] via 172.16.124.3, 00:04:20, Serial0/0/0
C        10.1.32.0 is directly connected, Loopback33
D        10.2.64.0 [90/20640000] via 172.16.124.2, 00:04:37, Serial0/0/0
D        10.3.64.0 [90/20640000] via 172.16.124.3, 00:04:21, Serial0/0/0
C        10.1.64.0 is directly connected, Loopback65
D        10.2.96.0 [90/20640000] via 172.16.124.2, 00:04:37, Serial0/0/0
D        10.3.96.0 [90/20640000] via 172.16.124.3, 00:04:21, Serial0/0/0
C        10.1.96.0 is directly connected, Loopback97
D        10.2.128.0 [90/20640000] via 172.16.124.2, 00:04:37, Serial0/0/0
D        10.3.128.0 [90/20640000] via 172.16.124.3, 00:04:21, Serial0/0/0
C        10.1.128.0 is directly connected, Loopback129
D        10.2.160.0 [90/20640000] via 172.16.124.2, 00:04:37, Serial0/0/0
D        10.3.160.0 [90/20640000] via 172.16.124.3, 00:04:21, Serial0/0/0
C        10.1.160.0 is directly connected, Loopback161
```

```
East# show ip route
<output omitted>
```

```
       172.16.0.0/29 is subnetted, 1 subnets
C         172.16.124.0 is directly connected, Serial0/0/0
       10.0.0.0/19 is subnetted, 18 subnets
C         10.2.0.0 is directly connected, Loopback1
D         10.3.0.0 [90/41152000] via 172.16.124.1, 00:01:31, Serial0/0/0
D         10.1.0.0 [90/40640000] via 172.16.124.1, 00:07:12, Serial0/0/0
C         10.2.32.0 is directly connected, Loopback33
D         10.3.32.0 [90/41152000] via 172.16.124.1, 00:01:31, Serial0/0/0
D         10.1.32.0 [90/40640000] via 172.16.124.1, 00:07:13, Serial0/0/0
C         10.2.64.0 is directly connected, Loopback65
D         10.3.64.0 [90/41152000] via 172.16.124.1, 00:01:32, Serial0/0/0
D         10.1.64.0 [90/40640000] via 172.16.124.1, 00:07:13, Serial0/0/0
C         10.2.96.0 is directly connected, Loopback97
D         10.3.96.0 [90/41152000] via 172.16.124.1, 00:01:32, Serial0/0/0
D         10.1.96.0 [90/40640000] via 172.16.124.1, 00:07:13, Serial0/0/0
C         10.2.128.0 is directly connected, Loopback129
D         10.3.128.0 [90/41152000] via 172.16.124.1, 00:01:32, Serial0/0/0
D         10.1.128.0 [90/40640000] via 172.16.124.1, 00:07:13, Serial0/0/0
C         10.2.160.0 is directly connected, Loopback161
D         10.3.160.0 [90/41152000] via 172.16.124.1, 00:01:32, Serial0/0/0
D         10.1.160.0 [90/40640000] via 172.16.124.1, 00:07:13, Serial0/0/0
```

West# **show ip route**

```
       172.16.0.0/29 is subnetted, 1 subnets
C         172.16.124.0 is directly connected, Serial0/0/0
       10.0.0.0/19 is subnetted, 18 subnets
D         10.2.0.0 [90/41152000] via 172.16.124.1, 00:02:00, Serial0/0/0
C         10.3.0.0 is directly connected, Loopback1
D         10.1.0.0 [90/40640000] via 172.16.124.1, 00:07:41, Serial0/0/0
D         10.2.32.0 [90/41152000] via 172.16.124.1, 00:02:00, Serial0/0/0
C         10.3.32.0 is directly connected, Loopback33
D         10.1.32.0 [90/40640000] via 172.16.124.1, 00:07:43, Serial0/0/0
D         10.2.64.0 [90/41152000] via 172.16.124.1, 00:02:01, Serial0/0/0
C         10.3.64.0 is directly connected, Loopback65
D         10.1.64.0 [90/40640000] via 172.16.124.1, 00:07:43, Serial0/0/0
D         10.2.96.0 [90/41152000] via 172.16.124.1, 00:02:01, Serial0/0/0
C         10.3.96.0 is directly connected, Loopback97
D         10.1.96.0 [90/40640000] via 172.16.124.1, 00:07:43, Serial0/0/0
D         10.2.128.0 [90/41152000] via 172.16.124.1, 00:02:01, Serial0/0/0
C         10.3.128.0 is directly connected, Loopback129
D         10.1.128.0 [90/40640000] via 172.16.124.1, 00:07:43, Serial0/0/0
D         10.2.160.0 [90/41152000] via 172.16.124.1, 00:02:01, Serial0/0/0
C         10.3.160.0 is directly connected, Loopback161
D         10.1.160.0 [90/40640000] via 172.16.124.1, 00:07:43, Serial0/0/0
```

Run the following TCL script on all routers to verify full connectivity. You can download this TCL script at www.ciscopress.com/title/1587132133 under the More Information section on the page.

```
foreach address {
10.1.1.1
10.1.33.1
10.1.65.1
10.1.97.1
10.1.129.1
10.1.161.1
172.16.124.1
10.2.1.1
10.2.33.1
10.2.65.1
10.2.97.1
10.2.129.1
10.2.161.1
172.16.124.2
10.3.1.1
10.3.33.1
10.3.65.1
10.3.97.1
10.3.129.1
10.3.161.1
172.16.124.3
} { ping $address }
```

If you have never used TCL scripts or need a refresher, see the TCL lab in the routing module.

You get ICMP echo replies for every address pinged. Make sure you run the TCL script on each router and get the same output listed in the section "TCL Script Output" for this lab before continuing.

Step 6: Using Nonbroadcast EIGRP Mode

Currently, we are using EIGRP in its default mode, which multicasts packets to the link-local address 224.0.0.10. However, not all Frame Relay configurations support multicast. EIGRP supports unicasts to remote destinations using nonbroadcast mode on a per-interface basis. If you are familiar with RIPv2, this mode is analogous to configuring RIPv2 with a passive interface and statically configuring neighbors out that interface.

To implement this functionality, do the following:

```
HQ(config)# router eigrp 1
HQ(config-router)# neighbor 172.16.124.2 serial 0/0/0
```

```
HQ(config-router)# neighbor 172.16.124.3 serial 0/0/0
```

```
East(config)# router eigrp 1
East(config-router)# neighbor 172.16.124.1 serial 0/0/0
```

```
West(config)# router eigrp 1
West(config-router)# neighbor 172.16.124.1 serial 0/0/0
```

HQ now has two **neighbor** statements, and the other two routers have one. Once you configure neighbor statements for a given interface, EIGRP automatically stops multicasting packets out that interface and starts unicasting packets instead. You can verify that all your changes have worked with the **show ip eigrp neighbors** command:

```
HQ# show ip eigrp neighbors
IP-EIGRP neighbors for process 1
```

H	Address	Interface	Hold Uptime	SRTT	RTO	Q	Seq
			(sec)	(ms)		Cnt	Num
1	172.16.124.2	Se0/0/0	153 00:00:28	65	390	0	9
0	172.16.124.3	Se0/0/0	158 00:00:28	1295	5000	0	9

```
East# show ip eigrp neighbors
IP-EIGRP neighbors for process 1
```

H	Address	Interface	Hold Uptime	SRTT	RTO	Q	Seq
			(sec)	(ms)		Cnt	Num
0	172.16.124.1	Se0/0/0	146 00:02:19	93	558	0	15

```
West# show ip eigrp neighbors
IP-EIGRP neighbors for process 1
```

H	Address	Interface	Hold Uptime	SRTT	RTO	Q	Seq
			(sec)	(ms)		Cnt	Num
0	172.16.124.1	Se0/0/0	160 00:03:00	59	354	0	15

Step 7: Implementing EIGRP Manual Summarization

Implement EIGRP manual summarization on each router. Each router should advertise only one network summarizing all of its loopbacks. Using the commands you learned in EIGRP Lab 2-3, configure the summary address on the serial interfaces.

What is the length of the network mask that is used to summarize all of the loopbacks on each router?

Look at the simplified EIGRP topology table on each router using the **show ip eigrp topology** command:

```
HQ# show ip eigrp topology
IP-EIGRP Topology Table for AS(1)/ID(10.1.12.1)


Codes: P - Passive, A - Active, U - Update, Q - Query, R - Reply,
       r - reply Status, s - sia Status


P 10.2.0.0/16, 1 successors, FD is 2297856
        via 172.16.124.2 (2297856/128256), Serial0/0/0
```

```
P 10.3.0.0/16, 1 successors, FD is 2297856
        via 172.16.124.3 (2297856/128256), Serial0/0/0
P 10.1.0.0/16, 1 successors, FD is 128256
        via Summary (128256/0), Null0
P 10.1.0.0/19, 1 successors, FD is 128256
        via Connected, Loopback1
P 10.1.32.0/19, 1 successors, FD is 128256
        via Connected, Loopback33
P 10.1.64.0/19, 1 successors, FD is 128256
        via Connected, Loopback65
P 10.1.96.0/19, 1 successors, FD is 128256
        via Connected, Loopback97
P 10.1.128.0/19, 1 successors, FD is 128256
        via Connected, Loopback129
P 10.1.160.0/19, 1 successors, FD is 128256
        via Connected, Loopback161
P 172.16.124.0/29, 1 successors, FD is 2169856
        via Connected, Serial0/0/0
East# show ip eigrp topology
IP-EIGRP Topology Table for AS(1)/ID(10.2.161.1)

Codes: P - Passive, A - Active, U - Update, Q - Query, R - Reply,
       r - reply Status, s - sia Status

P 10.2.0.0/16, 1 successors, FD is 128256
        via Summary (128256/0), Null0
P 10.2.0.0/19, 1 successors, FD is 128256
        via Connected, Loopback1
P 10.3.0.0/16, 1 successors, FD is 2809856
        via 172.16.124.1 (2809856/2297856), Serial0/0/0
P 10.1.0.0/16, 1 successors, FD is 2297856
        via 172.16.124.1 (2297856/128256), Serial0/0/0
P 10.2.32.0/19, 1 successors, FD is 128256
        via Connected, Loopback33
P 10.2.64.0/19, 1 successors, FD is 128256
        via Connected, Loopback65
P 10.2.96.0/19, 1 successors, FD is 128256
        via Connected, Loopback97
P 10.2.128.0/19, 1 successors, FD is 128256
        via Connected, Loopback129
P 10.2.160.0/19, 1 successors, FD is 128256
        via Connected, Loopback161
```

```
P 172.16.124.0/29, 1 successors, FD is 2169856
        via Connected, Serial0/0/0
East#
```

```
West# show ip eigrp topology
IP-EIGRP Topology Table for AS(1)/ID(172.16.124.3)

Codes: P - Passive, A - Active, U - Update, Q - Query, R - Reply,
       r - reply Status, s - sia Status

P 10.2.0.0/16, 1 successors, FD is 2809856
        via 172.16.124.1 (2809856/2297856), Serial0/0/0
P 10.3.0.0/16, 1 successors, FD is 128256
        via Summary (128256/0), Null0
P 10.3.0.0/19, 1 successors, FD is 128256
        via Connected, Loopback1
P 10.1.0.0/16, 1 successors, FD is 2297856
        via 172.16.124.1 (2297856/128256), Serial0/0/0
P 10.3.32.0/19, 1 successors, FD is 128256
        via Connected, Loopback33
P 10.3.64.0/19, 1 successors, FD is 128256
        via Connected, Loopback65
P 10.3.96.0/19, 1 successors, FD is 128256
        via Connected, Loopback97
P 10.3.128.0/19, 1 successors, FD is 128256
        via Connected, Loopback129
P 10.3.160.0/19, 1 successors, FD is 128256
        via Connected, Loopback161
P 172.16.124.0/29, 1 successors, FD is 2169856
        via Connected, Serial0/0/0
```

TCL Script Output

```
HQ# tclsh
HQ(tcl)# foreach address {
+>(tcl)# 10.1.1.1
+>(tcl)# 10.1.33.1
+>(tcl)# 10.1.65.1
+>(tcl)# 10.1.97.1
+>(tcl)# 10.1.129.1
+>(tcl)# 10.1.161.1
+>(tcl)# 172.16.124.1
+>(tcl)# 10.2.1.1
+>(tcl)# 10.2.33.1
+>(tcl)# 10.2.65.1
```

```
+>(tcl)# 10.2.97.1
+>(tcl)# 10.2.129.1
+>(tcl)# 10.2.161.1
+>(tcl)# 172.16.124.2
+>(tcl)# 10.3.1.1
+>(tcl)# 10.3.33.1
+>(tcl)# 10.3.65.1
+>(tcl)# 10.3.97.1
+>(tcl)# 10.3.129.1
+>(tcl)# 10.3.161.1
+>(tcl)# 172.16.124.3
+>(tcl)# } { ping $address }

Type escape sequence to abort.
Sending 5, 100-byte ICMP Echos to 10.1.1.1, timeout is 2 seconds:
!!!!!
Success rate is 100 percent (5/5), round-trip min/avg/max = 1/1/1 ms
Type escape sequence to abort.
Sending 5, 100-byte ICMP Echos to 10.1.33.1, timeout is 2 seconds:
!!!!!
Success rate is 100 percent (5/5), round-trip min/avg/max = 1/1/4 ms
Type escape sequence to abort.
Sending 5, 100-byte ICMP Echos to 10.1.65.1, timeout is 2 seconds:
!!!!!
Success rate is 100 percent (5/5), round-trip min/avg/max = 1/1/4 ms
Type escape sequence to abort.
Sending 5, 100-byte ICMP Echos to 10.1.97.1, timeout is 2 seconds:
!!!!!
Success rate is 100 percent (5/5), round-trip min/avg/max = 1/1/4 ms
Type escape sequence to abort.
Sending 5, 100-byte ICMP Echos to 10.1.129.1, timeout is 2 seconds:
!!!!!
Success rate is 100 percent (5/5), round-trip min/avg/max = 1/1/4 ms
Type escape sequence to abort.
Sending 5, 100-byte ICMP Echos to 10.1.161.1, timeout is 2 seconds:
!!!!!
Success rate is 100 percent (5/5), round-trip min/avg/max = 1/1/1 ms
Type escape sequence to abort.
Sending 5, 100-byte ICMP Echos to 172.16.124.1, timeout is 2 seconds:
!!!!!
Success rate is 100 percent (5/5), round-trip min/avg/max = 84/85/92 ms
Type escape sequence to abort.
Sending 5, 100-byte ICMP Echos to 10.2.1.1, timeout is 2 seconds:
!!!!!
```

```
Success rate is 100 percent (5/5), round-trip min/avg/max = 40/42/44 ms
Type escape sequence to abort.
Sending 5, 100-byte ICMP Echos to 10.2.33.1, timeout is 2 seconds:
!!!!!
Success rate is 100 percent (5/5), round-trip min/avg/max = 40/42/44 ms
Type escape sequence to abort.
Sending 5, 100-byte ICMP Echos to 10.2.65.1, timeout is 2 seconds:
!!!!!
Success rate is 100 percent (5/5), round-trip min/avg/max = 40/43/44 ms
Type escape sequence to abort.
Sending 5, 100-byte ICMP Echos to 10.2.97.1, timeout is 2 seconds:
!!!!!
Success rate is 100 percent (5/5), round-trip min/avg/max = 40/43/44 ms
Type escape sequence to abort.
Sending 5, 100-byte ICMP Echos to 10.2.129.1, timeout is 2 seconds:
!!!!!
Success rate is 100 percent (5/5), round-trip min/avg/max = 40/42/44 ms
Type escape sequence to abort.
Sending 5, 100-byte ICMP Echos to 10.2.161.1, timeout is 2 seconds:
!!!!!
Success rate is 100 percent (5/5), round-trip min/avg/max = 40/42/44 ms
Type escape sequence to abort.
Sending 5, 100-byte ICMP Echos to 172.16.124.2, timeout is 2 seconds:
!!!!!
Success rate is 100 percent (5/5), round-trip min/avg/max = 40/42/44 ms
Type escape sequence to abort.
Sending 5, 100-byte ICMP Echos to 10.3.1.1, timeout is 2 seconds:
!!!!!
Success rate is 100 percent (5/5), round-trip min/avg/max = 40/43/44 ms
Type escape sequence to abort.
Sending 5, 100-byte ICMP Echos to 10.3.33.1, timeout is 2 seconds:
!!!!!
Success rate is 100 percent (5/5), round-trip min/avg/max = 40/43/44 ms
Type escape sequence to abort.
Sending 5, 100-byte ICMP Echos to 10.3.65.1, timeout is 2 seconds:
!!!!!
Success rate is 100 percent (5/5), round-trip min/avg/max = 40/42/44 ms
Type escape sequence to abort.
Sending 5, 100-byte ICMP Echos to 10.3.97.1, timeout is 2 seconds:
!!!!!
Success rate is 100 percent (5/5), round-trip min/avg/max = 40/41/44 ms
Type escape sequence to abort.
Sending 5, 100-byte ICMP Echos to 10.3.129.1, timeout is 2 seconds:
!!!!!
```

```
Success rate is 100 percent (5/5), round-trip min/avg/max = 40/42/44 ms
Type escape sequence to abort.
Sending 5, 100-byte ICMP Echos to 10.3.161.1, timeout is 2 seconds:
!!!!!
Success rate is 100 percent (5/5), round-trip min/avg/max = 40/43/44 ms
Type escape sequence to abort.
Sending 5, 100-byte ICMP Echos to 172.16.124.3, timeout is 2 seconds:
!!!!!
Success rate is 100 percent (5/5), round-trip min/avg/max = 40/42/44 ms
HQ(tcl)# tclquit
```

```
East# tclsh
East(tcl)# foreach address {
+>(tcl)# 10.1.1.1
+>(tcl)# 10.1.33.1
+>(tcl)# 10.1.65.1
+>(tcl)# 10.1.97.1
+>(tcl)# 10.1.129.1
+>(tcl)# 10.1.161.1
+>(tcl)# 172.16.124.1
+>(tcl)# 10.2.1.1
+>(tcl)# 10.2.33.1
+>(tcl)# 10.2.65.1
+>(tcl)# 10.2.97.1
+>(tcl)# 10.2.129.1
+>(tcl)# 10.2.161.1
+>(tcl)# 172.16.124.2
+>(tcl)# 10.3.1.1
+>(tcl)# 10.3.33.1
+>(tcl)# 10.3.65.1
+>(tcl)# 10.3.97.1
+>(tcl)# 10.3.129.1
+>(tcl)# 10.3.161.1
+>(tcl)# 172.16.124.3
+>(tcl)# } { ping $address }

Type escape sequence to abort.
Sending 5, 100-byte ICMP Echos to 10.1.1.1, timeout is 2 seconds:
!!!!!
Success rate is 100 percent (5/5), round-trip min/avg/max = 40/42/44 ms
Type escape sequence to abort.
Sending 5, 100-byte ICMP Echos to 10.1.33.1, timeout is 2 seconds:
!!!!!
Success rate is 100 percent (5/5), round-trip min/avg/max = 40/42/44 ms
Type escape sequence to abort.
```

```
Sending 5, 100-byte ICMP Echos to 10.1.65.1, timeout is 2 seconds:
!!!!!
Success rate is 100 percent (5/5), round-trip min/avg/max = 40/43/44 ms
Type escape sequence to abort.
Sending 5, 100-byte ICMP Echos to 10.1.97.1, timeout is 2 seconds:
!!!!!
Success rate is 100 percent (5/5), round-trip min/avg/max = 40/43/44 ms
Type escape sequence to abort.
Sending 5, 100-byte ICMP Echos to 10.1.129.1, timeout is 2 seconds:
!!!!!
Success rate is 100 percent (5/5), round-trip min/avg/max = 40/42/44 ms
Type escape sequence to abort.
Sending 5, 100-byte ICMP Echos to 10.1.161.1, timeout is 2 seconds:
!!!!!
Success rate is 100 percent (5/5), round-trip min/avg/max = 40/41/44 ms
Type escape sequence to abort.
Sending 5, 100-byte ICMP Echos to 172.16.124.1, timeout is 2 seconds:
!!!!!
Success rate is 100 percent (5/5), round-trip min/avg/max = 40/42/44 ms
Type escape sequence to abort.
Sending 5, 100-byte ICMP Echos to 10.2.1.1, timeout is 2 seconds:
!!!!!
Success rate is 100 percent (5/5), round-trip min/avg/max = 1/1/4 ms
Type escape sequence to abort.
Sending 5, 100-byte ICMP Echos to 10.2.33.1, timeout is 2 seconds:
!!!!!
Success rate is 100 percent (5/5), round-trip min/avg/max = 1/1/4 ms
Type escape sequence to abort.
Sending 5, 100-byte ICMP Echos to 10.2.65.1, timeout is 2 seconds:
!!!!!
Success rate is 100 percent (5/5), round-trip min/avg/max = 1/1/4 ms
Type escape sequence to abort.
Sending 5, 100-byte ICMP Echos to 10.2.97.1, timeout is 2 seconds:
!!!!!
Success rate is 100 percent (5/5), round-trip min/avg/max = 1/1/4 ms
Type escape sequence to abort.
Sending 5, 100-byte ICMP Echos to 10.2.129.1, timeout is 2 seconds:
!!!!!
Success rate is 100 percent (5/5), round-trip min/avg/max = 1/1/4 ms
Type escape sequence to abort.
Sending 5, 100-byte ICMP Echos to 10.2.161.1, timeout is 2 seconds:
!!!!!
Success rate is 100 percent (5/5), round-trip min/avg/max = 1/1/1 ms
Type escape sequence to abort.
```

```
Sending 5, 100-byte ICMP Echos to 172.16.124.2, timeout is 2 seconds:
!!!!!
Success rate is 100 percent (5/5), round-trip min/avg/max = 84/84/88 ms
Type escape sequence to abort.
Sending 5, 100-byte ICMP Echos to 10.3.1.1, timeout is 2 seconds:
!!!!!
Success rate is 100 percent (5/5), round-trip min/avg/max = 84/84/84 ms
Type escape sequence to abort.
Sending 5, 100-byte ICMP Echos to 10.3.33.1, timeout is 2 seconds:
!!!!!
Success rate is 100 percent (5/5), round-trip min/avg/max = 84/85/92 ms
Type escape sequence to abort.
Sending 5, 100-byte ICMP Echos to 10.3.65.1, timeout is 2 seconds:
!!!!!
Success rate is 100 percent (5/5), round-trip min/avg/max = 84/84/84 ms
Type escape sequence to abort.
Sending 5, 100-byte ICMP Echos to 10.3.97.1, timeout is 2 seconds:
!!!!!
Success rate is 100 percent (5/5), round-trip min/avg/max = 84/84/88 ms
Type escape sequence to abort.
Sending 5, 100-byte ICMP Echos to 10.3.129.1, timeout is 2 seconds:
!!!!!
Success rate is 100 percent (5/5), round-trip min/avg/max = 84/84/84 ms
Type escape sequence to abort.
Sending 5, 100-byte ICMP Echos to 10.3.161.1, timeout is 2 seconds:
!!!!!
Success rate is 100 percent (5/5), round-trip min/avg/max = 84/84/84 ms
Type escape sequence to abort.
Sending 5, 100-byte ICMP Echos to 172.16.124.3, timeout is 2 seconds:
!!!!!
Success rate is 100 percent (5/5), round-trip min/avg/max = 84/84/88 ms
East(tcl)# tclquit
```
```
West# tclsh
West(tcl)# foreach address {
+>(tcl)# 10.1.1.1
+>(tcl)# 10.1.33.1
+>(tcl)# 10.1.65.1
+>(tcl)# 10.1.97.1
+>(tcl)# 10.1.129.1
+>(tcl)# 10.1.161.1
+>(tcl)# 172.16.124.1
+>(tcl)# 10.2.1.1
+>(tcl)# 10.2.33.1
+>(tcl)# 10.2.65.1
```

```
+>(tcl)# 10.2.97.1
+>(tcl)# 10.2.129.1
+>(tcl)# 10.2.161.1
+>(tcl)# 172.16.124.2
+>(tcl)# 10.3.1.1
+>(tcl)# 10.3.33.1
+>(tcl)# 10.3.65.1
+>(tcl)# 10.3.97.1
+>(tcl)# 10.3.129.1
+>(tcl)# 10.3.161.1
+>(tcl)# 172.16.124.3
+>(tcl)# } { ping $address }


Type escape sequence to abort.
Sending 5, 100-byte ICMP Echos to 10.1.1.1, timeout is 2 seconds:
!!!!!
Success rate is 100 percent (5/5), round-trip min/avg/max = 40/42/44 ms
Type escape sequence to abort.
Sending 5, 100-byte ICMP Echos to 10.1.33.1, timeout is 2 seconds:
!!!!!
Success rate is 100 percent (5/5), round-trip min/avg/max = 40/42/44 ms
Type escape sequence to abort.
Sending 5, 100-byte ICMP Echos to 10.1.65.1, timeout is 2 seconds:
!!!!!
Success rate is 100 percent (5/5), round-trip min/avg/max = 40/42/44 ms
Type escape sequence to abort.
Sending 5, 100-byte ICMP Echos to 10.1.97.1, timeout is 2 seconds:
!!!!!
Success rate is 100 percent (5/5), round-trip min/avg/max = 40/43/44 ms
Type escape sequence to abort.
Sending 5, 100-byte ICMP Echos to 10.1.129.1, timeout is 2 seconds:
!!!!!
Success rate is 100 percent (5/5), round-trip min/avg/max = 40/43/44 ms
Type escape sequence to abort.
Sending 5, 100-byte ICMP Echos to 10.1.161.1, timeout is 2 seconds:
!!!!!
Success rate is 100 percent (5/5), round-trip min/avg/max = 40/43/44 ms
Type escape sequence to abort.
Sending 5, 100-byte ICMP Echos to 172.16.124.1, timeout is 2 seconds:
!!!!!
Success rate is 100 percent (5/5), round-trip min/avg/max = 40/42/44 ms
Type escape sequence to abort.
Sending 5, 100-byte ICMP Echos to 10.2.1.1, timeout is 2 seconds:
!!!!!
```

```
Success rate is 100 percent (5/5), round-trip min/avg/max = 84/84/88 ms
Type escape sequence to abort.
Sending 5, 100-byte ICMP Echos to 10.2.33.1, timeout is 2 seconds:
!!!!!
Success rate is 100 percent (5/5), round-trip min/avg/max = 84/84/84 ms
Type escape sequence to abort.
Sending 5, 100-byte ICMP Echos to 10.2.65.1, timeout is 2 seconds:
!!!!!
Success rate is 100 percent (5/5), round-trip min/avg/max = 84/85/92 ms
Type escape sequence to abort.
Sending 5, 100-byte ICMP Echos to 10.2.97.1, timeout is 2 seconds:
!!!!!
Success rate is 100 percent (5/5), round-trip min/avg/max = 84/84/84 ms
Type escape sequence to abort.
Sending 5, 100-byte ICMP Echos to 10.2.129.1, timeout is 2 seconds:
!!!!!
Success rate is 100 percent (5/5), round-trip min/avg/max = 84/84/88 ms
Type escape sequence to abort.
Sending 5, 100-byte ICMP Echos to 10.2.161.1, timeout is 2 seconds:
!!!!!
Success rate is 100 percent (5/5), round-trip min/avg/max = 80/83/84 ms
Type escape sequence to abort.
Sending 5, 100-byte ICMP Echos to 172.16.124.2, timeout is 2 seconds:
!!!!!
Success rate is 100 percent (5/5), round-trip min/avg/max = 84/84/84 ms
Type escape sequence to abort.
Sending 5, 100-byte ICMP Echos to 10.3.1.1, timeout is 2 seconds:
!!!!!
Success rate is 100 percent (5/5), round-trip min/avg/max = 1/1/4 ms
Type escape sequence to abort.
Sending 5, 100-byte ICMP Echos to 10.3.33.1, timeout is 2 seconds:
!!!!!
Success rate is 100 percent (5/5), round-trip min/avg/max = 1/1/4 ms
Type escape sequence to abort.
Sending 5, 100-byte ICMP Echos to 10.3.65.1, timeout is 2 seconds:
!!!!!
Success rate is 100 percent (5/5), round-trip min/avg/max = 1/1/1 ms
Type escape sequence to abort.
Sending 5, 100-byte ICMP Echos to 10.3.97.1, timeout is 2 seconds:
!!!!!
Success rate is 100 percent (5/5), round-trip min/avg/max = 1/1/4 ms
Type escape sequence to abort.
Sending 5, 100-byte ICMP Echos to 10.3.129.1, timeout is 2 seconds:
!!!!!
```

```
Success rate is 100 percent (5/5), round-trip min/avg/max = 1/1/1 ms
Type escape sequence to abort.
Sending 5, 100-byte ICMP Echos to 10.3.161.1, timeout is 2 seconds:
!!!!!
Success rate is 100 percent (5/5), round-trip min/avg/max = 1/1/1 ms
Type escape sequence to abort.
Sending 5, 100-byte ICMP Echos to 172.16.124.3, timeout is 2 seconds:
!!!!!
Success rate is 100 percent (5/5), round-trip min/avg/max = 84/84/84 ms
West(tcl)# tclquit
```

Lab 2-6: EIGRP Authentication and Timers (2.7.5)

The objectives of this lab are as follows:

- Review basic configuration of EIGRP

- Configure and verify EIGRP authentication parameters

- Configure EIGRP hello interval and hold time

- Verify the hello interval and the hold time

Figure 2-6 illustrates the topology that will be used for this lab.

Figure 2-6   Topology Diagram

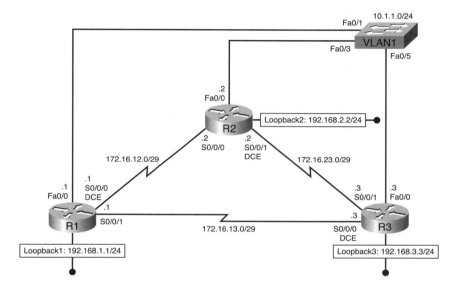

Scenario

As a network engineer, you have weighed the benefits of routing protocols and deployed EIGRP in your corporation's network. Recently, a new Chief Information Officer replaced the previous CIO and outlined a new network policy detailing more robust security measures. The CIO has also drawn up specifications to allow more frequent checking between neighboring routers so that fewer packets are lost in transit during times of instability.

Implement the CIO's specifications on your network.

Step 1: Addressing

Using the addressing scheme in Figure 2-6, apply IP addresses to the loopback, serial, and Fast Ethernet interfaces on R1, R2, and R3. Set the Frame Relay serial interface bandwidth on each router with the interface-level command **bandwidth** *bandwidth*. Specify the bandwidth as 64 Kbps on each serial interface. Specify the clock rate on the DCE end of each serial link using the command **clock rate 64000**.

You may cut and paste the following configurations into your routers to begin. Because your interfaces might be numbered differently, you may need to change the interface numbers. You can download these router configurations at www.ciscopress.com/title/1587132133 under the More Information section on the page.

```
R1:
!
interface Loopback1
 ip address 192.168.1.1 255.255.255.0
!
interface FastEthernet0/0
 ip address 10.1.1.1 255.255.255.0
 no shutdown
!
interface Serial0/0/0
 bandwidth 64
 ip address 172.16.12.1 255.255.255.248
 clock rate 64000
 no shutdown
!
interface Serial0/0/1
 bandwidth 64
 ip address 172.16.13.1 255.255.255.248
 no shutdown
!


end
```

```
R2:
!
interface Loopback2
 ip address 192.168.2.2 255.255.255.0
!
interface FastEthernet0/0
 ip address 10.1.1.2 255.255.255.0
 no shutdown
!
interface Serial0/0/0
 bandwidth 64
 ip address 172.16.12.2 255.255.255.248
 no shutdown
!
interface Serial0/0/1
 bandwidth 64
 ip address 172.16.23.2 255.255.255.248
 clock rate 64000
```

```
 no shutdown
!
end
```

R3:
```
!
interface Loopback3
 ip address 192.168.3.3 255.255.255.0
!
interface FastEthernet0/0
 ip address 10.1.1.3 255.255.255.0
 no shutdown
!
interface Serial0/0/0
 bandwidth 64
 ip address 172.16.13.3 255.255.255.248
 clock rate 64000
 no shutdown
!
interface Serial0/0/1
 bandwidth 64
 ip address 172.16.23.3 255.255.255.248
 no shutdown
!
end
```

Step 2: Configuring Basic EIGRP

Implement EIGRP AS 1 over the Fast Ethernet interfaces as you have configured it for the other EIGRP labs. Run EIGRP on all connections in the lab. Leave auto-summarization on. Advertise networks 10.0.0.0/8, 172.16.0.0/16, 192.168.1.0/24, 192.168.2.0/24, and 192.168.3.0/24 from their respective routers.

Verify your configuration by using the **show ip eigrp neighbors** command to check which routers have EIGRP adjacencies:

R1# **show ip eigrp neighbors**

IP-EIGRP neighbors for process 1

H	Address	Interface	Hold (sec)	Uptime	SRTT (ms)	RTO	Q Cnt	Seq Num
3	10.1.1.3	Fa0/0	14	00:00:13	1276	5000	0	15
2	172.16.13.3	Se0/0/1	12	00:00:17	28	2280	0	16
1	172.16.12.2	Se0/0/0	12	00:01:57	19	2280	0	35
0	10.1.1.2	Fa0/0	14	00:02:04	89	534	0	36

R2# **show ip eigrp neighbors**

IP-EIGRP neighbors for process 1

H	Address	Interface	Hold	Uptime	SRTT	RTO	Q	Seq

			(sec)	(ms)		Cnt	Num
3	10.1.1.3	Fa0/0	11 00:00:35	3	200	0	15
2	172.16.23.3	Se0/0/1	14 00:00:38	42	2280	0	17
1	172.16.12.1	Se0/0/0	14 00:02:18	15	2280	0	36
0	10.1.1.1	Fa0/0	10 00:02:26	1	200	0	34

```
R3# show ip eigrp neighbors
IP-EIGRP neighbors for process 1
```

H	Address	Interface	Hold Uptime	SRTT	RTO	Q	Seq
			(sec)	(ms)		Cnt	Num
3	10.1.1.2	Fa0/0	12 00:01:01	1028	5000	0	36
2	10.1.1.1	Fa0/0	12 00:01:01	4	200	0	34
1	172.16.23.2	Se0/0/1	11 00:01:03	834	5000	0	37
0	172.16.13.1	Se0/0/0	13 00:01:04	25	2280	0	35

Did you get the output you expected?

_____

Run the following TCL script on all routers to verify full connectivity. You can download this TCL script at www.ciscopress.com/title/1587132133 under the More Information section on the page.

```
foreach address {
10.1.1.1
172.16.12.1
172.16.13.1
192.168.1.1
10.1.1.2
172.16.12.2
172.16.23.2
192.168.2.2
10.1.1.3
172.16.13.3
172.16.23.3
192.168.3.3
} { ping $address }
```

If you have never used TCL scripts or need a refresher, see the TCL lab in the routing module.

You get ICMP echo replies for every address pinged. Make sure you run the TCL script on each router and that your results match the output in the section "TCL Script Output" for this lab before continuing.

Step 3: Configuring Authentication Keys

Before you configure a link to authenticate the EIGRP adjacencies, you must configure the keys that are used for the authentication. EIGRP uses generic router key chains that are available in Cisco IOS as storage locations for keys. These classify keys into groups and enable keys to be easily changed periodically without bringing down adjacencies.

Use the **key chain name** command in global configuration mode to create a chain of keys with the label EIGRP-KEYS:

```
R1# configure terminal
R1(config)# key chain EIGRP-KEYS
R1(config-keychain)# key 1
R1(config-keychain-key)# key-string cisco
```
```
R2# configure terminal
R2(config)# key chain EIGRP-KEYS
R2(config-keychain)# key 1
R2(config-keychain-key)# key-string cisco
```
```
R3# configure terminal
R3(config)# key chain EIGRP-KEYS
R3(config-keychain)# key 1
R3(config-keychain-key)# key-string cisco
```

Issue the **show key chain** command. You should have the same output on every router:

```
R1# show key chain
Key-chain EIGRP-KEYS:
    key 1 -- text "cisco"
        accept lifetime (always valid) - (always valid) [valid now]
        send lifetime (always valid) - (always valid) [valid now]
```

You can set a time span over which a key is sent to other routers and, separately, over which a key is accepted from other routers. Although lifetime values are not explored in the BSCI lab curriculum, you should keep it in mind for production networks when you are rolling from one set of authentication strings to another. For now, you simply want to authenticate the EIGRP adjacencies for security reasons.

Step 4: Configuring EIGRP Link Authentication

When configuring EIGRP link authentication, you first need to apply the authentication key chain to a specific autonomous system on an EIGRP interface. Although this does not engage EIGRP authentication on an interface, it associates a key chain with a particular autonomous system on an interface. The command that is entered on the interface is **ip authentication key-chain eigrp** *as-number key_chain_label*:

```
R1# configure terminal
R1(config)# interface serial 0/0/0
R1(config-if)# ip authentication key-chain eigrp 1 EIGRP-KEYS
```

Now, apply the key chain to the interface with the **ip authentication mode eigrp** *as_number* **md5** command:

```
R1(config-if)# ip authentication mode eigrp 1 md5
```

Apply these commands on all active EIGRP interfaces:

```
R1# configure terminal
R1(config)# interface serial 0/0/0
```

```
R1(config-if)# ip authentication key-chain eigrp 1 EIGRP-KEYS
R1(config-if)# ip authentication mode eigrp 1 md5
R1(config-if)# interface serial 0/0/1
R1(config-if)# ip authentication key-chain eigrp 1 EIGRP-KEYS
R1(config-if)# ip authentication mode eigrp 1 md5
R1(config-if)# interface fastethernet 0/0
R1(config-if)# ip authentication key-chain eigrp 1 EIGRP-KEYS
R1(config-if)# ip authentication mode eigrp 1 md5
```
```
R2# configure terminal
R2(config)# interface serial 0/0/0
R2(config-if)# ip authentication key-chain eigrp 1 EIGRP-KEYS
R2(config-if)# ip authentication mode eigrp 1 md5
R2(config-if)# interface serial 0/0/1
R2(config-if)# ip authentication key-chain eigrp 1 EIGRP-KEYS
R2(config-if)# ip authentication mode eigrp 1 md5
R2(config-if)# interface fastethernet 0/0
R2(config-if)# ip authentication key-chain eigrp 1 EIGRP-KEYS
R2(config-if)# ip authentication mode eigrp 1 md5
```
```
R3# configure terminal
R3(config)# interface serial 0/0/0
R3(config-if)# ip authentication key-chain eigrp 1 EIGRP-KEYS
R3(config-if)# ip authentication mode eigrp 1 md5
R3(config-if)# interface serial 0/0/1
R3(config-if)# ip authentication key-chain eigrp 1 EIGRP-KEYS
R3(config-if)# ip authentication mode eigrp 1 md5
R3(config-if)# interface fastethernet 0/0
R3(config-if)# ip authentication key-chain eigrp 1 EIGRP-KEYS
R3(config-if)# ip authentication mode eigrp 1 md5
```

Each of your EIGRP adjacencies should "flap" (go down and come back up) when you implement message digest algorithm 5 (MD5) authentication on one side of the link before the other side has been configured. In a production network, this causes some instability during a configuration, so make sure you implement it outside of peak usage times.

Check if this has been successfully implemented with the **show ip eigrp interfaces detail** command:

```
R1# show ip eigrp interfaces detail
IP-EIGRP interfaces for process 1

                Xmit Queue   Mean   Pacing Time   Multicast    Pending
Interface Peers Un/Reliable  SRTT   Un/Reliable   Flow Timer   Routes
Fa0/0      2       0/0        3        0/1            50           0
  Hello interval is 5 sec
  Next xmit serial <none>
  Un/reliable mcasts: 0/14  Un/reliable ucasts: 26/21
```

```
     Mcast exceptions: 3  CR packets: 3  ACKs suppressed: 3
     Retransmissions sent: 1  Out-of-sequence rcvd: 0
   Authentication mode is md5,  key-chain is "EIGRP-KEYS"
     Use multicast
Se0/0/0        1        0/0        4        0/12        50            0
     Hello interval is 5 sec
     Next xmit serial <none>
     Un/reliable mcasts: 0/0  Un/reliable ucasts: 10/28
     Mcast exceptions: 0  CR packets: 0  ACKs suppressed: 5
     Retransmissions sent: 0  Out-of-sequence rcvd: 0
   Authentication mode is md5,  key-chain is "EIGRP-KEYS"
     Use unicast
Se0/0/1        1        0/0        1        0/12        50            0
     Hello interval is 5 sec
     Next xmit serial <none>
     Un/reliable mcasts: 0/0  Un/reliable ucasts: 10/22
     Mcast exceptions: 0  CR packets: 0  ACKs suppressed: 8
     Retransmissions sent: 0  Out-of-sequence rcvd: 0
   Authentication mode is md5,  key-chain is "EIGRP-KEYS"
     Use unicast
```

R2# **show ip eigrp interfaces detail**

```
IP-EIGRP interfaces for process 1

                 Xmit Queue   Mean   Pacing Time   Multicast    Pending
Interface Peers  Un/Reliable  SRTT   Un/Reliable   Flow Timer   Routes
Fa0/0       2       0/0         4       0/10          50           0
     Hello interval is 5 sec
     Next xmit serial <none>
     Un/reliable mcasts: 0/7  Un/reliable ucasts: 34/15
     Mcast exceptions: 0  CR packets: 0  ACKs suppressed: 7
     Retransmissions sent: 1  Out-of-sequence rcvd: 0
   Authentication mode is md5,  key-chain is "EIGRP-KEYS"
Se0/0/0     1       0/0         1       0/12          50           0
     Hello interval is 5 sec
     Next xmit serial <none>
     Un/reliable mcasts: 0/0  Un/reliable ucasts: 19/17
     Mcast exceptions: 0  CR packets: 0  ACKs suppressed: 7
     Retransmissions sent: 0  Out-of-sequence rcvd: 0
   Authentication mode is md5,  key-chain is "EIGRP-KEYS"
Se0/0/1     1       0/0         3       0/12          50           0
     Hello interval is 5 sec
     Next xmit serial <none>
     Un/reliable mcasts: 0/0  Un/reliable ucasts: 11/9
```

```
    Mcast exceptions: 0  CR packets: 0  ACKs suppressed: 4
    Retransmissions sent: 0  Out-of-sequence rcvd: 0
    Authentication mode is md5,  key-chain is "EIGRP-KEYS"
R3# show ip eigrp interfaces detail
IP-EIGRP interfaces for process 1


                 Xmit Queue   Mean   Pacing Time   Multicast    Pending
Interface Peers  Un/Reliable  SRTT   Un/Reliable   Flow Timer   Routes
Fa0/0       2       0/0        2        0/1            50           0
  Hello interval is 5 sec
  Next xmit serial <none>
  Un/reliable mcasts: 0/13  Un/reliable ucasts: 22/12
  Mcast exceptions: 2  CR packets: 1  ACKs suppressed: 1
  Retransmissions sent: 1  Out-of-sequence rcvd: 0
  Authentication mode is md5,  key-chain is "EIGRP-KEYS"
  Use multicast
Se0/0/0     1       0/0        1        0/12           50           0
  Hello interval is 5 sec
  Next xmit serial <none>
  Un/reliable mcasts: 0/0  Un/reliable ucasts: 12/19
  Mcast exceptions: 0  CR packets: 0  ACKs suppressed: 7
  Retransmissions sent: 0  Out-of-sequence rcvd: 0
  Authentication mode is md5,  key-chain is "EIGRP-KEYS"
  Use unicast
Se0/0/1     1       0/0        4        0/12           50           0
  Hello interval is 5 sec
  Next xmit serial <none>
  Un/reliable mcasts: 0/0  Un/reliable ucasts: 3/15
  Mcast exceptions: 0  CR packets: 0  ACKs suppressed: 4
  Retransmissions sent: 0  Out-of-sequence rcvd: 0
  Authentication mode is md5,  key-chain is "EIGRP-KEYS"
  Use unicast
```

At this point, your interfaces are authenticating each adjacency with the EIGRP-KEYS key chain. Make sure that you verify the number of neighbors out each interface in the above output. Notice that the number of peers is the number of adjacencies established out that interface.

When EIGRP has a key chain associated with an autonomous system on a given interface and EIGRP is authenticating its adjacencies, you have successfully completed the initial work. Use the **debug eigrp packets** command to see the authenticated hellos:

```
R1# debug eigrp packets
EIGRP Packets debugging is on
    (UPDATE, REQUEST, QUERY, REPLY, HELLO, IPXSAP, PROBE, ACK, STUB, SIAQUERY,
SIAREPLY)
```

```
R1#
*Oct  4 16:10:51.090: EIGRP: Sending HELLO on Serial0/0/1
*Oct  4 16:10:51.090:    AS 1, Flags 0x0, Seq 0/0 idbQ 0/0 iidbQ un/rely 0/0
*Oct  4 16:10:51.190: EIGRP: received packet with MD5 authentication, key id = 1
*Oct  4 16:10:51.190: EIGRP: Received HELLO on Serial0/0/1 nbr 172.16.13.3
*Oct  4 16:10:51.190:    AS 1, Flags 0x0, Seq 0/0 idbQ 0/0 iidbQ un/rely 0/0 peerQ
un/rely 0/0
*Oct  4 16:10:51.854: EIGRP: received packet with MD5 authentication, key id = 1
*Oct  4 16:10:51.854: EIGRP: Received HELLO on FastEthernet0/0 nbr 10.1.1.2
*Oct  4 16:10:51.854:    AS 1, Flags 0x0, Seq 0/0 idbQ 0/0 iidbQ un/rely 0/0 peerQ
un/rely 0/0
*Oct  4 16:10:53.046: EIGRP: received packet with MD5 authentication, key id = 1
```

Issue the **undebug all** command to stop the debugging output.

Step 5: Manipulating EIGRP Timers

Your CIO also ordered you to change the hello and dead intervals on point-to-point serial interfaces so that dead neighbors are detected in roughly half the time that they are detected by default. To view the default timers, first use the **show ip eigrp interfaces detail** command:

```
R1# show ip eigrp interfaces detail
IP-EIGRP interfaces for process 1

                      Xmit Queue    Mean    Pacing Time    Multicast    Pending
Interface Peers      Un/Reliable    SRTT    Un/Reliable    Flow Timer   Routes
Fa0/0        2          0/0           1         0/1            50          0
  Hello interval is 5 sec
  Next xmit serial <none>
  Un/reliable mcasts: 0/20  Un/reliable ucasts: 41/27
  Mcast exceptions: 3  CR packets: 3  ACKs suppressed: 3
  Retransmissions sent: 1  Out-of-sequence rcvd: 0
  Authentication mode is md5,  key-chain is "EIGRP-KEYS"
  Use multicast
Se0/0/0      1          0/0          17        10/380          448         0
  Hello interval is 5 sec
  Next xmit serial <none>
  Un/reliable mcasts: 0/0  Un/reliable ucasts: 17/37
  Mcast exceptions: 0  CR packets: 0  ACKs suppressed: 6
  Retransmissions sent: 0  Out-of-sequence rcvd: 0
  Authentication mode is md5,  key-chain is "EIGRP-KEYS"
  Use unicast
Se0/0/1      1          0/0          11        10/380          416         0
  Hello interval is 5 sec
  Next xmit serial <none>
  Un/reliable mcasts: 0/0  Un/reliable ucasts: 18/31
```

```
    Mcast exceptions: 0  CR packets: 0  ACKs suppressed: 8
    Retransmissions sent: 0  Out-of-sequence rcvd: 0
    Authentication mode is md5,  key-chain is "EIGRP-KEYS"
    Use unicast
```

On all of your interfaces, you get the default hello interval of five seconds for point-to-point serial links regardless of the bandwidth, and five seconds for LAN interfaces. Recall that the default hold time is three times the length of the hello interval. If you change the EIGRP hello interval, the hold-time interval does not automatically change.

The hello interval determines how often *outgoing* EIGRP hellos are sent, while the hold-time monitors *incoming* hellos. You are more concerned with the hold time than the hello interval, because the hold time detects a dead neighbor. However, you also want the neighbors to send the same number of hellos as under normal circumstances before declaring a neighbor dead.

What is the hold time you will configure?

_____

_____

What is the hello interval you intend to configure?

_____

_____

Change both the hello interval and the hold time for AS 1 for Serial0/0/0 on R1 and R2 using the **ip hello-interval eigrp 1 2** and **ip hold-time eigrp 1 8** commands (use the "?" to investigate what each parameter does):

```
R1# configure terminal
R1(config)# interface serial 0/0/0
R1(config-if)# ip hello-interval eigrp 1 2
R1(config-if)# ip hold-time eigrp 1 8
R2# configure terminal
R2(config)# interface serial 0/0/0
R2(config-if)# ip hello-interval eigrp 1 2
R2(config-if)# ip hold-time eigrp 1 8
```

Verify that the hello interval has been successfully changed with the **show ip eigrp 1 interfaces detail serial0/0/0** command:

```
R1# show ip eigrp 1 interfaces detail serial 0/0/0
IP-EIGRP interfaces for process 1
```

Interface	Peers	Xmit Queue Un/Reliable	Mean SRTT	Pacing Time Un/Reliable	Multicast Flow Timer	Pending Routes
Se0/0/0	1	0/0	17	10/380	448	0

```
  Hello interval is 2 sec
  Next xmit serial <none>
```

```
   Un/reliable mcasts: 0/0  Un/reliable ucasts: 17/37

   Mcast exceptions: 0  CR packets: 0  ACKs suppressed: 6

   Retransmissions sent: 0  Out-of-sequence rcvd: 0

   Authentication mode is md5,  key-chain is "EIGRP-KEYS"

   Use unicast
```

```
R2# show ip eigrp 1 interfaces detail serial 0/0/0

IP-EIGRP interfaces for process 1


                      Xmit Queue   Mean   Pacing Time   Multicast    Pending
Interface     Peers   Un/Reliable  SRTT   Un/Reliable   Flow Timer   Routes
Se0/0/0         1       0/0         26      10/380         472          0
   Hello interval is 2 sec

   Next xmit serial <none>

   Un/reliable mcasts: 0/0  Un/reliable ucasts: 27/25

   Mcast exceptions: 0  CR packets: 0  ACKs suppressed: 8

   Retransmissions sent: 0  Out-of-sequence rcvd: 0

   Authentication mode is md5,  key-chain is "EIGRP-KEYS"
```

Verify that the hold time has been successfully changed with the **show ip eigrp neighbors** command:

```
R1# show ip eigrp neighbors

IP-EIGRP neighbors for process 1

H   Address            Interface      Hold Uptime    SRTT   RTO   Q   Seq
                                      (sec)          (ms)         Cnt Num
3   172.16.13.3        Se0/0/1         11 01:18:21    11   2280   0   85
2   10.1.1.3           Fa0/0           13 01:18:24     1    200   0   84
1   10.1.1.2           Fa0/0           12 01:23:31     1    200   0   74
0   172.16.12.2        Se0/0/0          6 01:23:39    17   2280   0   73
```

```
R2# show ip eigrp neighbors

IP-EIGRP neighbors for process 1

H   Address            Interface      Hold Uptime    SRTT   RTO   Q   Seq
                                      (sec)          (ms)         Cnt Num
3   172.16.23.3        Se0/0/1         13 01:20:38    16   2280   0   83
2   10.1.1.3           Fa0/0           14 01:20:38     1    200   0   81
1   10.1.1.1           Fa0/0           13 01:25:45     1    200   0  109
0   172.16.12.1        Se0/0/0          6 01:25:53    26   2280   0  110
```

Configure the same hello interval and hold time on each active serial interface in your topology:

```
R1# configure terminal

R1(config)# interface serial 0/0/1

R1(config-if)# ip hello-interval eigrp 1 2

R1(config-if)# ip hold-time eigrp 1 8
```

```
R2# configure terminal

R2(config)# interface serial 0/0/1

R2(config-if)# ip hello-interval eigrp 1 2
```

```
R2(config-if)# ip hold-time eigrp 1 8
```

```
R3# configure terminal
R3(config)# interface serial 0/0/0
R3(config-if)# ip hello-interval eigrp 1 2
R3(config-if)# ip hold-time eigrp 1 8
R3(config-if)# interface serial 0/0/1
R3(config-if)# ip hello-interval eigrp 1 2
R3(config-if)# ip hold-time eigrp 1 8
```

Make sure that all of your EIGRP neighbor relationships remain up during your configuration. Use the **show ip eigrp neighbors** command to verify the hold time, and the **show ip eigrp interfaces detail** command to verify the hello interval, as you just did.

Finally, run the TCL script again to make sure you still have full connectivity after making your changes to the EIGRP default configuration. Verify that you still have full connectivity by checking the output of the TCL script against the section that follows, "TCL Script Output." You should receive all ICMP echo replies back successfully.

TCL Script Output

```
R1# tclsh
R1(tcl)# foreach address {
+>(tcl)# 10.1.1.1
+>(tcl)# 172.16.12.1
+>(tcl)# 172.16.13.1
+>(tcl)# 192.168.1.1
+>(tcl)# 10.1.1.2
+>(tcl)# 172.16.12.2
+>(tcl)# 172.16.23.2
+>(tcl)# 192.168.2.2
+>(tcl)# 10.1.1.3
+>(tcl)# 172.16.13.3
+>(tcl)# 172.16.23.3
+>(tcl)# 192.168.3.3
+>(tcl)# } { ping $address }

Type escape sequence to abort.
Sending 5, 100-byte ICMP Echos to 10.1.1.1, timeout is 2 seconds:
!!!!!
Success rate is 100 percent (5/5), round-trip min/avg/max = 1/1/4 ms
Type escape sequence to abort.
Sending 5, 100-byte ICMP Echos to 172.16.12.1, timeout is 2 seconds:
!!!!!
Success rate is 100 percent (5/5), round-trip min/avg/max = 56/56/56 ms
Type escape sequence to abort.
Sending 5, 100-byte ICMP Echos to 172.16.13.1, timeout is 2 seconds:
```

```
!!!!!
Success rate is 100 percent (5/5), round-trip min/avg/max = 56/56/60 ms
Type escape sequence to abort.
Sending 5, 100-byte ICMP Echos to 192.168.1.1, timeout is 2 seconds:
!!!!!
Success rate is 100 percent (5/5), round-trip min/avg/max = 1/1/4 ms
Type escape sequence to abort.
Sending 5, 100-byte ICMP Echos to 10.1.1.2, timeout is 2 seconds:
!!!!!
Success rate is 100 percent (5/5), round-trip min/avg/max = 1/2/4 ms
Type escape sequence to abort.
Sending 5, 100-byte ICMP Echos to 172.16.12.2, timeout is 2 seconds:
!!!!!
Success rate is 100 percent (5/5), round-trip min/avg/max = 28/28/28 ms
Type escape sequence to abort.
Sending 5, 100-byte ICMP Echos to 172.16.23.2, timeout is 2 seconds:
!!!!!
Success rate is 100 percent (5/5), round-trip min/avg/max = 12/15/16 ms
Type escape sequence to abort.
Sending 5, 100-byte ICMP Echos to 192.168.2.2, timeout is 2 seconds:
!!!!!
Success rate is 100 percent (5/5), round-trip min/avg/max = 1/2/4 ms
Type escape sequence to abort.
Sending 5, 100-byte ICMP Echos to 10.1.1.3, timeout is 2 seconds:
!!!!!
Success rate is 100 percent (5/5), round-trip min/avg/max = 1/2/4 ms
Type escape sequence to abort.
Sending 5, 100-byte ICMP Echos to 172.16.13.3, timeout is 2 seconds:
!!!!!
Success rate is 100 percent (5/5), round-trip min/avg/max = 28/28/32 ms
Type escape sequence to abort.
Sending 5, 100-byte ICMP Echos to 172.16.23.3, timeout is 2 seconds:
!!!!!
Success rate is 100 percent (5/5), round-trip min/avg/max = 1/2/4 ms
Type escape sequence to abort.
Sending 5, 100-byte ICMP Echos to 192.168.3.3, timeout is 2 seconds:
!!!!!
Success rate is 100 percent (5/5), round-trip min/avg/max = 1/2/4 ms
R1(tcl)# tclquit
R1#
```

```
R2# tclsh
R2(tcl)#
R2(tcl)# foreach address {
+>(tcl)# 10.1.1.1
```

```
+>(tcl)# 172.16.12.1
+>(tcl)# 172.16.13.1
+>(tcl)# 192.168.1.1
+>(tcl)# 10.1.1.2
+>(tcl)# 172.16.12.2
+>(tcl)# 172.16.23.2
+>(tcl)# 192.168.2.2
+>(tcl)# 10.1.1.3
+>(tcl)# 172.16.13.3
+>(tcl)# 172.16.23.3
+>(tcl)# 192.168.3.3
+>(tcl)# } { ping $address }


Type escape sequence to abort.
Sending 5, 100-byte ICMP Echos to 10.1.1.1, timeout is 2 seconds:
!!!!!
Success rate is 100 percent (5/5), round-trip min/avg/max = 1/2/4 ms
Type escape sequence to abort.
Sending 5, 100-byte ICMP Echos to 172.16.12.1, timeout is 2 seconds:
!!!!!
Success rate is 100 percent (5/5), round-trip min/avg/max = 28/28/32 ms
Type escape sequence to abort.
Sending 5, 100-byte ICMP Echos to 172.16.13.1, timeout is 2 seconds:
!!!!!
Success rate is 100 percent (5/5), round-trip min/avg/max = 12/14/16 ms
Type escape sequence to abort.
Sending 5, 100-byte ICMP Echos to 192.168.1.1, timeout is 2 seconds:
!!!!!
Success rate is 100 percent (5/5), round-trip min/avg/max = 1/1/4 ms
Type escape sequence to abort.
Sending 5, 100-byte ICMP Echos to 10.1.1.2, timeout is 2 seconds:
!!!!!
Success rate is 100 percent (5/5), round-trip min/avg/max = 1/1/1 ms
Type escape sequence to abort.
Sending 5, 100-byte ICMP Echos to 172.16.12.2, timeout is 2 seconds:
!!!!!
Success rate is 100 percent (5/5), round-trip min/avg/max = 56/56/56 ms
Type escape sequence to abort.
Sending 5, 100-byte ICMP Echos to 172.16.23.2, timeout is 2 seconds:
!!!!!
Success rate is 100 percent (5/5), round-trip min/avg/max = 56/56/56 ms
Type escape sequence to abort.
Sending 5, 100-byte ICMP Echos to 192.168.2.2, timeout is 2 seconds:
!!!!!
```

```
Success rate is 100 percent (5/5), round-trip min/avg/max = 1/1/4 ms
Type escape sequence to abort.
Sending 5, 100-byte ICMP Echos to 10.1.1.3, timeout is 2 seconds:
!!!!!
Success rate is 100 percent (5/5), round-trip min/avg/max = 1/1/4 ms
Type escape sequence to abort.
Sending 5, 100-byte ICMP Echos to 172.16.13.3, timeout is 2 seconds:
!!!!!
Success rate is 100 percent (5/5), round-trip min/avg/max = 12/16/24 ms
Type escape sequence to abort.
Sending 5, 100-byte ICMP Echos to 172.16.23.3, timeout is 2 seconds:
!!!!!
Success rate is 100 percent (5/5), round-trip min/avg/max = 28/28/32 ms
Type escape sequence to abort.
Sending 5, 100-byte ICMP Echos to 192.168.3.3, timeout is 2 seconds:
!!!!!
Success rate is 100 percent (5/5), round-trip min/avg/max = 1/1/4 ms
R2(tcl)# tclquit
R2#
```

```
R3# tclsh
R3(tcl)#
R3(tcl)# foreach address {
+>(tcl)# 10.1.1.1
+>(tcl)# 172.16.12.1
+>(tcl)# 172.16.13.1
+>(tcl)# 192.168.1.1
+>(tcl)# 10.1.1.2
+>(tcl)# 172.16.12.2
+>(tcl)# 172.16.23.2
+>(tcl)# 192.168.2.2
+>(tcl)# 10.1.1.3
+>(tcl)# 172.16.13.3
+>(tcl)# 172.16.23.3
+>(tcl)# 192.168.3.3
+>(tcl)# } { ping $address }

Type escape sequence to abort.
Sending 5, 100-byte ICMP Echos to 10.1.1.1, timeout is 2 seconds:
!!!!!
Success rate is 100 percent (5/5), round-trip min/avg/max = 1/2/4 ms
Type escape sequence to abort.
Sending 5, 100-byte ICMP Echos to 172.16.12.1, timeout is 2 seconds:
!!!!!
Success rate is 100 percent (5/5), round-trip min/avg/max = 1/1/4 ms
```

```
Type escape sequence to abort.
Sending 5, 100-byte ICMP Echos to 172.16.13.1, timeout is 2 seconds:
!!!!!
Success rate is 100 percent (5/5), round-trip min/avg/max = 28/28/28 ms
Type escape sequence to abort.
Sending 5, 100-byte ICMP Echos to 192.168.1.1, timeout is 2 seconds:
!!!!!
Success rate is 100 percent (5/5), round-trip min/avg/max = 1/2/4 ms
Type escape sequence to abort.
Sending 5, 100-byte ICMP Echos to 10.1.1.2, timeout is 2 seconds:
!!!!!
Success rate is 100 percent (5/5), round-trip min/avg/max = 1/1/1 ms
Type escape sequence to abort.
Sending 5, 100-byte ICMP Echos to 172.16.12.2, timeout is 2 seconds:
!!!!!
Success rate is 100 percent (5/5), round-trip min/avg/max = 1/1/4 ms
Type escape sequence to abort.
Sending 5, 100-byte ICMP Echos to 172.16.23.2, timeout is 2 seconds:
!!!!!
Success rate is 100 percent (5/5), round-trip min/avg/max = 28/28/28 ms
Type escape sequence to abort.
Sending 5, 100-byte ICMP Echos to 192.168.2.2, timeout is 2 seconds:
!!!!!
Success rate is 100 percent (5/5), round-trip min/avg/max = 1/1/4 ms
Type escape sequence to abort.
Sending 5, 100-byte ICMP Echos to 10.1.1.3, timeout is 2 seconds:
!!!!!
Success rate is 100 percent (5/5), round-trip min/avg/max = 1/1/4 ms
Type escape sequence to abort.
Sending 5, 100-byte ICMP Echos to 172.16.13.3, timeout is 2 seconds:
!!!!!
Success rate is 100 percent (5/5), round-trip min/avg/max = 56/61/84 ms
Type escape sequence to abort.
Sending 5, 100-byte ICMP Echos to 172.16.23.3, timeout is 2 seconds:
!!!!!
Success rate is 100 percent (5/5), round-trip min/avg/max = 56/57/64 ms
Type escape sequence to abort.
Sending 5, 100-byte ICMP Echos to 192.168.3.3, timeout is 2 seconds:
!!!!!
Success rate is 100 percent (5/5), round-trip min/avg/max = 1/1/4 ms
R3(tcl)# tclquit
R3#
```

Lab 2-7: EIGRP Challenge Lab (2.7.6)

Implement the topology illustrated in Figure 2-7 according to the following requirements:

- Configure all interfaces shown in the Figure 2-7 with the IP addresses shown.

- Configure EIGRP AS 1 to route all networks shown in the diagram.

- Disable automatic-summarization.

- Have R4 summarize its loopback addresses to the most specific summary possible.

- R2 should filter R3's Loopback 3 interface from being advertised out.

- R1 should filter out R3's Loopback 2 interface from incoming updates.

- Do not multicast EIGRP hellos on the network between R1 and R2.

- Modify the hello timers on the link between R2 and R3 to send a hello packet every two seconds.

- Use message digest algorithm 5 (MD5) authentication with the key **cisco** over the link between R3 and R4.

Figure 2-7   Topology Diagram

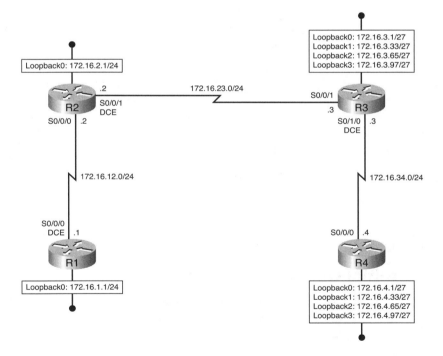

Lab 2-8: EIGRP Troubleshooting Lab (2.7.7)

In this lab, you troubleshoot existing configurations to get a working topology. Cut and paste the initial configurations into your routers. Your goal is to use troubleshooting techniques to fix anything in the scenario that prevents full IP connectivity. Full IP connectivity means every IP address in the scenario should be reachable from every router. If you don't know where to start, try pinging remote addresses and see which ones are reachable (either manually performing pings or using a TCL script). Figure 2-8 shows the topology for this lab, which must match the following requirements:

- Use the IP addressing scheme shown in Figure 2-8.

- All routers must participate in EIGRP AS 1.

- All networks in Figure 2-8 must be in EIGRP AS 1.

- Do not use any static routes, default routes, or other routing protocols.

- All IP addresses in the topology must be reachable from all routers.

Figure 2-8   Topology Diagram

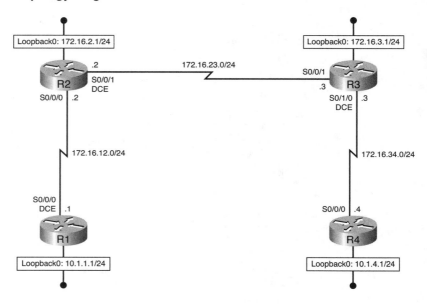

Initial Configurations

You can download these router configurations at www.ciscopress.com/title/1587132133 under the More Information section on the page.

```
R1# show run
hostname R1
!
interface Loopback0
 ip address 10.1.1.1 255.255.255.0
!
interface Serial0/0/0
 ip address 172.16.12.1 255.255.255.0
 clock rate 64000
 no shutdown
```

```
!
router eigrp 1
 network 10.1.1.0 0.0.0.255
 network 172.16.12.0 0.0.0.255
 auto-summary
end
```

```
R2# show run
hostname R2
!
interface Loopback0
 ip address 172.16.2.1 255.255.255.0
!
interface Serial0/0/0
 ip address 172.16.12.2 255.255.255.0
 no shutdown
!
interface Serial0/0/1
 ip address 172.16.23.2 255.255.255.0
 clock rate 64000
 no shutdown
!
router eigrp 1
 network 172.16.2.0 0.0.0.255
 network 172.16.12.0 0.0.0.255
 network 172.16.23.0 0.0.0.255
 no auto-summary
end
```

```
R3# show run
hostname R3
!
interface Loopback0
 ip address 172.16.3.1 255.255.255.0
!
interface Serial0/0/1
 ip address 172.16.23.3 255.255.255.0
 no shutdown
!
interface Serial0/1/0
 ip address 172.16.34.3 255.255.255.0
 clock rate 64000
 no shutdown
!
router eigrp 1
```

```
     network 172.16.23.0 0.0.0.255
     network 172.16.30.0 0.0.0.255
     network 172.16.34.0 0.0.0.255
     no auto-summary
   end
```

```
R4# show run
hostname R4
!
interface Loopback0
 ip address 10.1.4.1 255.255.255.0
!
interface Serial0/0/0
 ip address 172.16.34.4 255.255.255.0
 no shutdown
!
router eigrp 100
 network 10.1.4.0 0.0.0.255
 network 172.16.34.0 0.0.0.255
 auto-summary
end
```

Lab 3-1: Single-Area OSPF Link Costs and Interface Priorities (3.1 1.1)

The objectives of this lab are as follows:

- Configure single-area OSPF on a router

- Advertise loopback interfaces into OSPF

- Verify OSPF adjacencies

- Verify OSPF routing information exchange

- Modify OSPF link costs

- Change interface priorities

- Utilize debugging commands for troubleshooting OSPF

Figure 3-1 illustrates the topology that will be used for this lab.

Figure 3-1   Topology Diagram

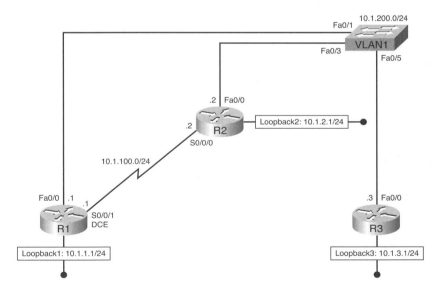

Scenario

You are responsible for configuring the new network to connect your company's engineering, marketing, and accounting departments, represented by the loopback interfaces on each of the three routers. The physical devices have just been installed and connected by Fast Ethernet and serial cables. Configure OSPF to allow full connectivity between all departments.

You will be using the same physical topology for the labs in this module, so save your configuration for use in the next lab exercise.

Step 1: Addressing

Using the addressing scheme in Figure 3-1, apply IP addresses to the Fast Ethernet interfaces on R1, R2, and R3. Create Loopback1 on R1, Loopback2 on R2, and Loopback3 on R3 and address them according to the topology in Figure 3-1:

```
R1# configure terminal
R1(config)# interface Loopback 1
R1(config-if)# description Engineering Department
R1(config-if)# ip address 10.1.1.1 255.255.255.0
R1(config-if)# exit
R1(config)# interface FastEthernet 0/0
R1(config-if)# ip address 10.1.200.1 255.255.255.0
R1(config-if)# no shutdown


R2# configure terminal
R2(config)# interface Loopback2
R2(config-if)# description Marketing Department
R2(config-if)# ip address 10.1.2.1 255.255.255.0
R2(config-if)# exit
R2(config)# interface FastEthernet 0/0
R2(config-if)# ip address 10.1.200.2 255.255.255.0
R2(config-if)# no shutdown


R3# configure terminal
R3(config)# interface Loopback3
R3(config-if)# description Accounting Department
R3(config-if)# ip address 10.1.3.1 255.255.255.0
R3(config-if)# exit
R3(config)# interface FastEthernet 0/0
R3(config-if)# ip address 10.1.200.3 255.255.255.0
R3(config-if)# no shutdown
```

Leave the switch in its default (blank) configuration. By default, all switchports are in VLAN1 and are not administratively down.

Also configure the serial interfaces with the IP addresses given in Figure 3-1. Remember to add the **clockrate** command where appropriate:

```
R1(config)# interface Serial 0/0/0
R1(config-if)# ip address 10.1.100.1 255.255.255.0
R1(config-if)# clockrate 64000
R1(config-if)# no shutdown
```

```
R2(config)# interface Serial 0/0/0
R2(config-if)# ip address 10.1.100.2 255.255.255.0
R2(config-if)# no shutdown
```

Verify that the line protocols of each interface are up and that you can reliably ping across each link.

Step 2: Adding Physical Interfaces to OSPF

After all your IP addressing is set up and you have local subnet connectivity, you can configure OSPF process 1. To enter the OSPF configuration prompt, use the command **router ospf** *process_number*. The process number is a locally significant number that does not affect how OSPF works. For this lab, use process number 1 on all your routers.

Next, add interfaces with the **network** *address wildcard_mask* **area** *area* command. The address can be any IP address. The mask is an inverse mask, similar to the kind used in an access list. The area is the OSPF area you want to put the interface into. For this lab, we will use area 0, the backbone area, for all interfaces. This command can be very confusing at first. What it means is that any interface with an IP that matches the address and wildcard mask combination in the network statement is added to the OSPF process in that area.

The command **network 10.1.200.1 0.0.0.0 area 0** adds any interface with the IP address of 10.1.200.1 to the OSPF process into area 0. The wildcard mask of 0.0.0.0 means that all 32 bits of the IP address have to be an exact match. A 0 bit in the wildcard mask means that the bit in that portion of the interface IP has to match the address. A 1 bit in the wildcard mask means that the bit in the interface IP does not have to match that portion of the IP address.

The command **network 10.1.100.0 0.0.0.255 area 0** means that any interface whose IP address matches 10.1.100.0 for the first 3 octets will match the command and add it to area 0. The last octet is all 1s because in the wildcard mask it is 255. This means that an interface with an IP of 10.1.100.1, 10.1.100.2, or 10.1.100.250 would match this address and wildcard combination and get added to OSPF.

The wildcard mask does not have to be the inverse of the subnet mask of an interface IP, although it can be helpful. An easy way to calculate a wildcard mask from the subnet mask is to subtract 255 minus the octet value for each octet. A subnet mask of 255.255.255.252 (/30) becomes 0.0.0.3 to capture all interfaces on that subnet. This is because 255 − 255 = 0, and 255 − 252 = 3.

When configuring OSPF, enter the commands on R1. Then exit to privileged EXEC mode and type **debug ip ospf adjacency**. This command lets you watch OSPF neighbors come up and see neighbor relationships:

```
R1(config)# router ospf 1
R1(config-router)# network 10.1.100.0 0.0.0.255 area 0
R1(config-router)# network 10.1.200.1 0.0.0.0 area 0
R1(config-router)# end
R1#
*Oct  2 09:19:16.351: %SYS-5-CONFIG_I: Configured from console by console
R1# debug ip ospf adjacency
OSPF adjacency events debugging is on
```

Now, add your network statements to the other two routers.

```
R2(config)# router ospf 1
R2(config-router)# network 10.1.100.0 0.0.0.255 area 0
R2(config-router)# network 10.1.200.0 0.0.0.255 area 0


R3(config)# router ospf 1
R3(config-router)# network 10.1.200.0 0.0.0.255 area 0
```

Observe the **debug** output on R1. When you are done looking at this, you can turn off debugging on R1 with **undebug all**.

What advantage is gained from adding networks with a wildcard mask instead of using classful network addresses?

_____

_____

_____

_____

Step 3: OSPF show Commands

Some **show** commands are very useful for OSPF. The **show ip protocols** command displays basic high-level routing protocol information. The following shows information about OSPF:

```
R1# show ip protocols
Routing Protocol is "ospf 1"
  Outgoing update filter list for all interfaces is not set
  Incoming update filter list for all interfaces is not set
  Router ID 10.1.1.1
  Number of areas in this router is 1. 1 normal 0 stub 0 nssa
  Maximum path: 4
  Routing for Networks:
    10.1.100.0 0.0.0.255 area 0
    10.1.200.1 0.0.0.0 area 0
  Reference bandwidth unit is 100 mbps
  Routing Information Sources:
    Gateway         Distance      Last Update
    10.1.2.1             110        00:04:21
  Distance: (default is 110)
```

Another useful command when looking at OSPF is **show ip ospf**:

```
R1# show ip ospf
```

```
Routing Process "ospf 1" with ID 10.1.1.1
Start time: 00:17:44.612, Time elapsed: 00:10:51.408
Supports only single TOS(TOS0) routes
Supports opaque LSA
Supports Link-local Signaling (LLS)
Supports area transit capability
Router is not originating router-LSAs with maximum metric
Initial SPF schedule delay 5000 msecs
Minimum hold time between two consecutive SPFs 10000 msecs
Maximum wait time between two consecutive SPFs 10000 msecs
Incremental-SPF disabled
Minimum LSA interval 5 secs
Minimum LSA arrival 1000 msecs
LSA group pacing timer 240 secs
Interface flood pacing timer 33 msecs
Retransmission pacing timer 66 msecs
Number of external LSA 0. Checksum Sum 0x000000
Number of opaque AS LSA 0. Checksum Sum 0x000000
Number of DCbitless external and opaque AS LSA 0
Number of DoNotAge external and opaque AS LSA 0
Number of areas in this router is 1. 1 normal 0 stub 0 nssa
Number of areas transit capable is 0
External flood list length 0
    Area BACKBONE(0)
        Number of interfaces in this area is 2
        Area has no authentication
        SPF algorithm last executed 00:03:21.132 ago
        SPF algorithm executed 5 times
        Area ranges are
        Number of LSA 4. Checksum Sum 0x021A30
        Number of opaque link LSA 0. Checksum Sum 0x000000
        Number of DCbitless LSA 0
        Number of indication LSA 0
        Number of DoNotAge LSA 0
        Flood list length 0
```

Notice the router ID listed in the show output. The router ID of R1 is 10.1.1.1, even though we have not added this loopback into the OSPF process. The router chooses the router ID using the highest IP on a loopback interface when OSPF is configured. If an additional higher IP address loopback interface is added after OSPF is turned on, it does not become the router ID unless the router is reloaded. If there are no loopback interfaces present on the router, the router takes the highest available IP address on an interface. If there are no IP addresses assigned to interfaces, the OSPF process does not start.

The **show ip ospf neighbor** command displays important neighbor status, including adjacency state, address, router ID, and connected interface:

```
R1# show ip ospf neighbor

Neighbor ID     Pri   State          Dead Time   Address      Interface
10.1.2.1          1   FULL/DR        00:00:33    10.1.200.2   FastEthernet0/0
10.1.3.1          1   FULL/DROTHER   00:00:32    10.1.200.3   FastEthernet0/0
10.1.2.1          0   FULL/  -       00:00:33    10.1.100.2   Serial0/0/0
```

If you need more detail, use **show ip ospf neighbor detail**, which shows more than just the standard one-line summaries of neighbors. However, in many instances, the regular command gives you all that you need.

Another helpful command is **show ip ospf interface** *interface_type number*. This command shows interface timers and network types. Here is the output for R1 f0/0:

```
R1# show ip ospf interface FastEthernet 0/0
FastEthernet0/0 is up, line protocol is up
  Internet Address 10.1.200.1/24, Area 0
  Process ID 1, Router ID 10.1.1.1, Network Type BROADCAST, Cost: 1
  Transmit Delay is 1 sec, State BDR, Priority 1
  Designated Router (ID) 10.1.2.1, Interface address 10.1.200.2
  Backup Designated router (ID) 10.1.1.1, Interface address 10.1.200.1
  Timer intervals configured, Hello 10, Dead 40, Wait 40, Retransmit 5
    oob-resync timeout 40
    Hello due in 00:00:09
  Supports Link-local Signaling (LLS)
  Index 2/2, flood queue length 0
  Next 0x0(0)/0x0(0)
  Last flood scan length is 0, maximum is 2
  Last flood scan time is 0 msec, maximum is 0 msec
  Neighbor Count is 2, Adjacent neighbor count is 2
    Adjacent with neighbor 10.1.2.1   (Designated Router)
    Adjacent with neighbor 10.1.3.1
  Suppress hello for 0 neighbor(s)
```

Another useful command is **show ip ospf database**, which displays the various LSAs in the OSPF database, organized by area and type.

```
R1# show ip ospf database

            OSPF Router with ID (10.1.1.1) (Process ID 1)


                Router Link States (Area 0)

Link ID        ADV Router      Age      Seq#        Checksum Link count
10.1.1.1       10.1.1.1        123      0x80000005 0x00546C 4
```

```
10.1.2.1         10.1.2.1         112        0x80000004 0x006C51 4
10.1.3.1         10.1.3.1         106        0x80000004 0x00F94C 2


                  Net Link States (Area 0)


Link ID          ADV Router       Age        Seq#       Checksum
10.1.200.2       10.1.2.1         725        0x80000002  0x00D74F
```

Step 4: Adding Loopback Interfaces to OSPF

All three routers have loopback interfaces, but they are not yet advertised in the routing process. You can verify this with **show ip route** on your three routers.

```
R1# show ip route
Codes: C - connected, S - static, R - RIP, M - mobile, B - BGP
       D - EIGRP, EX - EIGRP external, O - OSPF, IA - OSPF inter area
       N1 - OSPF NSSA external type 1, N2 - OSPF NSSA external type 2
       E1 - OSPF external type 1, E2 - OSPF external type 2
       i - IS-IS, su - IS-IS summary, L1 - IS-IS level-1, L2 - IS-IS level-2
       ia - IS-IS inter area, * - candidate default, U - per-user static route
       o - ODR, P - periodic downloaded static route


Gateway of last resort is not set


      10.0.0.0/24 is subnetted, 3 subnets
C        10.1.1.0 is directly connected, Loopback1
C        10.1.100.0 is directly connected, Serial0/0/0
C        10.1.200.0 is directly connected, FastEthernet0/0
R2# show ip route
Codes: C - connected, S - static, R - RIP, M - mobile, B - BGP
       D - EIGRP, EX - EIGRP external, O - OSPF, IA - OSPF inter area
       N1 - OSPF NSSA external type 1, N2 - OSPF NSSA external type 2
       E1 - OSPF external type 1, E2 - OSPF external type 2
       i - IS-IS, su - IS-IS summary, L1 - IS-IS level-1, L2 - IS-IS level-2
       ia - IS-IS inter area, * - candidate default, U - per-user static route
       o - ODR, P - periodic downloaded static route


Gateway of last resort is not set


      10.0.0.0/24 is subnetted, 3 subnets
C        10.1.2.0 is directly connected, Loopback2
C        10.1.100.0 is directly connected, Serial0/0/0
C        10.1.200.0 is directly connected, FastEthernet0/0
R3# show ip route
```

```
Codes: C - connected, S - static, R - RIP, M - mobile, B - BGP
       D - EIGRP, EX - EIGRP external, O - OSPF, IA - OSPF inter area
       N1 - OSPF NSSA external type 1, N2 - OSPF NSSA external type 2
       E1 - OSPF external type 1, E2 - OSPF external type 2
       i - IS-IS, su - IS-IS summary, L1 - IS-IS level-1, L2 - IS-IS level-2
       ia - IS-IS inter area, * - candidate default, U - per-user static route
       o - ODR, P - periodic downloaded static route


Gateway of last resort is not set


     10.0.0.0/24 is subnetted, 3 subnets
C       10.1.3.0 is directly connected, Loopback3
O       10.1.100.0 [110/65] via 10.1.200.2, 00:06:39, FastEthernet0/0
                   [110/65] via 10.1.200.1, 00:06:39, FastEthernet0/0
C       10.1.200.0 is directly connected, FastEthernet0/0
```

For each of the routers, the only loopback address that comes up is the locally connected one. You can add these into the routing process with the **network** command previously used to add the physical interfaces:

```
R1(config)# router ospf 1
R1(config-router)# network 10.1.1.0 0.0.0.255 area 0
```

```
R2(config)# router ospf 1
R2(config-router)# network 10.1.2.0 0.0.0.255 area 0
```

```
R3(config)# router ospf 1
R3(config-router)# network 10.1.3.0 0.0.0.255 area 0
```

Verify that these networks have been added to the routing table using the **show ip route** command:

```
R1# show ip route
Codes: C - connected, S - static, R - RIP, M - mobile, B - BGP
       D - EIGRP, EX - EIGRP external, O - OSPF, IA - OSPF inter area
       N1 - OSPF NSSA external type 1, N2 - OSPF NSSA external type 2
       E1 - OSPF external type 1, E2 - OSPF external type 2
       i - IS-IS, su - IS-IS summary, L1 - IS-IS level-1, L2 - IS-IS level-2
       ia - IS-IS inter area, * - candidate default, U - per-user static route
       o - ODR, P - periodic downloaded static route


Gateway of last resort is not set


     10.0.0.0/8 is variably subnetted, 5 subnets, 2 masks
O       10.1.2.1/32 [110/2] via 10.1.200.2, 00:00:03, FastEthernet0/0
O       10.1.3.1/32 [110/2] via 10.1.200.3, 00:00:03, FastEthernet0/0
C       10.1.1.0/24 is directly connected, Loopback1
```

```
C        10.1.100.0/24 is directly connected, Serial0/0/0
C        10.1.200.0/24 is directly connected, FastEthernet0/0
```

Now you can see the loopbacks of the other routers, but their subnet masks are incorrect because the default network type on loopback interfaces advertises them as /32 (host) routes. This is due to OSPF defaulting loopback interfaces as network type LOOPBACK. This can be verified by issuing the **show ip ospf interface lo1** on router 1. Notice the network type:

```
R1# show ip ospf interface lo1
Process ID 1, Router ID 10.1.2.1, Network Type LOOPBACK, Cost: 1
```

To change this, go to the interface configuration mode of each loopback and use the **ip ospf network point-to-point** command. After the routes propagate, you see the correct subnet masks associated with those loopback interfaces:

```
R1(config)# interface loopback1
R1(config-if)# ip ospf network point-to-point
```
```
R2(config)# interface loopback2
R2(config-if)# ip ospf network point-to-point
```
```
R3(config)# interface loopback3
R3(config-if)# ip ospf network point-to-point
```
```
R1# show ip route
Codes: C - connected, S - static, R - RIP, M - mobile, B - BGP
       D - EIGRP, EX - EIGRP external, O - OSPF, IA - OSPF inter area
       N1 - OSPF NSSA external type 1, N2 - OSPF NSSA external type 2
       E1 - OSPF external type 1, E2 - OSPF external type 2
       i - IS-IS, su - IS-IS summary, L1 - IS-IS level-1, L2 - IS-IS level-2
       ia - IS-IS inter area, * - candidate default, U - per-user static route
       o - ODR, P - periodic downloaded static route


Gateway of last resort is not set


     10.0.0.0/24 is subnetted, 5 subnets
O       10.1.3.0 [110/2] via 10.1.200.3, 00:00:01, FastEthernet0/0
O       10.1.2.0 [110/2] via 10.1.200.2, 00:00:01, FastEthernet0/0
C       10.1.1.0 is directly connected, Loopback1
C       10.1.100.0 is directly connected, Serial0/0/0
C       10.1.200.0 is directly connected, FastEthernet0/0
```

Step 5: Modifying Link Costs in OSPF

When you use the **show ip route** command on R1, you see that the most direct route to R2's loopback is through its Ethernet connection. Next to this route is a pair in the form [administrative distance / metric]. The administrative distance is 110, the default administrative distance of OSPF on Cisco routers. The metric depends on the link type. OSPF picks the route with the lowest metric, which is a sum of link costs. You can modify a single link cost by using the interface-level command **ip ospf cost** *cost*. Use this on both ends of the link. In the following commands, the link cost of the Ethernet connection between the three routers is changed to a cost of 50. Notice the change in the metrics in the routing table:

```
R1(config)# interface fastEthernet 0/0
R1(config-if)# ip ospf cost 50
```

```
R2(config)# interface fastEthernet 0/0
R2(config-if)# ip ospf cost 50
```

```
R3(config)# interface fastEthernet 0/0
R3(config-if)# ip ospf cost 50
```

```
R1# show ip route
Codes: C - connected, S - static, R - RIP, M - mobile, B - BGP
       D - EIGRP, EX - EIGRP external, O - OSPF, IA - OSPF inter area
       N1 - OSPF NSSA external type 1, N2 - OSPF NSSA external type 2
       E1 - OSPF external type 1, E2 - OSPF external type 2
       i - IS-IS, su - IS-IS summary, L1 - IS-IS level-1, L2 - IS-IS level-2
       ia - IS-IS inter area, * - candidate default, U - per-user static route
       o - ODR, P - periodic downloaded static route


Gateway of last resort is not set


     10.0.0.0/24 is subnetted, 5 subnets
O       10.1.3.0 [110/51] via 10.1.200.3, 00:01:40, FastEthernet0/0
O       10.1.2.0 [110/51] via 10.1.200.2, 00:01:40, FastEthernet0/0
C       10.1.1.0 is directly connected, Loopback1
C       10.1.100.0 is directly connected, Serial0/0/0
C       10.1.200.0 is directly connected, FastEthernet0/0
```

For reference, here are some default link costs (taken from Cisco.com):

- 56-kbps serial link—Default cost is 1785.

- 64-kbps serial link—Default cost is 1562.

- T1 (1.544-Mbps serial link)—Default cost is 64.

- E1 (2.048-Mbps serial link)—Default cost is 48.

- 4-Mbps Token Ring—Default cost is 25.

- Ethernet—Default cost is 10.

- 16-Mbps Token Ring—Default cost is 6.

- FDDI—Default cost is 1.

- X25—Default cost is 5208.

- Asynchronous—Default cost is 10,000.

- ATM—Default cost is 1.

Step 6: Modifying Interface Priorities

If you use the **show ip ospf neighbor detail** on any of the routers, you see that for the Ethernet network, R3 is the DR (designated router), and R2 is the BDR (backup designated router). This is determined by the interface priority for all routers in that network, which you see in the **show** output. The default priority is 1. If all the priorities are the same (which happens by default), the DR election is then based on router IDs. The highest router ID router becomes the DR, and the second highest becomes the BDR. All other routers become DROthers. If your routers do not have this behavior exactly, it may be because of the order the routers came up in.

Routers sometimes do not leave the DR position unless their interface goes down and another router takes over. In addition, OSPF has a timer associated with detecting neighbors for DR/BDR election. If your router's timer expired prior to bringing up another OSPF peer, the first router will elect itself the DR. It is okay if your routers are not exactly like the example. We will change OSPF priorities on R1 and R2 to make R1 the DR and R2 the BDR. To do this, use the interface-level command **ip ospf priority** number.

After changing this on both interfaces, look at the output of the **show ip ospf neighbor detail** command. You can also see the change with the **show ip ospf neighbor** command, but it requires more interpretation because it comes up with states per neighbor, rather than stating the DR and BDR on a neighbor adjacency network:

```
R1(config)# interface fastEthernet 0/0
R1(config-if)# ip ospf priority 10
R2(config)# interface fastEthernet 0/0
R2(config-if)# ip ospf priority 5
R1# show ip ospf neighbor detail
 Neighbor 10.1.2.1, interface address 10.1.200.2
    In the area 0 via interface FastEthernet0/0
    Neighbor priority is 5, State is FULL, 12 state changes
    DR is 10.1.200.1 BDR is 10.1.200.2
    Options is 0x52
    LLS Options is 0x1 (LR)
    Dead timer due in 00:00:37
    Neighbor is up for 00:01:32
    Index 3/3, retransmission queue length 0, number of retransmission 0
    First 0x0(0)/0x0(0) Next 0x0(0)/0x0(0)
    Last retransmission scan length is 0, maximum is 0
    Last retransmission scan time is 0 msec, maximum is 0 msec
 Neighbor 10.1.3.1, interface address 10.1.200.3
    In the area 0 via interface FastEthernet0/0
    Neighbor priority is 1, State is FULL, 12 state changes
    DR is 10.1.200.1 BDR is 10.1.200.2
    Options is 0x52
    LLS Options is 0x1 (LR)
    Dead timer due in 00:00:30
    Neighbor is up for 00:01:12
    Index 1/1, retransmission queue length 0, number of retransmission 3
    First 0x0(0)/0x0(0) Next 0x0(0)/0x0(0)
```

```
        Last retransmission scan length is 1, maximum is 1

        Last retransmission scan time is 0 msec, maximum is 0 msec

   Neighbor 10.1.2.1, interface address 10.1.100.2

      In the area 0 via interface Serial0/0/0

      Neighbor priority is 0, State is FULL, 12 state changes

      DR is 0.0.0.0 BDR is 0.0.0.0

      Options is 0x52

      LLS Options is 0x1 (LR)

      Dead timer due in 00:00:35

      Neighbor is up for 00:01:44

      Index 2/2, retransmission queue length 0, number of retransmission 2

      First 0x0(0)/0x0(0) Next 0x0(0)/0x0(0)

      Last retransmission scan length is 2, maximum is 2

      Last retransmission scan time is 0 msec, maximum is 0 msec
```

Note   To make a router take over as DR, you might need to use the **clear ip ospf process** command on all your routers after changing the priorities.

What is the purpose of a DR in OSPF?

_____

_____

_____

_____

What is the purpose of a BDR in OSPF?

_____

_____

_____

Challenge: Topology Change

OSPF, like many link-state routing protocols, is reasonably fast when it comes to convergence. To test this, you can have R3 ping R1's loopback with a large number of pings. Mid-ping, you can change the topology. By default, the pings take the path from R3 to R1 over Ethernet because it has the lowest total path cost. You can check this by performing a traceroute on R3 to the loopback of R1:

```
R3# traceroute 10.1.1.1

Type escape sequence to abort.
Tracing the route to 10.1.1.1

  1 10.1.200.1 0 msec 0 msec *
```

Read the next part carefully before trying out the commands on routers. First, start with having R3 ping R1's loopback with a high repeat number with **ping** *ip* **repeat** *number*. While this ping is going on, perform a **shutdown** on R1's f0/0 interface:

```
R3# ping 10.1.1.1 repeat 10000


R1(config)# interface fastEthernet 0/0
R1(config-if)# shutdown
```

Did you notice that some packets were dropped, but then the pings started returning again? Explain.

_____

_____

How do you think OSPF would have faired against other routing protocols, such as RIP? What about against EIGRP?

_____

_____

_____

TCL Script Verification

You can download this TCL script at www.ciscopress.com/title/1587132133 under the More Information section on the page.

```
foreach address {
10.1.1.1
10.1.2.1
10.1.3.1
10.1.100.1
10.1.100.2
10.1.200.1
10.1.200.2
10.1.200.3
} {
ping $address }
R1# tclsh
R1(tcl)#
R1(tcl)# foreach address {
+>(tcl)# 10.1.1.1
+>(tcl)# 10.1.2.1
+>(tcl)# 10.1.3.1
+>(tcl)# 10.1.100.1
+>(tcl)# 10.1.100.2
+>(tcl)# 10.1.200.1
+>(tcl)# 10.1.200.2
+>(tcl)# 10.1.200.3
```

```
+>(tcl)# } {
+>(tcl)# ping $address }

Type escape sequence to abort.
Sending 5, 100-byte ICMP Echos to 10.1.1.1, timeout is 2 seconds:
!!!!!
Success rate is 100 percent (5/5), round-trip min/avg/max = 1/1/1 ms
Type escape sequence to abort.
Sending 5, 100-byte ICMP Echos to 10.1.2.1, timeout is 2 seconds:
!!!!!
Success rate is 100 percent (5/5), round-trip min/avg/max = 1/2/4 ms
Type escape sequence to abort.
Sending 5, 100-byte ICMP Echos to 10.1.3.1, timeout is 2 seconds:
!!!!!
Success rate is 100 percent (5/5), round-trip min/avg/max = 1/2/4 ms
Type escape sequence to abort.
Sending 5, 100-byte ICMP Echos to 10.1.100.1, timeout is 2 seconds:
!!!!!
Success rate is 100 percent (5/5), round-trip min/avg/max = 56/57/64 ms
Type escape sequence to abort.
Sending 5, 100-byte ICMP Echos to 10.1.100.2, timeout is 2 seconds:
!!!!!
Success rate is 100 percent (5/5), round-trip min/avg/max = 28/28/28 ms
Type escape sequence to abort.
Sending 5, 100-byte ICMP Echos to 10.1.200.1, timeout is 2 seconds:
!!!!!
Success rate is 100 percent (5/5), round-trip min/avg/max = 1/1/1 ms
Type escape sequence to abort.
Sending 5, 100-byte ICMP Echos to 10.1.200.2, timeout is 2 seconds:
!!!!!
Success rate is 100 percent (5/5), round-trip min/avg/max = 1/2/4 ms
Type escape sequence to abort.
Sending 5, 100-byte ICMP Echos to 10.1.200.3, timeout is 2 seconds:
!!!!!
Success rate is 100 percent (5/5), round-trip min/avg/max = 1/2/4 ms

R2# tclsh
R2(tcl)#
R2(tcl)# foreach address {
+>(tcl)# 10.1.1.1
+>(tcl)# 10.1.2.1
+>(tcl)# 10.1.3.1
+>(tcl)# 10.1.100.1
+>(tcl)# 10.1.100.2
```

```
+>(tcl)# 10.1.200.1
+>(tcl)# 10.1.200.2
+>(tcl)# 10.1.200.3
+>(tcl)# } {
+>(tcl)# ping $address }

Type escape sequence to abort.
Sending 5, 100-byte ICMP Echos to 10.1.1.1, timeout is 2 seconds:
!!!!!
Success rate is 100 percent (5/5), round-trip min/avg/max = 1/2/4 ms
Type escape sequence to abort.
Sending 5, 100-byte ICMP Echos to 10.1.2.1, timeout is 2 seconds:
!!!!!
Success rate is 100 percent (5/5), round-trip min/avg/max = 1/1/4 ms
Type escape sequence to abort.
Sending 5, 100-byte ICMP Echos to 10.1.3.1, timeout is 2 seconds:
!!!!!
Success rate is 100 percent (5/5), round-trip min/avg/max = 1/2/4 ms
Type escape sequence to abort.
Sending 5, 100-byte ICMP Echos to 10.1.100.1, timeout is 2 seconds:
!!!!!
Success rate is 100 percent (5/5), round-trip min/avg/max = 28/29/32 ms
Type escape sequence to abort.
Sending 5, 100-byte ICMP Echos to 10.1.100.2, timeout is 2 seconds:
!!!!!
Success rate is 100 percent (5/5), round-trip min/avg/max = 56/57/64 ms
Type escape sequence to abort.
Sending 5, 100-byte ICMP Echos to 10.1.200.1, timeout is 2 seconds:
!!!!!
Success rate is 100 percent (5/5), round-trip min/avg/max = 1/1/4 ms
Type escape sequence to abort.
Sending 5, 100-byte ICMP Echos to 10.1.200.2, timeout is 2 seconds:
!!!!!
Success rate is 100 percent (5/5), round-trip min/avg/max = 1/1/4 ms
Type escape sequence to abort.
Sending 5, 100-byte ICMP Echos to 10.1.200.3, timeout is 2 seconds:
!!!!!
Success rate is 100 percent (5/5), round-trip min/avg/max = 1/1/4 ms

R3# tclsh
R3(tcl)#
R3(tcl)# foreach address {
+>(tcl)# 10.1.1.1
+>(tcl)# 10.1.2.1
```

```
+>(tcl)# 10.1.3.1
+>(tcl)# 10.1.100.1
+>(tcl)# 10.1.100.2
+>(tcl)# 10.1.200.1
+>(tcl)# 10.1.200.2
+>(tcl)# 10.1.200.3
+>(tcl)# } {
+>(tcl)# ping $address }

Type escape sequence to abort.
Sending 5, 100-byte ICMP Echos to 10.1.1.1, timeout is 2 seconds:
!!!!!
Success rate is 100 percent (5/5), round-trip min/avg/max = 1/2/4 ms
Type escape sequence to abort.
Sending 5, 100-byte ICMP Echos to 10.1.2.1, timeout is 2 seconds:
!!!!!
Success rate is 100 percent (5/5), round-trip min/avg/max = 1/1/4 ms
Type escape sequence to abort.
Sending 5, 100-byte ICMP Echos to 10.1.3.1, timeout is 2 seconds:
!!!!!
Success rate is 100 percent (5/5), round-trip min/avg/max = 1/1/4 ms
Type escape sequence to abort.
Sending 5, 100-byte ICMP Echos to 10.1.100.1, timeout is 2 seconds:
!!!!!
Success rate is 100 percent (5/5), round-trip min/avg/max = 1/2/4 ms
Type escape sequence to abort.
Sending 5, 100-byte ICMP Echos to 10.1.100.2, timeout is 2 seconds:
!!!!!
Success rate is 100 percent (5/5), round-trip min/avg/max = 12/14/16 ms
Type escape sequence to abort.
Sending 5, 100-byte ICMP Echos to 10.1.200.1, timeout is 2 seconds:
!!!!!
Success rate is 100 percent (5/5), round-trip min/avg/max = 1/1/4 ms
Type escape sequence to abort.
Sending 5, 100-byte ICMP Echos to 10.1.200.2, timeout is 2 seconds:
!!!!!
Success rate is 100 percent (5/5), round-trip min/avg/max = 1/1/1 ms
Type escape sequence to abort.
Sending 5, 100-byte ICMP Echos to 10.1.200.3, timeout is 2 seconds:
!!!!!
Success rate is 100 percent (5/5), round-trip min/avg/max = 1/1/4 ms
```

Lab 3-2: Multiple-Area OSPF with Stub Areas and Authentication (3.11.2)

The objectives of this lab are as follows:

- Configure multiple-area OSPF on a router

- Verify multiple-area behavior

- Configure OSPF stub, totally stubby, and not so stubby areas

- Configure OSPF authentication

Figure 3-2 illustrates the topology that will be used for this lab.

Figure 3-2   Topology Diagram

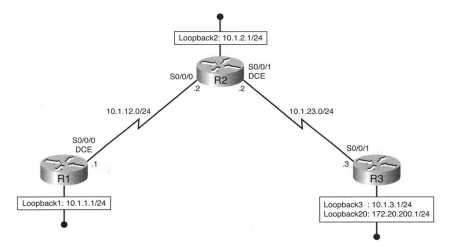

Scenario

You are responsible for configuring the new network to connect your company's engineering, marketing, and accounting departments, represented by loopback interfaces on each of the three routers. The physical devices have just been installed and connected by serial cables. Configure multiple-area OSPF to allow full connectivity between all departments.

R3 will also have a loopback representing a connection to another autonomous system that is not part of OSPF.

This topology may appear again in future labs, so save your configuration.

Step 1: Addressing

Set up the physical serial interfaces on R1, R2, and R3 with IP addresses and bring them up. Depending on which router models you have, you may need to add clock rates to the DCE end of each connection (newer equipment adds this automatically). Verify that you can ping across each serial link. Add the loopbacks shown in Figure 3-2 to each router:

```
R1# configure terminal
Enter configuration commands, one per line.  End with CNTL/Z.
```

```
R1(config)# interface loopback 1
R1(config-if)# ip address 10.1.1.1 255.255.255.0
R1(config-if)# interface serial 0/0/0
R1(config-if)# ip address 10.1.12.1 255.255.255.0
R1(config-if)# clockrate 64000
R1(config-if)# no shutdown
```
```
R2# configure terminal
Enter configuration commands, one per line.  End with CNTL/Z.
R2(config)# interface loopback 2
R2(config-if)# ip address 10.1.2.1 255.255.255.0
R2(config-if)# interface serial 0/0/0
R2(config-if)# ip address 10.1.12.2 255.255.255.0
R2(config-if)# no shutdown
R2(config-if)# interface serial 0/0/1
R2(config-if)# ip address 10.1.23.2 255.255.255.0
R2(config-if)# clockrate 64000
R2(config-if)# no shutdown
```
```
R3# configure terminal
Enter configuration commands, one per line.  End with CNTL/Z.
R3(config)# interface loopback 3
R3(config-if)# ip address 10.1.3.1 255.255.255.0
R3(config-if)# interface loopback 20
R3(config-if)# ip address 172.20.200.1 255.255.255.0
R3(config-if)# interface serial 0/0/1
R3(config-if)# ip address 10.1.23.1 255.255.255.0
R3(config-if)# no shutdown
```

Step 2: Adding Interfaces into OSPF

Create OSPF process 1 on all three routers. Configure the subnet of the serial link between R1 and R2 to be in OSPF area 0 using the **network** command. Add loopback 1 on R1 and loopback 2 on R2 into OSPF area 0. Verify that you can see OSPF neighbors in the **show ip ospf neighbors** output on both routers and that they can see each other's loopback with the **show ip route** command. Change the network type on the loopback interfaces so that they are advertised with the correct subnet:

```
R1(config)# router ospf 1
R1(config-router)# network 10.1.12.0 0.0.0.255 area 0
R1(config-router)# network 10.1.1.0 0.0.0.255 area 0
R1(config-router)# interface loopback 1
R1(config-if)# ip ospf network point-to-point
```
```
R2(config)# router ospf 1
R2(config-router)# network 10.1.12.0 0.0.0.255 area 0
R2(config-router)# network 10.1.2.0 0.0.0.255 area 0
```

```
R2(config-router)# interface loopback 2
R2(config-if)# ip ospf network point-to-point
```

```
R1# show ip ospf neighbor

Neighbor ID     Pri   State         Dead Time   Address       Interface
10.1.2.1          0   FULL/  -      00:00:38    10.1.12.2     Serial0/0/0


R1# show ip route
Codes: C - connected, S - static, R - RIP, M - mobile, B - BGP
       D - EIGRP, EX - EIGRP external, O - OSPF, IA - OSPF inter area
       N1 - OSPF NSSA external type 1, N2 - OSPF NSSA external type 2
       E1 - OSPF external type 1, E2 - OSPF external type 2
       i - IS-IS, su - IS-IS summary, L1 - IS-IS level-1, L2 - IS-IS level-2
       ia - IS-IS inter area, * - candidate default, U - per-user static route
       o - ODR, P - periodic downloaded static route


Gateway of last resort is not set


     10.0.0.0/24 is subnetted, 3 subnets
C       10.1.12.0 is directly connected, Serial0/0/0
O       10.1.2.0 [110/65] via 10.1.12.2, 00:00:10, Serial0/0/0
C       10.1.1.0 is directly connected, Loopback1
```

```
R2# show ip ospf neighbor

Neighbor ID     Pri   State         Dead Time   Address       Interface
10.1.1.1          0   FULL/  -      00:00:35    10.1.12.1     Serial0/0/0


R2# show ip route
Codes: C - connected, S - static, R - RIP, M - mobile, B - BGP
       D - EIGRP, EX - EIGRP external, O - OSPF, IA - OSPF inter area
       N1 - OSPF NSSA external type 1, N2 - OSPF NSSA external type 2
       E1 - OSPF external type 1, E2 - OSPF external type 2
       i - IS-IS, su - IS-IS summary, L1 - IS-IS level-1, L2 - IS-IS level-2
       ia - IS-IS inter area, * - candidate default, U - per-user static route
       o - ODR, P - periodic downloaded static route


Gateway of last resort is not set


     10.0.0.0/24 is subnetted, 4 subnets
C       10.1.12.0 is directly connected, Serial0/0/0
C       10.1.2.0 is directly connected, Loopback2
O       10.1.1.0 [110/65] via 10.1.12.1, 00:00:30, Serial0/0/0
C       10.1.23.0 is directly connected, Serial0/0/1
```

Add the subnet between R2 and R3 into OSPF area 23 using the **network** command. Add loopback 3 on R3 into area 23. Verify that this neighbor relationship comes up using the **show ip ospf neighbors** command:

```
R2(config)# router ospf 1
R2(config-router)# network 10.1.23.0 0.0.0.255 area 23
```

```
R3(config)# router ospf 1
R3(config-router)# network 10.1.23.0 0.0.0.255 area 23
R3(config-router)# network 10.1.3.0 0.0.0.255 area 23
R3(config-router)# interface loopback 3
R3(config-if)# ip ospf network point-to-point
```

```
R2# show ip ospf neighbor

Neighbor ID     Pri   State      Dead Time   Address      Interface
10.1.1.1          0   FULL/  -   00:00:36    10.1.12.1    Serial0/0/0
172.20.200.1      0   FULL/  -   00:00:36    10.1.23.3    Serial0/0/1
```

If you look at the output of the **show ip route** command on R1, you see a route to R3's loopback. Notice that it comes in as an inter-area route:

```
R1# show ip route
Codes: C - connected, S - static, R - RIP, M - mobile, B - BGP
       D - EIGRP, EX - EIGRP external, O - OSPF, IA - OSPF inter area
       N1 - OSPF NSSA external type 1, N2 - OSPF NSSA external type 2
       E1 - OSPF external type 1, E2 - OSPF external type 2
       i - IS-IS, su - IS-IS summary, L1 - IS-IS level-1, L2 - IS-IS level-2
       ia - IS-IS inter area, * - candidate default, U - per-user static route
       o - ODR, P - periodic downloaded static route

Gateway of last resort is not set

     10.0.0.0/24 is subnetted, 5 subnets
C       10.1.12.0 is directly connected, Serial0/0/0
O IA    10.1.3.0 [110/129] via 10.1.12.2, 00:00:28, Serial0/0/0
O       10.1.2.0 [110/65] via 10.1.12.2, 00:01:38, Serial0/0/0
C       10.1.1.0 is directly connected, Loopback1
O IA    10.1.23.0 [110/128] via 10.1.12.2, 00:01:38, Serial0/0/0
```

R2 has no inter-area routes because R2 is in both areas; it is an Area Border Router (ABR).

```
R2# show ip route
Codes: C - connected, S - static, R - RIP, M - mobile, B - BGP
       D - EIGRP, EX - EIGRP external, O - OSPF, IA - OSPF inter area
       N1 - OSPF NSSA external type 1, N2 - OSPF NSSA external type 2
       E1 - OSPF external type 1, E2 - OSPF external type 2
       i - IS-IS, su - IS-IS summary, L1 - IS-IS level-1, L2 - IS-IS level-2
       ia - IS-IS inter area, * - candidate default, U - per-user static route
```

```
        o - ODR, P - periodic downloaded static route

Gateway of last resort is not set

     10.0.0.0/24 is subnetted, 5 subnets
C        10.1.12.0 is directly connected, Serial0/0/0
O        10.1.3.0 [110/65] via 10.1.23.3, 00:00:50, Serial0/0/1
C        10.1.2.0 is directly connected, Loopback2
O        10.1.1.0 [110/65] via 10.1.12.1, 00:02:00, Serial0/0/0
C        10.1.23.0 is directly connected, Serial0/0/1
```

Verify that you can ping all interfaces from any router, with the exception of Loopback 20 on R3, which has not yet been configured as part of OSPF.

Step 3: Stub Areas

Under the OSPF process on R2 and R3, make area 23 the stub area using the **area** *area* **stub** command. The adjacency between the two routers may go down during the transition period, but it should come back up afterward. Confirm that it comes up by using the **show ip ospf neighbor** command:

```
R2(config)# router ospf 1
R2(config-router)# area 23 stub
```
```
R3(config)# router ospf 1
R3(config-router)# area 23 stub
```
```
R2# show ip ospf neighbor


Neighbor ID     Pri   State          Dead Time   Address         Interface
10.1.1.1          0   FULL/  -       00:00:36    10.1.12.1       Serial0/0/0
172.20.200.1      0   FULL/  -       00:00:36    10.1.23.3       Serial0/0/1
```
```
R3# show ip ospf neighbor


Neighbor ID     Pri   State          Dead Time   Address         Interface
10.1.2.1          0   FULL/  -       00:00:31    10.1.23.2       Serial0/0/1
```

Using the **show ip route** command, you can see that R3 now has a default route pointing toward R2. A stub area does not get any external routes. A stub area receives a default route and OSPF inter-area routes:

```
R3# show ip route
Codes: C - connected, S - static, R - RIP, M - mobile, B - BGP
       D - EIGRP, EX - EIGRP external, O - OSPF, IA - OSPF inter area
       N1 - OSPF NSSA external type 1, N2 - OSPF NSSA external type 2
       E1 - OSPF external type 1, E2 - OSPF external type 2
       i - IS-IS, su - IS-IS summary, L1 - IS-IS level-1, L2 - IS-IS level-2
       ia - IS-IS inter area, * - candidate default, U - per-user static route
       o - ODR, P - periodic downloaded static route
```

```
Gateway of last resort is 10.1.23.2 to network 0.0.0.0


      172.20.0.0/24 is subnetted, 1 subnets
C        172.20.200.0 is directly connected, Loopback20
      10.0.0.0/24 is subnetted, 5 subnets
O IA    10.1.12.0 [110/128] via 10.1.23.2, 00:00:56, Serial0/0/1
C        10.1.3.0 is directly connected, Loopback3
O IA    10.1.2.0 [110/65] via 10.1.23.2, 00:00:56, Serial0/0/1
O IA    10.1.1.0 [110/129] via 10.1.23.2, 00:00:56, Serial0/0/1
C        10.1.23.0 is directly connected, Serial0/0/1
O*IA 0.0.0.0/0 [110/65] via 10.1.23.2, 00:00:56, Serial0/0/1
```

Take a look at the output of the **show ip ospf** command to see what type each area is:

R2# **show ip ospf**

```
 Routing Process "ospf 1" with ID 10.1.2.1
 Supports only single TOS(TOS0) routes
 Supports opaque LSA
 Supports Link-local Signaling (LLS)
 Supports area transit capability
 It is an area border router
 Initial SPF schedule delay 5000 msecs
 Minimum hold time between two consecutive SPFs 10000 msecs
 Maximum wait time between two consecutive SPFs 10000 msecs
 Incremental-SPF disabled
 Minimum LSA interval 5 secs
 Minimum LSA arrival 1000 msecs
 LSA group pacing timer 240 secs
 Interface flood pacing timer 33 msecs
 Retransmission pacing timer 66 msecs
 Number of external LSA 0. Checksum Sum 0x000000
 Number of opaque AS LSA 0. Checksum Sum 0x000000
 Number of DCbitless external and opaque AS LSA 0
 Number of DoNotAge external and opaque AS LSA 0
 Number of areas in this router is 2. 1 normal 1 stub 0 nssa
 Number of areas transit capable is 0
 External flood list length 0
    Area BACKBONE(0)
        Number of interfaces in this area is 2
        Area has no authentication
        SPF algorithm last executed 00:02:11.680 ago
        SPF algorithm executed 5 times
        Area ranges are
```

```
        Number of LSA 4. Checksum Sum 0x01A85A
        Number of opaque link LSA 0. Checksum Sum 0x000000
        Number of DCbitless LSA 0
        Number of indication LSA 0
        Number of DoNotAge LSA 0
        Flood list length 0
    Area 23
        Number of interfaces in this area is 1
        It is a stub area
          generates stub default route with cost 1
        Area has no authentication
        SPF algorithm last executed 00:01:38.276 ago
        SPF algorithm executed 8 times
        Area ranges are
        Number of LSA 6. Checksum Sum 0x027269
        Number of opaque link LSA 0. Checksum Sum 0x000000
        Number of DCbitless LSA 0
        Number of indication LSA 0
        Number of DoNotAge LSA 0
        Flood list length 0
```

What advantages would be gained by having a router get a default route rather than a more specific route?

_____

_____

Why do all routers in a stub area need to know that its area is a stub?

_____

_____

_____

Step 4: Totally Stubby Areas

A modified version of a stubby area is a totally stubby area. A totally stubby area ABR only allows in a single, default route from the backbone. To configure this, you only need to change a command at the ABR, in our case, R2. Under the router OSPF process, enter the **area 23 stub no-summary** command. This replaces the existing stub command for area 23. The **no-summary** command tells the router that this area will not receive summary (inter-area) routes.

To see how this works, first issue the **show ip route** command on R3. Notice the inter-area routes in addition to the default route generated by R2. Also look at **show ip ospf database** on R2 to see what LSAs are in its OSPF database:

```
R3# show ip route
Codes: C - connected, S - static, R - RIP, M - mobile, B - BGP
       D - EIGRP, EX - EIGRP external, O - OSPF, IA - OSPF inter area
```

```
           N1 - OSPF NSSA external type 1, N2 - OSPF NSSA external type 2
           E1 - OSPF external type 1, E2 - OSPF external type 2
           i - IS-IS, su - IS-IS summary, L1 - IS-IS level-1, L2 - IS-IS level-2
           ia - IS-IS inter area, * - candidate default, U - per-user static route
           o - ODR, P - periodic downloaded static route


Gateway of last resort is 10.1.23.2 to network 0.0.0.0

     172.20.0.0/24 is subnetted, 1 subnets
C        172.20.200.0 is directly connected, Loopback20
     10.0.0.0/24 is subnetted, 5 subnets
O IA     10.1.12.0 [110/128] via 10.1.23.2, 00:00:56, Serial0/0/1
C        10.1.3.0 is directly connected, Loopback3
O IA     10.1.2.0 [110/65] via 10.1.23.2, 00:00:56, Serial0/0/1
O IA     10.1.1.0 [110/129] via 10.1.23.2, 00:00:56, Serial0/0/1
C        10.1.23.0 is directly connected, Serial0/0/1
O*IA 0.0.0.0/0 [110/65] via 10.1.23.2, 00:00:56, Serial0/0/1
R2# show ip ospf database


            OSPF Router with ID (10.1.2.1) (Process ID 1)


                Router Link States (Area 0)


Link ID          ADV Router       Age        Seq#        Checksum Link count
10.1.1.1         10.1.1.1         435        0x80000004  0x0056D6 3
10.1.2.1         10.1.2.1         358        0x80000003  0x0057D2 3


                Summary Net Link States (Area 0)


Link ID          ADV Router       Age        Seq#        Checksum
10.1.3.0         10.1.2.1         174        0x80000001  0x00EFEF
10.1.23.0        10.1.2.1         354        0x80000001  0x0009C3


                Router Link States (Area 23)


Link ID          ADV Router       Age        Seq#        Checksum Link count
10.1.2.1         10.1.2.1         188        0x80000004  0x00298C 2
172.20.200.1     172.20.200.1     188        0x80000004  0x00B762 3


                Summary Net Link States (Area 23)


Link ID          ADV Router       Age        Seq#        Checksum
0.0.0.0          10.1.2.1         207        0x80000001  0x003BF4
```

```
10.1.1.0          10.1.2.1          209          0x80000002 0x0022C0
10.1.2.0          10.1.2.1          209          0x80000002 0x00948D
10.1.12.0         10.1.2.1          209          0x80000002 0x009E3A
```

Now, enter the **stub no-summary** command on R2 (the ABR) under the OSPF process:

```
R2(config)# router ospf 1
R2(config-router)# area 23 stub no-summary
```

Go back to R3 and look at **show ip route** again. Notice that it only has one incoming route from OSPF. Also look at the **show ip ospf database** output to see which routes are in area 23:

```
R3# show ip route
Codes: C - connected, S - static, R - RIP, M - mobile, B - BGP
       D - EIGRP, EX - EIGRP external, O - OSPF, IA - OSPF inter area
       N1 - OSPF NSSA external type 1, N2 - OSPF NSSA external type 2
       E1 - OSPF external type 1, E2 - OSPF external type 2
       i - IS-IS, su - IS-IS summary, L1 - IS-IS level-1, L2 - IS-IS level-2
       ia - IS-IS inter area, * - candidate default, U - per-user static route
       o - ODR, P - periodic downloaded static route


Gateway of last resort is 10.1.23.2 to network 0.0.0.0


     172.20.0.0/24 is subnetted, 1 subnets
C       172.20.200.0 is directly connected, Loopback20
     10.0.0.0/24 is subnetted, 2 subnets
C       10.1.3.0 is directly connected, Loopback3
C       10.1.23.0 is directly connected, Serial0/0/1
O*IA 0.0.0.0/0 [110/65] via 10.1.23.2, 00:00:10, Serial0/0/1
```

```
R2# show ip ospf database


            OSPF Router with ID (10.1.2.1) (Process ID 1)


                Router Link States (Area 0)


Link ID         ADV Router        Age          Seq#          Checksum Link count
10.1.1.1        10.1.1.1          522          0x80000004    0x0056D6 3
10.1.2.1        10.1.2.1          445          0x80000003    0x0057D2 3


                Summary Net Link States (Area 0)


Link ID         ADV Router        Age          Seq#          Checksum
10.1.3.0        10.1.2.1          261          0x80000001    0x00EFEF
10.1.23.0       10.1.2.1          441          0x80000001    0x0009C3


                Router Link States (Area 23)
```

Link ID	ADV Router	Age	Seq#	Checksum	Link count
10.1.2.1	10.1.2.1	275	0x80000004	0x00298C	2
172.20.200.1	172.20.200.1	276	0x80000004	0x00B762	3

Summary Net Link States (Area 23)

Link ID	ADV Router	Age	Seq#	Checksum
0.0.0.0	10.1.2.1	68	0x80000002	0x0039F5

What advantages would there be in making an area totally stubby instead of a regular stub area? What are the disadvantages?

_____

_____

_____

Why did only the ABR need to know that the area was totally stubby rather than all routers in the area?

_____

_____

_____

Step 5: Not So Stubby Areas

Not so stubby areas (NSSAs) are similar to regular stub areas, except that they allow routes to be redistributed from an ASBR into that area with a special LSA type, which gets converted to a normal external route at the ABR. For this lab, you will change area 23 into an NSSA. NSSAs are not compatible with stub areas, so the first thing we must do is issue a **no area 23 stub** command on routers R2 and R3.

Next, we issue the **area** *area* **nssa** command on routers R2 and R3 to change area 23 to an NSSA. To generate an external route into the NSSA, use the **redistribute connected subnets** command on R3. This adds the previously unreachable loopback 20 into OSPF. Be sure to include the **subnets** keyword; otherwise, only classful networks are redistributed:

```
R2(config)# router ospf 1
R2(config-router)# no area 23 stub
R2(config-router)# area 23 nssa
R3(config)# router ospf 1
R3(config-router)# no area 23 stub
R3(config-router)# area 23 nssa
R3(config-router)# redistribute connected subnets
```

Take a look at the output of **show ip ospf** on R2. Notice that area 23 is an NSSA and that R2 is performing the LSA type 7 to type 5 translation. If there are multiple ABRs to an NSSA, the ABR with the highest router ID performs the translation:

```
R2# show ip ospf
 Routing Process "ospf 1" with ID 10.1.2.1
```

```
Supports only single TOS(TOS0) routes
Supports opaque LSA
Supports Link-local Signaling (LLS)
Supports area transit capability
It is an area border and autonomous system boundary router
Redistributing External Routes from,
Initial SPF schedule delay 5000 msecs
Minimum hold time between two consecutive SPFs 10000 msecs
Maximum wait time between two consecutive SPFs 10000 msecs
Incremental-SPF disabled
Minimum LSA interval 5 secs
Minimum LSA arrival 1000 msecs
LSA group pacing timer 240 secs
Interface flood pacing timer 33 msecs
Retransmission pacing timer 66 msecs
Number of external LSA 1. Checksum Sum 0x00CA2F
Number of opaque AS LSA 0. Checksum Sum 0x000000
Number of DCbitless external and opaque AS LSA 0
Number of DoNotAge external and opaque AS LSA 0
Number of areas in this router is 2. 1 normal 0 stub 1 nssa
Number of areas transit capable is 0
External flood list length 0
    Area BACKBONE(0)
        Number of interfaces in this area is 2
        Area has no authentication
        SPF algorithm last executed 00:03:11.636 ago
        SPF algorithm executed 9 times
        Area ranges are
        Number of LSA 4. Checksum Sum 0x01AC53
        Number of opaque link LSA 0. Checksum Sum 0x000000
        Number of DCbitless LSA 0
        Number of indication LSA 0
        Number of DoNotAge LSA 0
        Flood list length 0
    Area 23
        Number of interfaces in this area is 1
        It is a NSSA area
        Perform type-7/type-5 LSA translation
        Area has no authentication
        SPF algorithm last executed 00:00:16.408 ago
        SPF algorithm executed 16 times
        Area ranges are
```

```
        Number of LSA 6. Checksum Sum 0x025498
        Number of opaque link LSA 0. Checksum Sum 0x000000
        Number of DCbitless LSA 0
        Number of indication LSA 0
        Number of DoNotAge LSA 0
        Flood list length 0
```

Now look at the **show ip route** output on R2. Notice that the "external" route comes in as type N2 from R3. This is because it is a special NSSA external route:

```
R2# show ip route
Codes: C - connected, S - static, R - RIP, M - mobile, B - BGP
        D - EIGRP, EX - EIGRP external, O - OSPF, IA - OSPF inter area
        N1 - OSPF NSSA external type 1, N2 - OSPF NSSA external type 2
        E1 - OSPF external type 1, E2 - OSPF external type 2
        i - IS-IS, su - IS-IS summary, L1 - IS-IS level-1, L2 - IS-IS level-2
        ia - IS-IS inter area, * - candidate default, U - per-user static route
        o - ODR, P - periodic downloaded static route

Gateway of last resort is not set

     172.20.0.0/24 is subnetted, 1 subnets
O N2    172.20.200.0 [110/20] via 10.1.23.3, 00:00:41, Serial0/0/1
     10.0.0.0/24 is subnetted, 5 subnets
C       10.1.12.0 is directly connected, Serial0/0/0
O       10.1.3.0 [110/65] via 10.1.23.3, 00:00:47, Serial0/0/1
C       10.1.2.0 is directly connected, Loopback2
O       10.1.1.0 [110/65] via 10.1.12.1, 00:03:42, Serial0/0/0
C       10.1.23.0 is directly connected, Serial0/0/1
```

Look at the **show ip route** output on R1. Notice that now the route is a regular E2 external route because R2 has performed the type 7 to type 5 translation:

```
R1# show ip route
Codes: C - connected, S - static, R - RIP, M - mobile, B - BGP
        D - EIGRP, EX - EIGRP external, O - OSPF, IA - OSPF inter area
        N1 - OSPF NSSA external type 1, N2 - OSPF NSSA external type 2
        E1 - OSPF external type 1, E2 - OSPF external type 2
        i - IS-IS, su - IS-IS summary, L1 - IS-IS level-1, L2 - IS-IS level-2
        ia - IS-IS inter area, * - candidate default, U - per-user static route
        o - ODR, P - periodic downloaded static route

Gateway of last resort is not set

     172.20.0.0/24 is subnetted, 1 subnets
O E2    172.20.200.0 [110/20] via 10.1.12.2, 00:01:22, Serial0/0/0
     10.0.0.0/24 is subnetted, 5 subnets
C       10.1.12.0 is directly connected, Serial0/0/0
```

```
O IA    10.1.3.0 [110/129] via 10.1.12.2, 00:02:06, Serial0/0/0
O       10.1.2.0 [110/65] via 10.1.12.2, 00:04:22, Serial0/0/0
C       10.1.1.0 is directly connected, Loopback1
O IA    10.1.23.0 [110/128] via 10.1.12.2, 00:04:22, Serial0/0/0
```

If you look at the **show ip route** output on R3, you may notice that it no longer has a default route in it, but inter-area routes are coming in:

```
R3# show ip route
Codes: C - connected, S - static, R - RIP, M - mobile, B - BGP
       D - EIGRP, EX - EIGRP external, O - OSPF, IA - OSPF inter area
       N1 - OSPF NSSA external type 1, N2 - OSPF NSSA external type 2
       E1 - OSPF external type 1, E2 - OSPF external type 2
       i - IS-IS, su - IS-IS summary, L1 - IS-IS level-1, L2 - IS-IS level-2
       ia - IS-IS inter area, * - candidate default, U - per-user static route
       o - ODR, P - periodic downloaded static route


Gateway of last resort is not set


     172.20.0.0/24 is subnetted, 1 subnets
C       172.20.200.0 is directly connected, Loopback20
     10.0.0.0/24 is subnetted, 5 subnets
O IA    10.1.12.0 [110/128] via 10.1.23.2, 00:02:11, Serial0/0/1
C       10.1.3.0 is directly connected, Loopback3
O IA    10.1.2.0 [110/65] via 10.1.23.2, 00:02:11, Serial0/0/1
O IA    10.1.1.0 [110/129] via 10.1.23.2, 00:02:11, Serial0/0/1
C       10.1.23.0 is directly connected, Serial0/0/1
```

You can change this by making the area a totally not so stubby area. To configure this, issue the **area 23 nssa no-summary** command on R2, similar to converting a stub area into a totally stubby area. Then, check the routing table on R3 and notice that the inter-area routes have been replaced by a single default route:

```
R2(config)# router ospf 1
R2(config-router)# area 23 nssa no-summary
```

```
R3# show ip route
Codes: C - connected, S - static, R - RIP, M - mobile, B - BGP
       D - EIGRP, EX - EIGRP external, O - OSPF, IA - OSPF inter area
       N1 - OSPF NSSA external type 1, N2 - OSPF NSSA external type 2
       E1 - OSPF external type 1, E2 - OSPF external type 2
       i - IS-IS, su - IS-IS summary, L1 - IS-IS level-1, L2 - IS-IS level-2
       ia - IS-IS inter area, * - candidate default, U - per-user static route
       o - ODR, P - periodic downloaded static route


Gateway of last resort is 10.1.23.2 to network 0.0.0.0


     172.20.0.0/24 is subnetted, 1 subnets
```

```
C        172.20.200.0 is directly connected, Loopback20
      10.0.0.0/24 is subnetted, 2 subnets
C        10.1.3.0 is directly connected, Loopback3
C        10.1.23.0 is directly connected, Serial0/0/1
O*IA 0.0.0.0/0 [110/65] via 10.1.23.2, 00:00:20, Serial0/0/1
```

Also on R2, take a look at the **show ip ospf database** output to see the various LSA types.

R2# **show ip ospf database**

```
            OSPF Router with ID (10.1.2.1) (Process ID 1)

                Router Link States (Area 0)

Link ID          ADV Router       Age       Seq#       Checksum Link count
10.1.1.1         10.1.1.1         944       0x80000004 0x0056D6 3
10.1.2.1         10.1.2.1         383       0x80000004 0x005BCB 3

                Summary Net Link States (Area 0)

Link ID          ADV Router       Age       Seq#       Checksum
10.1.3.0         10.1.2.1         242       0x80000001 0x00EFEF
10.1.23.0        10.1.2.1         862       0x80000001 0x0009C3

                Router Link States (Area 23)

Link ID          ADV Router       Age       Seq#       Checksum Link count
10.1.2.1         10.1.2.1         257       0x80000007 0x00B0F7 2
172.20.200.1     172.20.200.1     209       0x80000007 0x003FCD 3

                Summary Net Link States (Area 23)

Link ID          ADV Router       Age       Seq#       Checksum
0.0.0.0          10.1.2.1         34        0x80000001 0x00C265

                Type-7 AS External Link States (Area 23)

Link ID          ADV Router       Age       Seq#       Checksum Tag
172.20.200.0     172.20.200.1     200       0x80000001 0x0076FC 0

                Type-5 AS External Link States

Link ID          ADV Router       Age       Seq#       Checksum Tag
172.20.200.0     10.1.2.1         199       0x80000001 0x00CA2F 0
```

Where would making an area an NSSA be useful?

_____

_____

Step 6: OSPF Interface Authentication

For security purposes, you can set OSPF interfaces to use authentication. For this lab, we will config-ure OSPF authentication on both serial links. We will configure the link between R2 and R3 for plain-text authentication and the link between R1 and R2 for MD5 authentication, which encrypts the pass-word for stronger security. Both passwords will be cisco. We will set up all of the authentication on a per-interface basis.

To set up plain-text authentication on an interface, go to the interface command prompt and type **ip ospf authentication**. Next, set a password with **ip ospf authentication-key** *key-string*. Configure this on both R2 and R3. Verify the authentication using the **show ip ospf interface** *interface* command. While configuring this, the adjacency may go down if the dead timer expires on one of the routers. The relationship comes back up once authentication is configured on both sides:

```
R2(config)# interface serial 0/0/1
R2(config-if)# ip ospf authentication
R2(config-if)# ip ospf authentication-key cisco
```
```
R3(config)# interface serial 0/0/1
R3(config-if)# ip ospf authentication
R3(config-if)# ip ospf authentication-key cisco
```
```
R2# show ip ospf interface serial 0/0/1
Serial0/0/1 is up, line protocol is up
  Internet Address 10.1.23.2/24, Area 23
  Process ID 1, Router ID 10.1.2.1, Network Type POINT_TO_POINT, Cost: 64
  Transmit Delay is 1 sec, State POINT_TO_POINT,
  Timer intervals configured, Hello 10, Dead 40, Wait 40, Retransmit 5
    oob-resync timeout 40
    Hello due in 00:00:09
  Supports Link-local Signaling (LLS)
  Index 1/3, flood queue length 0
  Next 0x0(0)/0x0(0)
  Last flood scan length is 1, maximum is 4
  Last flood scan time is 0 msec, maximum is 0 msec
  Neighbor Count is 1, Adjacent neighbor count is 1
    Adjacent with neighbor 172.20.200.1
  Suppress hello for 0 neighbor(s)
  Simple password authentication enabled
```

The commands are similar to those used to set up MD5 authentication on an interface. First, use the interface-level command **ip ospf authentication message-digest** to set the interface authentication type. Next, use the command **ip ospf message-digest-key key_number** *key-string*. Make sure that the key number is the same on both routers. In this case, use 1 for simplicity. Verify the configuration using the **show ip ospf interface** *interface* command. While configuring this, the adjacency may go down if the dead timer expires on one of the routers. The relationship comes back up once authentication is configured on both sides:

```
R1(config)# interface serial 0/0/0
R1(config-if)# ip ospf authentication message-digest
R1(config-if)# ip ospf message-digest-key 1 md5 cisco
```

```
R2(config)# interface serial 0/0/0
R2(config-if)# ip ospf authentication message-digest
R2(config-if)# ip ospf message-digest-key 1 md5 cisco
```

```
R1# show ip ospf interface serial 0/0/0
Serial0/0/0 is up, line protocol is up
  Internet Address 10.1.12.1/24, Area 0
  Process ID 1, Router ID 10.1.1.1, Network Type POINT_TO_POINT, Cost: 64
  Transmit Delay is 1 sec, State POINT_TO_POINT,
  Timer intervals configured, Hello 10, Dead 40, Wait 40, Retransmit 5
    oob-resync timeout 40
    Hello due in 00:00:08
  Supports Link-local Signaling (LLS)
  Index 1/1, flood queue length 0
  Next 0x0(0)/0x0(0)
  Last flood scan length is 1, maximum is 1
  Last flood scan time is 0 msec, maximum is 0 msec
  Neighbor Count is 0, Adjacent neighbor count is 0
  Suppress hello for 0 neighbor(s)
  Message digest authentication enabled
    Youngest key id is 1
```

Why is configuring authentication for OSPF, or any routing protocol, a good idea?

_____

_____

TCL Script Output

You can download this TCL script at www.ciscopress.com/title/1587132133 under the More Information section on the page.

```
foreach address {
10.1.1.1
10.1.2.1
10.1.3.1
172.20.200.1
10.1.12.1
10.1.12.2
10.1.23.2
10.1.23.3
} {
```

```
ping $address }
R1# tclsh
R1(tcl)#
R1(tcl)# foreach address {
+>(tcl)# 10.1.1.1
+>(tcl)# 10.1.2.1
+>(tcl)# 10.1.3.1
+>(tcl)# 172.20.200.1
+>(tcl)# 10.1.12.1
+>(tcl)# 10.1.12.2
+>(tcl)# 10.1.23.2
+>(tcl)# 10.1.23.3
+>(tcl)# } {
+>(tcl)# ping $address }

Type escape sequence to abort.
Sending 5, 100-byte ICMP Echos to 10.1.1.1, timeout is 2 seconds:
!!!!!
Success rate is 100 percent (5/5), round-trip min/avg/max = 1/1/1 ms
Type escape sequence to abort.
Sending 5, 100-byte ICMP Echos to 10.1.2.1, timeout is 2 seconds:
!!!!!
Success rate is 100 percent (5/5), round-trip min/avg/max = 28/28/32 ms
Type escape sequence to abort.
Sending 5, 100-byte ICMP Echos to 10.1.3.1, timeout is 2 seconds:
!!!!!
Success rate is 100 percent (5/5), round-trip min/avg/max = 28/29/32 ms
Type escape sequence to abort.
Sending 5, 100-byte ICMP Echos to 172.20.200.1, timeout is 2 seconds:
!!!!!
Success rate is 100 percent (5/5), round-trip min/avg/max = 28/29/32 ms
Type escape sequence to abort.
Sending 5, 100-byte ICMP Echos to 10.1.12.1, timeout is 2 seconds:
!!!!!
Success rate is 100 percent (5/5), round-trip min/avg/max = 56/56/56 ms
Type escape sequence to abort.
Sending 5, 100-byte ICMP Echos to 10.1.12.2, timeout is 2 seconds:
!!!!!
Success rate is 100 percent (5/5), round-trip min/avg/max = 28/33/56 ms
Type escape sequence to abort.
Sending 5, 100-byte ICMP Echos to 10.1.23.2, timeout is 2 seconds:
!!!!!
Success rate is 100 percent (5/5), round-trip min/avg/max = 28/28/32 ms
Type escape sequence to abort.
```

```
Sending 5, 100-byte ICMP Echos to 10.1.23.3, timeout is 2 seconds:
!!!!!
Success rate is 100 percent (5/5), round-trip min/avg/max = 28/28/32 ms

R2# tclsh
R2(tcl)#
R2(tcl)# foreach address {
+>(tcl)# 10.1.1.1
+>(tcl)# 10.1.2.1
+>(tcl)# 10.1.3.1
+>(tcl)# 172.20.200.1
+>(tcl)# 10.1.12.1
+>(tcl)# 10.1.12.2
+>(tcl)# 10.1.23.2
+>(tcl)# 10.1.23.3
+>(tcl)# } {
+>(tcl)# ping $address }

Type escape sequence to abort.
Sending 5, 100-byte ICMP Echos to 10.1.1.1, timeout is 2 seconds:
!!!!!
Success rate is 100 percent (5/5), round-trip min/avg/max = 28/28/32 ms
Type escape sequence to abort.
Sending 5, 100-byte ICMP Echos to 10.1.2.1, timeout is 2 seconds:
!!!!!
Success rate is 100 percent (5/5), round-trip min/avg/max = 1/1/4 ms
Type escape sequence to abort.
Sending 5, 100-byte ICMP Echos to 10.1.3.1, timeout is 2 seconds:
!!!!!
Success rate is 100 percent (5/5), round-trip min/avg/max = 1/2/4 ms
Type escape sequence to abort.
Sending 5, 100-byte ICMP Echos to 172.20.200.1, timeout is 2 seconds:
!!!!!
Success rate is 100 percent (5/5), round-trip min/avg/max = 1/2/4 ms
Type escape sequence to abort.
Sending 5, 100-byte ICMP Echos to 10.1.12.1, timeout is 2 seconds:
!!!!!
Success rate is 100 percent (5/5), round-trip min/avg/max = 28/28/32 ms
Type escape sequence to abort.
Sending 5, 100-byte ICMP Echos to 10.1.12.2, timeout is 2 seconds:
!!!!!
Success rate is 100 percent (5/5), round-trip min/avg/max = 56/57/64 ms
Type escape sequence to abort.
Sending 5, 100-byte ICMP Echos to 10.1.23.2, timeout is 2 seconds:
```

```
!!!!!
Success rate is 100 percent (5/5), round-trip min/avg/max = 1/3/4 ms
Type escape sequence to abort.
Sending 5, 100-byte ICMP Echos to 10.1.23.3, timeout is 2 seconds:
!!!!!
Success rate is 100 percent (5/5), round-trip min/avg/max = 1/2/4 ms

R3# tclsh
R3(tcl)#
R3(tcl)# foreach address {
+>(tcl)# 10.1.1.1
+>(tcl)# 10.1.2.1
+>(tcl)# 10.1.3.1
+>(tcl)# 172.20.200.1
+>(tcl)# 10.1.12.1
+>(tcl)# 10.1.12.2
+>(tcl)# 10.1.23.2
+>(tcl)# 10.1.23.3
+>(tcl)# } {
+>(tcl)# ping $address }

Type escape sequence to abort.
Sending 5, 100-byte ICMP Echos to 10.1.1.1, timeout is 2 seconds:
!!!!!
Success rate is 100 percent (5/5), round-trip min/avg/max = 28/32/48 ms
Type escape sequence to abort.
Sending 5, 100-byte ICMP Echos to 10.1.2.1, timeout is 2 seconds:
!!!!!
Success rate is 100 percent (5/5), round-trip min/avg/max = 1/2/4 ms
Type escape sequence to abort.
Sending 5, 100-byte ICMP Echos to 10.1.3.1, timeout is 2 seconds:
!!!!!
Success rate is 100 percent (5/5), round-trip min/avg/max = 1/1/4 ms
Type escape sequence to abort.
Sending 5, 100-byte ICMP Echos to 172.20.200.1, timeout is 2 seconds:
!!!!!
Success rate is 100 percent (5/5), round-trip min/avg/max = 1/1/4 ms
Type escape sequence to abort.
Sending 5, 100-byte ICMP Echos to 10.1.12.1, timeout is 2 seconds:
!!!!!
Success rate is 100 percent (5/5), round-trip min/avg/max = 28/29/32 ms
Type escape sequence to abort.
Sending 5, 100-byte ICMP Echos to 10.1.12.2, timeout is 2 seconds:
!!!!!
```

```
Success rate is 100 percent (5/5), round-trip min/avg/max = 1/2/4 ms
Type escape sequence to abort.
Sending 5, 100-byte ICMP Echos to 10.1.23.2, timeout is 2 seconds:
!!!!!
Success rate is 100 percent (5/5), round-trip min/avg/max = 1/2/4 ms
Type escape sequence to abort.
Sending 5, 100-byte ICMP Echos to 10.1.23.3, timeout is 2 seconds:
!!!!!
Success rate is 100 percent (5/5), round-trip min/avg/max = 1/3/4 ms
```

Lab 3-3: OSPF Virtual Links and Area Summarization (3.11.3)

The objectives of this lab are as follows:

- Configure multiple-area OSPF on a router

- Verify multiple-area behavior

- Create an OSPF virtual link

- Summarize an area

- Generate a default route into OSPF

Figure 3-3 illustrates the topology that will be used for this lab.

Figure 3-3   Topology Diagram

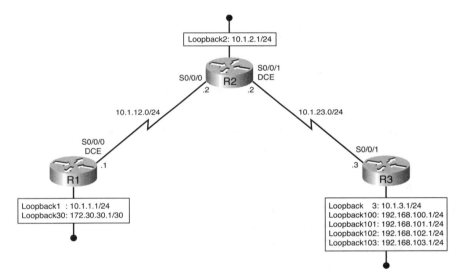

Scenario

You are responsible for configuring the new network to connect your company's engineering, marketing, and accounting departments, represented by loopback interfaces on each of the three routers. The physical devices have just been installed and connected by serial cables. Configure multiple-area OSPF to allow full connectivity between all departments.

In addition, R1 will also have a loopback interface representing a connection to the Internet. This connection will not be added into OSPF. R3 will have four additional loopback interfaces representing connections to branch offices.

This topology may appear again in future labs, so save your configuration when you are done.

Step 1: Addressing

Set up the physical serial interfaces on R1, R2, and R3 with IP addresses and bring them up. You may need to add clockrates to the DCE end of each connection. Verify that you can ping across each serial link. Add the loopbacks shown in the diagram to each router:

```
R1# configure terminal
Enter configuration commands, one per line.  End with CNTL/Z.
R1(config)# interface loopback 1
R1(config-if)# ip address 10.1.1.1 255.255.255.0
R1(config-if)# interface loopback 30
R1(config-if)# ip address 172.30.30.1 255.255.255.252
R1(config-if)# interface serial 0/0/0
R1(config-if)# ip address 10.1.12.1 255.255.255.0
R1(config-if)# clockrate 64000
R1(config-if)# no shutdown
```

```
R2# configure terminal
Enter configuration commands, one per line.  End with CNTL/Z.
R2(config)# interface loopback 2
R2(config-if)# ip address 10.1.2.1 255.255.255.0
R2(config-if)# interface serial 0/0/0
R2(config-if)# ip address 10.1.12.2 255.255.255.0
R2(config-if)# no shutdown
R2(config-if)# interface serial 0/0/1
R2(config-if)# ip address 10.1.23.2 255.255.255.0
R2(config-if)# clockrate 64000
R2(config-if)# no shutdown
```

```
R3# configure terminal
Enter configuration commands, one per line.  End with CNTL/Z.
R3(config)# interface loopback 3
R3(config-if)# ip address 10.1.3.1 255.255.255.0
R3(config-if)# interface loopback 100
R3(config-if)# ip address 192.168.100.1 255.255.255.0
R3(config-if)# interface loopback 101
R3(config-if)# ip address 192.168.101.1 255.255.255.0
R3(config-if)# interface loopback 102
R3(config-if)# ip address 192.168.102.1 255.255.255.0
R3(config-if)# interface loopback 103
R3(config-if)# ip address 192.168.103.1 255.255.255.0
R3(config-if)# interface serial 0/0/1
R3(config-if)# ip address 10.1.23.1 255.255.255.0
R3(config-if)# no shutdown
```

Step 2: Adding Interfaces into OSPF

Create OSPF process 1 on all three routers. Using the **network** command, configure the subnet of the serial link between R1 and R2 to be in OSPF area 0. Add loopback 1 on R1 and loopback 2 on R2 into OSPF area 0. Verify that you can see OSPF neighbors in the **show ip ospf neighbors** output on both routers and that they can see each other's loopback with the **show ip route** command. Change the network type on the loopback interfaces so that they are advertised with the correct subnet:

```
R1(config)# router ospf 1
R1(config-router)# network 10.1.12.0 0.0.0.255 area 0
R1(config-router)# network 10.1.1.0 0.0.0.255 area 0
R1(config-router)# interface loopback 1
R1(config-if)# ip ospf network point-to-point
```
```
R2(config)# router ospf 1
R2(config-router)# network 10.1.12.0 0.0.0.255 area 0
R2(config-router)# network 10.1.2.0 0.0.0.255 area 0
R2(config-router)# interface loopback 2
R2(config-if)# ip ospf network point-to-point
```
```
R1# show ip ospf neighbor


Neighbor ID     Pri   State           Dead Time   Address         Interface
10.1.2.1          0   FULL/  -        00:00:38    10.1.12.2       Serial0/0/0


R1# show ip route
Codes: C - connected, S - static, R - RIP, M - mobile, B - BGP
       D - EIGRP, EX - EIGRP external, O - OSPF, IA - OSPF inter area
       N1 - OSPF NSSA external type 1, N2 - OSPF NSSA external type 2
       E1 - OSPF external type 1, E2 - OSPF external type 2
       i - IS-IS, su - IS-IS summary, L1 - IS-IS level-1, L2 - IS-IS level-2
       ia - IS-IS inter area, * - candidate default, U - per-user static route
       o - ODR, P - periodic downloaded static route


Gateway of last resort is not set


     10.0.0.0/24 is subnetted, 3 subnets
C       10.1.12.0 is directly connected, Serial0/0/0
O       10.1.2.0 [110/65] via 10.1.12.2, 00:00:10, Serial0/0/0
C       10.1.1.0 is directly connected, Loopback1
```
```
R2# show ip ospf neighbor


Neighbor ID     Pri   State           Dead Time   Address         Interface
10.1.1.1          0   FULL/  -        00:00:35    10.1.12.1       Serial0/0/0


R2# show ip route
```

```
Codes: C - connected, S - static, R - RIP, M - mobile, B - BGP
       D - EIGRP, EX - EIGRP external, O - OSPF, IA - OSPF inter area
       N1 - OSPF NSSA external type 1, N2 - OSPF NSSA external type 2
       E1 - OSPF external type 1, E2 - OSPF external type 2
       i - IS-IS, su - IS-IS summary, L1 - IS-IS level-1, L2 - IS-IS level-2
       ia - IS-IS inter area, * - candidate default, U - per-user static route
       o - ODR, P - periodic downloaded static route

Gateway of last resort is not set

     10.0.0.0/24 is subnetted, 4 subnets
C       10.1.12.0 is directly connected, Serial0/0/0
C       10.1.2.0 is directly connected, Loopback2
O       10.1.1.0 [110/65] via 10.1.12.1, 00:00:30, Serial0/0/0
C       10.1.23.0 is directly connected, Serial0/0/1
```

Add the subnet between R2 and R3 into OSPF area 23 using the **network** command. Add loopback 3 on R3 into area 23. Verify that this neighbor relationship comes up using the **show ip ospf neighbors** command:

```
R2(config)# router ospf 1
R2(config-router)# network 10.1.23.0 0.0.0.255 area 23
```

```
R3(config)# router ospf 1
R3(config-router)# network 10.1.23.0 0.0.0.255 area 23
R3(config-router)# network 10.1.3.0 0.0.0.255 area 23
R3(config-router)# interface loopback 3
R3(config-if)# ip ospf network point-to-point
```

```
R2# show ip ospf neighbor


Neighbor ID     Pri   State           Dead Time   Address         Interface
10.1.1.1          0   FULL/  -        00:00:36    10.1.12.1       Serial0/0/0
172.20.200.1      0   FULL/  -        00:00:36    10.1.23.3       Serial0/0/1
```

Verify that you can ping all interfaces from any router, with the exception of loopback 30 on R1, and R3 loopbacks 100 through 103.

Step 3: Creating a Virtual Link

Add loopbacks 100 through 103 on R3 to the OSPF process in area 100 using the **network** command. Change the network type to advertise the correct subnet mask. If you look at the output of **show ip route** on R2, you see that the routes to those networks do not appear:

```
R3(config)# router ospf 1
R3(config-router)# network 192.168.100.0 0.0.3.255 area 100
R3(config-router)# interface loopback 100
R3(config-if)# ip ospf network point-to-point
R3(config-if)# interface loopback 101
R3(config-if)# ip ospf network point-to-point
```

```
R3(config-if)# interface loopback 102
R3(config-if)# ip ospf network point-to-point
R3(config-if)# interface loopback 103
R3(config-if)# ip ospf network point-to-point
```

```
R2# show ip route
Codes: C - connected, S - static, R - RIP, M - mobile, B - BGP
       D - EIGRP, EX - EIGRP external, O - OSPF, IA - OSPF inter area
       N1 - OSPF NSSA external type 1, N2 - OSPF NSSA external type 2
       E1 - OSPF external type 1, E2 - OSPF external type 2
       i - IS-IS, su - IS-IS summary, L1 - IS-IS level-1, L2 - IS-IS level-2
       ia - IS-IS inter area, * - candidate default, U - per-user static route
       o - ODR, P - periodic downloaded static route

Gateway of last resort is not set

     10.0.0.0/24 is subnetted, 5 subnets
C       10.1.12.0 is directly connected, Serial0/0/0
O       10.1.3.0 [110/65] via 10.1.23.3, 00:01:00, Serial0/0/1
C       10.1.2.0 is directly connected, Loopback2
O       10.1.1.0 [110/65] via 10.1.12.1, 00:03:10, Serial0/0/0
C       10.1.23.0 is directly connected, Serial0/0/1
```

The reason for this behavior is that area 100 is not connected to the backbone; it is only connected to area 23. If an area is not connected to the backbone, its routes are not advertised outside of its area.

What would happen if routes could pass between areas without going through the backbone?

You can get around this situation by creating what is called a virtual link. This is an OSPF feature that creates a logical extension of the backbone area across a regular area, without actually adding any physical interfaces into area 0. To create a virtual link, use the OSPF configuration command **area** *transit_area* **virtual-link** *router-id*. Use this command on both R2 and R3. After you see the adjacency over the virtual interface come up, issue the **show ip route** command on R2 and see the routes from area 100. You can verify the virtual link with the **show ip ospf neighbor** and **show ip ospf interface** commands:

```
R2(config)# router ospf 1
R2(config-router)# area 23 virtual-link 192.168.103.1
```

```
R3(config)# router ospf 1
R3(config-router)# area 23 virtual-link 10.1.2.1
```

```
R2# show ip route
Codes: C - connected, S - static, R - RIP, M - mobile, B - BGP
       D - EIGRP, EX - EIGRP external, O - OSPF, IA - OSPF inter area
```

```
          N1 - OSPF NSSA external type 1, N2 - OSPF NSSA external type 2
          E1 - OSPF external type 1, E2 - OSPF external type 2
          i - IS-IS, su - IS-IS summary, L1 - IS-IS level-1, L2 - IS-IS level-2
          ia - IS-IS inter area, * - candidate default, U - per-user static route
          o - ODR, P - periodic downloaded static route


Gateway of last resort is not set


     10.0.0.0/24 is subnetted, 5 subnets
C        10.1.12.0 is directly connected, Serial0/0/0
O        10.1.3.0 [110/65] via 10.1.23.3, 00:01:35, Serial0/0/1
C        10.1.2.0 is directly connected, Loopback2
O        10.1.1.0 [110/65] via 10.1.12.1, 00:01:35, Serial0/0/0
C        10.1.23.0 is directly connected, Serial0/0/1
O IA 192.168.102.0/24 [110/65] via 10.1.23.3, 00:00:05, Serial0/0/1
O IA 192.168.103.0/24 [110/65] via 10.1.23.3, 00:00:05, Serial0/0/1
O IA 192.168.100.0/24 [110/65] via 10.1.23.3, 00:00:57, Serial0/0/1
O IA 192.168.101.0/24 [110/65] via 10.1.23.3, 00:00:16, Serial0/0/1


R2# show ip ospf neighbor

Neighbor ID     Pri   State          Dead Time   Address      Interface
192.168.103.1    0    FULL/ -        -           10.1.23.3    OSPF_VL0
10.1.1.1         0    FULL/ -        00:00:30    10.1.12.1    Serial0/0/0
192.168.103.1    0    FULL/ -        00:00:30    10.1.23.3    Serial0/0/1


R2# show ip ospf interface
OSPF_VL0 is up, line protocol is up
  Internet Address 10.1.23.2/24, Area 0
  Process ID 1, Router ID 10.1.2.1, Network Type VIRTUAL_LINK, Cost: 64
  Configured as demand circuit.
  Run as demand circuit.
  DoNotAge LSA allowed.
  Transmit Delay is 1 sec, State POINT_TO_POINT,
  Timer intervals configured, Hello 10, Dead 40, Wait 40, Retransmit 5
    oob-resync timeout 40
    Hello due in 00:00:03
  Supports Link-local Signaling (LLS)
  Index 3/4, flood queue length 0
  Next 0x0(0)/0x0(0)
```

```
     Last flood scan length is 1, maximum is 1
     Last flood scan time is 0 msec, maximum is 0 msec
     Neighbor Count is 1, Adjacent neighbor count is 1
       Adjacent with neighbor 192.168.103.1   (Hello suppressed)
     Suppress hello for 1 neighbor(s)
<output omitted>
```

When are virtual links useful?

_____

_____

Why are virtual links a poor long-term solution?

_____

_____

_____

Step 4: Summarizing an Area

Loopbacks 100 through 103 can be summarized into one supernet of 192.168.100.0 /22. You can configure area 100 to be represented by this single summary route. To do this, configure R3 (the ABR) to summarize this area using the **area** *area* **range** *network mask* command:

```
R3(config)# router ospf 1
R3(config-router)# area 100 range 192.168.100.0 255.255.252.0
```

You can see the summary route on R2 with the **show ip route** and **show ip ospf database** commands:

```
R2# show ip route
Codes: C - connected, S - static, R - RIP, M - mobile, B - BGP
       D - EIGRP, EX - EIGRP external, O - OSPF, IA - OSPF inter area
       N1 - OSPF NSSA external type 1, N2 - OSPF NSSA external type 2
       E1 - OSPF external type 1, E2 - OSPF external type 2
       i - IS-IS, su - IS-IS summary, L1 - IS-IS level-1, L2 - IS-IS level-2
       ia - IS-IS inter area, * - candidate default, U - per-user static route
       o - ODR, P - periodic downloaded static route


Gateway of last resort is not set

     10.0.0.0/24 is subnetted, 5 subnets
C        10.1.12.0 is directly connected, Serial0/0/0
O        10.1.3.0 [110/65] via 10.1.23.3, 00:07:25, Serial0/0/1
C        10.1.2.0 is directly connected, Loopback2
O        10.1.1.0 [110/65] via 10.1.12.1, 00:07:25, Serial0/0/0
C        10.1.23.0 is directly connected, Serial0/0/1
O IA 192.168.100.0/22 [110/65] via 10.1.23.3, 00:00:01, Serial0/0/1
```

```
R2# show ip ospf database

            OSPF Router with ID (10.1.2.1) (Process ID 1)

                Router Link States (Area 0)

Link ID         ADV Router      Age         Seq#        Checksum Link count
10.1.1.1        10.1.1.1        969         0x80000002  0x00C668 3
10.1.2.1        10.1.2.1        498         0x80000005  0x00924E 4
192.168.103.1   192.168.103.1   5   (DNA)   0x80000002  0x00A573 1

                Summary Net Link States (Area 0)

Link ID         ADV Router      Age         Seq#        Checksum
10.1.3.0        10.1.2.1        537         0x80000001  0x00EFEF
10.1.3.0        192.168.103.1   11  (DNA)   0x80000001  0x00FD5E
10.1.23.0       10.1.2.1        557         0x80000001  0x0009C3
10.1.23.0       192.168.103.1   11  (DNA)   0x80000001  0x00996F
192.168.100.0   192.168.103.1   1   (DNA)   0x80000001  0x009C03

                Router Link States (Area 23)

Link ID         ADV Router      Age         Seq#        Checksum Link count
10.1.2.1        10.1.2.1        498         0x80000009  0x00D191 2
192.168.103.1   192.168.103.1   499         0x80000004  0x00A7DC 3

                Summary Net Link States (Area 23)

Link ID         ADV Router      Age         Seq#        Checksum
10.1.1.0        10.1.2.1        563         0x80000001  0x0006DB
10.1.2.0        10.1.2.1        563         0x80000001  0x0078A8
10.1.12.0       10.1.2.1        563         0x80000001  0x008255
192.168.100.0   192.168.103.1   51          0x80000002  0x009A04
```

Notice on R3 that OSPF has generated a summary route pointing toward null0:

```
R3# show ip route
Codes: C - connected, S - static, R - RIP, M - mobile, B - BGP
       D - EIGRP, EX - EIGRP external, O - OSPF, IA - OSPF inter area
       N1 - OSPF NSSA external type 1, N2 - OSPF NSSA external type 2
       E1 - OSPF external type 1, E2 - OSPF external type 2
       i - IS-IS, su - IS-IS summary, L1 - IS-IS level-1, L2 - IS-IS level-2
       ia - IS-IS inter area, * - candidate default, U - per-user static route
```

```
           o - ODR, P - periodic downloaded static route

Gateway of last resort is not set

     10.0.0.0/24 is subnetted, 5 subnets
O        10.1.12.0 [110/128] via 10.1.23.2, 00:01:18, Serial0/0/1
C        10.1.3.0 is directly connected, Loopback3
O        10.1.2.0 [110/65] via 10.1.23.2, 00:01:18, Serial0/0/1
O        10.1.1.0 [110/129] via 10.1.23.2, 00:01:18, Serial0/0/1
C        10.1.23.0 is directly connected, Serial0/0/1
C    192.168.102.0/24 is directly connected, Loopback102
C    192.168.103.0/24 is directly connected, Loopback103
C    192.168.100.0/24 is directly connected, Loopback100
C    192.168.101.0/24 is directly connected, Loopback101
O    192.168.100.0/22 is a summary, 00:01:19, Null0
```

This behavior is known as sending unknown traffic to the "bit bucket." This means that if the router advertising the summary route receives a packet destined for something covered by that summary but not in the routing table, it drops it.

What is the reasoning behind this behavior?

_____

_____

_____

_____

_____

Step 5: Generating a Default Route into OSPF

You can simulate loopback 30 on R1 to be a connection to the Internet. You do not necessarily need to advertise this specific network to the rest of the network. Rather, you can just have a default route for all unknown traffic to go here. To have R1 generate a default route, use the OSPF configuration command **default-information originate always**. The **always** keyword is necessary for generating a default route in this scenario. Without this keyword, a default route is generated only into OSPF if one exists in the routing table:

```
R1(config)# router ospf 1
R1(config-router)# default-information originate always
```

Verify that the default route appears on R2 and R3 with the **show ip route** command:

```
R2# show ip route
Codes: C - connected, S - static, R - RIP, M - mobile, B - BGP
       D - EIGRP, EX - EIGRP external, O - OSPF, IA - OSPF inter area
       N1 - OSPF NSSA external type 1, N2 - OSPF NSSA external type 2
       E1 - OSPF external type 1, E2 - OSPF external type 2
       i - IS-IS, su - IS-IS summary, L1 - IS-IS level-1, L2 - IS-IS level-2
```

```
             ia - IS-IS inter area, * - candidate default, U - per-user static route
             o - ODR, P - periodic downloaded static route


Gateway of last resort is 10.1.12.1 to network 0.0.0.0


       10.0.0.0/24 is subnetted, 5 subnets
C         10.1.12.0 is directly connected, Serial0/0/0
O         10.1.3.0 [110/65] via 10.1.23.3, 00:10:36, Serial0/0/1
C         10.1.2.0 is directly connected, Loopback2
O         10.1.1.0 [110/65] via 10.1.12.1, 00:00:19, Serial0/0/0
C         10.1.23.0 is directly connected, Serial0/0/1
O*E2 0.0.0.0/0 [110/1] via 10.1.12.1, 00:00:09, Serial0/0/0
O IA 192.168.100.0/22 [110/65] via 10.1.23.3, 00:00:19, Serial0/0/1
```

```
R3# show ip route
Codes: C - connected, S - static, R - RIP, M - mobile, B - BGP
       D - EIGRP, EX - EIGRP external, O - OSPF, IA - OSPF inter area
       N1 - OSPF NSSA external type 1, N2 - OSPF NSSA external type 2
       E1 - OSPF external type 1, E2 - OSPF external type 2
       i - IS-IS, su - IS-IS summary, L1 - IS-IS level-1, L2 - IS-IS level-2
       ia - IS-IS inter area, * - candidate default, U - per-user static route
       o - ODR, P - periodic downloaded static route


Gateway of last resort is 10.1.23.2 to network 0.0.0.0


       10.0.0.0/24 is subnetted, 5 subnets
O         10.1.12.0 [110/128] via 10.1.23.2, 00:00:35, Serial0/0/1
C         10.1.3.0 is directly connected, Loopback3
O         10.1.2.0 [110/65] via 10.1.23.2, 00:00:35, Serial0/0/1
O         10.1.1.0 [110/129] via 10.1.23.2, 00:00:35, Serial0/0/1
C         10.1.23.0 is directly connected, Serial0/0/1
C     192.168.102.0/24 is directly connected, Loopback102
C     192.168.103.0/24 is directly connected, Loopback103
C     192.168.100.0/24 is directly connected, Loopback100
C     192.168.101.0/24 is directly connected, Loopback101
O*E2 0.0.0.0/0 [110/1] via 10.1.23.2, 00:00:26, Serial0/0/1
O     192.168.100.0/22 is a summary, 00:03:28, Null0
```

You should be able to ping the interface connecting to the Internet from R2 or R3, despite never being advertised into OSPF:

```
R3# ping 172.30.30.1


Type escape sequence to abort.
Sending 5, 100-byte ICMP Echos to 172.30.30.1, timeout is 2 seconds:
!!!!!
Success rate is 100 percent (5/5), round-trip min/avg/max = 28/30/32 ms
```

Challenge: Configure OSPF Authentication

Configure OSPF authentication on the link between R2 and R3 for MD5 authentication, using key ID **1** and the password **cisco**:

_____

_____

_____

_____

TCL Connectivity Verification

You can download this TCL script at www.ciscopress.com/title/1587132133 under the More Information section on the page.

```
foreach address {
10.1.1.1
10.1.2.1
10.1.3.1
172.30.30.1
192.168.100.1
192.168.101.1
192.168.102.1
192.168.103.1
10.1.12.1
10.1.12.2
10.1.23.2
10.1.23.3
} {
ping $address }
R1# tclsh
R1(tcl)#
R1(tcl)# foreach address {
+>(tcl)# 10.1.1.1
+>(tcl)# 10.1.2.1
+>(tcl)# 10.1.3.1
+>(tcl)# 172.30.30.1
+>(tcl)# 192.168.100.1
+>(tcl)# 192.168.101.1
+>(tcl)# 192.168.102.1
+>(tcl)# 192.168.103.1
+>(tcl)# 10.1.12.1
+>(tcl)# 10.1.12.2
+>(tcl)# 10.1.23.2
+>(tcl)# 10.1.23.3
+>(tcl)# } {
+>(tcl)# ping $address }
```

```
Type escape sequence to abort.
Sending 5, 100-byte ICMP Echos to 10.1.1.1, timeout is 2 seconds:
!!!!!
Success rate is 100 percent (5/5), round-trip min/avg/max = 1/1/4 ms
Type escape sequence to abort.
Sending 5, 100-byte ICMP Echos to 10.1.2.1, timeout is 2 seconds:
!!!!!
Success rate is 100 percent (5/5), round-trip min/avg/max = 28/28/32 ms
Type escape sequence to abort.
Sending 5, 100-byte ICMP Echos to 10.1.3.1, timeout is 2 seconds:
!!!!!
Success rate is 100 percent (5/5), round-trip min/avg/max = 28/29/32 ms
Type escape sequence to abort.
Sending 5, 100-byte ICMP Echos to 172.30.30.1, timeout is 2 seconds:
!!!!!
Success rate is 100 percent (5/5), round-trip min/avg/max = 1/1/4 ms
Type escape sequence to abort.
Sending 5, 100-byte ICMP Echos to 192.168.100.1, timeout is 2 seconds:
!!!!!
Success rate is 100 percent (5/5), round-trip min/avg/max = 28/29/32 ms
Type escape sequence to abort.
Sending 5, 100-byte ICMP Echos to 192.168.101.1, timeout is 2 seconds:
!!!!!
Success rate is 100 percent (5/5), round-trip min/avg/max = 28/29/32 ms
Type escape sequence to abort.
Sending 5, 100-byte ICMP Echos to 192.168.102.1, timeout is 2 seconds:
!!!!!
Success rate is 100 percent (5/5), round-trip min/avg/max = 28/29/32 ms
Type escape sequence to abort.
Sending 5, 100-byte ICMP Echos to 192.168.103.1, timeout is 2 seconds:
!!!!!
Success rate is 100 percent (5/5), round-trip min/avg/max = 28/29/32 ms
Type escape sequence to abort.
Sending 5, 100-byte ICMP Echos to 10.1.12.1, timeout is 2 seconds:
!!!!!
Success rate is 100 percent (5/5), round-trip min/avg/max = 56/56/56 ms
Type escape sequence to abort.
Sending 5, 100-byte ICMP Echos to 10.1.12.2, timeout is 2 seconds:
!!!!!
Success rate is 100 percent (5/5), round-trip min/avg/max = 28/28/32 ms
Type escape sequence to abort.
Sending 5, 100-byte ICMP Echos to 10.1.23.2, timeout is 2 seconds:
!!!!!
Success rate is 100 percent (5/5), round-trip min/avg/max = 28/28/28 ms
Type escape sequence to abort.
Sending 5, 100-byte ICMP Echos to 10.1.23.3, timeout is 2 seconds:
```

```
!!!!!
Success rate is 100 percent (5/5), round-trip min/avg/max = 28/29/32 ms

R2# tclsh
R2(tcl)#
R2(tcl)# foreach address {
+>(tcl)# 10.1.1.1
+>(tcl)# 10.1.2.1
+>(tcl)# 10.1.3.1
+>(tcl)# 172.30.30.1
+>(tcl)# 192.168.100.1
+>(tcl)# 192.168.101.1
+>(tcl)# 192.168.102.1
+>(tcl)# 192.168.103.1
+>(tcl)# 10.1.12.1
+>(tcl)# 10.1.12.2
+>(tcl)# 10.1.23.2
+>(tcl)# 10.1.23.3
+>(tcl)# } {
+>(tcl)# ping $address }

Type escape sequence to abort.
Sending 5, 100-byte ICMP Echos to 10.1.1.1, timeout is 2 seconds:
!!!!!
Success rate is 100 percent (5/5), round-trip min/avg/max = 28/28/32 ms
Type escape sequence to abort.
Sending 5, 100-byte ICMP Echos to 10.1.2.1, timeout is 2 seconds:
!!!!!
Success rate is 100 percent (5/5), round-trip min/avg/max = 1/1/4 ms
Type escape sequence to abort.
Sending 5, 100-byte ICMP Echos to 10.1.3.1, timeout is 2 seconds:
!!!!!
Success rate is 100 percent (5/5), round-trip min/avg/max = 1/2/4 ms
Type escape sequence to abort.
Sending 5, 100-byte ICMP Echos to 172.30.30.1, timeout is 2 seconds:
!!!!!
Success rate is 100 percent (5/5), round-trip min/avg/max = 28/28/32 ms
Type escape sequence to abort.
Sending 5, 100-byte ICMP Echos to 192.168.100.1, timeout is 2 seconds:
!!!!!
Success rate is 100 percent (5/5), round-trip min/avg/max = 1/2/4 ms
Type escape sequence to abort.
Sending 5, 100-byte ICMP Echos to 192.168.101.1, timeout is 2 seconds:
!!!!!
Success rate is 100 percent (5/5), round-trip min/avg/max = 1/2/4 ms
Type escape sequence to abort.
```

```
Sending 5, 100-byte ICMP Echos to 192.168.102.1, timeout is 2 seconds:
!!!!!
Success rate is 100 percent (5/5), round-trip min/avg/max = 1/2/4 ms
Type escape sequence to abort.
Sending 5, 100-byte ICMP Echos to 192.168.103.1, timeout is 2 seconds:
!!!!!
Success rate is 100 percent (5/5), round-trip min/avg/max = 1/2/4 ms
Type escape sequence to abort.
Sending 5, 100-byte ICMP Echos to 10.1.12.1, timeout is 2 seconds:
!!!!!
Success rate is 100 percent (5/5), round-trip min/avg/max = 28/28/32 ms
Type escape sequence to abort.
Sending 5, 100-byte ICMP Echos to 10.1.12.2, timeout is 2 seconds:
!!!!!
Success rate is 100 percent (5/5), round-trip min/avg/max = 56/57/64 ms
Type escape sequence to abort.
Sending 5, 100-byte ICMP Echos to 10.1.23.2, timeout is 2 seconds:
!!!!!
Success rate is 100 percent (5/5), round-trip min/avg/max = 1/3/4 ms
Type escape sequence to abort.
Sending 5, 100-byte ICMP Echos to 10.1.23.3, timeout is 2 seconds:
!!!!!
Success rate is 100 percent (5/5), round-trip min/avg/max = 1/2/4 ms


R3# tclsh
R3(tcl)# foreach address {
+>(tcl)# 10.1.1.1
+>(tcl)# 10.1.2.1
+>(tcl)# 10.1.3.1
+>(tcl)# 172.30.30.1
+>(tcl)# 192.168.100.1
+>(tcl)# 192.168.101.1
+>(tcl)# 192.168.102.1
+>(tcl)# 192.168.103.1
+>(tcl)# 10.1.12.1
+>(tcl)# 10.1.12.2
+>(tcl)# 10.1.23.2
+>(tcl)# 10.1.23.3
+>(tcl)# } {
+>(tcl)# ping $address }

Type escape sequence to abort.
Sending 5, 100-byte ICMP Echos to 10.1.1.1, timeout is 2 seconds:
!!!!!
```

```
Success rate is 100 percent (5/5), round-trip min/avg/max = 28/28/32 ms
Type escape sequence to abort.
Sending 5, 100-byte ICMP Echos to 10.1.2.1, timeout is 2 seconds:
!!!!!
Success rate is 100 percent (5/5), round-trip min/avg/max = 1/2/4 ms
Type escape sequence to abort.
Sending 5, 100-byte ICMP Echos to 10.1.3.1, timeout is 2 seconds:
!!!!!
Success rate is 100 percent (5/5), round-trip min/avg/max = 1/1/1 ms
Type escape sequence to abort.
Sending 5, 100-byte ICMP Echos to 172.30.30.1, timeout is 2 seconds:
!!!!!
Success rate is 100 percent (5/5), round-trip min/avg/max = 28/29/32 ms
Type escape sequence to abort.
Sending 5, 100-byte ICMP Echos to 192.168.100.1, timeout is 2 seconds:
!!!!!
Success rate is 100 percent (5/5), round-trip min/avg/max = 1/1/4 ms
Type escape sequence to abort.
Sending 5, 100-byte ICMP Echos to 192.168.101.1, timeout is 2 seconds:
!!!!!
Success rate is 100 percent (5/5), round-trip min/avg/max = 1/1/4 ms
Type escape sequence to abort.
Sending 5, 100-byte ICMP Echos to 192.168.102.1, timeout is 2 seconds:
!!!!!
Success rate is 100 percent (5/5), round-trip min/avg/max = 1/1/4 ms
Type escape sequence to abort.
Sending 5, 100-byte ICMP Echos to 192.168.103.1, timeout is 2 seconds:
!!!!!
Success rate is 100 percent (5/5), round-trip min/avg/max = 1/1/1 ms
Type escape sequence to abort.
Sending 5, 100-byte ICMP Echos to 10.1.12.1, timeout is 2 seconds:
!!!!!
Success rate is 100 percent (5/5), round-trip min/avg/max = 28/29/32 ms
Type escape sequence to abort.
Sending 5, 100-byte ICMP Echos to 10.1.12.2, timeout is 2 seconds:
!!!!!
Success rate is 100 percent (5/5), round-trip min/avg/max = 1/2/4 ms
Type escape sequence to abort.
Sending 5, 100-byte ICMP Echos to 10.1.23.2, timeout is 2 seconds:
!!!!!
Success rate is 100 percent (5/5), round-trip min/avg/max = 1/2/4 ms
Type escape sequence to abort.
Sending 5, 100-byte ICMP Echos to 10.1.23.3, timeout is 2 seconds:
!!!!!
Success rate is 100 percent (5/5), round-trip min/avg/max = 1/2/4 ms
```

Lab 3-4: OSPF over Frame Relay Using a Router as the Frame Relay Switch (3.11.4a)

The objectives of this lab are as follows:

- Configure OSPF over Frame Relay

- Use non-broadcast and point-to-multipoint OSPF network types

- Modify default OSPF timers

Figure 3-4 illustrates the topology that will be used for this lab.

Figure 3-4   Topology Diagram

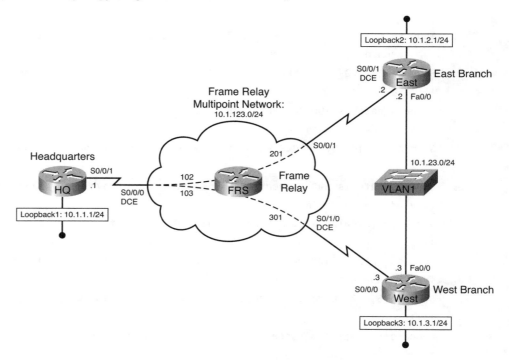

If you are using an Adtran as a Frame Relay switch, please skip this lab and go to Lab 3-5.

Note   Given the diversity of router models and the associated differing naming conventions for serial interfaces (S0, S0/0, S0/0/0), the actual interface numbers on your devices probably differ from those here. The same is true concerning which side of the link is DCE or DTE. You should always draw your own network diagram based upon your specific physical topology. If you are uncertain which side of the connection is DCE, use the **show controllers serial** *interface number* command:

```
HQ# show controllers serial0/0/0
Interface Serial0/0/0
Hardware is GT96K
DCE V.35, clock rate 2000000
```

Scenario

You are responsible for configuring the new network to connect your company's east branch and west branch through the company headquarters represented by loopback interfaces on each of the three routers. The physical devices have just been installed and connected over Frame Relay hub-and-spoke. Configure OSPF to allow full connectivity between all departments.

There will also be an Ethernet connection between East and West. This represents a backup line given by a service provider.

This topology may appear again in future labs, so save your configuration when you are done.

Step 1: Addressing

Set up the Frame Relay switch connecting the routers to have the data-link connection identifiers (DLCIs) indicated in the diagram between HQ and East and HQ and West.

Then configure the router physical interfaces with IP addresses. On the interfaces connected to the Frame Relay switch, configure Frame Relay encapsulation with Inverse ARP disabled and use Frame Relay map statements. Make sure you include the **broadcast** keyword in your map statements and local Frame Relay maps so that you can ping yourself. Also set up the loopback interfaces:

```
HQ# configure terminal
Enter configuration commands, one per line.  End with CNTL/Z.
HQ(config)# interface loopback 1
HQ(config-if)# ip address 10.1.1.1 255.255.255.0
HQ(config-if)# interface serial 0/0/1
HQ(config-if)# ip address 10.1.123.1 255.255.255.0
HQ(config-if)# encapsulation frame-relay
HQ(config-if)# no frame-relay inverse-arp
HQ(config-if)# frame-relay map ip 10.1.123.1 102
HQ(config-if)# frame-relay map ip 10.1.123.2 102 broadcast
HQ(config-if)# frame-relay map ip 10.1.123.3 103 broadcast
HQ(config-if)# no shutdown
```

```
EAST# configure terminal
Enter configuration commands, one per line. End with CNTL/Z.
EAST(config)# interface loopback 2
EAST(config-if)# ip address 10.1.2.1 255.255.255.0
EAST(config-if)# interface serial 0/0/1
EAST(config-if)# clock rate 2000000
EAST(config-if)# ip address 10.1.123.2 255.255.255.0
EAST(config-if)# encapsulation frame-relay
EAST(config-if)# no frame-relay inverse-arp
EAST(config-if)# frame-relay map ip 10.1.123.1 201 broadcast
EAST(config-if)# frame-relay map ip 10.1.123.2 201
EAST(config-if)# frame-relay map ip 10.1.123.3 201 broadcast
EAST(config-if)# no shutdown
EAST(config-if)# interface fastethernet 0/0
```

```
EAST(config-if)# ip address 10.1.23.2 255.255.255.0
EAST(config-if)# no shutdown
```

```
WEST# configure terminal
Enter configuration commands, one per line.  End with CNTL/Z.
WEST(config)# interface loopback 2
WEST(config-if)# ip address 10.1.3.1 255.255.255.0
WEST(config-if)# interface serial 0/0/1
WEST(config-if)# ip address 10.1.123.3 255.255.255.0
WEST(config-if)# encapsulation frame-relay
WEST(config-if)# no frame-relay inverse-arp
WEST(config-if)# frame-relay map ip 10.1.123.1 301 broadcast
WEST(config-if)# frame-relay map ip 10.1.123.2 301 broadcast
WEST(config-if)# frame-relay map ip 10.1.123.3 301
WEST(config-if)# no shutdown
WEST(config-if)# interface fastethernet 0/0
WEST(config-if)# ip address 10.1.23.3 255.255.255.0
WEST(config-if)# no shutdown
```

Verify that you have local subnet connectivity with **ping**.

Step 2: Setting Up NBMA OSPF

You can set up OSPF for hub-and-spoke over Frame Relay. HQ will be the hub; East and West will be the spokes. Create OSPF process 1 and add the Frame Relay interfaces on each router into area 0 with the **network** command. Also, add the loopback interfaces on each router into area 0. Then change the network type to allow the correct subnet mask to be advertised:

```
HQ(config)# router ospf 1
HQ(config-router)# network 10.1.123.0 0.0.0.255 area 0
HQ(config-router)# network 10.1.1.0 0.0.0.255 area 0
HQ(config-router)# interface loopback 1
HQ(config-if)# ip ospf network point-to-point
```

```
EAST(config)# router ospf 1
EAST(config-router)# network 10.1.123.0 0.0.0.255 area 0
EAST(config-router)# network 10.1.2.0 0.0.0.255 area 0
EAST(config-router)# interface loopback 2
EAST(config-if)# ip ospf network point-to-point
```

```
WEST(config)# router ospf 1
WEST(config-router)# network 10.1.123.0 0.0.0.255 area 0
WEST(config-router)# network 10.1.3.0 0.0.0.255 area 0
WEST(config-router)# interface loopback 3
WEST(config-if)# ip ospf network point-to-point
```

No Frame Relay adjacencies will be established yet because the default network type is non-broadcast. You can change this by adding neighbor statements. Before that, however, go on East and West and change their Frame Relay interfaces to have OSPF priority 0. This ensures that HQ becomes the

DR. Next, configure neighbor statements on HQ pointing toward East and West. Only the router starting the exchange needs neighbor statements (it is HQ in this case). Although it may take a little while because the hello timers are long on non-broadcast, the adjacencies will eventually come up. You can verify adjacency states with the **show ip ospf neighbor** command.

```
HQ(config)# router ospf 1
HQ(config-router)# neighbor 10.1.123.2
HQ(config-router)# neighbor 10.1.123.3
```
```
EAST(config)# interface serial 0/0/1
EAST(config-if)# ip ospf priority 0
```
```
WEST(config)# interface serial 0/0/0
WEST(config-if)# ip ospf priority 0
```
```
HQ# show ip ospf neighbor
```

Neighbor ID	Pri	State	Dead Time	Address	Interface
10.1.2.1	0	FULL/DROTHER	00:01:57	10.1.123.2	Serial0/0/1
10.1.3.1	0	FULL/DROTHER	00:01:57	10.1.123.3	Serial0/0/1

Non-broadcast networks are good for Frame Relay because you have the maximum level of control over neighbor relationships. All OSPF packets are unicast and go only to their intended destinations. Non-broadcast saves bandwidth because of the strict control you can have over which router becomes the DR.

Step 3: Changing the Network Type to Point-to-Multipoint

Point-to-multipoint is an OSPF area type that lends itself very well to a hub-and-spoke topology. Point-to-multipoint does not elect DRs or BDRs, so it does not need interface priorities. Instead, it treats the network as a collection of point-to-point networks and advertises host routes for any neighbors it has.

To configure this, first take off the configuration already there for a non-broadcast network, meaning the neighbor statements and interface priorities. The adjacencies time out after the dead timer expires:

```
HQ(config)# router ospf 1
HQ(config-router)# no neighbor 10.1.123.2
HQ(config-router)# no neighbor 10.1.123.3
```
```
EAST(config)# interface serial 0/0/1
EAST(config-if)# no ip ospf priority 0
```
```
WEST(config)# interface serial 0/0/0
WEST(config-if)# no ip ospf priority 0
```

After removing the old configuration, use the interface-level command **ip ospf network point-to-multipoint**. Verify that your adjacencies are active with the **show ip ospf neighbor** command:

```
HQ(config)# interface serial 0/0/1
HQ(config-if)# ip ospf network point-to-multipoint
```
```
EAST(config)# interface serial 0/0/1
EAST(config-if)# ip ospf network point-to-multipoint
```
```
WEST(config)# interface serial 0/0/0
```

```
WEST(config-if)# ip ospf network point-to-multipoint
```

```
HQ# show ip ospf neighbor


Neighbor ID     Pri   State         Dead Time   Address       Interface
10.1.3.1          0   FULL/  -      00:01:34    10.1.123.3    Serial0/0/1
10.1.2.1          0   FULL/  -      00:01:45    10.1.123.2    Serial0/0/1
```

Look at the routing table on one of the spoke routers. Notice how the routing table has host routes in it. This is part of point-to-multipoint behavior:

```
EAST# show ip route
Codes: C - connected, S - static, R - RIP, M - mobile, B - BGP
       D - EIGRP, EX - EIGRP external, O - OSPF, IA - OSPF inter area
       N1 - OSPF NSSA external type 1, N2 - OSPF NSSA external type 2
       E1 - OSPF external type 1, E2 - OSPF external type 2
       i - IS-IS, su - IS-IS summary, L1 - IS-IS level-1, L2 - IS-IS level-2
       ia - IS-IS inter area, * - candidate default, U - per-user static route
       o - ODR, P - periodic downloaded static route


Gateway of last resort is not set


     10.0.0.0/8 is variably subnetted, 7 subnets, 2 masks
O       10.1.3.0/24 [110/129] via 10.1.123.1, 00:01:07, Serial0/0/1
C       10.1.2.0/24 is directly connected, Loopback2
O       10.1.1.0/24 [110/65] via 10.1.123.1, 00:01:07, Serial0/0/1
C       10.1.23.0/24 is directly connected, FastEthernet0/0
C       10.1.123.0/24 is directly connected, Serial0/0/1
O       10.1.123.1/32 [110/64] via 10.1.123.1, 00:01:07, Serial0/0/1
O       10.1.123.3/32 [110/128] via 10.1.123.1, 00:01:07, Serial0/0/1
```

Look at the output of the **show ip ospf interface** *interface* command on your routers. Notice that the interface type is point-to-multipoint:

```
EAST# show ip ospf interface serial 0/0/1
Serial0/0/1 is up, line protocol is up
  Internet Address 10.1.123.2/24, Area 0
  Process ID 1, Router ID 10.1.2.1, Network Type POINT_TO_MULTIPOINT, Cost: 64
  Transmit Delay is 1 sec, State POINT_TO_MULTIPOINT,
  Timer intervals configured, Hello 30, Dead 120, Wait 120, Retransmit 5
    oob-resync timeout 120
    Hello due in 00:00:16
  Supports Link-local Signaling (LLS)
  Index 1/1, flood queue length 0
  Next 0x0(0)/0x0(0)
  Last flood scan length is 1, maximum is 1
  Last flood scan time is 0 msec, maximum is 0 msec
```

```
    Neighbor Count is 1, Adjacent neighbor count is 1
      Adjacent with neighbor 10.1.1.1
    Suppress hello for 0 neighbor(s)
```

What are some advantages to configuring a non-broadcast multiaccess (NBMA) network as point-to-multipoint instead of non-broadcast? What are some disadvantages?

_____

_____

_____

_____

Step 4: Changing OSPF Timers

Add the Ethernet link connecting East and West to the OSPF process using the **network** command:

```
EAST(config)# router ospf 1
EAST(config-router)# network 10.1.23.0 0.0.0.255 area 0
```
```
WEST(config)# router ospf 1
WEST(config-router)# network 10.1.23.0 0.0.0.255 area 0
```

Look at the interface OSPF properties with the **show ip ospf interface** *interface* command:

```
EAST# show ip ospf interface fastethernet 0/0
FastEthernet0/0 is up, line protocol is up
  Internet Address 10.1.23.2/24, Area 0
  Process ID 1, Router ID 10.1.2.1, Network Type BROADCAST, Cost: 1
  Transmit Delay is 1 sec, State BDR, Priority 1
  Designated Router (ID) 10.1.3.1, Interface address 10.1.23.3
  Backup Designated router (ID) 10.1.2.1, Interface address 10.1.23.2
  Timer intervals configured, Hello 10, Dead 40, Wait 40, Retransmit 5
    oob-resync timeout 40
    Hello due in 00:00:00
  Supports Link-local Signaling (LLS)
  Index 3/3, flood queue length 0
  Next 0x0(0)/0x0(0)
  Last flood scan length is 1, maximum is 1
  Last flood scan time is 0 msec, maximum is 0 msec
  Neighbor Count is 1, Adjacent neighbor count is 1
    Adjacent with neighbor 10.1.3.1  (Designated Router)
  Suppress hello for 0 neighbor(s)
```

Because it is an Ethernet link, it has the default network type of broadcast and the default network timers associated with a broadcast network. Sometimes, you may want to change the default timers to allow for better network convergence because lower dead timers mean that neighbors that go down are detected more quickly. The disadvantage of this is higher router CPU utilization and more bandwidth being consumed by hello packets.

You can change the default hello timer to any time you want with the **ip ospf hello-interval** *seconds* command. Change the hello interval to 5 seconds on both sides. Change the dead timer to 15 seconds with the **ip ospf dead-interval** *seconds* command. Verify this with the **show ip ospf interface** *interface* command:

```
EAST(config)# interface fastethernet 0/0
EAST(config-if)# ip ospf hello-interval 5
EAST(config-if)# ip ospf dead-interval 15
```

```
WEST(config)# interface fastethernet 0/0
WEST(config-if)# ip ospf hello-interval 5
WEST(config-if)# ip ospf dead-interval 15
```

```
EAST# show ip ospf int f0/0
FastEthernet0/0 is up, line protocol is up
  Internet Address 10.1.23.2/24, Area 0
  Process ID 1, Router ID 10.1.2.1, Network Type BROADCAST, Cost: 1
  Transmit Delay is 1 sec, State BDR, Priority 1
  Designated Router (ID) 10.1.3.1, Interface address 10.1.23.3
  Backup Designated router (ID) 10.1.2.1, Interface address 10.1.23.2
  Timer intervals configured, Hello 5, Dead 15, Wait 15, Retransmit 5
    oob-resync timeout 40
    Hello due in 00:00:01
  Supports Link-local Signaling (LLS)
  Index 3/3, flood queue length 0
  Next 0x0(0)/0x0(0)
  Last flood scan length is 1, maximum is 1
  Last flood scan time is 0 msec, maximum is 0 msec
  Neighbor Count is 1, Adjacent neighbor count is 1
    Adjacent with neighbor 10.1.3.1   (Designated Router)
  Suppress hello for 0 neighbor(s)
```

What are some downsides to changing the timers if they are not tuned correctly?

_____

_____

_____

_____

Challenge: Minimal Hello Intervals

Configure the serial link to have even lower convergence time in case of a failure. To configure this, use the variant of the dead-interval command **ip ospf dead-interval minimal hello-multiplier** *multiplier*. This command sets the dead interval to 1 second. The hello rate is the multiplier number of hellos per second. Configure the routers to send five hellos a second. Look at the dead time column of the **show ip ospf neighbor** command. Is it a different format than before for that connection?

_____

_____

_____

_____

TCL Connectivity Verification

You can download this TCL script at www.ciscopress.com/title/1587132133 under the More Information section on the page.

```
tclsh

foreach address {
10.1.1.1
10.1.2.1
10.1.3.1
10.1.123.1
10.1.123.2
10.1.123.3
10.1.23.2
10.1.23.3
} {
ping $address }
tclsh

foreach address {
10.1.1.1
10.1.2.1
10.1.3.1
10.1.123.1
10.1.123.2
10.1.123.3
10.1.23.2
10.1.23.3
} {
ping $address }

HQ# tclsh
HQ(tcl)#
HQ(tcl)# foreach address {
+>(tcl)# 10.1.1.1
+>(tcl)# 10.1.2.1
+>(tcl)# 10.1.3.1
```

```
+>(tcl)# 10.1.123.1
+>(tcl)# 10.1.123.2
+>(tcl)# 10.1.123.3
+>(tcl)# 10.1.23.2
+>(tcl)# 10.1.23.3
+>(tcl)# } {
+>(tcl)# ping $address }

Type escape sequence to abort.
Sending 5, 100-byte ICMP Echos to 10.1.1.1, timeout is 2 seconds:
!!!!!
Success rate is 100 percent (5/5), round-trip min/avg/max = 1/2/4 ms
Type escape sequence to abort.
Sending 5, 100-byte ICMP Echos to 10.1.2.1, timeout is 2 seconds:
!!!!!
Success rate is 100 percent (5/5), round-trip min/avg/max = 1/3/4 ms
Type escape sequence to abort.
Sending 5, 100-byte ICMP Echos to 10.1.3.1, timeout is 2 seconds:
!!!!!
Success rate is 100 percent (5/5), round-trip min/avg/max = 1/3/4 ms
Type escape sequence to abort.
Sending 5, 100-byte ICMP Echos to 10.1.123.1, timeout is 2 seconds:
!!!!!
Success rate is 0 percent (0/5)
Type escape sequence to abort.
Sending 5, 100-byte ICMP Echos to 10.1.123.2, timeout is 2 seconds:
!!!!!
Success rate is 100 percent (5/5), round-trip min/avg/max = 1/2/4 ms
Type escape sequence to abort.
Sending 5, 100-byte ICMP Echos to 10.1.123.3, timeout is 2 seconds:
!!!!!
Success rate is 100 percent (5/5), round-trip min/avg/max = 1/2/4 ms
Type escape sequence to abort.
Sending 5, 100-byte ICMP Echos to 10.1.23.2, timeout is 2 seconds:
!!!!!
Success rate is 100 percent (5/5), round-trip min/avg/max = 1/3/4 ms
Type escape sequence to abort.
Sending 5, 100-byte ICMP Echos to 10.1.23.3, timeout is 2 seconds:
!!!!!
Success rate is 100 percent (5/5), round-trip min/avg/max = 1/3/4 ms

EAST# tclsh
EAST(tcl)#
EAST(tcl)# foreach address {
+>10.1.1.1
```

```
+>10.1.2.1
+>10.1.3.1
+>10.1.123.1
+>10.1.123.2
+>10.1.123.3
+>10.1.23.2
+>10.1.23.3
+>} {
+>ping $address }

Type escape sequence to abort.
Sending 5, 100-byte ICMP Echos to 10.1.1.1, timeout is 2 seconds:
!!!!!
Success rate is 100 percent (5/5), round-trip min/avg/max = 1/3/4 ms
Type escape sequence to abort.
Sending 5, 100-byte ICMP Echos to 10.1.2.1, timeout is 2 seconds:
!!!!!
Success rate is 100 percent (5/5), round-trip min/avg/max = 1/1/4 ms
Type escape sequence to abort.
Sending 5, 100-byte ICMP Echos to 10.1.3.1, timeout is 2 seconds:
!!!!!
Success rate is 100 percent (5/5), round-trip min/avg/max = 1/1/4 ms
Type escape sequence to abort.
Sending 5, 100-byte ICMP Echos to 10.1.123.1, timeout is 2 seconds:
!!!!!
Success rate is 100 percent (5/5), round-trip min/avg/max = 1/2/4 ms
Type escape sequence to abort.
Sending 5, 100-byte ICMP Echos to 10.1.123.2, timeout is 2 seconds:
!!!!!
Success rate is 0 percent (0/5)
Type escape sequence to abort.
Sending 5, 100-byte ICMP Echos to 10.1.123.3, timeout is 2 seconds:
!!!!!
Success rate is 100 percent (5/5), round-trip min/avg/max = 1/1/4 ms
Type escape sequence to abort.
Sending 5, 100-byte ICMP Echos to 10.1.23.2, timeout is 2 seconds:
!!!!!
Success rate is 100 percent (5/5), round-trip min/avg/max = 1/1/4 ms
Type escape sequence to abort.
Sending 5, 100-byte ICMP Echos to 10.1.23.3, timeout is 2 seconds:
!!!!!
Success rate is 100 percent (5/5), round-trip min/avg/max = 1/2/4 ms

WEST# tclsh
WEST(tcl)#
```

```
WEST(tcl)# foreach address {
+>10.1.1.1
+>10.1.2.1
+>10.1.3.1
+>10.1.123.1
+>10.1.123.2
+>10.1.123.3
+>10.1.23.2
+>10.1.23.3
+>} {
+>ping $address }

Type escape sequence to abort.
Sending 5, 100-byte ICMP Echos to 10.1.1.1, timeout is 2 seconds:
!!!!!
Success rate is 100 percent (5/5), round-trip min/avg/max = 4/4/4 ms
Type escape sequence to abort.
Sending 5, 100-byte ICMP Echos to 10.1.2.1, timeout is 2 seconds:
!!!!!
Success rate is 100 percent (5/5), round-trip min/avg/max = 1/3/4 ms
Type escape sequence to abort.
Sending 5, 100-byte ICMP Echos to 10.1.3.1, timeout is 2 seconds:
!!!!!
Success rate is 100 percent (5/5), round-trip min/avg/max = 1/1/4 ms
Type escape sequence to abort.
Sending 5, 100-byte ICMP Echos to 10.1.123.1, timeout is 2 seconds:
!!!!!
Success rate is 100 percent (5/5), round-trip min/avg/max = 1/3/4 ms
Type escape sequence to abort.
Sending 5, 100-byte ICMP Echos to 10.1.123.2, timeout is 2 seconds:
!!!!!
Success rate is 100 percent (5/5), round-trip min/avg/max = 1/3/4 ms
Type escape sequence to abort.
Sending 5, 100-byte ICMP Echos to 10.1.123.3, timeout is 2 seconds:
!!!!!
Success rate is 0 percent (0/5)
Type escape sequence to abort.
Sending 5, 100-byte ICMP Echos to 10.1.23.2, timeout is 2 seconds:
!!!!!
Success rate is 100 percent (5/5), round-trip min/avg/max = 1/1/4 ms
Type escape sequence to abort.
Sending 5, 100-byte ICMP Echos to 10.1.23.3, timeout is 2 seconds:
!!!!!
Success rate is 100 percent (5/5), round-trip min/avg/max = 1/1/4 ms
```

Lab 3-5: OSPF Over Frame Relay Using an Adtran as the Frame Relay Switch (3.11.4b)

The objectives of this lab are as follows:

- Configure OSPF over Frame Relay

- Use non-broadcast and point-to-multipoint OSPF network types

- Modify default OSPF timers

Figure 3-5 illustrates the topology that will be used for this lab.

Figure 3-5   Topology Diagram

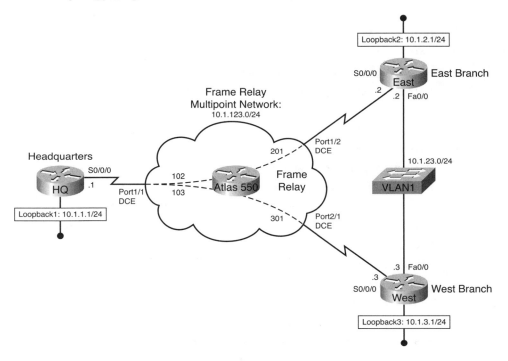

> **Note**   Given the diversity of router models and the associated differing naming conventions for serial interfaces (S0, S0/0, S0/0/0), the actual interface numbers on your devices probably differ from those here. The same is true concerning which side of the link is DCE or DTE. You should always draw your own network diagram based upon your specific physical topology. If you are uncertain which side of the connection is DCE, use the **show controllers serial** *interface number* command:
>
> ```
> HQ# show controllers serial0/0/0
> Interface Serial0/0/0
> Hardware is GT96K
> DCE V.35, clock rate 2000000
> ```

Scenario

You are responsible for configuring the new network to connect your company's east branch and west branch through the company headquarters represented by loopback interfaces on each of the three routers. The physical devices have just been installed and connected over Frame Relay hub-and-spoke. Configure OSPF to allow full connectivity between all departments.

There will also be an Ethernet connection between East and West. This represents a backup line given by a service provider.

This topology may appear again in future labs, so save your configuration when you are done.

Step 1: Addressing

Set up the Frame Relay switch connecting the routers to have the DLCIs indicated in the diagram between HQ and East and HQ and West.

Then configure the router physical interfaces with IP addresses. On the interfaces connected to the Frame Relay switch, configure Frame Relay encapsulation with Inverse ARP disabled and use Frame Relay map statements. Make sure you include the **broadcast** keyword in your map statements and local Frame Relay maps so that you can ping yourself. Also set up the loopback interfaces:

```
HQ# configure terminal
Enter configuration commands, one per line.  End with CNTL/Z.
HQ(config)# interface loopback 1
HQ(config-if)# ip address 10.1.1.1 255.255.255.0
HQ(config-if)# interface serial 0/0/0
HQ(config-if)# ip address 10.1.123.1 255.255.255.0
HQ(config-if)# encapsulation frame-relay ietf
HQ(config-if)# no frame-relay inverse-arp
HQ(config-if)# frame-relay map ip 10.1.123.1 102
HQ(config-if)# frame-relay map ip 10.1.123.2 102 broadcast
HQ(config-if)# frame-relay map ip 10.1.123.3 103 broadcast
HQ(config-if)# no shutdown
```

```
EAST# configure terminal
Enter configuration commands, one per line. End with CNTL/Z.
EAST(config)# interface loopback 2
EAST(config-if)# ip address 10.1.2.1 255.255.255.0
EAST(config-if)# interface serial 0/0/0
EAST(config-if)# ip address 10.1.123.2 255.255.255.0
EAST(config-if)# encapsulation frame-relay ietf
EAST(config-if)# no frame-relay inverse-arp
EAST(config-if)# frame-relay map ip 10.1.123.1 201 broadcast
EAST(config-if)# frame-relay map ip 10.1.123.2 201
EAST(config-if)# frame-relay map ip 10.1.123.3 201 broadcast
EAST(config-if)# no shutdown
EAST(config-if)# interface fastethernet 0/0
EAST(config-if)# ip address 10.1.23.2 255.255.255.0
EAST(config-if)# no shutdown
```

```
WEST# configure terminal
Enter configuration commands, one per line.  End with CNTL/Z.
WEST(config)# interface loopback 2
```

```
WEST(config-if)# ip address 10.1.3.1 255.255.255.0

WEST(config-if)# interface serial 0/0/0

WEST(config-if)# ip address 10.1.123.3 255.255.255.0

WEST(config-if)# encapsulation frame-relay ietf

WEST(config-if)# no frame-relay inverse-arp

WEST(config-if)# frame-relay map ip 10.1.123.1 301 broadcast

WEST(config-if)# frame-relay map ip 10.1.123.2 301 broadcast

WEST(config-if)# frame-relay map ip 10.1.123.3 301

WEST(config-if)# no shutdown

WEST(config-if)# interface fastethernet 0/0

WEST(config-if)# ip address 10.1.23.3 255.255.255.0

WEST(config-if)# no shutdown
```

Verify that you have local subnet connectivity with **ping**.

Step 2: Setting Up NBMA OSPF

You can set up OSPF for hub-and-spoke over Frame Relay. HQ will be the hub; East and West will be the spokes. Create OSPF process 1, and add the Frame Relay interfaces on each router into area 0 with the **network** command. Also, add the loopback interfaces on each router into area 0. Then change the network type to allow the correct subnet mask to be advertised:

```
HQ(config)# router ospf 1

HQ(config-router)# network 10.1.123.0 0.0.0.255 area 0

HQ(config-router)# network 10.1.1.0 0.0.0.255 area 0

HQ(config-router)# interface loopback 1

HQ(config-if)# ip ospf network point-to-point
```
```
EAST(config)# router ospf 1

EAST(config-router)# network 10.1.123.0 0.0.0.255 area 0

EAST(config-router)# network 10.1.2.0 0.0.0.255 area 0

EAST(config-router)# interface loopback 2

EAST(config-if)# ip ospf network point-to-point
```
```
WEST(config)# router ospf 1

WEST(config-router)# network 10.1.123.0 0.0.0.255 area 0

WEST(config-router)# network 10.1.3.0 0.0.0.255 area 0

WEST(config-router)# interface loopback 3

WEST(config-if)# ip ospf network point-to-point
```

No Frame Relay adjacencies will be established yet because the default network type is non-broadcast. You can change this by adding neighbor statements. Before that, however, go on East and West and change their Frame Relay interfaces to have OSPF priority 0. This ensures that HQ becomes the DR. Next, configure neighbor statements on HQ pointing toward East and West. Only the router starting the exchange needs neighbor statements (it is HQ in this case). Although it may take a little while because the hello timers are long on non-broadcast, the adjacencies will eventually come up. You can verify adjacency states with the **show ip ospf neighbor** command:

```
HQ(config)# router ospf 1

HQ(config-router)# neighbor 10.1.123.2
```

```
HQ(config-router)# neighbor 10.1.123.3
```

```
EAST(config)# interface serial 0/0/0
```
```
EAST(config-if)# ip ospf priority 0
```

```
WEST(config)# interface serial 0/0/0
```
```
WEST(config-if)# ip ospf priority 0
```

```
HQ# show ip ospf neighbor
```

```
Neighbor ID      Pri   State           Dead Time    Address        Interface
10.1.2.1          0    FULL/DROTHER    00:01:57     10.1.123.2     Serial0/0/0
10.1.3.1          0    FULL/DROTHER    00:01:57     10.1.123.3     Serial0/0/0
```

Non-broadcast networks are good for Frame Relay because you have the maximum level of control over neighbor relationships. All OSPF packets are unicast and go only to their intended destination. Non-broadcast saves bandwidth because of the strict control you can have over which router becomes the DR.

Step 3: Changing the Network Type to Point-to-Multipoint

Point-to-multipoint is an OSPF area type that lends itself very well to a hub-and-spoke topology. Point-to-multipoint does not elect DRs or BDRs, so it does not need interface priorities. Instead, it treats the network as a collection of point-to-point networks and advertises host routes for any neighbors it has.

To configure this, first take off the configuration already there for a non-broadcast network, meaning the neighbor statements and interface priorities. The adjacencies time out after the dead timer expires:

```
HQ(config)# router ospf 1
HQ(config-router)# no neighbor 10.1.123.2
HQ(config-router)# no neighbor 10.1.123.3
```

```
EAST(config)# interface serial 0/0/0
EAST(config-if)# no ip ospf priority 0
```

```
WEST(config)# interface serial 0/0/0
WEST(config-if)# no ip ospf priority 0
```

After removing the old configuration, use the interface-level command **ip ospf network point-to-multipoint**. Verify that your adjacencies are active with the **show ip ospf neighbor** command:

```
HQ(config)# interface serial 0/0/0
HQ(config-if)# ip ospf network point-to-multipoint
```

```
EAST(config)# interface serial 0/0/0
EAST(config-if)# ip ospf network point-to-multipoint
```

```
WEST(config)# interface serial 0/0/0
WEST(config-if)# ip ospf network point-to-multipoint
```

```
HQ# show ip ospf neighbor
```

```
Neighbor ID      Pri   State       Dead Time    Address        Interface
10.1.3.1          0    FULL/  -    00:01:34     10.1.123.3     Serial0/0/0
10.1.2.1          0    FULL/  -    00:01:45     10.1.123.2     Serial0/0/0
```

Look at the routing table on one of the spoke routers. Notice how the routing table has host routes in it. This is part of point-to-multipoint behavior:

```
EAST# show ip route
Codes: C - connected, S - static, R - RIP, M - mobile, B - BGP
       D - EIGRP, EX - EIGRP external, O - OSPF, IA - OSPF inter area
       N1 - OSPF NSSA external type 1, N2 - OSPF NSSA external type 2
       E1 - OSPF external type 1, E2 - OSPF external type 2
       i - IS-IS, su - IS-IS summary, L1 - IS-IS level-1, L2 - IS-IS level-2
       ia - IS-IS inter area, * - candidate default, U - per-user static route
       o - ODR, P - periodic downloaded static route


Gateway of last resort is not set


     10.0.0.0/8 is variably subnetted, 7 subnets, 2 masks
O       10.1.3.0/24 [110/129] via 10.1.123.1, 00:01:07, Serial0/0/0
C       10.1.2.0/24 is directly connected, Loopback2
O       10.1.1.0/24 [110/65] via 10.1.123.1, 00:01:07, Serial0/0/0
C       10.1.23.0/24 is directly connected, FastEthernet0/0
C       10.1.123.0/24 is directly connected, Serial0/0/0
O       10.1.123.1/32 [110/64] via 10.1.123.1, 00:01:07, Serial0/0/0
O       10.1.123.3/32 [110/128] via 10.1.123.1, 00:01:07, Serial0/0/0
```

Look at the output of the **show ip ospf interface** *interface* command on your routers. Notice that the interface type is point-to-multipoint:

```
EAST# show ip ospf interface serial 0/0/0
Serial0/0/0 is up, line protocol is up
  Internet Address 10.1.123.2/24, Area 0
  Process ID 1, Router ID 10.1.2.1, Network Type POINT_TO_MULTIPOINT, Cost: 64
  Transmit Delay is 1 sec, State POINT_TO_MULTIPOINT,
  Timer intervals configured, Hello 30, Dead 120, Wait 120, Retransmit 5
    oob-resync timeout 120
    Hello due in 00:00:16
  Supports Link-local Signaling (LLS)
  Index 1/1, flood queue length 0
  Next 0x0(0)/0x0(0)
  Last flood scan length is 1, maximum is 1
  Last flood scan time is 0 msec, maximum is 0 msec
  Neighbor Count is 1, Adjacent neighbor count is 1
    Adjacent with neighbor 10.1.1.1
  Suppress hello for 0 neighbor(s)
```

What are some advantages to configuring an NBMA network as point-to-multipoint instead of non-broadcast? What are some disadvantages?

_____

_____

_____

_____

Step 4: Changing OSPF Timers

Add the Ethernet link connecting East and West to the OSPF process using the **network** command:

```
EAST(config)# router ospf 1
EAST(config-router)# network 10.1.23.0 0.0.0.255 area 0
```
```
WEST(config)# router ospf 1
WEST(config-router)# network 10.1.23.0 0.0.0.255 area 0
```

Look at the interface OSPF properties with the **show ip ospf interface** *interface* command:

```
EAST# show ip ospf interface fastethernet 0/0
FastEthernet0/0 is up, line protocol is up
  Internet Address 10.1.23.2/24, Area 0
  Process ID 1, Router ID 10.1.2.1, Network Type BROADCAST, Cost: 1
  Transmit Delay is 1 sec, State BDR, Priority 1
  Designated Router (ID) 10.1.3.1, Interface address 10.1.23.3
  Backup Designated router (ID) 10.1.2.1, Interface address 10.1.23.2
  Timer intervals configured, Hello 10, Dead 40, Wait 40, Retransmit 5
    oob-resync timeout 40
    Hello due in 00:00:00
  Supports Link-local Signaling (LLS)
  Index 3/3, flood queue length 0
  Next 0x0(0)/0x0(0)
  Last flood scan length is 1, maximum is 1
  Last flood scan time is 0 msec, maximum is 0 msec
  Neighbor Count is 1, Adjacent neighbor count is 1
    Adjacent with neighbor 10.1.3.1  (Designated Router)
  Suppress hello for 0 neighbor(s)
```

Because it is an Ethernet link, it has the default network type of broadcast and the default network timers associated with a broadcast network. Sometimes, you may want to change the default timers to allow for better network convergence because lower dead timers mean that neighbors that go down are detected more quickly. The disadvantage of this is higher router CPU utilization and more bandwidth being consumed by hello packets.

You can change the default hello timer to any time you want with the **ip ospf hello-interval** *seconds* command. Change the hello interval to 5 seconds on both sides. Change the dead timer to 15 seconds with the **ip ospf dead-interval** *seconds* command. Verify this with the **show ip ospf interface** *interface* command:

```
EAST(config)# interface fastethernet 0/0
EAST(config-if)# ip ospf hello-interval 5
EAST(config-if)# ip ospf dead-interval 15
WEST(config)# interface fastethernet 0/0
WEST(config-if)# ip ospf hello-interval 5
WEST(config-if)# ip ospf dead-interval 15
EAST# show ip ospf int f0/0
FastEthernet0/0 is up, line protocol is up
  Internet Address 10.1.23.2/24, Area 0
  Process ID 1, Router ID 10.1.2.1, Network Type BROADCAST, Cost: 1
  Transmit Delay is 1 sec, State BDR, Priority 1
  Designated Router (ID) 10.1.3.1, Interface address 10.1.23.3
  Backup Designated router (ID) 10.1.2.1, Interface address 10.1.23.2
  Timer intervals configured, Hello 5, Dead 15, Wait 15, Retransmit 5
    oob-resync timeout 40
    Hello due in 00:00:01
  Supports Link-local Signaling (LLS)
  Index 3/3, flood queue length 0
  Next 0x0(0)/0x0(0)
  Last flood scan length is 1, maximum is 1
  Last flood scan time is 0 msec, maximum is 0 msec
  Neighbor Count is 1, Adjacent neighbor count is 1
    Adjacent with neighbor 10.1.3.1  (Designated Router)
  Suppress hello for 0 neighbor(s)
```

What are some downsides to changing the timers if they are not tuned correctly?

_____

_____

_____

_____

Challenge: Minimal Hello Intervals

Configure the serial link to have even lower convergence time in case of a failure. To configure this, use the variant of the dead-interval command **ip ospf dead-interval minimal hello-multiplier** *multiplier*. This command sets the dead interval to 1 second. The hello rate is the multiplier number of hellos per second. Configure the routers to send five hellos a second. Look at the dead time column of the **show ip ospf neighbor** command. Is it a different format than before for that connection?

_____

_____

_____

_____

TCL Connectivity Verification

You can download this TCL script at www.ciscopress.com/title/1587132133 under the More Information section on the page.

```
tclsh

foreach address {
10.1.1.1
10.1.2.1
10.1.3.1
10.1.123.1
10.1.123.2
10.1.123.3
10.1.23.2
10.1.23.3
} {
ping $address }

HQ# tclsh
HQ(tcl)#
HQ(tcl)# foreach address {
+>(tcl)# 10.1.1.1
+>(tcl)# 10.1.2.1
+>(tcl)# 10.1.3.1
+>(tcl)# 10.1.123.1
+>(tcl)# 10.1.123.2
+>(tcl)# 10.1.123.3
+>(tcl)# 10.1.23.2
+>(tcl)# 10.1.23.3
+>(tcl)# } {
+>(tcl)# ping $address }

Type escape sequence to abort.
Sending 5, 100-byte ICMP Echos to 10.1.1.1, timeout is 2 seconds:
!!!!!
Success rate is 100 percent (5/5), round-trip min/avg/max = 1/2/4 ms
Type escape sequence to abort.
Sending 5, 100-byte ICMP Echos to 10.1.2.1, timeout is 2 seconds:
!!!!!
Success rate is 100 percent (5/5), round-trip min/avg/max = 1/3/4 ms
Type escape sequence to abort.
Sending 5, 100-byte ICMP Echos to 10.1.3.1, timeout is 2 seconds:
!!!!!
Success rate is 100 percent (5/5), round-trip min/avg/max = 1/3/4 ms
Type escape sequence to abort.
```

```
Sending 5, 100-byte ICMP Echos to 10.1.123.1, timeout is 2 seconds:
!!!!!
Success rate is 0 percent (0/5)
Type escape sequence to abort.
Sending 5, 100-byte ICMP Echos to 10.1.123.2, timeout is 2 seconds:
!!!!!
Success rate is 100 percent (5/5), round-trip min/avg/max = 1/2/4 ms
Type escape sequence to abort.
Sending 5, 100-byte ICMP Echos to 10.1.123.3, timeout is 2 seconds:
!!!!!
Success rate is 100 percent (5/5), round-trip min/avg/max = 1/2/4 ms
Type escape sequence to abort.
Sending 5, 100-byte ICMP Echos to 10.1.23.2, timeout is 2 seconds:
!!!!!
Success rate is 100 percent (5/5), round-trip min/avg/max = 1/3/4 ms
Type escape sequence to abort.
Sending 5, 100-byte ICMP Echos to 10.1.23.3, timeout is 2 seconds:
!!!!!
Success rate is 100 percent (5/5), round-trip min/avg/max = 1/3/4 ms

EAST# tclsh
EAST(tcl)#
EAST(tcl)# foreach address {
+>10.1.1.1
+>10.1.2.1
+>10.1.3.1
+>10.1.123.1
+>10.1.123.2
+>10.1.123.3
+>10.1.23.2
+>10.1.23.3
+>} {
+>ping $address }

Type escape sequence to abort.
Sending 5, 100-byte ICMP Echos to 10.1.1.1, timeout is 2 seconds:
!!!!!
Success rate is 100 percent (5/5), round-trip min/avg/max = 1/3/4 ms
Type escape sequence to abort.
Sending 5, 100-byte ICMP Echos to 10.1.2.1, timeout is 2 seconds:
!!!!!
Success rate is 100 percent (5/5), round-trip min/avg/max = 1/1/4 ms
Type escape sequence to abort.
```

```
Sending 5, 100-byte ICMP Echos to 10.1.3.1, timeout is 2 seconds:
!!!!!
Success rate is 100 percent (5/5), round-trip min/avg/max = 1/1/4 ms
Type escape sequence to abort.
Sending 5, 100-byte ICMP Echos to 10.1.123.1, timeout is 2 seconds:
!!!!!
Success rate is 100 percent (5/5), round-trip min/avg/max = 1/2/4 ms
Type escape sequence to abort.
Sending 5, 100-byte ICMP Echos to 10.1.123.2, timeout is 2 seconds:
!!!!!
Success rate is 0 percent (0/5)
Type escape sequence to abort.
Sending 5, 100-byte ICMP Echos to 10.1.123.3, timeout is 2 seconds:
!!!!!
Success rate is 100 percent (5/5), round-trip min/avg/max = 1/1/4 ms
Type escape sequence to abort.
Sending 5, 100-byte ICMP Echos to 10.1.23.2, timeout is 2 seconds:
!!!!!
Success rate is 100 percent (5/5), round-trip min/avg/max = 1/1/4 ms
Type escape sequence to abort.
Sending 5, 100-byte ICMP Echos to 10.1.23.3, timeout is 2 seconds:
!!!!!
Success rate is 100 percent (5/5), round-trip min/avg/max = 1/2/4 ms

WEST# tclsh
WEST(tcl)#
WEST(tcl)# foreach address {
+>10.1.1.1
+>10.1.2.1
+>10.1.3.1
+>10.1.123.1
+>10.1.123.2
+>10.1.123.3
+>10.1.23.2
+>10.1.23.3
+>} {
+>ping $address }

Type escape sequence to abort.
Sending 5, 100-byte ICMP Echos to 10.1.1.1, timeout is 2 seconds:
!!!!!
Success rate is 100 percent (5/5), round-trip min/avg/max = 4/4/4 ms
```

```
Type escape sequence to abort.
Sending 5, 100-byte ICMP Echos to 10.1.2.1, timeout is 2 seconds:
!!!!!
Success rate is 100 percent (5/5), round-trip min/avg/max = 1/3/4 ms
Type escape sequence to abort.
Sending 5, 100-byte ICMP Echos to 10.1.3.1, timeout is 2 seconds:
!!!!!
Success rate is 100 percent (5/5), round-trip min/avg/max = 1/1/4 ms
Type escape sequence to abort.
Sending 5, 100-byte ICMP Echos to 10.1.123.1, timeout is 2 seconds:
!!!!!
Success rate is 100 percent (5/5), round-trip min/avg/max = 1/3/4 ms
Type escape sequence to abort.
Sending 5, 100-byte ICMP Echos to 10.1.123.2, timeout is 2 seconds:
!!!!!
Success rate is 100 percent (5/5), round-trip min/avg/max = 1/3/4 ms
Type escape sequence to abort.
Sending 5, 100-byte ICMP Echos to 10.1.123.3, timeout is 2 seconds:
!!!!!
Success rate is 0 percent (0/5)
Type escape sequence to abort.
Sending 5, 100-byte ICMP Echos to 10.1.23.2, timeout is 2 seconds:
!!!!!
Success rate is 100 percent (5/5), round-trip min/avg/max = 1/1/4 ms
Type escape sequence to abort.
Sending 5, 100-byte ICMP Echos to 10.1.23.3, timeout is 2 seconds:
!!!!!
Success rate is 100 percent (5/5), round-trip min/avg/max = 1/1/4 ms
```

Lab 3-6: OSPF Challenge Lab (3.11.5)

Implement the topology diagram in Figure 3-6 based on the following requirements:

- Configure all interfaces shown in the diagram with the IP addresses shown.

- Configure Open Shortest Path First (OSPF) with interfaces in the areas shown in the diagram.

- All IP addresses in the diagram must be reachable from every router.

- Have R2 summarize Area 20 with the most specific mask possible.

- The link between R1 and R2 should have the OSPF network type of broadcast, with R1 as the DR.

- R1 should always originate a default route.

- The link between R2 and R3 should have hello and dead timers that are double the default values.

- The link between R2 and R3 should have a link cost of 500.

- Area 34 should be a totally stubby area.

- Use Message Digest 5 (MD5) authentication over the link between R3 and R4 using **cisco** as a password.

- There is a hidden issue in the topology that you will need to correct in order to have full connectivity.

Figure 3-6   Topology Diagram

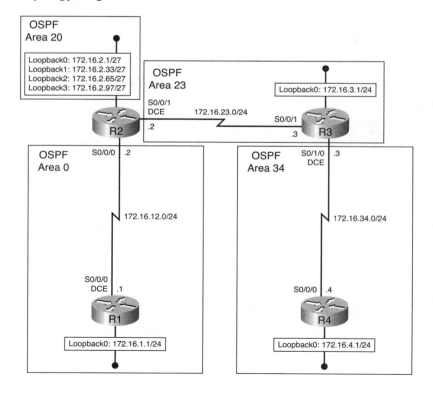

Lab 3-7: OSPF Troubleshooting Lab (3.11.6)

In this lab, you will troubleshoot existing configurations to get a working topology. Cut and paste the Initial Configurations from this lab into your four routers. Some of these configurations are correct. Some of these configurations are intentionally wrong. Your goal is to use troubleshooting techniques to fix anything in the scenario that prevents full IP connectivity. Full IP connectivity means every address in the scenario should be reachable from every router. If you don't know where to start, try pinging remote addresses and see which ones are reachable (either manually performing pings or using a TCL script).

The requirements for this lab are as follows:

- Use the IP addressing scheme shown in Figure 3-7.

- All routers must participate in OSPF.

- All interfaces must be in the OSPF areas shown in the diagram.

- Do not use static routes, default routes, or other routing protocols.

- All IP addresses in the topology must be reachable from all routers.

- The OSPF network type for the link between R2 and R3 is non-broadcast.

Figure 3-7   Topology Diagram

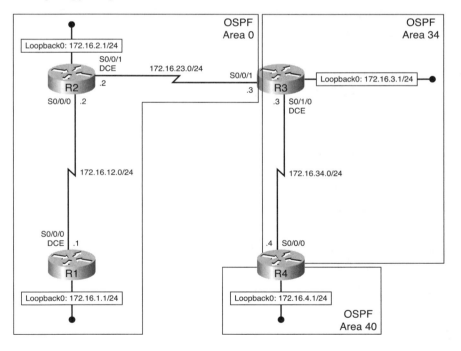

Initial Configurations

You can download these router configurations at www.ciscopress.com/title/1587132133 under the
More Information section on the page.

```
R1# show run
hostname R1
!
interface Loopback0
 ip address 172.16.1.1 255.255.255.0
!
interface Serial0/0/0
 ip address 172.16.12.1 255.255.255.0
 clock rate 64000
 no shutdown
!
router ospf 1
 network 172.16.1.0 0.0.0.255 area 0
 network 172.16.12.2 0.0.0.0 area 0
end
```

```
R2# show run
hostname R2
!
interface Loopback0
 ip address 172.16.2.1 255.255.255.0
!
interface Serial0/0/0
 ip address 172.16.12.2 255.255.255.0
 no shutdown
!
interface Serial0/0/1
 ip address 172.16.23.2 255.255.255.0
 ip ospf network non-broadcast
 clock rate 64000
 no shutdown
!
router ospf 1
 network 172.16.2.0 0.0.0.255 area 0
 network 172.16.12.0 0.0.0.255 area 0
 network 172.16.23.0 0.0.0.255 area 0
end
```

```
R3# show run
hostname R3
!
interface Loopback0
```

```
  ip address 172.16.3.1 255.255.255.0
!
interface Serial0/0/1
  ip address 172.16.23.3 255.255.255.0
  ip ospf network non-broadcast
  no shutdown
!
interface Serial0/1/0
  ip address 172.16.34.3 255.255.255.0
  clock rate 64000
  no shutdown
!
router ospf 1
  area 34 virtual-link 172.16.4.1
  network 172.16.3.0 0.0.0.255 area 34
  network 172.16.23.0 0.0.0.255 area 0
  network 172.16.34.0 0.0.0.255 area 34
end
```

```
R4# show run
hostname R4
!
interface Loopback0
  ip address 172.16.4.1 255.255.255.0
!
interface Serial0/0/0
  ip address 172.16.34.4 255.255.255.0
  no shutdown
!
router ospf 1
  area 34 virtual-link 172.16.34.3
  network 172.16.4.0 0.0.0.255 area 40
  network 172.16.34.0 0.0.0.255 area 34
end
```

Lab 4-1: Configuring Basic Integrated IS-IS (4.7.1)

The objectives of this lab are as follows:

- Configure and verify the operation of Integrated IS-IS on a router

- Configure a NET identifying a domain, area, and intermediate system

- Configure and verify Level 1 and Level 2 IS-IS adjacencies

- Verify and understand the IS-IS topology table

- Manipulate IS-IS adjacency timers

- Implement IS-IS domain and link authentication

Figure 4-1 illustrates the topology that will be used for this lab.

Figure 4-1   Topology Diagram

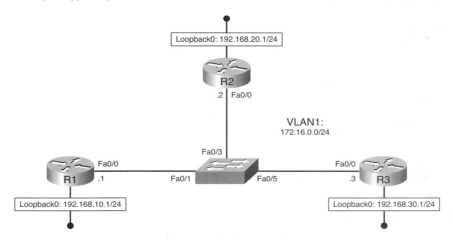

Scenario

The Intermediate System-to-Intermediate System (IS-IS) routing protocol has become increasingly popular with widespread usage among service providers. The International Travel Agency is considering implementing IS-IS because it is a link-state protocol that enables very fast convergence with large scalability and flexibility. But before making a final decision, management wants a nonproduction network set up to test the IS-IS routing protocol.

The backbone of the production ITA WAN consists of three routers connected by an Ethernet core. Because the routers are also connected to the Internet, authentication is needed to prevent unauthorized routers from participating in the IS-IS process.

Step 1: Addressing and Basic Connectivity

Build and configure the network according to the diagram, but do not configure IS-IS yet. Configure loopback interfaces and addresses as well.

Use **ping** to test connectivity between the directly connected Fast Ethernet interfaces. You could alternatively use the following Toolkit Command Language (TCL) script to ping across the Fast Ethernet link:

```
foreach address {
172.16.0.1
172.16.0.2
172.16.0.3 } { ping $address }
```

Step 2: Configuring Basic IS-IS

IS-IS (ISO/IEC 10589) is implemented with network service access point (NSAP) addresses consisting of three fields: area address, system ID, and NSEL (also known as N-selector, the service identifier or the process ID). The area address field can be from 1 to 13 octets, the system ID field is usually 6 octets (must be 6 for Cisco IOS Software), and the NSEL identifies a process on the device. It is a loose equivalent to a port or socket in IP. The NSEL is not used in routing decisions.

When the NSEL is set to 00, the NSAP is referred to as the network entity title (NET). NETs and NSAPs are represented in hexadecimal, and must start and end on a byte boundary, such as 49.0001.1111.1111.1111.00.

Level 1, or L1, IS-IS routing is based on system ID. Therefore, each router must have a unique system ID within the area. L1 IS-IS routing equates to intra-area routing. It is customary to use either a MAC address from the router or, for Integrated IS-IS, to code the IP address of a loopback address, for example, into the system ID.

Area addresses starting with 48, 49, 50, or 51 are private addresses. This group of addresses should not be advertised to other Connectionless Network Service (CLNS) networks. The area address must be the same for all routers in an area.

On a LAN, one of the routers is elected the designated intermediate system (DIS) based on interface priority. The default is 64. If all interface priorities are the same, the router with the highest subnetwork point of attachment (SNPA) address is selected. The (Ethernet) MAC address serves as the SNPA address for Ethernet LANs. The DIS serves the same purpose for IS-IS as the designated router does for Open Shortest Path First (OSPF) Protocol. The ITA network engineer decides that R1 is the DIS, so its priority must be set higher than R2 and R3.

Now, configure Integrated IS-IS on each router and set a priority of 100 on the FastEthernet 0/0 interface of R1 as follows:

```
R1(config)# router isis
R1(config-router)# net 49.0001.1111.1111.1111.00
R1(config-router)# interface fastethernet 0/0
R1(config-if)# ip router isis
R1(config-if)# isis priority 100
R1(config-if)# interface loopback 0
R1(config-if)# ip router isis
R2(config)# router isis
```

```
R2(config-router)# net 49.0001.2222.2222.2222.00
R2(config-router)# interface fastethernet 0/0
R2(config-if)# ip router isis
R2(config-if)# interface loopback 0
R2(config-if)# ip router isis
```

```
R3(config)# router isis
R3(config-router)# net 49.0001.3333.3333.3333.00
R3(config-router)# interface fastethernet 0/0
R3(config-if)# ip router isis
R3(config-if)# interface loopback 0
R3(config-if)# ip router isis
```

Identify parts of the NSAP/NET addresses:

Area address: _____

R1 system ID: _____

R2 system ID: _____

R3 system ID: _____

NSEL: _____

Step 3: Verifying IS-IS Adjacencies and Operation

Verify IS-IS operation using **show** commands on any of the three routers. The following is output for R1:

```
R1# show ip protocols
Routing Protocol is "isis"
  Invalid after 0 seconds, hold down 0, flushed after 0
  Outgoing update filter list for all interfaces is not set
  Incoming update filter list for all interfaces is not set
  Redistributing: isis
  Address Summarization:
    None
  Maximum path: 4
  Routing for Networks:
    FastEthernet0/0
    Loopback0
  Routing Information Sources:
    Gateway          Distance       Last Update
    192.168.30.1        115         00:00:36
    192.168.20.1        115         00:00:36
  Distance: (default is 115)
```

Because you are also working with the OSI connectionless protocol suite, use the **show clns protocols** command to see the IS-IS protocol output:

R1# **show clns protocols**

```
IS-IS Router: <Null Tag>
  System Id: 1111.1111.1111.00  IS-Type: level-1-2
  Manual area address(es):
        49.0001
  Routing for area address(es):
        49.0001
  Interfaces supported by IS-IS:
        FastEthernet0/0 - IP
        Loopback0 - IP
  Redistribute:
    static (on by default)
  Distance for L2 CLNS routes: 110
  RRR level: none
  Generate narrow metrics: level-1-2
  Accept narrow metrics:   level-1-2
  Generate wide metrics:   none
  Accept wide metrics:     none
R1#
```

Notice that the update timers are set to zero (0). Updates are not sent at regular intervals because they are event driven. The Last Update field indicates how long it has been since the last update in hours:minutes:seconds.

Issue the **show clns neighbors** command to view adjacencies:

R1# **show clns neighbors**

```
System Id     Interface   SNPA                 State   Holdtime   Type Protocol

R2            Fa0/0       0004.9ad2.d0c0       Up      9          L1L2 IS-IS
R3            Fa0/0       0002.16f4.1ba0       Up      29         L1L2 IS-IS
```

Neighbor ISs (intermediate systems) and neighbor ESs (end systems) are shown, if applicable. You can use the keyword **detail** to display comprehensive neighbor information:

R1# **show clns neighbors detail**

```
System Id     Interface   SNPA                 State   Holdtime   Type Protocol
R2            Fa0/0       0004.9ad2.d0c0       Up      24         L1L2 IS-IS
  Area Address(es): 49.0001
  IP Address(es):  172.16.0.2*
  Uptime: 00:07:30
  NSF capable
```

```
R3              Fa0/0        0002.16f4.1ba0      Up      27          L1L2 IS-IS
  Area Address(es): 49.0001
  IP Address(es):  172.16.0.3*
  Uptime: 00:07:00
  NSF capable
```

The system IDs of the IS neighbors are the hostnames of the respective neighbor routers. Starting with Cisco IOS Release 12.0(5), Cisco routers support dynamic hostname mapping. The feature is enabled by default. As seen in the sample output, the configured system ID of 2222.2222.2222 has been replaced by the hostname R2. Similarly, R3 replaces 3333.3333.3333.

The adjacency Type for both neighbors is L1L2. By default, Cisco IOS enables both L1 and L2 adjacency negotiation on IS-IS routers. You can use the router configuration mode command **is-type** or the interface configuration command **isis circuit-type** to specify how the router operates for L1 and L2 routing.

You can use the **show isis database** and **show clns interface fa0/0** commands to obtain DIS and related information. First, issue the **clear isis *** command on all routers to force IS-IS to refresh its link-state databases and recalculate all routes. A minute or two may be needed for all routers to update their respective IS-IS databases:

```
R1# clear isis *
```
```
R2# clear isis *
```
```
R3# clear isis *
```

Issue the **show isis database** command to view the content of the IS-IS database:

```
R1# show isis database
```

```
IS-IS Level-1 Link State Database:
LSPID           LSP Seq Num  LSP Checksum  LSP Holdtime    ATT/P/OL
R1.00-00      * 0x00000008   0x088F        1191            0/0/0
R1.01-00      * 0x00000002   0x9B60        1192            0/0/0
R2.00-00        0x00000001   0x8736        1190            0/0/0
R3.00-00        0x00000002   0x39A1        1195            0/0/0
IS-IS Level-2 Link State Database:
LSPID           LSP Seq Num  LSP Checksum  LSP Holdtime    ATT/P/OL
R1.00-00      * 0x00000017   0x4E1B        1195            0/0/0
R1.01-00      * 0x00000002   0x4D37        1192            0/0/0
R2.00-00        0x00000010   0xF4B9        1191            0/0/0
R3.00-00        0x00000002   0xD703        1195            0/0/0
```

IS-IS retains a separate database for L1 and L2 routing. Because IS-IS is a link-state protocol, the link-state database should be the same for the three routers.

As discussed earlier, if the priority for R1's FastEthernet 0/0 interface had not been increased, the DIS would have been elected on the basis of the highest SNPA. DIS election is preemptive, unlike OSPF behavior. The **isis priority 100** command ensured that R1 would be elected the DIS, regardless of router boot order. But how can it be determined from the **show isis database** output that R1 is indeed the DIS?

_____

_____

Look at the entries under the link-state protocol data unit ID (LSPID) column. The first six octets form the system ID. As mentioned earlier, because of the dynamic host mapping feature, the respective router names are listed instead of the numerical system ID. Following the system ID are two octets.

The first octet is the pseudonode ID, representing a LAN. The pseudonode ID is used to distinguish LAN IDs on the same DIS. When this value is nonzero, the associated LSP is a pseudonode link-state packet (LSP) originating from the DIS. The DIS is the only system that originates pseudonode LSPs. The DIS creates one pseudonode LSP for L1 and one for L2, as shown in the previous output.

The pseudonode ID varies upon reboot of the router as a function of the creation or deletion of virtual interfaces, such as loopback interfaces. The system ID and pseudonode ID together are referred to as the circuit ID. An example is R1.01.

A non-pseudonode LSP represents a router and is distinguished by the fact that the 2-byte value in the circuit ID is 00.

The second octet forms the LSP fragmentation number. The value 00 indicates that all data fits into a single LSP. If there had been more information that did not fit into the first LSP, IS-IS would have created additional LSPs with increasing LSP numbers, such as 01, 02, and so on. The asterisk (*) indicates that the LSP was originated by the local system.

Issue the **show clns interface fastethernet 0/0** command:

```
R1# show clns interface fastethernet 0/0
FastEthernet0/0 is up, line protocol is up
  Checksums enabled, MTU 1497, Encapsulation SAP
  ERPDUs enabled, min. interval 10 msec.
  CLNS fast switching enabled
  CLNS SSE switching disabled
  DEC compatibility mode OFF for this interface
  Next ESH/ISH in 8 seconds
  Routing Protocol: IS-IS
    Circuit Type: level-1-2
    Interface number 0x0, local circuit ID 0x1
    Level-1 Metric: 10, Priority: 100, Circuit ID: R1.01
    DR ID: R1.01
    Level-1 IPv6 Metric: 10
    Number of active level-1 adjacencies: 2
    Level-2 Metric: 10, Priority: 100, Circuit ID: R1.01
    DR ID: R1.01
```

```
Level-2 IPv6 Metric: 10
Number of active level-2 adjacencies: 2
Next IS-IS LAN Level-1 Hello in 803 milliseconds
Next IS-IS LAN Level-2 Hello in 2 seconds
```

Notice that the circuit ID, R1.01, which is made up of the system and pseudonode IDs, identifies the DIS. Circuit Types, Levels, Metric, and Priority information is also displayed.

You can obtain additional information about a specific LSP ID by appending the LSP ID and **detail** keyword to the **show isis database** command, as shown in the output. The hostname is case sensitive. You can also use this command to view the IS-IS database of a neighbor router by including its hostname in the command:

```
R1# show isis database R1.00-00 detail
IS-IS Level-1 LSP R1.00-00
LSPID               LSP Seq Num   LSP Checksum   LSP Holdtime      ATT/P/OL
R1.00-00        *  0x0000000B    0x0292         831               0/0/0
  Area Address: 49.0001
  NLPID:        0xCC
  Hostname: R1
  IP Address:   192.168.10.1
  Metric: 10         IP 172.16.0.0 255.255.255.0
  Metric: 10         IP 192.168.10.0 255.255.255.0
  Metric: 10         IS R1.02
  Metric: 10         IS R1.01


IS-IS Level-2 LSP R1.00-00
LSPID               LSP Seq Num   LSP Checksum   LSP Holdtime      ATT/P/OL
R1.00-00        *  0x0000000D    0x4703         709               0/0/0
  Area Address: 49.0001
  NLPID:        0xCC
  Hostname: R1
  IP Address:   192.168.10.1
  Metric: 10         IS R1.02
  Metric: 10         IS R1.01
  Metric: 20         IP 192.168.30.0 255.255.255.0
  Metric: 10         IP 192.168.10.0 255.255.255.0
  Metric: 10         IP 172.16.0.0 255.255.255.0
  Metric: 20         IP 192.168.20.0 255.255.255.0
```

The default IS-IS metric for every link is 10, but notice that the metrics for the 192.168.20.0 and 192.168.30.0 networks are both 20. This is because the networks are not directly connected, but are directly connected to neighbor routers.

Issue the **show isis topology** command to display the paths to the other intermediate systems:

```
R1# show isis topology
```

```
IS-IS paths to level-1 routers

System Id     Metric    Next-Hop       Interface     SNPA
R1            --
R2            10        R2             Fa0/0         0004.9ad2.d0c0
R3            10        R3             Fa0/0         0002.16f4.1ba0


IS-IS paths to level-2 routers

System Id     Metric    Next-Hop       Interface     SNPA
R1            --
R2            10        R2             Fa0/0         0004.9ad2.d0c0
R3            10        R3             Fa0/0         0002.16f4.1ba0
```

The highlighted entries in the SNPA column are the MAC addresses of the R2 and R3 FastEthernet 0/0 interfaces.

Issue the **show isis route** command to view the IS-IS L1 routing table:

```
R1# show isis route


IS-IS not running in OSI mode (*) (only calculating IP routes)


(*) Use "show isis topology" command to display paths to all routers
```

This command has no useful output because it is specific to OSI routing. Remember, IP IS-IS was enabled on each router. If CLNP were configured in the network, more interesting output would appear.

Issue the **show clns route** command to view the IS-IS L2 routing table:

```
R1# show clns route
Codes: C - connected, S - static, d - DecnetIV
       I - ISO-IGRP,  i - IS-IS,  e - ES-IS
       B - BGP,       b - eBGP-neighbor


C  49.0001.1111.1111.1111.00 [1/0], Local IS-IS NET
C  49.0001 [2/0], Local IS-IS Area
```

Again, there is no useful output because this command applies to OSI routing and not IP routing.

Issue the **show ip route** command to view the IP routing table:

```
R1# show ip route
<output omitted>


Gateway of last resort is not set
```

```
 i L1 192.168.30.0/24 [115/20] via 172.16.0.3, FastEthernet0/0
C    192.168.10.0/24 is directly connected, Loopback0
     172.16.0.0/24 is subnetted, 1 subnets
C       172.16.0.0 is directly connected, FastEthernet0/0
 i L1 192.168.20.0/24 [115/20] via 172.16.0.2, FastEthernet0/0
```

Notice how the routes to the 192.168.30.0 and 192.168.20.0 networks were learned.

The **show clns neighbors, show isis database, show clns interface, show isis topology, show isis route**, and **show clns route** commands illustrate the somewhat confusing nature of IS-IS verification and troubleshooting. There is no clear pattern as to whether incorporation of the keyword **isis** or **clns** in a **show** command applies to IP routing or to OSI routing.

Step 4: Converting to the IS-IS Backbone

L1 routers communicate with other L1 routers in the same area, while L2 routers route between L1 areas, forming an interdomain routing backbone. This lab scenario does not illustrate the typical multi-area composition of the set of L2 routers in an IS-IS domain, because the routers all reside in area 49.0001. Since the main function of the San Jose routers is to route between areas in the ITA internetwork, they should be configured as L2-only routers as follows:

```
R1(config)# router isis
R1(config-router)# is-type level-2-only
```

```
R2(config)# router isis
R2(config-router)# is-type level-2-only
```

```
R3(config)# router isis
R3(config-router)# is-type level-2-only
```

To see the effect of the **is-type** command, reenter the previous commands: **show ip protocols, show clns neighbors, show isis database, show clns interface fastethernet 0/0, show isis database R1.00-00 detail, show isis topology**, and **show ip route**. Here is the sample output:

```
R1# show ip protocols
Routing Protocol is "isis"
  Invalid after 0 seconds, hold down 0, flushed after 0
  Outgoing update filter list for all interfaces is not set
  Incoming update filter list for all interfaces is not set
  Redistributing: isis
  Address Summarization:
    None
  Maximum path: 4
  Routing for Networks:
    Loopback0
    FastEthernet0/0
  Routing Information Sources:
    Gateway         Distance      Last Update
    192.168.30.1         115      00:08:48
    192.168.20.1         115      00:00:09
```

```
        Distance: (default is 115)


R1# show clns neighbors


System Id    Interface    SNPA            State  Holdtime  Type  Protocol
R2           Fa0/0        0004.9ad2.d0c0  Up     26        L2    IS-IS
R3           Fa0/0        0002.16f4.1ba0  Up     22        L2    IS-IS


R1# show isis database


IS-IS Level-2 Link State Database:
LSPID           LSP Seq Num   LSP Checksum  LSP Holdtime   ATT/P/OL
R1.00-00      * 0x00000001    0x623C        1086           0/0/0
R1.01-00      * 0x0000000F    0x3344        1092           0/0/0
R2.00-00        0x00000001    0x13AA        1091           0/0/0
R3.00-00        0x00000002    0xD703        1096           0/0/0
```

If the LSP ID is seen with an LSP Holdtime of 0 followed by a parenthetical value, that rogue entry can be purged with the **clear isis *** command:

```
R1# show clns interface fastethernet 0/0
FastEthernet0/0 is up, line protocol is up
  Checksums enabled, MTU 1497, Encapsulation SAP
  ERPDUs enabled, min. interval 10 msec.
  CLNS fast switching enabled
  CLNS SSE switching disabled
  DEC compatibility mode OFF for this interface
  Next ESH/ISH in 16 seconds
  Routing Protocol: IS-IS
    Circuit Type: level-1-2
    DR ID: R1.02
    Level-2 IPv6 Metric: 10
    Interface number 0x0, local circuit ID 0x1
    Level-2 Metric: 10, Priority: 100, Circuit ID: R1.01
    Number of active level-2 adjacencies: 2
    Next IS-IS LAN Level-2 Hello in 2 seconds
```

Even though the Circuit Type is level-1-2, the entries following the Circuit Type show that only L2 operations are taking place:

```
R1# show isis database R1.00-00 detail


IS-IS Level-2 LSP R1.00-00
LSPID           LSP Seq Num   LSP Checksum  LSP Holdtime   ATT/P/OL
R1.00-00      * 0x00000001    0x623C        892            0/0/0
```

```
Area Address: 49.0001
NLPID:        0xCC
Hostname: R1
IP Address:   192.168.10.1
Metric: 10          IS R1.02
Metric: 10          IS R1.01
Metric: 10          IP 192.168.10.0 255.255.255.0
Metric: 10          IP 172.16.0.0 255.255.255.0
```

The output shows that the IDs, R1.02 and R1.01, are used to number the router interfaces participating in IS-IS:

R1# **show isis topology**

```
IS-IS paths to level-2 routers
System Id    Metric   Next-Hop        Interface    SNPA
R1           - -
R2           10       R2              Fa0/0        0004.9ad2.d0c0
R3           10       R3              Fa0/0        0002.16f4.1ba0
```

R1# **show ip route**

```
<output omitted>

Gateway of last resort is not set

i L2 192.168.30.0/24 [115/20] via 172.16.0.3, FastEthernet0/0
C    192.168.10.0/24 is directly connected, Loopback0
     172.16.0.0/24 is subnetted, 1 subnets
C       172.16.0.0 is directly connected, FastEthernet0/0
i L2 192.168.20.0/24 [115/20] via 172.16.0.2, FastEthernet0/0
```

This is also seen in the **show clns interface** output.

What types of routes are being placed into the routing table?

Step 5: Manipulating the IS-IS Interface Timers

The default value of the hello interval is 10 seconds, and the default value of the hello multiplier is 3. The hello multiplier specifies the number of IS-IS hello protocol data units (PDU) a neighbor must miss before the router declares the adjacency as down. With the default hello interval of 10 seconds, it takes 30 seconds for an adjacency to be declared down due to missed hello PDUs. The analogous OSPF settings are controlled by the **ip ospf hello-interval** and **ip ospf dead-interval** interface commands.

A decision is made to adjust the IS-IS timers so that the core routers detect network failures in less time. This will increase traffic, but this is much less of a concern on the high-speed core Ethernet segment than on a busy WAN link. It is determined that the need for quick convergence on the core outweighs the negative effect of extra control traffic. Change the hello interval on each router to 5 on each FastEthernet 0/0 interface:

```
R1(config)# interface fastethernet 0/0
R1(config-if)# isis hello-interval 5
R2(config)# interface fastethernet 0/0
R2(config-if)# isis hello-interval 5
R3(config)# interface fastethernet 0/0
R3(config-if)# isis hello-interval 5
```

How long will it take for an adjacency to be declared down with the new hello interval of 5?

Step 6: Implementing IS-IS L2 Core Authentication

There should not be any unauthorized routers forming adjacencies within the IS-IS core. Adding authentication to each IS-IS enabled interface can help to ensure this.

Configure interface authentication on R1:

```
R1(config)# interface FastEthernet 0/0
R1(config-if)# isis password cisco level-2
```

This command prevents unauthorized routers from forming L2 adjacencies with this router.

Important   Be sure to add the keyword **level-2**, which refers to the L2 database, not an encryption level. If you do not specify a keyword, the default is L1. Keep in mind that the passwords are exchanged in clear text and provide only limited security.

Wait 20 seconds and then issue the **show clns neighbors** command on R1.

Does R1 still show that it has IS-IS neighbors? Why or why not?

Issue the **debug isis adj-packets** command to verify that R1 does not recognize its neighbors, because it requires authentication that has not been configured on R2 and R3 yet:

```
R1# debug isis adj-packets
IS-IS Adjacency related packets debugging is on
03:22:28: ISIS-Adj: Sending L2 LAN IIH on FastEthernet0/0, length 1497
03:22:29: ISIS-Adj: Sending L2 LAN IIH on Loopback0, length 1514
03:22:30: ISIS-Adj: Sending L2 LAN IIH on FastEthernet0/0, length 1497
03:22:31: ISIS-Adj: Rec L2 IIH from 0004.9ad2.d0c0 (FastEthernet0/0), cir type L2,
    cir id 1111.1111.1111.01, length 1497
03:22:31: ISIS-Adj: Authentication failed
```

IS-IS routers do not communicate unless the authentication parameters match. However, many other interface-specific IS-IS parameters can vary on a given segment without disrupting communication, such as those set by the commands **isis hello-interval**, **isis hello-multiplier**, **isis retransmit-interval**, **isis retransmit-throttle-interval**, and **isis csnp-interval**. Of course, it makes sense for these parameters to coincide on a given segment.

Correct the authentication mismatch by configuring interface authentication on R2 and R3. After the configurations are complete, verify that the routers can communicate by using the **show clns neighbors** command on R1:

```
R2(config)# interface FastEthernet 0/0
R2(config-if)# isis password cisco level-2


R3(config)# interface FastEthernet 0/0
R3(config-if)# isis password cisco level-2


R1# show clns neighbors


System Id Interface  SNPA             State  Holdtime  Type Protocol
R2        Fa0/0      0004.9ad2.d0c0   Up     23        L2   IS-IS
R3        Fa0/0      0002.16f4.1ba0   Up     26        L2   IS-IS
```

In time, the system IDs resolve to the router names. This is done through the dynamic hostname mapping feature automatically enabled on Cisco routers. In the interim, the output may appear with the actual numerical ID for that system.

Step 7: Implementing IS-IS Domain Authentication

IS-IS provides two additional layers of authentication, area passwords for L1 and domain passwords for L2, to prevent unauthorized adjacencies between routers. The interface, area, and domain password options all use plain text authentication and, therefore, are of limited use. However, beginning with Cisco IOS Release 12.2(13)T, message digest algorithm 5 (MD5) authentication is available for IS-IS.

The command for L1 password authentication is **area-password password**. Using this command on all routers in an area prevents unauthorized routers from injecting false routing information into the L1 database.

The command for L2 password authentication is **domain-password password**. Using this command on all L2 routers in a domain prevents unauthorized routers from injecting false routing information into the L2 database. Because the core routers are operating at L2, implement domain password authentication as follows:

```
R1(config)# router isis
R1(config-router)# domain-password cisco
```

The password is case-sensitive. Time permitting, intentionally configure mismatched interface passwords. Do the same for area and domain passwords. By seeing the way in which the router responds, it will be easier for you to spot this error when you unintentionally mismatch passwords in a production network.

Refresh the IS-IS link-state database and recalculate all routes using the **clear isis *** command on all routers. It might take a minute or two for all routers to update their databases:

```
All_Router# clear isis *
```

Use the **show isis database** command to view the changes to the R1 link-state database:

```
R1# show isis database
```

```
IS-IS Level-2 Link State Database:
LSPID           LSP Seq Num  LSP Checksum  LSP Holdtime    ATT/P/OL
R1.00-00      * 0x00000004   0xDCB5        1155            0/0/0
R1.01-00      * 0x00000007   0xB4C1        1156            0/0/0
```

Change the other routers to reflect the new authentication policy:

```
R2(config)# router isis
R2(config-router)# domain-password cisco
R3(config)# router isis
R3(config-router)# domain-password cisco
```

View the R1 link-state database to verify that the LSPs were propagated:

```
R1# show isis database
```

```
IS-IS Level-2 Link State Database:
LSPID           LSP Seq Num  LSP Checksum  LSP Holdtime    ATT/P/OL
R1.00-00      * 0x00000001   0xE2B2        1189            0/0/0
R1.01-00      * 0x00000002   0xBEBC        1195            0/0/0
R2.00-00        0x00000002   0x5A59        1190            0/0/0
R3.00-00        0x00000002   0xF3DD        1185            0/0/0
```

The configuration of basic Integrated IS-IS routing protocol is now complete. In addition to enabling Integrated IS-IS, L2-specific routing was enabled, and the hello interval was changed to enable IS-IS to detect network failures faster. Two types of password authentication, interface and domain, were enabled to prevent unauthorized routers from forming adjacencies with these core routers.

Run the TCL script to verify full connectivity after implementing L2 authentication. You can download this TCL script at www.ciscopress.com/title/1587132133 under the More Information section on the page.

```
foreach address {
192.168.10.1
172.16.0.1
192.168.20.1
172.16.0.2
192.168.30.1
172.16.0.3 } { ping $address }
```

Save the R1 and R2 configurations for use with the next lab.

TCL Script Output

```
R1# tclsh
R1(tcl)# foreach address {
+>(tcl)# 192.168.10.1
+>(tcl)# 172.16.0.1
+>(tcl)# 192.168.20.1
+>(tcl)# 172.16.0.2
+>(tcl)# 192.168.30.1
+>(tcl)# 172.16.0.3 } { ping $address }

Type escape sequence to abort.
Sending 5, 100-byte ICMP Echos to 192.168.10.1, timeout is 2 seconds:
!!!!!
Success rate is 100 percent (5/5), round-trip min/avg/max = 1/1/4 ms
Type escape sequence to abort.
Sending 5, 100-byte ICMP Echos to 172.16.0.1, timeout is 2 seconds:
!!!!!
Success rate is 100 percent (5/5), round-trip min/avg/max = 1/1/1 ms
Type escape sequence to abort.
Sending 5, 100-byte ICMP Echos to 192.168.20.1, timeout is 2 seconds:
!!!!!
Success rate is 100 percent (5/5), round-trip min/avg/max = 1/1/4 ms
Type escape sequence to abort.
Sending 5, 100-byte ICMP Echos to 172.16.0.2, timeout is 2 seconds:
!!!!!
Success rate is 100 percent (5/5), round-trip min/avg/max = 1/1/4 ms
Type escape sequence to abort.
Sending 5, 100-byte ICMP Echos to 192.168.30.1, timeout is 2 seconds:
!!!!!
Success rate is 100 percent (5/5), round-trip min/avg/max = 1/1/4 ms
Type escape sequence to abort.
Sending 5, 100-byte ICMP Echos to 172.16.0.3, timeout is 2 seconds:
!!!!!
Success rate is 100 percent (5/5), round-trip min/avg/max = 1/1/1 ms
R1(tcl)#  tclquit
R2# tclsh
R2(tcl)# foreach address {
+>(tcl)# 192.168.10.1
+>(tcl)# 172.16.0.1
+>(tcl)# 192.168.20.1
+>(tcl)# 172.16.0.2
+>(tcl)# 192.168.30.1
+>(tcl)# 172.16.0.3 } { ping $address }
```

```
Type escape sequence to abort.
Sending 5, 100-byte ICMP Echos to 192.168.10.1, timeout is 2 seconds:
!!!!!
Success rate is 100 percent (5/5), round-trip min/avg/max = 1/2/4 ms
Type escape sequence to abort.
Sending 5, 100-byte ICMP Echos to 172.16.0.1, timeout is 2 seconds:
!!!!!
Success rate is 100 percent (5/5), round-trip min/avg/max = 1/2/4 ms
Type escape sequence to abort.
Sending 5, 100-byte ICMP Echos to 192.168.20.1, timeout is 2 seconds:
!!!!!
Success rate is 100 percent (5/5), round-trip min/avg/max = 1/1/1 ms
Type escape sequence to abort.
Sending 5, 100-byte ICMP Echos to 172.16.0.2, timeout is 2 seconds:
!!!!!
Success rate is 100 percent (5/5), round-trip min/avg/max = 1/1/4 ms
Type escape sequence to abort.
Sending 5, 100-byte ICMP Echos to 192.168.30.1, timeout is 2 seconds:
!!!!!
Success rate is 100 percent (5/5), round-trip min/avg/max = 1/1/4 ms
Type escape sequence to abort.
Sending 5, 100-byte ICMP Echos to 172.16.0.3, timeout is 2 seconds:
!!!!!
Success rate is 100 percent (5/5), round-trip min/avg/max = 1/1/4 ms
R2(tcl)#  tclquit
```

```
Type escape sequence to abort.
Sending 5, 100-byte ICMP Echos to 192.168.10.1, timeout is 2 seconds:
!!!!!
Success rate is 100 percent (5/5), round-trip min/avg/max = 1/2/4 ms
Type escape sequence to abort.
Sending 5, 100-byte ICMP Echos to 172.16.0.1, timeout is 2 seconds:
!!!!!
Success rate is 100 percent (5/5), round-trip min/avg/max = 1/2/4 ms
Type escape sequence to abort.
Sending 5, 100-byte ICMP Echos to 192.168.20.1, timeout is 2 seconds:
!!!!!
Success rate is 100 percent (5/5), round-trip min/avg/max = 1/2/4 ms
Type escape sequence to abort.
Sending 5, 100-byte ICMP Echos to 172.16.0.2, timeout is 2 seconds:
!!!!!
Success rate is 100 percent (5/5), round-trip min/avg/max = 1/1/4 ms
Type escape sequence to abort.
Sending 5, 100-byte ICMP Echos to 192.168.30.1, timeout is 2 seconds:
!!!!!
```

```
Success rate is 100 percent (5/5), round-trip min/avg/max = 1/1/1 ms
Type escape sequence to abort.
Sending 5, 100-byte ICMP Echos to 172.16.0.3, timeout is 2 seconds:
!!!!!
Success rate is 100 percent (5/5), round-trip min/avg/max = 1/1/4 ms
R3(tcl)# tclquit
```

Lab 4-2 Multi-Area Integrated IS-IS (4.7.2)

The objectives of this lab are as follows:

- Configure multi-area Integrated IS-IS

- Review configuration of IS-IS Level 1 and Level 2 intermediate systems

- Verify IS-IS adjacencies and view the IS-IS database

- Review IS-IS domain authentication

- Verify intra-area IS-IS operation

Figure 4-2 illustrates the topology that will be used for this lab.

Figure 4-2   Topology Diagram

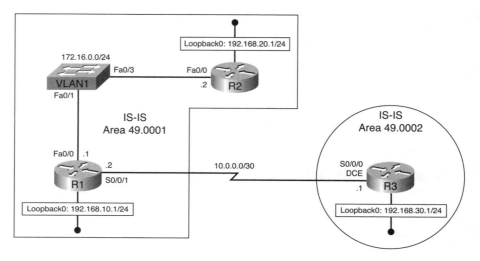

Scenario

Previous tests demonstrated that Integrated IS-IS works well with L2 routers in the International Travel Agency (ITA) Ethernet core. Management now wants to establish a point-to-point connection between a new R3 office and R1. R3 is in a different area from the core, so R2 will now be configured as an L1 router, R1 as an L1-L2 router, and R3 as an L2 router.

Start with the final configurations for R1 and R2 from the first IS-IS lab.

Step 1: Addressing and Initial Configuration

Load the R1 and R2 configurations from the previous lab. Add to the configuration of R1, the IP address for interface serial0/0/1:

```
R1(config)# interface serial 0/0/1
R1(config-if)# ip address 10.0.0.2 255.255.255.252
R1(config-if)# no shutdown
R1(config-if)# exit
```

Do not load the R3 configurations from the previous lab. You should start with a fresh configuration on R3, so clear and reload the router that is to be used as R3. Configure the IP address and clock rate on R3's serial interface. Configure the hostname, turn off Domain Name System (DNS) lookup, configure the IP address on the serial interface, and configure the loopback IP address on R3:

```
Router(config)# hostname R3
R3(config)# no ip domain-lookup
R3(config)# interface serial 0/0/0
R3(config-if)# ip address 10.0.0.1 255.255.255.252
R3(config-if)# clockrate 128000
R3(config-if)# no shutdown
R3(config-if)# interface loopback 0
R3(config-if)# ip address 192.168.30.1 255.255.255.0
```

Use **ping** to verify connectivity between the directly connected interfaces. R1 should also be able to reach the loopback address of R2 and vice versa.

Step 2: Verify IS-IS Initial Operation

Recall from Lab 4-1 that R1 was configured to be the DIS by setting the **isis priority** to 100 on the FastEthernet 0/0 interface. R1 and R2 were also configured to be L2-only routers. Verify the configuration by issuing the **show clns neighbors** and **show isis database** commands on either router:

Note   It is recommended to issue a **clear isis *** command to force IS-IS to update its database. An alternative way to force IS-IS to update its database is to save your configurations and reload the routers.

```
R1# show clns neighbors
```

System Id	Interface	SNPA	State	Holdtime	Type	Protocol
R2	Fa0/0	0004.9ad2.d0c0	Up	12	L2	IS-IS

```
R1# show isis database
```

IS-IS Level-2 Link State Database:

LSPID	LSP Seq Num	LSP Checksum	LSP Holdtime	ATT/P/OL
R1.00-00	* 0x00000014	0xBCC5	409	0/0/0
R1.01-00	* 0x00000015	0x1B0D	819	0/0/0
R2.00-00	0x00000016	0x326D	698	0/0/0

Notice that the neighbor Type is still L2. There is only one L2 link-state database, and R1 is still the DIS. LSPID R1.01-00 has a nonzero pseudonode ID. The LSPID may appear as R1.02-00, depending on the timing of the configuration of the loopback interface.

Step 3: Configure IS-IS Area 2

Configure IS-IS on R3, area 2, and on the Serial0/0/1 interface of R1:

```
R3(config)# router isis
R3(config-router)# net 49.0002.3333.3333.3333.00
R3(config-router)# interface serial 0/0/0
R3(config-if)# ip router isis
R3(config-if)# interface loopback 0
R3(config-if)# ip router isis
```
```
R1(config)# interface serial 0/0/1
R1(config-if)# ip router isis
```

Which IS-IS level is the link between R1 and R3?

Step 4: Verify IS-IS Multi-Area Operation

Verify IS-IS operation between R1 and R3 by pinging the loopback addresses on R1 and R2 from R3. The ping should be successful. Issue **show** commands on R3 as shown in the examples that follow:

```
R3# show clns neighbor
```

System Id	Interface	SNPA	State	Holdtime	Type	Protocol
R1	Se0/0/0	*HDLC*	Up	28	L2	IS-IS

Because serial interfaces do not have a MAC address, the encapsulation type for the serial link is listed in the SNPA column.

```
R3# show isis database
```

IS-IS Level-1 Link State Database:

LSPID	LSP Seq Num	LSP Checksum	LSP Holdtime	ATT/P/OL
R3.00-00	* 0x00000009	0x8FFA	1180	1/0/0

IS-IS Level-2 Link State Database:

LSPID	LSP Seq Num	LSP Checksum	LSP Holdtime	ATT/P/OL
R1.00-00	0x0000001C	0x25EC	1174	0/0/0
R1.01-00	0x00000017	0x170F	965	0/0/0
R2.00-00	0x00000018	0x2E6F	794	0/0/0
R3.00-00	* 0x00000008	0x4551	1176	0/0/0

By default, R3 is an L1-L2 router, so it retains a separate link-state database for each level. R1 is also identified as the DIS. R1 and R2 are not listed in the IS-IS L1 link-state database, because both were previously configured as L2-only routers:

```
R3# show clns interface serial 0/0/0
Serial0/0/0 is up, line protocol is up
  Checksums enabled, MTU 1500, Encapsulation HDLC
  ERPDUs enabled, min. interval 10 msec.
```

```
CLNS fast switching enabled
CLNS SSE switching disabled
DEC compatibility mode OFF for this interface
Next ESH/ISH in 26 seconds
Routing Protocol: IS-IS
  Circuit Type: level-1-2
  Interface number 0x0, local circuit ID 0x100
  Neighbor System-ID: R1
  Level-1 Metric: 10, Priority: 64, Circuit ID: R3.00
  Level-1 IPv6 Metric: 10
  Number of active level-1 adjacencies: 0
  Level-2 Metric: 10, Priority: 64, Circuit ID: R3.00
  Level-2 IPv6 Metric: 10
  Number of active level-2 adjacencies: 1
  Next IS-IS Hello in 5 seconds
  if state UP
```

Note that the circuit ID is R3.00.

From R1, **ping 192.168.30.1** on R3. The ping should not be successful:

```
R1# ping 192.168.30.1

Type escape sequence to abort.
Sending 5, 100-byte ICMP Echos to 192.168.30.1, timeout is 2 seconds:
.....
Success rate is 100 percent (5/5), round-trip min/avg/max = 1/2/4 ms
```

Why do you think the ping was unsuccessful?

Check the IP routing table of R1 and R3:

```
R1# show ip route
<output omitted>

Gateway of last resort is not set

C    192.168.10.0/24 is directly connected, FastEthernet0/1
     172.16.0.0/24 is subnetted, 1 subnets
C       172.16.0.0 is directly connected, FastEthernet0/0
i L2 192.168.20.0/24 [115/20] via 172.16.0.2, FastEthernet0/0
     10.0.0.0/30 is subnetted, 1 subnets
C       10.0.0.0 is directly connected, Serial0/0/1
```

```
R3# show ip route
<output omitted>
```

```
Gateway of last resort is not set

C    192.168.30.0/24 is directly connected, Loopback0
i L2 192.168.10.0/24 [115/20] via 10.0.0.2, Serial0/0/0
     172.16.0.0/24 is subnetted, 1 subnets
i L2    172.16.0.0 [115/20] via 10.0.0.2, Serial0/0/0
i L2 192.168.20.0/24 [115/30] via 10.0.0.2, Serial0/0/0
     10.0.0.0/30 is subnetted, 1 subnets
C       10.0.0.0 is directly connected, Serial0/0/0
```

Which IS-IS routes are missing on R1?

_____

All prior checks indicated that IS-IS was working properly between R1 and R3. However, there is no entry in the routing table for the 192.168.30.0 network. The next step will demonstrate why this is the case.

Step 5: Configure IS-IS Domain Authentication

During Step 3, you might have seen the following output message:

```
R1#
*Oct  9 23:56:53.275: %CLNS-4-AUTH_FAIL: ISIS: LSP authentication failed
```

Recall that domain password authentication was configured on both R1 and R2. If domain authentication is to be retained, R3 also needs to be configured appropriately, as follows:

```
R3(config)# router isis
R3(config-router)# domain-password cisco
```

What is this password used to authenticate?

_____

Now examine the routing table of either R1 or R2. A sample for R1 is shown here:

```
R1# show ip route
<output omitted>

Gateway of last resort is not set

i L2 192.168.30.0/24 [115/20] via 10.0.0.1, Serial0/0/1
C    192.168.10.0/24 is directly connected, FastEthernet0/1
     172.16.0.0/24 is subnetted, 1 subnets
C       172.16.0.0 is directly connected, FastEthernet0/0
i L2 192.168.20.0/24 [115/20] via 172.16.0.2, FastEthernet0/0
     10.0.0.0/30 is subnetted, 1 subnets
C       10.0.0.0 is directly connected, Serial0/0/1
```

The route to 192.168.30.0 now appears, and a ping from R1 or R2 to 192.168.30.1 should be successful:

```
R1# ping 192.168.30.1

Type escape sequence to abort.
Sending 5, 100-byte ICMP Echos to 192.168.30.1, timeout is 2 seconds:
!!!!!
Success rate is 100 percent (5/5), round-trip min/avg/max = 1/2/4 ms
```

Step 6: Reconfigure IS-IS Area 1

In the current state of configuration, to which IS-IS levels is each router speaking?

R1: _____

R2: _____

R3: L1-L2

In this topology, R1 is an L1-L2 router. However, R1 was previously configured as an L2-only router. Reconfigure R1 to be an L1-L2 router:

```
R1(config)# router isis
R1(config-router)# no is-type
R1(config-router)# ! this will set the router to its default level (L1L2)
```

or

```
R1(config-router)# is-type level-1-2
```

In this topology, R2 is an L1-only router. However, R2 was also configured as an L2-only router. Reconfigure R2 to be an L1-only router:

```
R2(config)# router isis
R2(config-router)# is-type level-1
```

Note that the **level-1** command does not use **–only**, which is required for the **is-type level-2-only** command

An interface password authentication for L2 was also configured on R1 and R2. Since R2 is now an L1-only router, making the link with R1 an L1 connection, the interface password authentication must be changed to L1:

```
R1(config)# interface fastethernet0/0
R1(config-if)# isis password cisco level-1
```

```
R2(config)# interface fastethernet0/0
R2(config-if)# isis password cisco level-1
```

Verify authentication from R1 with **ping 192.168.20.1**. The ping should be successful:

```
R1# ping 192.168.20.1
```

```
Type escape sequence to abort.
Sending 5, 100-byte ICMP Echos to 192.168.20.1, timeout is 2 seconds:
!!!!!
Success rate is 100 percent (5/5), round-trip min/avg/max = 1/2/4 ms
```

Issue the **clear isis *** command on all routers to force IS-IS to recalculate routers and to refresh its link-state databases. Wait a minute or two before issuing the **show** commands on R1 to verify that the changes were made:

```
R1# clear isis *
```

```
R1# show clns neighbors
```

System Id	Interface	SNPA	State	Holdtime	Type	Protocol
R2	Fa0/0	0004.9ad2.d0c0	Up	14	L1	IS-IS
R3	Se0/0/1	*HDLC*	Up	23	L2	IS-IS

R2 is shown as an L1 router. Although R3 is an L1-L2 router, it shows up as type L2 because of the interarea connection between R3 and R1:

```
R1# show isis database
```

IS-IS Level-1 Link State Database:

LSPID	LSP Seq Num	LSP Checksum	LSP Holdtime	ATT/P/OL
R1.00-00	* 0x00000002	0xDC22	1187	0/0/0
R1.01-00	* 0x00000002	0xBDFD	1188	0/0/0
R2.00-00	0x00000002	0x833B	1187	0/0/0

IS-IS Level-2 Link State Database:

LSPID	LSP Seq Num	LSP Checksum	LSP Holdtime	ATT/P/OL
R1.00-00	* 0x00000005	0xD732	1198	0/0/0
R3.00-00	0x00000004	0xD7B9	1193	0/0/0

The presence of L1 and L2 link-state databases confirm that R1 is now an L1-L2 router:

```
R1# show clns interface fastethernet 0/0
FastEthernet0/0 is up, line protocol is up
  Checksums enabled, MTU 1497, Encapsulation SAP
  ERPDUs enabled, min. interval 10 msec.
  CLNS fast switching enabled
  CLNS SSE switching disabled
  DEC compatibility mode OFF for this interface
  Next ESH/ISH in 36 seconds
  Routing Protocol: IS-IS
    Circuit Type: level-1-2
    Interface number 0x0, local circuit ID 0x1
    Level-1 Metric: 10, Priority: 100, Circuit ID: R1.01
    DR ID: R1.02
    Level-1 IPv6 Metric: 10
```

```
      Number of active level-1 adjacencies: 1
      Level-2 Metric: 10, Priority: 100, Circuit ID: R1.01
      DR ID: 0000.0000.0000.00
      Level-2 IPv6 Metric: 10
      Number of active level-2 adjacencies: 0
      Next IS-IS LAN Level-1 Hello in 938 milliseconds
      Next IS-IS LAN Level-2 Hello in 74 milliseconds
```

In addition to confirming that R1 is an L1-L2 router, the priority of 100 and the R1.01 circuit ID indicate that R1 is the DIS. This would be the same for R1.02, as noted in Step 2.

Issue the **show clns neighbors** command to obtain neighbor adjacency information for R2:

```
R2# show clns neighbors

System Id   Interface   SNPA            State  Holdtime  Type Protocol
R1          Fa0/0       0002.16de.3440  Up     4         L1   IS-IS
```

Although R1 is an L1-L2 router, the adjacency is an L1 connection.

```
R2# show isis database

IS-IS Level-1 Link State Database:
LSPID           LSP Seq Num    LSP Checksum  LSP Holdtime    ATT/P/OL
R1.00-00        0x0000001C     0xB02C        1024            1/0/0
R1.01-00        0x0000001C     0x8918        1112            0/0/0
R2.00-00      * 0x0000001B     0x5154        554             0/0/0
```

Only an L1 link-state database is maintained, confirming that R2 is now an L1-only router.

```
R2# show clns interface fastethernet 0/0
FastEthernet0/0 is up, line protocol is up
  Checksums enabled, MTU 1497, Encapsulation SAP
  ERPDUs enabled, min. interval 10 msec.
  CLNS fast switching enabled
  CLNS SSE switching disabled
  DEC compatibility mode OFF for this interface
  Next ESH/ISH in 41 seconds
  Routing Protocol: IS-IS
    Circuit Type: level-1-2
    Interface number 0x1, local circuit ID 0x2
    Level-1 Metric: 10, Priority: 64, Circuit ID: R1.01
    Number of active level-1 adjacencies: 1
    Next IS-IS LAN Level-1 Hello in 2 seconds
```

In addition to confirming R2 is an L1-only router, the circuit ID shows that R1 is the DIS.

Step 7: Reconfigure R3 IS-IS Operation

Issue the **show clns interface serial0/0/0** command on the R3 router:

```
R3# show clns interface serial 0/0/0
Serial0/0/0 is up, line protocol is up
  Checksums enabled, MTU 1500, Encapsulation HDLC
  ERPDUs enabled, min. interval 10 msec.
  CLNS fast switching enabled
  CLNS SSE switching disabled
  DEC compatibility mode OFF for this interface
  Next ESH/ISH in 22 seconds
  Routing Protocol: IS-IS
    Circuit Type: level-1-2
    Interface number 0x0, local circuit ID 0x100
    Neighbor System-ID: 1111.1111.1111
    Level-1 Metric: 10, Priority: 64, Circuit ID: R3.00
    Level-1 IPv6 Metric: 10
    Number of active level-1 adjacencies: 0
    Level-2 Metric: 10, Priority: 64, Circuit ID: R3.00
    Level-2 IPv6 Metric: 10
    Number of active level-2 adjacencies: 1
    Next IS-IS Hello in 6 seconds
    if state UP
```

Because R3 is presently an L1-L2 router, it maintains information for both levels. This is unnecessary, since R3 should be an L2-only router. Configure R3 for L2-only routing:

```
R3(config)# router isis
R3(config-router)# is-type level-2-only
```

Verify the configuration with the **show clns interface serial0/0/0** or **show isis database** command:

```
R3# show clns interface serial0/0/0
Serial0/0/0 is up, line protocol is up
  Checksums enabled, MTU 1500, Encapsulation HDLC
  ERPDUs enabled, min. interval 10 msec.
  CLNS fast switching enabled
  CLNS SSE switching disabled
  DEC compatibility mode OFF for this interface
  Next ESH/ISH in 24 seconds
  Routing Protocol: IS-IS
    Circuit Type: level-1-2
    Interface number 0x0, local circuit ID 0x100
    Neighbor System-ID: R1
    Level-2 Metric: 10, Priority: 64, Circuit ID: R3.00
    Level-2 IPv6 Metric: 10
    Number of active level-2 adjacencies: 1
```

```
      Next IS-IS Hello in 6 seconds
      if state UP
```

R3# **show isis database**

```
IS-IS Level-2 Link State Database:
LSPID            LSP Seq Num  LSP Checksum  LSP Holdtime    ATT/P/OL
R1.00-00         0x00000021   0x9F4E        1117            0/0/0
R3.00-00       * 0x00000021   0x9DD6        1119            0/0/0
```

Both outputs show only L2 information, confirming R3 is now an L2-only router.

A successful ping from R3 to 192.168.20.1 indicates that multi-area Integrated IS-IS with authentication has been properly configured:

R3# **ping 192.168.20.1**

```
Type escape sequence to abort.
Sending 5, 100-byte ICMP Echos to 192.168.20.1, timeout is 2 seconds:
!!!!!
Success rate is 100 percent (5/5), round-trip min/avg/max = 12/15/16 ms
```

Step 8: Verify IS-IS Intra-Area Operation

Issue the **show ip route** command on R2:

R2# **show ip route**

```
<output omitted>

Gateway of last resort is 172.16.0.1 to network 0.0.0.0

i L1 192.168.10.0/24 [115/20] via 172.16.0.1, FastEthernet0/0
     172.16.0.0/24 is subnetted, 1 subnets
C       172.16.0.0 is directly connected, FastEthernet0/0
C     192.168.20.0/24 is directly connected, Loopback0
     10.0.0.0/30 is subnetted, 1 subnets
i L1    10.0.0.0 [115/20] via 172.16.0.1, FastEthernet0/0
i*L1 0.0.0.0/0 [115/10] via 172.16.0.1, FastEthernet0/0
```

The R2 routing table shown would have included an entry for 192.168.30.0 as an L2 route if R2 had been left as an L2-only router. However, since it was changed to an L1-only router, it no longer has any L2 routes.

Note that the gateway of last resort has been set in the R2 routing table. L1-only routers, such as R2, always learn a default route from a neighboring L1-L2 router. In this case it was R1. This is a standard operating procedure for Integrated IS-IS. R2 learns to exit area 49.0001 via R1 because the attached bit (ATT) is set in the L1 non-pseudonode LSP sent by R1.

Issue the **show isis database** command on R2:

```
R2# show isis database

IS-IS Level-1 Link State Database:
LSPID           LSP Seq Num  LSP Checksum  LSP Holdtime      ATT/P/OL
R1.00-00        0x0000001F   0xAA2F        690               1/0/0
R1.01-00        0x0000001E   0x851A        900               0/0/0
R2.00-00      * 0x0000001E   0x4B57        934               0/0/0
```

The attached bit indicates that R1 is also an L2 router and can reach other areas.

The attached bit can also be seen in the R1 L1 link-state database:

```
R1# show isis database

IS-IS Level-1 Link State Database:
LSPID           LSP Seq Num  LSP Checksum  LSP Holdtime      ATT/P/OL
R1.00-00      * 0x0000001F   0xAA2F        640               1/0/0
R1.01-00      * 0x0000001E   0x851A        849               0/0/0
R2.00-00        0x0000001E   0x4B57        879               0/0/0
IS-IS Level-2 Link State Database:
LSPID           LSP Seq Num  LSP Checksum  LSP Holdtime      ATT/P/OL
R1.00-00      * 0x00000022   0x9D4F        583               0/0/0
R1.01-00      * 0x0000001D   0x5128        890               0/0/0
R3.00-00        0x00000022   0x9BD7        584               0/0/0
```

Verify that your configurations work completely with the following TCL script. You can download this TCL script at www.ciscopress.com/title/1587132133 under the More Information section on the page.

```
foreach address {
192.168.10.1
172.16.0.1
10.0.0.1
192.168.20.1
172.16.0.2
192.168.30.1
10.0.0.2 } { ping $address }
```

Save all configurations for future reference.

Reflection

Even though R2 and R3 were configured as L1-only and L2-only routers, respectively, they could have been left with the default setting of L1-L2. The result would have been each forming adjacencies for both levels, but unnecessarily. Why should unnecessary IS-IS adjacencies be eliminated?

_____

_____

_____

TCL Script Output

```
R1# tclsh
R1(tcl)#
R1(tcl)# foreach address {
+>(tcl)# 192.168.10.1
+>(tcl)# 172.16.0.1
+>(tcl)# 10.0.0.1
+>(tcl)# 192.168.20.1
+>(tcl)# 172.16.0.2
+>(tcl)# 192.168.30.1
+>(tcl)# 10.0.0.2 } { ping $address }

Type escape sequence to abort.
Sending 5, 100-byte ICMP Echos to 192.168.10.1, timeout is 2 seconds:
!!!!!
Success rate is 100 percent (5/5), round-trip min/avg/max = 1/1/4 ms
Type escape sequence to abort.
Sending 5, 100-byte ICMP Echos to 172.16.0.1, timeout is 2 seconds:
!!!!!
Success rate is 100 percent (5/5), round-trip min/avg/max = 1/1/4 ms
Type escape sequence to abort.
Sending 5, 100-byte ICMP Echos to 10.0.0.1, timeout is 2 seconds:
!!!!!
Success rate is 100 percent (5/5), round-trip min/avg/max = 12/14/16 ms
Type escape sequence to abort.
Sending 5, 100-byte ICMP Echos to 192.168.20.1, timeout is 2 seconds:
!!!!!
Success rate is 100 percent (5/5), round-trip min/avg/max = 1/2/4 ms
Type escape sequence to abort.
Sending 5, 100-byte ICMP Echos to 172.16.0.2, timeout is 2 seconds:
!!!!!
Success rate is 100 percent (5/5), round-trip min/avg/max = 1/2/4 ms
Type escape sequence to abort.
Sending 5, 100-byte ICMP Echos to 192.168.30.1, timeout is 2 seconds:
```

```
!!!!!
Success rate is 100 percent (5/5), round-trip min/avg/max = 12/15/16 ms
Type escape sequence to abort.
Sending 5, 100-byte ICMP Echos to 10.0.0.2, timeout is 2 seconds:
!!!!!
Success rate is 100 percent (5/5), round-trip min/avg/max = 28/29/32 ms
R1(tcl)#  tclquit
R1#
```

```
R2# tclsh
R2(tcl)#
R2(tcl)# foreach address {
+>(tcl)# 192.168.10.1
+>(tcl)# 172.16.0.1
+>(tcl)# 10.0.0.1
+>(tcl)# 192.168.20.1
+>(tcl)# 172.16.0.2
+>(tcl)# 192.168.30.1
+>(tcl)# 10.0.0.2 } { ping $address }

Type escape sequence to abort.
Sending 5, 100-byte ICMP Echos to 192.168.10.1, timeout is 2 seconds:
!!!!!
Success rate is 100 percent (5/5), round-trip min/avg/max = 1/1/4 ms
Type escape sequence to abort.
Sending 5, 100-byte ICMP Echos to 172.16.0.1, timeout is 2 seconds:
!!!!!
Success rate is 100 percent (5/5), round-trip min/avg/max = 1/1/4 ms
Type escape sequence to abort.
Sending 5, 100-byte ICMP Echos to 10.0.0.1, timeout is 2 seconds:
!!!!!
Success rate is 100 percent (5/5), round-trip min/avg/max = 12/13/16 ms
Type escape sequence to abort.
Sending 5, 100-byte ICMP Echos to 192.168.20.1, timeout is 2 seconds:
!!!!!
Success rate is 100 percent (5/5), round-trip min/avg/max = 1/1/4 ms
Type escape sequence to abort.
Sending 5, 100-byte ICMP Echos to 172.16.0.2, timeout is 2 seconds:
!!!!!
Success rate is 100 percent (5/5), round-trip min/avg/max = 1/1/1 ms
Type escape sequence to abort.
Sending 5, 100-byte ICMP Echos to 192.168.30.1, timeout is 2 seconds:
!!!!!
Success rate is 100 percent (5/5), round-trip min/avg/max = 12/14/16 ms
Type escape sequence to abort.
```

```
Sending 5, 100-byte ICMP Echos to 10.0.0.2, timeout is 2 seconds:
!!!!!
Success rate is 100 percent (5/5), round-trip min/avg/max = 1/2/4 ms
R2(tcl)#  tclquit
R2#
```

```
R3# tclsh
R3(tcl)# foreach address {
+>(tcl)# 192.168.10.1
+>(tcl)# 172.16.0.1
+>(tcl)# 10.0.0.1
+>(tcl)# 192.168.20.1
+>(tcl)# 172.16.0.2
+>(tcl)# 192.168.30.1
+>(tcl)# 10.0.0.2 } { ping $address }

Type escape sequence to abort.
Sending 5, 100-byte ICMP Echos to 192.168.10.1, timeout is 2 seconds:
!!!!!
Success rate is 100 percent (5/5), round-trip min/avg/max = 12/15/16 ms
Type escape sequence to abort.
Sending 5, 100-byte ICMP Echos to 172.16.0.1, timeout is 2 seconds:
!!!!!
Success rate is 100 percent (5/5), round-trip min/avg/max = 12/14/16 ms
Type escape sequence to abort.
Sending 5, 100-byte ICMP Echos to 10.0.0.1, timeout is 2 seconds:
!!!!!
Success rate is 100 percent (5/5), round-trip min/avg/max = 28/28/28 ms
Type escape sequence to abort.
Sending 5, 100-byte ICMP Echos to 192.168.20.1, timeout is 2 seconds:
!!!!!
Success rate is 100 percent (5/5), round-trip min/avg/max = 12/15/16 ms
Type escape sequence to abort.
Sending 5, 100-byte ICMP Echos to 172.16.0.2, timeout is 2 seconds:
!!!!!
Success rate is 100 percent (5/5), round-trip min/avg/max = 12/15/16 ms
Type escape sequence to abort.
Sending 5, 100-byte ICMP Echos to 192.168.30.1, timeout is 2 seconds:
!!!!!
Success rate is 100 percent (5/5), round-trip min/avg/max = 1/1/1 ms
Type escape sequence to abort.
Sending 5, 100-byte ICMP Echos to 10.0.0.2, timeout is 2 seconds:
!!!!!
Success rate is 100 percent (5/5), round-trip min/avg/max = 12/15/16 ms
R3(tcl)#  tclquit
```

Lab 4-3: Configuring IS-IS over Frame Relay: Router Used as Frame Switch (4.7.3a)

The objectives of this lab are as follows:

- Configure and verify Frame Relay point-to-point subinterfaces

- Configure and verify the operation of Integrated IS-IS over Frame Relay point-to-point subinterfaces

- Demonstrate mismatched Frame Relay interface types in IS-IS adjacencies

Figure 4-3 illustrates the topology that will be used for this lab.

Figure 4-3   Topology with a Cisco Router Acting as a Frame Relay Switch

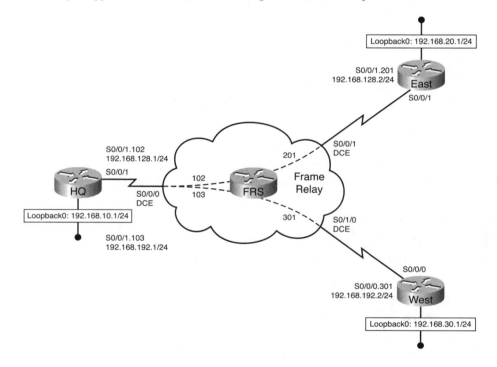

Scenario

International Travel Agency has just connected two regional offices to the headquarters using Frame Relay in a hub-and-spoke topology. You are asked to configure IS-IS routing over this network.

Step 1: Addressing and Basic Configuration

Cable the network and configure the hostnames according to the diagram in Figure 4-3. Turn off DNS lookup, and configure the IP address on the Fast Ethernet or loopback interfaces, whichever option was selected. Do not configure the serial interfaces and IS-IS routing for now. Until you configure Frame Relay, you will not be able to use **ping** to test connectivity.

Step 2: Frame Relay Configuration

HQ acts as the hub in this hub-and-spoke network. It reaches EAST and WEST via two separate permanent virtual circuits (PVC).

IS-IS can work only over nonbroadcast multiaccess (NBMA) clouds (such as Frame Relay) configured with a full mesh. Anything less than a full mesh can cause serious connectivity and routing issues. Even if a full mesh is configured, there is no guarantee that a full mesh will exist at all times. A failure in the underlying switched WAN network, or a misconfiguration on one or more routers, could break the full mesh either temporarily or permanently. Avoid NBMA multipoint configurations for IS-IS networks; use point-to-point subinterfaces instead.

Configure Frame Relay on HQ's serial interface as shown here:

```
HQ(config)# interface serial 0/0/1
HQ(config-if)# encapsulation frame-relay
HQ(config-if)# no shutdown
HQ(config-if)# interface s0/0/1.102 point-to-point
HQ(config-subif)# ip address 192.168.128.1 255.255.255.0
HQ(config-subif)# frame-relay interface-dlci 102
HQ(config-subif)# interface s0/0/1.103 point-to-point
HQ(config-subif)# ip address 192.168.192.1 255.255.255.0
HQ(config-subif)# frame-relay interface-dlci 103
```

Configure EAST's serial interface:

```
EAST(config)# interface serial 0/0/1
EAST(config-if)# encapsulation frame-relay
EAST(config-if)# no shutdown
EAST(config-if)# interface serial 0/0/1.201 point-to-point
EAST(config-subif)# ip address 192.168.128.2 255.255.255.0
EAST(config-subif)# frame-relay interface-dlci 201
```

Configure WEST's serial interface:

```
WEST(config)# interface serial 0/0/0
WEST(config-if)# encapsulation frame-relay
WEST(config-if)# no shutdown
WEST(config-if)# interface serial 0/0/0.301 point-to-point
WEST(config-subif)# ip address 192.168.192.2 255.255.255.0
WEST(config-subif)# frame-relay interface-dlci 301
```

Verify Frame Relay operation by pinging EAST and WEST from HQ.

Are you able to ping all the interfaces?

_____

_____

Issue **show frame-relay pvc** and **show frame-relay map** commands to troubleshoot connectivity problems:

HQ# **show frame-relay pvc**

PVC Statistics for interface Serial0/0/1 (Frame Relay DTE)

	Active	Inactive	Deleted	Static
Local	2	0	0	0
Switched	0	0	0	0
Unused	0	0	0	0

DLCI = 102, DLCI USAGE = LOCAL, PVC STATUS = ACTIVE, INTERFACE = Serial0/0/1.102

```
   input pkts 58          output pkts 52          in bytes 13130
   out bytes 13036        dropped pkts 0          in pkts dropped 0
   out pkts dropped 0             out bytes dropped 0
   in FECN pkts 0         in BECN pkts 0          out FECN pkts 0
   out BECN pkts 0        in DE pkts 0            out DE pkts 0
   out bcast pkts 32      out bcast bytes 10956
   5 minute input rate 0 bits/sec, 0 packets/sec
   5 minute output rate 0 bits/sec, 0 packets/sec
   pvc create time 00:37:48, last time pvc status changed 00:28:42
```

DLCI = 103, DLCI USAGE = LOCAL, PVC STATUS = ACTIVE, INTERFACE = Serial0/0/1.103

```
   input pkts 46          output pkts 48          in bytes 10322
   out bytes 11684        dropped pkts 0          in pkts dropped 0
   out pkts dropped 0             out bytes dropped 0
   in FECN pkts 0         in BECN pkts 0          out FECN pkts 0
   out BECN pkts 0        in DE pkts 0            out DE pkts 0
   out bcast pkts 28      out bcast bytes 9604
   5 minute input rate 0 bits/sec, 0 packets/sec
   5 minute output rate 0 bits/sec, 0 packets/sec
   pvc create time 00:37:14, last time pvc status changed 00:24:54
```

HQ# **show frame-relay map**
```
Serial0/0/1.102 (up): point-to-point dlci, dlci 102(0x66,0x1860), broadcast
          status defined, active
Serial0/0/1.103 (up): point-to-point dlci, dlci 103(0x67,0x1870), broadcast
          status defined, active
```

Which OSI Layer 3 protocols are forwarded over the PVCs you configured?

_____

_____

How does this differ from the way the output of the **show frame-relay map** command usually looks with multipoint subinterfaces configured? Refer to EIGRP Lab 2-4 if necessary.

_____

Which transport protocol does IS-IS use?

_____

Why will these packets be forwarded?

_____

Step 3: Configure and Verify IS-IS over Frame Relay

Like OSPF, IS-IS is configured by enabling an IS-IS process and specifying which interfaces are to participate in the IS-IS process. Configure IS-IS to run over this point-to-point network with the following commands:

```
HQ(config)# router isis
HQ(config-router)# net 49.0001.1111.1111.1111.00
HQ(config-router)# interface serial 0/0/1.102
HQ(config-if)# ip router isis
HQ(config-if)# interface serial 0/0/1.103
HQ(config-if)# ip router isis
HQ(config-if)# interface loopback 0
HQ(config-if)# ip router isis
```
```
EAST(config)# router isis
EAST(config-router)# net 49.0001.2222.2222.2222.00
EAST(config-router)# int serial 0/0/1.201
EAST(config-if)# ip router isis
EAST(config-if)# int loopback 0
EAST(config-if)# ip router isis
```
```
WEST(config)# router isis
WEST(config-router)# net 49.0001.3333.3333.3333.00
WEST(config-router)# int serial 0/0/0.301
WEST(config-if)# ip router isis
WEST(config-if)# int loopback 0
WEST(config-if)# ip router isis
```

Verify your IS-IS configuration by issuing the **show ip route** command on each of the routers:

```
WEST# show ip route
<output omitted>

Gateway of last resort is not set

C      192.168.192.0/24 is directly connected, Serial0/0/0.301
C      192.168.30.0/24 is directly connected, Loopback0
 i L1  192.168.128.0/24 [115/20] via 192.168.192.1, Serial0/0/0.301
 i L1  192.168.10.0/24 [115/20] via 192.168.192.1, Serial0/0/0.301
 i L1  192.168.20.0/24 [115/30] via 192.168.192.1, Serial0/0/0.301
```

If each router has a complete table, including routes to 192.168.10.0/24, 192.168.20.0/24, and 192.168.30.0/24, you have successfully configured IS-IS to operate over Frame Relay.

Test these routes by pinging the Fast Ethernet or loopback interfaces of each router from WEST's console.

Are you able to ping all the interfaces?

Finally, issue the **show isis database** and **show isis topology** commands:

```
HQ# show isis database

IS-IS Level-1 Link State Database:
LSPID          LSP Seq Num    LSP Checksum   LSP Holdtime    ATT/P/OL
HQ.00-00     * 0x00000007     0x3B7A         737             0/0/0
EAST.00-00     0x00000004     0xA0ED         736             0/0/0
WEST.00-00     0x00000003     0x7603         666             0/0/0
IS-IS Level-2 Link State Database:
LSPID          LSP Seq Num    LSP Checksum   LSP Holdtime    ATT/P/OL
HQ.00-00     * 0x00000009     0x2F3C         744             0/0/0
EAST.00-00     0x00000006     0x90E7         747             0/0/0
WEST.00-00     0x00000004     0x5B53         742             0/0/0
```

```
EAST# show isis topology

IS-IS paths to level-1 routers
System Id       Metric  Next-Hop     Interface       SNPA
HQ              10      HQ           Se0/0/1.201 DLCI 201
EAST            --
WEST            20      HQ           Se0/0/1.201 DLCI 201


IS-IS paths to level-2 routers
System Id       Metric  Next-Hop     Interface       SNPA
```

HQ	10	HQ	Se0/0/1.201 DLCI 201
EAST	--		
WEST	20	HQ	Se0/0/1.201 DLCI 201

Note that no pseudonode LSPs (with nonzero circuit IDs) appear in the **show isis database** output because we are using point-to-point links to connect the routers.

How is the subnetwork point of attachment (SNPA) expressed in a Frame Relay network?

Step 4: Verify IS-IS Connectivity

Run the following TCL script on all routers to verify full connectivity. You can download this TCL script at www.ciscopress.com/title/1587132133 under the More Information section on the page.

```
foreach address {
192.168.10.1
192.168.128.1
192.168.192.1
192.168.20.1
192.168.128.2
192.168.30.1
192.168.192.2 } { ping $address }
```

If you have never used TCL scripts before or need a refresher, see the TCL lab in the routing module.

You should get Internet Control Message Protocol (ICMP) echo replies for every address pinged. Check your TCL script output against the output in the section, "TCL Script Output," for this lab. Make sure you run the TCL script on each router and get the output recorded in the section, "TCL Script Output," for this lab before continuing.

Step 5: Demonstrate IS-IS Interface-Type Mismatch

A common error with IS-IS configuration is mismatched interface types in an NBMA environment (normally Frame Relay or ATM). To illustrate this, switch EAST's point-to-point interface to a multipoint interface. Remove the commands currently configured on Serial0/0/1.201 with their respective **no** commands. Then, create a multipoint subinterface on EAST named Serial0/0/1.2001. Place the same commands you removed from Serial0/0/1.201 on Serial0/0/1.2001:

```
EAST(config)# interface serial 0/0/1.201
EAST(config-subif)# no ip address
EAST(config-subif)# no ip router isis
EAST(config-subif)# no frame-relay interface-dlci 201
EAST(config-subif)# interface serial 0/0/1.2001 multipoint
EAST(config-subif)# ip address 192.168.128.2 255.255.255.0
EAST(config-subif)# ip router isis
EAST(config-subif)# frame-relay interface-dlci 201
```

Allow the Frame Relay PVC to become active. View the output of the **show clns neighbors** command on HQ and EAST:

```
HQ# show clns neighbors


System Id  Interface    SNPA           State  Holdtime  Type Protocol
WEST       Se0/0/1.103  DLCI 103       Up     27        L1L2 IS-IS
```

```
EAST# show clns neighbors


System Id  Interface    SNPA           State  Holdtime  Type Protocol
HQ         Se0/0/1.2001 DLCI 201       Up     258       IS   ES-IS
```

The output indicates mismatched interface types! Since Cisco IOS Release 12.1(1)T, an Integrated IS-IS mismatch is indicated in the following cases:

- EAST (multipoint) receives a point-to-point hello PDU, realizes it is the wrong hello type, and installs the neighbor as an ES. EAST shows HQ in the **show clns neighbors** command with protocol ES-IS.

- HQ (point-to-point) receives the LAN hello PDU, recognizes the mismatch, and ignores the neighbor. EAST does not appear in the output of the **show clns neighbors** command. The output of the **debug isis adj-packets** command shows the incoming LAN IIH PDU and EAST declaring the mismatch:

```
EAST# debug isis adj-packets
IS-IS Adjacency related packets debugging is on
00:31:58: ISIS-Adj: Sending L1 LAN IIH on Loopback0, length 1514
00:31:58: ISIS-Adj: Sending L2 LAN IIH on Loopback0, length 1514
00:31:59: ISIS-Adj: Encapsulation failed for L2 LAN IIH on Serial0/0/1.2001
00:31:59: ISIS-Adj: Encapsulation failed for L1 LAN IIH on Serial0/0/1.2001
00:32:01: ISIS-Adj: Sending L1 LAN IIH on Loopback0, length 1514
00:32:01: ISIS-Adj: Sending L2 LAN IIH on Loopback0, length 1514
00:32:02: ISIS-Adj: Encapsulation failed for L2 LAN IIH on Serial0/0/1.2001
00:32:03: ISIS-Adj: Encapsulation failed for L1 LAN IIH on Serial0/0/1.2001
00:32:04: ISIS-Adj: Sending L2 LAN IIH on Loopback0, length 1514
00:32:04: ISIS-Adj: Sending L1 LAN IIH on Loopback0, length 1514
00:32:04: ISIS-Adj: Rec serial IIH from DLCI 201 (Serial0/0/1.2001), cir type L1L2,
  cir id 00, length 1499
00:32:04: ISIS-Adj: Point-to-point IIH received on multi-point interface: ignored IIH
00:32:05: ISIS-Adj: Encapsulation failed for L2 LAN IIH on Serial0/0/1.2001
00:32:06: ISIS-Adj: Encapsulation failed for L1 LAN IIH on Serial0/0/1.2001
```

This completes the IS-IS over Frame Relay lab. Integrated IS-IS can be easily configured over a Frame Relay cloud. The only caveat is that IS-IS NBMA configurations, unlike OSPF, are essentially limited to point-to-point implementations. In an NBMA environment, mismatched interface types are a common problem; the symptoms are reflected in the output of the **show clns neighbors** and **debug isis adj-packets** commands.

Router as Frame Relay Switch Configuration

The following configuration enables a 2800 router with two WIC-2A/Ss or WIC-2Ts to act as a Frame Relay switch (FRS) for this lab. If you use a different model router (2600, 1700), the serial interfaces will be numbered differently. You can download this configuration at www.ciscopress.com/title/ 1587132133 under the More Information section on the page.

```
FRS# show run
!
hostname FRS
!
no ip domain-lookup
!
frame-relay switching
!
interface Serial0/0/0
 no ip address
 encapsulation frame-relay
 clockrate 128000
 frame-relay intf-type dce
 frame-relay route 102 interface Serial0/0/1 201
 frame-relay route 103 interface Serial0/1/0 301
 no shutdown
!
interface Serial0/0/1
 no ip address
 encapsulation frame-relay
 clockrate 128000
 frame-relay intf-type dce
 frame-relay route 201 interface Serial0/0/0 102
 no shutdown
!
interface Serial0/1/0
 no ip address
 encapsulation frame-relay
 clockrate 128000
 frame-relay intf-type dce
 frame-relay route 301 interface Serial0/0/0 103
 no shutdown
!
end
```

TCL Script Output

```
HQ# tclsh
HQ(tcl)# foreach address {
+>(tcl)# 192.168.10.1
+>(tcl)# 192.168.128.1
+>(tcl)# 192.168.192.1
+>(tcl)# 192.168.20.1
+>(tcl)# 192.168.128.2
+>(tcl)# 192.168.30.1
+>(tcl)# 192.168.192.2 } { ping $address }

Type escape sequence to abort.
Sending 5, 100-byte ICMP Echos to 192.168.10.1, timeout is 2 seconds:
!!!!!
Success rate is 100 percent (5/5), round-trip min/avg/max = 1/1/4 ms
Type escape sequence to abort.
Sending 5, 100-byte ICMP Echos to 192.168.128.1, timeout is 2 seconds:
!!!!!
Success rate is 100 percent (5/5), round-trip min/avg/max = 112/113/120 ms
Type escape sequence to abort.
Sending 5, 100-byte ICMP Echos to 192.168.192.1, timeout is 2 seconds:
!!!!!
Success rate is 100 percent (5/5), round-trip min/avg/max = 56/60/68 ms
Type escape sequence to abort.
Sending 5, 100-byte ICMP Echos to 192.168.20.1, timeout is 2 seconds:
!!!!!
Success rate is 100 percent (5/5), round-trip min/avg/max = 56/56/60 ms
Type escape sequence to abort.
Sending 5, 100-byte ICMP Echos to 192.168.128.2, timeout is 2 seconds:
!!!!!
Success rate is 100 percent (5/5), round-trip min/avg/max = 56/56/56 ms
Type escape sequence to abort.
Sending 5, 100-byte ICMP Echos to 192.168.30.1, timeout is 2 seconds:
!!!!!
Success rate is 100 percent (5/5), round-trip min/avg/max = 28/29/32 ms
Type escape sequence to abort.
Sending 5, 100-byte ICMP Echos to 192.168.192.2, timeout is 2 seconds:
!!!!!
Success rate is 100 percent (5/5), round-trip min/avg/max = 28/67/216 ms
HQ(tcl)#  tclquit
```

```
EAST# tclsh
EAST(tcl)# foreach address {
+>(tcl)# 192.168.10.1
```

```
+>(tcl)# 192.168.128.1
+>(tcl)# 192.168.192.1
+>(tcl)# 192.168.20.1
+>(tcl)# 192.168.128.2
+>(tcl)# 192.168.30.1
+>(tcl)# 192.168.192.2 } { ping $address }

Type escape sequence to abort.
Sending 5, 100-byte ICMP Echos to 192.168.10.1, timeout is 2 seconds:
!!!!!
Success rate is 100 percent (5/5), round-trip min/avg/max = 56/56/56 ms
Type escape sequence to abort.
Sending 5, 100-byte ICMP Echos to 192.168.128.1, timeout is 2 seconds:
!!!!!
Success rate is 100 percent (5/5), round-trip min/avg/max = 56/124/392 ms
Type escape sequence to abort.
Sending 5, 100-byte ICMP Echos to 192.168.192.1, timeout is 2 seconds:
!!!!!
Success rate is 100 percent (5/5), round-trip min/avg/max = 56/56/60 ms
Type escape sequence to abort.
Sending 5, 100-byte ICMP Echos to 192.168.20.1, timeout is 2 seconds:
!!!!!
Success rate is 100 percent (5/5), round-trip min/avg/max = 1/1/4 ms
Type escape sequence to abort.
Sending 5, 100-byte ICMP Echos to 192.168.128.2, timeout is 2 seconds:
!!!!!
Success rate is 100 percent (5/5), round-trip min/avg/max = 108/148/292 ms
Type escape sequence to abort.
Sending 5, 100-byte ICMP Echos to 192.168.30.1, timeout is 2 seconds:
!!!!!
Success rate is 100 percent (5/5), round-trip min/avg/max = 84/84/88 ms
Type escape sequence to abort.
Sending 5, 100-byte ICMP Echos to 192.168.192.2, timeout is 2 seconds:
!!!!!
Success rate is 100 percent (5/5), round-trip min/avg/max = 84/84/88 ms
EAST(tcl)#  tclquit
WEST# tclsh
WEST(tcl)# foreach address {
+>(tcl)# 192.168.10.1
+>(tcl)# 192.168.128.1
+>(tcl)# 192.168.192.1
+>(tcl)# 192.168.20.1
+>(tcl)# 192.168.128.2
+>(tcl)# 192.168.30.1
```

```
+>(tcl)# 192.168.192.2 } { ping $address }


Type escape sequence to abort.
Sending 5, 100-byte ICMP Echos to 192.168.10.1, timeout is 2 seconds:
!!!!!
Success rate is 100 percent (5/5), round-trip min/avg/max = 28/30/32 ms
Type escape sequence to abort.
Sending 5, 100-byte ICMP Echos to 192.168.128.1, timeout is 2 seconds:
!!!!!
Success rate is 100 percent (5/5), round-trip min/avg/max = 28/30/32 ms
Type escape sequence to abort.
Sending 5, 100-byte ICMP Echos to 192.168.192.1, timeout is 2 seconds:
!!!!!
Success rate is 100 percent (5/5), round-trip min/avg/max = 28/30/32 ms
Type escape sequence to abort.
Sending 5, 100-byte ICMP Echos to 192.168.20.1, timeout is 2 seconds:
!!!!!
Success rate is 100 percent (5/5), round-trip min/avg/max = 84/85/88 ms
Type escape sequence to abort.
Sending 5, 100-byte ICMP Echos to 192.168.128.2, timeout is 2 seconds:
!!!!!
Success rate is 100 percent (5/5), round-trip min/avg/max = 84/121/268 ms
Type escape sequence to abort.
Sending 5, 100-byte ICMP Echos to 192.168.30.1, timeout is 2 seconds:
!!!!!
Success rate is 100 percent (5/5), round-trip min/avg/max = 1/1/1 ms
Type escape sequence to abort.
Sending 5, 100-byte ICMP Echos to 192.168.192.2, timeout is 2 seconds:
!!!!!
Success rate is 100 percent (5/5), round-trip min/avg/max = 56/59/68 ms
WEST(tcl)#  tclquit
```

Lab 4-4: Configuring IS-IS over Frame Relay: Adtran Used as Frame Switch (4.7.3b)

The objectives of this lab are as follows:

- Configure and verify Frame Relay point-to-point subinterfaces

- Configure and verify the operation of Integrated IS-IS over Frame Relay point-to-point subinterfaces

- Demonstrate mismatched Frame Relay interface types in IS-IS adjacencies

This lab is a duplicate of Lab 4-3, in which a router is used as a Frame Relay switch. The only difference in this lab is that an Adtran device is used as the Frame Relay switch. It is useful to do one lab or the other; not both.

Figure 4-4 illustrates the topology that will be used for this lab.

Figure 4-4   Topology with an Adtran Acting as a Frame Relay Switch

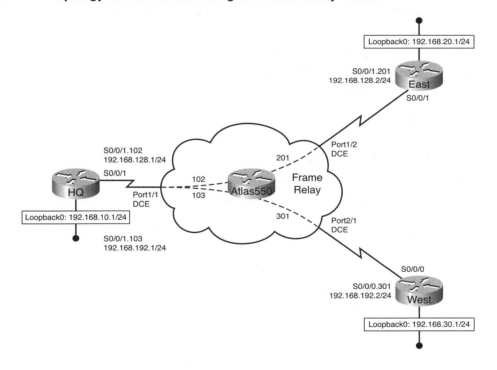

Scenario

International Travel Agency has just connected two regional offices to the headquarters using Frame Relay in a hub-and-spoke topology. You are asked to configure IS-IS routing over this network.

Step 1: Addressing and Basic Configuration

Cable the network and configure the hostnames according to the diagram. Turn off DNS lookup, and configure the IP address on the Fast Ethernet or loopback interfaces, whichever option was selected. Do not configure the serial interfaces and IS-IS routing for now. Until you configure Frame Relay, you will not be able to use **ping** to test connectivity.

Step 2: Frame Relay Configuration

HQ acts as the hub in this hub-and-spoke network. It reaches EAST and WEST via two separate PVCs.

IS-IS can work only over NBMA clouds (such as Frame Relay) configured with a full mesh. Anything less than a full mesh can cause serious connectivity and routing issues. Even if a full mesh is configured, there is no guarantee that a full mesh will exist at all times. A failure in the underlying switched WAN network, or a misconfiguration on one or more routers, could break the full mesh either temporarily or permanently. Avoid NBMA multipoint configurations for IS-IS networks; use point-to-point subinterfaces instead.

Configure Frame Relay on HQ's serial interface as shown here:

```
HQ(config)# interface serial 0/0/1
HQ(config-if)# encapsulation frame-relay ietf
HQ(config-if)# no shutdown
HQ(config-if)# interface s0/0/1.102 point-to-point
HQ(config-subif)# ip address 192.168.128.1 255.255.255.0
HQ(config-subif)# frame-relay interface-dlci 102
HQ(config-subif)# interface s0/0/1.103 point-to-point
HQ(config-subif)# ip address 192.168.192.1 255.255.255.0
HQ(config-subif)# frame-relay interface-dlci 103
```

Configure EAST's serial interface:

```
EAST(config)# interface serial 0/0/1
EAST(config-if)# encapsulation frame-relay ietf
EAST(config-if)# no shutdown
EAST(config-if)# interface serial 0/0/1.201 point-to-point
EAST(config-subif)# ip address 192.168.128.2 255.255.255.0
EAST(config-subif)# frame-relay interface-dlci 201
```

Configure WEST's serial interface:

```
WEST(config)# interface serial 0/0/0
WEST(config-if)# encapsulation frame-relay ietf
WEST(config-if)# no shutdown
WEST(config-if)# interface serial 0/0/0.301 point-to-point
WEST(config-subif)# ip address 192.168.192.2 255.255.255.0
WEST(config-subif)# frame-relay interface-dlci 301
```

Verify Frame Relay operation by pinging EAST and WEST from HQ.

Are you able to ping all the interfaces?

_____

_____

Issue **show frame-relay pvc** and **show frame-relay map** commands to troubleshoot connectivity problems:

HQ# `show frame-relay pvc`

PVC Statistics for interface Serial0/0/1 (Frame Relay DTE)

	Active	Inactive	Deleted	Static
Local	2	0	0	0
Switched	0	0	0	0
Unused	0	0	0	0

DLCI = 102, DLCI USAGE = LOCAL, PVC STATUS = ACTIVE, INTERFACE = Serial0/0/1.102

```
  input pkts 58            output pkts 52           in bytes 13130
  out bytes 13036          dropped pkts 0           in pkts dropped 0
  out pkts dropped 0               out bytes dropped 0
  in FECN pkts 0           in BECN pkts 0           out FECN pkts 0
  out BECN pkts 0          in DE pkts 0             out DE pkts 0
  out bcast pkts 32        out bcast bytes 10956
  5 minute input rate 0 bits/sec, 0 packets/sec
  5 minute output rate 0 bits/sec, 0 packets/sec
  pvc create time 00:37:48, last time pvc status changed 00:28:42
```

DLCI = 103, DLCI USAGE = LOCAL, PVC STATUS = ACTIVE, INTERFACE = Serial0/0/1.103

```
  input pkts 46            output pkts 48           in bytes 10322
  out bytes 11684          dropped pkts 0           in pkts dropped 0
  out pkts dropped 0               out bytes dropped 0
  in FECN pkts 0           in BECN pkts 0           out FECN pkts 0
  out BECN pkts 0          in DE pkts 0             out DE pkts 0
  out bcast pkts 28        out bcast bytes 9604
  5 minute input rate 0 bits/sec, 0 packets/sec
  5 minute output rate 0 bits/sec, 0 packets/sec
  pvc create time 00:37:14, last time pvc status changed 00:24:54
```

HQ# `show frame-relay map`
```
Serial0/0/1.102 (up): point-to-point dlci, dlci 102(0x66,0x1860), broadcast
          status defined, active
Serial0/0/1.103 (up): point-to-point dlci, dlci 103(0x67,0x1870), broadcast
          status defined, active
```

Which OSI Layer 3 protocols are forwarded over the PVCs you configured?

_____

_____

How does this differ from the way the output of the **show frame-relay map** command usually looks with multipoint subinterfaces configured? Refer to EIGRP Lab 2-5 if necessary.

_____

Which transport protocol does IS-IS use?

_____

Why will these packets be forwarded?

_____

Step 3: Configure and Verify IS-IS over Frame Relay

Like OSPF, IS-IS is configured by enabling an IS-IS process and specifying which interfaces are to participate in the IS-IS process. Configure IS-IS to run over this point-to-point network with the following commands:

```
HQ(config)# router isis
HQ(config-router)# net 49.0001.1111.1111.1111.00
HQ(config-router)# interface serial 0/0/1.102
HQ(config-if)# ip router isis
HQ(config-if)# interface serial 0/0/1.103
HQ(config-if)# ip router isis
HQ(config-if)# interface loopback 0
HQ(config-if)# ip router isis
```
```
EAST(config)# router isis
EAST(config-router)# net 49.0001.2222.2222.2222.00
EAST(config-router)# int serial 0/0/1.201
EAST(config-if)# ip router isis
EAST(config-if)# int loopback 0
EAST(config-if)# ip router isis
```
```
WEST(config)# router isis
WEST(config-router)# net 49.0001.3333.3333.3333.00
WEST(config-router)# int serial 0/0/0.301
WEST(config-if)# ip router isis
WEST(config-if)# int loopback 0
WEST(config-if)# ip router isis
```

Verify your IS-IS configuration by issuing the **show ip route** command on each of the routers:

```
WEST# show ip route
<output omitted>

Gateway of last resort is not set

C    192.168.192.0/24 is directly connected, Serial0/0/0.301
C    192.168.30.0/24 is directly connected, Loopback0
 i L1 192.168.128.0/24 [115/20] via 192.168.192.1, Serial0/0/0.301
 i L1 192.168.10.0/24 [115/20] via 192.168.192.1, Serial0/0/0.301
 i L1 192.168.20.0/24 [115/30] via 192.168.192.1, Serial0/0/0.301
```

If each router has a complete table, including routes to 192.168.10.0/24, 192.168.20.0/24, and 192.168.30.0/24, you have successfully configured IS-IS to operate over Frame Relay.

Test these routes by pinging the Fast Ethernet or loopback interfaces of each router from WEST's console.

Are you able to ping all the interfaces?

Finally, issue the **show isis database** and **show isis topology** commands:

```
HQ# show isis database

IS-IS Level-1 Link State Database:
LSPID           LSP Seq Num  LSP Checksum  LSP Holdtime    ATT/P/OL
HQ.00-00      * 0x00000007   0x3B7A        737             0/0/0
EAST.00-00      0x00000004   0xA0ED        736             0/0/0
WEST.00-00      0x00000003   0x7603        666             0/0/0
IS-IS Level-2 Link State Database:
LSPID           LSP Seq Num  LSP Checksum  LSP Holdtime    ATT/P/OL
HQ.00-00      * 0x00000009   0x2F3C        744             0/0/0
EAST.00-00      0x00000006   0x90E7        747             0/0/0
WEST.00-00      0x00000004   0x5B53        742             0/0/0
EAST# show isis topology

IS-IS paths to level-1 routers
System Id       Metric  Next-Hop        Interface    SNPA
HQ              10      HQ              Se0/0/1.201  DLCI 201
EAST            --
WEST            20      HQ              Se0/0/1.201  DLCI 201

IS-IS paths to level-2 routers
System Id       Metric  Next-Hop        Interface    SNPA
```

HQ	10	HQ	Se0/0/1.201 DLCI 201
EAST	--		
WEST	20	HQ	Se0/0/1.201 DLCI 201

Note that no pseudonode LSPs (with nonzero circuit IDs) appear in the **show isis database** output because we are using point-to-point links to connect the routers.

How is the subnetwork point of attachment (SNPA) expressed in a Frame Relay network?

Step 4: Verify IS-IS Connectivity

Run the following TCL script on all routers to verify full connectivity. You can download this TCL script at www.ciscopress.com/title/1587132133 under the More Information section on the page.

```
foreach address {
192.168.10.1
192.168.128.1
192.168.192.1
192.168.20.1
192.168.128.2
192.168.30.1
192.168.192.2 } { ping $address }
```

If you have never used TCL scripts before or need a refresher, see the TCL lab in the routing module.

You should get ICMP echo replies for every address pinged. Check your TCL script output against the output in the section, "TCL Script Output," for this lab. Make sure you run the TCL script on each router and get the output recorded in the section, "TCL Script Output," before continuing.

Step 5: Demonstrate IS-IS Interface-Type Mismatch

A common error with IS-IS configuration is mismatched interface types in an NBMA environment (normally Frame Relay or ATM). To illustrate this, switch EAST's point-to-point interface to a multipoint interface. Remove the commands currently configured on Serial0/0/1.201 with their respective **no** commands. Then, create a multipoint subinterface on EAST named Serial0/0/1.2001. Place the same commands you removed from Serial0/0/1.201 on Serial0/0/1.2001:

```
EAST(config)# interface serial 0/0/1.201
EAST(config-subif)# no ip address
EAST(config-subif)# no ip router isis
EAST(config-subif)# no frame-relay interface-dlci 201
EAST(config-subif)# interface serial 0/0/1.2001 multipoint
EAST(config-subif)# ip address 192.168.128.2 255.255.255.0
EAST(config-subif)# ip router isis
EAST(config-subif)# frame-relay interface-dlci 201
```

Allow the Frame Relay PVC to become active. View the output of the **show clns neighbors** command on HQ and EAST:

```
HQ# show clns neighbors

System Id  Interface   SNPA              State  Holdtime  Type Protocol
WEST       Se0/0/1.103  DLCI 103          Up     27        L1L2 IS-IS
```

```
EAST# show clns neighbors

System Id  Interface   SNPA              State  Holdtime  Type Protocol
HQ         Se0/0/1.2001 DLCI 201          Up     258       IS   ES-IS
```

The output indicates mismatched interface types! Since Cisco IOS Release 12.1(1)T, an Integrated IS-IS mismatch is indicated in the following cases:

- EAST (multipoint) receives a point-to-point hello PDU, realizes it is the wrong hello type, and installs the neighbor as an ES. EAST shows HQ in the **show clns neighbors** command with protocol ES-IS.

- HQ (point-to-point) receives the LAN hello PDU, recognizes the mismatch, and ignores the neighbor. EAST does not appear in the output of the **show clns neighbors** command. The output of the **debug isis adj-packets** command shows the incoming LAN IIH PDU and EAST declaring the mismatch:

```
EAST# debug isis adj-packets
IS-IS Adjacency related packets debugging is on
00:31:58: ISIS-Adj: Sending L1 LAN IIH on Loopback0, length 1514
00:31:58: ISIS-Adj: Sending L2 LAN IIH on Loopback0, length 1514
00:31:59: ISIS-Adj: Encapsulation failed for L2 LAN IIH on Serial0/0/1.2001
00:31:59: ISIS-Adj: Encapsulation failed for L1 LAN IIH on Serial0/0/1.2001
00:32:01: ISIS-Adj: Sending L1 LAN IIH on Loopback0, length 1514
00:32:01: ISIS-Adj: Sending L2 LAN IIH on Loopback0, length 1514
00:32:02: ISIS-Adj: Encapsulation failed for L2 LAN IIH on Serial0/0/1.2001
00:32:03: ISIS-Adj: Encapsulation failed for L1 LAN IIH on Serial0/0/1.2001
00:32:04: ISIS-Adj: Sending L2 LAN IIH on Loopback0, length 1514
00:32:04: ISIS-Adj: Sending L1 LAN IIH on Loopback0, length 1514
00:32:04: ISIS-Adj: Rec serial IIH from DLCI 201 (Serial0/0/1.2001), cir type L1L2,
  cir id 00, length 1499
00:32:04: ISIS-Adj: Point-to-point IIH received on multi-point interface: ignored IIH
00:32:05: ISIS-Adj: Encapsulation failed for L2 LAN IIH on Serial0/0/1.2001
00:32:06: ISIS-Adj: Encapsulation failed for L1 LAN IIH on Serial0/0/1.2001
```

This completes the IS-IS over Frame Relay lab. Integrated IS-IS can be easily configured over a Frame Relay cloud. The only caveat is that IS-IS NBMA configurations, unlike OSPF, are essentially limited to point-to-point implementations. In an NBMA environment, mismatched interface types are a common problem; the symptoms are reflected in the output of the **show clns neighbors** and **debug isis adj-packets** commands.

TCL Script Output

```
HQ# tclsh
HQ(tcl)# foreach address {
+>(tcl)# 192.168.10.1
+>(tcl)# 192.168.128.1
+>(tcl)# 192.168.192.1
+>(tcl)# 192.168.20.1
+>(tcl)# 192.168.128.2
+>(tcl)# 192.168.30.1
+>(tcl)# 192.168.192.2 } { ping $address }

Type escape sequence to abort.
Sending 5, 100-byte ICMP Echos to 192.168.10.1, timeout is 2 seconds:
!!!!!
Success rate is 100 percent (5/5), round-trip min/avg/max = 1/1/4 ms
Type escape sequence to abort.
Sending 5, 100-byte ICMP Echos to 192.168.128.1, timeout is 2 seconds:
!!!!!
Success rate is 100 percent (5/5), round-trip min/avg/max = 112/113/120 ms
Type escape sequence to abort.
Sending 5, 100-byte ICMP Echos to 192.168.192.1, timeout is 2 seconds:
!!!!!
Success rate is 100 percent (5/5), round-trip min/avg/max = 56/60/68 ms
Type escape sequence to abort.
Sending 5, 100-byte ICMP Echos to 192.168.20.1, timeout is 2 seconds:
!!!!!
Success rate is 100 percent (5/5), round-trip min/avg/max = 56/56/60 ms
Type escape sequence to abort.
Sending 5, 100-byte ICMP Echos to 192.168.128.2, timeout is 2 seconds:
!!!!!
Success rate is 100 percent (5/5), round-trip min/avg/max = 56/56/56 ms
Type escape sequence to abort.
Sending 5, 100-byte ICMP Echos to 192.168.30.1, timeout is 2 seconds:
!!!!!
Success rate is 100 percent (5/5), round-trip min/avg/max = 28/29/32 ms
Type escape sequence to abort.
Sending 5, 100-byte ICMP Echos to 192.168.192.2, timeout is 2 seconds:
!!!!!
Success rate is 100 percent (5/5), round-trip min/avg/max = 28/67/216 ms
HQ(tcl)#  tclquit
```

```
EAST# tclsh
EAST(tcl)# foreach address {
+>(tcl)# 192.168.10.1
```

```
+>(tcl)# 192.168.128.1
+>(tcl)# 192.168.192.1
+>(tcl)# 192.168.20.1
+>(tcl)# 192.168.128.2
+>(tcl)# 192.168.30.1
+>(tcl)# 192.168.192.2 } { ping $address }

Type escape sequence to abort.
Sending 5, 100-byte ICMP Echos to 192.168.10.1, timeout is 2 seconds:
!!!!!
Success rate is 100 percent (5/5), round-trip min/avg/max = 56/56/56 ms
Type escape sequence to abort.
Sending 5, 100-byte ICMP Echos to 192.168.128.1, timeout is 2 seconds:
!!!!!
Success rate is 100 percent (5/5), round-trip min/avg/max = 56/124/392 ms
Type escape sequence to abort.
Sending 5, 100-byte ICMP Echos to 192.168.192.1, timeout is 2 seconds:
!!!!!
Success rate is 100 percent (5/5), round-trip min/avg/max = 56/56/60 ms
Type escape sequence to abort.
Sending 5, 100-byte ICMP Echos to 192.168.20.1, timeout is 2 seconds:
!!!!!
Success rate is 100 percent (5/5), round-trip min/avg/max = 1/1/4 ms
Type escape sequence to abort.
Sending 5, 100-byte ICMP Echos to 192.168.128.2, timeout is 2 seconds:
!!!!!
Success rate is 100 percent (5/5), round-trip min/avg/max = 108/148/292 ms
Type escape sequence to abort.
Sending 5, 100-byte ICMP Echos to 192.168.30.1, timeout is 2 seconds:
!!!!!
Success rate is 100 percent (5/5), round-trip min/avg/max = 84/84/88 ms
Type escape sequence to abort.
Sending 5, 100-byte ICMP Echos to 192.168.192.2, timeout is 2 seconds:
!!!!!
Success rate is 100 percent (5/5), round-trip min/avg/max = 84/84/88 ms
EAST(tcl)#  tclquit
```
```
WEST# tclsh
WEST(tcl)# foreach address {
+>(tcl)# 192.168.10.1
+>(tcl)# 192.168.128.1
+>(tcl)# 192.168.192.1
+>(tcl)# 192.168.20.1
+>(tcl)# 192.168.128.2
+>(tcl)# 192.168.30.1
```

```
+>(tcl)# 192.168.192.2 } { ping $address }

Type escape sequence to abort.
Sending 5, 100-byte ICMP Echos to 192.168.10.1, timeout is 2 seconds:
!!!!!
Success rate is 100 percent (5/5), round-trip min/avg/max = 28/30/32 ms
Type escape sequence to abort.
Sending 5, 100-byte ICMP Echos to 192.168.128.1, timeout is 2 seconds:
!!!!!
Success rate is 100 percent (5/5), round-trip min/avg/max = 28/30/32 ms
Type escape sequence to abort.
Sending 5, 100-byte ICMP Echos to 192.168.192.1, timeout is 2 seconds:
!!!!!
Success rate is 100 percent (5/5), round-trip min/avg/max = 28/30/32 ms
Type escape sequence to abort.
Sending 5, 100-byte ICMP Echos to 192.168.20.1, timeout is 2 seconds:
!!!!!
Success rate is 100 percent (5/5), round-trip min/avg/max = 84/85/88 ms
Type escape sequence to abort.
Sending 5, 100-byte ICMP Echos to 192.168.128.2, timeout is 2 seconds:
!!!!!
Success rate is 100 percent (5/5), round-trip min/avg/max = 84/121/268 ms
Type escape sequence to abort.
Sending 5, 100-byte ICMP Echos to 192.168.30.1, timeout is 2 seconds:
!!!!!
Success rate is 100 percent (5/5), round-trip min/avg/max = 1/1/1 ms
Type escape sequence to abort.
Sending 5, 100-byte ICMP Echos to 192.168.192.2, timeout is 2 seconds:
!!!!!
Success rate is 100 percent (5/5), round-trip min/avg/max = 56/59/68 ms
WEST(tcl)#  tclquit
```

CHAPTER 5

Route Optimization

 ## Lab 5-1: Redistribution Between RIP and OSPF (5.6.1)

The objectives of this lab are as follows:

- Review configuration and verification of Routing Information Protocol (RIP) and OSPF

- Configure passive interfaces in both RIP and OSPF

- Filter routing updates using distribute lists

- Redistribute static routes into RIP

- Redistribute RIP routes into OSPF

- Redistribute OSPF routes into RIP

- Originate a default route into OSPF

- Set a default seed metric

- Modify OSPF external network types

- Configure summary addresses

Figure 5-1 illustrates the topology that will be used for this lab.

Figure 5-1   Topology Diagram

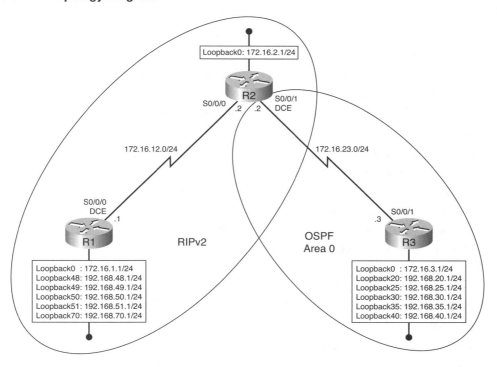

Scenario

Two online booksellers, Example.com and Example.net, have merged and now need a short-term solution to interdomain routing. Because these companies provide client services to Internet users, it is essential to have minimal downtime during the transition.

Example.com is a small firm running RIP, while Example.net has a somewhat larger network running OSPF. The diagram identifies R2 as the router that will bridge the two networks. Since it is imperative that the two booksellers continuously deliver Internet services, you should bridge these two routing domains without interfering with each router's path through its own routing domain to the Internet.

The CIO determines that it is preferable to keep the two protocol domains pictured in Figure 5-1 during the transition period, because the network engineers on each side need to understand the other's network before deploying a long-term solution. Redistribution will not be your long-term solution, but will suffice as a short-term solution.

Configure the topology in a lab to verify the short-term solution. In this scenario, R1 and R2 are running RIPv2, but the 172.16.23.0/24 network between R2 and R3 is running OSPF. You need to configure R2 to enable these two routing protocols to interact to allow full connectivity between all networks.

Step 1: Assign Addresses

Configure all loopback interfaces on the three routers in Figure 5-1. Configure the serial interfaces with the IP addresses, bring them up, and set a DCE clockrate where appropriate:

```
R1(config)# interface Loopback 0
R1(config-if)# ip address 172.16.1.1 255.255.255.0
R1(config-if)# interface Loopback 48
R1(config-if)# ip address 192.168.48.1 255.255.255.0
R1(config-if)# interface Loopback 49
R1(config-if)# ip address 192.168.49.1 255.255.255.0
R1(config-if)# interface Loopback 50
R1(config-if)# ip address 192.168.50.1 255.255.255.0
R1(config-if)# interface Loopback 51
R1(config-if)# ip address 192.168.51.1 255.255.255.0
R1(config-if)# interface Loopback 70
R1(config-if)# ip address 192.168.70.1 255.255.255.0
R1(config-if)# interface Serial 0/0/0
R1(config-if)# ip address 172.16.12.1 255.255.255.0
R1(config-if)# no fair-queue
R1(config-if)# clock rate 64000
R1(config-if)# no shutdown
```

```
R2(config)# interface Loopback 0
R2(config-if)# ip address 172.16.2.1 255.255.255.0
R2(config-if)# interface Serial 0/0/0
R2(config-if)# ip address 172.16.12.2 255.255.255.0
R2(config-if)# no fair-queue
R2(config-if)# no shutdown
R2(config-if)# interface Serial 0/0/1
```

```
R2(config-if)# ip address 172.16.23.2 255.255.255.0
R2(config-if)# clock rate 2000000
R2(config-if)# no shutdown
R3(config)# interface Loopback 0
R3(config-if)# ip address 172.16.3.1 255.255.255.0
R3(config-if)# interface Loopback 20
R3(config-if)# ip address 192.168.20.1 255.255.255.0
R3(config-if)# interface Loopback 25
R3(config-if)# ip address 192.168.25.1 255.255.255.0
R3(config-if)# interface Loopback 30
R3(config-if)# ip address 192.168.30.1 255.255.255.0
R3(config-if)# interface Loopback 35
R3(config-if)# ip address 192.168.35.1 255.255.255.0
R3(config-if)# interface Loopback 40
R3(config-if)# ip address 192.168.40.1 255.255.255.0
R3(config-if)# interface Serial 0/0/1
R3(config-if)# ip address 172.16.23.3 255.255.255.0
R3(config-if)# no shutdown
```

Be sure you can ping across the serial links when you are done.

TCL scripting is heavily used in the route optimization labs to show full or partial connectivity. If you are unfamiliar with TCL scripting or need a refresher, refer to "Lab 1-2: TCL Script Reference and Demonstration (1.5.1)" in Chapter 1, "Scalable Network Design."

The TCL shell is only available on Cisco IOS Software Release 12.3(2)T or later, and only in specific Cisco IOS feature sets. Refer to the Cisco.com Feature Navigator for more information at http://www.cisco.com/go/fn/.

You will be checking full and partial connectivity throughout this lab with the following TCL script. You can download this TCL script at www.ciscopress.com/title/1587132133 under the More Information section on the page.

```
foreach address {
172.16.1.1
192.168.48.1
192.168.49.1
192.168.50.1
192.168.51.1
192.168.70.1
172.16.12.1
172.16.2.1
172.16.12.2
172.16.23.2
172.16.3.1
192.168.20.1
192.168.25.1
192.168.30.1
```

```
192.168.35.1
192.168.40.1
172.16.23.3
} { ping $address }
```

At this point, the only pings you should receive back are those connected networks to the router from which you are pinging.

Step 2: Configure RIPv2

Configuring RIPv2 on a router is fairly simple:

1. Type the global configuration command **router rip** to enter RIP configuration mode.

2. Enable RIP version 2 with the **version 2** command.

3. Enter the **no auto-summary** command to disable automatic summarization at classful network boundaries.

4. Add the networks you want using the **network** *network* command.

Unlike Enhanced Interior Gateway Routing Protocol (EIGRP) and OSPF, you cannot use a wildcard version of the **network** command, and you have to add the whole network. This is an inherited command from the classful protocol RIPv1. Classful protocols do not support subnets, so subnet or wildcard masks are unnecessary.

Which major networks do you need to add into RIP that are depicted in the topology in Figure 5-1?

_____

_____

_____

_____

_____

_____

From which routers will these networks be advertised?

_____

Apply the following commands to R1 and R2:

```
R1(config)# router rip
R1(config-router)# version 2
R1(config-router)# no auto-summary
R1(config-router)# network 172.16.0.0
R1(config-router)# network 192.168.48.0
R1(config-router)# network 192.168.49.0
R1(config-router)# network 192.168.50.0
R1(config-router)# network 192.168.51.0
R1(config-router)# network 192.168.70.0
R2(config)# router rip
```

```
R2(config-router)# version 2
R2(config-router)# no auto-summary
R2(config-router)# network 172.16.0.0
```

Verify RIP entering routes from the other routers into the routing table using the **show ip route rip** command on each router. You can also verify which routes this router learns by RIP advertisements with the **show ip rip database** command:

```
R1# show ip route rip
     172.16.0.0/24 is subnetted, 4 subnets
R        172.16.23.0 [120/1] via 172.16.12.2, 00:00:03, Serial0/0/0
R        172.16.2.0 [120/1] via 172.16.12.2, 00:00:03, Serial0/0/0
```
```
R2# show ip route rip
     172.16.0.0/24 is subnetted, 4 subnets
R        172.16.1.0 [120/1] via 172.16.12.1, 00:00:29, Serial0/0/0
R     192.168.51.0/24 [120/1] via 172.16.12.1, 00:00:29, Serial0/0/0
R     192.168.50.0/24 [120/1] via 172.16.12.1, 00:00:29, Serial0/0/0
R     192.168.49.0/24 [120/1] via 172.16.12.1, 00:00:29, Serial0/0/0
R     192.168.70.0/24 [120/1] via 172.16.12.1, 00:00:29, Serial0/0/0
R     192.168.48.0/24 [120/1] via 172.16.12.1, 00:00:29, Serial0/0/0
```

You can also verify which routes are coming in from RIP advertisements with the **show ip rip database** command:

```
R1# show ip rip database
172.16.0.0/16       auto-summary
172.16.1.0/24       directly connected, Loopback0
172.16.2.0/24
     [1] via 172.16.12.2, 00:00:06, Serial0/0/0
172.16.12.0/24      directly connected, Serial0/0/0
172.16.23.0/24
     [1] via 172.16.12.2, 00:00:06, Serial0/0/0
192.168.48.0/24     auto-summary
192.168.48.0/24     directly connected, Loopback48
192.168.49.0/24     auto-summary
192.168.49.0/24     directly connected, Loopback49
192.168.50.0/24     auto-summary
192.168.50.0/24     directly connected, Loopback50
192.168.51.0/24     auto-summary
192.168.51.0/24     directly connected, Loopback51
192.168.70.0/24     auto-summary
192.168.70.0/24     directly connected, Loopback70
```
```
R2# show ip rip database
172.16.0.0/16       auto-summary
172.16.1.0/24
```

```
        [1] via 172.16.12.1, 00:00:10, Serial0/0/0
172.16.2.0/24     directly connected, Loopback0
172.16.12.0/24    directly connected, Serial0/0/0
172.16.23.0/24    directly connected, Serial0/0/1
192.168.48.0/24    auto-summary
192.168.48.0/24
        [1] via 172.16.12.1, 00:00:10, Serial0/0/0
192.168.49.0/24    auto-summary
192.168.49.0/24
        [1] via 172.16.12.1, 00:00:10, Serial0/0/0
192.168.50.0/24    auto-summary
192.168.50.0/24
        [1] via 172.16.12.1, 00:00:10, Serial0/0/0
192.168.51.0/24    auto-summary
192.168.51.0/24
        [1] via 172.16.12.1, 00:00:10, Serial0/0/0
192.168.70.0/24    auto-summary
192.168.70.0/24
        [1] via 172.16.12.1, 00:00:10, Serial0/0/0
```

Step 3: Configure Passive Interfaces in RIP

Look again at the RIP routes in the routing table on R1. Notice that the serial interface of R2 connecting to R3 is there, even though you do not have a RIP neighbor on that interface:

```
R1# show ip route rip
      172.16.0.0/24 is subnetted, 4 subnets
R        172.16.23.0 [120/1] via 172.16.12.2, 00:00:03, Serial0/0/0
R        172.16.2.0 [120/1] via 172.16.12.2, 00:00:03, Serial0/0/0
```

This is because the entire class B network 172.16.0.0 /16 was added to RIP on R2. If you execute the **show ip protocols** command, you can see that RIP updates are being sent out both serial interfaces:

```
R2# show ip protocols
Routing Protocol is "rip"
  Outgoing update filter list for all interfaces is not set
  Incoming update filter list for all interfaces is not set
  Sending updates every 30 seconds, next due in 13 seconds
  Invalid after 180 seconds, hold down 180, flushed after 240
  Redistributing: rip
  Default version control: send version 2, receive version 2
```

Interface	Send	Recv	Triggered RIP	Key-chain
Serial0/0/0	2	2		
Serial0/0/1	2	2		
Loopback0	2	2		

```
Automatic network summarization is not in effect
```

```
Maximum path: 4
Routing for Networks:
   172.16.0.0
Routing Information Sources:
   Gateway          Distance      Last Update
   172.16.12.1          120       00:00:26
Distance: (default is 120)
```

You do not want to send RIP updates out that serial interface toward R3 for security reasons. You can disable updates being sent with the RIP configuration command **passive-interface** *interface_type interface_number*. Disable the serial interface to R3 on R2. Observe that that interface is no longer listed under **show ip protocols** for RIP:

```
R2(config)# router rip
R2(config-router)# passive-interface serial 0/0/1
```

```
R2# show ip protocols
Routing Protocol is "rip"
  Outgoing update filter list for all interfaces is not set
  Incoming update filter list for all interfaces is not set
  Sending updates every 30 seconds, next due in 23 seconds
  Invalid after 180 seconds, hold down 180, flushed after 240
  Redistributing: rip
  Default version control: send version 2, receive version 2
    Interface             Send  Recv  Triggered RIP  Key-chain
    Serial0/0/0            2     2
    Loopback0             2     2
  Automatic network summarization is not in effect
  Maximum path: 4
  Routing for Networks:
     172.16.0.0
  Passive Interface(s):
     Serial0/0/1
  Routing Information Sources:
     Gateway          Distance      Last Update
     172.16.12.1          120       00:00:17
  Distance: (default is 120)
```

Looking at R1's routing table, notice that the network is still there from RIP:

```
R1# show ip route rip
     172.16.0.0/24 is subnetted, 4 subnets
R       172.16.23.0 [120/1] via 172.16.12.2, 00:00:19, Serial0/0/0
R       172.16.2.0 [120/1] via 172.16.12.2, 00:00:19, Serial0/0/0
```

Making an interface in RIP passive only disables updates from being sent through RIP; it does not affect interfaces being received through it.

What are some reasons you would want to disable RIP sending updates out a particular interface?

_____

_____

_____

_____

_____

Putting a RIPv2 interface in passive mode saves the router from sending multicast RIP packets out an interface that has no neighbors.

Does RIPv2 send advertisements out loopback interfaces?

_____

_____

_____

If you are unsure, monitor the output of the **debug ip rip** command to verify your answer. Place any loopbacks out of which RIPv2 is sending advertisements in passive state with the **passive-interface** command, as described previously:

```
R1(config)# router rip
R1(config-router)# passive-interface loopback 0
R1(config-router)# passive-interface loopback 48
R1(config-router)# passive-interface loopback 49
R1(config-router)# passive-interface loopback 50
R1(config-router)# passive-interface loopback 51
R1(config-router)# passive-interface loopback 70
R2(config)# router rip
R2(config-router)# passive-interface loopback 0
```

If you are running RIPv2, you should implement the use of passive interfaces as a common practice to save CPU processor cycles and bandwidth on interfaces that do not have multicast RIPv2 neighbors.

Step 4: Summarize a Supernet with RIP

Notice that you can see all prefixes from R1 in R2's routing table:

```
R2# show ip route rip
     172.16.0.0/24 is subnetted, 4 subnets
R       172.16.1.0 [120/1] via 172.16.12.1, 00:00:29, Serial0/0/0
R     192.168.51.0/24 [120/1] via 172.16.12.1, 00:00:29, Serial0/0/0
R     192.168.50.0/24 [120/1] via 172.16.12.1, 00:00:29, Serial0/0/0
R     192.168.49.0/24 [120/1] via 172.16.12.1, 00:00:29, Serial0/0/0
R     192.168.70.0/24 [120/1] via 172.16.12.1, 00:00:29, Serial0/0/0
R     192.168.48.0/24 [120/1] via 172.16.12.1, 00:00:29, Serial0/0/0
```

In preparing for redistribution, you want to redistribute the minimum number of destination prefixes into each of the routing protocols.

Which RIP routes should you summarize because they are contiguous, and which mask should you use?

_____

_____

Under normal circumstances, you could simply summarize the four consecutive class-C networks with the **ip summary address rip** command on R1's Serial0/0/0 interface. However, the Cisco IOS does not allow you to summarize to a mask length that is less than the classful network prefix (in this case, 24 bits). If you do, you receive the following error message:

```
R1(config-if)# ip summary-address rip 192.168.48.0 255.255.252.0
Summary mask must be greater or equal to major net
```

Recall from the EIGRP labs that summary routes display in the summarizing device's routing table as having the next hop being the Null0 interface. The routing protocol advertises these routes as pointing toward the redistributing router.

To get around the **ip summary-address rip** message error, create a static route on R1 to summarize the networks of loopbacks 48 through 51. Then redistribute the route on R1:

```
R1(config)# ip route 192.168.48.0 255.255.252.0 null0
R1(config)# router rip
R1(config-router)# redistribute static
```

This solution might seem unusual, but in fact you are modeling the internal workings of other routing protocols like EIGRP or OSPF to overcome RIP's limitations. It is helpful to understand how EIGRP and OSPF handle summary routes internally because it can apply to other applications.

Verify with the **show ip route** command on R1 and R2 that the RIP supernet has been added to the routing table:

```
R1# show ip route
<output omitted>

Gateway of last resort is not set

     172.16.0.0/24 is subnetted, 4 subnets
R       172.16.23.0 [120/1] via 172.16.12.2, 00:00:27, Serial0/0/0
C       172.16.12.0 is directly connected, Serial0/0/0
C       172.16.1.0 is directly connected, Loopback0
R       172.16.2.0 [120/1] via 172.16.12.2, 00:00:27, Serial0/0/0
C    192.168.51.0/24 is directly connected, Loopback51
C    192.168.50.0/24 is directly connected, Loopback50
C    192.168.49.0/24 is directly connected, Loopback49
C    192.168.70.0/24 is directly connected, Loopback70
C    192.168.48.0/24 is directly connected, Loopback48
```

```
S    192.168.48.0/22 is directly connected, Null0
```

```
R2# show ip route
<output omitted>

Gateway of last resort is not set


     172.16.0.0/24 is subnetted, 4 subnets
C        172.16.23.0 is directly connected, Serial0/0/1
C        172.16.12.0 is directly connected, Serial0/0/0
R        172.16.1.0 [120/1] via 172.16.12.1, 00:00:05, Serial0/0/0
C        172.16.2.0 is directly connected, Loopback0
R    192.168.51.0/24 [120/1] via 172.16.12.1, 00:00:05, Serial0/0/0
R    192.168.50.0/24 [120/1] via 172.16.12.1, 00:00:05, Serial0/0/0
R    192.168.49.0/24 [120/1] via 172.16.12.1, 00:00:05, Serial0/0/0
R    192.168.70.0/24 [120/1] via 172.16.12.1, 00:00:07, Serial0/0/0
R    192.168.48.0/24 [120/1] via 172.16.12.1, 00:00:07, Serial0/0/0
R    192.168.48.0/22 [120/1] via 172.16.12.1, 00:00:07, Serial0/0/0
```

Will this route to Null0 affect routing to prefixes with longer addresses on R1? Explain.

_____

_____

_____

_____

Step 5: Suppress Routes Using Prefix Lists

Sometimes you may not want to advertise certain networks out a particular interface, or you may want to filter updates as they come in. This is possible with some routing protocols, such as RIP or EIGRP. However, link-state protocols are less flexible because every router in an area is required to have a synchronized database as a condition for full adjacency.

In this scenario, you want to filter updates from R1 to R2, allowing only the networks Loopback 0 and Loopback 70 and the summary route to be advertised. Suppress the more specific prefixes so that routing tables are kept small, and CPU processor cycles on the routers are not wasted.

Distribute lists use either access lists or prefix lists to filter routes by network address. They can also be configured to filter subnet masks. You can only use standard access lists to filter for the network address of the destination network without regard to subnet address. In this scenario, you have two networks with the same destination network address—192.168.48.0. The 22-bit summary and the 24-bit major network address both have the same address, so standard access lists will not accomplish the filtering correctly. Prefix lists or extended access lists are appropriate workarounds. On R1, use a prefix list as a distribution filter to prevent the more specific routes to Loopbacks 48 through 51. Allow all other destination networks including the summary route. Table 5-1 lists, in order, the commands used for this prefix list.

Table 5-1   Line-by-Line Evaluation of Prefix List RIP-OUT

Line Number	Prefix List Instruction	Description
Line 1:	**ip prefix-list RIP-OUT permit 192.168.48.0/22**	Permits the summary route and nothing else, because no other route can match that network address with a mask of exactly 22 bits.
Line 2:	**ip prefix-list RIP-OUT deny 192.168.48.0/22 le 24**	Denies all prefixes with a network address in the 192.168.48.0/22 block of addresses that have subnet masks from 22 bits to 24 bits. This removes exactly four network addresses matching both 22, 23, and 24 bits in length of the subnet mask. This line would deny the 192.168.48.0/22 summary route you created if Line 1 of the prefix list did not explicitly permit the summary route.
Line 3:	**ip prefix-list RIP-OUT permit 0.0.0.0/0 le 32**	Allows all IPv4 prefixes that are not explicitly denied in previous statements of the prefix list.

Apply this access list with the **distribute-list** command from the RIP configuration prompt on R1:

```
R1(config)# router rip
R1(config-router)# distribute-list prefix RIP-OUT out serial0/0/0
```

On R1 use the command **clear ip route** (Otherwise you will have to wait for the RIP timers to expire.) Then verify that the filtering has taken place using the **show ip route rip** and **show ip rip database** commands on R2:

```
R2# show ip route rip
     172.16.0.0/24 is subnetted, 4 subnets
R       172.16.1.0 [120/1] via 172.16.12.1, 00:00:12, Serial0/0/0
R    192.168.70.0/24 [120/1] via 172.16.12.1, 00:00:12, Serial0/0/0
R    192.168.48.0/22 [120/1] via 172.16.12.1, 00:00:12, Serial0/0/0
R2# show ip rip database
172.16.0.0/16     auto-summary
172.16.1.0/24
    [1] via 172.16.12.1, 00:00:11, Serial0/0/0
172.16.2.0/24     directly connected, Loopback0
172.16.12.0/24    directly connected, Serial0/0/0
172.16.23.0/24    directly connected, Serial0/0/1
```

```
192.168.48.0/22
    [1] via 172.16.12.1, 00:00:11, Serial0/0/0
192.168.70.0/24    auto-summary
192.168.70.0/24
    [1] via 172.16.12.1, 00:00:11, Serial0/0/0
```

Why would you want to filter updates getting sent out or coming in?

_____

_____

_____

_____

Step 6: Configure OSPF

Configure single-area OSPF between R2 and R3. On R2, include just the serial link connecting to R3. On R3, include the serial link and all loopback interfaces. Make sure that you change the network type for the loopback interfaces. Verify that your adjacencies come up with the **show ip ospf neighbors** command. Also make sure that you have routes from OSPF populating the routing tables with the **show ip route ospf** command:

```
R2(config)# router ospf 1
R2(config-router)# network 172.16.23.0 0.0.0.255 area 0
```

```
R3(config)# router ospf 1
R3(config-router)# network 172.16.0.0 0.0.255.255 area 0
R3(config-router)# network 192.168.0.0 0.0.255.255 area 0
```

```
R2# show ip ospf neighbor
```

Neighbor ID	Pri	State	Dead Time	Address	Interface
192.168.40.1	0	FULL/ -	00:00:37	172.16.23.3	Serial0/0/1

```
R3# show ip ospf neighbor
```

Neighbor ID	Pri	State	Dead Time	Address	Interface
172.16.2.1	0	FULL/ -	00:00:39	172.16.23.2	Serial0/0/1

```
R2# show ip route ospf
     192.168.30.0/32 is subnetted, 1 subnets
O       192.168.30.1 [110/65] via 172.16.23.3, 00:04:41, Serial0/0/1
     192.168.25.0/32 is subnetted, 1 subnets
O       192.168.25.1 [110/65] via 172.16.23.3, 00:04:41, Serial0/0/1
     192.168.40.0/32 is subnetted, 1 subnets
O       192.168.40.1 [110/65] via 172.16.23.3, 00:04:41, Serial0/0/1
     172.16.0.0/16 is variably subnetted, 5 subnets, 2 masks
O       172.16.3.1/32 [110/65] via 172.16.23.3, 00:00:20, Serial0/0/1
     192.168.20.0/32 is subnetted, 1 subnets
```

```
O          192.168.20.1 [110/65] via 172.16.23.3, 00:04:41, Serial0/0/1
        192.168.35.0/32 is subnetted, 1 subnets
O          192.168.35.1 [110/65] via 172.16.23.3, 00:04:41, Serial0/0/1
```

```
R3# show ip route ospf

R3#
! note that the above output is blank
```

The **network 192.168.0.0 0.0.255.255 area 0** command allows OSPF to involve interfaces that have IP addresses in that range.

A common misconception is that OSPF advertises the entire range of the network given in the router's network statement; it certainly does not. However, it does advertise any connected subnets in that entire range of addresses to adjacent routers. You can verify this by viewing the output of the **show ip route** command on R2. Do you see a 192.168.0.0/16 supernet?

_____

_____

R2 is the only router with all routes in the topology (except for those that were filtered out) because it is involved with both routing protocols.

Step 7: Configure Passive Interfaces in OSPF

As discussed before, passive interfaces save CPU cycles, router memory, and link bandwidth by preventing broadcast/multicast routing updates on interfaces that have no neighbors. In link-state protocols, adjacencies must be formed before routers exchange routing information. The **passive-interface** command in OSPF configuration mode prevents an interface from sending multicast Hello packets out that interface.

OSPF included R3's loopback interfaces in its **network** statements shown in Step 6.

On R3, configure Loopback0 as a passive interface in OSPF. At the OSPF configuration prompt, use the **passive-interface** _interface_type interface_number_ command:

```
R3(config-router)# passive-interface loopback 0
```

How is this different from the RIP version of this command?

_____

_____

_____

_____

_____

_____

The Cisco IOS provides a quick way of selecting interfaces for passive mode. Use the **passive-interface default** command to make all interfaces passive. Then use the **no passive-interface** *interface interface_number* command to bring the Serial0/0/1 interface out of passive mode:

```
R3(config)# router ospf 1

R3(config-router)# passive-interface default

R3(config-router)#

*Oct 15 01:49:44.174: %OSPF-5-ADJCHG: Process 1, Nbr 172.16.2.1 on Serial0/0/1 from
FULL to DOWN, Neighbor Down: Interface down or detached

R3(config-router)# no passive-interface serial 0/0/1

R3(config-router)#

*Oct 15 01:49:55.438: %OSPF-5-ADJCHG: Process 1, Nbr 172.16.2.1 on Serial0/0/1 from
LOADING to FULL, Loading Done
```

You can verify the application of this command by issuing the **show ip protocols** command:

```
R3# show ip protocols
Routing Protocol is "ospf 1"
  Outgoing update filter list for all interfaces is not set
  Incoming update filter list for all interfaces is not set
  Router ID 192.168.40.1
  Number of areas in this router is 1. 1 normal 0 stub 0 nssa
  Maximum path: 4
  Routing for Networks:
    172.16.0.0 0.0.255.255 area 0
    192.168.0.0 0.0.255.255 area 0
  Reference bandwidth unit is 100 mbps
  Passive Interface(s):
    FastEthernet0/0
    FastEthernet0/1
    Serial0/0/0
    Serial0/1/0
    Serial0/1/1
    Loopback0
    Loopback20
    Loopback25
    Loopback30
    Loopback35
    Loopback40
    VoIP-Null0
  Routing Information Sources:
    Gateway         Distance      Last Update
  Distance: (default is 110)
```

Step 8: Allow One-Way Redistribution

On R2, configure OSPF to redistribute into RIP under the RIP configuration prompt with the **redistribute ospf** *process* **metric** *metric* command, where *process* is the OSPF process number, and *metric* is the default metric with which you want to originate the routes into RIP. If you do not specify a default metric in RIP, it gives routes an infinite metric, and they are not advertised:

```
R2(config)# router rip
R2(config-router)# redistribute ospf 1 metric 4
```

Verify the redistribution with the **show ip protocols** command:

```
R2# show ip protocols
Routing Protocol is "rip"
  Outgoing update filter list for all interfaces is not set
  Incoming update filter list for all interfaces is not set
  Sending updates every 30 seconds, next due in 24 seconds
  Invalid after 180 seconds, hold down 180, flushed after 240
  Redistributing: rip, ospf 1
  Default version control: send version 2, receive version 2
    Interface              Send  Recv  Triggered RIP  Key-chain
    Serial0/0/0              2     2
  Automatic network summarization is not in effect
  Maximum path: 4
  Routing for Networks:
    172.16.0.0
  Passive Interface(s):
    Serial0/0/1
    Loopback0
  Routing Information Sources:
    Gateway         Distance      Last Update
    172.16.12.1          120      00:00:19
  Distance: (default is 120)
...
<output omitted>
```

If you look at the routing table on R1 with the **show ip route** command, you see that it has all the routes in the topology. However, pinging a loopback on R3 from R1 shows that R1 has a route to R3, but R3 does not have a route back to R1. You can verify this with the **traceroute** command on R1:

```
R1# show ip route rip
      192.168.30.0/32 is subnetted, 1 subnets
R        192.168.30.1 [120/4] via 172.16.12.2, 00:00:02, Serial0/0/0
      192.168.25.0/32 is subnetted, 1 subnets
R        192.168.25.1 [120/4] via 172.16.12.2, 00:00:02, Serial0/0/0
      192.168.40.0/32 is subnetted, 1 subnets
R        192.168.40.1 [120/4] via 172.16.12.2, 00:00:02, Serial0/0/0
```

```
       172.16.0.0/24 is subnetted, 4 subnets
R         172.16.23.0 [120/1] via 172.16.12.2, 00:00:02, Serial0/0/0
R         172.16.2.0 [120/1] via 172.16.12.2, 00:00:02, Serial0/0/0
R         172.16.3.1/32 [120/4] via 172.16.12.2, 00:00:24, Serial0/0/0
       192.168.20.0/32 is subnetted, 1 subnets
R         192.168.20.1 [120/4] via 172.16.12.2, 00:00:02, Serial0/0/0
       192.168.35.0/32 is subnetted, 1 subnets
R         192.168.35.1 [120/4] via 172.16.12.2, 00:00:02, Serial0/0/0

R1# ping 192.168.30.1


Type escape sequence to abort.
Sending 5, 100-byte ICMP Echos to 192.168.30.1, timeout is 2 seconds:
.....
Success rate is 0 percent (0/5)


R1# traceroute 192.168.30.1


Type escape sequence to abort.
Tracing the route to 192.168.30.1


  1 172.16.12.2 12 msec 12 msec 16 msec
  2  *   *   *
  3  *   *   *
  4  *   *   *
<remaining output omitted>
```

To alleviate this problem, you can originate a default route into OSPF that points toward R2 so that the pings are routed back toward R2. R2 uses its information from RIPv2 to send pings back to R1.

Issue the **default-information originate always** command under the OSPF configuration prompt to force R2 to advertise a default route in OSPF. Verify that this route shows up in R3's routing table:

```
R2(config)# router ospf 1
R2(config-router)# default-information originate always
R3# show ip route ospf
O*E2 0.0.0.0/0 [110/1] via 172.16.23.2, 00:05:13, Serial0/0/1
```

You should now have full connectivity between all networks illustrated in Figure 5-1. Try using the TCL script and comparing it with the output shown in the section, "TCL Script Output: Steps 8 and 9" (all successful).

Step 9: Redistribute Between Two Routing Protocols

You can substitute this default route in with actual, more specific routes. First, take away the default route advertisement with the **no default-information originate always** command under the OSPF configuration prompt on R2. Next, use the **redistribute rip** command. You do not need to specify a default metric in OSPF. Notice the warning:

```
R2(config)# router ospf 1

R2(config-router)# no default-information originate always

R2(config-router)# redistribute rip

% Only classful networks will be redistributed
```

If you display the routing table on R3, the only external OSPF route that came in was the 192.168.70.0 /24 network:

```
R3# show ip route ospf

O E2 192.168.70.0/24 [110/20] via 172.16.23.2, 00:00:51, Serial0/0/1

O E2 192.168.48.0/22 [110/20] via 172.16.23.2, 00:00:51, Serial0/0/1
```

This is because, by default, OSPF only accepts classful networks when redistributing into it. The only classful network coming into R2 from RIP is the class C network 192.168.70.0. You can modify this behavior by adding the **subnets** keyword to the **redistribute** command. Verify this with the **show ip route ospf** command on R3:

```
R2(config)# router ospf 1

R2(config-router)# redistribute rip subnets
```

```
R3# show ip route ospf
     172.16.0.0/24 is subnetted, 5 subnets
O E2    172.16.12.0 [110/20] via 172.16.23.2, 00:00:01, Serial0/0/1
O E2    172.16.1.0 [110/20] via 172.16.23.2, 00:00:01, Serial0/0/1
O E2    172.16.2.0 [110/20] via 172.16.23.2, 00:00:01, Serial0/0/1
O E2 192.168.70.0/24 [110/20] via 172.16.23.2, 00:04:19, Serial0/0/1
O E2 192.168.48.0/22 [110/20] via 172.16.23.2, 00:04:19, Serial0/0/1
```

You should again have full connectivity between all networks shown in Figure 5-1. Run the TCL script from each router. Verify your output against the output in the section, "TCL Script Output: Steps 8 and 9."

Step 10: Set a Default Seed Metric

Under any routing protocol, you can specify a default seed metric to be used for redistribution, instead of or in addition to setting metrics on a per-protocol basis. Seed metrics is a protocol-independent feature of Cisco IOS Software that is usually used when redistributing into distance-vector protocols.

Notice that the metric listed in the R3 routing table just shown is 20.

On R2, under the OSPF configuration prompt, issue the **default-metric** *metric* command to configure a default metric for redistributed routes. You can override the global creation of a default seed metric on a per-protocol basis by using the **metric** argument in a redistribution command. You can also use the **metric** command under other routing protocols. Verify the new metric in R3's routing table. It may take a little while for the new metric to propagate:

```
R2(config)# router ospf 1
R2(config-router)# default-metric 10000
```

```
R3# show ip route ospf
       172.16.0.0/24 is subnetted, 5 subnets
O E2    172.16.12.0 [110/10000] via 172.16.23.2, 00:02:56, Serial0/0/1
O E2    172.16.1.0 [110/10000] via 172.16.23.2, 00:02:56, Serial0/0/1
O E2    172.16.2.0 [110/10000] via 172.16.23.2, 00:02:56, Serial0/0/1
O E2 192.168.70.0/24 [110/10000] via 172.16.23.2, 00:02:56, Serial0/0/1
O E2 192.168.48.0/22 [110/10000] via 172.16.23.2, 00:02:56, Serial0/0/1
```

Step 11: Change the OSPF External Network Type

In this last step, take a look at R3's routing table. Notice that the external (redistributed) routes have O E2 as their type. Also notice that the metric is exactly the same as the seed metric given in the previous step. O means OSPF, and E2 means external, type 2. In OSPF, there are two external metric types, and E2 is the default. External type 1 metrics increase like a usual route, whereas external type 2 metrics do not increase as they get advertised through the OSPF domain.

Where would an external type 1 metric be useful?

_____

_____

_____

_____

Where would an external type 2 metric be useful?

_____

_____

You can change this type using the **metric-type** argument with the **redistribute** command. Change it to type 1 for RIP redistributed routes, and then display R3's routing table again:

```
R2(config)# router ospf 1
R2(config-router)# redistribute rip sub metric-type 1
```

```
R3# show ip route ospf
       172.16.0.0/24 is subnetted, 5 subnets
O E1    172.16.12.0 [110/10064] via 172.16.23.2, 00:03:05, Serial0/0/1
O E1    172.16.1.0 [110/10064] via 172.16.23.2, 00:03:05, Serial0/0/1
O E1    172.16.2.0 [110/10064] via 172.16.23.2, 00:03:05, Serial0/0/1
O E1 192.168.70.0/24 [110/10064] via 172.16.23.2, 00:03:05, Serial0/0/1
O E1 192.168.48.0/22 [110/10064] via 172.16.23.2, 00:03:05, Serial0/0/1
```

Which attributes of the routes changed?

_____

_____

Challenge: Use Extended Access Lists for Filtering

On R1, configure a distribute list to filter 192.168.20.0 /24 and 192.168.25.0 /27 from inbound updates from R2. Pay special attention to the subnet masks. Do not filter out 192.168.25.0 /24. Use an extended access list to accomplish this. Refer to Step 5 for more details.

_____

_____

_____

_____

_____

_____

_____

_____

_____

_____

_____

_____

_____

_____

_____

_____

_____

_____

_____

TCL Script Output: Steps 8 and 9

```
R1# tclsh
R1(tcl)# foreach address {
+>(tcl)# 172.16.1.1
+>(tcl)# 192.168.48.1
+>(tcl)# 192.168.49.1
+>(tcl)# 192.168.50.1
+>(tcl)# 192.168.51.1
+>(tcl)# 192.168.70.1
+>(tcl)# 172.16.12.1
+>(tcl)# 172.16.2.1
+>(tcl)# 172.16.12.2
+>(tcl)# 172.16.23.2
+>(tcl)# 172.16.3.1
+>(tcl)# 192.168.20.1
+>(tcl)# 192.168.25.1
+>(tcl)# 192.168.30.1
+>(tcl)# 192.168.35.1
+>(tcl)# 192.168.40.1
+>(tcl)# 172.16.23.3
+>(tcl)# } { ping $address }

Type escape sequence to abort.
Sending 5, 100-byte ICMP Echos to 172.16.1.1, timeout is 2 seconds:
!!!!!
Success rate is 100 percent (5/5), round-trip min/avg/max = 1/1/4 ms
Type escape sequence to abort.
Sending 5, 100-byte ICMP Echos to 192.168.48.1, timeout is 2 seconds:
!!!!!
Success rate is 100 percent (5/5), round-trip min/avg/max = 1/1/4 ms
Type escape sequence to abort.
Sending 5, 100-byte ICMP Echos to 192.168.49.1, timeout is 2 seconds:
!!!!!
Success rate is 100 percent (5/5), round-trip min/avg/max = 1/1/4 ms
Type escape sequence to abort.
Sending 5, 100-byte ICMP Echos to 192.168.50.1, timeout is 2 seconds:
!!!!!
Success rate is 100 percent (5/5), round-trip min/avg/max = 1/1/1 ms
Type escape sequence to abort.
Sending 5, 100-byte ICMP Echos to 192.168.51.1, timeout is 2 seconds:
!!!!!
Success rate is 100 percent (5/5), round-trip min/avg/max = 1/1/4 ms
Type escape sequence to abort.
```

```
Sending 5, 100-byte ICMP Echos to 192.168.70.1, timeout is 2 seconds:
!!!!!
Success rate is 100 percent (5/5), round-trip min/avg/max = 1/2/4 ms
Type escape sequence to abort.
Sending 5, 100-byte ICMP Echos to 172.16.12.1, timeout is 2 seconds:
!!!!!
Success rate is 100 percent (5/5), round-trip min/avg/max = 56/57/64 ms
Type escape sequence to abort.
Sending 5, 100-byte ICMP Echos to 172.16.2.1, timeout is 2 seconds:
!!!!!
Success rate is 100 percent (5/5), round-trip min/avg/max = 28/28/32 ms
Type escape sequence to abort.
Sending 5, 100-byte ICMP Echos to 172.16.12.2, timeout is 2 seconds:
!!!!!
Success rate is 100 percent (5/5), round-trip min/avg/max = 28/28/32 ms
Type escape sequence to abort.
Sending 5, 100-byte ICMP Echos to 172.16.23.2, timeout is 2 seconds:
!!!!!
Success rate is 100 percent (5/5), round-trip min/avg/max = 28/28/32 ms
Type escape sequence to abort.
Sending 5, 100-byte ICMP Echos to 172.16.3.1, timeout is 2 seconds:
!!!!!
Success rate is 100 percent (5/5), round-trip min/avg/max = 28/28/32 ms
Type escape sequence to abort.
Sending 5, 100-byte ICMP Echos to 192.168.20.1, timeout is 2 seconds:
!!!!!
Success rate is 100 percent (5/5), round-trip min/avg/max = 28/29/32 ms
Type escape sequence to abort.
Sending 5, 100-byte ICMP Echos to 192.168.25.1, timeout is 2 seconds:
!!!!!
Success rate is 100 percent (5/5), round-trip min/avg/max = 28/29/32 ms
Type escape sequence to abort.
Sending 5, 100-byte ICMP Echos to 192.168.30.1, timeout is 2 seconds:
!!!!!
Success rate is 100 percent (5/5), round-trip min/avg/max = 28/29/32 ms
Type escape sequence to abort.
Sending 5, 100-byte ICMP Echos to 192.168.35.1, timeout is 2 seconds:
!!!!!
Success rate is 100 percent (5/5), round-trip min/avg/max = 28/28/32 ms
Type escape sequence to abort.
Sending 5, 100-byte ICMP Echos to 192.168.40.1, timeout is 2 seconds:
!!!!!
Success rate is 100 percent (5/5), round-trip min/avg/max = 28/30/32 ms
Type escape sequence to abort.
```

```
Sending 5, 100-byte ICMP Echos to 172.16.23.3, timeout is 2 seconds:
!!!!!
Success rate is 100 percent (5/5), round-trip min/avg/max = 28/29/32 ms
R1(tcl)# tclquit
```
```
R2# tclsh
R2(tcl)# foreach address {
+>(tcl)# 172.16.1.1
+>(tcl)# 192.168.48.1
+>(tcl)# 192.168.49.1
+>(tcl)# 192.168.50.1
+>(tcl)# 192.168.51.1
+>(tcl)# 192.168.70.1
+>(tcl)# 172.16.12.1
+>(tcl)# 172.16.2.1
+>(tcl)# 172.16.12.2
+>(tcl)# 172.16.23.2
+>(tcl)# 172.16.3.1
+>(tcl)# 192.168.20.1
+>(tcl)# 192.168.25.1
+>(tcl)# 192.168.30.1
+>(tcl)# 192.168.35.1
+>(tcl)# 192.168.40.1
+>(tcl)# 172.16.23.3
+>(tcl)# } { ping $address }

Type escape sequence to abort.
Sending 5, 100-byte ICMP Echos to 172.16.1.1, timeout is 2 seconds:
!!!!!
Success rate is 100 percent (5/5), round-trip min/avg/max = 28/28/32 ms
Type escape sequence to abort.
Sending 5, 100-byte ICMP Echos to 192.168.48.1, timeout is 2 seconds:
!!!!!
Success rate is 100 percent (5/5), round-trip min/avg/max = 28/28/28 ms
Type escape sequence to abort.
Sending 5, 100-byte ICMP Echos to 192.168.49.1, timeout is 2 seconds:
!!!!!
Success rate is 100 percent (5/5), round-trip min/avg/max = 28/28/32 ms
Type escape sequence to abort.
Sending 5, 100-byte ICMP Echos to 192.168.50.1, timeout is 2 seconds:
!!!!!
Success rate is 100 percent (5/5), round-trip min/avg/max = 28/28/32 ms
Type escape sequence to abort.
Sending 5, 100-byte ICMP Echos to 192.168.51.1, timeout is 2 seconds:
!!!!!
```

```
Success rate is 100 percent (5/5), round-trip min/avg/max = 28/28/32 ms
Type escape sequence to abort.
Sending 5, 100-byte ICMP Echos to 192.168.70.1, timeout is 2 seconds:
!!!!!
Success rate is 100 percent (5/5), round-trip min/avg/max = 28/28/32 ms
Type escape sequence to abort.
Sending 5, 100-byte ICMP Echos to 172.16.12.1, timeout is 2 seconds:
!!!!!
Success rate is 100 percent (5/5), round-trip min/avg/max = 28/28/28 ms
Type escape sequence to abort.
Sending 5, 100-byte ICMP Echos to 172.16.2.1, timeout is 2 seconds:
!!!!!
Success rate is 100 percent (5/5), round-trip min/avg/max = 1/1/4 ms
Type escape sequence to abort.
Sending 5, 100-byte ICMP Echos to 172.16.12.2, timeout is 2 seconds:
!!!!!
Success rate is 100 percent (5/5), round-trip min/avg/max = 56/57/64 ms
Type escape sequence to abort.
Sending 5, 100-byte ICMP Echos to 172.16.23.2, timeout is 2 seconds:
!!!!!
Success rate is 100 percent (5/5), round-trip min/avg/max = 1/2/4 ms
Type escape sequence to abort.
Sending 5, 100-byte ICMP Echos to 172.16.3.1, timeout is 2 seconds:
!!!!!
Success rate is 100 percent (5/5), round-trip min/avg/max = 1/2/4 ms
Type escape sequence to abort.
Sending 5, 100-byte ICMP Echos to 192.168.20.1, timeout is 2 seconds:
!!!!!
Success rate is 100 percent (5/5), round-trip min/avg/max = 1/2/4 ms
Type escape sequence to abort.
Sending 5, 100-byte ICMP Echos to 192.168.25.1, timeout is 2 seconds:
!!!!!
Success rate is 100 percent (5/5), round-trip min/avg/max = 1/2/4 ms
Type escape sequence to abort.
Sending 5, 100-byte ICMP Echos to 192.168.30.1, timeout is 2 seconds:
!!!!!
Success rate is 100 percent (5/5), round-trip min/avg/max = 1/2/4 ms
Type escape sequence to abort.
Sending 5, 100-byte ICMP Echos to 192.168.35.1, timeout is 2 seconds:
!!!!!
Success rate is 100 percent (5/5), round-trip min/avg/max = 1/2/4 ms
Type escape sequence to abort.
Sending 5, 100-byte ICMP Echos to 192.168.40.1, timeout is 2 seconds:
!!!!!
```

```
Success rate is 100 percent (5/5), round-trip min/avg/max = 1/2/4 ms
Type escape sequence to abort.
Sending 5, 100-byte ICMP Echos to 172.16.23.3, timeout is 2 seconds:
!!!!!
Success rate is 100 percent (5/5), round-trip min/avg/max = 1/2/4 ms
R2(tcl)# tclquit
```
```
R3# tclsh
R3(tcl)# foreach address {
+>(tcl)# 172.16.1.1
+>(tcl)# 192.168.48.1
+>(tcl)# 192.168.49.1
+>(tcl)# 192.168.50.1
+>(tcl)# 192.168.51.1
+>(tcl)# 192.168.70.1
+>(tcl)# 172.16.12.1
+>(tcl)# 172.16.2.1
+>(tcl)# 172.16.12.2
+>(tcl)# 172.16.23.2
+>(tcl)# 172.16.3.1
+>(tcl)# 192.168.20.1
+>(tcl)# 192.168.25.1
+>(tcl)# 192.168.30.1
+>(tcl)# 192.168.35.1
+>(tcl)# 192.168.40.1
+>(tcl)# 172.16.23.3
+>(tcl)# } { ping $address }

Type escape sequence to abort.
Sending 5, 100-byte ICMP Echos to 172.16.1.1, timeout is 2 seconds:
!!!!!
Success rate is 100 percent (5/5), round-trip min/avg/max = 28/29/32 ms
Type escape sequence to abort.
Sending 5, 100-byte ICMP Echos to 192.168.48.1, timeout is 2 seconds:
!!!!!
Success rate is 100 percent (5/5), round-trip min/avg/max = 28/30/32 ms
Type escape sequence to abort.
Sending 5, 100-byte ICMP Echos to 192.168.49.1, timeout is 2 seconds:
!!!!!
Success rate is 100 percent (5/5), round-trip min/avg/max = 28/29/32 ms
Type escape sequence to abort.
Sending 5, 100-byte ICMP Echos to 192.168.50.1, timeout is 2 seconds:
!!!!!
Success rate is 100 percent (5/5), round-trip min/avg/max = 28/29/32 ms
Type escape sequence to abort.
```

```
Sending 5, 100-byte ICMP Echos to 192.168.51.1, timeout is 2 seconds:
!!!!!
Success rate is 100 percent (5/5), round-trip min/avg/max = 28/30/32 ms
Type escape sequence to abort.
Sending 5, 100-byte ICMP Echos to 192.168.70.1, timeout is 2 seconds:
!!!!!
Success rate is 100 percent (5/5), round-trip min/avg/max = 28/29/32 ms
Type escape sequence to abort.
Sending 5, 100-byte ICMP Echos to 172.16.12.1, timeout is 2 seconds:
!!!!!
Success rate is 100 percent (5/5), round-trip min/avg/max = 28/28/32 ms
Type escape sequence to abort.
Sending 5, 100-byte ICMP Echos to 172.16.2.1, timeout is 2 seconds:
!!!!!
Success rate is 100 percent (5/5), round-trip min/avg/max = 1/2/4 ms
Type escape sequence to abort.
Sending 5, 100-byte ICMP Echos to 172.16.12.2, timeout is 2 seconds:
!!!!!
Success rate is 100 percent (5/5), round-trip min/avg/max = 1/2/4 ms
Type escape sequence to abort.
Sending 5, 100-byte ICMP Echos to 172.16.23.2, timeout is 2 seconds:
!!!!!
Success rate is 100 percent (5/5), round-trip min/avg/max = 1/2/4 ms
Type escape sequence to abort.
Sending 5, 100-byte ICMP Echos to 172.16.3.1, timeout is 2 seconds:
!!!!!
Success rate is 100 percent (5/5), round-trip min/avg/max = 1/1/4 ms
Type escape sequence to abort.
Sending 5, 100-byte ICMP Echos to 192.168.20.1, timeout is 2 seconds:
!!!!!
Success rate is 100 percent (5/5), round-trip min/avg/max = 1/1/1 ms
Type escape sequence to abort.
Sending 5, 100-byte ICMP Echos to 192.168.25.1, timeout is 2 seconds:
!!!!!
Success rate is 100 percent (5/5), round-trip min/avg/max = 1/1/4 ms
Type escape sequence to abort.
Sending 5, 100-byte ICMP Echos to 192.168.30.1, timeout is 2 seconds:
!!!!!
Success rate is 100 percent (5/5), round-trip min/avg/max = 1/1/1 ms
Type escape sequence to abort.
Sending 5, 100-byte ICMP Echos to 192.168.35.1, timeout is 2 seconds:
!!!!!
Success rate is 100 percent (5/5), round-trip min/avg/max = 1/1/4 ms
Type escape sequence to abort.
```

```
Sending 5, 100-byte ICMP Echos to 192.168.40.1, timeout is 2 seconds:
!!!!!
Success rate is 100 percent (5/5), round-trip min/avg/max = 1/1/1 ms
Type escape sequence to abort.
Sending 5, 100-byte ICMP Echos to 172.16.23.3, timeout is 2 seconds:
!!!!!
Success rate is 100 percent (5/5), round-trip min/avg/max = 1/3/4 ms
R3(tcl)# tclquit
```

Lab 5-2   Redistribution Between EIGRP and OSPF (5.6.2)

The objectives of this lab are as follows:

- Review EIGRP and OSPF configuration

- Redistribute into EIGRP

- Redistribute into OSPF

- Summarize routes in EIGRP

- Filter routes using route maps

- Modify EIGRP distances

- Modify OSPF distances

- Create passive interfaces in EIGRP

- Summarize in OSPF at an ABR and an ASBR

Figure 5-2 illustrates the topology that will be used for this lab.

Figure 5-2   Topology Diagram

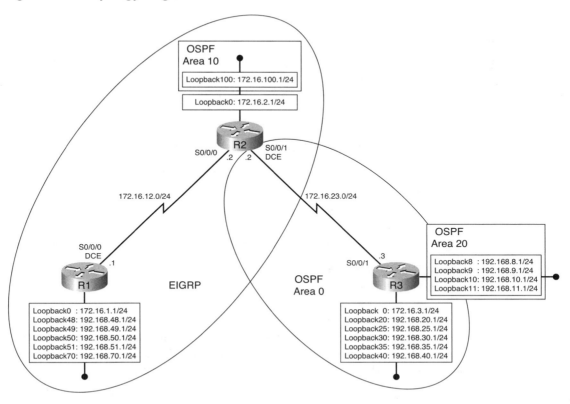

Scenario

Model the same physical topology as Lab 5-1. R1 is running EIGRP, and R3 is running OSPF. Add R2 to enable these two routing protocols to interact, allowing full connectivity between all networks.

Step 1: Additional Addressing

Start with the final configurations of Lab 5-1.

On R1 and R2, remove the RIPv2 configuration and the static route with the following commands:

```
R1(config)# no router rip
R1(config)# no ip route 192.168.48.0 255.255.252.0 null0
R1(config)# no ip prefix-list 100
```

```
R2(config)# no router rip
R2(config)# router ospf 1
R2(config-router)# no default-information originate
R2(config-router)# no redistribute rip
R2(config-router)# no default-metric 10000
```

Configure the additional loopback interfaces on R2 and R3 as shown in Figure 5-2:

```
R2(config)# interface loopback 100
R2(config-if)# ip address 172.16.100.1 255.255.255.0
```

```
R3(config)# interface loopback 8
R3(config-if)# ip address 192.168.8.1 255.255.255.0
R3(config-if)# interface loopback 9
R3(config-if)# ip address 192.168.9.1 255.255.255.0
R3(config-if)# interface loopback 10
R3(config-if)# ip address 192.168.10.1 255.255.255.0
R3(config-if)# interface loopback 11
R3(config-if)# ip address 192.168.11.1 255.255.255.0
```

Step 2: Configuring EIGRP

Prepare serial interfaces for running EIGRP with the **bandwidth** command:

```
R1# configure terminal
R1(config)# interface serial 0/0/0
R1(config-if)# bandwidth 64
```

```
R2# configure terminal
R2(config)# interface serial 0/0/0
R2(config-if)# bandwidth 64
```

Configure R1 and R2 to run EIGRP in autonomous system 1. On R1, add in all connected interfaces either with classful **network** commands or with wildcard masks. Use a classful **network** statement on R2. Make sure you disable automatic summarization. Verify the configuration with the **show ip eigrp neighbors** and **show ip route eigrp** commands on both routers.

```
R1(config)# router eigrp 1
R1(config-router)# no auto-summary
R1(config-router)# network 172.16.0.0
R1(config-router)# network 192.168.1.0
R1(config-router)# network 192.168.48.0
R1(config-router)# network 192.168.49.0
```

```
R1(config-router)# network 192.168.50.0
R1(config-router)# network 192.168.51.0
R1(config-router)# network 192.168.70.0
```

or

```
R1(config)# router eigrp 1
R1(config-router)# no auto-summary
R1(config-router)# network 172.16.0.0
R1(config-router)# network 192.168.0.0 0.0.255.255
```

```
R2(config)# router eigrp 1
R2(config-router)# no auto-summary
R2(config-router)# network 172.16.0.0
```

```
R1# show ip eigrp neighbors
IP-EIGRP neighbors for process 1
H    Address              Interface      Hold Uptime    SRTT   RTO   Q   Seq
                                         (sec)          (ms)         Cnt Num
0    172.16.12.2          Se0/0/0          11 00:00:30    36   216   0   3
```

```
R2# show ip eigrp neighbors
IP-EIGRP neighbors for process 1
H    Address              Interface      Hold Uptime    SRTT   RTO   Q   Seq
                                         (sec)          (ms)         Cnt Num
0    172.16.12.1          Se0/0/0          11 00:01:53  1604  5000   0   2
```

```
R1# show ip route eigrp
     172.16.0.0/24 is subnetted, 4 subnets
D       172.16.23.0 [95/41024000] via 172.16.12.2, 00:01:38, Serial0/0/0
D       172.16.2.0 [95/40640000] via 172.16.12.2, 00:01:16, Serial0/0/0
```

```
R2# show ip route eigrp
     172.16.0.0/24 is subnetted, 5 subnets
D       172.16.1.0 [90/40640000] via 172.16.12.1, 00:01:08, Serial0/0/0
D    192.168.70.0/24 [90/40640000] via 172.16.12.1, 00:01:08, Serial0/0/0
D    192.168.51.0/24 [90/40640000] via 172.16.12.1, 00:01:08, Serial0/0/0
D    192.168.50.0/24 [90/40640000] via 172.16.12.1, 00:01:08, Serial0/0/0
D    192.168.49.0/24 [90/40640000] via 172.16.12.1, 00:01:08, Serial0/0/0
D    192.168.48.0/24 [90/40640000] via 172.16.12.1, 00:01:08, Serial0/0/0
```

Step 3: Create Passive Interfaces in EIGRP

Execute the **show ip eigrp interfaces** command on R2:

```
R2# show ip eigrp interfaces
IP-EIGRP interfaces for process 1

                       Xmit Queue   Mean   Pacing Time   Multicast    Pending
Interface      Peers   Un/Reliable  SRTT   Un/Reliable   Flow Timer   Routes
Se0/0/0          1        0/0       1604      0/15          6431          0
```

Se0/0/1	0	0/0	0	0/1	0	0
Lo0	0	0/0	0	0/1	0	0
Lo100	0	0/0	0	0/1	0	0
R2#						

Because you used the classful **network** command, both serial interfaces are involved with EIGRP. To stop EIGRP from sending hello packets out the serial interface going to R3, use the **passive-interface** *interface_type interface_number* command. Verify the change with the **show ip eigrp interfaces** and **show ip protocols** commands:

```
R2(config)# router eigrp 1
R2(config-router)# passive-interface serial 0/0/1


R2# show ip eigrp interfaces
IP-EIGRP interfaces for process 1

                     Xmit Queue    Mean   Pacing Time   Multicast    Pending
Interface    Peers   Un/Reliable   SRTT   Un/Reliable   Flow Timer   Routes
Se0/0/0        1        0/0        1604      0/15          6431         0
Lo0            0        0/0          0       0/1             0          0
Lo100          0        0/0          0       0/1             0          0


R2# show ip protocols
Routing Protocol is "ospf 1"
<output omitted>
...
Routing Protocol is "eigrp 1"
  Outgoing update filter list for all interfaces is not set
  Incoming update filter list for all interfaces is not set
  Default networks flagged in outgoing updates
  Default networks accepted from incoming updates
  EIGRP metric weight K1=1, K2=0, K3=1, K4=0, K5=0
  EIGRP maximum hopcount 100
  EIGRP maximum metric variance 1
  Redistributing: eigrp 1
  EIGRP NSF-aware route hold timer is 240s
  Automatic network summarization is not in effect
  Maximum path: 4
  Routing for Networks:
    172.16.0.0
  Passive Interface(s):
    Serial0/0/1
  Routing Information Sources:
    Gateway           Distance      Last Update
    172.16.12.1           90        00:27:57
  Distance: internal 90 external 170
```

How does preventing hello packets out of an interface affect EIGRP's update capabilities out that interface?

Is this behavior more like RIP or OSPF in regard to the **passive-interface** command?

Step 4: Manually Summarize with EIGRP

You can have EIGRP summarize routes sent out an interface to make routing updates more efficient by using the **ip summary-address eigrp** *as network mask* command. Have R1 advertise one supernet for Loopbacks 48 and 49 to R2. Do not summarize Loopbacks 50 and 51 in this statement because these will be summarized in Step 9. Verify the configuration with the **show ip route eigrp** and **show ip route 192.168.48.0 255.255.254.0** commands on R1. Notice the administrative distance for this route:

```
R1(config)# interface serial 0/0/0
R1(config-if)# ip summary-address eigrp 1 192.168.48.0 255.255.254.0


R1# show ip route eigrp
      172.16.0.0/24 is subnetted, 5 subnets
D        172.16.23.0 [90/41024000] via 172.16.12.2, 00:45:21, Serial0/0/0
D        172.16.2.0 [90/40640000] via 172.16.12.2, 00:45:21, Serial0/0/0
D     192.168.48.0/23 is a summary, 04:27:07, Null0


R1# show ip route 192.168.48.0 255.255.254.0
Routing entry for 192.168.48.0/23, supernet
  Known via "eigrp 1", distance 5, metric 128256, type internal
  Redistributing via eigrp 1
  Routing Descriptor Blocks:
  * directly connected, via Null0
      Route metric is 128256, traffic share count is 1
      Total delay is 5000 microseconds, minimum bandwidth is 10000000 Kbit
      Reliability 255/255, minimum MTU 1514 bytes
      Loading 1/255, Hops 0
```

Why does EIGRP make the administrative distance different for summary routes?

_____

_____

_____

_____

_____

Step 5: Additional OSPF Configuration

OSPF is already partially configured on R2 and R3. You need to add the Area 10 configuration to R2 and the Area 20 configuration to R3 to complete the configuration.

Verify that your adjacencies come up with the **show ip ospf neighbors** command, and make sure that you have routes from OSPF populating the R2's routing table using the **show ip route ospf** command:

```
R2(config)# router ospf 1
R2(config-router)# network 172.16.100.0 0.0.0.255 area 10
```

```
R3(config)# router ospf 1
R3(config-router)# network 192.168.8.0 0.0.3.255 area 20
```

```
R2# show ip route ospf
      192.168.30.0/32 is subnetted, 1 subnets
O        192.168.30.1 [110/65] via 172.16.23.3, 00:00:44, Serial0/0/1
      192.168.8.0/32 is subnetted, 1 subnets
O IA     192.168.8.1 [110/65] via 172.16.23.3, 00:00:44, Serial0/0/1
      192.168.25.0/32 is subnetted, 1 subnets
O        192.168.25.1 [110/65] via 172.16.23.3, 00:00:44, Serial0/0/1
      192.168.9.0/32 is subnetted, 1 subnets
O IA     192.168.9.1 [110/65] via 172.16.23.3, 00:00:44, Serial0/0/1
      192.168.10.0/32 is subnetted, 1 subnets
O IA     192.168.10.1 [110/65] via 172.16.23.3, 00:00:44, Serial0/0/1
      192.168.40.0/32 is subnetted, 1 subnets
O        192.168.40.1 [110/65] via 172.16.23.3, 00:00:44, Serial0/0/1
      172.16.0.0/16 is variably subnetted, 4 subnets, 2 masks
O        172.16.3.1/32 [110/65] via 172.16.23.3, 00:00:44, Serial0/0/1
      192.168.11.0/32 is subnetted, 1 subnets
O IA     192.168.11.1 [110/65] via 172.16.23.3, 00:00:44, Serial0/0/1
      192.168.20.0/32 is subnetted, 1 subnets
O        192.168.20.1 [110/65] via 172.16.23.3, 00:00:46, Serial0/0/1
      192.168.35.0/32 is subnetted, 1 subnets
O        192.168.35.1 [110/65] via 172.16.23.3, 00:00:46, Serial0/0/1
```

```
R3# show ip route ospf
O IA     172.16.100.1/32 [110/1563] via 172.16.23.2, 00:00:15, Serial0/0/1
```

Notice that OSPF advertised /32 destination prefixes for the remote loopback interfaces (for example, R2 has a route to 192.168.20.1/32 in its routing table). Override this default behavior by using the **ip**

ospf network point-to-point command on the OSPF loopback interfaces on R2 and R3. You can paste in the following configurations to save time. You can download these router configurations at www.ciscopress.com/title/1587132133 under the More Information section on the page.

R2:
```
!
interface loopback 0
 ip ospf network point-to-point
!
interface loopback 100
 ip ospf network point-to-point
!
```

R3:
```
!
interface loopback 0
 ip ospf network point-to-point
!
interface loopback 8
 ip ospf network point-to-point
!
interface loopback 9
 ip ospf network point-to-point
!
interface loopback 10
 ip ospf network point-to-point
!
interface loopback 11
 ip ospf network point-to-point
!
interface loopback 20
 ip ospf network point-to-point
!
interface loopback 25
 ip ospf network point-to-point
!
interface loopback 30
 ip ospf network point-to-point
!
interface loopback 35
 ip ospf network point-to-point
!
interface loopback 40
 ip ospf network point-to-point
!
```

Verify the configuration with the **show ip route** command on R2. You should notice that the routes now each show on one line with the /24 major network mask:

```
R2# show ip route
<output omitted>


Gateway of last resort is not set


O    192.168.30.0/24 [110/65] via 172.16.23.3, 02:35:03, Serial0/0/1
O IA 192.168.8.0/24 [110/65] via 172.16.23.3, 02:35:03, Serial0/0/1
O    192.168.25.0/24 [110/65] via 172.16.23.3, 02:35:03, Serial0/0/1
O IA 192.168.9.0/24 [110/65] via 172.16.23.3, 02:35:03, Serial0/0/1
O IA 192.168.10.0/24 [110/65] via 172.16.23.3, 02:35:03, Serial0/0/1
O    192.168.40.0/24 [110/65] via 172.16.23.3, 02:35:03, Serial0/0/1
     172.16.0.0/24 is subnetted, 4 subnets
C       172.16.100.0 is directly connected, Loopback100
C       172.16.23.0 is directly connected, Serial0/0/1
C       172.16.12.0 is directly connected, Serial0/0/0
C       172.16.2.0 is directly connected, Loopback0
O       172.16.3.0 [110/65] via 172.16.23.3, 02:35:04, Serial0/0/1
O IA 192.168.11.0/24 [110/65] via 172.16.23.3, 02:35:04, Serial0/0/1
O    192.168.20.0/24 [110/65] via 172.16.23.3, 02:35:04, Serial0/0/1
D    192.168.51.0/24 [90/40640000] via 172.16.12.1, 03:17:13, Serial0/0/0
D    192.168.50.0/24 [90/40640000] via 172.16.12.1, 03:17:13, Serial0/0/0
O    192.168.35.0/24 [110/65] via 172.16.23.3, 02:35:04, Serial0/0/1
D    192.168.48.0/23 [90/40640000] via 172.16.12.1, 02:45:07, Serial0/0/0
```

Notice that R2 is the only router with knowledge of all routes in the topology at this point because it is involved with both routing protocols.

Step 6: Summarize OSPF Areas at the ABR

Review R2's routing table shown at the end of Step 5. Notice the inter-area routes for R3's loopbacks in Area 20. You can summarize this into a single inter-area route using the **area** *area* **range** *network mask* command. Verify the summarization with the **show ip route ospf** command on R2:

```
R3(config)# router ospf 1
R3(config-router)# area 20 range 192.168.8.0 255.255.252.0


R2# show ip route ospf
O    192.168.30.0/24 [110/65] via 172.16.23.3, 02:38:46, Serial0/0/1
O    192.168.25.0/24 [110/65] via 172.16.23.3, 02:38:46, Serial0/0/1
O    192.168.40.0/24 [110/65] via 172.16.23.3, 02:38:46, Serial0/0/1
     172.16.0.0/24 is subnetted, 4 subnets
O       172.16.3.0 [110/65] via 172.16.23.3, 02:38:46, Serial0/0/1
```

```
O     192.168.20.0/24 [110/65] via 172.16.23.3, 02:38:46, Serial0/0/1
O     192.168.35.0/24 [110/65] via 172.16.23.3, 02:38:46, Serial0/0/1
O IA 192.168.8.0/22 [110/65] via 172.16.23.3, 00:00:07, Serial0/0/1
```

Where can you summarize in OSPF?

_____

_____

_____

_____

Compare and contrast OSPF and EIGRP in terms of where summarization takes place?

_____

_____

Explain the synchronization requirement in OSPF that eliminates other routers as points of summarization.

_____

_____

_____

_____

Why or why not does EIGRP have this requirement?

_____

_____

_____

_____

_____

Step 7: Mutually Redistribute Between OSPF and EIGRP

You can configure redistribution between OSPF and EIGRP on R2. Under the OSPF process on R2, issue the command **redistribute eigrp 1 subnets**. You need to redistribute the connected routes (172.16.2.0/24 and 172.16.100.0/24) that R2 has not learned through EIGRP even though they are involved in the EIGRP process. The **subnets** command is necessary because, by default, OSPF only redistributes classful networks. A default seed metric is not required for OSPF. Under the EIGRP process, issue the command **redistribute ospf 1 metric 10000 100 255 1 1500**, which tells EIGRP to redistribute OSPF process 1 with the following metrics: bandwidth of 10000, delay of 100, reliability of 255/255, load of 1/255, and a MTU of 1500. Like RIP, EIGRP requires a seed metric. You can also set a default seed metric with the **default-metric** command:

```
R2(config)# router ospf 1
R2(config-router)# redistribute eigrp 1 subnets
R2(config-router)# redistribute connected subnets
R2(config-router)# exit
```

```
R2(config)# router eigrp 1
R2(config-router)# redistribute ospf 1 metric 10000 100 255 1 1500
```

Or:

```
R2(config-router)# default-metric 10000 100 255 1 1500
R2(config-router)# redistribute ospf 1
```

Execute the **show ip protocols** command on the redistributing router, R2. Compare your output with the following:

```
R2# show ip protocols
Routing Protocol is "ospf 1"
  Outgoing update filter list for all interfaces is not set
  Incoming update filter list for all interfaces is not set
  Router ID 172.16.2.1
  It is an autonomous system boundary router
  Redistributing External Routes from,
    eigrp 1, includes subnets in redistribution
  Number of areas in this router is 1. 1 normal 0 stub 0 nssa
  Maximum path: 4
  Routing for Networks:
    172.16.23.0 0.0.0.255 area 0
 Reference bandwidth unit is 100 mbps
  Routing Information Sources:
    Gateway         Distance      Last Update
    192.168.40.1         110       01:33:07
  Distance: (default is 110)


Routing Protocol is "eigrp 1"
  Outgoing update filter list for all interfaces is not set
  Incoming update filter list for all interfaces is not set
  Default networks flagged in outgoing updates
  Default networks accepted from incoming updates
  EIGRP metric weight K1=1, K2=0, K3=1, K4=0, K5=0
  EIGRP maximum hopcount 100
  EIGRP maximum metric variance 1
  Redistributing: ospf 1, eigrp 1
  EIGRP NSF-aware route hold timer is 240s
  Automatic network summarization is not in effect
  Maximum path: 4
  Routing for Networks:
    172.16.0.0
  Passive Interface(s):
    Serial0/0/1
```

```
Routing Information Sources:
    Gateway          Distance       Last Update
    172.16.12.1            90        00:40:04
Distance: internal 90 external 170
```

Display the routing tables on R1 and R3 so that you can see the redistributed routes. Redistributed OSPF routes display on R1 as D EX, which means that they are external EIGRP routes. Redistributed EIGRP routes are tagged in R3's routing table as O E2, which means that they are OSPF external type 2. Type 2 is the default OSPF external type:

```
R1# show ip route
<output omitted>

Gateway of last resort is not set

D EX 192.168.30.0/24 [170/40537600] via 172.16.12.2, 00:00:05, Serial0/0/0
D EX 192.168.25.0/24 [170/40537600] via 172.16.12.2, 00:00:05, Serial0/0/0
D EX 192.168.40.0/24 [170/40537600] via 172.16.12.2, 00:00:05, Serial0/0/0
     172.16.0.0/24 is subnetted, 5 subnets
D        172.16.100.0 [90/40640000] via 172.16.12.2, 00:38:02, Serial0/0/0
D        172.16.23.0 [90/2681856] via 172.16.12.2, 00:38:02, Serial0/0/0
C        172.16.12.0 is directly connected, Serial0/0/0
C        172.16.1.0 is directly connected, Loopback0
D        172.16.2.0 [90/40640000] via 172.16.12.2, 00:38:02, Serial0/0/0
D EX     172.16.3.0 [170/40537600] via 172.16.12.2, 00:00:06, Serial0/0/0
D EX 192.168.20.0/24 [170/40537600] via 172.16.12.2, 00:00:06, Serial0/0/0
C    192.168.51.0/24 is directly connected, Loopback51
C    192.168.50.0/24 is directly connected, Loopback50
D EX 192.168.35.0/24 [170/40537600] via 172.16.12.2, 00:00:06, Serial0/0/0
C    192.168.49.0/24 is directly connected, Loopback49
C    192.168.70.0/24 is directly connected, Loopback70
C    192.168.48.0/24 is directly connected, Loopback48
D EX 192.168.8.0/22 [170/40537600] via 172.16.12.2, 00:00:07, Serial0/0/0
D    192.168.48.0/23 is a summary, 04:19:50, Null0
R3# show ip route
<output omitted>

Gateway of last resort is not set

C    192.168.30.0/24 is directly connected, Loopback30
C    192.168.8.0/24 is directly connected, Loopback8
C    192.168.25.0/24 is directly connected, Loopback25
C    192.168.9.0/24 is directly connected, Loopback9
C    192.168.10.0/24 is directly connected, Loopback10
C    192.168.40.0/24 is directly connected, Loopback40
     172.16.0.0/24 is subnetted, 5 subnets
```

```
C          172.16.23.0 is directly connected, Serial0/0/1
O E2       172.16.12.0 [110/20] via 172.16.23.2, 00:41:48, Serial0/0/1
O E2       172.16.1.0 [110/20] via 172.16.23.2, 00:41:48, Serial0/0/1
O E2       172.16.2.0 [110/20] via 172.16.23.2, 00:41:48, Serial0/0/1
O IA       172.16.100.0 [110/1563] via 172.16.23.2, 00:41:48, Serial0/0/1
C          172.16.3.0 is directly connected, Loopback0
C       192.168.11.0/24 is directly connected, Loopback11
C       192.168.20.0/24 is directly connected, Loopback20
O E2    192.168.51.0/24 [110/20] via 172.16.23.2, 00:41:48, Serial0/0/1
O E2    192.168.50.0/24 [110/20] via 172.16.23.2, 00:41:48, Serial0/0/1
C       192.168.35.0/24 is directly connected, Loopback35
O E2    192.168.70.0/24 [110/20] via 172.16.23.2, 00:41:48, Serial0/0/1
O       192.168.8.0/22 is a summary, 01:34:48, Null0
O E2    192.168.48.0/23 [110/20] via 172.16.23.2, 00:41:48, Serial0/0/1
```

Verify full connectivity with the following TCL script. You can download this TCL script at www.cis-copress.com/title/1587132133 under the More Information section on the page.

```
foreach address {
172.16.1.1
192.168.48.1
192.168.49.1
192.168.50.1
192.168.51.1
192.168.70.1
172.16.12.1
172.16.2.1
172.16.100.1
172.16.12.2
172.16.23.2
172.16.3.1
192.168.20.1
192.168.25.1
192.168.30.1
192.168.35.1
192.168.40.1
192.168.8.1
192.168.9.1
192.168.10.1
192.168.11.1
172.16.23.3
} { ping $address }
```

The TCL script output should match the output shown in the section, "TCL Script Output," for this lab. This output corresponds to full connectivity by showing all ICMP echo replies.

Step 8: Filter Redistribution with Route Maps

One way to filter prefixes is with a route map. When used for filtering prefixes, a route map works like an access list. It has multiple statements that are read in a sequential order. Each statement can be a deny or permit and can have a match clause for a variety of attributes, such as the route or a route tag. You can also include route attributes in each statement that will be set if the match clause is met. This example filters R3's Loopbacks 25 and 30 networks from getting redistributed into EIGRP on R2. Display R1's routing table and verify that those two routes currently appear there:

```
R1# show ip route eigrp
D EX 192.168.30.0/24 [170/40537600] via 172.16.12.2, 00:04:28, Serial0/0/0
D EX 192.168.25.0/24 [170/40537600] via 172.16.12.2, 00:04:28, Serial0/0/0
D EX 192.168.40.0/24 [170/40537600] via 172.16.12.2, 00:04:28, Serial0/0/0
     172.16.0.0/24 is subnetted, 5 subnets
D        172.16.23.0 [90/2681856] via 172.16.12.2, 00:42:25, Serial0/0/0
D        172.16.2.0 [90/40640000] via 172.16.12.2, 00:42:25, Serial0/0/0
D EX     172.16.3.0 [170/40537600] via 172.16.12.2, 00:04:28, Serial0/0/0
D EX 192.168.20.0/24 [170/40537600] via 172.16.12.2, 00:04:28, Serial0/0/0
D EX 192.168.35.0/24 [170/40537600] via 172.16.12.2, 00:04:28, Serial0/0/0
D EX 192.168.8.0/22 [170/40537600] via 172.16.12.2, 00:04:28, Serial0/0/0
D    192.168.48.0/23 is a summary, 04:24:12, Null0
```

There are multiple ways to configure this filtering. For this exercise, configure an access list that matches these two network addresses and a route map that denies based on a match for that access list. Configure the access list as follows:

```
R2(config)# access-list 1 permit 192.168.25.0
R2(config)# access-list 1 permit 192.168.30.0
```

Now configure a route map with a statement that denies based on a match with this access list. Then add a permit statement without a match statement, which acts as an explicit permit all:

```
R2(config)# route-map SELECTED-DENY deny 10
R2(config-route-map)# match ip address 1
R2(config-route-map)# route-map SELECTED-DENY permit 20
```

Finally, apply this route map by redoing the **redistribute** command with the route map under the EIGRP process:

```
R2(config)# router eigrp 1
R2(config-router)# redistribute ospf 1 route-map SELECTED-DENY metric 64 100 255 1
   1500
```

If you previously configured a default metric under EIGRP, you can simply use:

```
R2(config-router)# redistribute ospf 1 route-map SELECTED-DENY
```

Verify that these routes are filtered out in R1's routing table:

```
R1# show ip route eigrp
D EX 192.168.40.0/24 [170/40537600] via 172.16.12.2, 00:07:24, Serial0/0/0
     172.16.0.0/24 is subnetted, 5 subnets
D        172.16.23.0 [90/41024000] via 172.16.12.2, 00:45:21, Serial0/0/0
```

```
D        172.16.2.0 [90/40640000] via 172.16.12.2, 00:45:21, Serial0/0/0
D EX     172.16.3.0 [170/40537600] via 172.16.12.2, 00:07:24, Serial0/0/0
D EX 192.168.20.0/24 [170/40537600] via 172.16.12.2, 00:07:24, Serial0/0/0
D EX 192.168.35.0/24 [170/40537600] via 172.16.12.2, 00:07:24, Serial0/0/0
D EX 192.168.8.0/22 [170/40537600] via 172.16.12.2, 00:07:24, Serial0/0/0
D        192.168.48.0/23 is a summary, 04:27:07, Null0
```

Step 9: Summarize External Routes into OSPF at the ASBR

You can summarize routes redistributed into OSPF without the **area range** command, which is used for internal summarization. Instead, use the OSPF configuration prompt command **summary-address** *network mask*. However, before you make any changes, display R3's routing table:

```
R3# show ip route ospf
     172.16.0.0/24 is subnetted, 6 subnets
O E2    172.16.12.0 [110/20] via 172.16.23.2, 00:00:07, Serial0/0/1
O E2    172.16.1.0 [110/20] via 172.16.23.2, 00:00:07, Serial0/0/1
O E2    172.16.2.0 [110/20] via 172.16.23.2, 00:00:07, Serial0/0/1
O IA    172.16.100.0 [110/1563] via 172.16.23.2, 00:00:07, Serial0/0/1
O E2 192.168.70.0/24 [110/20] via 172.16.23.2, 00:00:07, Serial0/0/1
O       192.168.8.0/22 is a summary, 00:00:07, Null0
O E2 192.168.51.0/24 [110/20] via 172.16.23.2, 00:00:07, Serial0/0/1
O E2 192.168.50.0/24 [110/20] via 172.16.23.2, 00:00:07, Serial0/0/1
O E2 192.168.48.0/23 [110/20] via 172.16.23.2, 00:00:07, Serial0/0/1
```

Notice the three external routes for R1's Loopback interfaces 48 through 51. Two of the loopbacks are already summarized to one /23.

Which mask should you use to summarize all four of the loopbacks to one prefix?

_____

You can summarize this all into one supernet on R2 as follows:

```
R2(config)# router ospf 1
R2(config-router)# summary-address 192.168.48.0 255.255.252.0
```

Verify this action in R3's routing table.

```
R3# show ip route ospf
     172.16.0.0/24 is subnetted, 5 subnets
O E2    172.16.12.0 [110/20] via 172.16.23.2, 01:40:45, Serial0/0/1
O E2    172.16.1.0 [110/20] via 172.16.23.2, 00:48:54, Serial0/0/1
O E2    172.16.2.0 [110/20] via 172.16.23.2, 01:40:45, Serial0/0/1
O IA    172.16.100.0 [110/1563] via 172.16.23.2, 01:40:45, Serial0/0/1
O E2 192.168.70.0/24 [110/20] via 172.16.23.2, 00:48:54, Serial0/0/1
O       192.168.8.0/22 is a summary, 01:41:55, Null0
O E2 192.168.48.0/22 [110/20] via 172.16.23.2, 00:00:08, Serial0/0/1
```

What would happen if Loopback 50 on R1 were to become unreachable by R2?

_____

_____

Would data destined for 192.168.50.0/24 from R3 still be sent to R2?

_____

Would data destined for 192.168.50.0/24 from R2 continue to be sent to R1?

_____

_____

If you are unsure of the outcome, shut down the interface on R1. Execute the ICMP **traceroute** command to 192.168.50.1 from R3 and then from R2. Check your output against the output and analysis in the section, "Exploring Black Hole Operation," for this lab. Remember to issue the **no shutdown** command when you are done checking.

Is this a desirable outcome? Explain.

_____

_____

_____

_____

Step 10: Modifying EIGRP Distances

By default, EIGRP uses an administrative distance of 90 for internal routes and 170 for external routes. You can see this in R1's routing table and in the output of the **show ip protocols** command.

```
R1# show ip route eigrp
D EX 192.168.40.0/24 [170/40537600] via 172.16.12.2, 00:04:03, Serial0/0/0
        172.16.0.0/24 is subnetted, 5 subnets
D        172.16.23.0 [90/41024000] via 172.16.12.2, 00:04:03, Serial0/0/0
D        172.16.2.0 [90/40640000] via 172.16.12.2, 00:04:03, Serial0/0/0
D EX     172.16.3.0 [170/40537600] via 172.16.12.2, 00:04:03, Serial0/0/0
D EX 192.168.20.0/24 [170/40537600] via 172.16.12.2, 00:04:03, Serial0/0/0
D EX 192.168.35.0/24 [170/40537600] via 172.16.12.2, 00:04:03, Serial0/0/0
D EX 192.168.8.0/22 [170/40537600] via 172.16.12.2, 00:04:03, Serial0/0/0
D    192.168.48.0/23 is a summary, 3d17h, Null0
D EX 192.168.48.0/22 [170/40537600] via 172.16.12.2, 00:04:03, Serial0/0/0


R1# show ip protocols
R1#show ip proto
Routing Protocol is "eigrp 1"
   ...
```

```
        Routing Information Sources:
          Gateway          Distance      Last Update
          172.16.12.2            95      00:02:13
        Distance: internal 90 external 170
```

You can change the administrative distance with the **distance eigrp** *internal external*. This command is only applicable locally. Change the distances to 95 for internal routes and 165 for external routes:

```
R1(config)# router eigrp 1
R1(config-router)# distance eigrp 95 165
```

Verify the change in the routing table with the **show ip route eigrp** and **show ip protocols** commands:

```
R1# show ip route eigrp
D EX 192.168.40.0/24 [165/40537600] via 172.16.12.2, 00:04:03, Serial0/0/0
        172.16.0.0/24 is subnetted, 5 subnets
D          172.16.23.0 [95/41024000] via 172.16.12.2, 00:04:03, Serial0/0/0
D          172.16.2.0 [95/40640000] via 172.16.12.2, 00:04:03, Serial0/0/0
D EX      172.16.3.0 [165/40537600] via 172.16.12.2, 00:04:03, Serial0/0/0
D EX 192.168.20.0/24 [165/40537600] via 172.16.12.2, 00:04:03, Serial0/0/0
D EX 192.168.35.0/24 [165/40537600] via 172.16.12.2, 00:04:03, Serial0/0/0
D EX 192.168.8.0/22 [165/40537600] via 172.16.12.2, 00:04:03, Serial0/0/0
D     192.168.48.0/23 is a summary, 3d17h, Null0
D EX 192.168.48.0/22 [165/40537600] via 172.16.12.2, 00:04:03, Serial0/0/0


R1# show ip protocols
Routing Protocol is "eigrp 1"
  ...
    Routing Information Sources:
      Gateway          Distance      Last Update
      172.16.12.2            95      00:00:00
    Distance: internal 95 external 165
```

Step 11: Modifying OSPF Distances

You can also modify individual OSPF distances. By default, all OSPF distances are 110, but you can change the intra-area, inter-area, and external route distances using the **distance ospf intra-area** *distance* **inter-area** *distance* **external** *distance* command. All the command arguments are optional, so you can change only what you need to. For this example, change the intra-area distance to 105, inter-area distance to 115, and external routes to 175 on R3. Before changing anything, display R3's routing table:

```
R3# show ip route ospf
        172.16.0.0/24 is subnetted, 5 subnets
O E2    172.16.12.0 [110/20] via 172.16.23.2, 01:40:45, Serial0/0/1
O E2    172.16.1.0 [110/20] via 172.16.23.2, 00:48:54, Serial0/0/1
O E2    172.16.2.0 [110/20] via 172.16.23.2, 01:40:45, Serial0/0/1
O IA    172.16.100.0 [110/1563] via 172.16.23.2, 01:40:45, Serial0/0/1
```

```
O E2 192.168.70.0/24 [110/20] via 172.16.23.2, 00:48:54, Serial0/0/1
O     192.168.8.0/22 is a summary, 01:41:55, Null0
O E2 192.168.48.0/22 [110/20] via 172.16.23.2, 00:00:08, Serial0/0/1
```

Change the distance and then verify the change in the routing table. Unfortunately, the only information you can get from the output of the **show ip protocols** command is the default distance, which is the intra-area distance:

```
R3(config)# router ospf 1
R3(config-router)# distance ospf intra-area 105 inter-area 115 external 175
```

```
R3# show ip route ospf
      172.16.0.0/24 is subnetted, 6 subnets
O E2    172.16.12.0 [175/20] via 172.16.23.2, 00:00:05, Serial0/0/1
O E2    172.16.1.0 [175/20] via 172.16.23.2, 00:00:05, Serial0/0/1
O E2    172.16.2.0 [175/20] via 172.16.23.2, 00:00:05, Serial0/0/1
O IA    172.16.100.0 [115/1563] via 172.16.23.2, 00:00:05, Serial0/0/1
O E2 192.168.70.0/24 [175/20] via 172.16.23.2, 00:00:05, Serial0/0/1
O     192.168.8.0/22 is a summary, 00:00:05, Null0
O E2 192.168.48.0/22 [175/20] via 172.16.23.2, 00:00:05, Serial0/0/1
```

```
R3# show ip protocols
Routing Protocol is "ospf 1"
  Outgoing update filter list for all interfaces is not set
  Incoming update filter list for all interfaces is not set
  Router ID 192.168.40.1
  It is an area border router
  Number of areas in this router is 2. 2 normal 0 stub 0 nssa
  Maximum path: 4
  Routing for Networks:
    172.16.0.0 0.0.255.255 area 0
    192.168.8.0 0.0.3.255 area 20
    192.168.0.0 0.0.255.255 area 0
  Reference bandwidth unit is 100 mbps
  Passive Interface(s):
    FastEthernet0/0
    FastEthernet0/1
    Serial0/0/0
    Serial0/1/0
    Serial0/1/1
    Loopback0
    Loopback8
    Loopback9
    Loopback10
    Loopback11
```

```
        Passive Interface(s):
          Loopback20
          Loopback25
          Loopback30
          Loopback35
          Loopback40
          VoIP-Null0
        Routing Information Sources:
          Gateway         Distance       Last Update
          (this router)        110       00:03:04
          172.16.2.1           110       00:03:04
        Distance: (default is 105)
```

Challenge: Change Administrative Distance on R2

The previous two steps demonstrated using the **distance** command in a fairly inconsequential environment. In which types of scenarios would the **distance** command be more valuable?

_____

_____

On R2, you are running both EIGRP and OSPF. Imagine a fourth router, R4, connected to both R1 and R3. R4 is redistributing between the two routing protocols.

Using the default administrative distances for EIGRP and OSPF, which protocol would be preferred in the routing table for destination prefixes and why?

- _____

  _____

- _____

  _____

Instead of adding the 172.16.10.0/24 networks natively to EIGRP using a **network** statement, add the networks using the **redistribute connected** command in EIGRP configuration mode on R1.

With the default administrative distances set, what would the administrative distance be for that prefix on R2 in EIGRP and in OSPF? Explain why.

_____

_____

How could you make the EIGRP path prefer this route? Is there more than one way?

_____

_____

_____

_____

The general-purpose **distance** command could be used as follows to manipulate the external OSPF distance:

_____

_____

The gateway-specific **distance** command could be used as follows to manipulate the distance in OSPF:

_____

_____

The **distance** command will be used in more detail in Lab 5-4.

Could using the **distance** command in this situation cause asymmetric routing? Explain.

_____

_____

_____

_____

_____

_____

TCL Script Output

```
R1# tclsh
R1(tcl)# foreach address {
+>(tcl)# 172.16.1.1
+>(tcl)# 192.168.48.1
+>(tcl)# 192.168.49.1
+>(tcl)# 192.168.50.1
+>(tcl)# 192.168.51.1
+>(tcl)# 192.168.70.1
+>(tcl)# 172.16.12.1
+>(tcl)# 172.16.2.1
+>(tcl)# 172.16.100.1
+>(tcl)# 172.16.12.2
+>(tcl)# 172.16.23.2
+>(tcl)# 172.16.3.1
+>(tcl)# 192.168.20.1
+>(tcl)# 192.168.25.1
+>(tcl)# 192.168.30.1
+>(tcl)# 192.168.35.1
+>(tcl)# 192.168.40.1
```

```
+>(tcl)# 192.168.8.1
+>(tcl)# 192.168.9.1
+>(tcl)# 192.168.10.1
+>(tcl)# 192.168.11.1
+>(tcl)# 172.16.23.3
+>(tcl)#} { ping $address }

Type escape sequence to abort.
Sending 5, 100-byte ICMP Echos to 172.16.1.1, timeout is 2 seconds:
!!!!!
Success rate is 100 percent (5/5), round-trip min/avg/max = 1/1/1 ms
Type escape sequence to abort.
Sending 5, 100-byte ICMP Echos to 192.168.48.1, timeout is 2 seconds:
!!!!!
Success rate is 100 percent (5/5), round-trip min/avg/max = 1/1/4 ms
Type escape sequence to abort.
Sending 5, 100-byte ICMP Echos to 192.168.49.1, timeout is 2 seconds:
!!!!!
Success rate is 100 percent (5/5), round-trip min/avg/max = 1/1/4 ms
Type escape sequence to abort.
Sending 5, 100-byte ICMP Echos to 192.168.50.1, timeout is 2 seconds:
!!!!!
Success rate is 100 percent (5/5), round-trip min/avg/max = 1/2/4 ms
Type escape sequence to abort.
Sending 5, 100-byte ICMP Echos to 192.168.51.1, timeout is 2 seconds:
!!!!!
Success rate is 100 percent (5/5), round-trip min/avg/max = 1/1/4 ms
Type escape sequence to abort.
Sending 5, 100-byte ICMP Echos to 192.168.70.1, timeout is 2 seconds:
!!!!!
Success rate is 100 percent (5/5), round-trip min/avg/max = 1/1/4 ms
Type escape sequence to abort.
Sending 5, 100-byte ICMP Echos to 172.16.12.1, timeout is 2 seconds:
!!!!!
Success rate is 100 percent (5/5), round-trip min/avg/max = 56/57/64 ms
Type escape sequence to abort.
Sending 5, 100-byte ICMP Echos to 172.16.2.1, timeout is 2 seconds:
!!!!!
Success rate is 100 percent (5/5), round-trip min/avg/max = 28/28/28 ms
Type escape sequence to abort.
Sending 5, 100-byte ICMP Echos to 172.16.100.1, timeout is 2 seconds:
!!!!!
```

```
Success rate is 100 percent (5/5), round-trip min/avg/max = 28/28/28 ms
Type escape sequence to abort.
Sending 5, 100-byte ICMP Echos to 172.16.12.2, timeout is 2 seconds:
!!!!!
Success rate is 100 percent (5/5), round-trip min/avg/max = 28/28/28 ms
Type escape sequence to abort.
Sending 5, 100-byte ICMP Echos to 172.16.23.2, timeout is 2 seconds:
!!!!!
Success rate is 100 percent (5/5), round-trip min/avg/max = 28/28/32 ms
Type escape sequence to abort.
Sending 5, 100-byte ICMP Echos to 172.16.3.1, timeout is 2 seconds:
!!!!!
Success rate is 100 percent (5/5), round-trip min/avg/max = 28/28/32 ms
Type escape sequence to abort.
Sending 5, 100-byte ICMP Echos to 192.168.20.1, timeout is 2 seconds:
!!!!!
Success rate is 100 percent (5/5), round-trip min/avg/max = 28/29/32 ms
Type escape sequence to abort.
Sending 5, 100-byte ICMP Echos to 192.168.25.1, timeout is 2 seconds:
!!!!!
Success rate is 100 percent (5/5), round-trip min/avg/max = 28/28/32 ms
Type escape sequence to abort.
Sending 5, 100-byte ICMP Echos to 192.168.30.1, timeout is 2 seconds:
!!!!!
Success rate is 100 percent (5/5), round-trip min/avg/max = 28/30/32 ms
Type escape sequence to abort.
Sending 5, 100-byte ICMP Echos to 192.168.35.1, timeout is 2 seconds:
!!!!!
Success rate is 100 percent (5/5), round-trip min/avg/max = 28/29/32 ms
Type escape sequence to abort.
Sending 5, 100-byte ICMP Echos to 192.168.40.1, timeout is 2 seconds:
!!!!!
Success rate is 100 percent (5/5), round-trip min/avg/max = 28/29/32 ms
Type escape sequence to abort.
Sending 5, 100-byte ICMP Echos to 192.168.8.1, timeout is 2 seconds:
!!!!!
Success rate is 100 percent (5/5), round-trip min/avg/max = 28/30/32 ms
Type escape sequence to abort.
Sending 5, 100-byte ICMP Echos to 192.168.9.1, timeout is 2 seconds:
!!!!!
Success rate is 100 percent (5/5), round-trip min/avg/max = 28/29/32 ms
Type escape sequence to abort.
```

```
Sending 5, 100-byte ICMP Echos to 192.168.10.1, timeout is 2 seconds:
!!!!!
Success rate is 100 percent (5/5), round-trip min/avg/max = 28/29/32 ms
Type escape sequence to abort.
Sending 5, 100-byte ICMP Echos to 192.168.11.1, timeout is 2 seconds:
!!!!!
Success rate is 100 percent (5/5), round-trip min/avg/max = 28/28/32 ms
Type escape sequence to abort.
Sending 5, 100-byte ICMP Echos to 172.16.23.3, timeout is 2 seconds:
!!!!!
Success rate is 100 percent (5/5), round-trip min/avg/max = 28/30/32 ms
R1(tcl)# tclquit
```

```
R2# tclsh
R2(tcl)# foreach address {
+>(tcl)# 172.16.1.1
+>(tcl)# 192.168.48.1
+>(tcl)# 192.168.49.1
+>(tcl)# 192.168.50.1
+>(tcl)# 192.168.51.1
+>(tcl)# 192.168.70.1
+>(tcl)# 172.16.12.1
+>(tcl)# 172.16.2.1
+>(tcl)# 172.16.100.1
+>(tcl)# 172.16.12.2
+>(tcl)# 172.16.23.2
+>(tcl)# 172.16.3.1
+>(tcl)# 192.168.20.1
+>(tcl)# 192.168.25.1
+>(tcl)# 192.168.30.1
+>(tcl)# 192.168.35.1
+>(tcl)# 192.168.40.1
+>(tcl)# 192.168.8.1
+>(tcl)# 192.168.9.1
+>(tcl)# 192.168.10.1
+>(tcl)# 192.168.11.1
+>(tcl)# 172.16.23.3
+>(tcl)# } { ping $address }
*Oct 16 20:19:07.306: %SYS-5-CONFIG_I: Configured from console by console
+>(tcl)#} { ping $address }

Type escape sequence to abort.
Sending 5, 100-byte ICMP Echos to 172.16.1.1, timeout is 2 seconds:
!!!!!
Success rate is 100 percent (5/5), round-trip min/avg/max = 28/28/32 ms
```

```
Type escape sequence to abort.
Sending 5, 100-byte ICMP Echos to 192.168.48.1, timeout is 2 seconds:
!!!!!
Success rate is 100 percent (5/5), round-trip min/avg/max = 28/28/32 ms
Type escape sequence to abort.
Sending 5, 100-byte ICMP Echos to 192.168.49.1, timeout is 2 seconds:
!!!!!
Success rate is 100 percent (5/5), round-trip min/avg/max = 28/28/32 ms
Type escape sequence to abort.
Sending 5, 100-byte ICMP Echos to 192.168.50.1, timeout is 2 seconds:
!!!!!
Success rate is 100 percent (5/5), round-trip min/avg/max = 28/28/32 ms
Type escape sequence to abort.
Sending 5, 100-byte ICMP Echos to 192.168.51.1, timeout is 2 seconds:
!!!!!
Success rate is 100 percent (5/5), round-trip min/avg/max = 28/28/28 ms
Type escape sequence to abort.
Sending 5, 100-byte ICMP Echos to 192.168.70.1, timeout is 2 seconds:
!!!!!
Success rate is 100 percent (5/5), round-trip min/avg/max = 28/28/32 ms
Type escape sequence to abort.
Sending 5, 100-byte ICMP Echos to 172.16.12.1, timeout is 2 seconds:
!!!!!
Success rate is 100 percent (5/5), round-trip min/avg/max = 28/28/32 ms
Type escape sequence to abort.
Sending 5, 100-byte ICMP Echos to 172.16.2.1, timeout is 2 seconds:
!!!!!
Success rate is 100 percent (5/5), round-trip min/avg/max = 1/1/4 ms
Type escape sequence to abort.
Sending 5, 100-byte ICMP Echos to 172.16.100.1, timeout is 2 seconds:
!!!!!
Success rate is 100 percent (5/5), round-trip min/avg/max = 1/1/4 ms
Type escape sequence to abort.
Sending 5, 100-byte ICMP Echos to 172.16.12.2, timeout is 2 seconds:
!!!!!
Success rate is 100 percent (5/5), round-trip min/avg/max = 56/56/60 ms
Type escape sequence to abort.
Sending 5, 100-byte ICMP Echos to 172.16.23.2, timeout is 2 seconds:
!!!!!
Success rate is 100 percent (5/5), round-trip min/avg/max = 56/56/56 ms
Type escape sequence to abort.
Sending 5, 100-byte ICMP Echos to 172.16.3.1, timeout is 2 seconds:
!!!!!
Success rate is 100 percent (5/5), round-trip min/avg/max = 28/28/32 ms
```

```
Type escape sequence to abort.
Sending 5, 100-byte ICMP Echos to 192.168.20.1, timeout is 2 seconds:
!!!!!
Success rate is 100 percent (5/5), round-trip min/avg/max = 28/28/32 ms
Type escape sequence to abort.
Sending 5, 100-byte ICMP Echos to 192.168.25.1, timeout is 2 seconds:
!!!!!
Success rate is 100 percent (5/5), round-trip min/avg/max = 28/28/32 ms
Type escape sequence to abort.
Sending 5, 100-byte ICMP Echos to 192.168.30.1, timeout is 2 seconds:
!!!!!
Success rate is 100 percent (5/5), round-trip min/avg/max = 28/28/32 ms
Type escape sequence to abort.
Sending 5, 100-byte ICMP Echos to 192.168.35.1, timeout is 2 seconds:
!!!!!
Success rate is 100 percent (5/5), round-trip min/avg/max = 28/28/28 ms
Type escape sequence to abort.
Sending 5, 100-byte ICMP Echos to 192.168.40.1, timeout is 2 seconds:
!!!!!
Success rate is 100 percent (5/5), round-trip min/avg/max = 28/28/32 ms
Type escape sequence to abort.
Sending 5, 100-byte ICMP Echos to 192.168.8.1, timeout is 2 seconds:
!!!!!
Success rate is 100 percent (5/5), round-trip min/avg/max = 28/28/32 ms
Type escape sequence to abort.
Sending 5, 100-byte ICMP Echos to 192.168.9.1, timeout is 2 seconds:
!!!!!
Success rate is 100 percent (5/5), round-trip min/avg/max = 28/28/32 ms
Type escape sequence to abort.
Sending 5, 100-byte ICMP Echos to 192.168.10.1, timeout is 2 seconds:
!!!!!
Success rate is 100 percent (5/5), round-trip min/avg/max = 28/28/28 ms
Type escape sequence to abort.
Sending 5, 100-byte ICMP Echos to 192.168.11.1, timeout is 2 seconds:
!!!!!
Success rate is 100 percent (5/5), round-trip min/avg/max = 28/28/28 ms
Type escape sequence to abort.
Sending 5, 100-byte ICMP Echos to 172.16.23.3, timeout is 2 seconds:
!!!!!
Success rate is 100 percent (5/5), round-trip min/avg/max = 28/28/32 ms
R2(tcl)# tclquit
```

```
R3# tclsh
R3(tcl)# foreach address {
+>(tcl)# 172.16.1.1
```

```
+>(tcl)# 192.168.48.1
+>(tcl)# 192.168.49.1
+>(tcl)# 192.168.50.1
+>(tcl)# 192.168.51.1
+>(tcl)# 192.168.70.1
+>(tcl)# 172.16.12.1
+>(tcl)# 172.16.2.1
+>(tcl)# 172.16.100.1
+>(tcl)# 172.16.12.2
+>(tcl)# 172.16.23.2
+>(tcl)# 172.16.3.1
+>(tcl)# 192.168.20.1
+>(tcl)# 192.168.25.1
+>(tcl)# 192.168.30.1
+>(tcl)# 192.168.35.1
+>(tcl)# 192.168.40.1
+>(tcl)# 192.168.8.1
+>(tcl)# 192.168.9.1
+>(tcl)# 192.168.10.1
+>(tcl)# 192.168.11.1
+>(tcl)# 172.16.23.3
+>(tcl)# } { ping $address }


Type escape sequence to abort.
Sending 5, 100-byte ICMP Echos to 172.16.1.1, timeout is 2 seconds:
!!!!!
Success rate is 100 percent (5/5), round-trip min/avg/max = 56/56/56 ms
Type escape sequence to abort.
Sending 5, 100-byte ICMP Echos to 192.168.48.1, timeout is 2 seconds:
!!!!!
Success rate is 100 percent (5/5), round-trip min/avg/max = 56/56/56 ms
Type escape sequence to abort.
Sending 5, 100-byte ICMP Echos to 192.168.49.1, timeout is 2 seconds:
!!!!!
Success rate is 100 percent (5/5), round-trip min/avg/max = 56/56/56 ms
Type escape sequence to abort.
Sending 5, 100-byte ICMP Echos to 192.168.50.1, timeout is 2 seconds:
!!!!!
Success rate is 100 percent (5/5), round-trip min/avg/max = 56/56/56 ms
Type escape sequence to abort.
Sending 5, 100-byte ICMP Echos to 192.168.51.1, timeout is 2 seconds:
!!!!!
Success rate is 100 percent (5/5), round-trip min/avg/max = 56/56/56 ms
Type escape sequence to abort.
```

```
Sending 5, 100-byte ICMP Echos to 192.168.70.1, timeout is 2 seconds:
!!!!!
Success rate is 100 percent (5/5), round-trip min/avg/max = 56/57/60 ms
Type escape sequence to abort.
Sending 5, 100-byte ICMP Echos to 172.16.12.1, timeout is 2 seconds:
!!!!!
Success rate is 100 percent (5/5), round-trip min/avg/max = 56/56/56 ms
Type escape sequence to abort.
Sending 5, 100-byte ICMP Echos to 172.16.2.1, timeout is 2 seconds:
!!!!!
Success rate is 100 percent (5/5), round-trip min/avg/max = 28/28/32 ms
Type escape sequence to abort.
Sending 5, 100-byte ICMP Echos to 172.16.100.1, timeout is 2 seconds:
!!!!!
Success rate is 100 percent (5/5), round-trip min/avg/max = 28/28/32 ms
Type escape sequence to abort.
Sending 5, 100-byte ICMP Echos to 172.16.12.2, timeout is 2 seconds:
!!!!!
Success rate is 100 percent (5/5), round-trip min/avg/max = 28/28/32 ms
Type escape sequence to abort.
Sending 5, 100-byte ICMP Echos to 172.16.23.2, timeout is 2 seconds:
!!!!!
Success rate is 100 percent (5/5), round-trip min/avg/max = 28/28/28 ms
Type escape sequence to abort.
Sending 5, 100-byte ICMP Echos to 172.16.3.1, timeout is 2 seconds:
!!!!!
Success rate is 100 percent (5/5), round-trip min/avg/max = 1/1/4 ms
Type escape sequence to abort.
Sending 5, 100-byte ICMP Echos to 192.168.20.1, timeout is 2 seconds:
!!!!!
Success rate is 100 percent (5/5), round-trip min/avg/max = 1/1/4 ms
Type escape sequence to abort.
Sending 5, 100-byte ICMP Echos to 192.168.25.1, timeout is 2 seconds:
!!!!!
Success rate is 100 percent (5/5), round-trip min/avg/max = 1/1/1 ms
Type escape sequence to abort.
Sending 5, 100-byte ICMP Echos to 192.168.30.1, timeout is 2 seconds:
!!!!!
Success rate is 100 percent (5/5), round-trip min/avg/max = 1/1/4 ms
Type escape sequence to abort.
Sending 5, 100-byte ICMP Echos to 192.168.35.1, timeout is 2 seconds:
!!!!!
Success rate is 100 percent (5/5), round-trip min/avg/max = 1/1/1 ms
Type escape sequence to abort.
```

```
Sending 5, 100-byte ICMP Echos to 192.168.40.1, timeout is 2 seconds:
!!!!!
Success rate is 100 percent (5/5), round-trip min/avg/max = 1/1/4 ms
Type escape sequence to abort.
Sending 5, 100-byte ICMP Echos to 192.168.8.1, timeout is 2 seconds:
!!!!!
Success rate is 100 percent (5/5), round-trip min/avg/max = 1/1/4 ms
Type escape sequence to abort.
Sending 5, 100-byte ICMP Echos to 192.168.9.1, timeout is 2 seconds:
!!!!!
Success rate is 100 percent (5/5), round-trip min/avg/max = 1/1/4 ms
Type escape sequence to abort.
Sending 5, 100-byte ICMP Echos to 192.168.10.1, timeout is 2 seconds:
!!!!!
Success rate is 100 percent (5/5), round-trip min/avg/max = 1/1/1 ms
Type escape sequence to abort.
Sending 5, 100-byte ICMP Echos to 192.168.11.1, timeout is 2 seconds:
!!!!!
Success rate is 100 percent (5/5), round-trip min/avg/max = 1/1/4 ms
Type escape sequence to abort.
Sending 5, 100-byte ICMP Echos to 172.16.23.3, timeout is 2 seconds:
!!!!!
Success rate is 100 percent (5/5), round-trip min/avg/max = 56/57/64 ms
R3(tcl)# tclquit
```

Exploring Black Hole Operation

Configure R1 and shut down the Loopback 50 interface:

```
R1(config)# interface loopback 50
R1(config-if)# shutdown
```

On R2, you *should* see the following output:

```
R2# show ip route

Gateway of last resort is not set

O    192.168.30.0/24 [110/65] via 172.16.23.3, 18:53:52, Serial0/0/1
O    192.168.25.0/24 [110/65] via 172.16.23.3, 18:53:52, Serial0/0/1
O    192.168.40.0/24 [110/65] via 172.16.23.3, 18:53:52, Serial0/0/1
     172.16.0.0/24 is subnetted, 5 subnets
C       172.16.100.0 is directly connected, Loopback100
C       172.16.23.0 is directly connected, Serial0/0/1
C       172.16.12.0 is directly connected, Serial0/0/0
D       172.16.1.0 [90/40640000] via 172.16.12.1, 18:54:06, Serial0/0/0
```

```
C        172.16.2.0 is directly connected, Loopback0
O        172.16.3.0 [110/65] via 172.16.23.3, 18:53:53, Serial0/0/1
O     192.168.20.0/24 [110/65] via 172.16.23.3, 18:53:53, Serial0/0/1
D     192.168.51.0/24 [90/40640000] via 172.16.12.1, 18:54:07, Serial0/0/0
O     192.168.35.0/24 [110/65] via 172.16.23.3, 18:53:53, Serial0/0/1
D     192.168.70.0/24 [90/40640000] via 172.16.12.1, 18:54:07, Serial0/0/0
O IA 192.168.8.0/22 [110/65] via 172.16.23.3, 18:53:54, Serial0/0/1
D     192.168.48.0/23 [90/40640000] via 172.16.12.1, 18:54:08, Serial0/0/0
O     192.168.48.0/22 is a summary, 17:16:44, Null0
```

Notice the absence of 192.168.50.0/24 in a specific route in R2's routing table. Begin debugging all incoming IP packets on R2, and then issue the **ping 192.168.50.1** command:

```
R2# debug ip packet

R2# ping 192.168.50.1

(cleaned up so as to be readable)

Type escape sequence to abort.
Sending 5, 100-byte ICMP Echos to 192.168.50.1, timeout is 2 seconds:
.....
Success rate is 0 percent (0/5)


*Oct 17 16:39:14.147: IP: s=172.16.2.1 (local), d=192.168.50.1 (Null0), len 100,
sending

...


R2# undebug all

R2# traceroute 192.168.50.1

Type escape sequence to abort.
Tracing the route to 192.168.50.1

  1  *  *  *
  2  *  *  *
  3  *  *  *
  4  *  *  *
  5  *  *  *
  6  *  *  *
  7  *  *  *
  8  *  *  *
  9  *  *  *
  <output omitted>
```

The summary route, pointing to the Null0 interface as the next hop, acts as a "catch all" for any traffic generated by R2 or forwarded to R2 with the destination network 192.168.48.0/24. R2 sends traffic to the Null0 virtual interface as shown by the highlighted IP packet debugging output.

R2 is not able to ping R1's shutdown loopback interface because the 192.168.50.0/24 route no longer exists in the routing table.

Is network 192.168.50.0/24, or a supernet thereof, in the routing table of R3?

```
R3# show ip route 192.168.50.1
Routing entry for 192.168.48.0/22, supernet
  Known via "ospf 1", distance 110, metric 20, type extern 2, forward metric 1562
  Last update from 172.16.23.2 on Serial0/0/1, 00:39:17 ago
  Routing Descriptor Blocks:
  * 172.16.23.2, from 172.16.2.1, 00:39:17 ago, via Serial0/0/1
      Route metric is 20, traffic share count is 1
```

Begin debugging all IP and ICMP packets on R3. Ping the address 192.168.50.1 from R3. Try to trace the route from R3 to 192.168.50.1:

```
R3# debug ip packet
R3# debug ip icmp

R3# ping 192.168.50.1
(cleaned up so as to be readable)

Type escape sequence to abort.
Sending 5, 100-byte ICMP Echos to 192.168.50.1, timeout is 2 seconds:
U.U.U
Success rate is 0 percent (0/5)


*Oct 17 16:49:21.023: IP: tableid=0, s=172.16.23.3 (local), d=192.168.50.1
(Serial0/0/1), routed via FIB

*Oct 17 16:49:21.047: ICMP: dst (172.16.23.3) host unreachable rcv from 172.16.23.2


R3# undebug all

R3# traceroute 192.168.50.1

Type escape sequence to abort.
Tracing the route to 192.168.50.1

 1 172.16.23.2 12 msec 12 msec 16 msec
 2 172.16.23.2 !H  !H  *
```

Analyze the process indicated by the ICMP responses. You might also want to refer to debugging messages for ICMP and IP packets on R2:

1. R3 generates an ICMP Echo Request (ping) to 192.168.50.1.

2. R3 looks up the (next hop address, outgoing interface) pair for the longest matching prefix containing 192.168.50.1 in the IP routing table and finds (172.16.23.2, Serial0/0/1).

3. R3 routes the IP packet to (172.16.23.2, Serial0/0/1).

4. R2 receives the IP packet from R3 on interface Serial0/0/1.

5. R2 looks up the (next hop address, outgoing interface) pair for the longest prefix matching containing 192.168.50.1 in the IP routing table. The longest matching prefix that the routing table returns is 192.168.48.0/22, for which the routing table responds with (null, Null0) because it has no next-hop address or physical outgoing interface.

6. R2 realizes that this packet was routed remotely to it, but that it has no route, so it sends an ICMP Type 3, Code 1 (host unreachable) packet to the source address of the packet, 172.16.23.3.[1]

7. R2 looks up the (next hop address, outgoing interface) pair for 172.16.23.3 and resolves it to (172.16.23.3, Serial0/0/1).

8. R2 then routes the ICMP packet for destination 172.16.23.3, normally 172.16.23.3 through Serial0/0/1.

9. R3 receives a packet destined for its local address 172.16.23.3 and reads the packet, sending the ICMP "Host Unreachable" message to the **ping** output.

Notice that R2 sends R3 an ICMP Type 3, Code 1 reply indicating that it does not have a route to the host 192.168.50.1. This ICMP "Host Unreachable" message is not only sent in response to pings or traceroutes (also a form of ICMP) but for *all IP traffic*. If you were to telnet to 192.168.50.1, you would receive the following message based on the ICMP response from R2:

```
R3# telnet 192.168.50.1
Trying 192.168.50.1 ...
% Destination unreachable; gateway or host down

R3#
```

This is not an example of Telnet timing out, but of intelligent network protocols responding to routing issues in the network.

This summarization problem is a classic example of a "black hole" in a domain, which simply means traffic passing through the network destined for that subnet is discarded at some point along the way. Thankfully, ICMP informs sources of when their traffic is being discarded.

Do not forget to issue the **no shutdown** command on R1's Loopback 50 interface to re-enable routing to this network:

```
R1(config)# interface loopback 50
R1(config-if)# no shutdown
```

Lab 5-3: Redistribution Between EIGRP and IS-IS (5.6.3)

The objectives of this lab are as follows:

- Review basic configuration of EIGRP and IS-IS

- Redistribute into EIGRP

- Redistribute into IS-IS

- Use a standard access list to select routes for filtering

- Use a prefix list to select routes for filtering

- Examine the differences between using access lists and prefix lists for filtering routes

- Filter routes using route maps

- Summarize routes in IS-IS

Figure 5-3 illustrates the topology that will be used for this lab.

Figure 5-3   Topology Diagram

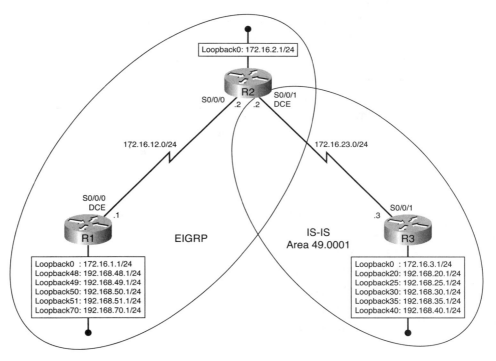

Scenario

R1 is running EIGRP, and R3 is running IS-IS. Configure R2 to enable these two routing protocols to interact to allow full connectivity between all networks. Then filter routes from each of the routing protocols using various methods.

Step 1: Assign Addresses

Configure all loopback interfaces on the three routers given in the diagram, and configure the serial interfaces with the IP addresses. Issue the **no shutdown** command on the physical interfaces, and set a clock rate where appropriate:

```
R1# configure terminal
R1(config)# interface loopback 0
R1(config-if)# ip address 172.16.1.1 255.255.255.0
R1(config-if)# interface loopback 48
R1(config-if)# ip address 192.168.48.1 255.255.255.0
R1(config-if)# interface loopback 49
R1(config-if)# ip address 192.168.49.1 255.255.255.0
R1(config-if)# interface loopback 50
R1(config-if)# ip address 192.168.50.1 255.255.255.0
R1(config-if)# interface loopback 51
R1(config-if)# ip address 192.168.51.1 255.255.255.0
R1(config-if)# interface loopback 70
R1(config-if)# ip address 192.168.70.1 255.255.255.0
R1(config-if)# interface serial 0/0/0
R1(config-if)# bandwidth 64
R1(config-if)# ip address 172.16.12.1 255.255.255.0
R1(config-if)# clock rate 64000
R1(config-if)# no shutdown
```

```
R2# configure terminal
R2(config)# interface loopback 0
R2(config-if)# ip address 172.16.2.1 255.255.255.0
R2(config-if)# interface serial 0/0/0
R2(config-if)# bandwidth 64
R2(config-if)# ip address 172.16.12.2 255.255.255.0
R2(config-if)# no shutdown
R2(config-if)# interface serial 0/0/1
R2(config-if)# bandwidth 64
R2(config-if)# ip address 172.16.23.2 255.255.255.0
R2(config-if)# clock rate 64000
R2(config-if)# no shutdown
```

```
R3# configure terminal
R3(config)# interface loopback 0
R3(config-if)# ip address 172.16.3.1 255.255.255.0
R3(config-if)# interface loopback 20
R3(config-if)# ip address 192.168.20.1 255.255.255.0
R3(config-if)# interface loopback 25
R3(config-if)# ip address 192.168.25.1 255.255.255.0
R3(config-if)# interface loopback 30
R3(config-if)# ip address 192.168.30.1 255.255.255.0
```

```
R3(config-if)# interface loopback 35
R3(config-if)# ip address 192.168.35.1 255.255.255.0
R3(config-if)# interface loopback 40
R3(config-if)# ip address 192.168.40.1 255.255.255.0
R3(config-if)# interface serial 0/0/0
R3(config-if)# bandwidth 64
R3(config-if)# ip address 172.16.23.3 255.255.255.0
R3(config-if)# no shutdown
```

Be sure you can ping across the serial links when you are done.

Step 2: Configure EIGRP

Configure R1 and R2 to run EIGRP in autonomous system 1. On R1, add in all connected interfaces either with classful **network** commands or with wildcard masks. Use a classful **network** statement on R2. Make sure that you disable automatic summarization. Verify the configuration with the **show ip eigrp neighbors** and **show ip route eigrp** commands on both routers. Issue the **passive-interface** command on R2 to prevent Hello packets from being sent out Serial0/0/1 to R3.

```
R1(config)# router eigrp 1
R1(config-router)# no auto-summary
R1(config-router)# network 172.16.0.0
R1(config-router)# network 192.168.1.0
R1(config-router)# network 192.168.48.0
R1(config-router)# network 192.168.49.0
R1(config-router)# network 192.168.50.0
R1(config-router)# network 192.168.51.0
R1(config-router)# network 192.168.70.0
```

Or:

```
R1(config)# router eigrp 1
R1(config-router)# no auto-summary
R1(config-router)# network 172.16.0.0
R1(config-router)# network 192.168.0.0 0.0.255.255
```

```
R2(config)# router eigrp 1
R2(config-router)# no auto-summary
R2(config-router)# network 172.16.0.0
R2(config-router)# passive-interface Serial0/0/1
```

```
R1# show ip eigrp neighbors
IP-EIGRP neighbors for process 1
H   Address              Interface       Hold Uptime   SRTT   RTO  Q   Seq
                                         (sec)         (ms)        Cnt Num
0   172.16.12.2          Se0/0/0          10 00:00:45   30   2280  0   5


R1# show ip route eigrp
     172.16.0.0/24 is subnetted, 5 subnets
D       172.16.23.0 [90/41024000] via 172.16.12.2, 00:00:48, Serial0/0/0
```

```
D         172.16.2.0 [90/40640000] via 172.16.12.2, 00:00:48, Serial0/0/0
D         172.16.100.0 [90/40640000] via 172.16.12.2, 00:00:48, Serial0/0/0
```

```
R2# show ip eigrp neighbors
IP-EIGRP neighbors for process 1
H   Address              Interface       Hold Uptime    SRTT   RTO  Q  Seq
                                         (sec)          (ms)        Cnt Num
0   172.16.12.1          Se0/0/0          11 00:00:54    25   2280  0  2
```

```
R2# show ip route eigrp
      172.16.0.0/24 is subnetted, 5 subnets
D         172.16.1.0 [90/40640000] via 172.16.12.1, 00:00:57, Serial0/0/0
D     192.168.51.0/24 [90/40640000] via 172.16.12.1, 00:00:57, Serial0/0/0
D     192.168.50.0/24 [90/40640000] via 172.16.12.1, 00:00:57, Serial0/0/0
D     192.168.49.0/24 [90/40640000] via 172.16.12.1, 00:00:57, Serial0/0/0
D     192.168.70.0/24 [90/40640000] via 172.16.12.1, 00:00:57, Serial0/0/0
D     192.168.48.0/24 [90/40640000] via 172.16.12.1, 00:00:57, Serial0/0/0
```

Step 3: Configure IS-IS

Configure IS-IS Area 49.0001 on R2 and R3. Assign R2 a NET of 49.0001.2222.2222.2222.00 and R3 a NET of 49.0001.3333.3333.3333.00. Configure both to be level 2-only routers. Add in the serial interface connecting the two on both routers and all of R3's loopback interfaces. Verify the configuration with the **show isis neighbors** and **show ip route isis** commands:

```
R2(config)# router isis
R2(config-router)# net 49.0001.2222.2222.2222.00
R2(config-router)# interface serial 0/0/1
R2(config-if)# ip router isis
R2(config-if)# isis circuit-type level-2-only
```

```
R3(config)# router isis
R3(config-router)# net 49.0001.3333.3333.3333.00
R3(config-router)# interface loopback 0
R3(config-if)# ip router isis
R3(config-if)# interface loopback 20
R3(config-if)# ip router isis
R3(config-if)# interface loopback 25
R3(config-if)# ip router isis
R3(config-if)# interface loopback 30
R3(config-if)# ip router isis
R3(config-if)# interface loopback 35
R3(config-if)# ip router isis
R3(config-if)# interface loopback 40
R3(config-if)# ip router isis
R3(config-if)# interface serial 0/0/1
R3(config-if)# ip router isis
```

```
R3(config-if)# isis circuit-type level-2-only
```

```
R2# show isis neighbors


System Id       Type Interface IP Address      State Holdtime Circuit Id
R3              L2   Se0/0/1   172.16.23.3      UP    24       00
```

```
R2# show ip route isis
i L2 192.168.30.0/24 [115/20] via 172.16.23.3, Serial0/0/1
i L2 192.168.25.0/24 [115/20] via 172.16.23.3, Serial0/0/1
i L2 192.168.40.0/24 [115/20] via 172.16.23.3, Serial0/0/1
     172.16.0.0/24 is subnetted, 6 subnets
i L2    172.16.3.0 [115/20] via 172.16.23.3, Serial0/0/1
i L2 192.168.20.0/24 [115/20] via 172.16.23.3, Serial0/0/1
i L2 192.168.35.0/24 [115/20] via 172.16.23.3, Serial0/0/1
```

```
R3# show isis neighbors


System Id       Type Interface IP Address      State Holdtime Circuit Id
R2              L2   Se0/0/1   172.16.23.2      UP    28       00
```

```
R3# show ip route isis

R3#
```

Note that R3 has not received any remote network advertisements from R2, so there are no IS-IS routes in the routing table.

Will IS-IS send Hello packets and LSPs out the Serial0/0/0 interface on R2? Explain.

_____

_____

_____

Note In general, link-state protocols develop adjacencies with a form of Hello packet before routing information is sent out an interface. These adjacencies eliminate the need for periodic updates, decrease the convergence time, and allow neighboring routers to notify each other when a link in the network changes state.

When you apply a network statement in router configuration mode, you are actually performing two actions. First, you are selecting the interfaces out which that protocol sends Hello packets. Second, you are selecting IP subnets for the protocol to advertise. For example, if you enter **network 172.16.0.0** in OSPF configuration mode on a router, you instruct OSPF to send Hello packets out of the interfaces with IP addresses within that major network. You also instructed EIGRP to advertise any and all subnets of 172.16.0.0/16 to its neighbors.

An alternate, more intuitive way to accomplish the same two steps in OSPF is to apply the **ip ospf** *process* **area** *area* command to a router interface. This per-interface OSPF configuration was introduced in Cisco IOS Release 12.3(11)T. This is analogous to the way that you configure IS-IS in a per-interface manner with the **ip router isis command**. Remember that IS-IS selects networks for advertisement based on the IP subnets of interfaces that have the **ip router isis** command applied.

Be sure you understand this methodology and its results thoroughly because it is used not only by IS-IS, but by PIM multicast routing protocols and IPv6 routing protocols such as RIPng, OSPFv3, IS-IS for IPv6, and EIGRP for IPv6.

Step 4: Mutually Redistribute Between IS-IS and EIGRP

Configure redistribution between IS-IS and EIGRP on R2. Under the IS-IS process, issue the **redistribute eigrp 1** command. A default seed metric is not required for IS-IS.

Under the EIGRP process, issue the **redistribute isis metric 64 100 255 1 1500** command. This command tells EIGRP to redistribute IS-IS routes with the following metrics: 64 Kbps bandwidth, 100 milliseconds delay, 255/255 reliability ratio, 1/255 load ratio, and 1500 bytes MTU. Because every link advertisement sent in EIGRP has these metric fields, a seed metric is required. Seed metrics populate these fields on route advertisements when you redistribute into EIGRP. You can also set a default seed metric with the **default-metric** command. With IS-IS redistribution, you can specify which level you want the routes to go to or come from, but for now we will use the defaults because we are only dealing with level 2:

```
R2(config)# router isis
R2(config-router)# redistribute eigrp 1
R2(config-router)# router eigrp 1
R2(config-router)# redistribute isis metric 64 100 255 1 1500
```

Verify the redistribution with the **show ip route** command on R1 and R3:

```
R1# show ip route
<output omitted>


Gateway of last resort is not set


D EX 192.168.30.0/24 [170/40537600] via 172.16.12.2, 00:00:04, Serial0/0/0
D EX 192.168.25.0/24 [170/40537600] via 172.16.12.2, 00:00:04, Serial0/0/0
D EX 192.168.40.0/24 [170/40537600] via 172.16.12.2, 00:00:04, Serial0/0/0
     172.16.0.0/24 is subnetted, 6 subnets
D        172.16.23.0 [90/41024000] via 172.16.12.2, 00:00:26, Serial0/0/0
C        172.16.12.0 is directly connected, Serial0/0/0
C        172.16.1.0 is directly connected, Loopback0
D        172.16.2.0 [90/40640000] via 172.16.12.2, 00:00:26, Serial0/0/0
D EX     172.16.3.0 [170/40537600] via 172.16.12.2, 00:00:05, Serial0/0/0
D        172.16.100.0 [90/40640000] via 172.16.12.2, 00:00:27, Serial0/0/0
D EX 192.168.20.0/24 [170/40537600] via 172.16.12.2, 00:00:05, Serial0/0/0
C    192.168.51.0/24 is directly connected, Loopback51
C    192.168.50.0/24 is directly connected, Loopback50
D EX 192.168.35.0/24 [170/40537600] via 172.16.12.2, 00:00:07, Serial0/0/0
C    192.168.49.0/24 is directly connected, Loopback49
C    192.168.70.0/24 is directly connected, Loopback70
C    192.168.48.0/24 is directly connected, Loopback48
R3# show ip route
<output omitted>


Gateway of last resort is not set
```

```
C       192.168.30.0/24 is directly connected, Loopback30
C       192.168.8.0/24 is directly connected, Loopback8
C       192.168.25.0/24 is directly connected, Loopback25
C       192.168.9.0/24 is directly connected, Loopback9
C       192.168.10.0/24 is directly connected, Loopback10
C       192.168.40.0/24 is directly connected, Loopback40
        172.16.0.0/24 is subnetted, 6 subnets
C          172.16.23.0 is directly connected, Serial0/0/1
i L2       172.16.12.0 [115/10] via 172.16.23.2, Serial0/0/1
i L2       172.16.1.0 [115/10] via 172.16.23.2, Serial0/0/1
i L2       172.16.2.0 [115/10] via 172.16.23.2, Serial0/0/1
C          172.16.3.0 is directly connected, Loopback0
C       192.168.11.0/24 is directly connected, Loopback11
C       192.168.20.0/24 is directly connected, Loopback20
i L2 192.168.51.0/24 [115/10] via 172.16.23.2, Serial0/0/1
i L2 192.168.50.0/24 [115/10] via 172.16.23.2, Serial0/0/1
C       192.168.35.0/24 is directly connected, Loopback35
i L2 192.168.49.0/24 [115/10] via 172.16.23.2, Serial0/0/1
i L2 192.168.70.0/24 [115/10] via 172.16.23.2, Serial0/0/1
i L2 192.168.48.0/24 [115/10] via 172.16.23.2, Serial0/0/1
```

Verify full connectivity with the following TCL script. You can download this TCL script at www.ciscopress.com/title/1587132133 under the More Information section on the page.

```
foreach address {
172.16.1.1
192.168.48.1
192.168.49.1
192.168.50.1
192.168.51.1
192.168.70.1
172.16.12.1
172.16.2.1
172.16.12.2
172.16.23.2
172.16.3.1
192.168.20.1
192.168.25.1
192.168.30.1
192.168.35.1
192.168.40.1
172.16.23.3
} { ping $address }
```

You should receive the TCL script output shown in the section, "TCL Script Output," for this lab. This output corresponds to full connectivity by showing all ICMP echo replies.

Step 5: Filter Network Addresses with Route Maps

You are given the requirement to prevent R3 from receiving LSPs advertising R1's Loopback 0 and Loopback 70 interfaces. All of R1's other loopback networks must be reachable by R3.

At what points within your network topology could you employ a filter to fulfill this requirement?

_____

_____

_____

_____

Because all the IS-IS link-state databases in an area must be fully synchronized, where must you apply this route map? (Note that IS-IS does not support the **distribute-list** command.)

_____

_____

_____

_____

_____

What kind of route filters does IS-IS support if it does not support distribute lists?

_____

One way to filter prefixes is with a route map. When used for filtering prefixes, a route map works like an access list. It has multiple statements that are read in a sequential order. Each statement can be a deny or permit and can have a match clause for a variety of attributes, such as the route or a route tag. You can also include route attributes in each statement that will be set if the match clause is met.

Use a route map on R2 to prevent traffic from entering the IS-IS routing domain. First configure a standard access list that permits the network address of the two subnets associated with the interfaces for Step 5's requirement:

```
R2(config)# ip access-list standard SELECT-EIGRP
R2(config-std-nacl)# permit 172.16.1.0
R2(config-std-nacl)# permit 192.168.70.0
R2(config-std-nacl)# exit
```

Then create a route map, the first statement of which denies all network addresses permitted by the access list you just configured. The final statement permits advertisement of any network not previously denied in the route map:

```
R2(config)# route-map EIGRP-to-ISIS deny 10
R2(config-route-map)# match ip address SELECT-EIGRP
R2(config-route-map)# route-map EIGRP-to-ISIS permit 20
```

Finally, apply this route map to the **redistribute** statement in R2's IS-IS configuration menu.

```
R2(config)# router isis
R2(config-router)# redistribute eigrp 1 route-map EIGRP-to-ISIS
```

Verify the operation of this route map by displaying all IS-IS routes in R3's routing table and in R2's topology database.

```
R3# show ip route isis
      172.16.0.0/24 is subnetted, 5 subnets
i L2     172.16.12.0 [115/10] via 172.16.23.2, Serial0/0/1
i L2     172.16.2.0 [115/10] via 172.16.23.2, Serial0/0/1
i L2 192.168.51.0/24 [115/10] via 172.16.23.2, Serial0/0/1
i L2 192.168.50.0/24 [115/10] via 172.16.23.2, Serial0/0/1
i L2 192.168.49.0/24 [115/10] via 172.16.23.2, Serial0/0/1
i L2 192.168.48.0/24 [115/10] via 172.16.23.2, Serial0/0/1
```

```
R2# show isis database detail
IS-IS Level-1 Link State Database:
LSPID                  LSP Seq Num  LSP Checksum  LSP Holdtime      ATT/P/OL
R2.00-00             * 0x00000046   0xD064        552               0/0/0
  Area Address: 49.0001
  NLPID:        0xCC
  Hostname: R2
IS-IS Level-2 Link State Database:
LSPID                  LSP Seq Num  LSP Checksum  LSP Holdtime      ATT/P/OL
R2.00-00             * 0x00000082   0xF55A        1118              0/0/0
  Area Address: 49.0001
  NLPID:        0xCC
  Hostname: R2
  IP Address:   172.16.23.2
  Metric: 10       IP 172.16.23.0 255.255.255.0
  Metric: 10       IS R3.00
  Metric: 0        IP-External 172.16.2.0 255.255.255.0
  Metric: 0        IP-External 172.16.12.0 255.255.255.0
  Metric: 0        IP-External 192.168.48.0 255.255.255.0
  Metric: 0        IP-External 192.168.49.0 255.255.255.0
  Metric: 0        IP-External 192.168.50.0 255.255.255.0
  Metric: 0        IP-External 192.168.51.0 255.255.255.0
R3.00-00               0x0000007D   0xAADF        923               0/0/0
  Area Address: 49.0001
  NLPID:        0xCC
  Hostname: R3
  IP Address:   172.16.3.1
  Metric: 10       IP 172.16.23.0 255.255.255.0
  Metric: 10       IS R2.00
  Metric: 10       IP 172.16.3.0 255.255.255.0
  Metric: 10       IP 192.168.20.0 255.255.255.0
```

```
    Metric: 10          IP 192.168.25.0 255.255.255.0
    Metric: 10          IP 192.168.30.0 255.255.255.0
    Metric: 10          IP 192.168.35.0 255.255.255.0
    Metric: 10          IP 192.168.40.0 255.255.255.0
```

You could also verify that matches to each of the statements in the access list are occurring by issuing the **show access-list** command on R2:

```
R2# show access-list
Standard IP access list 1
    10 deny    any
Standard IP access list SELECT-EIGRP
    20 permit 192.168.70.0 (1 match)
    10 permit 172.16.1.0 (1 match)
```

Could this route filtering be configured any other way using the same two tools? If so, write out the configuration in complete form.

_____

_____

_____

_____

_____

_____

Would the following configuration fulfill the requirements given at the beginning of this step? Explain.

```
ip access-list standard DENY-EIGRP
 10 deny 172.16.1.0
 20 deny 192.168.70.0
!
route-map DENY-EIGRP-TO-ISIS permit 10
 match ip address DENY-EIGRP
!
router isis
 redistribute eigrp 1 route-map DENY-EIGRP-TO-ISIS
```

_____

_____

If there is anything wrong with the preceding configuration, what would you have to change to make the example work according to the requirement? Give any configuration changes in complete form.

Enter the **permit any** command at the end of the DENY-EIGRP access list.

___

Step 6: Filter Prefixes with Route Maps

Filter the subnets associated with R3's loopbacks 25 and 30 on R2 from getting redistributed into EIGRP. Display R1's routing table to verify that those two routes appear there:

```
R1# show ip route eigrp
 D EX 192.168.30.0/24 [170/40537600] via 172.16.12.2, 07:21:48, Serial0/0/0
 D EX 192.168.25.0/24 [170/40537600] via 172.16.12.2, 07:21:48, Serial0/0/0
 D EX 192.168.40.0/24 [170/40537600] via 172.16.12.2, 07:21:48, Serial0/0/0
       172.16.0.0/24 is subnetted, 5 subnets
 D        172.16.23.0 [90/41024000] via 172.16.12.2, 07:22:11, Serial0/0/0
 D        172.16.2.0 [90/40640000] via 172.16.12.2, 07:22:11, Serial0/0/0
 D EX     172.16.3.0 [170/40537600] via 172.16.12.2, 07:21:48, Serial0/0/0
 D EX 192.168.20.0/24 [170/40537600] via 172.16.12.2, 07:21:48, Serial0/0/0
 D EX 192.168.35.0/24 [170/40537600] via 172.16.12.2, 07:21:48, Serial0/0/0
```

There are multiple ways to configure a solution using route maps. A prefix list matches network prefixes, including network masks. It is read sequentially like an access list. For this example, configure a prefix list that matches the networks on loopbacks 25 and 30, and a route map that denies based on a match for that prefix list. First, configure a prefix list that matches only these two prefixes:

```
R2(config)# ip prefix-list MATCH-25-30 permit 192.168.25.0/24
R2(config)# ip prefix-list MATCH-25-30 permit 192.168.30.0/24
```

Now configure a route map with a statement that denies based on a match with this prefix list. Then add a permit statement without a match statement, which acts as an implicit permit:

```
R2(config)# route-map ISIS-to-EIGRP deny 10
R2(config-route-map)# match ip address prefix-list MATCH-25-30
R2(config-route-map)# route-map ISIS-to-EIGRP permit 20
```

Finally, apply this route map under the EIGRP process by replacing the **redistribute isis** statement with a statement including the route map:

```
R2(config)# router eigrp 1
R2(config-router)# redistribute isis route-map ISIS-TO-EIGRP
```

```
R2# show run | section router
 ip router isis
router eigrp 1
 redistribute isis level-2 metric 64 100 255 1 1500 route-map ISIS-TO-EIGRP
 passive-interface Serial0/0/1
```

```
 network 172.16.0.0
 no auto-summary
router isis
 net 49.0001.2222.2222.2222.00
 redistribute eigrp 1 route-map EIGRP-to-ISIS
```

Notice that adding the **redistribute isis route-map** *route-map* command does not negate the seed metrics configured previously. You have simply added the route map parameter to the group of other parameters in the redistribution statement.

Verify that these routes are filtered out in R1's routing table. Also verify that the prefix lists are matching route advertisements to be denied from IS-IS by using the **show ip prefix-list detail** command on R2:

```
R1# show ip route eigrp
D EX 192.168.40.0/24 [170/40537600] via 172.16.12.2, 00:09:19, Serial0/0/0
        172.16.0.0/24 is subnetted, 5 subnets
D        172.16.23.0 [90/41024000] via 172.16.12.2, 1d00h, Serial0/0/0
D        172.16.2.0 [90/40640000] via 172.16.12.2, 1d00h, Serial0/0/0
D EX     172.16.3.0 [170/40537600] via 172.16.12.2, 00:09:19, Serial0/0/0
D EX 192.168.20.0/24 [170/40537600] via 172.16.12.2, 00:09:19, Serial0/0/0
D EX 192.168.35.0/24 [170/40537600] via 172.16.12.2, 00:09:19, Serial0/0/0
R2# show ip prefix-list detail
Prefix-list with the last deletion/insertion: MATCH-25-30
ip prefix-list MATCH-25-30:
   count: 2, range entries: 0, sequences: 5 - 10, refcount: 3
   seq 5 permit 192.168.25.0/24 (hit count: 1, refcount: 2)
   seq 10 permit 192.168.30.0/24 (hit count: 1, refcount: 1)
```

Would the following configuration produce the same result as the above prefix list example? Explain.

```
ip prefix-list DENY-25-30 deny 192.168.25.0/24
ip prefix-list DENY-25-30 deny 192.168.30.0/24
!
route-map DENY-ISIS-TO-EIGRP permit 10
 match ip address prefix-list DENY-25-30
!
router eigrp 1
 redistribute isis metric 64 100 255 1 1500 route-map DENY-ISIS-TO-EIGRP
```

_____

_____

If the previous configuration does not perform as required, is there a way that you could amend the configuration to correct the behavior? If yes, record your answer in complete form.

_____

Why is it better to filter on an entire prefix (including network mask) rather than just a network address?

_____

_____

Can you filter based on a network or subnet mask using an access list? Explain.

_____

_____

_____

_____

If you can configure an access list to match the same prefixes and masks as the MATCH-25-30 prefix list matches, show how that access list would be defined and applied. Record your answer in complete form.

_____

_____

_____

Step 7: Summarize Addresses in IS-IS

You can summarize R1's loopback interfaces 48 through 51 into one supernet to get advertised to R3 through IS-IS. Under the IS-IS configuration prompt, use the **summary-address** *address mask* command. You can specify additional arguments specifying the level to summarize into, but this lab uses the default. Before configuring, display the routing table on R3:

```
R3# show ip route isis
     172.16.0.0/24 is subnetted, 5 subnets
i L2    172.16.12.0 [115/10] via 172.16.23.2, Serial0/0/1
i L2    172.16.1.0 [115/10] via 172.16.23.2, Serial0/0/1
i L2    172.16.2.0 [115/10] via 172.16.23.2, Serial0/0/1
i L2 192.168.51.0/24 [115/10] via 172.16.23.2, Serial0/0/1
i L2 192.168.50.0/24 [115/10] via 172.16.23.2, Serial0/0/1
i L2 192.168.49.0/24 [115/10] via 172.16.23.2, Serial0/0/1
i L2 192.168.70.0/24 [115/10] via 172.16.23.2, Serial0/0/1
i L2 192.168.48.0/24 [115/10] via 172.16.23.2, Serial0/0/1
```

Now enter the command on R2 and check the routing table on R3. Also utilize the **show ip protocols** command to view any IS-IS summary addresses:

```
R2(config)# router isis
R2(config-router)# summary-address 192.168.48.0 255.255.252.0


R2# show ip route isis
i L2 192.168.30.0/24 [115/20] via 172.16.23.3, Serial0/0/1
i L2 192.168.25.0/24 [115/20] via 172.16.23.3, Serial0/0/1
```

```
i L2 192.168.40.0/24 [115/20] via 172.16.23.3, Serial0/0/1
       172.16.0.0/24 is subnetted, 5 subnets
i L2    172.16.3.0 [115/20] via 172.16.23.3, Serial0/0/1
i L2 192.168.20.0/24 [115/20] via 172.16.23.3, Serial0/0/1
i L2 192.168.35.0/24 [115/20] via 172.16.23.3, Serial0/0/1
i su 192.168.48.0/22 [115/0] via 0.0.0.0, Null0
```

```
R2# show ip protocols
<output omitted>

Routing Protocol is "isis"
  Invalid after 0 seconds, hold down 0, flushed after 0
  Outgoing update filter list for all interfaces is not set
  Incoming update filter list for all interfaces is not set
  Redistributing: eigrp 1, isis
  Address Summarization:
    192.168.48.0/255.255.252.0 into level-2
  Maximum path: 4
  Routing for Networks:
    Serial0/0/1
  Routing Information Sources:
    Gateway          Distance      Last Update
    (this router)        115       00:25:18
    172.16.3.1           115       00:12:51
  Distance: (default is 115)
```

```
R3# show ip route isis
       172.16.0.0/24 is subnetted, 5 subnets
i L2    172.16.12.0 [115/10] via 172.16.23.2, Serial0/0/1
i L2    172.16.2.0 [115/10] via 172.16.23.2, Serial0/0/1
i L2 192.168.48.0/22 [115/10] via 172.16.23.2, Serial0/0/1
```

TCL Script Output

```
R1# tclsh
R1(tcl)# foreach address {
+>(tcl)# 172.16.1.1
+>(tcl)# 192.168.48.1
+>(tcl)# 192.168.49.1
+>(tcl)# 192.168.50.1
+>(tcl)# 192.168.51.1
+>(tcl)# 192.168.70.1
+>(tcl)# 172.16.12.1
+>(tcl)# 172.16.2.1
+>(tcl)# 172.16.12.2
```

```
+>(tcl)# 172.16.23.2
+>(tcl)# 172.16.3.1
+>(tcl)# 192.168.20.1
+>(tcl)# 192.168.25.1
+>(tcl)# 192.168.30.1
+>(tcl)# 192.168.35.1
+>(tcl)# 192.168.40.1
+>(tcl)# 172.16.23.3
+>(tcl)# } { ping $address }

Type escape sequence to abort.
Sending 5, 100-byte ICMP Echos to 172.16.1.1, timeout is 2 seconds:
!!!!!
Success rate is 100 percent (5/5), round-trip min/avg/max = 1/1/4 ms
Type escape sequence to abort.
Sending 5, 100-byte ICMP Echos to 192.168.48.1, timeout is 2 seconds:
!!!!!
Success rate is 100 percent (5/5), round-trip min/avg/max = 1/1/4 ms
Type escape sequence to abort.
Sending 5, 100-byte ICMP Echos to 192.168.49.1, timeout is 2 seconds:
!!!!!
Success rate is 100 percent (5/5), round-trip min/avg/max = 1/1/1 ms
Type escape sequence to abort.
Sending 5, 100-byte ICMP Echos to 192.168.50.1, timeout is 2 seconds:
!!!!!
Success rate is 100 percent (5/5), round-trip min/avg/max = 1/1/4 ms
Type escape sequence to abort.
Sending 5, 100-byte ICMP Echos to 192.168.51.1, timeout is 2 seconds:
!!!!!
Success rate is 100 percent (5/5), round-trip min/avg/max = 1/1/1 ms
Type escape sequence to abort.
Sending 5, 100-byte ICMP Echos to 192.168.70.1, timeout is 2 seconds:
!!!!!
Success rate is 100 percent (5/5), round-trip min/avg/max = 1/2/4 ms
Type escape sequence to abort.
Sending 5, 100-byte ICMP Echos to 172.16.12.1, timeout is 2 seconds:
!!!!!
Success rate is 100 percent (5/5), round-trip min/avg/max = 56/58/68 ms
Type escape sequence to abort.
Sending 5, 100-byte ICMP Echos to 172.16.2.1, timeout is 2 seconds:
!!!!!
Success rate is 100 percent (5/5), round-trip min/avg/max = 28/29/32 ms
Type escape sequence to abort.
Sending 5, 100-byte ICMP Echos to 172.16.12.2, timeout is 2 seconds:
```

```
!!!!!
Success rate is 100 percent (5/5), round-trip min/avg/max = 28/28/32 ms
Type escape sequence to abort.
Sending 5, 100-byte ICMP Echos to 172.16.23.2, timeout is 2 seconds:
!!!!!
Success rate is 100 percent (5/5), round-trip min/avg/max = 28/28/32 ms
Type escape sequence to abort.
Sending 5, 100-byte ICMP Echos to 172.16.3.1, timeout is 2 seconds:
!!!!!
Success rate is 100 percent (5/5), round-trip min/avg/max = 56/56/56 ms
Type escape sequence to abort.
Sending 5, 100-byte ICMP Echos to 192.168.20.1, timeout is 2 seconds:
!!!!!
Success rate is 100 percent (5/5), round-trip min/avg/max = 56/56/60 ms
Type escape sequence to abort.
Sending 5, 100-byte ICMP Echos to 192.168.25.1, timeout is 2 seconds:
!!!!!
Success rate is 100 percent (5/5), round-trip min/avg/max = 56/56/60 ms
Type escape sequence to abort.
Sending 5, 100-byte ICMP Echos to 192.168.30.1, timeout is 2 seconds:
!!!!!
Success rate is 100 percent (5/5), round-trip min/avg/max = 56/88/216 ms
Type escape sequence to abort.
Sending 5, 100-byte ICMP Echos to 192.168.35.1, timeout is 2 seconds:
!!!!!
Success rate is 100 percent (5/5), round-trip min/avg/max = 56/56/60 ms
Type escape sequence to abort.
Sending 5, 100-byte ICMP Echos to 192.168.40.1, timeout is 2 seconds:
!!!!!
Success rate is 100 percent (5/5), round-trip min/avg/max = 56/56/60 ms
Type escape sequence to abort.
Sending 5, 100-byte ICMP Echos to 172.16.23.3, timeout is 2 seconds:
!!!!!
Success rate is 100 percent (5/5), round-trip min/avg/max = 56/56/56 ms
R1(tcl)# tclquit
R2# tclsh
R2(tcl)# foreach address {
+>(tcl)# 172.16.1.1
+>(tcl)# 192.168.48.1
+>(tcl)# 192.168.49.1
+>(tcl)# 192.168.50.1
+>(tcl)# 192.168.51.1
+>(tcl)# 192.168.70.1
+>(tcl)# 172.16.12.1
```

```
+>(tcl)# 172.16.2.1
+>(tcl)# 172.16.12.2
+>(tcl)# 172.16.23.2
+>(tcl)# 172.16.3.1
+>(tcl)# 192.168.20.1
+>(tcl)# 192.168.25.1
+>(tcl)# 192.168.30.1
+>(tcl)# 192.168.35.1
+>(tcl)# 192.168.40.1
+>(tcl)# 172.16.23.3
+>(tcl)# } { ping $address }

Type escape sequence to abort.
Sending 5, 100-byte ICMP Echos to 172.16.1.1, timeout is 2 seconds:
!!!!!
Success rate is 100 percent (5/5), round-trip min/avg/max = 28/28/28 ms
Type escape sequence to abort.
Sending 5, 100-byte ICMP Echos to 192.168.48.1, timeout is 2 seconds:
!!!!!
Success rate is 100 percent (5/5), round-trip min/avg/max = 28/28/32 ms
Type escape sequence to abort.
Sending 5, 100-byte ICMP Echos to 192.168.49.1, timeout is 2 seconds:
!!!!!
Success rate is 100 percent (5/5), round-trip min/avg/max = 28/28/32 ms
Type escape sequence to abort.
Sending 5, 100-byte ICMP Echos to 192.168.50.1, timeout is 2 seconds:
!!!!!
Success rate is 100 percent (5/5), round-trip min/avg/max = 28/28/32 ms
Type escape sequence to abort.
Sending 5, 100-byte ICMP Echos to 192.168.51.1, timeout is 2 seconds:
!!!!!
Success rate is 100 percent (5/5), round-trip min/avg/max = 28/28/32 ms
Type escape sequence to abort.
Sending 5, 100-byte ICMP Echos to 192.168.70.1, timeout is 2 seconds:
!!!!!
Success rate is 100 percent (5/5), round-trip min/avg/max = 28/28/32 ms
Type escape sequence to abort.
Sending 5, 100-byte ICMP Echos to 172.16.12.1, timeout is 2 seconds:
!!!!!
Success rate is 100 percent (5/5), round-trip min/avg/max = 28/28/32 ms
Type escape sequence to abort.
Sending 5, 100-byte ICMP Echos to 172.16.2.1, timeout is 2 seconds:
!!!!!
Success rate is 100 percent (5/5), round-trip min/avg/max = 1/1/4 ms
```

```
Type escape sequence to abort.
Sending 5, 100-byte ICMP Echos to 172.16.12.2, timeout is 2 seconds:
!!!!!
Success rate is 100 percent (5/5), round-trip min/avg/max = 56/57/64 ms
Type escape sequence to abort.
Sending 5, 100-byte ICMP Echos to 172.16.23.2, timeout is 2 seconds:
!!!!!
Success rate is 100 percent (5/5), round-trip min/avg/max = 56/57/64 ms
Type escape sequence to abort.
Sending 5, 100-byte ICMP Echos to 172.16.3.1, timeout is 2 seconds:
!!!!!
Success rate is 100 percent (5/5), round-trip min/avg/max = 28/28/28 ms
Type escape sequence to abort.
Sending 5, 100-byte ICMP Echos to 192.168.20.1, timeout is 2 seconds:
!!!!!
Success rate is 100 percent (5/5), round-trip min/avg/max = 28/28/32 ms
Type escape sequence to abort.
Sending 5, 100-byte ICMP Echos to 192.168.25.1, timeout is 2 seconds:
!!!!!
Success rate is 100 percent (5/5), round-trip min/avg/max = 28/28/32 ms
Type escape sequence to abort.
Sending 5, 100-byte ICMP Echos to 192.168.30.1, timeout is 2 seconds:
!!!!!
Success rate is 100 percent (5/5), round-trip min/avg/max = 28/28/32 ms
Type escape sequence to abort.
Sending 5, 100-byte ICMP Echos to 192.168.35.1, timeout is 2 seconds:
!!!!!
Success rate is 100 percent (5/5), round-trip min/avg/max = 28/28/28 ms
Type escape sequence to abort.
Sending 5, 100-byte ICMP Echos to 192.168.40.1, timeout is 2 seconds:
!!!!!
Success rate is 100 percent (5/5), round-trip min/avg/max = 28/28/32 ms
Type escape sequence to abort.
Sending 5, 100-byte ICMP Echos to 172.16.23.3, timeout is 2 seconds:
!!!!!
Success rate is 100 percent (5/5), round-trip min/avg/max = 28/28/32 ms
R2(tcl)# tclquit
R3# tclsh
R3(tcl)# foreach address {
+>(tcl)# 172.16.1.1
+>(tcl)# 192.168.48.1
+>(tcl)# 192.168.49.1
+>(tcl)# 192.168.50.1
+>(tcl)# 192.168.51.1
```

```
+>(tcl)# 192.168.70.1
+>(tcl)# 172.16.12.1
+>(tcl)# 172.16.2.1
+>(tcl)# 172.16.12.2
+>(tcl)# 172.16.23.2
+>(tcl)# 172.16.3.1
+>(tcl)# 192.168.20.1
+>(tcl)# 192.168.25.1
+>(tcl)# 192.168.30.1
+>(tcl)# 192.168.35.1
+>(tcl)# 192.168.40.1
+>(tcl)# 172.16.23.3
+>(tcl)# } { ping $address }

Type escape sequence to abort.
Sending 5, 100-byte ICMP Echos to 172.16.1.1, timeout is 2 seconds:
!!!!!
Success rate is 100 percent (5/5), round-trip min/avg/max = 56/56/56 ms
Type escape sequence to abort.
Sending 5, 100-byte ICMP Echos to 192.168.48.1, timeout is 2 seconds:
!!!!!
Success rate is 100 percent (5/5), round-trip min/avg/max = 56/56/56 ms
Type escape sequence to abort.
Sending 5, 100-byte ICMP Echos to 192.168.49.1, timeout is 2 seconds:
!!!!!
Success rate is 100 percent (5/5), round-trip min/avg/max = 56/56/60 ms
Type escape sequence to abort.
Sending 5, 100-byte ICMP Echos to 192.168.50.1, timeout is 2 seconds:
!!!!!
Success rate is 100 percent (5/5), round-trip min/avg/max = 56/56/56 ms
Type escape sequence to abort.
Sending 5, 100-byte ICMP Echos to 192.168.51.1, timeout is 2 seconds:
!!!!!
Success rate is 100 percent (5/5), round-trip min/avg/max = 56/56/56 ms
Type escape sequence to abort.
Sending 5, 100-byte ICMP Echos to 192.168.70.1, timeout is 2 seconds:
!!!!!
Success rate is 100 percent (5/5), round-trip min/avg/max = 56/56/56 ms
Type escape sequence to abort.
Sending 5, 100-byte ICMP Echos to 172.16.12.1, timeout is 2 seconds:
!!!!!
Success rate is 100 percent (5/5), round-trip min/avg/max = 56/56/56 ms
Type escape sequence to abort.
Sending 5, 100-byte ICMP Echos to 172.16.2.1, timeout is 2 seconds:
```

```
!!!!!
Success rate is 100 percent (5/5), round-trip min/avg/max = 28/28/32 ms
Type escape sequence to abort.
Sending 5, 100-byte ICMP Echos to 172.16.12.2, timeout is 2 seconds:
!!!!!
Success rate is 100 percent (5/5), round-trip min/avg/max = 28/28/32 ms
Type escape sequence to abort.
Sending 5, 100-byte ICMP Echos to 172.16.23.2, timeout is 2 seconds:
!!!!!
Success rate is 100 percent (5/5), round-trip min/avg/max = 28/28/32 ms
Type escape sequence to abort.
Sending 5, 100-byte ICMP Echos to 172.16.3.1, timeout is 2 seconds:
!!!!!
Success rate is 100 percent (5/5), round-trip min/avg/max = 1/1/4 ms
Type escape sequence to abort.
Sending 5, 100-byte ICMP Echos to 192.168.20.1, timeout is 2 seconds:
!!!!!
Success rate is 100 percent (5/5), round-trip min/avg/max = 1/1/4 ms
Type escape sequence to abort.
Sending 5, 100-byte ICMP Echos to 192.168.25.1, timeout is 2 seconds:
!!!!!
Success rate is 100 percent (5/5), round-trip min/avg/max = 1/1/4 ms
Type escape sequence to abort.
Sending 5, 100-byte ICMP Echos to 192.168.30.1, timeout is 2 seconds:
!!!!!
Success rate is 100 percent (5/5), round-trip min/avg/max = 1/1/4 ms
Type escape sequence to abort.
Sending 5, 100-byte ICMP Echos to 192.168.35.1, timeout is 2 seconds:
!!!!!
Success rate is 100 percent (5/5), round-trip min/avg/max = 1/1/4 ms
Type escape sequence to abort.
Sending 5, 100-byte ICMP Echos to 192.168.40.1, timeout is 2 seconds:
!!!!!
Success rate is 100 percent (5/5), round-trip min/avg/max = 1/1/4 ms
Type escape sequence to abort.
Sending 5, 100-byte ICMP Echos to 172.16.23.3, timeout is 2 seconds:
!!!!!
Success rate is 100 percent (5/5), round-trip min/avg/max = 56/57/64 ms
R3(tcl)# tclquit
```

Lab 5-4: Manipulating Administrative Distances (5.6.4)

The objectives of this lab are as follows:

- Configure RIP on a router
- Configure OSPF on a router
- Manipulate administrative distances
- Compare routing protocol behaviors

Figure 5-4 illustrates the topology that will be used for this lab.

Figure 5-4   Topology Diagram

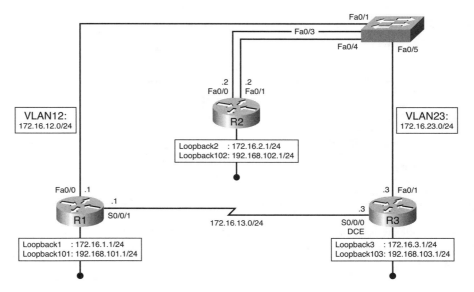

Scenario

In this lab, you will compare two routing protocols in how efficient they are at selecting routes, as well as what happens when you manipulate administrative distances in the routing table.

Pre-Lab: Review of Administrative Distances

Fill in Table 5-2 with all the administrative distances you can recall from your reading.

Table 5-2   Administrative Distances

Protocol	Administrative Distance
Connected	_____
Static	_____
EIGRP Summary Route	_____
External BGP	_____
EIGRP	_____
IGRP	_____
OSPF	_____
IS-IS	_____
RIP	_____
EGP	_____
External EIGRP	_____
Internal BGP	_____
Unknown	_____

Of the Interior Gateway Protocols (IGPs) you have studied, which one is considered most trusted on a Cisco router and why?

_____

_____

Step 1: Configure Addressing

Configure all loopback interfaces on the three routers in the diagram. Configure the serial interface with the IP addresses. Bring them up, and set a clockrate where appropriate. Additionally, set up routers R1 and R2 to be in one VLAN and routers R2 and R3 to be in a different VLAN:

```
R1# configure terminal
R1(config)# interface loopback 1
R1(config-if)# ip address 172.16.1.1 255.255.255.0
R1(config-if)# interface loopback 101
R1(config-if)# ip address 192.168.101.1 255.255.255.0
R1(config-if)# interface fastethernet 0/0
R1(config-if)# ip address 172.16.12.1 255.255.255.0
R1(config-if)# no shutdown
R1(config-if)# interface serial 0/0/1
```

```
R1(config-if)# bandwidth 64
R1(config-if)# ip address 172.16.13.1 255.255.255.0
R1(config-if)# no shutdown
R2# configure terminal
R2(config)# interface loopback 2
R2(config-if)# ip address 172.16.2.1 255.255.255.0
R2(config-if)# interface loopback 102
R2(config-if)# ip address 192.168.102.1 255.255.255.0
R2(config-if)# interface fastethernet 0/0
R2(config-if)# ip address 172.16.12.2 255.255.255.0
R2(config-if)# no shutdown
R2(config-if)# interface fastethernet 0/1
R2(config-if)# ip address 172.16.23.2 255.255.255.0
R2(config-if)# no shutdown
R3# configure terminal
R3(config)# interface loopback 3
R3(config-if)# ip address 172.16.3.1 255.255.255.0
R3(config-if)# interface loopback 103
R3(config-if)# ip address 192.168.103.1 255.255.255.0
R3(config-if)# interface fastethernet 0/1
R3(config-if)# ip address 172.16.23.3 255.255.255.0
R3(config-if)# no shutdown
R3(config-if)# interface serial 0/0/1
R3(config-if)# bandwidth 64
R3(config-if)# ip address 172.16.13.3 255.255.255.0
R3(config-if)# clock rate 64000
R3(config-if)# no shutdown
```

Be sure you can ping across the local subnets.

Step 2: Configure RIP

Configure RIPv2 on all three routers for the major networks. Disable automatic summarization:

```
R1(config)# router rip
R1(config-router)# version 2
R1(config-router)# no auto-summary
R1(config-router)# network 172.16.0.0
R1(config-router)# network 192.168.101.0
R2(config)# router rip
R2(config-router)# version 2
R2(config-router)# no auto-summary
R2(config-router)# network 172.16.0.0
R2(config-router)# network 192.168.102.0
R3(config)# router rip
R3(config-router)# version 2
```

```
R3(config-router)# no auto-summary
R3(config-router)# network 172.16.0.0
R3(config-router)# network 192.168.103.0
```

Verify the configuration using the **show ip route rip** command on each router:

```
R1# show ip route rip
     172.16.0.0/24 is subnetted, 6 subnets
R        172.16.23.0 [100/1] via 172.16.13.3, 00:02:29, Serial0/0/1
                     [100/1] via 172.16.12.2, 00:02:15, FastEthernet0/0
R        172.16.2.0 [100/1] via 172.16.12.2, 00:02:15, FastEthernet0/0
R        172.16.3.0 [100/1] via 172.16.13.3, 00:02:29, Serial0/0/1
R        192.168.102.0/24 [100/1] via 172.16.12.2, 00:02:15, FastEthernet0/0
R        192.168.103.0/24 [100/1] via 172.16.13.3, 00:02:29, Serial0/0/1
```

```
R2# show ip route rip
     172.16.0.0/24 is subnetted, 6 subnets
R        172.16.13.0 [100/1] via 172.16.23.3, 00:02:18, FastEthernet0/1
                     [100/1] via 172.16.12.1, 00:02:20, FastEthernet0/0
R        172.16.1.0 [100/1] via 172.16.12.1, 00:02:20, FastEthernet0/0
R        172.16.3.0 [100/1] via 172.16.23.3, 00:02:18, FastEthernet0/1
R        192.168.103.0/24 [100/1] via 172.16.23.3, 00:02:18, FastEthernet0/1
R        192.168.101.0/24 [100/1] via 172.16.12.1, 00:02:20, FastEthernet0/0
```

```
R3# show ip route rip
     172.16.0.0/24 is subnetted, 6 subnets
R        172.16.12.0 [100/1] via 172.16.23.2, 00:02:32, FastEthernet0/1
                     [100/1] via 172.16.13.1, 00:02:47, Serial0/0/0
R        172.16.1.0 [100/1] via 172.16.13.1, 00:02:47, Serial0/0/0
R        172.16.2.0 [100/1] via 172.16.23.2, 00:02:32, FastEthernet0/1
R        192.168.102.0/24 [100/1] via 172.16.23.2, 00:02:32, FastEthernet0/1
R        192.168.101.0/24 [100/1] via 172.16.13.1, 00:02:47, Serial0/0/0
```

Notice that on R1, RIP chooses the serial interface as the best next hop for R3's loopback interface. Verify that each router is receiving RIP routes from other routers using the **show ip protocols** command:

```
R1# show ip protocols
Routing Protocol is "rip"
  Outgoing update filter list for all interfaces is not set
  Incoming update filter list for all interfaces is not set
  Sending updates every 30 seconds, next due in 26 seconds
  Invalid after 180 seconds, hold down 180, flushed after 240
  Redistributing: rip
  Default version control: send version 2, receive version 2
    Interface           Send  Recv  Triggered RIP  Key-chain
    FastEthernet0/0       2     2
    Serial0/0/1          2     2
    Loopback1            2     2
```

```
     Loopback101              2      2
  Automatic network summarization is not in effect
  Maximum path: 4
  Routing for Networks:
     172.16.0.0
     192.168.101.0
  Routing Information Sources:
     Gateway          Distance      Last Update
     172.16.12.2         120        00:00:21
     172.16.13.3         120        00:00:03
  Distance: (default is 120)
```
R2# **show ip protocols**
```
Routing Protocol is "rip"
  Outgoing update filter list for all interfaces is not set
  Incoming update filter list for all interfaces is not set
  Sending updates every 30 seconds, next due in 23 seconds
  Invalid after 180 seconds, hold down 180, flushed after 240
  Redistributing: rip
  Default version control: send version 2, receive version 2
     Interface           Send  Recv  Triggered RIP  Key-chain
     FastEthernet0/0       2     2
     FastEthernet0/1       2     2
     Loopback2             2     2
     Loopback102           2     2
  Automatic network summarization is not in effect
  Maximum path: 4
  Routing for Networks:
     172.16.0.0
     192.168.102.0
  Routing Information Sources:
     Gateway          Distance      Last Update
     172.16.23.3         120        00:00:02
     172.16.12.1         120        00:00:24
  Distance: (default is 120)
```
R3# **show ip protocols**
```
Routing Protocol is "rip"
  Outgoing update filter list for all interfaces is not set
  Incoming update filter list for all interfaces is not set
  Sending updates every 30 seconds, next due in 22 seconds
  Invalid after 180 seconds, hold down 180, flushed after 240
  Redistributing: rip
  Default version control: send version 2, receive version 2
     Interface           Send  Recv  Triggered RIP  Key-chain
     FastEthernet0/1       2     2
```

```
    Serial0/0/0              2      2
    Loopback3               2      2
    Loopback103             2      2
Automatic network summarization is not in effect
Maximum path: 4
Routing for Networks:
   172.16.0.0
   192.168.103.0
Routing Information Sources:
   Gateway          Distance      Last Update
   172.16.23.2         120        00:00:06
   172.16.13.1         120        00:00:17
Distance: (default is 120)
```

Step 3: Configure OSPF

Configure OSPF on all the routers as well. Include the entire major network in area 0 on all three routers. Remember to change the network types on the loopback interfaces:

```
R1(config)# interface loopback 1
R1(config-if)# ip ospf network point-to-point
R1(config-if)# interface loopback 101
R1(config-if)# ip ospf network point-to-point
R1(config-if)# router ospf 1
R1(config-router)# network 172.16.0.0 0.0.255.255 area 0
R1(config-router)# network 192.168.101.0 0.0.0.255 area 0
```
```
R2(config)# interface loopback 2
R2(config-if)# ip ospf network point-to-point
R2(config-if)# interface loopback 102
R1(config-if)# ip ospf network point-to-point
R2(config-if)# router ospf 1
R2(config-router)# network 172.16.0.0 0.0.255.255 area 0
R2(config-router)# network 192.168.102.0 0.0.0.255 area 0
```
```
R3(config)# interface loopback 3
R3(config-if)# ip ospf network point-to-point
R3(config-if)# interface loopback 103
R3(config-if)# ip ospf network point-to-point
R3(config-if)# router ospf 1
R3(config-router)# network 172.16.0.0 0.0.255.255 area 0
R3(config-router)# network 192.168.103.0 0.0.0.255 area 0
```

Verify the configuration using the **show ip ospf neighbor** and **show ip route** commands on each router:

```
R1# show ip ospf neighbor
```

```
Neighbor ID      Pri   State      Dead Time   Address      Interface
192.168.103.1    0     FULL/  -   00:00:39    172.16.13.3  Serial0/0/1
192.168.102.1    1     FULL/DR    00:00:39    172.16.12.2  FastEthernet0/0

R1# show ip route
<output omitted>

Gateway of last resort is not set

      172.16.0.0/24 is subnetted, 6 subnets
O        172.16.23.0 [110/2] via 172.16.12.2, 00:00:48, FastEthernet0/0
C        172.16.12.0 is directly connected, FastEthernet0/0
C        172.16.13.0 is directly connected, Serial0/0/1
C        172.16.1.0 is directly connected, Loopback1
O        172.16.2.0 [110/2] via 172.16.12.2, 00:00:48, FastEthernet0/0
O        172.16.3.0 [110/3] via 172.16.12.2, 00:00:48, FastEthernet0/0
O     192.168.102.0/24 [110/2] via 172.16.12.2, 00:00:48, FastEthernet0/0
O     192.168.103.0/24 [110/3] via 172.16.12.2, 00:00:49, FastEthernet0/0
C     192.168.101.0/24 is directly connected, Loopback101
R2# show ip ospf neighbor

Neighbor ID      Pri   State      Dead Time   Address      Interface
192.168.103.1    1     FULL/DR    00:00:31    172.16.23.3  FastEthernet0/1
192.168.101.1    1     FULL/BDR   00:00:34    172.16.12.1  FastEthernet0/0

R2# show ip route
<output omitted>

Gateway of last resort is not set

      172.16.0.0/24 is subnetted, 6 subnets
C        172.16.23.0 is directly connected, FastEthernet0/1
C        172.16.12.0 is directly connected, FastEthernet0/0
O        172.16.13.0 [110/1563] via 172.16.23.3, 00:01:19, FastEthernet0/1
                     [110/1563] via 172.16.12.1, 00:01:19, FastEthernet0/0
O        172.16.1.0 [110/2] via 172.16.12.1, 00:01:19, FastEthernet0/0
C        172.16.2.0 is directly connected, Loopback2
O        172.16.3.0 [110/2] via 172.16.23.3, 00:01:19, FastEthernet0/1
C     192.168.102.0/24 is directly connected, Loopback102
O     192.168.103.0/24 [110/2] via 172.16.23.3, 00:01:20, FastEthernet0/1
O     192.168.101.0/24 [110/2] via 172.16.12.1, 00:01:20, FastEthernet0/0
R3# show ip ospf neighbor
```

```
Neighbor ID       Pri   State       Dead Time   Address        Interface
192.168.101.1      0    FULL/  -    00:00:36    172.16.13.1    Serial0/0/0
192.168.102.1      1    FULL/BDR    00:00:33    172.16.23.2    FastEthernet0/1
```

R3# **show ip route**

```
Gateway of last resort is not set

     172.16.0.0/24 is subnetted, 6 subnets
C        172.16.23.0 is directly connected, FastEthernet0/1
O        172.16.12.0 [110/2] via 172.16.23.2, 00:02:10, FastEthernet0/1
C        172.16.13.0 is directly connected, Serial0/0/0
O        172.16.1.0 [110/3] via 172.16.23.2, 00:02:10, FastEthernet0/1
O        172.16.2.0 [110/2] via 172.16.23.2, 00:02:10, FastEthernet0/1
C        172.16.3.0 is directly connected, Loopback3
O     192.168.102.0/24 [110/2] via 172.16.23.2, 00:02:10, FastEthernet0/1
C     192.168.103.0/24 is directly connected, Loopback103
O     192.168.101.0/24 [110/3] via 172.16.23.2, 00:02:11, FastEthernet0/1
```

Notice that all the OSPF routes have replaced the RIP routes in the routing table. This is because OSPF has an administrative distance of 110, and RIP has an administrative distance of 120.

What is the best next hop on R1 for 172.16.3.1 with only RIP running?

_____

_____

What is the best next hop on R1 for 172.16.3.1 with OSPF running?

_____

_____

On R1, the best next hop for R3's loopback is now through the VLAN between R1 and R2. This is because the sum of the costs for the two Ethernet links is still less than that of the single serial link. This is one of the reasons why RIP's metric of a hop count is not very effective.

Which metric does R1 use to make routing decisions about crossing the serial link to R3 to reach R3's 172.16.3.1? Use the following information for your answer:

R1# **show ip ospf database router adv-router 192.168.103.1**

```
        OSPF Router with ID (192.168.101.1) (Process ID 1)


        Router Link States (Area 0)


  LS age: 433
  Options: (No TOS-capability, DC)
```

```
LS Type: Router Links
Link State ID: 192.168.103.1
Advertising Router: 192.168.103.1
LS Seq Number: 80000003
Checksum: 0xE87F
Length: 84
Number of Links: 5

  Link connected to: a Stub Network
   (Link ID) Network/subnet number: 192.168.103.0
   (Link Data) Network Mask: 255.255.255.0
    Number of TOS metrics: 0
      TOS 0 Metrics: 1

   Link connected to: a Stub Network
    (Link ID) Network/subnet number: 172.16.3.0
    (Link Data) Network Mask: 255.255.255.0
    Number of TOS metrics: 0
      TOS 0 Metrics: 1

  Link connected to: another Router (point-to-point)
   (Link ID) Neighboring Router ID: 192.168.101.1
   (Link Data) Router Interface address: 172.16.13.3
    Number of TOS metrics: 0
      TOS 0 Metrics: 1562

   Link connected to: a Stub Network
    (Link ID) Network/subnet number: 172.16.13.0
    (Link Data) Network Mask: 255.255.255.0
    Number of TOS metrics: 0
      TOS 0 Metrics: 1562

  Link connected to: a Transit Network
   (Link ID) Designated Router address: 172.16.23.3
   (Link Data) Router Interface address: 172.16.23.3
    Number of TOS metrics: 0
      TOS 0 Metrics: 1
```

Step 4: Modify a Routing Protocol's Distance

The **distance** command is a protocol-independent way to manipulate routing protocol distances. This command is different from the routing protocol-specific commands such as **distance ospf** and **distance eigrp**. This command lets you completely change a routing protocol's distances, or change only routes from a certain neighbor or those matching an access list, or a combination of any two of these three options.

Try applying the **distance** *distance* command, which changes the distance of every route. In the previous output of the **show ip route** command, you may have noticed that OSPF marks routes it injects into the routing table with a default administrative distance of 110. RIP injects routes into the routing table with a default administrative distance of 120.

What do you think would happen if the administrative distance on each router for RIP were set to 100?

_____

On all three routers, change the distance of RIP to 100. Then look at the output of the **show ip route** command:

```
R1(config)# router rip
R1(config-router)# distance 100
```

```
R2(config)# router rip
R2(config-router)# distance 100
```

```
R3(config)# router rip
R3(config-router)# distance 100
```

```
R1# show ip route
<output omitted>


Gateway of last resort is not set


     172.16.0.0/24 is subnetted, 6 subnets
R       172.16.23.0 [100/1] via 172.16.13.3, 00:00:17, Serial0/0/1
                    [100/1] via 172.16.12.2, 00:00:09, FastEthernet0/0
C       172.16.12.0 is directly connected, FastEthernet0/0
C       172.16.13.0 is directly connected, Serial0/0/1
C       172.16.1.0 is directly connected, Loopback1
R       172.16.2.0 [100/1] via 172.16.12.2, 00:00:09, FastEthernet0/0
R       172.16.3.0 [100/1] via 172.16.13.3, 00:00:17, Serial0/0/1
R     192.168.102.0/24 [100/1] via 172.16.12.2, 00:00:10, FastEthernet0/0
R     192.168.103.0/24 [100/1] via 172.16.13.3, 00:00:18, Serial0/0/1
C     192.168.101.0/24 is directly connected, Loopback101
```

```
R2# show ip route
<output omitted>
```

```
Gateway of last resort is not set


     172.16.0.0/24 is subnetted, 6 subnets
C       172.16.23.0 is directly connected, FastEthernet0/1
C       172.16.12.0 is directly connected, FastEthernet0/0
R       172.16.13.0 [100/1] via 172.16.23.3, 00:00:07, FastEthernet0/1
                     [100/1] via 172.16.12.1, 00:00:07, FastEthernet0/0
R       172.16.1.0 [100/1] via 172.16.12.1, 00:00:07, FastEthernet0/0
C       172.16.2.0 is directly connected, Loopback2
R       172.16.3.0 [100/1] via 172.16.23.3, 00:00:07, FastEthernet0/1
C     192.168.102.0/24 is directly connected, Loopback102
R     192.168.103.0/24 [100/1] via 172.16.23.3, 00:00:08, FastEthernet0/1
R     192.168.101.0/24 [100/1] via 172.16.12.1, 00:00:08, FastEthernet0/0
```

R3# **show ip route**

```
<output omitted>


Gateway of last resort is not set


     172.16.0.0/24 is subnetted, 6 subnets
C       172.16.23.0 is directly connected, FastEthernet0/1
R       172.16.12.0 [100/1] via 172.16.23.2, 00:00:07, FastEthernet0/1
                     [100/1] via 172.16.13.1, 00:00:02, Serial0/0/0
C       172.16.13.0 is directly connected, Serial0/0/0
R       172.16.1.0 [100/1] via 172.16.13.1, 00:00:02, Serial0/0/0
R       172.16.2.0 [100/1] via 172.16.23.2, 00:00:07, FastEthernet0/1
C       172.16.3.0 is directly connected, Loopback3
R     192.168.102.0/24 [100/1] via 172.16.23.2, 00:00:08, FastEthernet0/1
C     192.168.103.0/24 is directly connected, Loopback103
R     192.168.101.0/24 [100/1] via 172.16.13.1, 00:00:03, Serial0/0/0
```

Notice that *all* the routes have become RIP routes because RIP now has a lower distance than OSPF. You can display the new default distance for RIP using the **show ip protocols** command:

R1# **show ip protocols**

```
Routing Protocol is "rip"
  Outgoing update filter list for all interfaces is not set
  Incoming update filter list for all interfaces is not set
  Sending updates every 30 seconds, next due in 11 seconds
  Invalid after 180 seconds, hold down 180, flushed after 240
  Redistributing: rip
  Default version control: send version 2, receive version 2
     Interface        Send  Recv  Triggered RIP  Key-chain
     FastEthernet0/0    2     2
     Serial0/0/1        2     2
     Loopback1          2     2
```

```
     Loopback101           2      2
  Automatic network summarization is not in effect
  Maximum path: 4
  Routing for Networks:
     172.16.0.0
     192.168.101.0
  Routing Information Sources:
     Gateway           Distance       Last Update
     172.16.13.3          100         00:00:14
     172.16.12.2          100         00:00:22
  Distance: (default is 100)
<output omitted>
```

Step 5: Modify Distance Based on Route Source

You can also modify administrative distance based on route source using the **distance** *distance address wildcard* command, where *address* and *wildcard* represent the peer advertising the route. For OSPF, the address is the router ID.

On all three routers, change the OSPF administrative distance to 85 for any routes being advertised from routers with IDs in the range of 192.168.100.0/21. Verify the change with the **show ip protocols** and **show ip route** commands:

```
R1(config)# router ospf 1
R1(config-router)# distance 85 192.168.100.0 0.0.3.255
```
```
R2(config)# router ospf 1
R2(config-router)# distance 85 192.168.100.0 0.0.3.255
```
```
R3(config)# router ospf 1
R3(config-router)# distance 85 192.168.100.0 0.0.3.255
```
```
R1# show ip route
<output omitted>

Gateway of last resort is not set

     172.16.0.0/24 is subnetted, 6 subnets
O       172.16.23.0 [85/2] via 172.16.12.2, 00:00:31, FastEthernet0/0
C       172.16.12.0 is directly connected, FastEthernet0/0
C       172.16.13.0 is directly connected, Serial0/0/1
C       172.16.1.0 is directly connected, Loopback1
O       172.16.2.0 [85/2] via 172.16.12.2, 00:00:31, FastEthernet0/0
O       172.16.3.0 [85/3] via 172.16.12.2, 00:00:31, FastEthernet0/0
O     192.168.102.0/24 [85/2] via 172.16.12.2, 00:00:31, FastEthernet0/0
O     192.168.103.0/24 [85/3] via 172.16.12.2, 00:00:32, FastEthernet0/0
C     192.168.101.0/24 is directly connected, Loopback101
R2# show ip route
```

```
<output omitted>

Gateway of last resort is not set

     172.16.0.0/24 is subnetted, 6 subnets
C        172.16.23.0 is directly connected, FastEthernet0/1
C        172.16.12.0 is directly connected, FastEthernet0/0
O        172.16.13.0 [85/1563] via 172.16.23.3, 00:00:53, FastEthernet0/1
                     [85/1563] via 172.16.12.1, 00:00:53, FastEthernet0/0
O        172.16.1.0 [85/2] via 172.16.12.1, 00:00:53, FastEthernet0/0
C        172.16.2.0 is directly connected, Loopback2
O        172.16.3.0 [85/2] via 172.16.23.3, 00:00:53, FastEthernet0/1
C    192.168.102.0/24 is directly connected, Loopback102
O    192.168.103.0/24 [85/2] via 172.16.23.3, 00:00:54, FastEthernet0/1
O    192.168.101.0/24 [85/2] via 172.16.12.1, 00:00:54, FastEthernet0/0
```

```
R3# show ip route
<output omitted>

Gateway of last resort is not set

     172.16.0.0/24 is subnetted, 6 subnets
C        172.16.23.0 is directly connected, FastEthernet0/1
O        172.16.12.0 [85/2] via 172.16.23.2, 00:01:15, FastEthernet0/1
C        172.16.13.0 is directly connected, Serial0/0/0
O        172.16.1.0 [85/3] via 172.16.23.2, 00:01:15, FastEthernet0/1
O        172.16.2.0 [85/2] via 172.16.23.2, 00:01:15, FastEthernet0/1
C        172.16.3.0 is directly connected, Loopback3
O    192.168.102.0/24 [85/2] via 172.16.23.2, 00:01:15, FastEthernet0/1
C    192.168.103.0/24 is directly connected, Loopback103
O    192.168.101.0/24 [85/3] via 172.16.23.2, 00:01:16, FastEthernet0/1
```

```
R1# show ip protocols
Routing Protocol is "ospf 1"
  Outgoing update filter list for all interfaces is not set
  Incoming update filter list for all interfaces is not set
  Router ID 192.168.101.1
  Number of areas in this router is 1. 1 normal 0 stub 0 nssa
  Maximum path: 4
  Routing for Networks:
    172.16.0.0 0.0.255.255 area 0
    192.168.101.0 0.0.0.255 area 0
 Reference bandwidth unit is 100 mbps
```

```
Routing Information Sources:
    Gateway          Distance        Last Update
    192.168.103.1        85          00:05:47
    192.168.102.1        85          00:05:47
Distance: (default is 110)
    Address          Wild mask      Distance  List
    192.168.100.0        0.0.3.255       85
```

Routers R2 and R3 should have an entry similar to the one highlighted for R1.

Step 6: Modify Distance Based on an Access List

You can also modify administrative distance based on which routes match an access list using the **distance** *distance address wildcard acl* command. The way routes are listed in an access list is similar to how they are listed when filtering based on a route. For this lab, make an access list containing all the subnets of 172.16.0.0/16. Set the address and wildcard to be any IP or any route source. On all three routers, change the distances of the affected routes to 65. Verify the change with the **show ip protocols** and **show ip route** commands.

```
R1(config)# access-list 1 permit 172.16.0.0 0.0.255.255
R1(config)# router rip
R1(config-router)# distance 65 0.0.0.0 255.255.255.255 1
```
```
R2(config)# access-list 1 permit 172.16.0.0 0.0.255.255
R2(config)# router rip
R2(config-router)# distance 65 0.0.0.0 255.255.255.255 1
```
```
R3(config)# access-list 1 permit 172.16.0.0 0.0.255.255
R3(config)# router rip
R3(config-router)# distance 65 0.0.0.0 255.255.255.255 1
```
```
R1# show ip protocols
Routing Protocol is "rip"
  Outgoing update filter list for all interfaces is not set
  Incoming update filter list for all interfaces is not set
  Sending updates every 30 seconds, next due in 22 seconds
  Invalid after 180 seconds, hold down 180, flushed after 240
  Redistributing: rip
  Default version control: send version 2, receive version 2
    Interface           Send  Recv  Triggered RIP  Key-chain
    FastEthernet0/0       2     2
    Serial0/0/1          2     2
    Loopback1            2     2
    Loopback101          2     2
  Automatic network summarization is not in effect
  Maximum path: 4
  Routing for Networks:
    172.16.0.0
    192.168.101.0
```

```
Routing Information Sources:
    Gateway          Distance       Last Update
    172.16.12.2          64         00:00:11
    172.16.13.3          64         00:00:12
Distance: (default is 100)
    Address          Wild mask          Distance  List
    0.0.0.0          255.255.255.255          65  1
<remaining output omitted>
```

R1# **show ip route**

```
<output omitted>


Gateway of last resort is not set


     172.16.0.0/24 is subnetted, 6 subnets
R       172.16.23.0 [64/1] via 172.16.13.3, 00:00:20, Serial0/0/1
                    [64/1] via 172.16.12.2, 00:00:19, FastEthernet0/0
C       172.16.12.0 is directly connected, FastEthernet0/0
C       172.16.13.0 is directly connected, Serial0/0/1
C       172.16.1.0 is directly connected, Loopback1
R       172.16.2.0 [64/1] via 172.16.12.2, 00:00:19, FastEthernet0/0
R       172.16.3.0 [64/1] via 172.16.13.3, 00:00:20, Serial0/0/1
O     192.168.102.0/24 [85/2] via 172.16.12.2, 00:09:09, FastEthernet0/0
O     192.168.103.0/24 [85/3] via 172.16.12.2, 00:09:09, FastEthernet0/0
C     192.168.101.0/24 is directly connected, Loopback101
```

R2# **show ip protocols**

```
Routing Protocol is "rip"
  Outgoing update filter list for all interfaces is not set
  Incoming update filter list for all interfaces is not set
  Sending updates every 30 seconds, next due in 27 seconds
  Invalid after 180 seconds, hold down 180, flushed after 240
  Redistributing: rip
  Default version control: send version 2, receive version 2
    Interface           Send  Recv  Triggered RIP  Key-chain
    FastEthernet0/0      2     2
    FastEthernet0/1      2     2
    Loopback2            2     2
    Loopback102          2     2
  Automatic network summarization is not in effect
  Maximum path: 4
  Routing for Networks:
    172.16.0.0
    192.168.102.0
```

```
Routing Information Sources:
    Gateway         Distance        Last Update
    172.16.23.3          65         00:00:06
    172.16.12.1          65         00:00:22
Distance: (default is 100)
    Address          Wild mask           Distance  List
    0.0.0.0          255.255.255.255           65  1
<remaining output omitted>


R2# show ip route
Codes: C - connected, S - static, R - RIP, M - mobile, B - BGP
       D - EIGRP, EX - EIGRP external, O - OSPF, IA - OSPF inter area
       N1 - OSPF NSSA external type 1, N2 - OSPF NSSA external type 2
       E1 - OSPF external type 1, E2 - OSPF external type 2
       i - IS-IS, su - IS-IS summary, L1 - IS-IS level-1, L2 - IS-IS level-2
       ia - IS-IS inter area, * - candidate default, U - per-user static route
       o - ODR, P - periodic downloaded static route


Gateway of last resort is not set


     172.16.0.0/24 is subnetted, 6 subnets
C       172.16.23.0 is directly connected, FastEthernet0/1
C       172.16.12.0 is directly connected, FastEthernet0/0
R       172.16.13.0 [65/1] via 172.16.23.3, 00:00:10, FastEthernet0/1
                    [65/1] via 172.16.12.1, 00:00:00, FastEthernet0/0
R       172.16.1.0 [65/1] via 172.16.12.1, 00:00:00, FastEthernet0/0
C       172.16.2.0 is directly connected, Loopback2
R       172.16.3.0 [65/1] via 172.16.23.3, 00:00:10, FastEthernet0/1
C     192.168.102.0/24 is directly connected, Loopback102
O     192.168.103.0/24 [85/2] via 172.16.23.3, 00:09:35, FastEthernet0/1
O     192.168.101.0/24 [85/2] via 172.16.12.1, 00:09:35, FastEthernet0/0

R3# show ip protocols
Routing Protocol is "rip"
  Outgoing update filter list for all interfaces is not set
  Incoming update filter list for all interfaces is not set
  Sending updates every 30 seconds, next due in 15 seconds
  Invalid after 180 seconds, hold down 180, flushed after 240
  Redistributing: rip
  Default version control: send version 2, receive version 2
    Interface            Send  Recv  Triggered RIP  Key-chain
    FastEthernet0/1        2     2
    Serial0/0/0           2     2
    Loopback3             2     2
    Loopback103           2     2
```

```
Automatic network summarization is not in effect
Maximum path: 4
Routing for Networks:
   172.16.0.0
   192.168.103.0
Routing Information Sources:
   Gateway          Distance        Last Update
   172.16.23.2           65         00:00:24
   172.16.13.1           65         00:00:16
Distance: (default is 100)
      Address            Wild mask          Distance  List
      0.0.0.0            255.255.255.255          65  1
<remaining output omitted>
```

```
R3# show ip route
<output omitted>

Gateway of last resort is not set

      172.16.0.0/24 is subnetted, 6 subnets
C        172.16.23.0 is directly connected, FastEthernet0/1
R        172.16.12.0 [65/1] via 172.16.23.2, 00:00:00, FastEthernet0/1
                     [65/1] via 172.16.13.1, 00:00:19, Serial0/0/0
C        172.16.13.0 is directly connected, Serial0/0/0
R        172.16.1.0 [65/1] via 172.16.13.1, 00:00:19, Serial0/0/0
R        172.16.2.0 [65/1] via 172.16.23.2, 00:00:00, FastEthernet0/1
C        172.16.3.0 is directly connected, Loopback3
O     192.168.102.0/24 [85/2] via 172.16.23.2, 00:09:43, FastEthernet0/1
C     192.168.103.0/24 is directly connected, Loopback103
O     192.168.101.0/24 [85/3] via 172.16.23.2, 00:09:43, FastEthernet0/1
```

Challenge

Attempt this exercise based on what you know about OSPF, Dijkstra's algorithm, and the **distance** command. Using only the **distance** command, write out the commands necessary to confuse the routers in this topology so that packets destined for 172.16.3.1 would continually bounce between R1 to R2?

_____

_____

Because it is possible to intentionally break routing in this way, what degree of caution should be exercised when manipulating administrative distances in a production network?

_____

Lab 5-5: Configuring the Cisco IOS DHCP Server (5.6.5)

The objectives of this lab are as follows:

- Configure and verify the operation of the Cisco IOS DHCP server

- Configure an IP Helper address

- Review the EIGRP configuration

Figure 5-5 illustrates the topology that will be used for this lab.

Figure 5-5   Topology Diagram

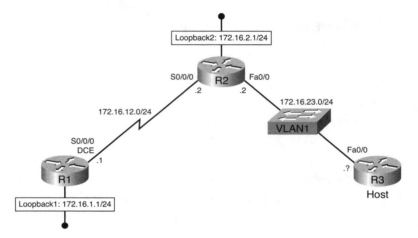

Scenario

In this lab, R3 will not be assigned an IP address. Instead, it gets one from Dynamic Host Configuration Protocol (DHCP). R1 will demonstrate the use of the **ip helper-address** command.

Step 1: Assign IP Addresses

Configure the serial link between R1 and R2 with the addresses shown in the diagram. Configure R2's Fast Ethernet address, but leave R3's Fast Ethernet interface shutdown without an IP address. Also configure the loopback interfaces with the IP addresses in Figure 5-5.

```
R1# configure terminal
R1(config)# interface loopback 1
R1(config-if)# ip address 172.16.1.1 255.255.255.0
R1(config-if)# interface serial 0/0/0
R1(config-if)# bandwidth 64
R1(config-if)# ip address 172.16.12.1 255.255.255.0
R1(config-if)# clock rate 64000
R1(config-if)# no shutdown
```

```
R1(config-if)# exit
R2# configure terminal
R2(config)# interface loopback 2
R2(config-if)# ip address 172.16.2.1 255.255.255.0
R2(config-if)# interface fastethernet 0/0
R2(config-if)# ip address 172.16.23.2 255.255.255.0
R2(config-if)# no shutdown
R2(config-if)# interface serial 0/0/0
R2(config-if)# bandwidth 64
R2(config-if)# ip address 172.16.12.2 255.255.255.0
R2(config-if)# clock rate 64000
R2(config-if)# no shutdown
```

Verify local subnet connectivity across the serial link with **ping**.

Step 2: Configure EIGRP

Configure R1 and R2 to run EIGRP in autonomous system 1. Disable automatic summarization and include the entire major network in EIGRP. Verify the configuration with the **show ip eigrp neighbors** and **show ip route** commands:

```
R1(config)# router eigrp 1
R1(config-router)# network 172.16.0.0
R1(config-router)# no auto-summary
R1(config-router)# exit
R2(config)# router eigrp 1
R2(config-router)# network 172.16.0.0
R2(config-router)# no auto-summary
R2(config-router)# exit
R1# show ip eigrp neighbors
IP-EIGRP neighbors for process 1
H   Address              Interface       Hold Uptime   SRTT   RTO  Q   Seq
                                         (sec)         (ms)        Cnt Num
0   172.16.12.2          Se0/0/0           12 00:03:18 1600   5000 0   3


R1# show ip route eigrp
     172.16.0.0/24 is subnetted, 4 subnets
D       172.16.23.0 [90/40514560] via 172.16.12.2, 00:03:18, Serial0/0/0
D       172.16.2.0 [90/40640000] via 172.16.12.2, 00:03:18, Serial0/0/0
R2# show ip eigrp neighbors
IP-EIGRP neighbors for process 1
H   Address              Interface       Hold Uptime   SRTT   RTO  Q   Seq
                                         (sec)         (ms)        Cnt Num
0   172.16.12.1          Se0/0/0           10 00:04:22   20   2280 0   2
```

```
R2# show ip route eigrp
     172.16.0.0/24 is subnetted, 4 subnets
D        172.16.1.0 [90/40640000] via 172.16.12.1, 00:04:21, Serial0/0/0
```

Step 3: Configure a DHCP Pool

On R2, configure a DHCP pool for the subnet connecting R2 and R3. A DHCP pool is a pool of addresses that the router gives out for DHCP requests. The Cisco IOS DHCP server is running by default. Therefore, to enable the router to act as a DHCP server, you simply create DHCP address pools. You can also tell the router an address or range of addresses that will not be given out in DHCP offers. Before you configure DHCP, add the following configuration line in global configuration mode on R2:

```
R2(config)# ip dhcp excluded-address 172.16.23.1 172.16.23.100
```

Now you can create the pool using the **ip dhcp pool** *name* command. This command creates a configuration submenu. Once in this menu, you can enter various attributes about which information the router gives out. Set the network of IP addresses to be leased with the **network** *address mask* command. This command also implicitly configures which interface issues and receives DHCP server packets because the interface must be directly connected to the subnet to be leased. Set the default gateway of hosts that will be receiving DHCP information with the **default-router** *address* command. There are other DHCP options you can set as well, such as the lifetime of the DHCP lease in days with **lease** *days* [*hours* [*minutes*]], and the domain name with **domain-name** *name*. For more DHCP options, consult the Cisco IOS documentation or use the inline help system.

Configure the network to be the subnet connecting R2 and R3. The default gateway is R2's IP address on that subnet, the domain name is Cisco.com, and the lease time is 1 day, 5 hours, and 36 minutes:

```
R2(config)# ip dhcp pool VLAN1-POOL
R2(dhcp-config)# network 172.16.23.0 255.255.255.0
R2(dhcp-config)# default-router 172.16.23.2
R2(dhcp-config)# domain-name Cisco.com
R2(dhcp-config)# lease 1 5 36
```

Before you bring the interface to active state, issue the following debugging commands on R2 and R3, respectively:

```
R2# debug ip dhcp server events
R2# debug ip dhcp server packets
R3# debug ip packet detail
```

Make R3 a host by disabling IP routing because IP routing is on by default. Use the global configuration command **no ip routing**. Because you have configured the DHCP service on R2, configure R3 as a DHCP client and bring the interface state to active.

Instruct R3 to request a DHCP lease with the **ip address dhcp** command entered in interface configuration mode. Finally, bring up the interface with the **no shutdown** command. The interface gets an IP address from DHCP after a few seconds. You receive a message on the console line referring to this event.

```
R3# configure terminal
R3(config)# no ip routing
R3(config)# interface fastethernet 0/0
```

```
R3(config-if)# ip address dhcp
R3(config-if)# no shutdown
```

At this point, DHCP debug messages similar to the output shown below flood the console output of R2 and R3. Examine both the debug output and Figure 5-6. Do the debug messages correlate with the DHCP communication diagram in Figure 5-6? If not, in what way do they differ?

Figure 5-6   DHCP Communication Diagram

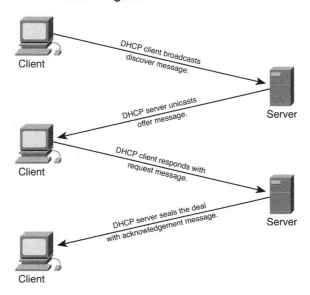

```
R2#
*Oct 24 16:44:19.015: DHCPD: Sending notification of DISCOVER:
*Oct 24 16:44:19.015:    DHCPD: htype 1 chaddr 0018.b9cd.bef0
*Oct 24 16:44:19.015:    DHCPD: remote id 020a0000ac10170200000000
*Oct 24 16:44:19.015:    DHCPD: circuit id 00000000
*Oct 24 16:44:19.015: DHCPD: DHCPDISCOVER received from client
   0063.6973.636f.2d30.3031.382e.6239.6364.2e62.6566.302d.4661.302f.30 on interface
   FastEthernet0/0.
*Oct 24 16:44:19.015: DHCPD: Seeing if there is an internally specified pool class:
*Oct 24 16:44:19.015:    DHCPD: htype 1 chaddr 0018.b9cd.bef0
*Oct 24 16:44:19.015:    DHCPD: remote id 020a0000ac10170200000000
*Oct 24 16:44:19.015:    DHCPD: circuit id 00000000
*Oct 24 16:44:19.015: DHCPD: Allocate an address without class information
   (172.16.23.0)
*Oct 24 16:44:21.015: DHCPD: Adding binding to radix tree (172.16.23.101)
*Oct 24 16:44:21.015: DHCPD: Adding binding to hash tree
*Oct 24 16:44:21.015: DHCPD: assigned IP address 172.16.23.101 to client
   0063.6973.636f.2d30.3031.382e.6239.6364.2e62.6566.302d.4661.302f.30.
*Oct 24 16:44:21.015: DHCPD: Sending DHCPOFFER to client
   0063.6973.636f.2d30.3031.382e.6239.6364.2e62.6566.302d.4661.302f.30 (172.16.23.101).
*Oct 24 16:44:21.015: DHCPD: broadcasting BOOTREPLY to client 0018.b9cd.bef0.
```

```
*Oct 24 16:44:21.019: DHCPD: DHCPREQUEST received from client
0063.6973.636f.2d30.3031.382e.6239.6364.2e62.6566.302d.4661.302f.30.

*Oct 24 16:44:21.019: DHCPD: Sending notification of ASSIGNMENT:

*Oct 24 16:44:21.019:  DHCPD: address 172.16.23.101 mask 255.255.255.0

*Oct 24 16:44:21.019:   DHCPD: htype 1 chaddr 0018.b9cd.bef0

*Oct 24 16:44:21.019:   DHCPD: lease time remaining (secs) = 106560

*Oct 24 16:44:21.019: DHCPD: Appending default domain from pool

*Oct 24 16:44:21.019: DHCPD: Using hostname 'R3.Cisco.com.' for dynamic update (from
  hostname option)

*Oct 24 16:44:21.019: DHCPD: Sending DHCPACK to client
0063.6973.636f.2d30.3031.382e.6239.6364.2e62.6566.302d.4661.302f.30 (172.16.23.101).

*Oct 24 16:44:21.019: DHCPD: broadcasting BOOTREPLY to client 0018.b9cd.bef0.
```
```
R3#

*Oct 24 16:45:19.627: %SYS-5-CONFIG_I: Configured from console by console

*Oct 24 16:45:21.263: %LINK-3-UPDOWN: Interface FastEthernet0/0, changed state to up

*Oct 24 16:45:22.263: %LINEPROTO-5-UPDOWN: Line protocol on Interface
FastEthernet0/0, changed state to up

*Oct 24 16:45:29.267: IP: s=0.0.0.0 (local), d=255.255.255.255 (FastEthernet0/0), len
  604, sending broad/multicast

*Oct 24 16:45:29.267:     UDP src=68, dst=67

*Oct 24 16:45:31.267: IP: s=172.16.23.2 (FastEthernet0/0), d=255.255.255.255, len
  328, rcvd 2

*Oct 24 16:45:31.267:     UDP src=67, dst=68

*Oct 24 16:45:31.267: IP: s=0.0.0.0 (local), d=255.255.255.255 (FastEthernet0/0), len
  604, sending broad/multicast

*Oct 24 16:45:31.267:     UDP src=68, dst=67

*Oct 24 16:45:31.271: IP: s=172.16.23.2 (FastEthernet0/0), d=255.255.255.255, len
  334, rcvd 2

*Oct 24 16:45:31.271:     UDP src=67, dst=68

*Oct 24 16:45:35.283: %DHCP-6-ADDRESS_ASSIGN: Interface FastEthernet0/0 assigned DHCP
  address 172.16.23.101, mask 255.255.255.0, hostname R3
```

Notice the correlation between the IP packets sent and received on R3 with the debug messages turned on.

What is the source IP address that the DHCP client sees before it receives a DHCP lease?

_____

How does the DHCP server communicate the information back to the client? How does it identify the specific DHCP client?

_____

_____

_____

_____

Until DHCP completes, the DHCP client broadcasts to all IP speakers on the Layer 2 segment, sourcing its IP address as 0.0.0.0. Thus, these packets can pass throughout a broadcast domain and over the entire span of a VLAN.

Rogue DHCP servers can be a major problem in some campus networks. Rogue DHCP servers lease IP addresses to clients because they receive the broadcast packet before the primary DHCP server. The rogue DHCP server needs to be identified by the system administrator and disabled.

Step 4: Verify DHCP Lease on Client

To make sure that an IP is received and assigned to the interface, use the **show ip interface brief** command. Display the IP routing table on R3:

```
R3# show ip interface brief
Interface              IP-Address      OK? Method Status                Protocol
FastEthernet0/0        172.16.23.101   YES DHCP   up                    up
FastEthernet0/1        unassigned      YES NVRAM  administratively down down
Serial0/0/0            unassigned      YES NVRAM  administratively down down
Serial0/0/1            unassigned      YES NVRAM  administratively down down
Serial0/1/0            unassigned      YES NVRAM  administratively down down
Serial0/1/1            unassigned      YES NVRAM  administratively down down


R3# show ip route
<output omitted>


Gateway of last resort is 172.16.23.2 to network 0.0.0.0


     172.16.0.0/24 is subnetted, 1 subnets
C       172.16.23.0 is directly connected, FastEthernet0/0
S*   0.0.0.0/0 [254/0] via 172.16.23.2
```

The administrative distance of the default gateway obtained through DHCP is 254, which is just 255 (Unreachable) − 1.

Consider the following scenario. Suppose this router were running any of the IGPs discussed in this module, and the routing protocol discovered that remote network 172.16.1.0/24 was accessible through a path other than through R2. Would R3 prefer the path through that IGP, or would it continue to send traffic destined to the 172.16.1.0/24 network to its DHCP default gateway? Explain.

_____

_____

Assume the IGP did not inject a route into the routing table for 172.16.1.0/24, but did receive a default route through the routing protocol, such as an IS-IS route to the L2 router for that area that did not point to R2. Would R3 prefer the path through that IGP, or would it continue to send traffic destined to the 172.16.1.0/24 network to its DHCP default gateway? Explain.

_____

_____

Because there is an IP address on the interface, try pinging R1's Loopback 1 interface from R3. It should be successful, indicating that R3 has a default gateway to send packets to, and that R1 has a route back to R3's assigned address:

```
R3# ping 172.16.1.1

Type escape sequence to abort.
Sending 5, 100-byte ICMP Echos to 172.16.1.1, timeout is 2 seconds:
.!!!!
Success rate is 80 percent (4/5), round-trip min/avg/max = 28/28/32 ms
```

The first packet was dropped because the Layer 2 encapsulation procedure needs to wait for the ARP request to be sent back before encapsulating the IP packet in an Ethernet frame. All further packets succeed.

Notice that the IP address assigned to the interface is outside of the excluded range (172.16.23.1–172.16.23.100) due to the command you applied earlier.

Step 5: Verify DHCP Configuration on Server

Investigate and verify DHCP server operation with the **show ip dhcp binding**, **show ip dhcp pool**, and **show ip dhcp server statistic** commands on R2, as follows:

```
R2# show ip dhcp ?
  binding    DHCP address bindings
  conflict   DHCP address conflicts
  database   DHCP database agents
  import     Show Imported Parameters
  pool       DHCP pools information
  relay      Miscellaneous DHCP relay information
  server     Miscellaneous DHCP server information

R2# show ip dhcp binding
Bindings from all pools not associated with VRF:
IP address          Client-ID/           Lease expiration        Type
                    Hardware address/
                    User name
172.16.23.101       0063.6973.636f.2d30.  Oct 25 2006 10:20 PM    Automatic
                    3031.382e.6239.6364.
                    2e62.6566.302d.4661.
                    302f.30

R2# show ip dhcp pool

Pool VLAN1-POOL :
 Utilization mark (high/low)    : 100 / 0
```

```
    Subnet size (first/next)      : 0 / 0
    Total addresses               : 254
    Leased addresses              : 1
    Pending event                 : none
    1 subnet is currently in the pool :
    Current index          IP address range                 Leased addresses
    172.16.23.102          172.16.23.1      - 172.16.23.254      1
```

```
R2# show ip dhcp server statistics
Memory usage           23714
Address pools          1
Database agents        0
Automatic bindings     1
Manual bindings        0
Expired bindings       0
Malformed messages     0
Secure arp entries     0

Message                Received
BOOTREQUEST            0
DHCPDISCOVER           1
DHCPREQUEST            1
DHCPDECLINE            0
DHCPRELEASE            0
DHCPINFORM             0

Message                Sent
BOOTREPLY              0
DHCPOFFER              1
DHCPACK                1
DHCPNAK                0
```

Notice especially that in the output of the **show ip dhcp pool** command, the value of the current index represents the next IP address that will be selected dynamically for a DHCP client on that subnet.

Step 6: DHCPRELEASE and DHCPRENEW

With debug messaging for DHCP left on for R2, issue the **shutdown** command for R3's FastEthernet0/0 interface:

```
R3(config)# interface fastethernet 0/0
R3(config-if)# shutdown
```

```
R2#
*Oct 24 18:04:57.475: DHCPD: DHCPRELEASE message received from client
0063.6973.636f.2d30.3031.382e.6239.6364.2e62.6566.302d.4661.302f.30 (172.16.23.101).
```

```
*Oct 24 18:04:57.475: DHCPD: Sending notification of TERMINATION:

*Oct 24 18:04:57.475:  DHCPD: address 172.16.23.101 mask 255.255.255.0

*Oct 24 18:04:57.475:  DHCPD: reason flags: RELEASE

*Oct 24 18:04:57.475:   DHCPD: htype 1 chaddr 0018.b9cd.bef0

*Oct 24 18:04:57.475:   DHCPD: lease time remaining (secs) = 101724

*Oct 24 18:04:57.475: DHCPD: returned 172.16.23.101 to address pool VLAN1-POOL.

*Oct 24 18:04:58.991: DHCPD: DHCPRELEASE message received from client
0063.6973.636f.2d30.3031.382e.6239.6364.2e62.6566.302d.4661.302f.30 (172.16.23.101).

*Oct 24 18:04:58.991: DHCPD: Finding a relay for client
  0063.6973.636f.2d30.3031.382e.6239.6364.2e62.6566.302d.4661.302f.30 on interface
  FastEthernet0/0.

*Oct 24 18:04:58.991: DHCPD: Seeing if there is an internally specified pool class:

*Oct 24 18:04:58.991:   DHCPD: htype 1 chaddr 0018.b9cd.bef0

*Oct 24 18:04:58.991:   DHCPD: remote id 020a0000ac10170200000000

*Oct 24 18:04:58.991:   DHCPD: circuit id 00000000

*Oct 24 18:05:00.991: DHCPD: DHCPRELEASE message received from client
0063.6973.636f.2d30.3031.382e.6239.6364.2e62.6566.302d.4661.302f.30 (172.16.23.101).

*Oct 24 18:05:00.991: DHCPD: Finding a relay for client
  0063.6973.636f.2d30.3031.382e.6239.6364.2e62.6566.302d.4661.302f.30 on interface
  FastEthernet0/0.

*Oct 24 18:05:00.991: DHCPD: Seeing if there is an internally specified pool class:

*Oct 24 18:05:00.991:   DHCPD: htype 1 chaddr 0018.b9cd.bef0

*Oct 24 18:05:00.991:   DHCPD: remote id 020a0000ac10170200000000

*Oct 24 18:05:00.991:   DHCPD: circuit id 00000000
```

Notice that just before the interface went offline, it sent several DHCPRELEASE messages to the DHCP server to notify it that it would not need the DHCP address for an indefinite period of time.

Issue the **no shutdown** command for the FastEthernet0/0 interface on R3:

```
R3(config)# interface fastethernet 0/0

R3(config-if)# no shutdown
```

```
R2#

*Oct 24 18:05:27.555: DHCPD: Sending notification of DISCOVER:

*Oct 24 18:05:27.555:   DHCPD: htype 1 chaddr 0018.b9cd.bef0

*Oct 24 18:05:27.555:   DHCPD: remote id 020a0000ac10170200000000

*Oct 24 18:05:27.555:   DHCPD: circuit id 00000000

*Oct 24 18:05:27.555: DHCPD: DHCPDISCOVER received from client
  0063.6973.636f.2d30.3031.382e.6239.6364.2e62.6566.302d.4661.302f.30 on interface
  FastEthernet0/0.

*Oct 24 18:05:27.555: DHCPD: Seeing if there is an internally specified pool class:

*Oct 24 18:05:27.555:   DHCPD: htype 1 chaddr 0018.b9cd.bef0

*Oct 24 18:05:27.555:   DHCPD: remote id 020a0000ac10170200000000

*Oct 24 18:05:27.555:   DHCPD: circuit id 00000000

*Oct 24 18:05:27.555: DHCPD: Allocate an address without class information
  (172.16.23.0)

*Oct 24 18:05:29.555: DHCPD: Adding binding to radix tree (172.16.23.102)

*Oct 24 18:05:29.555: DHCPD: Adding binding to hash tree

*Oct 24 18:05:29.555: DHCPD: assigned IP address 172.16.23.102 to client
0063.6973.636f.2d30.3031.382e.6239.6364.2e62.6566.302d.4661.302f.30.
```

```
*Oct 24 18:05:29.555: DHCPD: Sending DHCPOFFER to client
0063.6973.636f.2d30.3031.382e.6239.6364.2e62.6566.302d.4661.302f.30 (172.16.23.102).

*Oct 24 18:05:29.555: DHCPD: broadcasting BOOTREPLY to client 0018.b9cd.bef0.

*Oct 24 18:05:29.555: DHCPD: DHCPREQUEST received from client
0063.6973.636f.2d30.3031.382e.6239.6364.2e62.6566.302d.4661.302f.30.

*Oct 24 18:05:29.555: DHCPD: Sending notification of ASSIGNMENT:

*Oct 24 18:05:29.555:  DHCPD: address 172.16.23.102 mask 255.255.255.0

*Oct 24 18:05:29.555:   DHCPD: htype 1 chaddr 0018.b9cd.bef0

*Oct 24 18:05:29.559:   DHCPD: lease time remaining (secs) = 106560

*Oct 24 18:05:29.559: DHCPD: Appending default domain from pool

*Oct 24 18:05:29.559: DHCPD: Using hostname 'R3.Cisco.com.' for dynamic update (from
hostname option)

*Oct 24 18:05:29.559: DHCPD: Sending DHCPACK to client
0063.6973.636f.2d30.3031.382e.6239.6364.2e62.6566.302d.4661.302f.30 (172.16.23.102).

*Oct 24 18:05:29.559: DHCPD: broadcasting BOOTREPLY to client 0018.b9cd.bef0.

*Oct 24 18:05:37.983: DHCPD: checking for expired leases.
```

You should see the change in IP address with the **show ip interface brief** command:

```
R3# show ip interface brief
Interface                IP-Address      OK? Method Status                Protocol
FastEthernet0/0          172.16.23.102   YES DHCP   up                    up
FastEthernet0/1          unassigned      YES NVRAM  administratively down  down
Serial0/0/0              unassigned      YES NVRAM  administratively down  down
Serial0/0/1              unassigned      YES NVRAM  administratively down  down
Serial0/1/0              unassigned      YES NVRAM  administratively down  down
Serial0/1/1              unassigned      YES NVRAM  administratively down  down
```

You can also manually release a DHCP binding with the **release dhcp** *interface_type interface_number* command in privileged EXEC mode. Notice the debug output on R2 is almost precisely the same as when the **no shutdown** command was issued because both procedures are carried out by DHCPRELEASE:

```
R2#

*Oct 24 18:31:06.351: DHCPD: DHCPRELEASE message received from client
0063.6973.636f.2d30.3031.382e.6239.6364.2e62.6566.302d.4661.302f.30 (172.16.23.102).

*Oct 24 18:31:06.351: DHCPD: Sending notification of TERMINATION:

*Oct 24 18:31:06.351:  DHCPD: address 172.16.23.102 mask 255.255.255.0

*Oct 24 18:31:06.351:  DHCPD: reason flags: RELEASE

*Oct 24 18:31:06.351:   DHCPD: htype 1 chaddr 0018.b9cd.bef0

*Oct 24 18:31:06.351:    DHCPD: lease time remaining (secs) = 106453

*Oct 24 18:31:06.351: DHCPD: returned 172.16.23.102 to address pool VLAN1-POOL.

*Oct 24 18:31:08.351: DHCPD: DHCPRELEASE message received from client
0063.6973.636f.2d30.3031.382e.6239.6364.2e62.6566.302d.4661.302f.30 (172.16.23.102).

*Oct 24 18:31:08.351: DHCPD: Finding a relay for client
   0063.6973.636f.2d30.3031.382e.6239.6364.2e62.6566.302d.4661.302f.30 on interface
   FastEthernet0/0.

*Oct 24 18:31:08.351: DHCPD: Seeing if there is an internally specified pool class:

*Oct 24 18:31:08.351:   DHCPD: htype 1 chaddr 0018.b9cd.bef0
```

```
*Oct 24 18:31:08.351:    DHCPD: remote id 020a0000ac10170200000000
*Oct 24 18:31:08.351:    DHCPD: circuit id 00000000
```

You can manually issue the DHCPREQUEST command for an interface to request a DHCP binding using the **release dhcp** *interface_type interface_number* command in privileged EXEC mode. If you already have a DHCP address, this command renews the DHCP lease. Without a DHCP lease, this command sends a DHCPREQUEST:

```
R3# renew dhcp fastethernet 0/0
```

```
R2#
*Oct 24 18:36:16.839: DHCPD: Sending notification of DISCOVER:
*Oct 24 18:36:16.839:    DHCPD: htype 1 chaddr 0018.b9cd.bef0
*Oct 24 18:36:16.839:    DHCPD: remote id 020a0000ac10170200000000
*Oct 24 18:36:16.839:    DHCPD: circuit id 00000000
*Oct 24 18:36:16.839: DHCPD: DHCPDISCOVER received from client
   0063.6973.636f.2d30.3031.382e.6239.6364.2e62.6566.302d.4661.302f.30 on interface
   FastEthernet0/0.
*Oct 24 18:36:16.839: DHCPD: Seeing if there is an internally specified pool class:
*Oct 24 18:36:16.839:    DHCPD: htype 1 chaddr 0018.b9cd.bef0
*Oct 24 18:36:16.839:    DHCPD: remote id 020a0000ac10170200000000
*Oct 24 18:36:16.839:    DHCPD: circuit id 00000000
*Oct 24 18:36:16.839: DHCPD: Allocate an address without class information
(172.16.23.0)
*Oct 24 18:36:18.839: DHCPD: Adding binding to radix tree (172.16.23.103)
*Oct 24 18:36:18.839: DHCPD: Adding binding to hash tree
*Oct 24 18:36:18.839: DHCPD: assigned IP address 172.16.23.103 to client
0063.6973.636f.2d30.3031.382e.6239.6364.2e62.6566.302d.4661.302f.30.
*Oct 24 18:36:18.839: DHCPD: Sending DHCPOFFER to client
0063.6973.636f.2d30.3031.382e.6239.6364.2e62.6566.302d.4661.302f.30 (172.16.23.103).
*Oct 24 18:36:18.839: DHCPD: broadcasting BOOTREPLY to client 0018.b9cd.bef0.
*Oct 24 18:36:18.843: DHCPD: DHCPREQUEST received from client
0063.6973.636f.2d30.3031.382e.6239.6364.2e62.6566.302d.4661.302f.30.
*Oct 24 18:36:18.843: DHCPD: Sending notification of ASSIGNMENT:
*Oct 24 18:36:18.843:    DHCPD: address 172.16.23.103 mask 255.255.255.0
*Oct 24 18:36:18.843:    DHCPD: htype 1 chaddr 0018.b9cd.bef0
*Oct 24 18:36:18.843:    DHCPD: lease time remaining (secs) = 106560
*Oct 24 18:36:18.843: DHCPD: Appending default domain from pool
*Oct 24 18:36:18.843: DHCPD: Using hostname 'R3.Cisco.com.' for dynamic update (from
hostname option)
*Oct 24 18:36:18.843: DHCPD: Sending DHCPACK to client
0063.6973.636f.2d30.3031.382e.6239.6364.2e62.6566.302d.4661.302f.30 (172.16.23.103).
*Oct 24 18:36:18.843: DHCPD: broadcasting BOOTREPLY to client 0018.b9cd.bef0.
```

Similar commands to manually release and renew DHCP assignments also exist in Microsoft Windows, Mac, and UNIX/Linux operating systems.

In Windows, for example, these commands are:

```
C:\> ipconfig /release [adapter]
C:\> ipconfig /renew   [adapter]
```

Step 7: Configure the IP Helper Address

In Cisco IOS, the **ip helper-address** *address* command enables forwarding of special UDP broadcast packets as unicast packets to a specific address. Normally, routers do not forward broadcast packets. The ability to forward is useful if there is a remote TFTP or DHCP server. To demonstrate forwarding we will set up R1's loopback interface to simulate the network with hosts on it, and R2's loopback interface will simulate the server with all of the UDP services on it. To configure this, go to R1's loopback interface and use the **ip helper-address** *address* command. Verify the configuration with the **show ip helper-address** command:

```
R1(config)# interface loopback 1
R1(config-if)#ip helper-address 172.16.2.1


R1# show ip helper-address
Interface                Helper-Address  VPN VRG Name      VRG State
Loopback1                172.16.2.1        0  None         Unknown
```

The Cisco IOS Release 12.4 Configuration Guide states:

> All of the following conditions must be met in order for a User Datagram Protocol (UDP) or IP packet to be helped by the **ip helper-address** command:
>
> - The MAC address of the received frame must be all-ones broadcast address (ffff.ffff.ffff).
>
> - The IP destination address must be one of the following: all-ones broadcast (255.255.255.255), subnet broadcast for the receiving interface, or major-net broadcast for the receiving interface if the **no ip classless** command is also configured.
>
> - The IP time-to-live (TTL) value must be at least 2.
>
> - The IP protocol must be UDP (17).
>
> - The UDP destination port must be TFTP, Domain Name System (DNS), Time, NetBIOS, ND, BOOTP or DHCP packet, or a UDP port specified by the **ip forward-protocol udp** command.
>
> The UDP protocols that will be forwarded by default are:
>
> - Trivial File Transfer Protocol (TFTP) (port 69)
>
> - Domain Naming System (port 53)
>
> - Time service (port 37)
>
> - NetBIOS Name Server (port 137)
>
> - NetBIOS Datagram Server (port 138)
>
> - Boot Protocol (BOOTP) client and server packets (ports 67 and 68)
>
> - TACACS service (port 49)
>
> - IEN-116 Name Service (port 42)

You can add a port to this list with the global configuration command **ip forward-protocol udp** *port*. You can also leave out the port number if you want to forward all UDP packets, although this could be a security risk. The following example forwards the arbitrary UDP port 50000:

```
R1(config)# ip forward-protocol udp 50000
```

Which network services require these protocols to obtain necessary information?

_____

_____

_____

Will the following IP packets be forwarded to R2? Each field refers to the tuple (Destination MAC, Destination IP, Protocol number, Destination port, TTL). Give a reason for each answer.

- **(ffff.ffff.ffff, 255.255.255.255, 17, 69, 2)**—_____

- **(ffff.ffff.ffff, 172.16.1.255, 18, 69, 3)**—_____

   _____

- **(ffff.ffff.ffff, 172.16.2.255, 17, 67, 3)**—_____

   _____

   _____

   _____

   _____

- **(ffff.ffff.ffff, 172.16.255.255, 17, 138, 1)**—_____

- **(ffff.ffff.ffff, 172.16.255.255, 17, 37, 8)**—_____

- **(0001.0de1.934a, 172.16.2.1, 19, 30, 8)**—_____

   _____

Challenge: Apply Per-Protocol Forwarding

Allow R1 to forward mySQL via UDP to R2's loopback interface.

_____

Hint   If you don't know the UDP port number for mySQL, use the **show ip port-map** command.

_____

_____

_____

[1] For more information about how routers respond to unreachable hosts, see RFC 792 (ICMP) at http://www.ietf.org/rfc/rfc0792.txt and RFC 2463 (ICMPv6) at http://www.ietf.org/rfc/rfc2463.txt.

Lab 6-1: Configuring BGP with Default Routing (6.7.1)

In this lab, you will configure BGP to exchange routing information with two Internet service providers (ISP).

Figure 6-1 illustrates the topology that will be used for this lab.

Figure 6-1   Topology Diagram

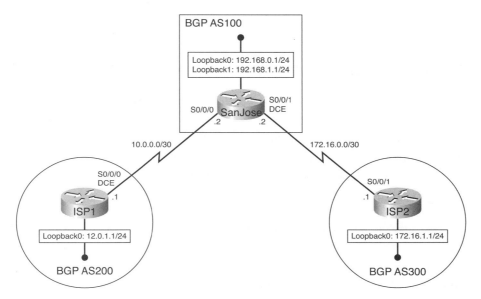

Scenario

The International Travel Agency relies extensively on the Internet for sales. The company has contracted with two ISPs for Internet connectivity with fault tolerance. You need to configure Border Gateway Protocol (BGP), which runs between the San Jose boundary router and the two ISP routers.

Step 1: Assign IP Addresses

Configure the network according to the diagram, but do not configure a routing protocol. Configure a loopback interface with an IP address for each ISP route shown in Figure 6-1. These loopbacks simulate real networks that can be reached through the ISP. Configure two loopback interfaces with the IP addresses for the San Jose router. These loopbacks simulate the connections between the core routers.

Use **ping** to test the connectivity between the directly connected routers. Note that router ISP1 cannot reach router ISP2.

Step 2: Configure the ISPs

Configure the ISP routers, and the International Travel Agency's boundary router, San Jose. On the ISP1 router, enter the following configuration:

```
ISP1(config)# router bgp 200
ISP1(config-router)# neighbor 10.0.0.2 remote-as 100
ISP1(config-router)# network 12.0.1.0 mask 255.255.255.0
```

On ISP2, configure BGP:

```
ISP2(config)# router bgp 300
ISP2(config-router)# neighbor 172.16.0.2 remote-as 100
ISP2(config-router)# network 172.16.1.0 mask 255.255.255.0
```

Step 3: Configure SanJose BGP

Configure the SanJose router to run BGP with both providers:

```
SanJose(config)# router bgp 100
SanJose(config-router)# neighbor 10.0.0.1 remote-as 200
SanJose(config-router)# neighbor 172.16.0.1 remote-as 300
SanJose(config-router)# network 192.168.0.0
SanJose(config-router)# network 192.168.1.0
```

To verify the configuration, check the routing table for SanJose with the **show ip route** command:

```
SanJose# show ip route

Gateway of last resort is not set

      172.16.0.0/16 is variably subnetted, 2 subnets, 2 masks
C        172.16.0.0/30 is directly connected, Serial0/0/1
B        172.16.1.0/24 [20/0] via 172.16.0.1, 00:00:03
      10.0.0.0/30 is subnetted, 1 subnets
C        10.0.0.0 is directly connected, Serial0/0/0
C     192.168.0.0/24 is directly connected, Loopback0
      12.0.0.0/24 is subnetted, 1 subnets
B        12.0.1.0 [20/0] via 10.0.0.1, 00:00:42
C     192.168.1.0/24 is directly connected, Loopback1
```

SanJose has routes to the loopback networks at each ISP router. Verify that SanJose has connectivity to these networks by pinging each loopback address from its console. One way to do this is to create your own Toolkit Command Language (TCL) script. If these pings are not successful, troubleshoot.

Step 4: Verify BGP on the SanJose Router

To verify the operation of SanJose, issue the **show ip bgp** command:

```
SanJose# show ip bgp
BGP table version is 5, local router ID is 192.168.1.1
Status codes: s suppressed, d damped, h history, * valid, > best, i - internal
Origin codes: i - IGP, e - EGP, ? - incomplete

    Network          Next Hop          Metric LocPrf Weight Path
*> 12.0.1.0/24       10.0.0.1              0             0 200 i
*> 172.16.1.0/24     172.16.0.1            0             0 300 i
*> 192.168.0.0       0.0.0.0               0         32768 i
*> 192.168.1.0       0.0.0.0               0         32768 i
```

What is the local router ID?

_____

Which table version is displayed?

_____

An asterisk (*) next to a route indicates that it is the best route. An angle bracket (>) indicates that the route is inserted into the routing table.

On the ISP1 router, issue the **shutdown** command on Loopback 0. Then on SanJose, issue the **show ip bgp** command again.

Which table version is displayed?

_____

The **shutdown** command causes a routing table update, so the version should be one higher than the last.

Bring ISP1 router Loopback0 back up by issuing the **no shutdown** command.

On SanJose, issue the **show ip bgp neighbors** command. The following is a partial sample output of the command:

```
BGP neighbor is 172.16.0.1, remote AS 300, external link
Index 2, Offset 0, Mask 0x4
BGP version 4, remote router ID 172.16.1.1
BGP state = Established, table version = 5, up for 00:02:24
Last read 00:00:24, hold time is 180
```

Based on the output of this command, what is the BGP state between this router and ISP2?

_____

How long has this connection been up?

_____

Step 5: Filter Routes

Check ISP2's routing table using the **show ip route** command. ISP2 should have a route that belongs to ISP1, network 12.0.1.0.

If SanJose advertises a route belonging to ISP1, ISP2 installs that route in its table. ISP2 might then attempt to route transit traffic through the International Travel Agency. Configure the SanJose router so that it advertises only International Travel Agency networks 192.168.0.0 and 192.168.1.0 to both providers. On the SanJose router, configure the following access list:

```
SanJose(config)# access-list 1 permit 192.168.0.0 0.0.1.255
```

Then apply this access list as a route filter using the **distribute-list** keyword with the BGP **neighbor** statement:

```
SanJose(config)# router bgp 100
SanJose(config-router)# neighbor 10.0.0.1 distribute-list 1 out
SanJose(config-router)# neighbor 172.16.0.1 distribute-list 1 out
```

After you configured the route filter, check the routing table for ISP2 again. The route to 12.0.1.0, ISP1, should still be in the table.

Return to SanJose and issue the **clear ip bgp *** command. Wait until the routers reach the Established state, which might take several moments, and then recheck the ISP2 routing table. The route to ISP1 should no longer be in the routing table.

The route to ISP2, network 172.16.1.0, should not be in the routing table for ISP1.

Step 6: Configure the Primary and Backup Routes Using Floating Static Routes

Now that bidirectional communication has been established with each ISP via BGP, it is time to configure the primary and backup routes. This can be done with floating static routes or BGP.

To look at the floating static route method, issue the **show ip_route** command on the SanJose router:

```
SanJose# show ip route
Gateway of last resort is not set

     172.16.0.0/16 is variably subnetted, 2 subnets, 2 masks
C       172.16.0.0/30 is directly connected, Serial0/0/1
B       172.16.1.0/24 [20/0] via 172.16.0.1, 00:07:37
     10.0.0.0/30 is subnetted, 1 subnets
C       10.0.0.0 is directly connected, Serial0/0/0
C    192.168.0.0/24 is directly connected, Loopback0
     12.0.0.0/24 is subnetted, 1 subnets
B       12.0.1.0 [20/0] via 10.0.0.1, 00:07:42
C    192.168.1.0/24 is directly connected, Loopback1
```

Notice that there is no gateway of last resort defined. This is a huge problem, because SanJose is the border router for the corporate network. Assume that ISP1 is the primary provider, and ISP2 acts as the backup. Configure static routes to reflect this policy:

```
SanJose(config)# ip route 0.0.0.0 0.0.0.0 10.0.0.1 210
SanJose(config)# ip route 0.0.0.0 0.0.0.0 172.16.0.1 220
```

Now verify that a default route is defined using the **show ip_route** command:

```
SanJose# show ip route


Gateway of last resort is 10.0.0.1 to network 0.0.0.0


     172.16.0.0/16 is variably subnetted, 2 subnets, 2 masks
C        172.16.0.0/30 is directly connected, Serial0/0/1
B        172.16.1.0/24 [20/0] via 172.16.0.1, 00:16:34
     10.0.0.0/30 is subnetted, 1 subnets
C        10.0.0.0 is directly connected, Serial0/0/0
C    192.168.0.0/24 is directly connected, Loopback0
     12.0.0.0/24 is subnetted, 1 subnets
B        12.0.1.0 [20/0] via 10.0.0.1, 00:16:39
C    192.168.1.0/24 is directly connected, Loopback1
S*   0.0.0.0/0 [210/0] via 10.0.0.1
```

Test this default route by creating an unadvertised loopback on the router for ISP1:

```
ISP1# configure terminal
ISP1(config)# int loopback 100
ISP1(config-if)# ip address 210.210.210.1 255.255.255.0
```

Issue the **clear ip bgp 10.0.0.1** command to reestablish a conversation with the 10.0.0.1 BGP speaker:

```
SanJose# clear ip bgp 10.0.0.1
```

Wait until the BGP conversation is reestablished with the 10.0.0.1 host.

Issue the **show ip route** command to ensure that the newly added 210.210.210.0/24 network does not appear in the routing table:

```
SanJose# show ip route


Gateway of last resort is 10.0.0.1 to network 0.0.0.0


     172.16.0.0/16 is variably subnetted, 2 subnets, 2 masks
C        172.16.0.0/30 is directly connected, Serial0/0/1
B        172.16.1.0/24 [20/0] via 172.16.0.1, 00:27:40
     10.0.0.0/30 is subnetted, 1 subnets
C        10.0.0.0 is directly connected, Serial0/0/0
C    192.168.0.0/24 is directly connected, Loopback0
     12.0.0.0/24 is subnetted, 1 subnets
```

```
B       12.0.1.0 [20/0] via 10.0.0.1, 00:27:45
C    192.168.1.0/24 is directly connected, Loopback1
S*   0.0.0.0/0 [210/0] via 10.0.0.1
```

Ping the 210.210.210.1 loopback interface originating from the 192.168.1.1 SanJose interface:

```
SanJose# ping
Protocol [ip]:
Target IP address: 210.210.210.1
Repeat count [5]:
Datagram size [100]:
Timeout in seconds [2]:
Extended commands [n]: y
Source address or interface: 192.168.1.1
Type of service [0]:
Set DF bit in IP header? [no]:
Validate reply data? [no]:
Data pattern [0xABCD]:
Loose, Strict, Record, Timestamp, Verbose[none]:
Sweep range of sizes [n]:
Type escape sequence to abort.
Sending 5, 100-byte ICMP Echos to 210.210.210.1, timeout is 2 seconds:
!!!!!
Success rate is 100 percent (5/5), round-trip min/avg/max = 32/32/36 ms
```

Step 7: Configure Primary and Backup Routes Using Static Routes

Another method for configuring primary and backup routes is to use the **default-network** command instead of a 0.0.0.0/0 route.

Remove the floating static routes configured in Step 6:

```
SanJose(config)# no ip route 0.0.0.0 0.0.0.0 10.0.0.1 210
SanJose(config)# no ip route 0.0.0.0 0.0.0.0 172.16.0.1 220
```

The network that was added in the last step, 210.210.210.0/24, should now be advertised on the ISP1 router:

```
ISP1(config)# router bgp 200
ISP1(config-router)# network 210.210.210.0
```

```
ISP1# clear ip bgp 10.0.0.2
```

Configure the SanJose router a **default-network** statement to reestablish a gateway of last resort. Make sure that the classful network 210.210.210.0 /24 appears in the routing table and is followed with the **ip default-network** statement:

```
SanJose# show ip route


Gateway of last resort is not set

B    210.210.210.0/24 [20/0] via 10.0.0.1, 00:04:51
     172.16.0.0/16 is variably subnetted, 2 subnets, 2 masks
C       172.16.0.0/30 is directly connected, Serial0/0/1
B       172.16.1.0/24 [20/0] via 172.16.0.1, 00:21:19
     10.0.0.0/30 is subnetted, 1 subnets
C       10.0.0.0 is directly connected, Serial0/0/0
C    192.168.0.0/24 is directly connected, Loopback0
     12.0.0.0/24 is subnetted, 1 subnets
B       12.0.1.0 [20/0] via 10.0.0.1, 00:04:51
C    192.168.1.0/24 is directly connected, Loopback1


SanJose(config)# ip default-network 210.210.210.0
```

Wait a few moments, and then reexamine the routing table on SanJose:

```
SanJose# show ip route


Gateway of last resort is 10.0.0.1 to network 210.210.210.0

B*   210.210.210.0/24 [20/0] via 10.0.0.1, 00:04:28
     172.16.0.0/16 is variably subnetted, 2 subnets, 2 masks
C       172.16.0.0/30 is directly connected, Serial0/0/1
B       172.16.1.0/24 [20/0] via 172.16.0.1, 00:20:56
     10.0.0.0/30 is subnetted, 1 subnets
C       10.0.0.0 is directly connected, Serial0/0/0
C    192.168.0.0/24 is directly connected, Loopback0
     12.0.0.0/24 is subnetted, 1 subnets
B       12.0.1.0 [20/0] via 10.0.0.1, 00:04:28
C    192.168.1.0/24 is directly connected, Loopback1
```

This establishes ISP1 as the only default route. This route can be manipulated with policy routing. Correct this by adding a backup route to the 172.16.0.1 host on ISP2:

```
SanJose(config)# ip route 0.0.0.0 0.0.0.0 172.16.0.1 220
```

External BGP (EBGP)-learned routes have an administrative distance of 20 and are preferred to any routes with an administrative distance greater than 20, such as the default route defined above with an administrative distance of 220. The default route acts as a backup if the 210.210.210.0 /24 network is unavailable because of a fault or misconfiguration, or during the short period after a **clear ip bgp 10.0.0.1** command is issued.

Verify that this newly added route establishes a consistent default route while the BGP conversation between SanJose and ISP1 reestablishes. Notice that the routing table includes two candidate default routes (*), only one of which is used because of different administrative distances:

```
SanJose# show ip route

Codes: C - connected, S - static, I - IGRP, R - RIP, M - mobile,
B - BGP D - EIGRP, EX - EIGRP external, O - OSPF, IA - OSPF inter area N1 - OSPF
    NSSA external type 1, N2 - OSPF NSSA external
type 2 E1 - OSPF external type 1, E2 - OSPF external type 2,
E - EGP i - IS-IS, L1 - IS-IS level-1, L2 - IS-IS level-2, ia - IS-IS inter area *
- candidate default, U - per-user static route, o - ODR  P - periodic downloaded
    static route


Gateway of last resort is 10.0.0.1 to network 210.210.210.0


B*    210.210.210.0/24 [20/0] via 10.0.0.1, 00:19:17
      172.16.0.0/16 is variably subnetted, 2 subnets, 2 masks
C        172.16.0.0/30 is directly connected, Serial0/0/1
B        172.16.1.0/24 [20/0] via 172.16.0.1, 00:35:45
      10.0.0.0/30 is subnetted, 1 subnets
C        10.0.0.0 is directly connected, Serial0/0/0
C     192.168.0.0/24 is directly connected, Loopback0
      12.0.0.0/24 is subnetted, 1 subnets
B        12.0.1.0 [20/0] via 10.0.0.1, 00:19:17
C     192.168.1.0/24 is directly connected, Loopback1
S*    0.0.0.0/0 [220/0] via 172.16.0.1


SanJose# clear ip bgp 10.0.0.1
SanJose# show ip route


Gateway of last resort is 172.16.0.1 to network 0.0.0.0


      172.16.0.0/16 is variably subnetted, 2 subnets, 2 masks
C        172.16.0.0/30 is directly connected, Serial0/0/1
B        172.16.1.0/24 [20/0] via 172.16.0.1, 00:45:31
      10.0.0.0/30 is subnetted, 1 subnets
C        10.0.0.0 is directly connected, Serial0/0/0
C     192.168.0.0/24 is directly connected, Loopback0
C     192.168.1.0/24 is directly connected, Loopback1
S*    0.0.0.0/0 [220/0] via 172.16.0.1


SanJose# show ip route
Gateway of last resort is 10.0.0.1 to network 210.210.210.0
B*    210.210.210.0/24 [20/0] via 10.0.0.1, 00:01:03
      172.16.0.0/16 is variably subnetted, 2 subnets, 2 masks
C        172.16.0.0/30 is directly connected, Serial0/0/1
```

```
B        172.16.1.0/24 [20/0] via 172.16.0.1, 00:46:42
      10.0.0.0/30 is subnetted, 1 subnets
C        10.0.0.0 is directly connected, Serial0/0/0
C     192.168.0.0/24 is directly connected, Loopback0
      12.0.0.0/24 is subnetted, 1 subnets
B        12.0.1.0 [20/0] via 10.0.0.1, 00:01:03
C     192.168.1.0/24 is directly connected, Loopback1
S*    0.0.0.0/0 [220/0] via 172.16.0.1
```

As expected, while the BGP conversation was down between SanJose and ISP1, the route to ISP2 was added as the gateway of last resort. However, once BGP reestablished the conversation between SanJose and ISP1, the default route of 210.210.210.0 was again set as the gateway of last resort on SanJose.

TCL Verification

You can download this TCL script at www.ciscopress.com/title/1587132133 under the More Information section on the page.

```
ISP1# tclsh
ISP1(tcl)#
ISP1(tcl)# foreach address {
+>12.0.1.1
+>192.168.0.1
+>192.168.1.1
+>172.16.1.1
+>10.0.0.1
+>10.0.0.2
+>172.16.0.1
+>172.16.1.1
+>210.210.210.1
+>} {
+>ping $address }

Type escape sequence to abort.
Sending 5, 100-byte ICMP Echos to 12.0.1.1, timeout is 2 seconds:
!!!!!
Success rate is 100 percent (5/5), round-trip min/avg/max = 1/1/1 ms
Type escape sequence to abort.
Sending 5, 100-byte ICMP Echos to 192.168.0.1, timeout is 2 seconds:
!!!!!
Success rate is 100 percent (5/5), round-trip min/avg/max = 28/28/32 ms
Type escape sequence to abort.
Sending 5, 100-byte ICMP Echos to 192.168.1.1, timeout is 2 seconds:
!!!!!
Success rate is 100 percent (5/5), round-trip min/avg/max = 28/28/28 ms
```

```
Type escape sequence to abort.
Sending 5, 100-byte ICMP Echos to 172.16.1.1, timeout is 2 seconds:
.....
Success rate is 0 percent (0/5)
Type escape sequence to abort.
Sending 5, 100-byte ICMP Echos to 10.0.0.1, timeout is 2 seconds:
!!!!!
Success rate is 100 percent (5/5), round-trip min/avg/max = 56/58/64 ms
Type escape sequence to abort.
Sending 5, 100-byte ICMP Echos to 10.0.0.2, timeout is 2 seconds:
!!!!!
Success rate is 100 percent (5/5), round-trip min/avg/max = 28/28/32 ms
Type escape sequence to abort.
Sending 5, 100-byte ICMP Echos to 172.16.0.1, timeout is 2 seconds:
.....
Success rate is 0 percent (0/5)
Type escape sequence to abort.
Sending 5, 100-byte ICMP Echos to 172.16.1.1, timeout is 2 seconds:
.....
Success rate is 0 percent (0/5)
Type escape sequence to abort.
Sending 5, 100-byte ICMP Echos to 210.210.210.1, timeout is 2 seconds:
!!!!!
Success rate is 100 percent (5/5), round-trip min/avg/max = 1/1/4 ms
ISP1(tcl)# tclquit
```

```
SanJose# tclsh
SanJose(tcl)#
SanJose(tcl)# foreach address {
+>12.0.1.1
+>192.168.0.1
+>192.168.1.1
+>172.16.1.1
+>10.0.0.1
+>10.0.0.2
+>172.16.0.1
+>172.16.1.1
+>210.210.210.1
+>} {
+>ping $address }

Type escape sequence to abort.
Sending 5, 100-byte ICMP Echos to 12.0.1.1, timeout is 2 seconds:
!!!!!
Success rate is 100 percent (5/5), round-trip min/avg/max = 28/28/32 ms
```

```
Type escape sequence to abort.
Sending 5, 100-byte ICMP Echos to 192.168.0.1, timeout is 2 seconds:
!!!!!
Success rate is 100 percent (5/5), round-trip min/avg/max = 1/1/4 ms
Type escape sequence to abort.
Sending 5, 100-byte ICMP Echos to 192.168.1.1, timeout is 2 seconds:
!!!!!
Success rate is 100 percent (5/5), round-trip min/avg/max = 1/1/4 ms
Type escape sequence to abort.
Sending 5, 100-byte ICMP Echos to 172.16.1.1, timeout is 2 seconds:
!!!!!
Success rate is 100 percent (5/5), round-trip min/avg/max = 28/28/32 ms
Type escape sequence to abort.
Sending 5, 100-byte ICMP Echos to 10.0.0.1, timeout is 2 seconds:
!!!!!
Success rate is 100 percent (5/5), round-trip min/avg/max = 28/28/32 ms
Type escape sequence to abort.
Sending 5, 100-byte ICMP Echos to 10.0.0.2, timeout is 2 seconds:
!!!!!
Success rate is 100 percent (5/5), round-trip min/avg/max = 56/57/64 ms
Type escape sequence to abort.
Sending 5, 100-byte ICMP Echos to 172.16.0.1, timeout is 2 seconds:
!!!!!
Success rate is 100 percent (5/5), round-trip min/avg/max = 28/28/28 ms
Type escape sequence to abort.
Sending 5, 100-byte ICMP Echos to 172.16.1.1, timeout is 2 seconds:
!!!!!
Success rate is 100 percent (5/5), round-trip min/avg/max = 28/28/28 ms
Type escape sequence to abort.
Sending 5, 100-byte ICMP Echos to 210.210.210.1, timeout is 2 seconds:
!!!!!
Success rate is 100 percent (5/5), round-trip min/avg/max = 28/28/32 ms
SanJose(tcl)# tclquit
```

```
ISP2# tclsh
ISP2(tcl)#
ISP2(tcl)# foreach address {
+>12.0.1.1
+>192.168.0.1
+>192.168.1.1
+>172.16.1.1
+>10.0.0.1
+>10.0.0.2
+>172.16.0.1
+>172.16.1.1
```

```
+>210.210.210.1
+>} {
+>ping $address }

Type escape sequence to abort.
Sending 5, 100-byte ICMP Echos to 12.0.1.1, timeout is 2 seconds:
.....
Success rate is 0 percent (0/5)
Type escape sequence to abort.
Sending 5, 100-byte ICMP Echos to 192.168.0.1, timeout is 2 seconds:
!!!!!
Success rate is 100 percent (5/5), round-trip min/avg/max = 28/28/32 ms
Type escape sequence to abort.
Sending 5, 100-byte ICMP Echos to 192.168.1.1, timeout is 2 seconds:
!!!!!
Success rate is 100 percent (5/5), round-trip min/avg/max = 28/28/32 ms
Type escape sequence to abort.
Sending 5, 100-byte ICMP Echos to 172.16.1.1, timeout is 2 seconds:
!!!!!
Success rate is 100 percent (5/5), round-trip min/avg/max = 1/1/1 ms
Type escape sequence to abort.
Sending 5, 100-byte ICMP Echos to 10.0.0.1, timeout is 2 seconds:
.....
Success rate is 0 percent (0/5)
Type escape sequence to abort.
Sending 5, 100-byte ICMP Echos to 10.0.0.2, timeout is 2 seconds:
.....
Success rate is 0 percent (0/5)
Type escape sequence to abort.
Sending 5, 100-byte ICMP Echos to 172.16.0.1, timeout is 2 seconds:
!!!!!
Success rate is 100 percent (5/5), round-trip min/avg/max = 56/57/64 ms
Type escape sequence to abort.
Sending 5, 100-byte ICMP Echos to 172.16.1.1, timeout is 2 seconds:
!!!!!
Success rate is 100 percent (5/5), round-trip min/avg/max = 1/1/1 ms
Type escape sequence to abort.
Sending 5, 100-byte ICMP Echos to 210.210.210.1, timeout is 2 seconds:
.....
Success rate is 0 percent (0/5)
ISP2(tcl)# tclquit
```

Lab 6-2: Using the AS_PATH Attribute (6.7.2)

In this lab, you will use BGP commands to prevent private AS numbers from being advertised to the outside world. You will also use the AS_PATH attribute to filter BGP routes based on their source AS numbers.

Figure 6-2 illustrates the topology that will be used for this lab.

Figure 6-2   Topology Diagram

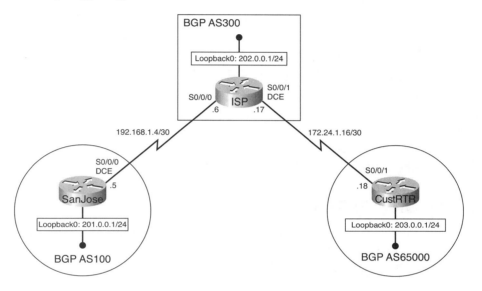

Scenario

The International Travel Agency's ISP has been assigned an AS number of 300. This provider uses BGP to exchange routing information with several customer networks. Each customer network is assigned an AS number from the private range, such as AS 65000. Configure ISP to remove the private AS numbers within the AS_Path information from CustRtr. In addition, the ISP would like to prevent its customer networks from receiving route information from International Travel Agency's AS 100. Use the AS_PATH attribute to implement this policy.

Step 1: IP Addressing

Build and configure the network according to the diagram, but do not configure a routing protocol.

Use **ping** to test the connectivity between the directly connected routers. Note that SanJose cannot reach the customer network for CustRtr. It cannot reach it by the IP address in the link leading to CustRtr nor the loopback interface 202.0.0.1/24.

Note   SanJose will not be able to reach the customer network for ISP, CustRtr. It will not be able to reach it by the IP address in the link leading to the CustRtr, nor the loopback interface, 202.0.0.1/24.

Step 2: Configure BGP

Configure BGP for normal operation. Enter the appropriate BGP commands on each router so that they identify their BGP neighbors and advertise their loopback networks:

```
SanJose(config)# router bgp 100
SanJose(config-router)# neighbor 192.168.1.6 remote-as 300
SanJose(config-router)# network 201.0.0.0
```
```
ISP(config)# router bgp 300
ISP(config-router)# neighbor 192.168.1.5 remote-as 100
ISP(config-router)# neighbor 172.24.1.18 remote-as 65000
ISP(config-router)# network 202.0.0.0
```
```
CustRtr(config)# router bgp 65000
CustRtr(config-router)# neighbor 172.24.1.17 remote-as 300
CustRtr(config-router)# network 203.0.0.0
```

Verify that these routers have established the appropriate neighbor relationships by issuing the **show ip bgp neighbors** command on each router.

Step 3: Remove the Private AS

Check SanJose's routing table by using the **show ip route** command. SanJose should have a route to both 202.0.0.0 and 203.0.0.0. Troubleshoot, if necessary.

Ping the 203.0.0.1 address from SanJose. Why does this fail?

_____

_____

Ping again, this time as an extended **ping**, sourcing from the Loopback 0 interface as follows:

```
SanJose# ping
Protocol [ip]:
Target IP address: 203.0.0.1
Repeat count [5]:
Datagram size [100]:
Timeout in seconds [2]:
Extended commands [n]: y
Source address or interface: 201.0.0.1
Type of service [0]:
Set DF bit in IP header? [no]:
Validate reply data? [no]:
Data pattern [0xABCD]:
Loose, Strict, Record, Timestamp, Verbose[none]:
Sweep range of sizes [n]:
Type escape sequence to abort.
Sending 5, 100-byte ICMP Echos to 203.0.0.1, timeout is 2 seconds:
!!!!!
Success rate is 100 percent (5/5), round-trip min/avg/max = 64/64/68 ms
```

Check the BGP table from SanJose by using the **show ip bgp** command. Note the AS path for the 203.0.0.0 network. The AS 65000 should be listed in the path to 203.0.0.0. Why is this a problem?

```
SanJose# show ip bgp

BGP table version is 4, local router ID is 201.0.0.1
Status codes: s suppressed, d damped, h history, * valid, > best, i - internal
Origin codes: i - IGP, e - EGP, ? - incomplete


   Network          Next Hop            Metric LocPrf Weight Path
*> 201.0.0.0        0.0.0.0                  0          32768 i
*> 202.0.0.0        192.168.1.6              0              0 300 i
*> 203.0.0.0        192.168.1.6                             0 300 65000 i
```

Configure ISP to strip the private AS numbers from BGP routes exchanged with SanJose. Use the following commands:

```
ISP(config)# router bgp 300
ISP(config-router)# neighbor 192.168.1.5 remove-private-as
```

After issuing these commands, use the **clear ip bgp *** command on SanJose to reestablish the BGP relationship between the three routers.

Wait several seconds, and then return to SanJose to check its routing table.

Does SanJose still have a route to 203.0.0.0?

Using extended **ping**, SanJose should be able to ping 203.0.0.1.

Now check the BGP table on SanJose. The AS_PATH to the 203.0.0.0 network should be AS 300:

```
SanJose# show ip bgp
BGP table version is 8, local router ID is 201.0.0.1
Status codes: s suppressed, d damped, h history, * valid, > best, i - internal
Origin codes: i - IGP, e - EGP, ? - incomplete


   Network          Next Hop            Metric LocPrf Weight Path
*> 201.0.0.0        0.0.0.0                  0          32768 i
*> 202.0.0.0        192.168.1.6              0              0 300 i
*> 203.0.0.0        192.168.1.6                             0 300 i
```

Step 4: Use the AS_PATH Attribute to Filter Routes

As a final configuration, use the AS_PATH attribute to filter routes based on their origin. In a complex environment, this attribute can be used to enforce routing policy. In this case, the provider router, ISP, must be configured so that it does not propagate routes that originate from AS 100 to the customer router, CustRtr.

First, configure a special kind of access list to match BGP routes with an AS_PATH attribute that both begins and ends with the number 100. Enter the following commands on ISP:

```
ISP(config)# ip as-path access-list 1 deny ^100$
ISP(config)# ip as-path access-list 1 permit .*
```

AS-path access lists are read like regular access lists, in that they are read through in order and have an implicit deny at the end. Rather than matching an address in each statement, like a conventional access-list, they match on something called regular expressions. Regular expressions are a way of matching text patterns, and have many uses. In this case, we will use them in the AS-path access list to match text patterns in AS-paths.

The first command above uses the ^ character to indicate that the AS_PATH must begin with the given number 100. The $ character indicates that the AS_PATH attribute must also end with 100. Essentially, this statement matches only paths that are sourced from AS 100. Other paths, which might include AS 100 along the way, will not match this list.

In the second statement, the . character is a wildcard, and the * symbol stands for a repetition of the wildcard. Together, .* matches any value of the AS_PATH attribute, which in effect permits any update that has not been denied by the previous **access-list** statement.

For more details on configuring regular expressions on Cisco routers, use the following link:

http://www.cisco.com/univercd/cc/td/doc/product/software/ ios122/122cgcr/ftersv_c/ftsappx/tcfaapre.htm

Now that the access list has been configured, apply it as follows:

```
ISP(config)# router bgp 300
ISP(config-router)# neighbor 172.24.1.18 filter-list 1 out
```

The **out** keyword specifies that the list is applied to routing information sent to this neighbor.

Use the **clear ip bgp *** command to reset the routing information. Wait several seconds, and then check the routing table for ISP. The route to 201.0.0.0 should be in the routing table.

Check the routing table for CustRtr. It should not have a route to 201.0.0.0 in its routing table.

Return to ISP and verify that the filter is working as intended. Issue the command **show ip bgp regexp ^100$**.

The output of this command shows all matches for the regular expressions that were used in the access list. The path to 201.0.0.0 matches the access list and is filtered from updates to CustRtr:

```
ISP# show ip bgp regexp ^100$
BGP table version is 4, local router ID is 202.0.0.1
Status codes: s suppressed, d damped, h history, * valid, > best, i - internal
Origin codes: i - IGP, e - EGP, ? - incomplete

   Network          Next Hop            Metric LocPrf Weight Path
*> 201.0.0.0        192.168.1.5              0             0 100 i
```

TCL Output

You can download these TCL scripts at www.ciscopress.com/title/1587132133 under the More Information section on the page.

```
tclsh

foreach address {
201.0.0.1
202.0.0.1
203.0.0.1
```

```
192.168.1.5
192.168.1.6
172.24.1.17
172.24.1.18
} {
ping $address }

SanJose# tclsh
SanJose(tcl)#
SanJose(tcl)# foreach address {
+>201.0.0.1
+>202.0.0.1
+>203.0.0.1
+>192.168.1.5
+>192.168.1.6
+>172.24.1.17
+>172.24.1.18
+>} {
+>ping $address }

Type escape sequence to abort.
Sending 5, 100-byte ICMP Echos to 201.0.0.1, timeout is 2 seconds:
!!!!!
Success rate is 100 percent (5/5), round-trip min/avg/max = 1/1/1 ms
Type escape sequence to abort.
Sending 5, 100-byte ICMP Echos to 202.0.0.1, timeout is 2 seconds:
!!!!!
Success rate is 100 percent (5/5), round-trip min/avg/max = 28/28/32 ms
Type escape sequence to abort.
Sending 5, 100-byte ICMP Echos to 203.0.0.1, timeout is 2 seconds:
.....
Success rate is 0 percent (0/5)
Type escape sequence to abort.
Sending 5, 100-byte ICMP Echos to 192.168.1.5, timeout is 2 seconds:
!!!!!
Success rate is 100 percent (5/5), round-trip min/avg/max = 56/57/64 ms
Type escape sequence to abort.
Sending 5, 100-byte ICMP Echos to 192.168.1.6, timeout is 2 seconds:
!!!!!
Success rate is 100 percent (5/5), round-trip min/avg/max = 28/28/28 ms
Type escape sequence to abort.
Sending 5, 100-byte ICMP Echos to 172.24.1.17, timeout is 2 seconds:
.....
Success rate is 0 percent (0/5)
```

```
Type escape sequence to abort.
Sending 5, 100-byte ICMP Echos to 172.24.1.18, timeout is 2 seconds:
.....
Success rate is 0 percent (0/5)
SanJose(tcl)# tclquit
```

```
ISP# tclsh
ISP(tcl)#
ISP(tcl)# foreach address {
+>201.0.0.1
+>202.0.0.1
+>203.0.0.1
+>192.168.1.5
+>192.168.1.6
+>172.24.1.17
+>172.24.1.18
+>} {
+>ping $address }

Type escape sequence to abort.
Sending 5, 100-byte ICMP Echos to 201.0.0.1, timeout is 2 seconds:
!!!!!
Success rate is 100 percent (5/5), round-trip min/avg/max = 28/28/28 ms
Type escape sequence to abort.
Sending 5, 100-byte ICMP Echos to 202.0.0.1, timeout is 2 seconds:
!!!!!
Success rate is 100 percent (5/5), round-trip min/avg/max = 1/1/1 ms
Type escape sequence to abort.
Sending 5, 100-byte ICMP Echos to 203.0.0.1, timeout is 2 seconds:
!!!!!
Success rate is 100 percent (5/5), round-trip min/avg/max = 28/28/32 ms
Type escape sequence to abort.
Sending 5, 100-byte ICMP Echos to 192.168.1.5, timeout is 2 seconds:
!!!!!
Success rate is 100 percent (5/5), round-trip min/avg/max = 28/28/32 ms
Type escape sequence to abort.
Sending 5, 100-byte ICMP Echos to 192.168.1.6, timeout is 2 seconds:
!!!!!
Success rate is 100 percent (5/5), round-trip min/avg/max = 56/57/64 ms
Type escape sequence to abort.
Sending 5, 100-byte ICMP Echos to 172.24.1.17, timeout is 2 seconds:
!!!!!
Success rate is 100 percent (5/5), round-trip min/avg/max = 56/58/68 ms
Type escape sequence to abort.
Sending 5, 100-byte ICMP Echos to 172.24.1.18, timeout is 2 seconds:
!!!!!
```

```
Success rate is 100 percent (5/5), round-trip min/avg/max = 28/28/32 ms
ISP(tcl)# tclquit
```
```
CustRtr# tclsh
CustRtr(tcl)#
CustRtr(tcl)# foreach address {
+>201.0.0.1
+>202.0.0.1
+>203.0.0.1
+>192.168.1.5
+>192.168.1.6
+>172.24.1.17
+>172.24.1.18
+>} {
+>ping $address }

Type escape sequence to abort.
Sending 5, 100-byte ICMP Echos to 201.0.0.1, timeout is 2 seconds:
.....
Success rate is 0 percent (0/5)
Type escape sequence to abort.
Sending 5, 100-byte ICMP Echos to 202.0.0.1, timeout is 2 seconds:
!!!!!
Success rate is 100 percent (5/5), round-trip min/avg/max = 28/28/32 ms
Type escape sequence to abort.
Sending 5, 100-byte ICMP Echos to 203.0.0.1, timeout is 2 seconds:
!!!!!
Success rate is 100 percent (5/5), round-trip min/avg/max = 1/1/4 ms
Type escape sequence to abort.
Sending 5, 100-byte ICMP Echos to 192.168.1.5, timeout is 2 seconds:
.....
Success rate is 0 percent (0/5)
Type escape sequence to abort.
Sending 5, 100-byte ICMP Echos to 192.168.1.6, timeout is 2 seconds:
.....
Success rate is 0 percent (0/5)
Type escape sequence to abort.
Sending 5, 100-byte ICMP Echos to 172.24.1.17, timeout is 2 seconds:
!!!!!
Success rate is 100 percent (5/5), round-trip min/avg/max = 28/28/32 ms
Type escape sequence to abort.
Sending 5, 100-byte ICMP Echos to 172.24.1.18, timeout is 2 seconds:
!!!!!
Success rate is 100 percent (5/5), round-trip min/avg/max = 56/57/64 ms
CustRtr(tcl)# tclquit
```

Lab 6-3: Configuring IBGP and EBGP Sessions, Local Preference, and MED (6.7.3)

In this lab, you will configure both Internal BGP (IBGP) and External BGP (EBGP). For IBGP peers in this lab to correctly exchange routing information, the **next-hop-self** command must be used along with the **Local-Preference** and **MED** attributes. This is to ensure that the flat-rate, unlimited-use T1 link is used for sending and receiving data to and from the AS 200 on ISP. The metered T1 should only be used in the event that the primary T1 link has failed. Traffic sent across the metered T1 link offers the same bandwidth of the primary link but at a huge expense. Ensure that this link is not used unnecessarily.

Figure 6-3 illustrates the topology that will be used for this lab.

Figure 6-3   Topology Diagram

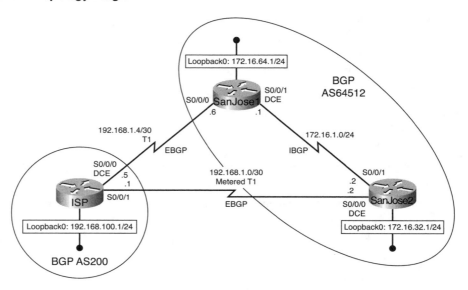

Scenario

The International Travel Agency runs BGP on its SanJose1 and SanJose2 routers externally with ISP, AS 200. IBGP is run internally between SanJose1 and SanJose2. Your job is to configure both EBGP and IBGP for this internetwork to allow for redundancy.

Step 1: IP Addressing

Build and configure the network according to the diagram in Figure 6-3, but do not configure a routing protocol. Configure a loopback interface on the SanJose1 and SanJose2 routers as shown. These loopbacks will be used with BGP **neighbor** statements for increased stability.

Use **ping** to test the connectivity between the directly connected routers. Note that the ISP router cannot reach the segment between SanJose1 and SanJose2. Both SanJose routers should be able to ping each other and their local ISP serial link IP address.

Step 2: Configure EIGRP

Configure EIGRP between the SanJose1 and SanJose2 routers with the same commands:

```
(config)# router eigrp 64512
(config-router)# no auto-summary
(config-router)# network 172.16.0.0
```

Step 3: Configure IBGP

Configure IBGP between the SanJose1 and SanJose2 routers. On the SanJose1 router, enter the following configuration:

```
SanJose1(config)# router bgp 64512
SanJose1(config-router)# neighbor 172.16.32.1 remote-as 64512
SanJose1(config-router)# neighbor 172.16.32.1 update-source loopback0
```

If multiple pathways to the neighbor exist, the router can use any IP interface to communicate by way of BGP. The **update-source loopback0** command instructs the router to use interface Loopback 0 for TCP connections. This command offers greater fault tolerance if one of the potentially numerous links within the corporate EIGRP WAN cloud fails. For simplicity in the lab environment, only one link needs to be configured.

Step 4: Verify BGP Neighbors

Complete the IBGP configuration on SanJose2 using the following commands:

```
SanJose2(config)# router bgp 64512
SanJose2(config-router)# neighbor 172.16.64.1 remote-as 64512
SanJose2(config-router)# neighbor 172.16.64.1 update-source lo0
```

Verify that SanJose1 and SanJose2 become BGP neighbors by issuing the **show ip bgp neighbors** command on SanJose1. View the following partial output. If the BGP state is not established, troubleshoot the connection.

The link between SanJose1 and SanJose2 should indicate an internal link as shown in the following:

```
SanJose2# show ip bgp neighbors
BGP neighbor is 172.16.64.1,  remote AS 64512, internal link
        BGP version 4, remote router ID 172.16.64.1
        BGP state = Established, up for 00:00:01
```

Step 5: Configure EBGP

Configure ISP to run EBGP with SanJose1 and SanJose2. Enter the following commands on ISP:

```
ISP(config)# router bgp 200
ISP(config-router)# neighbor 192.168.1.6 remote-as 64512
ISP(config-router)# neighbor 192.168.1.2 remote-as 64512
ISP(config-router)# network 192.168.100.0
```

Because EBGP sessions are almost always established over point-to-point links, there is no reason to use the **update-source** keyword in this configuration. Only one path exists between the peers. If this path goes down, alternative paths are not available.

Step 6: Verify BGP Neighbors

Configure SanJose1 as an EBGP peer to ISP:

```
SanJose1(config)# ip route 172.16.0.0 255.255.0.0 null0
SanJose1(config)# router bgp 64512
SanJose1(config-router)# neighbor 192.168.1.5 remote-as 200
SanJose1(config-router)# network 172.16.0.0
```

Use the **show ip bgp neighbors** command to verify that SanJose1 and ISP have reached the Established state. Troubleshoot if necessary.

Step 7: View BGP Summary Output

Configure SanJose2 as an EBGP peer to ISP:

```
SanJose2(config)# ip route 172.16.0.0 255.255.0.0 null0
SanJose2(config)# router bgp 64512
SanJose2(config-router)# neighbor 192.168.1.1 remote-as 200
SanJose2(config-router)# network 172.16.0.0
```

In Step 6, the **show ip bgp neighbors** command was used to verify that SanJose1 and ISP had reached the Established state. A useful alternative command is **show ip bgp summary**. The output should be similar to the following:

```
SanJose2# show ip bgp summary

BGP router identifier 172.16.32.1, local AS number 64512
BGP table version is 2, main routing table version 2
1 network entries and 1 paths using 137 bytes of memory
1 BGP path attribute entries using 60 bytes of memory
0 BGP route-map cache entries using 0 bytes of memory
0 BGP filter-list cache entries using 0 bytes of memory
BGP activity 2/1 prefixes, 2/1 paths, scan interval 15 secs

Neighbor        V    AS MsgRcvd MsgSent   TblVer  InQ OutQ Up/Down   State/PfxRcd
172.16.64.1     4 64512      21      24        2    0    0 00:03:02             0
192.168.1.1     4   200      14      15        2    0    0 00:03:36             0
```

Step 8: Verify Which Path Traffic Takes

Test whether ISP can ping the Loopback 0 address of 172.16.64.1 on SanJose1 and the serial link between SanJose1 and SanJose2, 172.16.1.1.

Now ping from ISP to the Loopback 0 address of 172.16.32.1 on SanJose2 and the serial link between SanJose1 and SanJose2. This time try 172.16.1.2.

You should see successful pings to each IP address on SanJose2 router. Ping attempts to 172.16.64.1 and 172.16.1.1 should fail.

Why is this the case?

_____

_____

Issue the **show ip bgp** command on ISP to verify BGP routes and metrics:

```
ISP# show ip bgp

BGP table version is 3, local router ID is 192.168.100.1
Status codes: s suppressed, d damped, h history, * valid, > best, i - internal
Origin codes: i - IGP, e - EGP, ? - incomplete

   Network          Next Hop          Metric LocPrf Weight  Path
*  172.16.0.0       192.168.1.6                        0 64512 i
*>                  192.168.1.2            0            0 64512 i
*> 192.168.100.0    0.0.0.0               0        32768 i
```

Notice that ISP has two valid routes to the 172.16.0.0 network, as indicated by the *. However, the link to SanJose2, the metered T1, has been selected as the best path. While that may be better for the ISP, a premium is paid for each megabyte transferred across this link.

Was this a malicious attempt by the ISP to get more money? Why did the ISP prefer the link to SanJose2 over SanJose1?

_____

_____

Would changing the bandwidth metric on each link help to correct this issue?

_____

BGP operates differently than all other protocols. Unlike other routing protocols that may use complex algorithms involving factors such as bandwidth, delay, reliability, and load to formulate a metric, BGP is policy-based. BGP determines the best path based upon variables, such as AS_Path, Weight, Local Preference, MED, and so on. If all things are equal, BGP prefers the route leading to the BGP speaker with the lowest IP address. This was not a malicious attempt by the ISP to get additional funds. In fact, this ISP router was configured from the beginning. The SanJose2 router with address 192.168.1.2 was preferred to the higher IP address of the SanJose1 router, 192.168.1.6.

At this point, the ISP router should be able to get to each network connected to SanJose1 and SanJose2 from the loopback address 192.168.100.1:

```
ISP# ping
Protocol [ip]:
Target IP address: 172.16.64.1
Repeat count [5]:
Datagram size [100]:
```

```
Timeout in seconds [2]:
Extended commands [n]: y
Source address or interface: 192.168.100.1
Type of service [0]:
Set DF bit in IP header? [no]:
Validate reply data? [no]:
Data pattern [0xABCD]:
Loose, Strict, Record, Timestamp, Verbose[none]:
Sweep range of sizes [n]:
Type escape sequence to abort.
Sending 5, 100-byte ICMP Echos to 172.16.64.1, timeout is 2 seconds:
!!!!!
Success rate is 100 percent (5/5), round-trip min/avg/max = 48/48/52 ms
ISP# ping
Protocol [ip]:
Target IP address: 172.16.1.1
Repeat count [5]:
Datagram size [100]:
Timeout in seconds [2]:
Extended commands [n]: y
Source address or interface: 192.168.100.1
Type of service [0]:
Set DF bit in IP header? [no]:
Validate reply data? [no]:
Data pattern [0xABCD]:
Loose, Strict, Record, Timestamp, Verbose[none]:
Sweep range of sizes [n]:
Type escape sequence to abort.
Sending 5, 100-byte ICMP Echos to 172.16.1.1, timeout is 2 seconds:
!!!!!
Success rate is 100 percent (5/5), round-trip min/avg/max = 48/48/48 ms
ISP# ping
Protocol [ip]:
Target IP address: 172.16.32.1
Repeat count [5]:
Datagram size [100]:
Timeout in seconds [2]:
Extended commands [n]: y
Source address or interface: 192.168.100.1
Type of service [0]:
Set DF bit in IP header? [no]:
Validate reply data? [no]:
Data pattern [0xABCD]:
Loose, Strict, Record, Timestamp, Verbose[none]:
```

```
Sweep range of sizes [n]:
Type escape sequence to abort.
Sending 5, 100-byte ICMP Echos to 172.16.32.1, timeout is 2 seconds:
!!!!!
Success rate is 100 percent (5/5), round-trip min/avg/max = 32/33/36 ms
ISP# ping
Protocol [ip]:
Target IP address: 172.16.1.2
Repeat count [5]:
Datagram size [100]:
Timeout in seconds [2]:
Extended commands [n]: y
Source address or interface: 192.168.100.1
Type of service [0]:
Set DF bit in IP header? [no]:
Validate reply data? [no]:
Data pattern [0xABCD]:
Loose, Strict, Record, Timestamp, Verbose[none]:
Sweep range of sizes [n]:
Type escape sequence to abort.
Sending 5, 100-byte ICMP Echos to 172.16.1.2, timeout is 2 seconds:
!!!!!
Success rate is 100 percent (5/5), round-trip min/avg/max = 32/36/56 ms
```

Complete reachability was proven between the ISP router and both SanJose1 and SanJose2.

```
ISP# ping 172.16.1.1

Type escape sequence to abort.
Sending 5, 100-byte ICMP Echos to 172.16.1.1, timeout is 2 seconds:
.....
Success rate is 0 percent (0/5)
ISP# ping 172.16.64.1

Type escape sequence to abort.
Sending 5, 100-byte ICMP Echos to 172.16.64.1, timeout is 2 seconds:
.....
Success rate is 0 percent (0/5)
```

Why did the ping requests fail?

_____

_____

_____

Step 9: BGP Next-Hop_Self

Before the ISP can successfully ping the internal serial interfaces of autonomous system 64512, two issues need to be resolved. First, SanJose1 does not know about the link between the ISP and SanJose2. Second, SanJose2 is unaware of the link between the ISP and SanJose1. This can be resolved by an advertisement of these serial links via BGP on the ISP router. This can also be resolved via Enhanced Interior Gateway Routing Protocol (EIGRP) on each of the SanJose routers. The preferred method is for the ISP to advertise these links. If they are advertised and then, at a future date, a BGP link is activated to another ISP in addition to ISP at AS 200, there is a risk of becoming a transit AS.

Issue the following commands on the ISP router:

```
ISP(config)# router bgp 200
ISP(config-router)# network 192.168.1.0 mask 255.255.255.252
ISP(config-router)# network 192.168.1.4 mask 255.255.255.252
```

Clear the IP BGP conversation with the **clear ip bgp *** command on ISP. Wait for the conversations to reestablish with each SanJose router. Issue the **show ip bgp** command to verify that the ISP router can see its own WAN links through BGP:

```
ISP# show ip bgp
BGP table version is 5, local router ID is 192.168.100.1
Status codes: s suppressed, d damped, h history, * valid, > best, i – internal
Origin codes: i - IGP, e - EGP, ? - incomplete


   Network          Next Hop          Metric LocPrf Weight Path
*  172.16.0.0       192.168.1.6                          0 64512 i
*>                  192.168.1.2            0              0 64512 i
*> 192.168.1.0/30   0.0.0.0               0          32768 i
*> 192.168.1.4/30   0.0.0.0               0          32768 i
*> 192.168.100.0    0.0.0.0               0          32768 i
```

Verify on SanJose1 and SanJose2 that the opposite WAN link is included in the routing table. The output from SanJose2 is as follows:

```
SanJose2# show ip route
Gateway of last resort is not set


     172.16.0.0/24 is subnetted, 3 subnets
C       172.16.32.0 is directly connected, Loopback0
C       172.16.1.0 is directly connected, Serial0/0/1
D       172.16.64.0 [90/20640000] via 172.16.1.1, 00:57:10, Serial0/0/1
     192.168.1.0/30 is subnetted, 2 subnets
C       192.168.1.0 is directly connected, Serial0/0/0
B       192.168.1.4 [20/0] via 192.168.1.1, 00:04:23
B    192.168.100.0/24 [20/0] via 192.168.1.1, 00:04:23
```

The next issue to consider is BGP policy routing between autonomous systems. BGP routers do not increment the next-hop address to their IBGP peers. The SanJose2 router is passing a policy to

SanJose1 and vice versa. The policy for routing from AS 64512 to AS 200 is to forward packets to the 192.168.1.1 interface. SanJose1 has a similar yet opposite policy: forwarding requests to the 192.168.1.5 interface. If either WAN link fails, it is critical that the opposite router become a valid gateway. This is only achieved if the **next-hop-self** command is configured on SanJose1 and SanJose2.

This is the output before the **next-hop-self** command was issued:

```
SanJose2# show ip bgp
BGP table version is 11, local router ID is 172.16.32.1
Status codes: s suppressed, d damped, h history, * valid, > best, i – internal
Origin codes: i - IGP, e - EGP, ? - incomplete

   Network          Next Hop          Metric LocPrf Weight Path
*> 172.16.0.0       0.0.0.0                0          32768 i
*  i192.168.1.0/30  192.168.1.5            0     100      0 200 i
*>                  192.168.1.1            0              0 200 i
*  i192.168.1.4/30  192.168.1.5            0     100      0 200 i
*>                  192.168.1.1            0              0 200 i
*  i192.168.100.0   192.168.1.5            0     100      0 200 i
*>                  192.168.1.1            0              0 200 i
```

```
SanJose1(config)# router bgp 64512
SanJose1(config-router)# neighbor 172.16.32.1 next-hop-self
```

```
SanJose2(config)# router bgp 64512
SanJose2(config-router)# neighbor 172.16.64.1 next-hop-self
```

After issuing these commands, reset BGP operation on either router with the **clear ip bgp *** command.

After the routers have returned to established BGP speakers, issue the **show ip bgp** command to validate that the next hop has also been corrected:

```
SanJose2# show ip bgp
BGP table version is 11, local router ID is 172.16.32.1
Status codes: s suppressed, d damped, h history, * valid, > best, i - internal
Origin codes: i - IGP, e - EGP, ? - incomplete

   Network          Next Hop          Metric LocPrf Weight Path
*> 172.16.0.0       0.0.0.0                0          32768 i
*  i192.168.1.0/30  172.16.64.1            0     100      0 200 i
*>                  192.168.1.1            0              0 200 i
*  i192.168.1.4/30  172.16.64.1            0     100      0 200 i
*>                  192.168.1.1            0              0 200 i
*  i192.168.100.0   172.16.64.1            0     100      0 200 i
*>                  192.168.1.1            0              0 200 i
```

Step 10: Set BGP Local Preference

At this point, everything looks good, with the exception of default routes, the outbound flow of data, and inbound packet flow.

Because the local preference value is shared between IBGP neighbors, configure a simple route map that references the local preference value on SanJose1 and SanJose2. This policy adjusts outbound traffic to prefer the link off the SanJose1 router instead of the metered T1 off SanJose2.

Issue the following commands on SanJose1 and SanJose2:

```
SanJose1(config)# route-map PRIMARY_T1_IN permit 10
SanJose1(config-route-map)# set local-preference 150
SanJose1(config-route-map)# exit
SanJose1(config)# router bgp 64512
SanJose1(config-router)# neighbor 192.168.1.5 route-map PRIMARY_T1_IN in
```

```
SanJose2(config)# route-map SECONDARY_T1_IN permit 10
SanJose2(config-route-map)# set local-preference 125
SanJose2(config-route-map)# router bgp 64512
SanJose2(config-router)# neighbor 192.168.1.1 route-map SECONDARY_T1_IN in
```

Do not forget to use the **clear ip bgp** * command after configuring this new policy. Once the conversations have been reestablished, issue the **show ip bgp** command on SanJose1 and SanJose2:

```
SanJose1# show ip bgp
```

```
BGP table version is 8, local router ID is 172.16.64.1
Status codes: s suppressed, d damped, h history, * valid, > best, i - internal
Origin codes: i - IGP, e - EGP, ? - incomplete
```

Network	Next Hop	Metric	LocPrf	Weight	Path
*>i172.16.0.0	172.16.32.1	0	100	0	i
*> 192.168.1.0/30	192.168.1.5	0	150	0	200 i
*> 192.168.1.4/30	192.168.1.5	0	150	0	200 i
*> 192.168.100.0	192.168.1.5	0	150	0	200 i

```
SanJose2# show ip bgp
```

```
BGP table version is 11, local router ID is 172.16.32.1
Status codes: s suppressed, d damped, h history, * valid, > best, i - internal
Origin codes: i - IGP, e - EGP, ? - incomplete
```

Network	Next Hop	Metric	LocPrf	Weight	Path
*> 172.16.0.0	0.0.0.0	0		32768	i
*>i192.168.1.0/30	172.16.64.1	0	150	0	200 i
*	192.168.1.1	0	125	0	200 i
*>i192.168.1.4/30	172.16.64.1	0	150	0	200 i
*	192.168.1.1	0	125	0	200 i
*>i192.168.100.0	172.16.64.1	0	150	0	200 i
*	192.168.1.1	0	125	0	200 i

This now indicates that routing to the loopback segment for ISP 192.168.100.0 /24 can be reached only through the link common to SanJose1 and ISP.

Step 11: Set BGP MED

How will traffic return from network 192.168.100.0 /24? Will it be routed through SanJose1 or SanJose2?

_____

_____

The simplest solution is to issue the **show ip bgp** command on the ISP router. What if access was not given to the ISP router? Would there be a simple way to verify before receiving the monthly bill? Traffic returning from the Internet should not be passed across the metered T1. How can it be checked instantly?

_____

_____

_____

Use an extended **ping** in this situation. Compare your output to the following:

```
SanJose2# ping
Protocol [ip]:
Target IP address: 192.168.100.1
Repeat count [5]: 2
Datagram size [100]:
Timeout in seconds [2]:
Extended commands [n]: y
Source address or interface: 172.16.32.1
Type of service [0]:
Set DF bit in IP header? [no]:
Validate reply data? [no]:
Data pattern [0xABCD]:
Loose, Strict, Record, Timestamp, Verbose[none]: record
Number of hops [ 9 ]:
Loose, Strict, Record, Timestamp, Verbose[RV]:
Sweep range of sizes [n]:
Type escape sequence to abort.
Sending 5, 100-byte ICMP Echos to 192.168.100.1, timeout is 2 seconds:
Packet has IP options:  Total option bytes= 39, padded length=40
  Record route: <*>
    (0.0.0.0)
    (0.0.0.0)
    (0.0.0.0)
    (0.0.0.0)
    (0.0.0.0)
```

```
   (0.0.0.0)
   (0.0.0.0)
   (0.0.0.0)
   (0.0.0.0)

Reply to request 0 (48 ms).  Received packet has options
 Total option bytes= 40, padded length=40
 Record route:
   (172.16.1.2)
   (192.168.1.6)
   (192.168.100.1)
   (192.168.1.1)
   (172.16.32.1) <*>
   (0.0.0.0)
   (0.0.0.0)
   (0.0.0.0)
   (0.0.0.0)
 End of list

Reply to request 1 (48 ms).  Received packet has options
 Total option bytes= 40, padded length=40
 Record route:
   (172.16.1.2)
   (192.168.1.6)
   (192.168.100.1)
   (192.168.1.1)
   (172.16.32.1) <*>
   (0.0.0.0)
   (0.0.0.0)
   (0.0.0.0)
   (0.0.0.0)
 End of list
```

If the **record** option has not been used before this, the important thing to note is that each of the IP addresses in brackets is an outgoing interface. The output can be interpreted as follows:

1. A ping that is sourced from 172.16.32.1 exits SanJose2 through the Serial0/0/1 interface, 172.16.1.2. It then arrives on the Serial0/0/1 interface on SanJose1.

2. SanJose1 routes the packet out the Serial0/0/0 interface to arrive on the Serial0/0/0 interface of ISP.

3. The target of 192.168.100.1 is reached: 192.168.100.1. The transit information in the echo request is transcribed into the echo reply, and the reply packet is sent.

4. The packet is next forwarded out the Serial0/0/1 interface for ISP and arrives on the Serial0/0/0 interface for SanJose2.

5. SanJose2 then forwards the packet out the last interface, Loopback 0, 172.16.32.1.

Although the unlimited use of the T1 from SanJose1 is preferred here, ISP prefers the link from SanJose2 for all return traffic.

The next step is to create a new policy to force router ISP to return all traffic via SanJose1. Create a second route map utilizing the MED (metric) that is shared between EBGP neighbors:

```
SanJose1(config)# route-map PRIMARY_T1_MED_OUT permit 10
SanJose1(config-route-map)# set Metric 50
SanJose1(config-route-map)# exit
SanJose1(config)# router bgp 64512
SanJose1(config-router)# neighbor 192.168.1.5 route-map PRIMARY_T1_MED_OUT out
```

```
SanJose2(config)# route-map SECONDARY_T1_MED_OUT permit 10
SanJose2(config-route-map)# set Metric 75
SanJose2(config-route-map)# exit
SanJose2(config)# router bgp 64512
SanJose2(config-router)# neighbor 192.168.1.1 route-map SECONDARY_T1_MED_OUT out
```

As before, do not forget to use the **clear ip bgp *** command after issuing this new policy. Issuing the **show ip bgp** command as follows on SanJose1 or SanJose2 does not indicate anything about this newly defined policy:

```
SanJose1# show ip bgp
BGP table version is 10, local router ID is 172.16.64.1
Status codes: s suppressed, d damped, h history, * valid, > best, i - internal
Origin codes: i - IGP, e - EGP, ? - incomplete

   Network          Next Hop          Metric LocPrf Weight Path
*>i172.16.0.0       172.16.32.1            0    100      0 i
*>  192.168.1.0/30  192.168.1.5           0    150      0 200 i
*>  192.168.1.4/30  192.168.1.5           0    150      0 200 i
*>  192.168.100.0   192.168.1.5           0    150      0 200 i
```

Now reissue an extended **ping** with a **record** option:

```
SanJose2# ping
Protocol [ip]:
Target IP address: 192.168.100.1
Repeat count [5]: 2
Datagram size [100]:
Timeout in seconds [2]:
Extended commands [n]: y
Source address or interface: 172.16.32.1
Type of service [0]:
Set DF bit in IP header? [no]:
Validate reply data? [no]:
```

```
Data pattern [0xABCD]:
Loose, Strict, Record, Timestamp, Verbose[none]: record
Number of hops [ 9 ]:
Loose, Strict, Record, Timestamp, Verbose[RV]:
Sweep range of sizes [n]:
Type escape sequence to abort.
Sending 5, 100-byte ICMP Echos to 192.168.100.1, timeout is 2 seconds:
Packet has IP options:  Total option bytes= 39, padded length=40
 Record route: <*>
    (0.0.0.0)
    (0.0.0.0)
    (0.0.0.0)
    (0.0.0.0)
    (0.0.0.0)
    (0.0.0.0)
    (0.0.0.0)
    (0.0.0.0)
    (0.0.0.0)
Reply to request 0 (64 ms).  Received packet has options
 Total option bytes= 40, padded length=40
 Record route:
    (172.16.1.2)
    (192.168.1.6)
    (192.168.100.1)
    (192.168.1.5)
    (172.16.1.1)
    (172.16.32.1) <*>
    (0.0.0.0)
    (0.0.0.0)
    (0.0.0.0)
 End of list
Reply to request 1 (64 ms).  Received packet has options
 Total option bytes= 40, padded length=40
 Record route:
    (172.16.1.2)
    (192.168.1.6)
    (192.168.100.1)
    (192.168.1.5)
    (172.16.1.1)
    (172.16.32.1) <*>
    (0.0.0.0)
    (0.0.0.0)
    (0.0.0.0)
 End of list
```

Does the output look correct? Does the 192.168.1.5 above mean that the ISP now prefers SanJose1 for return traffic?

There may not be a chance to telnet to the ISP router and to issue the **show ip bgp** command. However, the command on the opposite side of the newly configured policy MED is clear, showing that the lower value is considered best. The ISP now prefers the route with the lower MED value to AS 64512. This is just opposite from the **local-preference** command configured earlier:

```
BGP table version is 12, local router ID is 192.168.100.1

Status codes: s suppressed, d damped, h history, * valid, > best, i - internal
Origin codes: i - IGP, e - EGP, ? - incomplete

    Network          Next Hop          Metric LocPrf Weight Path
*   172.16.0.0       192.168.1.2          75             0 64512 i
*>                   192.168.1.6          50             0 64512 i
*>  192.168.1.0/30   0.0.0.0               0         32768 i
*>  192.168.1.4/30   0.0.0.0               0         32768 i
*>  192.168.100.0    0.0.0.0               0         32768 i
```

Step 12: Establish a Default Network

The final step is to establish a default route that uses a policy statement that adjusts to changes in the network. Configure both SanJose1 and SanJose2 to use the 192.168.100.0/24 network as the default network. The following output includes the routing table before the command was issued, the actual command syntax, and then the routing table after the command was issued. Do the same on the SanJose2 router.

```
SanJose1# show ip route
! Note: Prior to Default-Network Statement
Gateway of last resort is not set
     172.16.0.0/16 is variably subnetted, 4 subnets, 2 masks
D       172.16.32.0/24 [90/20640000] via 172.16.1.2, 02:43:46, Serial0/1
B       172.16.0.0/16 [200/0] via 172.16.32.1, 00:12:32
C       172.16.1.0/24 is directly connected, Serial0/1
C       172.16.64.0/24 is directly connected, Loopback0
     192.168.1.0/30 is subnetted, 2 subnets
B       192.168.1.0 [20/0] via 192.168.1.5, 00:14:05
C       192.168.1.4 is directly connected, Serial0/0
B    192.168.100.0/24 [20/0] via 192.168.1.5, 00:14:05

SanJose1(config)# ip default-network 192.168.100.0
SanJose1# show ip route
Gateway of last resort is 192.168.1.5 to network 192.168.100.0
     172.16.0.0/16 is variably subnetted, 4 subnets, 2 masks
D       172.16.32.0/24 [90/20640000] via 172.16.1.2, 02:44:09, Serial0/1
B       172.16.0.0/16 [200/0] via 172.16.32.1, 00:12:55
C       172.16.1.0/24 is directly connected, Serial0/1
```

```
C          172.16.64.0/24 is directly connected, Loopback0
        192.168.1.0/30 is subnetted, 2 subnets
B          192.168.1.0 [20/0] via 192.168.1.5, 00:14:28
C          192.168.1.4 is directly connected, Serial0/0
B*    192.168.100.0/24 [20/0] via 192.168.1.5, 00:14:29
```

What would be required to add a future T3 link on SanJose2 and for it to have preference for incoming and outgoing traffic?

_____

_____

A newly added route would be as easy as adding another route map for local preference with a value of 175 and a route map referencing a MED (metric) value of 35. Issue the **clear ip bgp *** command to complete the lab is.

TCL Verification

You can download this TCL script at www.ciscopress.com/title/1587132133 under the More Information section on the page.

```
tclsh

foreach address {
192.168.100.1
172.16.64.1
172.16.32.1
192.168.1.1
192.168.1.2
192.168.1.5
192.168.1.6
172.16.1.1
172.16.1.2
} {
ping $address }


ISP# tclsh
ISP(tcl)#
ISP(tcl)# foreach address {
+>192.168.100.1
+>172.16.64.1
+>172.16.32.1
+>192.168.1.1
+>192.168.1.2
+>192.168.1.5
+>192.168.1.6
+>172.16.1.1
```

```
+>172.16.1.2
+>} {
+>ping $address }

Type escape sequence to abort.
Sending 5, 100-byte ICMP Echos to 192.168.100.1, timeout is 2 seconds:
!!!!!
Success rate is 100 percent (5/5), round-trip min/avg/max = 1/1/4 ms
Type escape sequence to abort.
Sending 5, 100-byte ICMP Echos to 172.16.64.1, timeout is 2 seconds:
!!!!!
Success rate is 100 percent (5/5), round-trip min/avg/max = 28/28/28 ms
Type escape sequence to abort.
Sending 5, 100-byte ICMP Echos to 172.16.32.1, timeout is 2 seconds:
!!!!!
Success rate is 100 percent (5/5), round-trip min/avg/max = 56/56/56 ms
Type escape sequence to abort.
Sending 5, 100-byte ICMP Echos to 192.168.1.1, timeout is 2 seconds:
!!!!!
Success rate is 100 percent (5/5), round-trip min/avg/max = 56/57/64 ms
Type escape sequence to abort.
Sending 5, 100-byte ICMP Echos to 192.168.1.2, timeout is 2 seconds:
!!!!!
Success rate is 100 percent (5/5), round-trip min/avg/max = 28/28/32 ms
Type escape sequence to abort.
Sending 5, 100-byte ICMP Echos to 192.168.1.5, timeout is 2 seconds:
!!!!!
Success rate is 100 percent (5/5), round-trip min/avg/max = 56/56/56 ms
Type escape sequence to abort.
Sending 5, 100-byte ICMP Echos to 192.168.1.6, timeout is 2 seconds:
!!!!!
Success rate is 100 percent (5/5), round-trip min/avg/max = 28/28/32 ms
Type escape sequence to abort.
Sending 5, 100-byte ICMP Echos to 172.16.1.1, timeout is 2 seconds:
!!!!!
Success rate is 100 percent (5/5), round-trip min/avg/max = 28/28/28 ms
Type escape sequence to abort.
Sending 5, 100-byte ICMP Echos to 172.16.1.2, timeout is 2 seconds:
!!!!!
Success rate is 100 percent (5/5), round-trip min/avg/max = 56/56/60 ms
ISP(tcl)# tclquit
SanJose1# tclsh
SanJose1(tcl)#
SanJose1(tcl)# foreach address {
```

```
+>192.168.100.1
+>172.16.64.1
+>172.16.32.1
+>192.168.1.1
+>192.168.1.2
+>192.168.1.5
+>192.168.1.6
+>172.16.1.1
+>172.16.1.2
+>} {
+>ping $address }

Type escape sequence to abort.
Sending 5, 100-byte ICMP Echos to 192.168.100.1, timeout is 2 seconds:
!!!!!
Success rate is 100 percent (5/5), round-trip min/avg/max = 28/28/32 ms
Type escape sequence to abort.
Sending 5, 100-byte ICMP Echos to 172.16.64.1, timeout is 2 seconds:
!!!!!
Success rate is 100 percent (5/5), round-trip min/avg/max = 1/1/4 ms
Type escape sequence to abort.
Sending 5, 100-byte ICMP Echos to 172.16.32.1, timeout is 2 seconds:
!!!!!
Success rate is 100 percent (5/5), round-trip min/avg/max = 28/28/32 ms
Type escape sequence to abort.
Sending 5, 100-byte ICMP Echos to 192.168.1.1, timeout is 2 seconds:
!!!!!
Success rate is 100 percent (5/5), round-trip min/avg/max = 28/28/28 ms
Type escape sequence to abort.
Sending 5, 100-byte ICMP Echos to 192.168.1.2, timeout is 2 seconds:
!!!!!
Success rate is 100 percent (5/5), round-trip min/avg/max = 40/43/44 ms
Type escape sequence to abort.
Sending 5, 100-byte ICMP Echos to 192.168.1.5, timeout is 2 seconds:
!!!!!
Success rate is 100 percent (5/5), round-trip min/avg/max = 28/28/32 ms
Type escape sequence to abort.
Sending 5, 100-byte ICMP Echos to 192.168.1.6, timeout is 2 seconds:
!!!!!
Success rate is 100 percent (5/5), round-trip min/avg/max = 56/58/68 ms
Type escape sequence to abort.
Sending 5, 100-byte ICMP Echos to 172.16.1.1, timeout is 2 seconds:
!!!!!
Success rate is 100 percent (5/5), round-trip min/avg/max = 56/56/56 ms
```

```
Type escape sequence to abort.
Sending 5, 100-byte ICMP Echos to 172.16.1.2, timeout is 2 seconds:
!!!!!
Success rate is 100 percent (5/5), round-trip min/avg/max = 28/28/28 ms
SanJose1(tcl)# tclquit
```

```
SanJose2# tclsh
SanJose2(tcl)#
SanJose2(tcl)# foreach address {
+>192.168.100.1
+>172.16.64.1
+>172.16.32.1
+>192.168.1.1
+>192.168.1.2
+>192.168.1.5
+>192.168.1.6
+>172.16.1.1
+>172.16.1.2
+>} {
+>ping $address }

Type escape sequence to abort.
Sending 5, 100-byte ICMP Echos to 192.168.100.1, timeout is 2 seconds:
!!!!!
Success rate is 100 percent (5/5), round-trip min/avg/max = 56/56/56 ms
Type escape sequence to abort.
Sending 5, 100-byte ICMP Echos to 172.16.64.1, timeout is 2 seconds:
!!!!!
Success rate is 100 percent (5/5), round-trip min/avg/max = 28/28/32 ms
Type escape sequence to abort.
Sending 5, 100-byte ICMP Echos to 172.16.32.1, timeout is 2 seconds:
!!!!!
Success rate is 100 percent (5/5), round-trip min/avg/max = 1/1/4 ms
Type escape sequence to abort.
Sending 5, 100-byte ICMP Echos to 192.168.1.1, timeout is 2 seconds:
!!!!!
Success rate is 100 percent (5/5), round-trip min/avg/max = 28/28/32 ms
Type escape sequence to abort.
Sending 5, 100-byte ICMP Echos to 192.168.1.2, timeout is 2 seconds:
!!!!!
Success rate is 100 percent (5/5), round-trip min/avg/max = 56/56/56 ms
Type escape sequence to abort.
Sending 5, 100-byte ICMP Echos to 192.168.1.5, timeout is 2 seconds:
!!!!!
Success rate is 100 percent (5/5), round-trip min/avg/max = 56/56/56 ms
```

```
Type escape sequence to abort.
Sending 5, 100-byte ICMP Echos to 192.168.1.6, timeout is 2 seconds:
!!!!!
Success rate is 100 percent (5/5), round-trip min/avg/max = 28/30/36 ms
Type escape sequence to abort.
Sending 5, 100-byte ICMP Echos to 172.16.1.1, timeout is 2 seconds:
!!!!!
Success rate is 100 percent (5/5), round-trip min/avg/max = 28/28/32 ms
Type escape sequence to abort.
Sending 5, 100-byte ICMP Echos to 172.16.1.2, timeout is 2 seconds:
!!!!!
Success rate is 100 percent (5/5), round-trip min/avg/max = 56/57/64 ms
SanJose2(tcl)# tclquit
```

Lab 6-4: BGP Route Reflectors and Route Filters (6.7.4)

In this lab, you will configure IBGP routers to use a route reflector and a simple route filter.

Figure 6-4 illustrates the topology that will be used for this lab.

Figure 6-4   Topology Diagram

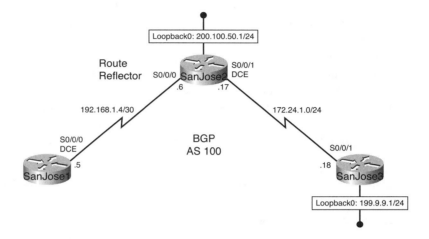

Scenario

The International Travel Agency maintains a full-mesh IBGP network that has quickly scaled beyond 100 routers. The company wants to implement route reflectors to work around the full-mesh IBGP requirement. Configure a small cluster and observe how BGP operates in this configuration. Use IP prefix filters to control the updates between IBGP peers.

Step 1: Configure RIPv2

Build and configure the network according to the diagram, and use Routing Information Protocol Version 2 (RIPv2) as the Interior Gateway Protocol (IGP). Do not configure the 199.9.9.0 network under the RIP process. Use **ping** to test connectivity among all interfaces. Each router should have a complete routing table:

```
SanJose1(config)# router rip

SanJose1(config-router)# version 2

SanJose1(config-router)# no auto-summary

SanJose1(config-router)# network 192.168.1.0
```

```
SanJose2(config)# router rip

SanJose2(config-router)# version 2

SanJose2(config-router)# no auto-summary

SanJose2(config-router)# network 172.24.0.0

SanJose2(config-router)# network 192.168.1.0

SanJose2(config-router)# network 200.100.50.0
```

```
SanJose3(config)# router rip

SanJose3(config-router)# version 2
```

```
SanJose3(config-router)# no auto-summary
SanJose3(config-router)# network 172.24.0.0
```

Step 2: IBGP Peers and Route Reflectors

In this lab, you will configure a route reflector. By default, a router that receives an EBGP route will advertise it to its IBGP peers. However, if it receives it through IBGP, it will not advertise it to its IBGP peers. This is a loop-prevention mechanism. However, because of this behavior, the only way for all IBGP routers to receive a route once it is originated into the AS is to have a full mesh of IBGP peers. This can get messy with a large number of peers. To get around this limitation of IBGP, we can use a route reflector. A route reflector allows a topology to get around the IBGP limitation of having to have a full mesh. To do this, a route reflector specifies its neighbors as route reflector clients. When a route reflector receives an update from a route reflector client, it can pass it on to its other clients. This greatly simplifies configuration because only the route reflector needs to know all the other peers. The clients don't even know that they are clients. To them, it is just a normal IBGP peering relationship. You can even set up multiple route reflectors in a more advanced configuration for redundancy.

Configure the IBGP peers for BGP. Later, you will configure SanJose2 as the route reflector. However, first configure it to peer with both of the other routers:

```
SanJose2(config)# router bgp 100
SanJose2(config-router)# neighbor 192.168.1.5 remote-as 100
SanJose2(config-router)# neighbor 172.24.1.18 remote-as 100
SanJose2(config-router)# network 200.100.50.0
SanJose2(config-router)# network 172.24.1.0 mask 255.255.255.0
SanJose2(config-router)# network 192.168.1.4 mask 255.255.255.252
```

After SanJose2 is configured, configure the other two routers as route reflector clients. Remember that to set up clients simply configure peering between the client and the server. IBGP does not need to be configured to a full mesh.

Issue the following commands on SanJose1:

```
SanJose1(config)# router bgp 100
SanJose1(config-router)# neighbor 192.168.1.6 remote-as 100
```

Issue the following commands on SanJose3:

```
SanJose3(config)# router bgp 100
SanJose3(config-router)# neighbor 172.24.1.17 remote-as 100
```

Verify that SanJose2 has established a peering relationship with both SanJose1 and SanJose3. Troubleshoot as necessary.

SanJose1 and SanJose3 should not have established a connection. Why?

_____

_____

_____

_____

Step 3: Inject an External Route into BGP

To observe the full effect of using a route reflector, configure SanJose3 to inject external routing information into BGP:

```
SanJose3(config)# int lo0
SanJose3(config-if)# ip address 199.9.9.1 255.255.255.0
SanJose3(config)# router bgp 100
SanJose3(config-router)# network 199.9.9.0
```

This configuration forces SanJose3 to inject the external route 199.9.9.0 into BGP. Use the **show ip route** command to check if SanJose2 has picked up this route through BGP. SanJose2 should have a route to 199.9.9.0.

Is the next hop for this route 172.24.1.18?

_____

Verify that you can ping 199.9.9.1 from SanJose3. If not, troubleshoot.

Now check the routing table of SanJose1. There should not be a route to 199.9.9.0. Why?

_____

Remember that SanJose1 is not configured to peer with SanJose3. To eliminate the need for a full IBGP mesh, SanJose2 must be configured as a route reflector. Issue the following commands on SanJose2:

```
SanJose2(config)# router bgp 100
SanJose2(config-router)# neighbor 192.168.1.5 route-reflector-client
SanJose2(config-router)# neighbor 172.24.1.18 route-reflector-client
```

Verify that an IBGP cluster was successfully created by issuing the **show ip protocols** command on SanJose2. The output of this command should indicate that SanJose2 is a route reflector.

How many clients does SanJose2 have?

_____

Issue the **show ip protocols** command on SanJose1. The output of this command does not include information about route reflectors. Remember that SanJose1 is a client and not a route reflector server, so it is unaware of route reflection.

Finally, verify that route reflection is working by checking the routing table on SanJose1. SanJose1 will have a route to network 199.9.9.0.

Is 172.24.1.18 the IP address of the next hop of this route on the SanJose1 table?

_____

Notice that SanJose1 is not directly connected to the IP network for the next hop. Why?

Hint: From which router did SanJose1 learn the route?

_____

Ping 199.9.9.1 from SanJose1. This ping should be successful.

Notice that SanJose1 pings 199.9.9.1 even though the next-hop address is not on a directly connected network. For example, the next-hop address could be 172.24.1.18.

Step 4: Inject a Summary Address into BGP

For the purpose of this lab, configure SanJose3 to inject a summary address into BGP:

```
SanJose3(config)# router bgp 100
SanJose3(config-router)# aggregate-address 199.0.0.0 255.0.0.0
```

BGP should now send the supernet route 199.0.0.0/8 to SanJose2 with the attribute ATOMIC_AGGREGATE set.

On SanJose2, issue the following command:

```
SanJose2# show ip bgp 199.0.0.0
BGP routing table entry for 199.0.0.0/8, version 6
Paths: (1 available, best # 1)
Bestpath transition flag: 0x208
                Advertised to non peer-group peers:
                192.168.1.5
  Local, (aggregated by 100 172.24.1.18), (Received from a RR-client)
    172.24.1.18 from 172.24.1.18 (172.24.1.18)
      Origin IGP, localpref 100, valid, internal, atomic-aggregate, best,
      ref 2
```

According to the output of this command, what address aggregated this route?

_____

What indicates that route reflection is involved in this process?

_____

Is there an indication that the ATOMIC_AGGREGATE attribute has been set?

_____

SanJose2 should, in turn, reflect this route to SanJose1. Check both the routing table and BGP table on SanJose1 to be sure. Both the route to 199.9.9.0 and the supernet route 199.0.0.0 should be installed in the SanJose1 routing table and the BGP table.

The International Travel Agency has decided to filter specific routes to the 199.0.0.0/8 address space. Configure a route filter to prevent SanJose2 from sending the 199.9.9.0/24 route to its other clients, in this case to SanJose1.

Issue the following commands on SanJose2:

```
SanJose2(config)# ip prefix-list supernetonly permit 199.0.0.0/8
SanJose2(config)# ip prefix-list supernetonly permit 172.24.1.0/24
SanJose2(config)# ip prefix-list supernetonly permit 200.100.50.0/24
SanJose2(config)# router bgp 100
SanJose2(config-router)# neighbor 192.168.1.5 prefix-list supernetonly out
```

Return to SanJose1, issue the **clear ip bgp** * command, and verify that the prefix list has done its job by issuing a **show ip bgp** command. Troubleshoot as necessary.

Unlike before, where routes to 199.9.9.0 and 199.0.0.0 were present, now only one route to 199.0.0.0 in the routing and BGP tables should be seen. Troubleshoot as necessary.

TCL Verification

You can download this TCL script at www.ciscopress.com/title/1587132133 under the More Information section on the page.

```
SanJose1# tclsh

SanJose1(tcl)#

SanJose1(tcl)# foreach address {

+>200.100.50.1

+>199.9.9.1

+>192.168.1.5

+>192.168.1.6

+>172.24.1.17

+>172.24.1.18

+>} {

+>ping $address }


Type escape sequence to abort.

Sending 5, 100-byte ICMP Echos to 200.100.50.1, timeout is 2 seconds:

!!!!!

Success rate is 100 percent (5/5), round-trip min/avg/max = 28/28/32 ms

Type escape sequence to abort.

Sending 5, 100-byte ICMP Echos to 199.9.9.1, timeout is 2 seconds:

!!!!!

Success rate is 100 percent (5/5), round-trip min/avg/max = 56/56/60 ms

Type escape sequence to abort.

Sending 5, 100-byte ICMP Echos to 192.168.1.5, timeout is 2 seconds:

!!!!!

Success rate is 100 percent (5/5), round-trip min/avg/max = 56/57/64 ms

Type escape sequence to abort.

Sending 5, 100-byte ICMP Echos to 192.168.1.6, timeout is 2 seconds:

!!!!!

Success rate is 100 percent (5/5), round-trip min/avg/max = 28/28/32 ms

Type escape sequence to abort.

Sending 5, 100-byte ICMP Echos to 172.24.1.17, timeout is 2 seconds:

!!!!!

Success rate is 100 percent (5/5), round-trip min/avg/max = 28/28/28 ms

Type escape sequence to abort.

Sending 5, 100-byte ICMP Echos to 172.24.1.18, timeout is 2 seconds:

!!!!!
```

```
Success rate is 100 percent (5/5), round-trip min/avg/max = 56/56/56 ms
SanJose1(tcl)# tclquit
```

```
SanJose2# tclsh
SanJose2(tcl)#
SanJose2(tcl)# foreach address {
+>200.100.50.1
+>199.9.9.1
+>192.168.1.5
+>192.168.1.6
+>172.24.1.17
+>172.24.1.18
+>} {
+>ping $address }

Type escape sequence to abort.
Sending 5, 100-byte ICMP Echos to 200.100.50.1, timeout is 2 seconds:
!!!!!
Success rate is 100 percent (5/5), round-trip min/avg/max = 1/1/1 ms
Type escape sequence to abort.
Sending 5, 100-byte ICMP Echos to 199.9.9.1, timeout is 2 seconds:
!!!!!
Success rate is 100 percent (5/5), round-trip min/avg/max = 28/28/32 ms
Type escape sequence to abort.
Sending 5, 100-byte ICMP Echos to 192.168.1.5, timeout is 2 seconds:
!!!!!
Success rate is 100 percent (5/5), round-trip min/avg/max = 28/28/28 ms
Type escape sequence to abort.
Sending 5, 100-byte ICMP Echos to 192.168.1.6, timeout is 2 seconds:
!!!!!
Success rate is 100 percent (5/5), round-trip min/avg/max = 56/58/64 ms
Type escape sequence to abort.
Sending 5, 100-byte ICMP Echos to 172.24.1.17, timeout is 2 seconds:
!!!!!
Success rate is 100 percent (5/5), round-trip min/avg/max = 56/58/64 ms
Type escape sequence to abort.
Sending 5, 100-byte ICMP Echos to 172.24.1.18, timeout is 2 seconds:
!!!!!
Success rate is 100 percent (5/5), round-trip min/avg/max = 28/28/28 ms
SanJose2(tcl)# tclquit
```

```
SanJose3# tclsh
SanJose3(tcl)#
SanJose3(tcl)# foreach address {
+>200.100.50.1
+>199.9.9.1
```

```
+>192.168.1.5
+>192.168.1.6
+>172.24.1.17
+>172.24.1.18
+>} {
+>ping $address }

Type escape sequence to abort.
Sending 5, 100-byte ICMP Echos to 200.100.50.1, timeout is 2 seconds:
!!!!!
Success rate is 100 percent (5/5), round-trip min/avg/max = 28/28/32 ms
Type escape sequence to abort.
Sending 5, 100-byte ICMP Echos to 199.9.9.1, timeout is 2 seconds:
!!!!!
Success rate is 100 percent (5/5), round-trip min/avg/max = 1/1/4 ms
Type escape sequence to abort.
Sending 5, 100-byte ICMP Echos to 192.168.1.5, timeout is 2 seconds:
!!!!!
Success rate is 100 percent (5/5), round-trip min/avg/max = 56/56/56 ms
Type escape sequence to abort.
Sending 5, 100-byte ICMP Echos to 192.168.1.6, timeout is 2 seconds:
!!!!!
Success rate is 100 percent (5/5), round-trip min/avg/max = 28/28/32 ms
Type escape sequence to abort.
Sending 5, 100-byte ICMP Echos to 172.24.1.17, timeout is 2 seconds:
!!!!!
Success rate is 100 percent (5/5), round-trip min/avg/max = 28/28/32 ms
Type escape sequence to abort.
Sending 5, 100-byte ICMP Echos to 172.24.1.18, timeout is 2 seconds:
!!!!!
Success rate is 100 percent (5/5), round-trip min/avg/max = 56/63/92 ms
SanJose3(tcl)# tclquit
```

CHAPTER 7

IP Multicasting

Lab 7-1: Implementing IGMP and IGMP Snooping (7.5.1)

The objectives of this lab are as follows:

- Configure Internet Group Management Protocol (IGMP) to join interfaces to a multicast group
- Verify the operation of IGMP at Layer 3
- Analyze IGMP packets and packets sent to multicast groups
- Enable Protocol Independent Multicast dense mode (PIM-DM)
- Verify the operation of IGMP snooping on a Catalyst switch

Figure 7-1 illustrates the topology that will be used for this lab.

Figure 7-1   Topology Diagram for Lab 7-1

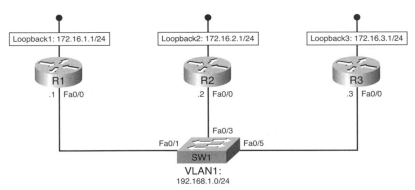

Scenario

Configure IGMP to listen to the multicast group 229.7.7.7 on R2 and R3. Send multicast traffic from R1 to the LAN segment. Configure IGMP snooping to efficiently send multicast traffic through the switch.

Review IGMP, PIM-DM, and IGMP snooping in your course materials before completing this lab.

Overview

This set of multicast labs builds skills in working with multicast features and routing protocols so that the student can confidently configure PIM in sparse-dense mode. Sparse-dense mode is simply PIM sparse mode (PIM-SM) with a dense mode fallback control mechanism.

To grasp the principles involved in sparse-dense mode, students must understand the principles involved with IGMP and PIM routing protocols at Layer 3. Thus, considerable lab time will be spent understanding IGMP as well as each of the PIM protocols. IGMP snooping greatly improves multicast efficiency at Layer 2 and therefore receives thorough treatment.

Step 1: Configure Hosts on a LAN

Configure the basic addressing scheme in the diagram on each router. Disable IP routing using the **no ip routing** command. This command forces a router to act as a host connected to a specific VLAN via the switch. Routing between networks is not performed:

```
R1# configure terminal
R1(config)# no ip routing
R1(config)# interface fastethernet 0/0
R1(config-if)# ip address 192.168.1.1 255.255.255.0
R1(config-if)# no shutdown
R1(config-if)# interface loopback 1
R1(config-if)# ip address 172.16.1.1 255.255.255.0
```

```
R2# configure terminal
R2(config)# no ip routing
R2(config)# interface fastethernet 0/0
R2(config-if)# ip address 192.168.1.2 255.255.255.0
R2(config-if)# no shutdown
R2(config-if)# interface loopback 2
R2(config-if)# ip address 172.16.2.1 255.255.255.0
```

```
R3# configure terminal
R3(config)# no ip routing
R3(config)# interface fastethernet 0/0
R3(config-if)# ip address 192.168.1.3 255.255.255.0
R3(config-if)# no shutdown
R3(config-if)# interface loopback 3
R3(config-if)# ip address 172.16.3.1 255.255.255.0
```

With routing disabled, will the routers redirect packets between remote addresses on connected subnets?

_____

Reload the switch with a blank configuration file and erase the vlan.dat file in flash memory. By default, all connected ports are assigned to VLAN 1.

Step 2: Subscribe Interfaces to Multicast Groups with IGMP

In IP multicast, hosts use the IGMP to join and leave groups and to respond to membership queries.

Debug IP IGMP and all IP packets on all routers. This allows you to see any IGMP messages sent or received by any of the routers.

```
R1# debug ip igmp
R1# debug ip packet
```

```
R2# debug ip igmp
R2# debug ip packet
```

```
R3# debug ip igmp
R3# debug ip packet
```

On R1, issue the **ip igmp join-group** *group_address* command in interface configuration mode for FastEthernet 0/0:

```
R1# configure terminal
R1(config)# interface fastethernet 0/0
R1(config-if)# ip igmp join-group 229.7.7.7
```

```
*Nov  3 20:54:57.114: IGMP(0): WAVL Insert group: 229.7.7.7 interface:
FastEthernet0/0Successful
*Nov  3 20:54:57.114: IGMP(0): Send v2 Report for 229.7.7.7 on FastEthernet0/0
*Nov  3 20:54:57.114: IP: s=192.168.1.1 (local), d=229.7.7.7 (FastEthernet0/0), len
28, sending broad/multicast
```

The **ip igmp join-group** command sends an IGMPv2 join message to the group-specific address, which is then propagated to all reachable members of the specified group. This message states that multicast traffic destined for the group should be forwarded to the local router's IP address. Because none of the other routers are listening to the 229.7.7.7 group at this point, R2 and R3 do not receive a broadcast sent to the group.

Issue the **show ip igmp interface** *interface_type interface_number* command on R1:

```
R1# show ip igmp interface fastethernet 0/0
FastEthernet0/0 is up, line protocol is up
  Internet address is 192.168.1.1/24
  IGMP is enabled on interface
  Current IGMP host version is 2
  Current IGMP router version is 2
  IGMP query interval is 60 seconds
  IGMP querier timeout is 120 seconds
  IGMP max query response time is 10 seconds
  Last member query count is 2
  Last member query response interval is 1000 ms
  Inbound IGMP access group is not set
  IGMP activity: 1 joins, 0 leaves
  Multicast routing is disabled on interface
  Multicast TTL threshold is 0
  Multicast groups joined by this system (number of users):
      229.7.7.7(1)
```

Which version of IGMP is R1's FastEthernet interface using?

_____

Remove the **ip igmp join-group** command from R1's FastEthernet 0/0 interface because it is not used for the remainder of this lab:

```
R1(config)# interface fastethernet 0/0
R1(config-if)# no ip igmp join-group 229.7.7.7
```

```
*Nov  3 20:59:10.582: IGMP(0): IGMP delete group 229.7.7.7 on FastEthernet0/0
*Nov  3 20:59:10.582: IGMP(0): Send Leave for 229.7.7.7 on FastEthernet0/0
*Nov  3 20:59:10.582: IP: s=192.168.1.1 (local), d=224.0.0.2 (FastEthernet0/0), len
28, sending broad/multicast
```

Note that the IGMPv2 leave messages are sent to 224.0.0.2, the link-local multicast group representing all routers on the subnet.

Use R1 as the originator of multicast traffic to the group 229.7.7.7, but do not subscribe it to the group. Use IGMP to subscribe R2 and R3 to the 229.7.7.7 group. If you turned debugging off on R2 and R3, re-enable debugging on both routers to watch the IGMP messages. Keep debugging on for IGMP and IP packets through the end of Step 4:

```
R2# debug ip igmp

R2# debug ip packet
```

```
R3# debug ip igmp

R3# debug ip packet
```

```
R2(config-if)# ip igmp join-group 229.7.7.7

*Nov  4 04:59:59.340: IGMP(0): WAVL Insert group: 229.7.7.7 interface: FastEther-
net0/0Successful

*Nov  4 04:59:59.340: IGMP(0): Send v2 Report for 229.7.7.7 on FastEthernet0/0

*Nov  4 04:59:59.340: IP: s=192.168.1.2 (local), d=229.7.7.7 (FastEthernet0/0), len
28, sending broad/multicast
```

```
R3(config-if)# ip igmp join-group 229.7.7.7

*Nov  4 05:02:11.696: IGMP(0): WAVL Insert group: 229.7.7.7 interface: FastEther-
net0/0Successful

*Nov  4 05:02:11.700: IGMP(0): Send v2 Report for 229.7.7.7 on FastEthernet0/0

*Nov  4 05:02:11.700: IP: s=192.168.1.3 (local), d=229.7.7.7 (FastEthernet0/0), len
28, sending broad/multicast
```

Display the IGMP groups to which R2 and R3 have subscribed with the **show ip igmp groups** and **show ip igmp membership** commands. Verify that the specified groups are being received:

```
R2# show ip igmp groups

IGMP Connected Group Membership

Group Address Interface       Uptime    Expires  Last Reporter  Group Accounted

229.7.7.7     FastEthernet0/0 00:07:56  stopped  192.168.1.2
```

```
R2# show ip igmp membership

Flags: A  - aggregate, T - tracked
       L  - Local, S - static, V - virtual, R - Reported through v3
       I  - v3lite, U - Urd, M - SSM (S,G) channel
       1,2,3 - The version of IGMP the group is in
Channel/Group-Flags:
       / - Filtering entry (Exclude mode (S,G), Include mode (*,G))
Reporter:
       <mac-or-ip-address> - last reporter if group is not explicitly tracked
       <n>/<m>     - <n> reporter in include mode, <m> reporter in exclude
```

```
Channel/Group                Reporter          Uptime  Exp.  Flags  Interface
*,229.7.7.7                  192.168.1.2       00:08:27 stop  2LA    Fa0/0
```

```
R3# show ip igmp groups
IGMP Connected Group Membership
Group Address Interface       Uptime   Expires   Last Reporter Group Accounted
229.7.7.7      FastEthernet0/0 00:09:00 stopped   192.168.1.3
```

```
R3# show ip igmp membership
Flags: A  - aggregate, T - tracked
       L  - Local, S - static, V - virtual, R - Reported through v3
       I  - v3lite, U - Urd, M - SSM (S,G) channel
       1,2,3 - The version of IGMP the group is in
Channel/Group-Flags:
       / - Filtering entry (Exclude mode (S,G), Include mode (*,G))
Reporter:
       <mac-or-ip-address> - last reporter if group is not explicitly tracked
       <n>/<m>        - <n> reporter in include mode, <m> reporter in exclude


Channel/Group                Reporter          Uptime  Exp.  Flags  Interface
*,229.7.7.7                  192.168.1.3       00:09:27 stop  2LA    Fa0/0
```

From R1, ping the multicast group 229.7.7.7. The output should appear similar to the following with debugging turned on:

```
R1# ping 229.7.7.7


Type escape sequence to abort.
Sending 1, 100-byte ICMP Echos to 229.7.7.7, timeout is 2 seconds:


*Nov  4 16:10:18.413: IP: s=192.168.1.1 (local), d=229.7.7.7 (FastEthernet0/0), len
100, sending broad/multicast
*Nov  4 16:10:18.413: IP: s=172.16.1.1 (local), d=229.7.7.7 (Loopback1), len 100,
sending broad/multicast
*Nov  4 16:10:18.413: IP: s=192.168.1.3 (FastEthernet0/0), d=192.168.1.1, len 100,
rcvd 1
*Nov  4 16:10:18.413: IP: s=192.168.1.2 (FastEthernet0/0), d=192.168.1.1, len 100,
rcvd 1
Reply to request 0 from 192.168.1.3, 1 ms
Reply to request 0 from 192.168.1.2, 1 ms
```

The preceding output indicates the expected result of a successful multicast ping—echo replies from all members of the multicast group. Notice that the ping is sent out all interfaces, including the loopback interface on R1. Because there could technically be multicast listeners to that group on other connected subnets or even remote networks, multicasts must be flooded out all interfaces, unless a multicast routing protocol informs the router that this is unnecessary.

If R2 and R3 received the multicast ping, how did SW1 treat the ping at OSI Layer 2?

_____

_____

To which address did R2 and R3 send their replies?

_____

_____

_____

Is this a unicast or multicast address?

_____

Ping from R2 to the multicast group. From which hosts do you expect replies?

_____

_____

If the output of your ping has only one reply, as demonstrated in the following output, re-issue the ping. With unicast pings, the first ping usually times out due to the delay at Layer 2 caused by the Address Resolution Protocol (ARP) request from the source to the destination.

R2# **ping 229.7.7.7**

Type escape sequence to abort.

Sending 1, 100-byte ICMP Echos to 229.7.7.7, timeout is 2 seconds:

Reply to request 0 from 192.168.1.2, 1 ms

For R3 to send the ICMP echo reply to 192.168.1.2, it needs to locate a MAC address for that IP address via ARP. Thus, the ARP request from the multicast listener to the multicast receiver may cause the ICMP echo to time out at the source. Try to ping again with the same command. You should now receive all ICMP echo replies, as follows:

R2# **ping 229.7.7.7**

Type escape sequence to abort.

Sending 1, 100-byte ICMP Echos to 229.7.7.7, timeout is 2 seconds:

*Nov 4 16:19:28.117: IP: s=192.168.1.2 (local), d=229.7.7.7 (FastEthernet0/0), len 100, sending broad/multicast

*Nov 4 16:19:28.117: IP: s=172.16.2.1 (local), d=229.7.7.7 (Loopback2), len 100, sending broad/multicast

*Nov 4 16:19:28.117: IP: s=192.168.1.2 (FastEthernet0/0), d=229.7.7.7, len 100, rcvd 1

*Nov 4 16:19:28.117: IP: tableid=0, s=192.168.1.2 (local), d=192.168.1.2 (FastEthernet0/0), routed via RIB

*Nov 4 16:19:28.117: IP: s=192.168.1.2 (local), d=192.168.1.2 (FastEthernet0/0), len 100, sending

*Nov 4 16:19:28.121: IP: s=192.168.1.3 (FastEthernet0/0), d=192.168.1.2, len 100, rcvd 1

```
*Nov  4 16:19:28.121: IP: s=192.168.1.2 (FastEthernet0/0), d=192.168.1.2, len 100,
rcvd 1
Reply to request 0 from 192.168.1.3, 4 ms
Reply to request 0 from 192.168.1.2, 4 ms
```

For more information on IP multicast and IGMP, see RFC 1112 and RFC 2236:
http://www.ietf.org/rfc/rfc1112.txt and http://www.ietf.org/rfc/rfc2236.txt.

Step 3: Verify IGMP Snooping on the Switch

Up to this point, multicast has been simplified to be multicast hosts on a broadcast, multi-access medium of a switched VLAN. The switch treated these multicast packets as broadcasts at Layer 2 and forwarded them to every host on the VLAN, regardless of whether that host was subscribed to the group. Sending traffic to every host on the subnet effectively reduces multicasting to broadcasting with a different destination address. Multicast switching in an enterprise network should be designed in a more intelligent way at Layer 2.

Layer 2 switches can use IGMP snooping to constrain the flooding of multicast traffic by dynamically configuring Layer 2 interfaces. Multicast traffic is then forwarded to only those interfaces associated with IP multicast devices. IGMP snooping requires the LAN switch to snoop on the IGMP transmissions between the host and the router and to track multicast groups and member ports. When the switch receives an IGMP report from a host for a particular multicast group, the switch adds the host port number to the forwarding table entry. When it receives an IGMP Leave Group message from a host, it removes the host port from the table entry. It also periodically deletes entries if it does not receive IGMP membership reports from the multicast clients.

The multicast router sends out periodic IGMP general queries to all VLANs. When IGMP snooping is enabled, the switch responds to the router queries with only one join request per MAC multicast group, and the switch creates one entry per VLAN in the Layer 2 forwarding table for each MAC group from which it receives an IGMP join request. All hosts interested in this multicast traffic send join requests and are added to the forwarding table entry.

Layer 2 multicast groups learned through IGMP snooping are dynamic. However, you can statically configure MAC multicast groups by using the **ip igmp snooping vlan static** global configuration command. If you specify group membership for a multicast group address statically, your setting supersedes any automatic manipulation by IGMP snooping. Multicast group membership lists can consist of both user-defined and IGMP snooping-learned settings.

If a port spanning-tree, a port group, or a VLAN ID change occurs, the IGMP snooping-learned multicast groups from this port on the VLAN are deleted.

IGMP snooping is enabled on Catalyst switches by default.

Issue the **show ip igmp snooping** command on SW1:

```
SW1# show ip igmp snooping
vlan 1
----------
  IGMP snooping is globally enabled
  IGMP snooping is enabled on this Vlan
  IGMP snooping immediate-leave is disabled on this Vlan
  IGMP snooping mrouter learn mode is pim-dvmrp on this Vlan
  IGMP snooping is running in IGMP_ONLY mode on this Vlan
```

Notice that IGMP snooping is enabled by default globally and on a per-VLAN basis on SW1. In this case, IGMP snooping identifies a switchport as a multicast router port only if it sees PIM or Distance Vector Multicast Routing Protocol (DVMRP) messages sent toward the switch on that port.

IGMP snooping only subscribes other switchports to multicast groups at Layer 2 if it sees IGMP messages sent to the multicast router. Until you configure a supported multicast routing protocol (PIM or DVMRP) on the multicast router R1, IGMP snooping does not create MAC address table entries for the multicast groups. Verify this with the **show mac-address-table multicast** command on SW1:

```
SW1# show mac-address-table multicast

Vlan    Mac Address     Type     Ports
----    -----------     ----     -----

SW1#
```

Step 4: Configure a Multicast-Enabled Router on the VLAN

First, enable IP routing on R1 with the **ip routing** command:

```
R1(config)# ip routing
```

Enable multicast routing on R1 using the **ip multicast-routing** command in global configuration mode, which is similar to the **ip routing** command. The **ip multicast-routing** command allows R1 to start obtaining current information on multicast groups, sources, destination, and routing patterns:

```
R1(config)# ip multicast-routing
```

Enable PIM-DM on R1's FastEthernet 0/0 interface with the **ip pim dense-mode** command. Identify the output with debugging turned on:

```
R1(config-if)# ip pim dense-mode
R1(config-if)#

*Nov  5 00:28:24.687: IP: s=192.168.1.1 (local), d=224.0.0.13 (FastEthernet0/0), len
54, sending broad/multicast
```

PIM attempts to make adjacencies out interfaces on which it is enabled. The multicast packet to 224.0.0.13 equates with a PIM Hello packet to all PIM-enabled routers on the subnet:

```
R1(config-if)#

*Nov  5 00:28:24.687: IGMP(0): Send v2 init  Query on FastEthernet0/0
*Nov  5 00:28:24.687: IP: s=192.168.1.1 (local), d=224.0.0.1 (FastEthernet0/0), len
28, sending broad/multicast
```

Next, IGMP sends the initial IGMP query to the multicast group referencing all devices on the subnet 224.0.0.1. Each IGMP-enabled interface connected to the VLAN should now send an IGMP join message to 192.168.1.1 indicating which multicast groups it wishes to join:

```
*Nov  5 00:28:24.691: IGMP(0): WAVL Insert group: 224.0.1.40 interface: FastEther-
net0/0Successful
*Nov  5 00:28:24.691: IGMP(0): Send v2 Report for 224.0.1.40 on FastEthernet0/0
*Nov  5 00:28:24.691: IGMP(0): Received v2 Report on FastEthernet0/0 from 192.168.1.1
for 224.0.1.40
R1(config-if)#

*Nov  5 00:28:24.691: IGMP(0): Received Group record for group 224.0.1.40, mode 2
from 192.168.1.1 for 0 sources
```

```
*Nov  5 00:28:24.691: IGMP(0): Switching to EXCLUDE mode for 224.0.1.40 on FastEther-
net0/0

*Nov  5 00:28:24.691: IGMP(0): Updating EXCLUDE group timer for 224.0.1.40

*Nov  5 00:28:25.331: IGMP(0): MRT Add/Update FastEthernet0/0 for (*,224.0.1.40) by 0

*Nov  5 00:28:24.691: IP: s=192.168.1.1 (local), d=224.0.1.40 (FastEthernet0/0), len
28, sending broad/multicast
```

All PIM routers automatically subscribe to the 224.0.1.40 group. Therefore, R1 sends an IGMP join message on its FastEthernet interface for the 224.0.1.40 group. Then, R1 receives its own message and implicitly joins its FastEthernet interface to the group. You will learn more about the 224.0.1.40 group in Lab 7-4.

The relevant parts of the remaining output are highlighted:

```
*Nov  5 00:28:25.331: IP: s=192.168.1.2 (FastEthernet0/0), d=229.7.7.7, len 28,
rcvd 0

*Nov  5 00:28:25.331: IGMP(0): Received v2 Report on FastEthernet0/0 from
192.168.1.2 for 229.7.7.7

*Nov  5 00:28:25.331: IGMP(0): Received Group record for group 229.7.7.7, mode 2
from 192.168.1.2 for 0 sources

*Nov  5 00:28:25.331: IGMP(0): WAVL Insert group: 229.7.7.7 interface:
FastEthernet0/0Successful

*Nov  5 00:28:25.331: IGMP(0): Switching to EXCLUDE mode for 229.7.7.7 on
FastEthernet0/0

*Nov  5 00:28:25.331: IGMP(0): Updating EXCLUDE group timer for 229.7.7.7

*Nov  5 00:28:25.331: IGMP(0): MRT Add/Update FastEthernet0/0 for (*,229.7.7.7) by 0

*Nov  5 00:28:25.687: %PIM-5-DRCHG: DR change from neighbor 0.0.0.0 to 192.168.1.1 on
interface FastEthernet0/0 (vrf default)

*Nov  5 00:28:53.979: IP: s=192.168.1.1 (local), d=224.0.0.13 (FastEthernet0/0), len
54, sending broad/multicast

*Nov  5 00:29:23.415: IP: s=192.168.1.1 (local), d=224.0.0.13 (FastEthernet0/0), len
54, sending broad/multicast

*Nov  5 00:29:23.695: IGMP(0): Send v2 general Query on FastEthernet0/0

*Nov  5 00:29:23.695: IGMP(0): Set report delay time to 4.6 seconds for 224.0.1.40 on
FastEthernet0/0

*Nov  5 00:29:23.695: IP: s=192.168.1.1 (local), d=224.0.0.1 (FastEthernet0/0), len
28, sending broad/multicast

*Nov  5 00:29:28.695: IGMP(0): Send v2 Report for 224.0.1.40 on FastEthernet0/0

*Nov  5 00:29:28.695: IGMP(0): Received v2 Report on FastEthernet0/0 from 192.168.1.1
for 224.0.1.40

*Nov  5 00:29:28.695: IGMP(0): Received Group record for group 224.0.1.40, mode 2
from 192.168.1.1 for 0 sources

*Nov  5 00:29:28.695: IGMP(0): Updating EXCLUDE group timer for 224.0.1.40

*Nov  5 00:29:28.695: IP: s=192.168.1.1 (local), d=224.0.1.40 (FastEthernet0/0), len
28, sending broad/multicast

*Nov  5 00:29:29.331: IP: s=192.168.1.2 (FastEthernet0/0), d=229.7.7.7, len 28, rcvd
0

*Nov  5 00:29:29.331: IGMP(0): Received v2 Report on FastEthernet0/0 from
192.168.1.2 for 229.7.7.7

*Nov  5 00:29:29.331: IGMP(0): Received Group record for group 229.7.7.7, mode 2
from 192.168.1.2 for 0 sources
```

```
*Nov  5 00:29:29.331: IGMP(0): Updating EXCLUDE group timer for 229.7.7.7
```

```
*Nov  5 00:29:29.331: IGMP(0): MRT Add/Update FastEthernet0/0 for (*,229.7.7.7) by 0
```

```
*Nov  5 00:29:53.111: IP: s=192.168.1.1 (local), d=224.0.0.13 (FastEthernet0/0), len
54, sending broad/multicast
```

```
*Nov  5 00:30:22.819: IP: s=192.168.1.1 (local), d=224.0.0.13 (FastEthernet0/0), len
54, sending broad/multicast
```

```
*Nov  5 00:30:23.695: IGMP(0): Send v2 general Query on FastEthernet0/0
```

```
*Nov  5 00:30:23.695: IGMP(0): Set report delay time to 4.8 seconds for 224.0.1.40 on
FastEthernet0/0
```

```
*Nov  5 00:30:23.695: IP: s=192.168.1.1 (local), d=224.0.0.1 (FastEthernet0/0), len
28, sending broad/multicast
```

```
*Nov  5 00:30:27.331: IP: s=192.168.1.2 (FastEthernet0/0), d=229.7.7.7, len 28, rcvd
0
```

```
*Nov  5 00:30:27.331: IGMP(0): Received v2 Report on FastEthernet0/0 from
192.168.1.2 for 229.7.7.7
```

```
*Nov  5 00:30:27.331: IGMP(0): Received Group record for group 229.7.7.7, mode 2
from 192.168.1.2 for 0 sources
```

```
*Nov  5 00:30:27.331: IGMP(0): Updating EXCLUDE group timer for 229.7.7.7
```

```
*Nov  5 00:30:27.331: IGMP(0): MRT Add/Update FastEthernet0/0 for (*,229.7.7.7) by 0
```

```
*Nov  5 00:30:28.695: IGMP(0): Send v2 Report for 224.0.1.40 on FastEthernet0/0
```

```
*Nov  5 00:30:28.695: IGMP(0): Received v2 Report on FastEthernet0/0 from 192.168.1.1
for 224.0.1.40
```

```
*Nov  5 00:30:28.695: IGMP(0): Received Group record for group 224.0.1.40, mode 2
from 192.168.1.1 for 0 sources
```

```
*Nov  5 00:30:28.695: IGMP(0): Updating EXCLUDE group timer for 224.0.1.40
```

```
*Nov  5 00:30:28.695: IP: s=192.168.1.1 (local), d=224.0.1.40 (FastEthernet0/0), len
28, sending broad/multicast
```

```
*Nov  5 00:30:52.155: IP: s=192.168.1.1 (local), d=224.0.0.13 (FastEthernet0/0), len
54, sending broad/multicast
```

```
*Nov  5 00:31:22.079: IP: s=192.168.1.1 (local), d=224.0.0.13 (FastEthernet0/0), len
54, sending broad/multicast
```

```
*Nov  5 00:31:23.695: IGMP(0): Send v2 general Query on FastEthernet0/0
```

```
*Nov  5 00:31:23.695: IGMP(0): Set report delay time to 9.8 seconds for 224.0.1.40 on
FastEthernet0/0
```

```
*Nov  5 00:31:23.695: IP: s=192.168.1.1 (local), d=224.0.0.1 (FastEthernet0/0), len
28, sending broad/multicast
```

```
*Nov  5 00:31:27.503: IP: s=192.168.1.3 (FastEthernet0/0), d=229.7.7.7, len 28, rcvd
0
```

```
*Nov  5 00:31:27.503: IGMP(0): Received v2 Report on FastEthernet0/0 from
192.168.1.3 for 229.7.7.7
```

```
*Nov  5 00:31:27.503: IGMP(0): Received Group record for group 229.7.7.7, mode 2
from 192.168.1.3 for 0 sources
```

```
*Nov  5 00:31:27.503: IGMP(0): Updating EXCLUDE group timer for 229.7.7.7
```

```
*Nov  5 00:31:27.503: IGMP(0): MRT Add/Update FastEthernet0/0 for (*,229.7.7.7) by 0
```

The highlighted messages indicate the IGMP queries and responses. In each case, R1 sends a periodic IGMP query to all devices on the subnet. R2 and R3 periodically respond to those queries as necessary, requesting that multicast traffic to the 229.7.7.7 group be allowed onto this subnet. PIM-DM periodically floods traffic to a Layer 2 segment and then prunes that traffic from that segment if no listeners are configured.

At this point, disable debugging on all routers:

```
Router# undebug all
```

Step 5: Verify Multicast Operation at Layer 2

Which IP multicast groups do you expect to see in the IGMP records on R1?

_____

_____

_____

_____

_____

On R1, issue the **show ip igmp groups** command to display the multicast groups for which IGMP has currently recorded information from connected interfaces:

```
R1# show ip igmp groups
IGMP Connected Group Membership
Group Address    Interface        Uptime    Expires   Last Reporter  Group Accounted
229.7.7.7        FastEthernet0/0  00:02:19  00:02:19  192.168.1.3
224.0.1.40       FastEthernet0/0  00:02:22  00:02:22  192.168.1.1
```

Display the IGMP membership for the IGMP groups reported by R1 using the **show ip igmp membership** command.

```
R1# show ip igmp membership
Flags: A  - aggregate, T - tracked
       L  - Local, S - static, V - virtual, R - Reported through v3
       I  - v3lite, U - Urd, M - SSM (S,G) channel
       1,2,3 - The version of IGMP the group is in
Channel/Group-Flags:
       / - Filtering entry (Exclude mode (S,G), Include mode (*,G))
Reporter:
       <mac-or-ip-address> - last reporter if group is not explicitly tracked
       <n>/<m>      - <n> reporter in include mode, <m> reporter in exclude

       Channel/Group              Reporter         Uptime   Exp.  Flags  Interface
       *,229.7.7.7                192.168.1.3      00:02:20 02:20 2A     Fa0/0
       *,224.0.1.40               192.168.1.1      00:02:23 02:23 2LA    Fa0/0
```

Display the IGMP status on R1's FastEthernet 0/0 interface with the **show ip igmp interface** command:

```
R1# show ip igmp interface
FastEthernet0/0 is up, line protocol is up
  Internet address is 192.168.1.1/24
  IGMP is enabled on interface
```

```
Current IGMP host version is 2
Current IGMP router version is 2
IGMP query interval is 60 seconds
IGMP querier timeout is 120 seconds
IGMP max query response time is 10 seconds
Last member query count is 2
Last member query response interval is 1000 ms
Inbound IGMP access group is not set
IGMP activity: 2 joins, 0 leaves
Multicast routing is enabled on interface
Multicast TTL threshold is 0
Multicast designated router (DR) is 192.168.1.1 (this system)
IGMP querying router is 192.168.1.1 (this system)
Multicast groups joined by this system (number of users):
    224.0.1.40(1)
```

Step 6: Verify IGMP Snooping

On SW1, issue the **show mac-address-table multicast** command:

```
SW1# show mac-address-table multicast

Vlan    Mac Address       Type    Ports
----    -----------       ----    -----
   1    0100.5e00.0128    IGMP    Fa0/1
   1    0100.5e07.0707    IGMP    Fa0/1, Fa0/3, Fa0/5
```

These MAC addresses are not unique to one IP multicast group because there is a 1:32 correlation between each MAC address and the IP multicast groups it represents.

Consider the binary form of the group address for 229.7.7.7 as shown in Figure 7-2:

Figure 7-2   Multicast Group Addressing at OSI Layers 2 and 3

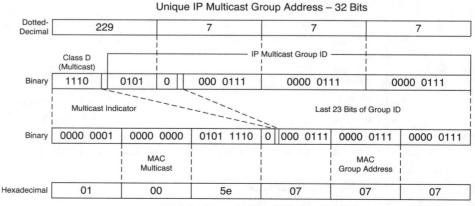

Because the center set of boxed bits in the binary representation of the IP address is not mapped to any bits in the MAC address, the MAC addresses of multicast groups are not unique to an IP multicast group. Class D addresses with any value in those 5 bits and a constant sequence of bits in the 23 least-significant digits all map to the same MAC address.

List at least three IP multicast groups with which the following MAC addresses correspond.

0100.5e00.0128

0100.5e07.0707

_____

_____

_____

_____

_____

_____

_____

_____

_____

_____

_____

_____

_____

Although all 32 groups are forwarded at Layer 2 to the Layer 3 interfaces of the routers and hosts, IGMP only reads IP packets for groups to which the interface has subscribed or for which it is in a forwarding state. All other multicast traffic is dropped.

As discussed in Step 3, statically subscribe FastEthernet 0/9 on SW1 to the multicast MAC group of 0100.5e07.07.07 via the **ip igmp snooping vlan static** global configuration command. This configuration does not affect the remainder of the lab:

```
SW1(config)# ip igmp snooping vlan 1 static 0100.5e07.0707 interface fastethernet 0/9
```

Reissue the **show mac address-table multicast** command on SW1:

```
SW1# show mac-address-table multicast
Vlan    Mac Address      Type       Ports
----    -----------      ----       -----
   1    0100.5e00.0128   IGMP       Fa0/1
   1    0100.5e07.0707   USER       Fa0/1, Fa0/3, Fa0/5,
                                    Fa0/9
```

Notice that the Type field for the 0100.5e07.0707 entry now indicates that it is a statically configured group address. Statically configured addresses override mappings dynamically learned via IGMP snooping.

Step 7: Verify Multicast Operation at Layer 3

Verify that multicast route state has been recorded on R1 using the **show ip mroute** command:

```
R1# show ip mroute
IP Multicast Routing Table
Flags: D - Dense, S - Sparse, B - Bidir Group, s - SSM Group, C - Connected,
       L - Local, P - Pruned, R - RP-bit set, F - Register flag,
       T - SPT-bit set, J - Join SPT, M - MSDP created entry,
       X - Proxy Join Timer Running, A - Candidate for MSDP Advertisement,
       U - URD, I - Received Source Specific Host Report,
       Z - Multicast Tunnel, z - MDT-data group sender,
       Y - Joined MDT-data group, y - Sending to MDT-data group
Outgoing interface flags: H - Hardware switched, A - Assert winner
 Timers: Uptime/Expires
 Interface state: Interface, Next-Hop or VCD, State/Mode


(*, 229.7.7.7), 00:06:48/00:02:11, RP 0.0.0.0, flags: DC
  Incoming interface: Null, RPF nbr 0.0.0.0
  Outgoing interface list:
    FastEthernet0/0, Forward/Dense, 00:06:48/00:00:00


(*, 224.0.1.40), 00:07:33/00:02:15, RP 0.0.0.0, flags: DCL
  Incoming interface: Null, RPF nbr 0.0.0.0
  Outgoing interface list:
    FastEthernet0/0, Forward/Dense, 00:07:33/00:00:00
```

The **show ip mroute** command shows multicast state with reference to each multicast group. Multicast routes are more complex than unicast routes because the router needs to identify incoming interfaces that it considers the "upstream interface" to specific multicast sources using a reverse-path check. The multicast router must also store the outgoing interfaces that should forward the multicast traffic for each source and group.

Without PIM communicating between routers, much of the interface and RPF neighbor information the multicast routing table shown above is default information, such as RPF neighbors of 0.0.0.0. You will see a more complex router state in the next lab.

Notice in the output shown that all traffic to the 229.7.7.7 group should be forwarded out FastEthernet 0/0. Verify this by pinging from R1 to 229.7.7.7:

```
R1# ping 229.7.7.7
Type escape sequence to abort.
Sending 1, 100-byte ICMP Echos to 229.7.7.7, timeout is 2 seconds:

Reply to request 0 from 192.168.1.3, 1 ms
Reply to request 0 from 192.168.1.2, 1 ms
```

Lab 7-2: Routing IP Multicast with PIM Dense Mode (7.5.2)

The objectives of this lab are as follows:

- Implement IGMP

- Review configuration of Enhanced Interior Gateway Routing Protocol (EIGRP)

- Implement and verify PIM-DM operation and adjacencies

- Verify IGMP operation of PIM-DM flooding and pruning

- Explore the multicast routing table

Figure 7-3 illustrates the topology that will be used for this lab.

Figure 7-3   Topology Diagram for Lab 7-2

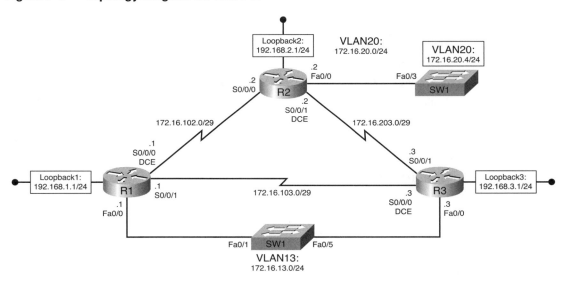

Scenario

A community action organization, CrushASodaCan.com, contracted you as a consultant to set up IP multicast in their network. At the end of the week, the public relations department wants to multicast a live video feed of the CEO crushing a soda can to encourage citizens to compact their recyclable material before sending it to the recycling center. As a consultant working on this network, you are concerned about the use of the network resources.

The three remote sites are connected by a full mesh of serial leased lines. Sites 1 and 3 (R1 and R3) are also connected via FastEthernet.

The multicast source is a host on VLAN 20, which connects at Layer 3 to R2's FastEthernet interface. A remote network at each site represented by a loopback interface should receive the press feed of the CEO's message. While performing testing in this scenario, you will use a switched virtual interface (SVI) on SW1 to simulate the multicast source. At each multicast group member interface network, you should prefer the shortest cost path to the multicast source according to the underlying unicast routing table.

Step 1: Configure Addressing and Implement IGMP

Paste in the following initial configurations. You can download these configurations at www.cisco-press.com/title/1587132133 under the More Information section on the page.

R1:

```
!
hostname R1
!
interface Loopback1
 ip address 192.168.1.1 255.255.255.0
!
interface FastEthernet0/0
 ip address 172.16.13.1 255.255.255.0
 no shutdown
!
interface Serial0/0/0
 bandwidth 64
 ip address 172.16.102.1 255.255.255.248
 clock rate 64000
 no shutdown
!
interface Serial0/0/1
 bandwidth 64
 ip address 172.16.103.1 255.255.255.248
 no shutdown
!
end
```

R2:

```
!
hostname R2
!
interface Loopback2
 ip address 192.168.2.1 255.255.255.0
!
interface FastEthernet0/0
 ip address 172.16.20.2 255.255.255.0
 no shutdown
!
interface Serial0/0/0
 bandwidth 64
 ip address 172.16.102.2 255.255.255.248
 no shutdown
!
interface Serial0/0/1
```

```
 bandwidth 128
 ip address 172.16.203.2 255.255.255.248
 clock rate 128000
 no shutdown
!
end
```

R3:

```
!
hostname R3
!
interface Loopback3
 ip address 192.168.3.1 255.255.255.0
!
interface FastEthernet0/0
 ip address 172.16.13.3 255.255.255.0
 no shutdown
!
interface Serial0/0/0
 bandwidth 64
 ip address 172.16.103.3 255.255.255.248
 clock rate 64000
 no shutdown
!
interface Serial0/0/1
 bandwidth 128
 ip address 172.16.203.3 255.255.255.248
 no shutdown
!
end
```

SW1:

```
!
hostname SW1
!
interface FastEthernet0/1
 switchport access vlan 13
 switchport mode access
!
interface FastEthernet0/3
 switchport access vlan 20
 switchport mode access
!
interface FastEthernet0/5
```

```
 switchport access vlan 13
 switchport mode access
!
end
```

Use an SVI on SW1 to simulate a multicast source on the VLAN 20 subnet. This will be used to generate a repeated multicast ping to simulate the multicast traffic while you set up the network. Assign the SVI the IP address 172.16.20.4/24 with a default gateway of 172.16.20.2:

```
SW1# configure terminal
SW1(config)# ip default-gateway 172.16.20.2
SW1(config)# interface vlan 20
SW1(config-if)# ip address 172.16.20.4 255.255.255.0
SW1(config-if)# no shutdown
```

Using IGMP, subscribe each of the loopback interfaces on the three routers to the multicast group 232.32.32.32:

```
R1# configure terminal
R1(config)# interface loopback 1
R1(config-if)# ip igmp join-group 232.32.32.32
```

```
R2# configure terminal
R2(config)# interface loopback 2
R2(config-if)# ip igmp join-group 232.32.32.32
```

```
R3# configure terminal
R3(config)# interface loopback 3
R3(config-if)# ip igmp join-group 232.32.32.32
```

Verify that each of the interfaces has subscribed to the multicast group using the **show ip igmp groups** command:

```
R1# show ip igmp groups
IGMP Connected Group Membership
Group Address     Interface      Uptime     Expires   Last Reporter   Group Accounted
232.32.32.32      Loopback1      00:02:13   stopped   192.168.1.1
```

```
R2# show ip igmp groups
IGMP Connected Group Membership
Group Address     Interface      Uptime     Expires   Last Reporter   Group Accounted
232.32.32.32      Loopback2      00:02:15   stopped   192.168.1.2
```

```
R3# show ip igmp groups
IGMP Connected Group Membership
Group Address     Interface      Uptime     Expires   Last Reporter   Group Accounted
232.32.32.32      Loopback3      00:02:17   stopped   192.168.1.3
```

Step 2: Configure EIGRP

Configure EIGRP on each router with the following configuration:

```
router eigrp 1
 network 192.168.0.0 0.0.255.255
 network 172.16.0.0
```

After the EIGRP adjacencies form, run the following TCL script to verify full unicast connectivity. You can download this TCL script at www.ciscopress.com/title/1587132133 under the More Information section on the page.

```
foreach address {
192.168.1.1
172.16.13.1
172.16.102.1
172.16.103.1
192.168.2.1
172.16.20.2
172.16.102.2
172.16.203.2
192.168.3.1
172.16.13.3
172.16.103.3
172.16.203.3
172.16.20.4
} { ping $address }
```

Compare the output you receive with the output in the section, "TCL Script Output: Unicast," for this lab (all pings successful). Make sure you have ICMP replies from the host. If your host has a reachable default gateway of R2's FastEthernet 0/0 interface and if all routers have full connectivity between all subnets, you should be able to ping the host and receive all replies.

Step 3: Implement PIM-DM

Ping the 232.32.32.32 multicast address from the VLAN 20 SVI on SW1 discussed in Step 2.

```
SW1# ping 232.32.32.32

Type escape sequence to abort.
Sending 1, 100-byte ICMP Echos to 232.32.32.32, timeout is 2 seconds:

SW1#
```

Did you receive ICMP echo replies from the loopback interfaces subscribed to this group via IGMP?

Why does the host not receive ICMP replies?

_____

_____

_____

List at least three responsibilities of an IP multicast routing protocol.

_____

_____

_____

_____

_____

_____

Routing protocols are primarily useful for "introducing" multicast sources to their receivers, a procedure known as *source discovery*. In unicast IP networks, a Layer 3 device must know the next downstream hop or interface to route a unicast packet to a destination network. Similarly, an IP multicast router must know the tree along which multicast data from a source should flow to the receivers.

Protocol Independent Multicast (PIM) has two modes: sparse mode (SM) and dense mode (DM). Cisco IOS Software supports both modes. PIM-DM is designed for networks in which devices on almost every subnet subscribe to the available groups. PIM-DM is useful in lab settings and in situations in which most of the Layer 2 segments involved have subscriptions to the multicast groups. PIM-SM is designed for multicast networks in which multicast groups do not have subscribers on many subnets.

Note   Cisco does not recommend implementing PIM-DM in production networks because of the inefficiency inherent in the push-based model. Though a multicast group does not have subscribers on many subnets in the network, multicast packets are still periodically flooded and pruned throughout the entire multicast network.

PIM-DM creates (S, G) multicast trees rooted at each source that form shortest-cost paths to the receivers throughout the network. Each multicast router uses the unicast IP routing table to track which interfaces are upstream with reference to each multicast source. PIM-DM also analyzes the downstream subscriptions to assign forwarding state to outgoing interfaces. When a PIM router receives a packet for a multicast group, it must determine which interfaces for that group are in a forwarding state before sending the packet.

To enable multicast routing, issue the **ip multicast-routing** command in global configuration mode.

```
R1(config)# ip multicast-routing
```

```
R2(config)# ip multicast-routing
```

```
R3(config)# ip multicast-routing
```

To enable PIM-DM on the Loopback2 and FastEthernet 0/0 interfaces on R2, issue the **ip pim dense-mode** command in interface configuration mode:

```
R2(config)# interface loopback 2
R2(config-if)# ip pim dense-mode
R2(config-if)# interface fastethernet 0/0
R2(config-if)# ip pim dense-mode
```

Recall the behavior of IGMP when PIM-DM was configured on R1's FastEthernet interface in Lab 7-1. Will IGMP queries be sent over VLAN 20?

_____

_____

Now that multicast routing and PIM-DM are enabled on R2, will a ping from SW1 to the 232.32.32.32 group receive any replies? Explain.

_____

_____

_____

_____

_____

_____

Verify your answer by pinging the multicast group from SW1:

```
SW1# ping 232.32.32.32

Type escape sequence to abort.
Sending 1, 100-byte ICMP Echos to 232.32.32.32, timeout is 2 seconds:

Reply to request 0 from 172.16.20.2, 4 ms
```

Why was the first packet dropped?

_____

_____

Why did the host not receive replies from the other loopback interfaces in your topology?

_____

_____

_____

In Lab 7-1, you demonstrated that without IGMP snooping Layer 2 multicast traffic traveling over Ethernet is treated as broadcast traffic. The switch then forwards multicast traffic to all ports that would normally receive a broadcast from the same source. However, at OSI Layer 3, multicast traffic is discarded unless the router receives directives from IGMP to send traffic out certain egress interfaces. If IGMP had registered such messages, the state would be shown in the IP multicast routing table.

Display the multicast routing table to check for egress interfaces to forward multicast traffic to group 232.32.32.32:

```
R2# show ip mroute
IP Multicast Routing Table
Flags: D - Dense, S - Sparse, B - Bidir Group, s - SSM Group, C - Connected,
       L - Local, P - Pruned, R - RP-bit set, F - Register flag,
       T - SPT-bit set, J - Join SPT, M - MSDP created entry,
       X - Proxy Join Timer Running, A - Candidate for MSDP Advertisement,
       U - URD, I - Received Source Specific Host Report,
       Z - Multicast Tunnel, z - MDT-data group sender,
       Y - Joined MDT-data group, y - Sending to MDT-data group
Outgoing interface flags: H - Hardware switched, A - Assert winner
 Timers: Uptime/Expires
 Interface state: Interface, Next-Hop or VCD, State/Mode


(*, 232.32.32.32), 00:25:11/stopped, RP 0.0.0.0, flags: DCL
  Incoming interface: Null, RPF nbr 0.0.0.0
  Outgoing interface list:
    Loopback2, Forward/Dense, 00:25:11/00:00:00


(172.16.20.4, 232.32.32.32), 00:00:07/00:02:55, flags: LT
  Incoming interface: FastEthernet0/0, RPF nbr 0.0.0.0
  Outgoing interface list:
    Loopback2, Forward/Dense, 00:00:07/00:00:00


(*, 224.0.1.40), 00:25:12/00:02:32, RP 0.0.0.0, flags: DCL
  Incoming interface: Null, RPF nbr 0.0.0.0
  Outgoing interface list:
    Loopback2, Forward/Dense, 00:25:12/00:00:00
```

Because IGMP only queries interfaces that are running PIM-DM, the subscriptions for the remote loopback interfaces have not been reported to R2 and are, therefore, in a nonforwarding state. Only R2's Loopback2 interface will receive multicast packets destined for 232.32.32.32.

You can resolve this issue by applying the **ip pim dense-mode** command to each remaining interface in the topology:

```
R1(config)# interface loopback 1
R1(config-if)# ip pim dense-mode
R1(config-if)# interface fastethernet 0/0
R1(config-if)# ip pim dense-mode
R1(config-if)# interface serial 0/0/0
R1(config-if)# ip pim dense-mode
R1(config-if)# interface serial 0/0/1
```

```
R1(config-if)# ip pim dense-mode
```
```
R2(config)# interface serial 0/0/0
R2(config-if)# ip pim dense-mode
R2(config-if)# interface serial 0/0/1
R2(config-if)# ip pim dense-mode
```
```
R3(config)# interface loopback 3
R3(config-if)# ip pim dense-mode
R3(config-if)# interface fastethernet 0/0
R3(config-if)# ip pim dense-mode
R3(config-if)# interface serial 0/0/0
R3(config-if)# ip pim dense-mode
R3(config-if)# interface serial 0/0/1
R3(config-if)# ip pim dense-mode
```

Ping the multicast group from SW1 again. You should receive replies from each router. Note that you will not receive replies from the IP address of the interface on which the multicast packet was received but rather from whichever interface on the responding router encapsulated the return packet:

```
SW1# ping 232.32.32.32

Type escape sequence to abort.
Sending 1, 100-byte ICMP Echos to 232.32.32.32, timeout is 2 seconds:

Reply to request 0 from 172.16.20.2, 4 ms
Reply to request 0 from 172.16.102.1, 32 ms
Reply to request 0 from 172.16.203.3, 32 ms
```

Based on your understanding of IP unicast routing, why are the ICMP echo replies sent from the interfaces shown in the preceding ping output?

_____

_____

_____

_____

Step 4: Verify PIM Adjacencies

This step explores PIM adjacencies and how PIM functions over various Layer 2 media.

Issue the **show ip pim neighbor** command to display all the routers on the connected Layer 3 subnets:

```
R1# show ip pim neighbor
PIM Neighbor Table
Mode: B - Bidir Capable, DR - Designated Router, N - Default DR Priority,
      S - State Refresh Capable
Neighbor          Interface               Uptime/Expires    Ver   DR
```

```
Address                                                     Prio/Mode
172.16.13.3      FastEthernet0/0      00:02:29/00:01:42 v2   1 / DR S
172.16.102.2     Serial0/0/0          00:02:30/00:01:40 v2   1 / S
172.16.103.3     Serial0/0/1          00:02:29/00:01:43 v2   1 / S
```

```
R2# show ip pim neighbor
PIM Neighbor Table
Mode: B - Bidir Capable, DR - Designated Router, N - Default DR Priority,
      S - State Refresh Capable
Neighbor         Interface            Uptime/Expires    Ver   DR
Address                                                     Prio/Mode
172.16.102.1     Serial0/0/0          00:03:16/00:01:25 v2   1 / S
172.16.203.3     Serial0/0/1          00:03:18/00:01:24 v2   1 / S
```

```
R3# show ip pim neighbor
PIM Neighbor Table
Mode: B - Bidir Capable, DR - Designated Router, N - Default DR Priority,
      S - State Refresh Capable
Neighbor         Interface            Uptime/Expires    Ver   DR
Address                                                     Prio/Mode
172.16.13.1      FastEthernet0/0      00:03:00/00:01:42 v2   1 / S
172.16.103.1     Serial0/0/0          00:03:31/00:01:41 v2   1 / S
172.16.203.2     Serial0/0/1          00:03:03/00:01:38 v2   1 / S
```

Consider the adjacency between R1 and R3 on VLAN 13. If more than one multicast router exists on a multi-access VLAN, is it necessary for both devices to query for IGMP subscriptions on the VLAN?

Recall the idea of a designated router (DR) in OSPF or a designated intermediate system (DIS) in IS-IS. These link-state protocols allow Layer 3 devices running those protocols to become adjacent only with the master device for that multi-access Layer 2 medium. This behavior decreases network control traffic and provides an authoritative source for routing information on that network segment.

A similar situation exists for IGMP control traffic on multi-access media, such as Ethernet. Rather than have each multicast router on a subnet running its own IGMP queries, PIM-DM elects one router to handle the IGMP querying for the entire network segment. PIM elects a DR for that subnet by selecting the PIM-DM router with the highest IP address.

From a practical perspective, do you need a DR on a point-to-point medium? Explain.

Display detailed information about PIM-enabled interfaces with the **show ip pim interface detail** command on R1:

```
R1# show ip pim interface detail
Loopback1 is up, line protocol is up
  Internet address is 192.168.1.1/24
```

```
   Multicast switching: fast
   Multicast packets in/out: 919/0
   Multicast TTL threshold: 0
  PIM: enabled
    PIM version: 2, mode: dense
    PIM DR: 192.168.1.1 (this system)
    PIM neighbor count: 0
    PIM Hello/Query interval: 30 seconds
    PIM Hello packets in/out: 77/78
    PIM State-Refresh processing: enabled
    PIM State-Refresh origination: disabled
    PIM NBMA mode: disabled
    PIM ATM multipoint signalling: disabled
    PIM domain border: disabled
   Multicast Tagswitching: disabled
Serial0/0/0 is up, line protocol is up
   Internet address is 172.16.102.1/29
   Multicast switching: fast
   Multicast packets in/out: 917/0
   Multicast TTL threshold: 0
  PIM: enabled
    PIM version: 2, mode: dense
    PIM DR: 0.0.0.0
    PIM neighbor count: 1
    PIM Hello/Query interval: 30 seconds
    PIM Hello packets in/out: 77/78
    PIM State-Refresh processing: enabled
    PIM State-Refresh origination: disabled
    PIM NBMA mode: disabled
    PIM ATM multipoint signalling: disabled
    PIM domain border: disabled
   Multicast Tagswitching: disabled
Serial0/0/1 is up, line protocol is up
   Internet address is 172.16.103.1/29
   Multicast switching: fast
   Multicast packets in/out: 920/0
   Multicast TTL threshold: 0
  PIM: enabled
    PIM version: 2, mode: dense
    PIM DR: 0.0.0.0
    PIM neighbor count: 1
    PIM Hello/Query interval: 30 seconds
    PIM Hello packets in/out: 77/78
    PIM State-Refresh processing: enabled
```

```
      PIM State-Refresh origination: disabled
      PIM NBMA mode: disabled
      PIM ATM multipoint signalling: disabled
      PIM domain border: disabled
   Multicast Tagswitching: disabled
FastEthernet0/0 is up, line protocol is up
   Internet address is 172.16.13.1/24
   Multicast switching: fast
   Multicast packets in/out: 918/0
   Multicast TTL threshold: 0
   PIM: enabled
     PIM version: 2, mode: dense
     PIM DR: 172.16.13.3
     PIM neighbor count: 1
     PIM Hello/Query interval: 30 seconds
     PIM Hello packets in/out: 76/77
     PIM State-Refresh processing: enabled
     PIM State-Refresh origination: disabled
     PIM NBMA mode: disabled
     PIM ATM multipoint signalling: disabled
     PIM domain border: disabled
   Multicast Tagswitching: disabled
```

Notice that the two serial interfaces use the default DR address 0.0.0.0 as the DR for the interface. Because a multicast packet is received by either 0 or 1 remote routers on a serial segment, PIM does not need to set up a complex neighbor relationship.

Step 5: Verify Multicast Routing Operation

On each router, use the **mrinfo** command to view information about the connected multicast-enabled routers:

```
R1# mrinfo
172.16.13.1 [version  12.4] [flags: PMA]:
   192.168.1.1 -> 0.0.0.0 [1/0/pim/querier/leaf]
   172.16.13.1 -> 172.16.13.3 [1/0/pim]
   172.16.102.1 -> 172.16.102.2 [1/0/pim]
   172.16.103.1 -> 172.16.103.3 [1/0/pim]
```
```
R2# mrinfo
172.16.20.2 [version  12.4] [flags: PMA]:
   192.168.2.1 -> 0.0.0.0 [1/0/pim/querier/leaf]
   172.16.20.2 -> 0.0.0.0 [1/0/pim/querier/leaf]
   172.16.102.2 -> 172.16.102.1 [1/0/pim]
   172.16.203.2 -> 172.16.203.3 [1/0/pim]
```
```
R3# mrinfo
```

```
172.16.13.3 [version  12.4] [flags: PMA]:
  192.168.3.1 -> 0.0.0.0 [1/0/pim/querier/leaf]
  172.16.13.3 -> 172.16.13.1 [1/0/pim/querier]
  172.16.103.3 -> 172.16.103.1 [1/0/pim]
  172.16.203.3 -> 172.16.203.2 [1/0/pim]
```

Each router realizes that the loopback interfaces are topological leaves in which PIM will never establish an adjacency with any other routers. These routers also record the neighboring multicast router addresses and the multicast routing protocols they utilize.

Use the **show ip multicast interface** command to display statistics about the multicast traffic passing through the router. You should receive similar output on each router:

```
R1# show ip multicast interface
Loopback1 is up, line protocol is up
  Internet address is 192.168.1.1/24
  Multicast routing: enabled
  Multicast switching: fast
  Multicast packets in/out: 512/0
  Multicast TTL threshold: 0
  Multicast Tagswitching: disabled
FastEthernet0/0 is up, line protocol is up
  Internet address is 172.16.13.1/24
  Multicast routing: enabled
  Multicast switching: fast
  Multicast packets in/out: 524/6
  Multicast TTL threshold: 0
  Multicast Tagswitching: disabled
Serial0/0/0 is up, line protocol is up
  Internet address is 172.16.102.1/29
  Multicast routing: enabled
  Multicast switching: fast
  Multicast packets in/out: 519/0
  Multicast TTL threshold: 0
  Multicast Tagswitching: disabled
Serial0/0/1 is up, line protocol is up
  Internet address is 172.16.103.1/29
  Multicast routing: enabled
  Multicast switching: fast
  Multicast packets in/out: 516/6
  Multicast TTL threshold: 0
  Multicast Tagswitching: disabled
```

Based on the preceding output and your knowledge of PIM-DM and this topology, which interfaces appear to be forwarding multicasts to 232.32.32.32 on R1?

_____

_____

Generate a stream of multicast data to the group by issuing an extended ping from SW1 with a repeat count of 100:

```
SW1# ping
Protocol [ip]:
Target IP address: 232.32.32.32
Repeat count [1]: 100
Datagram size [100]:
Timeout in seconds [2]:
Extended commands [n]:
Sweep range of sizes [n]:
Type escape sequence to abort.
Sending 100, 100-byte ICMP Echos to 232.32.32.32, timeout is 2 seconds:

Reply to request 0 from 172.16.20.2, 8 ms
Reply to request 0 from 172.16.102.1, 36 ms
Reply to request 0 from 172.16.203.3, 36 ms
Reply to request 1 from 172.16.20.2, 4 ms
Reply to request 1 from 172.16.102.1, 28 ms
Reply to request 1 from 172.16.203.3, 28 ms
Reply to request 2 from 172.16.20.2, 8 ms
Reply to request 2 from 172.16.102.1, 32 ms
Reply to request 2 from 172.16.203.3, 32 ms
...
```

On each of the routers, you should see that PIM and IGMP have communicated to install the 232.32.32.32 multicast group in the multicast routing table. Verify this with the **show ip mroute** command on each router:

```
R1# show ip mroute
IP Multicast Routing Table
Flags: D - Dense, S - Sparse, B - Bidir Group, s - SSM Group, C - Connected,
       L - Local, P - Pruned, R - RP-bit set, F - Register flag,
       T - SPT-bit set, J - Join SPT, M - MSDP created entry,
       X - Proxy Join Timer Running, A - Candidate for MSDP Advertisement,
       U - URD, I - Received Source Specific Host Report,
       Z - Multicast Tunnel, z - MDT-data group sender,
       Y - Joined MDT-data group, y - Sending to MDT-data group
Outgoing interface flags: H - Hardware switched, A - Assert winner
 Timers: Uptime/Expires
 Interface state: Interface, Next-Hop or VCD, State/Mode
```

```
(*, 232.32.32.32), 02:34:00/stopped, RP 0.0.0.0, flags: DCL
  Incoming interface: Null, RPF nbr 0.0.0.0
  Outgoing interface list:
    Serial0/0/0, Forward/Dense, 00:31:23/00:00:00
    FastEthernet0/0, Forward/Dense, 02:33:31/00:00:00
    Serial0/0/1, Forward/Dense, 02:33:31/00:00:00
    Loopback1, Forward/Dense, 02:34:00/00:00:00


(172.16.20.4, 232.32.32.32), 00:00:09/00:03:00, flags: LT
  Incoming interface: Serial0/0/0, RPF nbr 172.16.102.2
  Outgoing interface list:
    Loopback1, Forward/Dense, 00:00:09/00:00:00
    Serial0/0/1, Prune/Dense, 00:00:09/00:02:52
    FastEthernet0/0, Prune/Dense, 00:00:09/00:02:49


(*, 224.0.1.40), 02:34:01/00:02:43, RP 0.0.0.0, flags: DCL
  Incoming interface: Null, RPF nbr 0.0.0.0
  Outgoing interface list:
    Serial0/0/0, Forward/Dense, 00:31:24/00:00:00
    FastEthernet0/0, Forward/Dense, 02:33:33/00:00:00
    Serial0/0/1, Forward/Dense, 02:33:33/00:00:00
    Loopback1, Forward/Dense, 02:34:02/00:00:00
```

```
R2# show ip mroute
IP Multicast Routing Table
Flags: D - Dense, S - Sparse, B - Bidir Group, s - SSM Group, C - Connected,
       L - Local, P - Pruned, R - RP-bit set, F - Register flag,
       T - SPT-bit set, J - Join SPT, M - MSDP created entry,
       X - Proxy Join Timer Running, A - Candidate for MSDP Advertisement,
       U - URD, I - Received Source Specific Host Report,
       Z - Multicast Tunnel, z - MDT-data group sender,
       Y - Joined MDT-data group, y - Sending to MDT-data group
Outgoing interface flags: H - Hardware switched, A - Assert winner
 Timers: Uptime/Expires
 Interface state: Interface, Next-Hop or VCD, State/Mode


(*, 232.32.32.32), 00:32:01/stopped, RP 0.0.0.0, flags: DCL
  Incoming interface: Null, RPF nbr 0.0.0.0
  Outgoing interface list:
    Serial0/0/0, Forward/Dense, 00:31:33/00:00:00
    Serial0/0/1, Forward/Dense, 00:31:33/00:00:00
    Loopback2, Forward/Dense, 00:32:01/00:00:00


(172.16.20.4, 232.32.32.32), 00:00:48/00:02:58, flags: LT
  Incoming interface: FastEthernet0/0, RPF nbr 0.0.0.0
```

```
Outgoing interface list:
   Loopback2, Forward/Dense, 00:00:50/00:00:00
   Serial0/0/1, Forward/Dense, 00:00:50/00:00:00
   Serial0/0/0, Prune/Dense, 00:00:50/00:00:00


(*, 224.0.1.40), 00:32:03/00:02:47, RP 0.0.0.0, flags: DCL
  Incoming interface: Null, RPF nbr 0.0.0.0
  Outgoing interface list:
    Serial0/0/0, Forward/Dense, 00:31:34/00:00:00
    Serial0/0/1, Forward/Dense, 00:31:34/00:00:00
    Loopback2, Forward/Dense, 00:32:23/00:00:00
```

```
R3# show ip mroute
IP Multicast Routing Table
Flags: D - Dense, S - Sparse, B - Bidir Group, s - SSM Group, C - Connected,
       L - Local, P - Pruned, R - RP-bit set, F - Register flag,
       T - SPT-bit set, J - Join SPT, M - MSDP created entry,
       X - Proxy Join Timer Running, A - Candidate for MSDP Advertisement,
       U - URD, I - Received Source Specific Host Report,
       Z - Multicast Tunnel, z - MDT-data group sender,
       Y - Joined MDT-data group, y - Sending to MDT-data group
Outgoing interface flags: H - Hardware switched, A - Assert winner
 Timers: Uptime/Expires
 Interface state: Interface, Next-Hop or VCD, State/Mode


(*, 232.32.32.32), 02:34:45/stopped, RP 0.0.0.0, flags: DCL
  Incoming interface: Null, RPF nbr 0.0.0.0
  Outgoing interface list:
    Serial0/0/1, Forward/Dense, 00:32:05/00:00:00
    FastEthernet0/0, Forward/Dense, 02:34:13/00:00:00
    Serial0/0/0, Forward/Dense, 02:34:43/00:00:00
    Loopback3, Forward/Dense, 02:34:45/00:00:00


(172.16.20.4, 232.32.32.32), 00:00:52/00:02:59, flags: LT
  Incoming interface: Serial0/0/1, RPF nbr 172.16.203.2
  Outgoing interface list:
    Loopback3, Forward/Dense, 00:00:52/00:00:00
    Serial0/0/0, Prune/Dense, 00:00:51/00:02:11, A
    FastEthernet0/0, Forward/Dense, 00:00:48/00:02:11, A


(*, 224.0.1.40), 02:34:46/00:02:58, RP 0.0.0.0, flags: DCL
  Incoming interface: Null, RPF nbr 0.0.0.0
  Outgoing interface list:
    Serial0/0/1, Forward/Dense, 00:32:06/00:00:00
```

```
FastEthernet0/0, Forward/Dense, 02:34:15/00:00:00
Serial0/0/0, Forward/Dense, 02:34:46/00:00:00
Loopback3, Forward/Dense, 02:34:47/00:00:00
```

The two timers shown on the first line of the (S, G) entry on each router indicate the time since the first multicast to that group and the time when the entry expires. All the expiration timers for (172.16.20.4, 232.32.32.32) state display as roughly 3 minutes while SW1 sends the multicast pings. Thus, each time the router receives a multicast packet matching the (S, G) entry (172.16.20.4, 232.32.32.32), IGMP resets the expiration timer to 3 minutes.

By default, IGMP sends a general query every 60 seconds on each PIM interface. A general query requests any devices running IGMP on that subnet to report any groups to which they subscribe to the querying router. If no membership reports are heard for a particular group on that interface over three times the query interval, the multicast router declares that there is no active member of the group on the interface. The router stops sending multicasts to that group on that egress interface. If a router does not receive multicasts from an (S, G) pair for 3 minutes, the multicast routing table deletes the (S, G) entry.

The IP multicast routing table also indicates whether the PIM interfaces negotiated to flood multicast data to that group out an interface or pruned (S, G) multicast traffic from being sent out that interface.

Based on the IP multicast routing tables shown previously, which PIM interfaces on each router are forwarding traffic from 172.16.20.4 to 232.32.32.32?

_____

_____

_____

Step 6: Verify PIM-DM Flood-and-Prune Behavior

To view the flood-and-prune behavior of PIM-DM, wait for the multicast stream from 172.16.20.4 to complete and for the (S, G) state in the multicast routing tables to expire. Then issue the **debug ip igmp** and **debug ip pim** commands on all routers.

PIM relies on the unicast IP routing table to construct shortest-path trees from the sources to the multicast subscribers. PIM neighbors send control messages to determine which neighbor is closer to the source in terms of the unicast routing information on each neighbor. PIM neighbors on the subnet elect a particular router as the forwarder for that (S, G) pair using Assert messages. Each Assert message carries the best administrative distance and metric that the advertising router has to the source. The PIM router with the best administrative distance and metric is elected as the forwarder for that (S, G) or (*, G) entry. The forwarder then prunes that (S, G) pair from being forwarded by any other routers on the subnet.

Do not confuse the DR with the forwarder. Although both are elected on multi-access networks, the role of DR does not include the responsibility to forward multicast traffic. As defined by IGMPv1, a DR is elected based on highest IP address to control the IGMP querying. Thus, a DR exists to identify which receivers exist on a subnet by polling for listeners to any group. There can only be one DR on a subnet at a time.

In contrast, every multi-access subnet elects forwarders individually for each (S, G) and (*, G) pair. The forwarder is elected based on best administrative distance and metric to the source. The forwarder is the metrically closest router on the subnet to the source.

Display the unicast routing table entry for 172.16.20.4 on each router:

```
R1# show ip route 172.16.20.4
Routing entry for 172.16.20.0/24
  Known via "eigrp 1", distance 90, metric 20517120, type internal
  Redistributing via eigrp 1
  Last update from 172.16.13.3 on FastEthernet0/0, 00:42:57 ago
  Routing Descriptor Blocks:
  * 172.16.13.3, from 172.16.13.3, 00:42:57 ago, via FastEthernet0/0
      Route metric is 20517120, traffic share count is 1
      Total delay is 20200 microseconds, minimum bandwidth is 128 Kbit
      Reliability 255/255, minimum MTU 1500 bytes
      Loading 1/255, Hops 2
```

```
R2# show ip route 172.16.20.4
Routing entry for 172.16.20.0/24
  Known via "connected", distance 0, metric 0 (connected, via interface)
  Redistributing via eigrp 1
  Routing Descriptor Blocks:
  * directly connected, via FastEthernet0/0
      Route metric is 0, traffic share count is 1
```

```
R3# show ip route 172.16.20.4
Routing entry for 172.16.20.0/24
  Known via "eigrp 1", distance 90, metric 20514560, type internal
  Redistributing via eigrp 1
  Last update from 172.16.203.2 on Serial0/0/1, 00:43:31 ago
  Routing Descriptor Blocks:
  * 172.16.203.2, from 172.16.203.2, 00:43:31 ago, via Serial0/0/1
      Route metric is 20514560, traffic share count is 1
      Total delay is 20100 microseconds, minimum bandwidth is 128 Kbit
      Reliability 255/255, minimum MTU 1500 bytes
      Loading 1/255, Hops 1
```

Begin the same extended ping on SW1 to the multicast group. Examine the debugging messages shown on each router:

```
R1# debug ip pim
*Nov  6 00:43:28.731: PIM(0): Send v2 Assert on Serial0/0/0 for 232.32.32.32, source
172.16.20.4, metric [90/20517120]

*Nov  6 00:43:28.735: PIM(0): Assert metric to source 172.16.20.4 is [90/20517120]

*Nov  6 00:43:28.735: PIM(0): We win, our metric [90/20517120]

*Nov  6 00:43:28.735: PIM(0): Prune Serial0/0/0/232.32.32.32 from (172.16.20.4/32,
232.32.32.32)

*Nov  6 00:43:28.735: PIM(0): Pruning immediately Serial0/0/0 (p2p)

*Nov  6 00:43:28.743: PIM(0): Send v2 Assert on Serial0/0/1 for 232.32.32.32, source
172.16.20.4, metric [90/20517120]

*Nov  6 00:43:28.743: PIM(0): Assert metric to source 172.16.20.4 is [90/20517120]
```

```
*Nov  6 00:43:28.743: PIM(0): We win, our metric [90/20517120]

*Nov  6 00:43:28.743: PIM(0): Prune Serial0/0/1/232.32.32.32 from (172.16.20.4/32,
232.32.32.32)

*Nov  6 00:43:28.743: PIM(0): Pruning immediately Serial0/0/1 (p2p)


!... continues below ...
```

Because R1 has not yet received any PIMv2 assert messages from its neighbors on either Serial0/0/0 or Serial0/0/1, it has elected itself as the forwarder for (172.16.20.4/32, 232.32.32.32) on both interfaces and pruned other traffic flows.

On a point-to-point link, a PIM-DM router must assert itself as being the forwarder on the subnet for the group, unless another router sends an assert message with a lower metric to the source. This behavior allows PIM-DM to succeed in the simple case of a single multicast router on a subnet. In this case, the router cannot wait for other multicast routers to respond to the assert message before flooding multicast data; it must simply begin sending data until another router with a lower metric to the source prunes it.

Notice that the metrics used for route calculation are the EIGRP and composite metrics for the unicast IP routes to those source networks from the unicast routing table:

```
!... continued from above ...


*Nov  6 00:43:28.751: PIM(0): Received v2 Assert on Serial0/0/1 from 172.16.103.3

*Nov  6 00:43:28.751: PIM(0): Assert metric to source 172.16.20.4 is [90/20514560]

*Nov  6 00:43:28.751: PIM(0): We lose, our metric [90/20517120]

*Nov  6 00:43:28.751: PIM(0): (172.16.20.4/32, 232.32.32.32) oif Serial0/0/1 in Prune
state

*Nov  6 00:43:28.751: PIM(0): Received v2 Assert on Serial0/0/0 from 172.16.102.2

*Nov  6 00:43:28.751: PIM(0): Assert metric to source 172.16.20.4 is [0/0]

*Nov  6 00:43:28.751: PIM(0): We lose, our metric [90/20517120]

*Nov  6 00:43:28.751: PIM(0): (172.16.20.4/32, 232.32.32.32) oif Serial0/0/0 in Prune
state

*Nov  6 00:43:29.663: PIM(0): Received v2 Assert on Serial0/0/0 from 172.16.102.2

*Nov  6 00:43:29.663: PIM(0): Assert metric to source 172.16.20.4 is [0/0]

*Nov  6 00:43:29.663: PIM(0): We lose, our metric [90/20517120]

*Nov  6 00:43:29.663: PIM(0): (172.16.20.4/32, 232.32.32.32) oif Serial0/0/0 in Prune
state

*Nov  6 00:43:29.751: PIM(0): Received v2 Assert on Serial0/0/1 from 172.16.103.3

*Nov  6 00:43:29.751: PIM(0): Assert metric to source 172.16.20.4 is [90/20514560]

*Nov  6 00:43:29.751: PIM(0): We lose, our metric [90/20517120]

*Nov  6 00:43:29.751: PIM(0): (172.16.20.4/32, 232.32.32.32) oif Serial0/0/1 in Prune
state
```

PIM selects the router with the lowest administrative distance to be the designated forwarder for the subnet for the (S, G) pair. In the case of a tie, PIM prefers the router with the lowest metric.

Step 7: Explore the Multicast Routing Table

Verify the state you predicted at the end of Step 5 about forwarding and pruning interfaces against the following output of the **show ip mroute** *source_address group_address* command:

```
R1# show ip mroute 172.16.20.4 232.32.32.32
<output omitted>


(172.16.20.4, 232.32.32.32), 00:01:07/00:02:58, flags: LT
  Incoming interface: FastEthernet0/0, RPF nbr 172.16.13.3
  Outgoing interface list:
    Loopback1, Forward/Dense, 00:01:07/00:00:00
    Serial0/0/1, Prune/Dense, 00:01:07/00:01:55
    Serial0/0/0, Prune/Dense, 00:01:07/00:01:55
R2# show ip mroute 172.16.20.4 232.32.32.32
<output omitted>


(172.16.20.4, 232.32.32.32), 00:01:21/00:02:58, flags: LT
  Incoming interface: FastEthernet0/0, RPF nbr 0.0.0.0
  Outgoing interface list:
    Loopback2, Forward/Dense, 00:01:21/00:00:00
    Serial0/0/0, Prune/Dense, 00:01:20/00:01:42, A
    Serial0/0/1, Forward/Dense, 00:01:21/00:00:00
R3# show ip mroute 172.16.20.4 232.32.32.32
<output omitted>


(172.16.20.4, 232.32.32.32), 00:01:22/00:02:59, flags: LT
  Incoming interface: Serial0/0/1, RPF nbr 172.16.203.2
  Outgoing interface list:
    Loopback3, Forward/Dense, 00:01:22/00:00:00
    Serial0/0/0, Prune/Dense, 00:01:22/00:01:40, A
    FastEthernet0/0, Forward/Dense, 00:01:22/00:00:00
```

How does PIM decide which incoming interface to use for each group?

_____

_____

Because PIM does not use its own topological algorithm to locate multicast sources, it must have a way of determining which interface faces the upstream neighbor of the tree stemming from the multicast source. PIM uses the reverse-path forwarding (RPF) check to find the interface closest to the source in terms of destination-based unicast routing.

Cisco IOS allows you to run RPF checks for specific sources with the **show ip rpf** *source_address* command. Use this command on R1 to find the incoming interface for the (172.16.20.4, 232.32.32.32) pair:

```
R1# show ip rpf 172.16.20.4
RPF information for ? (172.16.20.4)
  RPF interface: FastEthernet0/0
  RPF neighbor: ? (172.16.13.3)
  RPF route/mask: 172.16.20.0/24
  RPF type: unicast (eigrp 1)
  RPF recursion count: 0
  Doing distance-preferred lookups across tables
```

Although the multicast routing table includes RPF information, the **show ip rpf** command can be useful when debugging hidden multicast issues.

Use this output from R1 to answer the questions that follow:

```
R1# show ip mroute 172.16.20.4 232.32.32.32
<output omitted>

(172.16.20.4, 232.32.32.32), 00:01:07/00:02:58, flags: LT
  Incoming interface: FastEthernet0/0, RPF nbr 172.16.13.3
  Outgoing interface list:
    Loopback1, Forward/Dense, 00:01:07/00:00:00
    Serial0/0/1, Prune/Dense, 00:01:07/00:01:55
    Serial0/0/0, Prune/Dense, 00:01:07/00:01:55
```

What is the incoming interface for the (S, G) pair (172.16.20.4, 232.32.32.32)?

_____

How does Cisco IOS assign this interface as the incoming interface?

_____

_____

Which neighboring router appears to R1 as being the next hop upstream toward the multicast source 172.16.20.4?

_____

Challenge

If your simulation of the (S, G) pair (172.16.20.4, 232.32.32.32) correctly models the CEO's presentation to be shown later in the week, do you think the presentation will be available on the loopback interfaces at all three sites?

_____

_____

Why does Cisco not recommend using PIM-DM in production networks?

_____

_____

_____

_____

_____

TCL Script Output: Unicast

```
R1# tclsh
R1(tcl)# foreach address {
+>(tcl)# 192.168.1.1
+>(tcl)# 172.16.13.1
+>(tcl)# 172.16.102.1
+>(tcl)# 172.16.103.1
+>(tcl)# 192.168.2.1
+>(tcl)# 172.16.20.2
+>(tcl)# 172.16.102.2
+>(tcl)# 172.16.203.2
+>(tcl)# 192.168.3.1
+>(tcl)# 172.16.13.3
+>(tcl)# 172.16.103.3
+>(tcl)# 172.16.203.3
+>(tcl)# 172.16.20.4
+>(tcl)# } { ping $address }

Type escape sequence to abort.
Sending 5, 100-byte ICMP Echos to 192.168.1.1, timeout is 2 seconds:
!!!!!
Success rate is 100 percent (5/5), round-trip min/avg/max = 1/1/1 ms
Type escape sequence to abort.
Sending 5, 100-byte ICMP Echos to 172.16.13.1, timeout is 2 seconds:
!!!!!
Success rate is 100 percent (5/5), round-trip min/avg/max = 1/2/4 ms
Type escape sequence to abort.
Sending 5, 100-byte ICMP Echos to 172.16.102.1, timeout is 2 seconds:
!!!!!
Success rate is 100 percent (5/5), round-trip min/avg/max = 56/56/60 ms
Type escape sequence to abort.
Sending 5, 100-byte ICMP Echos to 172.16.103.1, timeout is 2 seconds:
!!!!!
Success rate is 100 percent (5/5), round-trip min/avg/max = 56/56/60 ms
```

```
Type escape sequence to abort.
Sending 5, 100-byte ICMP Echos to 192.168.2.1, timeout is 2 seconds:
!!!!!
Success rate is 100 percent (5/5), round-trip min/avg/max = 28/28/32 ms
Type escape sequence to abort.
Sending 5, 100-byte ICMP Echos to 172.16.20.2, timeout is 2 seconds:
!!!!!
Success rate is 100 percent (5/5), round-trip min/avg/max = 28/29/32 ms
Type escape sequence to abort.
Sending 5, 100-byte ICMP Echos to 172.16.102.2, timeout is 2 seconds:
!!!!!
Success rate is 100 percent (5/5), round-trip min/avg/max = 28/28/32 ms
Type escape sequence to abort.
Sending 5, 100-byte ICMP Echos to 172.16.203.2, timeout is 2 seconds:
!!!!!
Success rate is 100 percent (5/5), round-trip min/avg/max = 28/29/32 ms
Type escape sequence to abort.
Sending 5, 100-byte ICMP Echos to 192.168.3.1, timeout is 2 seconds:
!!!!!
Success rate is 100 percent (5/5), round-trip min/avg/max = 1/2/4 ms
Type escape sequence to abort.
Sending 5, 100-byte ICMP Echos to 172.16.13.3, timeout is 2 seconds:
!!!!!
Success rate is 100 percent (5/5), round-trip min/avg/max = 1/2/4 ms
Type escape sequence to abort.
Sending 5, 100-byte ICMP Echos to 172.16.103.3, timeout is 2 seconds:
!!!!!
Success rate is 100 percent (5/5), round-trip min/avg/max = 28/28/32 ms
Type escape sequence to abort.
Sending 5, 100-byte ICMP Echos to 172.16.203.3, timeout is 2 seconds:
!!!!!
Success rate is 100 percent (5/5), round-trip min/avg/max = 1/1/4 ms
Type escape sequence to abort.
Sending 5, 100-byte ICMP Echos to 172.16.20.4, timeout is 2 seconds:
!!!!!
Success rate is 100 percent (5/5), round-trip min/avg/max = 28/28/32 ms
R1(tcl)# tclquit
R2# tclsh
R2(tcl)# foreach address {
+>(tcl)# 192.168.1.1
+>(tcl)# 172.16.13.1
```

```
+>(tcl)# 172.16.102.1
+>(tcl)# 172.16.103.1
+>(tcl)# 192.168.2.1
+>(tcl)# 172.16.20.2
+>(tcl)# 172.16.102.2
+>(tcl)# 172.16.203.2
+>(tcl)# 192.168.3.1
+>(tcl)# 172.16.13.3
+>(tcl)# 172.16.103.3
+>(tcl)# 172.16.203.3
+>(tcl)# 172.16.20.4
+>(tcl)# } { ping $address }


Type escape sequence to abort.
Sending 5, 100-byte ICMP Echos to 192.168.1.1, timeout is 2 seconds:
!!!!!
Success rate is 100 percent (5/5), round-trip min/avg/max = 28/28/32 ms
Type escape sequence to abort.
Sending 5, 100-byte ICMP Echos to 172.16.13.1, timeout is 2 seconds:
!!!!!
Success rate is 100 percent (5/5), round-trip min/avg/max = 28/28/28 ms
Type escape sequence to abort.
Sending 5, 100-byte ICMP Echos to 172.16.102.1, timeout is 2 seconds:
!!!!!
Success rate is 100 percent (5/5), round-trip min/avg/max = 28/28/32 ms
Type escape sequence to abort.
Sending 5, 100-byte ICMP Echos to 172.16.103.1, timeout is 2 seconds:
!!!!!
Success rate is 100 percent (5/5), round-trip min/avg/max = 28/28/32 ms
Type escape sequence to abort.
Sending 5, 100-byte ICMP Echos to 192.168.2.1, timeout is 2 seconds:
!!!!!
Success rate is 100 percent (5/5), round-trip min/avg/max = 1/1/4 ms
Type escape sequence to abort.
Sending 5, 100-byte ICMP Echos to 172.16.20.2, timeout is 2 seconds:
!!!!!
Success rate is 100 percent (5/5), round-trip min/avg/max = 1/1/1 ms
Type escape sequence to abort.
Sending 5, 100-byte ICMP Echos to 172.16.102.2, timeout is 2 seconds:
!!!!!
Success rate is 100 percent (5/5), round-trip min/avg/max = 56/57/64 ms
Type escape sequence to abort.
```

```
Sending 5, 100-byte ICMP Echos to 172.16.203.2, timeout is 2 seconds:
!!!!!
Success rate is 100 percent (5/5), round-trip min/avg/max = 56/58/68 ms
Type escape sequence to abort.
Sending 5, 100-byte ICMP Echos to 192.168.3.1, timeout is 2 seconds:
!!!!!
Success rate is 100 percent (5/5), round-trip min/avg/max = 28/28/32 ms
Type escape sequence to abort.
Sending 5, 100-byte ICMP Echos to 172.16.13.3, timeout is 2 seconds:
!!!!!
Success rate is 100 percent (5/5), round-trip min/avg/max = 28/28/32 ms
Type escape sequence to abort.
Sending 5, 100-byte ICMP Echos to 172.16.103.3, timeout is 2 seconds:
!!!!!
Success rate is 100 percent (5/5), round-trip min/avg/max = 40/42/44 ms
Type escape sequence to abort.
Sending 5, 100-byte ICMP Echos to 172.16.203.3, timeout is 2 seconds:
!!!!!
Success rate is 100 percent (5/5), round-trip min/avg/max = 28/28/28 ms
Type escape sequence to abort.
Sending 5, 100-byte ICMP Echos to 172.16.20.4, timeout is 2 seconds:
!!!!!
Success rate is 100 percent (5/5), round-trip min/avg/max = 1/1/4 ms
R2(tcl)# tclquit
```
```
R3# tclsh
R3(tcl)# foreach address {
+>(tcl)# 192.168.1.1
+>(tcl)# 172.16.13.1
+>(tcl)# 172.16.102.1
+>(tcl)# 172.16.103.1
+>(tcl)# 192.168.2.1
+>(tcl)# 172.16.20.2
+>(tcl)# 172.16.102.2
+>(tcl)# 172.16.203.2
+>(tcl)# 192.168.3.1
+>(tcl)# 172.16.13.3
+>(tcl)# 172.16.103.3
+>(tcl)# 172.16.203.3
+>(tcl)# 172.16.20.4
+>(tcl)# } { ping $address }

Type escape sequence to abort.
Sending 5, 100-byte ICMP Echos to 192.168.1.1, timeout is 2 seconds:
!!!!!
```

```
Success rate is 100 percent (5/5), round-trip min/avg/max = 1/2/4 ms
Type escape sequence to abort.
Sending 5, 100-byte ICMP Echos to 172.16.13.1, timeout is 2 seconds:
!!!!!
Success rate is 100 percent (5/5), round-trip min/avg/max = 1/2/4 ms
Type escape sequence to abort.
Sending 5, 100-byte ICMP Echos to 172.16.102.1, timeout is 2 seconds:
!!!!!
Success rate is 100 percent (5/5), round-trip min/avg/max = 1/2/4 ms
Type escape sequence to abort.
Sending 5, 100-byte ICMP Echos to 172.16.103.1, timeout is 2 seconds:
!!!!!
Success rate is 100 percent (5/5), round-trip min/avg/max = 28/28/32 ms
Type escape sequence to abort.
Sending 5, 100-byte ICMP Echos to 192.168.2.1, timeout is 2 seconds:
!!!!!
Success rate is 100 percent (5/5), round-trip min/avg/max = 28/28/32 ms
Type escape sequence to abort.
Sending 5, 100-byte ICMP Echos to 172.16.20.2, timeout is 2 seconds:
!!!!!
Success rate is 100 percent (5/5), round-trip min/avg/max = 28/28/32 ms
Type escape sequence to abort.
Sending 5, 100-byte ICMP Echos to 172.16.102.2, timeout is 2 seconds:
!!!!!
Success rate is 100 percent (5/5), round-trip min/avg/max = 28/28/32 ms
Type escape sequence to abort.
Sending 5, 100-byte ICMP Echos to 172.16.203.2, timeout is 2 seconds:
!!!!!
Success rate is 100 percent (5/5), round-trip min/avg/max = 28/28/32 ms
Type escape sequence to abort.
Sending 5, 100-byte ICMP Echos to 192.168.3.1, timeout is 2 seconds:
!!!!!
Success rate is 100 percent (5/5), round-trip min/avg/max = 1/1/1 ms
Type escape sequence to abort.
Sending 5, 100-byte ICMP Echos to 172.16.13.3, timeout is 2 seconds:
!!!!!
Success rate is 100 percent (5/5), round-trip min/avg/max = 1/1/1 ms
Type escape sequence to abort.
Sending 5, 100-byte ICMP Echos to 172.16.103.3, timeout is 2 seconds:
!!!!!
Success rate is 100 percent (5/5), round-trip min/avg/max = 56/56/60 ms
Type escape sequence to abort.
Sending 5, 100-byte ICMP Echos to 172.16.203.3, timeout is 2 seconds:
!!!!!
```

```
Success rate is 100 percent (5/5), round-trip min/avg/max = 56/58/64 ms
Type escape sequence to abort.
Sending 5, 100-byte ICMP Echos to 172.16.20.4, timeout is 2 seconds:
!!!!!
Success rate is 100 percent (5/5), round-trip min/avg/max = 28/28/32 ms
R3(tcl)#  tclquit
```

Lab 7-3: Routing IP Multicast with PIM Sparse Mode (7.5.3)

The objectives of this lab are as follows:

- Implement and verify PIM-SM operation and adjacencies

- Implement and verify the use of a static rendezvous point

- Observe the shared tree and source tree

- Debug the PIM-SM operation to discover SPT shared tree to shortest-path tree transition

Figure 7-4 illustrates the topology that will be used for this lab.

Figure 7-4   Topology Diagram for Lab 7-3

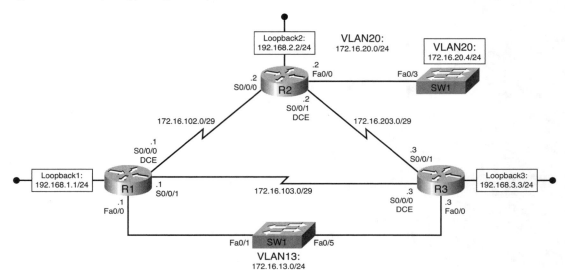

Scenario

Your successful assistance in configuring IP multicast routing has allowed CrushASodaCan.com to become a community action organization with a wide base of interested citizens. Because of your help, the organization can now preview their TV commercials via the network before releasing them to the public. CrushASodaCan.com also projects high growth rates in terms of volunteer workers using their network. Unfortunately, the flooding and pruning with PIM-DM that you configured for them cannot handle the new demands being made on the network. So they have hired you again as a consultant to solve this. You decide to implement PIM sparse mode (PIM-SM) to create a subscription-based multicast topology in CrushASodaCan.com's network.

Step 1: Load Initial Configurations

Begin with the final configurations from Lab 7-2. You can download these router configurations at www.ciscopress.com/title/1587132133 under the More Information section on the page.

R1:

!

```
hostname R1
!
interface Loopback1
 ip address 192.168.1.1 255.255.255.0
 ip pim dense-mode
 ip igmp join-group 232.32.32.32
!
interface FastEthernet0/0
 ip address 172.16.13.1 255.255.255.0
 ip pim dense-mode
 no shutdown
!
interface Serial0/0/0
 bandwidth 64
 ip address 172.16.102.1 255.255.255.248
 ip pim dense-mode
 clock rate 64000
 no shutdown
!
interface Serial0/0/1
 bandwidth 64
 ip address 172.16.103.1 255.255.255.248
 ip pim dense-mode
 no shutdown
!
router eigrp 1
 network 172.16.0.0
 network 192.168.0.0 0.0.255.255
 auto-summary
!
end
```

R2:
```
!
hostname R2
!
interface Loopback2
 ip address 192.168.2.1 255.255.255.0
 ip pim dense-mode
 ip igmp join-group 232.32.32.32
!
interface FastEthernet0/0
 ip address 172.16.20.2 255.255.255.0
```

```
 ip pim dense-mode
 no shutdown
!
interface Serial0/0/0
 bandwidth 64
 ip address 172.16.102.2 255.255.255.248
 ip pim dense-mode
 no shutdown
!
interface Serial0/0/1
 bandwidth 128
 ip address 172.16.203.2 255.255.255.248
 ip pim dense-mode
 clock rate 128000
 no shutdown
!
router eigrp 1
 network 172.16.0.0
 network 192.168.0.0 0.0.255.255
 auto-summary
!
end
```

R3:

```
!
hostname R3
!
interface Loopback3
 ip address 192.168.3.1 255.255.255.0
 ip pim dense-mode
 ip igmp join-group 232.32.32.32
!
interface FastEthernet0/0
 ip address 172.16.13.3 255.255.255.0
 ip pim dense-mode
 no shutdown
!
interface Serial0/0/0
 bandwidth 64
 ip address 172.16.103.3 255.255.255.248
 ip pim dense-mode
 clock rate 64000
 no shutdown
!
```

```
interface Serial0/0/1
 bandwidth 128
 ip address 172.16.203.3 255.255.255.248
 ip pim dense-mode
 no shutdown
!
router eigrp 1
 network 172.16.0.0
 network 192.168.0.0 0.0.255.255
 auto-summary
!
end
```
```
SW1# show run
!
hostname SW1
!
interface FastEthernet0/1
 switchport access vlan 13
 switchport mode access
!
interface FastEthernet0/3
 switchport access vlan 20
 switchport mode access
!
interface FastEthernet0/5
 switchport access vlan 13
 switchport mode access
!
interface Vlan20
 ip address 172.16.20.4 255.255.255.0
 no shutdown
!
ip default-gateway 172.16.20.2
!
end
```

Verify that each of the loopback interfaces subscribed to the multicast group using the **show ip igmp groups** command:

```
R1# show ip igmp groups
IGMP Connected Group Membership
Group Address    Interface      Uptime    Expires   Last Reporter   Group Accounted
232.32.32.32     Loopback1      00:05:45  00:01:59  192.168.1.1
224.0.1.40       Loopback1      00:05:45  00:01:59  192.168.1.1
R2# show ip igmp groups
```

```
IGMP Connected Group Membership
Group Address     Interface       Uptime    Expires   Last Reporter  Group Accounted
232.32.32.32      Loopback2       00:05:12  00:02:37  192.168.2.1
224.0.1.40        Loopback2       00:05:12  00:02:40  192.168.2.1
```

```
R3# show ip igmp groups
IGMP Connected Group Membership
Group Address     Interface       Uptime    Expires   Last Reporter  Group Accounted
232.32.32.32      Loopback3       00:05:27  00:02:23  192.168.3.1
224.0.1.40        Loopback3       00:05:27  00:02:21  192.168.3.1
```

Step 3: Implement PIM-SM

Planning is important when creating PIM-SM networks. Because traffic is not simply flooded out all PIM interfaces as it is in dense mode networks, you make sure to place the rendezvous point (RP) in a central location.

CrushASodaCan.com's management decided the RP should be placed on R1. This location allows you to observe the cutover from the shared tree to the source tree because R2 and R3 have shorter paths to 172.16.20.4 than those through R1.

Before enabling PIM-SM on the interfaces, set the static RP address as R1's Loopback1 address using the **ip pim rp-address** *rp-address* [*access-list*] command. You can either assign a router to be the global RP for all multicast groups or have it be on a per-group basis using an access list. In this case, map R1 as the RP only for the 232.32.32.32 multicast group. This command must be used on all routers running PIM-SM:

```
R1# configure terminal
R1(config)# access-list 32 permit 232.32.32.32
R1(config)# ip pim rp-address 192.168.1.1 32
```

```
R2# configure terminal
R2(config)# access-list 32 permit 232.32.32.32
R2(config)# ip pim rp-address 192.168.1.1
```

```
R3# configure terminal
R3(config)# access-list 32 permit 232.32.32.32
R3(config)# ip pim rp-address 192.168.1.1
```

What is the purpose of the RP in PIM-SM?

_____

_____

Given the fact that an RP can be set for specific groups, can you have more than one static RP in a multicast network? Explain.

_____

PIM-SM has more redundant ways of configuring RPs and mapping agents. Notice in this example that each multicast router has a static RP address pointing to a specific router on the network and a static mapping agent of itself. A mapping agent is simply a device that provides a mapping of a group to an RP. You have statically the group-to-RP mapping on every router, so each router acts as its own mapping agent.

In PIM-DM, all (S, G) entries are present in *every* IP multicast routing table on the multicast network while the source is broadcasting. If you were using many groups or many sources for each group, the size of the multicast routing table would dramatically increase from the one in Lab 7-2.

PIM-SM rendezvous points introduce multicast sources by acting as the network receptionist that knows the location of all multicast sources. PIM-SM creates a shared distribution tree represented by (*, G) in each multicast routing table. This shared tree is calculated using the RPF upstream interface to the RP for that group. Thus, the shared tree is essentially a shortest-path tree to the RP address.

PIM-SM reduces the amount of multicast state in the network by using (*, G) shared tree entries on routers through which no sources are sending traffic for a given group G. When a node in the topology subscribes to a multicast group, that node's upstream multicast router registers with the RP and forwards traffic down the shared tree to the receiver until it discovers a shorter path to the source in its unicast routing table. At that point, the multicast router prunes the stream from the shared tree and begins receiving the stream via its shortest unicast path to the source represented by its (S, G) entry.

PIM-SM is designed for sparsely populated multicast networks in which it is not necessary to flood multicast traffic to every subnet. Sparse mode is a general-purpose multicast mode that should be used in most circumstances.

As you did in Lab 7-2, issue a repeated ping from SW1 to generate the (S, G) state in PIM-DM before you apply PIM-SM to the interfaces:

```
SW1# ping
Protocol [ip]:
Target IP address: 232.32.32.32
Repeat count [1]: 100
Datagram size [100]:
Timeout in seconds [2]:
Extended commands [n]:
Sweep range of sizes [n]:
Type escape sequence to abort.
Sending 100, 100-byte ICMP Echos to 232.32.32.32, timeout is 2 seconds:

Reply to request 0 from 172.16.20.2, 8 ms
Reply to request 0 from 172.16.102.1, 36 ms
Reply to request 0 from 172.16.203.3, 36 ms
Reply to request 1 from 172.16.20.2, 4 ms
Reply to request 1 from 172.16.102.1, 28 ms
Reply to request 1 from 172.16.203.3, 28 ms
Reply to request 2 from 172.16.20.2, 8 ms
Reply to request 2 from 172.16.102.1, 32 ms
Reply to request 2 from 172.16.203.3, 32 ms
```

Display the multicast routing table on each router with the **show ip mroute** command:

R1# **show ip mroute**

IP Multicast Routing Table

Flags: D - Dense, S - Sparse, B - Bidir Group, s - SSM Group, C - Connected,

      L - Local, P - Pruned, R - RP-bit set, F - Register flag,

      T - SPT-bit set, J - Join SPT, M - MSDP created entry,

      X - Proxy Join Timer Running, A - Candidate for MSDP Advertisement,

      U - URD, I - Received Source Specific Host Report,

      Z - Multicast Tunnel, z - MDT-data group sender,

      Y - Joined MDT-data group, y - Sending to MDT-data group

Outgoing interface flags: H - Hardware switched, A - Assert winner

 Timers: Uptime/Expires

 Interface state: Interface, Next-Hop or VCD, State/Mode

(*, 232.32.32.32), 01:42:56/00:03:04, RP 192.168.1.1, flags: SJCL

  Incoming interface: Null, RPF nbr 0.0.0.0

  Outgoing interface list:

    FastEthernet0/0, Forward/Dense, 01:42:26/00:00:00

    Serial0/0/1, Forward/Dense, 01:42:27/00:00:00

    Serial0/0/0, Forward/Dense, 01:42:28/00:00:00

    Loopback1, Forward/Dense, 01:42:56/00:00:00

(172.16.20.4, 232.32.32.32), 00:01:20/00:02:59, flags: LT

  Incoming interface: FastEthernet0/0, RPF nbr 172.16.13.3

  Outgoing interface list:

    Loopback1, Forward/Dense, 00:01:20/00:00:00

    Serial0/0/0, Prune/Dense, 00:01:20/00:01:39

    Serial0/0/1, Prune/Dense, 00:01:20/00:01:39

(*, 224.0.1.40), 00:57:27/00:02:49, RP 0.0.0.0, flags: DCL

  Incoming interface: Null, RPF nbr 0.0.0.0

  Outgoing interface list:

    Serial0/0/1, Forward/Dense, 00:57:27/00:00:00

    Serial0/0/0, Forward/Dense, 00:57:35/00:00:00

    FastEthernet0/0, Forward/Dense, 00:57:35/00:00:00

    Loopback1, Forward/Dense, 00:57:35/00:00:00

R2# **show ip mroute**

IP Multicast Routing Table

Flags: D - Dense, S - Sparse, B - Bidir Group, s - SSM Group, C - Connected,

      L - Local, P - Pruned, R - RP-bit set, F - Register flag,

      T - SPT-bit set, J - Join SPT, M - MSDP created entry,

      X - Proxy Join Timer Running, A - Candidate for MSDP Advertisement,

      U - URD, I - Received Source Specific Host Report,

```
        Z - Multicast Tunnel, z - MDT-data group sender,
        Y - Joined MDT-data group, y - Sending to MDT-data group
Outgoing interface flags: H - Hardware switched, A - Assert winner
 Timers: Uptime/Expires
 Interface state: Interface, Next-Hop or VCD, State/Mode


(*, 232.32.32.32), 01:43:06/stopped, RP 192.168.1.1, flags: SJCLF
  Incoming interface: Serial0/0/1, RPF nbr 172.16.203.3
  Outgoing interface list:
    Serial0/0/0, Forward/Dense, 01:43:02/00:00:00
    Loopback2, Forward/Dense, 01:43:06/00:00:00


(172.16.20.4, 232.32.32.32), 00:01:24/00:02:59, flags: LFT
  Incoming interface: FastEthernet0/0, RPF nbr 0.0.0.0
  Outgoing interface list:
    Serial0/0/1, Forward/Dense, 00:01:26/00:00:00
    Loopback2, Forward/Dense, 00:01:26/00:00:00
    Serial0/0/0, Forward/Dense, 00:01:26/00:00:00, A


(*, 224.0.1.40), 00:55:42/00:02:41, RP 0.0.0.0, flags: DCL
  Incoming interface: Null, RPF nbr 0.0.0.0
  Outgoing interface list:
    Serial0/0/1, Forward/Dense, 00:55:42/00:00:00
    Serial0/0/0, Forward/Dense, 00:55:42/00:00:00
    Loopback2, Forward/Dense, 00:55:42/00:00:00
```

```
R3# show ip mroute
IP Multicast Routing Table
Flags: D - Dense, S - Sparse, B - Bidir Group, s - SSM Group, C - Connected,
       L - Local, P - Pruned, R - RP-bit set, F - Register flag,
       T - SPT-bit set, J - Join SPT, M - MSDP created entry,
       X - Proxy Join Timer Running, A - Candidate for MSDP Advertisement,
       U - URD, I - Received Source Specific Host Report,
       Z - Multicast Tunnel, z - MDT-data group sender,
       Y - Joined MDT-data group, y - Sending to MDT-data group
Outgoing interface flags: H - Hardware switched, A - Assert winner
 Timers: Uptime/Expires
 Interface state: Interface, Next-Hop or VCD, State/Mode


(*, 232.32.32.32), 01:43:06/00:03:26, RP 192.168.1.1, flags: SJCL
  Incoming interface: FastEthernet0/0, RPF nbr 172.16.13.1
  Outgoing interface list:
    Serial0/0/1, Forward/Dense, 01:42:37/00:00:00
```

```
    Serial0/0/0, Forward/Dense, 01:43:04/00:00:00
    Loopback3, Forward/Dense, 01:43:06/00:00:00


(172.16.20.4, 232.32.32.32), 00:01:26/00:02:58, flags: LT
  Incoming interface: Serial0/0/1, RPF nbr 172.16.203.2
  Outgoing interface list:
    FastEthernet0/0, Forward/Dense, 00:01:28/00:00:00, A
    Loopback3, Forward/Dense, 00:01:28/00:00:00
    Serial0/0/0, Forward/Dense, 00:01:28/00:00:00, A


(*, 224.0.1.40), 01:43:07/00:02:30, RP 0.0.0.0, flags: DCL
  Incoming interface: Null, RPF nbr 0.0.0.0
  Outgoing interface list:
    FastEthernet0/0, Forward/Dense, 01:42:35/00:00:00
    Serial0/0/1, Forward/Dense, 01:42:38/00:00:00
    Serial0/0/0, Forward/Dense, 01:43:20/00:00:00
    Loopback3, Forward/Dense, 01:43:21/00:00:00
```

Notice that R1 has 0.0.0.0 as the RPF neighbor of the (*, G) entry, indicating that it is the RP for the 232.32.32.32 multicast group. R2 and R3 listen to multicast traffic on the shared tree coming from their RPF neighbor for that (*, G) entry in their multicast routing tables.

Enable PIM-SM on all interfaces using the **ip pim sparse-mode** command in interface configuration mode:

```
R1(config)# interface loopback 1
R1(config-if)# ip pim sparse-mode
R1(config-if)# interface fastethernet 0/0
R1(config-if)# ip pim sparse-mode
R1(config-if)# interface serial 0/0/0
R1(config-if)# ip pim sparse-mode
R1(config-if)# interface serial 0/0/1
R1(config-if)# ip pim sparse-mode
R2(config)# interface loopback 2
R2(config-if)# ip pim sparse-mode
R2(config-if)# interface fastethernet 0/0
R2(config-if)# ip pim sparse-mode
R2(config-if)# interface serial 0/0/0
R2(config-if)# ip pim sparse-mode
R2(config-if)# interface serial 0/0/1
R2(config-if)# ip pim sparse-mode
R3(config)# interface loopback 3
R3(config-if)# ip pim sparse-mode
R3(config-if)# interface fastethernet 0/0
R3(config-if)# ip pim sparse-mode
R3(config-if)# interface serial 0/0/0
```

```
R3(config-if)# ip pim sparse-mode
R3(config-if)# interface serial 0/0/1
R3(config-if)# ip pim sparse-mode
```

Now that multicast routing and PIM-SM are enabled on R2, do you think a ping from SW1 to the 232.32.32.32 group will receive any replies? Explain.

_____

_____

Verify your answer by pinging the multicast group from SW1. You will not necessarily receive replies from the IP address of the interface on which the multicast packet was received but rather from whichever interface on the responding router encapsulated the return packet:

```
SW1# ping 232.32.32.32

Type escape sequence to abort.
Sending 1, 100-byte ICMP Echos to 232.32.32.32, timeout is 2 seconds:

Reply to request 0 from 172.16.20.2, 4 ms
Reply to request 0 from 172.16.102.1, 32 ms
Reply to request 0 from 172.16.203.3, 32 ms
```

Based on your understanding of IP unicast routing, why are the ICMP echo replies sent from the interfaces shown in the preceding output?

_____

_____

Step 4: Verify PIM Adjacencies

In this step, we explore PIM adjacencies and how PIM functions over various Layer 2 media.

Issue the **show ip pim neighbor** command to display all adjacent PIM routers:

```
R1# show ip pim neighbor
PIM Neighbor Table
Mode: B - Bidir Capable, DR - Designated Router, N - Default DR Priority,
      S - State Refresh Capable
Neighbor         Interface          Uptime/Expires      Ver    DR
Address                                                        Prio/Mode
172.16.13.3      FastEthernet0/0    00:07:22/00:01:19 v2    1 / DR S
172.16.102.2     Serial0/0/0        00:07:23/00:01:22 v2    1 / S
172.16.103.3     Serial0/0/1        00:07:23/00:01:29 v2    1 / S
R2# show ip pim neighbor
PIM Neighbor Table
Mode: B - Bidir Capable, DR - Designated Router, N - Default DR Priority,
      S - State Refresh Capable
Neighbor         Interface          Uptime/Expires      Ver    DR
```

```
Address                                                        Prio/Mode
172.16.102.1       Serial0/0/0              00:08:27/00:01:20 v2    1 / S
172.16.203.3       Serial0/0/1              00:08:29/00:01:22 v2    1 / S
```

```
R3# show ip pim neighbor
PIM Neighbor Table
Mode: B - Bidir Capable, DR - Designated Router, N - Default DR Priority,
      S - State Refresh Capable
Neighbor           Interface               Uptime/Expires     Ver    DR
Address                                                              Prio/Mode
172.16.13.1        FastEthernet0/0         00:08:28/00:01:23 v2    1 / S
172.16.103.1       Serial0/0/0             00:08:59/00:01:19 v2    1 / S
172.16.203.2       Serial0/0/1             00:08:32/00:01:39 v2    1 / S
```

PIM-DM uses a designated router (DR) as the source of IGMPv1 queries. PIM-SM also supports this type of behavior because it is required in the IGMPv1 protocol.

Which router is the IGMP querier for the 172.16.13.0/24 subnet?

Display information about PIM-enabled interfaces with the **show ip pim interface** command:

```
R1# show ip pim interface
```

Address	Interface	Ver/Mode	Nbr Count	Query Intvl	DR Prior	DR
192.168.1.1	Loopback1	v2/S	0	30	1	192.168.1.1
172.16.13.1	FastEthernet0/0	v2/S	1	30	1	172.16.13.3
172.16.102.1	Serial0/0/0	v2/S	1	30	1	0.0.0.0
172.16.103.1	Serial0/0/1	v2/S	1	30	1	0.0.0.0

```
R2# show ip pim interface
```

Address	Interface	Ver/Mode	Nbr Count	Query Intvl	DR Prior	DR
192.168.2.1	Loopback2	v2/S	0	30	1	192.168.2.1
172.16.20.2	FastEthernet0/0	v2/S	0	30	1	172.16.20.2
172.16.102.2	Serial0/0/0	v2/S	1	30	1	0.0.0.0
172.16.203.2	Serial0/0/1	v2/S	1	30	1	0.0.0.0

```
R3# show ip pim interface
```

Address	Interface	Ver/Mode	Nbr Count	Query Intvl	DR Prior	DR
192.168.3.1	Loopback3	v2/S	0	30	1	192.168.3.1
172.16.13.3	FastEthernet0/0	v2/S	1	30	1	172.16.13.3
172.16.103.3	Serial0/0/0	v2/S	1	30	1	0.0.0.0
172.16.203.3	Serial0/0/1	v2/S	1	30	1	0.0.0.0

The serial interfaces use the default DR address 0.0.0.0 as the DR for the interface. Because a multicast is received by either 0 or 1 remote routers on a serial segment, PIM does need not to set up a complex neighbor relationship.

The Ver/Mode column displays the PIM version and mode running on each interface. S refers to sparse mode. D is used for dense mode, and SD indicates the hybrid sparse-dense mode.

Step 5: Verify Multicast Routing Operation

On each router, use the **mrinfo** command to view information about the connected multicast-enabled routers:

```
R1# mrinfo
172.16.13.1 [version  12.4] [flags: PMA]:
  192.168.1.1 -> 0.0.0.0 [1/0/pim/querier/leaf]
  172.16.13.1 -> 172.16.13.3 [1/0/pim]
  172.16.102.1 -> 172.16.102.2 [1/0/pim]
  172.16.103.1 -> 172.16.103.3 [1/0/pim]
```

```
R2# mrinfo
172.16.20.2 [version  12.4] [flags: PMA]:
  192.168.2.1 -> 0.0.0.0 [1/0/pim/querier/leaf]
  172.16.20.2 -> 0.0.0.0 [1/0/pim/querier/leaf]
  172.16.102.2 -> 172.16.102.1 [1/0/pim]
  172.16.203.2 -> 172.16.203.3 [1/0/pim]
```

```
R3# mrinfo
172.16.13.3 [version  12.4] [flags: PMA]:
  192.168.3.1 -> 0.0.0.0 [1/0/pim/querier/leaf]
  172.16.13.3 -> 172.16.13.1 [1/0/pim/querier]
  172.16.103.3 -> 172.16.103.1 [1/0/pim]
  172.16.203.3 -> 172.16.203.2 [1/0/pim]
```

Each router realizes that the loopback interfaces are topological leaves in which PIM will never establish an adjacency with any other routers. These routers also record the neighboring multicast router addresses and the multicast routing protocols they utilize.

As discussed in the previous step, IGMPv1 requires the multicast routing protocol to elect a querier on a multi-access network.

Based on the information in the output of the **mrinfo** command, which interface is the querier on VLAN 13?

_____

_____

Generate a stream of multicast data to the group by issuing an extended ping from SW1 with a repeat count of 100:

```
SW1# ping
Protocol [ip]:
```

```
Target IP address: 232.32.32.32
Repeat count [1]: 100
Datagram size [100]:
Timeout in seconds [2]:
Extended commands [n]:
Sweep range of sizes [n]:
Type escape sequence to abort.
Sending 100, 100-byte ICMP Echos to 232.32.32.32, timeout is 2 seconds:

Reply to request 0 from 172.16.20.2, 8 ms
Reply to request 0 from 172.16.102.1, 36 ms
Reply to request 0 from 172.16.203.3, 36 ms
Reply to request 1 from 172.16.20.2, 4 ms
Reply to request 1 from 172.16.102.1, 28 ms
Reply to request 1 from 172.16.203.3, 28 ms
Reply to request 2 from 172.16.20.2, 8 ms
Reply to request 2 from 172.16.102.1, 32 ms
Reply to request 2 from 172.16.203.3, 32 ms
...
```

On each of the routers, you should see that PIM and IGMP have communicated to install the 232.32.32.32 multicast group in the multicast routing table. Verify this with the **show ip mroute** command on each router:

```
R1# show ip mroute
IP Multicast Routing Table
Flags: D - Dense, S - Sparse, B - Bidir Group, s - SSM Group, C - Connected,
       L - Local, P - Pruned, R - RP-bit set, F - Register flag,
       T - SPT-bit set, J - Join SPT, M - MSDP created entry,
       X - Proxy Join Timer Running, A - Candidate for MSDP Advertisement,
       U - URD, I - Received Source Specific Host Report,
       Z - Multicast Tunnel, z - MDT-data group sender,
       Y - Joined MDT-data group, y - Sending to MDT-data group
Outgoing interface flags: H - Hardware switched, A - Assert winner
 Timers: Uptime/Expires
 Interface state: Interface, Next-Hop or VCD, State/Mode


(*, 232.32.32.32), 02:26:04/00:03:21, RP 192.168.1.1, flags: SJCL
  Incoming interface: Null, RPF nbr 0.0.0.0
  Outgoing interface list:
    FastEthernet0/0, Forward/Sparse, 02:25:34/00:03:21
    Serial0/0/1, Forward/Sparse, 02:25:34/00:00:00
    Serial0/0/0, Forward/Sparse, 02:25:35/00:00:00
    Loopback1, Forward/Sparse, 02:26:04/00:02:43
```

```
(172.16.20.4, 232.32.32.32), 00:00:14/00:02:59, flags: T
  Incoming interface: FastEthernet0/0, RPF nbr 172.16.13.3
  Outgoing interface list:
    Loopback1, Forward/Sparse, 00:00:14/00:02:45
    Serial0/0/1, Forward/Sparse, 00:00:14/00:02:45


(*, 224.0.1.40), 01:40:34/00:02:45, RP 0.0.0.0, flags: DCL
  Incoming interface: Null, RPF nbr 0.0.0.0
  Outgoing interface list:
    Serial0/0/1, Forward/Sparse, 01:40:34/00:00:00
    Serial0/0/0, Forward/Sparse, 01:40:34/00:00:00
    FastEthernet0/0, Forward/Sparse, 01:40:36/00:00:00
    Loopback1, Forward/Sparse, 01:40:36/00:02:44
```

```
R2# show ip mroute
IP Multicast Routing Table
Flags: D - Dense, S - Sparse, B - Bidir Group, s - SSM Group, C - Connected,
       L - Local, P - Pruned, R - RP-bit set, F - Register flag,
       T - SPT-bit set, J - Join SPT, M - MSDP created entry,
       X - Proxy Join Timer Running, A - Candidate for MSDP Advertisement,
       U - URD, I - Received Source Specific Host Report,
       Z - Multicast Tunnel, z - MDT-data group sender,
       Y - Joined MDT-data group, y - Sending to MDT-data group
Outgoing interface flags: H - Hardware switched, A - Assert winner
 Timers: Uptime/Expires
 Interface state: Interface, Next-Hop or VCD, State/Mode


(*, 232.32.32.32), 02:26:14/stopped, RP 192.168.1.1, flags: SJCLF
  Incoming interface: Serial0/0/1, RPF nbr 172.16.203.3
  Outgoing interface list:
    Serial0/0/0, Forward/Sparse, 02:26:10/00:00:00
    Loopback2, Forward/Sparse, 02:26:14/00:02:32


(172.16.20.4, 232.32.32.32), 00:00:19/00:03:28, flags: LFT
  Incoming interface: FastEthernet0/0, RPF nbr 0.0.0.0
  Outgoing interface list:
    Serial0/0/1, Forward/Sparse, 00:00:20/00:03:09, A
    Loopback2, Forward/Sparse, 00:00:20/00:02:39
    Serial0/0/0, Forward/Sparse, 00:00:20/00:02:39, A


(*, 224.0.1.40), 01:38:49/00:02:34, RP 0.0.0.0, flags: DCL
  Incoming interface: Null, RPF nbr 0.0.0.0
  Outgoing interface list:
    Serial0/0/1, Forward/Sparse, 01:38:49/00:00:00
```

```
        Serial0/0/0, Forward/Sparse, 01:38:49/00:00:00
        Loopback2, Forward/Sparse, 01:38:49/00:02:34
```

R3# **show ip mroute**

```
IP Multicast Routing Table
Flags: D - Dense, S - Sparse, B - Bidir Group, s - SSM Group, C - Connected,
       L - Local, P - Pruned, R - RP-bit set, F - Register flag,
       T - SPT-bit set, J - Join SPT, M - MSDP created entry,
       X - Proxy Join Timer Running, A - Candidate for MSDP Advertisement,
       U - URD, I - Received Source Specific Host Report,
       Z - Multicast Tunnel, z - MDT-data group sender,
       Y - Joined MDT-data group, y - Sending to MDT-data group
Outgoing interface flags: H - Hardware switched, A - Assert winner
 Timers: Uptime/Expires
 Interface state: Interface, Next-Hop or VCD, State/Mode


(*, 232.32.32.32), 02:26:16/00:02:47, RP 192.168.1.1, flags: SJCL
  Incoming interface: FastEthernet0/0, RPF nbr 172.16.13.1
  Outgoing interface list:
    Serial0/0/1, Forward/Sparse, 00:30:25/00:02:32
    Loopback3, Forward/Sparse, 02:26:16/00:02:23


(172.16.20.4, 232.32.32.32), 00:00:24/00:03:29, flags: LT
  Incoming interface: Serial0/0/1, RPF nbr 172.16.203.2
  Outgoing interface list:
    FastEthernet0/0, Forward/Sparse, 00:00:25/00:03:06
    Loopback3, Forward/Sparse, 00:00:25/00:02:34


(*, 224.0.1.40), 02:26:17/00:02:22, RP 0.0.0.0, flags: DCL
  Incoming interface: Null, RPF nbr 0.0.0.0
  Outgoing interface list:
    Loopback3, Forward/Sparse, 02:26:17/00:02:22
```

Multicast forwarding state refers to the current set of (S, G) and (*, G) entries in the multicast routing table. In general, "state" is defined as a stored set of properties at a given point in time. In unicast tables, the state for a destination network is referred to as the route to that network. A unicast IP route is essentially stored in the unicast routing table as a destination network address and mask, along with the next-hop routing information.

Multicast routing tables contain significantly more information than unicast routing tables because a multicast routing table must track many time-based variables for sources and group members. For instance, a multicast router must track the time when the last packet from a source is received, the outgoing interface list, and the RPF neighbors for each source-based and shared tree it maintains. These variables are not stored in a PIM topology table but in the multicast routing table natively. Multicast routing state is subject to quick changes based on source registrations and group subscriptions.

In PIM-DM, the IP multicast routing table indicates whether the PIM interfaces negotiated to flood multicast data to that group out an interface or pruned (S, G) multicast traffic from being sent out that interface.

In the multicast tables generated above, notice that PIM-SM does not refer to interfaces as pruned.

Why does PIM-SM not need to record the interfaces over which the router will prune (S, G) streams from flowing?

_____

_____

_____

_____

_____

_____

_____

_____

When a PIM-SM router receives an explicit join message from IGMP on an interface, it adds that interface to the outgoing interface list of the source-based tree. The source-based tree is also known as the shortest-path tree and is represented in the routing table by an (S, G) entry. Since PIM-SM is a registration-based multicast service, it simply drops from the list the interfaces to which it does not need to send data.

Based on the preceding output of the **show ip mroute** command shown:

- Trace the (*, G) shared tree on the following diagram (Figure 7-5). Be sure to reference the RPF interfaces for the (*, G) traffic.

- Trace the (172.16.20.4, 232.32.32.32) source-based tree.

Figure 7-5   Sparse-Mode Multicast Trees

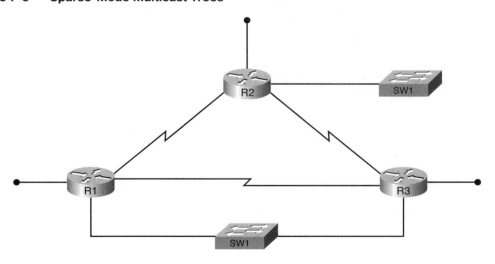

From which PIM neighbor will each loopback interface receive data?

■   _____

■   _____

■   _____

Step 6: Verify PIM-SM Registration and SPT Cutover

You are interested in viewing how sources register with the RP. You are also interested in exploring pruning data from the shared tree and the cutover to the source tree. Wait for the multicast stream from 172.16.20.4 to complete and for the (S, G) state in the multicast routing tables to expire. Then issue the **debug ip igmp** and **debug ip pim** commands on all routers.

PIM relies on the unicast IP routing table to construct shortest-path trees from the sources to the multicast subscribers. PIM interfaces send control messages to determine which neighbor is closer to the source in terms of the unicast routing information on each neighbor. PIM-SM neighbors elect a particular router on the subnet as the forwarder for that (S, G) pair and then prune that (S, G) pair from being forwarded by any other routers on the subnet.

Display the unicast routing table entry for 172.16.20.4 on each router:

```
R1# show ip route 172.16.20.4
Routing entry for 172.16.20.0/24
  Known via "eigrp 1", distance 90, metric 20517120, type internal
  Redistributing via eigrp 1
  Last update from 172.16.13.3 on FastEthernet0/0, 03:05:58 ago
  Routing Descriptor Blocks:
  * 172.16.13.3, from 172.16.13.3, 03:05:58 ago, via FastEthernet0/0
      Route metric is 20517120, traffic share count is 1
      Total delay is 20200 microseconds, minimum bandwidth is 128 Kbit
      Reliability 255/255, minimum MTU 1500 bytes
      Loading 1/255, Hops 2
```

```
R2# show ip route 172.16.20.4
Routing entry for 172.16.20.0/24
  Known via "connected", distance 0, metric 0 (connected, via interface)
  Redistributing via eigrp 1
  Routing Descriptor Blocks:
  * directly connected, via FastEthernet0/0
      Route metric is 0, traffic share count is 1
```

```
R3# show ip route 172.16.20.4
Routing entry for 172.16.20.0/24
  Known via "eigrp 1", distance 90, metric 20514560, type internal
  Redistributing via eigrp 1
  Last update from 172.16.203.2 on Serial0/0/1, 03:06:09 ago
  Routing Descriptor Blocks:
  * 172.16.203.2, from 172.16.203.2, 03:06:09 ago, via Serial0/0/1
      Route metric is 20514560, traffic share count is 1
```

```
        Total delay is 20100 microseconds, minimum bandwidth is 128 Kbit
        Reliability 255/255, minimum MTU 1500 bytes
        Loading 1/255, Hops 1
```

Recall from the previous lab: What does PIM use to select the forwarder for a multicast routing entry on a point-to-point link?

_____

Begin the same extended ping on SW1 to the multicast group. Examine the debugging messages shown on R1:

```
R1# debug ip pim

*Nov  6 16:10:08.879: PIM(0): Received v2 Register on FastEthernet0/0 from
172.16.203.2

*Nov  6 16:10:08.879:        for 172.16.20.4, group 232.32.32.32

*Nov  6 16:10:08.883: PIM(0): Insert (172.16.20.4,232.32.32.32) join in nbr
172.16.13.3's queue

*Nov  6 16:10:08.883: PIM(0): Forward decapsulated data packet for 232.32.32.32 on
FastEthernet0/0

*Nov  6 16:10:08.883: PIM(0): Forward decapsulated data packet for 232.32.32.32 on
Serial0/0/1

*Nov  6 16:10:08.883: PIM(0): Forward decapsulated data packet for 232.32.32.32 on
Serial0/0/0

*Nov  6 16:10:08.883: PIM(0): Forward decapsulated data packet for 232.32.32.32 on
Loopback1

!... continued below ...
```

Initially, R2 begins encapsulating multicast packets from 172.16.20.4 in unicast PIMv2 register packets and sends those unicast messages to the RP. This packet is sent via R2's shortest path to 192.168.1.1 and received on R1's FastEthernet 0/0 interface.

The RP sends a PIM control message to the downstream neighbor in the shared tree informing R3 to record (172.16.20.4, 232.32.32.32) state in its multicast routing table. R1 then forwards the newly decapsulated _multicast_ packets to 232.32.32.32 down the shared tree:

```
!... continued from above ...

R1#

*Nov  6 16:10:08.883: PIM(0): Building Join/Prune packet for nbr 172.16.13.3

*Nov  6 16:10:08.883: PIM(0): Adding v2 (172.16.20.4/32, 232.32.32.32), S-bit Join

*Nov  6 16:10:08.883: PIM(0): Send v2 join/prune to 172.16.13.3 (FastEthernet0/0)

*Nov  6 16:10:08.907: PIM(0): Received v2 Assert on Serial0/0/0 from 172.16.102.2

*Nov  6 16:10:08.907: PIM(0): Assert metric to source 172.16.20.4 is [0/0]

*Nov  6 16:10:08.907: PIM(0): We lose, our metric [90/20517120]

*Nov  6 16:10:08.907: PIM(0): Prune Serial0/0/0/224.0.0.2 from (172.16.20.4/32,
232.32.32.32) - deleted

!... continued below ...
```

Because Loopback1 has received the first multicast packet from SW1, R1 cuts over to the SPT. R1 builds and sends a join packet for R3 because R3 is its RPF neighbor for source 172.16.20.4. As soon as PIM routers accumulate state about the (S, G) pair, they can begin to cut over to the source-based tree.

By default, when a PIM router with a connected multicast leaf node receives the first packet from a source to a group via the shared tree, it cuts over to the shortest-path tree (SPT). You can also manually configure this as a bandwidth threshold using the **ip pim spt-threshold** command. When the (S, G) stream reaches the threshold bandwidth (in kbps), the PIM router switches to the SPT.

The cutover process is initiated on R2 and R3 by the first (172.16.20.4, 232.32.32.32) multicast packet. R1 and R2 compare administrative distances and metrics regarding their shortest path to the source, and R2, the winner, sends a prune message to R1 indicating that it should not send traffic out Serial0/0/0 to 232.32.32.32. R2's SPT state process completes:

```
!... continued from above ...

R1#

*Nov  6 16:10:10.879: PIM(0): Received v2 Register on FastEthernet0/0 from
172.16.203.2

*Nov  6 16:10:10.879:        for 172.16.20.4, group 232.32.32.32

*Nov  6 16:10:10.879: PIM(0): Forward decapsulated data packet for 232.32.32.32 on
FastEthernet0/0

*Nov  6 16:10:10.879: PIM(0): Forward decapsulated data packet for 232.32.32.32 on
Serial0/0/1

*Nov  6 16:10:10.879: PIM(0): Forward decapsulated data packet for 232.32.32.32 on
Serial0/0/0

*Nov  6 16:10:10.879: PIM(0): Forward decapsulated data packet for 232.32.32.32 on
Loopback1

*Nov  6 16:10:10.891: PIM(0): Received v2 Join/Prune on FastEthernet0/0 from
172.16.13.3, to us

*Nov  6 16:10:10.895: PIM(0): Prune-list: (172.16.20.4/32, 232.32.32.32) RPT-bit set

!... continued below ...
```

R2 continues encapsulating multicast data in unicast packets and sending them to the RP via R3.

Because all the multicast receivers have now obtained (S, G) SPT state for (172.16.20.4, 232.32.32.32), R3 decides it does not need R1 to continue sending this traffic down the shared tree. R3 sends a prune message to R1 via the Ethernet link between them.

```
!... continued from above ...

R1#

*Nov  6 16:10:10.903: PIM(0): Received v2 Assert on Serial0/0/0 from 172.16.102.2

*Nov  6 16:10:10.903: PIM(0): Assert metric to source 172.16.20.4 is [0/0]

*Nov  6 16:10:10.979: PIM(0): Insert (172.16.20.4,232.32.32.32) join in nbr
172.16.13.3's queue

*Nov  6 16:10:10.979: PIM(0): Building Join/Prune packet for nbr 172.16.13.3

*Nov  6 16:10:10.979: PIM(0): Adding v2 (172.16.20.4/32, 232.32.32.32), S-bit Join

*Nov  6 16:10:10.979: PIM(0): Send v2 join/prune to 172.16.13.3 (FastEthernet0/0)

*Nov  6 16:10:12.879: PIM(0): Received v2 Register on FastEthernet0/0 from
172.16.203.2

*Nov  6 16:10:12.879:        for 172.16.20.4, group 232.32.32.32

*Nov  6 16:10:12.879: PIM(0): Send v2 Register-Stop to 172.16.203.2 for 172.16.20.4,
group 232.32.32.32
```

The first two messages indicate that R2 sent a periodic Assert message on the serial link between them. The Insert, Building, Adding, and Send messages represent R1 acting as a standard multicast router and sending a join message to its upstream SPT neighbor, which requests (S, G) traffic to continue.

R2 sends another Register packet to the RP with an encapsulated multicast packet. R1, acting as the RP, checks its routing table for outgoing interfaces on the shared tree. Since all downstream branches of the shared tree have been pruned, indicating that R2 and R3 have switched over to the SPT, R1 sends a Register-Stop message to R2 telling it to stop forwarding multicast packets as unicasts to the RP.

At this point, all multicast routers are listening directly to the source via their shortest path to 172.16.20.4, and the current receivers do not need the RP or the shared tree because they are listening directly to the source via the SPT. It would not be unusual if the router acting as the RP was still a part of the SPT, as it is in this case, because R1's Loopback1 interface subscribes to the 232.32.32.32 group. However, R1 is acting simply as a subscriber to the group and no longer as the RP.

Why does R2 initially encapsulate the multicast data in a unicast packet?

_____

_____

_____

_____

_____

According to the debugging output shown previously, what happens to the multicast data once it reaches the RP?

_____

_____

If R2 simply forwarded the data to all receivers via multicast packets, does that sound similar to another multicast routing protocol or procedure?

_____

_____

Conclusion

Why is PIM-SM more efficient?

_____

_____

_____

Why did the routers cut over to the SPT?

_____

_____

_____

Issue the **show ip mroute** command on all routers. Compare the output to the output in Step 3 before you implemented PIM-SM:

R1# **show ip mroute**

(*, 232.32.32.32), 04:27:40/stopped, RP 192.168.1.1, flags: SJCL
  Incoming interface: Null, RPF nbr 0.0.0.0
  Outgoing interface list:
    FastEthernet0/0, Forward/Sparse, 04:27:10/00:02:45
    Serial0/0/1, Forward/Sparse, 04:27:11/00:00:00
    Serial0/0/0, Forward/Sparse, 04:27:12/00:00:00
    Loopback1, Forward/Sparse, 04:27:40/00:02:04

(172.16.20.4, 232.32.32.32), 00:00:05/00:02:58, flags: T
  Incoming interface: FastEthernet0/0, RPF nbr 172.16.13.3
  Outgoing interface list:
    Loopback1, Forward/Sparse, 00:00:05/00:02:54
    Serial0/0/1, Forward/Sparse, 00:00:05/00:02:54

(*, 224.0.1.40), 03:42:11/00:02:01, RP 0.0.0.0, flags: DCL
  Incoming interface: Null, RPF nbr 0.0.0.0
  Outgoing interface list:
    Serial0/0/1, Forward/Sparse, 03:42:11/00:00:00
    Serial0/0/0, Forward/Sparse, 03:42:11/00:00:00
    FastEthernet0/0, Forward/Sparse, 03:42:12/00:00:00
    Loopback1, Forward/Sparse, 03:42:12/00:02:00

R2# **show ip mroute**

(*, 232.32.32.32), 04:28:00/stopped, RP 192.168.1.1, flags: SJCLF
  Incoming interface: Serial0/0/1, RPF nbr 172.16.203.3
  Outgoing interface list:
    Serial0/0/0, Forward/Sparse, 04:27:56/00:00:00
    Loopback2, Forward/Sparse, 04:28:00/00:02:49

(172.16.20.4, 232.32.32.32), 00:00:19/00:03:18, flags: LFT
  Incoming interface: FastEthernet0/0, RPF nbr 0.0.0.0
  Outgoing interface list:
    Serial0/0/1, Forward/Sparse, 00:00:20/00:03:09, A
    Loopback2, Forward/Sparse, 00:00:20/00:02:48

```
      Serial0/0/0, Forward/Sparse, 00:00:20/00:02:39, A

(*, 224.0.1.40), 03:40:35/00:02:43, RP 0.0.0.0, flags: DCL
  Incoming interface: Null, RPF nbr 0.0.0.0
  Outgoing interface list:
    Serial0/0/1, Forward/Sparse, 03:40:35/00:00:00
    Serial0/0/0, Forward/Sparse, 03:40:35/00:00:00
    Loopback2, Forward/Sparse, 03:40:35/00:02:43
```
```
R3# show ip mroute
<output omitted>

(*, 232.32.32.32), 04:28:01/00:02:47, RP 192.168.1.1, flags: SJCL
  Incoming interface: FastEthernet0/0, RPF nbr 172.16.13.1
  Outgoing interface list:
    Serial0/0/1, Forward/Sparse, 02:32:10/00:02:46
    Loopback3, Forward/Sparse, 04:28:01/00:02:37

(172.16.20.4, 232.32.32.32), 00:00:23/00:03:28, flags: LT
  Incoming interface: Serial0/0/1, RPF nbr 172.16.203.2
  Outgoing interface list:
    FastEthernet0/0, Forward/Sparse, 00:00:24/00:03:07
    Loopback3, Forward/Sparse, 00:00:24/00:02:36

(*, 224.0.1.40), 04:28:02/00:02:31, RP 0.0.0.0, flags: DCL
  Incoming interface: Null, RPF nbr 0.0.0.0
  Outgoing interface list:
    Loopback3, Forward/Sparse, 04:28:02/00:02:31
```

Does the implementation of PIM-SM in CrushASodaCan.com's multicast network save bandwidth compared to the PIM-DM implementation? Explain.

_____

_____

Although not part of this lab activity, could the implementation of PIM-SM also save memory by decreasing multicast routing state? Explain.

_____

_____

_____

_____

Lab 7-4: Routing IP Multicast with PIM Sparse-Dense Mode (7.5.4)

The objectives of this lab are as follows:

- Configure multiple multicast sources and groups via IGMP

- Configure and verify PIM sparse-dense mode operation and adjacencies

- Configure and verify automatic rendezvous points and mapping agents

- Force PIM sparse-dense mode to fail over to dense mode operation

Figure 7-6 illustrates the topology that will be used for this lab.

Figure 7-6   Topology Diagram

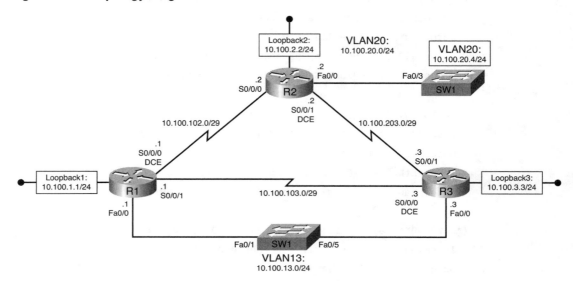

Scenario

After the incredible community response to CrushASodaCan.com TV spots, a skeptical citizen began questioning the usefulness of crushing aluminum cans before recycling them. After conducting a thorough case study, he founded the organization JustRecycleTheCan.org and began producing TV announcements encouraging citizens to recycle but informing them that it is unnecessary to crush cans before committing them to the safe care of a recycle bin.

The founder of JustRecycleTheCan.org has contracted you to implement multicast on his network so that he can also preview TV spots before releasing them to the public. However, he requests that you implement PIM in a more redundant, scalable manner than you did for CrushASodaCan.com.

Fully configure multicast routing on his network according to the requests of the founder of the organization. Verify that if the route to the rendezvous point (RP) is lost, multicast receivers on remote networks can still receive multicast streams.

Step 1: Configure Addressing and Implement IGMP

Paste in the following initial configurations. You can download these router configurations at www.ciscopress.com/title/1587132133 under the More Information section on the page.

R1:

```
!
hostname R1
!
interface Loopback1
 ip address 10.100.1.1 255.255.255.0
!
interface FastEthernet0/0
 ip address 10.100.13.1 255.255.255.0
 no shutdown
!
interface Serial0/0/0
 bandwidth 64
 ip address 10.100.102.1 255.255.255.248
 clock rate 64000
 no shutdown
!
interface Serial0/0/1
 bandwidth 64
 ip address 10.100.103.1 255.255.255.248
 no shutdown
!
end
```

R2:

```
!
hostname R2
!
interface Loopback2
 ip address 10.100.2.2 255.255.255.0
!
interface FastEthernet0/0
 ip address 10.100.20.2 255.255.255.0
 no shutdown
!
interface Serial0/0/0
 bandwidth 64
 ip address 10.100.102.2 255.255.255.248
 no shutdown
!
interface Serial0/0/1
```

```
 bandwidth 128
 ip address 10.100.203.2 255.255.255.248
 clock rate 128000
 no shutdown
!
end
```

R3:
```
!
hostname R3
!
interface Loopback3
 ip address 10.100.3.3 255.255.255.0
!
interface FastEthernet0/0
 ip address 10.100.13.3 255.255.255.0
 no shutdown
!
interface Serial0/0/0
 bandwidth 64
 ip address 10.100.103.3 255.255.255.248
 clock rate 64000
 no shutdown
!
interface Serial0/0/1
 bandwidth 128
 ip address 10.100.203.3 255.255.255.248
 no shutdown
!
end
```

SW1:
```
!
hostname SW1
!
interface FastEthernet0/1
 switchport access vlan 13
 switchport mode access
!
interface FastEthernet0/3
 switchport access vlan 20
 switchport mode access
!
interface FastEthernet0/5
```

```
 switchport access vlan 13
 switchport mode access
!
end
```

Use a switched virtual interface (SVI) on SW1 to simulate a multicast source on the VLAN 20 subnet. Use this SVI to send a repeated multicast ping that simulates multicast traffic while you set up the network. Assign the SVI the IP address 10.100.20.4/24 with a default gateway of 10.100.20.2:

```
SW1# configure terminal
SW1(config)# ip default-gateway 10.100.20.2
SW1(config)# interface vlan 20
SW1(config-if)# ip address 10.100.20.4 255.255.255.0
SW1(config-if)# no shutdown
```

Using IGMP, subscribe each of the loopback interfaces on the three routers to the multicast groups 225.25.25.25. Subscribe R1 and R3 loopbacks to 226.26.26.26 as well:

```
R1# configure terminal
R1(config)# interface loopback 1
R1(config-if)# ip igmp join-group 225.25.25.25
R1(config-if)# ip igmp join-group 226.26.26.26
```
```
R2# configure terminal
R2(config)# interface loopback 2
R2(config-if)# ip igmp join-group 225.25.25.25
```
```
R3# configure terminal
R3(config)# interface loopback 3
R3(config-if)# ip igmp join-group 225.25.25.25
R3(config-if)# ip igmp join-group 226.26.26.26
```

Verify that each of the interfaces has subscribed to the multicast group using the **show ip igmp groups** command:

```
R1# show ip igmp groups
IGMP Connected Group Membership
Group Address    Interface    Uptime     Expires    Last Reporter   Group Accounted
226.26.26.26     Loopback1    00:01:51   00:02:03   10.100.1.1
225.25.25.25     Loopback1    00:01:51   00:02:03   10.100.1.1
```
```
R2# show ip igmp groups
IGMP Connected Group Membership
Group Address    Interface    Uptime     Expires    Last Reporter   Group Accounted
225.25.25.25     Loopback2    00:01:51   00:02:03   10.100.2.2
```
```
R3# show ip igmp groups
IGMP Connected Group Membership
Group Address    Interface    Uptime     Expires    Last Reporter   Group Accounted
226.26.26.26     Loopback3    00:01:51   00:02:03   10.100.3.3
225.25.25.25     Loopback3    00:01:51   00:02:03   10.100.3.3
```

Step 2: Configure Single-Area OSPF

Configure single-area OSPF on each router with the following configuration:

```
router ospf 1
 network 10.0.0.0 0.255.255.255 area 0
```

After you apply this configuration and the OSPF adjacencies form, run the following TCL script to verify full unicast connectivity. You can download this TCL script at www.ciscopress.com/title/1587132133 under the More Information section on the page.

```
foreach address {
10.100.1.1
10.100.13.1
10.100.102.1
10.100.103.1
10.100.2.2
10.100.20.2
10.100.102.2
10.100.203.2
10.100.3.3
10.100.13.3
10.100.103.3
10.100.203.3
10.100.20.4
} { ping $address }
```

Compare the output you receive with the output found in the section, "TCL Script Output," for this lab (all pings successful). Make sure that you have ICMP replies from the SVI interface on SW1. If SW1 has a reachable default gateway of R2's FastEthernet 0/0 interface, and if all routers have full connectivity between all subnets, you should be able to ping the SVI address and receive all replies.

Step 3: Implement PIM Sparse-Dense Mode

First, enable your routers to accumulate and maintain multicast state using the **ip multicast-routing** command in global configuration mode:

```
R1(config)# ip multicast-routing
```

```
R2(config)# ip multicast-routing
```

```
R3(config)# ip multicast-routing
```

Next, enable PIM sparse-dense mode on all interfaces using the **ip pim sparse-dense-mode** command in interface configuration mode:

```
R1(config)# interface loopback 1
R1(config-if)# ip pim sparse-dense-mode
R1(config-if)# interface fastethernet 0/0
R1(config-if)# ip pim sparse-dense-mode
```

```
R1(config-if)# interface serial 0/0/0
R1(config-if)# ip pim sparse-dense-mode
R1(config-if)# interface serial 0/0/1
R1(config-if)# ip pim sparse-dense-mode
R2(config)# interface loopback 2
R2(config-if)# ip pim sparse-dense-mode
R2(config-if)# interface fastethernet 0/0
R2(config-if)# ip pim sparse-dense-mode
R2(config-if)# interface serial 0/0/0
R2(config-if)# ip pim sparse-dense-mode
R2(config-if)# interface serial 0/0/1
R2(config-if)# ip pim sparse-dense-mode
R3(config)# interface loopback 1
R3(config-if)# ip pim sparse-dense-mode
R3(config-if)# interface fastethernet 0/0
R3(config-if)# ip pim sparse-dense-mode
R3(config-if)# interface serial 0/0/0
R3(config-if)# ip pim sparse-dense-mode
R3(config-if)# interface serial 0/0/1
R3(config-if)# ip pim sparse-dense-mode
```

After completing the previous two labs, you should have an idea of how PIM-SM operates. The following questions test your understanding of the concepts.

What is the purpose of the PIM-SM rendezvous point?

_____

_____

_____

_____

If no rendezvous points are reachable in an PIM-SM network, what functionality is lost? (Hint: Will PIMv2 Register messages be sent?)

_____

_____

If you implement PIM-SM with a static RP as in Lab 7-3, which routers identify the RP? Which routers identify the group-to-RP mappings?

_____

_____

Other than configuring a static RP globally for a network or on a per-group basis, which other ways can you configure an RP in sparse mode or sparse-dense mode? Why are other methods useful?

_____

_____

_____

_____

_____

As demonstrated in Lab 7-3, it is important to locate RPs in locations that are reachable via a unicast routing protocol when available. In this lab, you will configure two RP candidates for the 225.25.25.25 multicast group. Allow only R1 to be elected as the RP for the 226.26.26.26 group but discover all RP candidates dynamically. Use PIM sparse-dense mode and Auto-RP to achieve this functionality.

PIM sparse-dense mode manages multicast groups dynamically between sparse mode and dense mode. Sparse-dense mode applies sparse mode processes and algorithms to any multicast groups for which it can discover an RP via static configuration, Auto-RP, or the more advanced Bootstrap Router (BSR) process. All multicast groups for which a sparse-dense mode router cannot discover an RP run in PIM-DM. This applies to PIM-SM networks as well. This process is referred to as dense mode fall-back and can be disabled with the **no ip pim dm-fallback** command in global configuration mode.

Without additional configuration, will the multicast groups 225.25.25.25 and 226.26.26.26 effectively operate in sparse mode or dense mode? Explain.

_____

_____

_____

_____

Will a ping from SW1 to the 225.25.25.25 group receive any replies? Explain.

_____

Issue a stream of multicast pings from the SVI on SW1 to generate the (S, G) state on your routers:

```
SW1# ping
Protocol [ip]:
Target IP address: 225.25.25.25
Repeat count [1]: 1
Datagram size [100]:
Timeout in seconds [2]:
Extended commands [n]:
Sweep range of sizes [n]:
Type escape sequence to abort.
Sending 1, 100-byte ICMP Echos to 225.25.25.25, timeout is 2 seconds:
```

```
Reply to request 0 from 10.100.20.2, 8 ms
Reply to request 0 from 10.100.13.1, 32 ms
Reply to request 0 from 10.100.203.3, 20 ms
```

Display the multicast routing table on each router with the **show ip mroute** command:

```
R1# show ip mroute
IP Multicast Routing Table
Flags: D - Dense, S - Sparse, B - Bidir Group, s - SSM Group, C - Connected,
       L - Local, P - Pruned, R - RP-bit set, F - Register flag,
       T - SPT-bit set, J - Join SPT, M - MSDP created entry,
       X - Proxy Join Timer Running, A - Candidate for MSDP Advertisement,
       U - URD, I - Received Source Specific Host Report,
       Z - Multicast Tunnel, z - MDT-data group sender,
       Y - Joined MDT-data group, y - Sending to MDT-data group
Outgoing interface flags: H - Hardware switched, A - Assert winner
 Timers: Uptime/Expires
 Interface state: Interface, Next-Hop or VCD, State/Mode


(*, 226.26.26.26), 00:49:00/00:02:48, RP 0.0.0.0, flags: DCL
  Incoming interface: Null, RPF nbr 0.0.0.0
  Outgoing interface list:
    Serial0/0/0, Forward/Sparse-Dense, 00:47:56/00:00:00
    Serial0/0/1, Forward/Sparse-Dense, 00:48:30/00:00:00
    FastEthernet0/0, Forward/Sparse-Dense, 00:48:38/00:00:00
    Loopback1, Forward/Sparse-Dense, 00:49:00/00:00:00


(*, 225.25.25.25), 00:50:35/stopped, RP 0.0.0.0, flags: DCL
  Incoming interface: Null, RPF nbr 0.0.0.0
  Outgoing interface list:
    Serial0/0/0, Forward/Sparse-Dense, 00:47:57/00:00:00
    Serial0/0/1, Forward/Sparse-Dense, 00:48:31/00:00:00
    FastEthernet0/0, Forward/Sparse-Dense, 00:48:39/00:00:00
    Loopback1, Forward/Sparse-Dense, 00:50:35/00:00:00


(10.100.20.4, 225.25.25.25), 00:00:43/00:02:58, flags: LT
  Incoming interface: FastEthernet0/0, RPF nbr 10.100.13.3
  Outgoing interface list:
    Loopback1, Forward/Sparse-Dense, 00:00:51/00:00:00
    Serial0/0/1, Prune/Sparse-Dense, 00:00:51/00:02:11
    Serial0/0/0, Prune/Sparse-Dense, 00:00:51/00:02:11


(*, 224.0.1.40), 00:50:43/00:02:47, RP 0.0.0.0, flags: DCL
  Incoming interface: Null, RPF nbr 0.0.0.0
  Outgoing interface list:
```

```
    Serial0/0/0, Forward/Sparse-Dense, 00:48:05/00:00:00
    Serial0/0/1, Forward/Sparse-Dense, 00:48:39/00:00:00
    FastEthernet0/0, Forward/Sparse-Dense, 00:48:47/00:00:00
    Loopback1, Forward/Sparse-Dense, 00:50:43/00:00:00
```

R2# **show ip mroute**

```
<output omitted>

(*, 225.25.25.25), 00:00:45/stopped, RP 0.0.0.0, flags: DL
  Incoming interface: Null, RPF nbr 0.0.0.0
  Outgoing interface list:
    Serial0/0/1, Forward/Sparse-Dense, 00:00:45/00:00:00
    Serial0/0/0, Forward/Sparse-Dense, 00:00:45/00:00:00

(10.100.20.4, 225.25.25.25), 00:00:45/00:03:01, flags: LT
  Incoming interface: FastEthernet0/0, RPF nbr 0.0.0.0
  Outgoing interface list:
    Serial0/0/0, Prune/Sparse-Dense, 00:00:45/00:02:17, A
    Serial0/0/1, Forward/Sparse-Dense, 00:00:46/00:00:00

(*, 224.0.1.40), 00:48:03/00:02:48, RP 0.0.0.0, flags: DCL
  Incoming interface: Null, RPF nbr 0.0.0.0
  Outgoing interface list:
    Serial0/0/1, Forward/Sparse-Dense, 00:47:56/00:00:00
    Serial0/0/0, Forward/Sparse-Dense, 00:48:00/00:00:00
    FastEthernet0/0, Forward/Sparse-Dense, 00:48:03/00:00:00
```

R3# **show ip mroute**

```
<output omitted>

(*, 226.26.26.26), 00:00:03/00:02:58, RP 0.0.0.0, flags: DCL
  Incoming interface: Null, RPF nbr 0.0.0.0
  Outgoing interface list:
    Serial0/0/1, Forward/Sparse-Dense, 00:00:03/00:00:00
    Serial0/0/0, Forward/Sparse-Dense, 00:00:03/00:00:00
    FastEthernet0/0, Forward/Sparse-Dense, 00:00:03/00:00:00
    Loopback3, Forward/Sparse-Dense, 00:00:03/00:00:00

(*, 225.25.25.25), 00:00:05/00:02:55, RP 0.0.0.0, flags: DCL
  Incoming interface: Null, RPF nbr 0.0.0.0
  Outgoing interface list:
    Serial0/0/1, Forward/Sparse-Dense, 00:00:05/00:00:00
    Serial0/0/0, Forward/Sparse-Dense, 00:00:05/00:00:00
    FastEthernet0/0, Forward/Sparse-Dense, 00:00:05/00:00:00
    Loopback3, Forward/Sparse-Dense, 00:00:05/00:00:00
```

```
(10.100.20.4, 225.25.25.25), 00:03:26/00:02:56, flags: LT
  Incoming interface: Serial0/0/1, RPF nbr 10.100.203.2
  Outgoing interface list:
    FastEthernet0/0, Forward/Sparse-Dense, 00:03:27/00:00:00
    Serial0/0/0, Prune/Sparse-Dense, 00:00:22/00:02:40, A

(*, 224.0.1.40), 00:51:23/00:02:05, RP 0.0.0.0, flags: DCL
  Incoming interface: Null, RPF nbr 0.0.0.0
  Outgoing interface list:
    Serial0/0/1, Forward/Sparse-Dense, 00:50:37/00:00:00
    Serial0/0/0, Forward/Sparse-Dense, 00:51:15/00:00:00
    FastEthernet0/0, Forward/Sparse-Dense, 00:51:23/00:00:00
```

Referring to the preceding output, in which mode is PIM operating if it is not relying on the shared tree to connect it with receivers?

_____

How is this indicated in the multicast routing tables?

_____

_____

If your output differs from that shown above, verify that you have configured PIM sparse-dense mode correctly on all interfaces by using the **show ip pim interface** command. Make sure that all PIM adjacencies are active by using the **show ip pim neighbor** command.

Step 4: Configure PIM Auto-RP

PIM now operates successfully, but you can configure the routers to use bandwidth more efficiently by forcing multicast groups to use PIM-SM.

PIM-SM rendezvous points introduce multicast sources by acting as a network receptionist that knows the location of all multicast sources for specific groups. PIM-SM creates shared distribution trees for multicast groups represented by (*, G) in each multicast routing table. This shared tree is calculated using the RPF upstream interface to the RP for that group. Thus, the shared tree is essentially a shortest-path tree to the RP address.

When you configured the interfaces in sparse-dense mode, every router implicitly subscribed to the RP Discovery group 224.0.1.40. Use the **show ip igmp groups** command to verify this. Each router applies the information it receives about group-to-RP mappings via the RP Discovery group to its multicast routing table entries:

```
R1# show ip igmp groups
IGMP Connected Group Membership
Group Address    Interface        Uptime    Expires    Last Reporter   Group Accounted
226.26.26.26     Loopback1        00:42:38  00:02:14   10.100.1.1
225.25.25.25     Loopback1        00:42:38  00:02:09   10.100.1.1
```

```
224.0.1.40        FastEthernet0/0           00:41:44  00:02:10  10.100.13.3
224.0.1.40        Loopback1                 00:42:38  00:02:13  10.100.1.1
```

When configuring interfaces running only PIM-SM, you also need to apply the **ip pim autorp listener** command to each sparse mode interface. This command allows RP mapping messages to be read by multicast routers and propagated throughout the network in dense mode fashion. Because sparse-dense mode acts in a PIM-DM fashion without an RP for the group, you achieve the same functionality without applying the command.

By default, sparse-dense mode also enables the installation of RP mapping information into the multicast routing table. Verify this with the **show ip pim autorp** command:

```
R1# show ip pim autorp
AutoRP Information:
  AutoRP is enabled.


PIM AutoRP Statistics: Sent/Received
  RP Announce: 0/0, RP Discovery: 0/0
```

Enable the advertisement of Auto-RP information for the specified groups on R1 and R3. Configure R1 to candidate as an RP for both groups. Allow R3 to only apply as a candidate for the 226.26.26.26 group. Configure access lists to control the groups for which Auto-RP information is sent. Finally, apply these access lists with the **ip pim send-rp-announce** {*interface-type interface-number* | *ip-address*} **scope** *ttl-value* [**group-list** *access-list*] command. The RP candidates should be the loopback interfaces on R1 and R3. Use a time-to-live (TTL) value of 3 so that RP announcements are not discarded anywhere in your existing network. The scope determines the number of times a multicast packet is routed at Layer 3 before being discarded because the TTL has reached 0:

```
R1(config)# access-list 1 permit 225.25.25.25
R1(config)# access-list 1 permit 226.26.26.26
R1(config)# ip pim send-rp-announce Loopback 1 scope 3 group-list 1
R3(config)# access-list 3 permit 226.26.26.26
R3(config)# ip pim send-rp-announce Loopback 3 scope 3 group-list 3
```

Enable PIM Auto-RP debugging with the **debug ip pim auto-rp** command on R1 and R3. The following excerpt shows that Auto-RP announcements are sent periodically, indicating that the announcements are being flooded from the local router:

```
R1# debug ip pim auto-rp
*Nov  7 16:08:05.803: Auto-RP(0): Build RP-Announce for 10.100.1.1, PIMv2/v1, ttl 3,
ht 181
*Nov  7 16:08:05.803: Auto-RP(0):  Build announce entry for (225.25.25.25/32)
*Nov  7 16:08:05.803: Auto-RP(0):  Build announce entry for (226.26.26.26/32)
*Nov  7 16:08:05.803: Auto-RP(0): Send RP-Announce packet on FastEthernet0/0
*Nov  7 16:08:05.803: Auto-RP(0): Send RP-Announce packet on Serial0/0/0
*Nov  7 16:08:05.803: Auto-RP(0): Send RP-Announce packet on Serial0/0/1
*Nov  7 16:08:05.803: Auto-RP: Send RP-Announce packet on Loopback1
```

Continue debugging Auto-RP messages while you configure the mapping agent.

PIM-SM networks using Auto-RP also need one or more mapping agents to inform routers that are listening to the Auto-RP group of the group-to-RP mappings. Configure R1 as the mapping agent for this network using the **ip pim send-rp-discovery** [*interface-type interface-number*] **scope** *ttl-value* command to generate group-to-RP mapping messages from R1:

```
R1(config)# ip pim send-rp-discovery Loopback 1 scope 3
```

You should see the following debug output on R1:

```
R1#
*Nov  7 16:26:08.803: Auto-RP(0): Build RP-Announce for 10.100.1.1, PIMv2/v1, ttl 3,
ht 181
*Nov  7 16:26:08.803: Auto-RP(0):  Build announce entry for (225.25.25.25/32)
*Nov  7 16:26:08.803: Auto-RP(0):  Build announce entry for (226.26.26.26/32)
*Nov  7 16:26:08.803: Auto-RP(0): Send RP-Announce packet on FastEthernet0/0
*Nov  7 16:26:08.803: Auto-RP(0): Send RP-Announce packet on Serial0/0/0
*Nov  7 16:26:08.803: Auto-RP(0): Send RP-Announce packet on Serial0/0/1
*Nov  7 16:26:08.803: Auto-RP: Send RP-Announce packet on Loopback1
!  ... continued below ...
```

Because you previously configured R1 as an RP candidate, it advertises itself as an RP for the 225.25.25.25 and 226.26.26.26 groups. However, no router will select R1 as the confirmed RP for those groups until it hears from the mapping agent. R1 continues to multicast its announcements of RP candidacy out all interfaces:

```
!  ... continued from above ...
R1#
*Nov  7 16:26:08.803: Auto-RP(0): Received RP-announce, from 10.100.1.1, RP_cnt 1, ht
181
*Nov  7 16:26:08.803: Auto-RP(0): Added with (225.25.25.25/32, RP:10.100.1.1), PIMv2
v1
*Nov  7 16:26:08.803: Auto-RP(0): Added with (226.26.26.26/32, RP:10.100.1.1), PIMv2
v1
*Nov  7 16:26:08.807: Auto-RP(0): Build RP-Discovery packet
*Nov  7 16:26:08.807: Auto-RP:  Build mapping (225.25.25.25/32, RP:10.100.1.1),
PIMv2 v1,
*Nov  7 16:26:08.807: Auto-RP:  Build mapping (226.26.26.26/32, RP:10.100.1.1),
PIMv2 v1.
*Nov  7 16:26:08.811: Auto-RP(0): Send RP-discovery packet on FastEthernet0/0 (1 RP
entries)
*Nov  7 16:26:08.811: Auto-RP(0): Send RP-discovery packet on Serial0/0/0 (1 RP
entries)
*Nov  7 16:26:08.811: Auto-RP(0): Send RP-discovery packet on Serial0/0/1 (1 RP
entries)
*Nov  7 16:26:08.811: Auto-RP: Send RP-discovery packet on Loopback1 (1 RP entries)
!  ... continued below ...
```

The router acting as a mapping agent, which in this case is also R1, receives the candidacy announcement that the Auto-RP process on R1 just sent to the 224.0.1.39 Auto-RP announcement group.

R1, acting as an RP mapping agent, elects R1 as the RP for both groups because it has not received any other RP announcements with higher source IP addresses. The mapping agent sends the two group-to-RP mappings via multicast to all Auto-RP listeners in the network. The mappings are sent to the Auto-RP discovery group 224.0.1.40:

```
!  ... continued from above ...

R1#

*Nov  7 16:26:08.819: Auto-RP(0): Received RP-announce, from 10.100.1.1, RP_cnt 1,
ht 181

*Nov  7 16:26:08.819: Auto-RP(0): Update (225.25.25.25/32, RP:10.100.1.1), PIMv2 v1

*Nov  7 16:26:08.819: Auto-RP(0): Update (226.26.26.26/32, RP:10.100.1.1), PIMv2 v1

*Nov  7 16:26:08.819: Auto-RP(0): Received RP-announce, from 10.100.1.1, RP_cnt 1,
ht 181

*Nov  7 16:26:08.819: Auto-RP(0): Update (225.25.25.25/32, RP:10.100.1.1), PIMv2 v1

*Nov  7 16:26:08.823: Auto-RP(0): Update (226.26.26.26/32, RP:10.100.1.1), PIMv2 v1

   ... continued below ...
```

The Auto-RP messages that R1 sent previously are received back again on different interfaces because of the dense-mode flooding throughout the network. R1 simply installs the group-to-RP mappings in its table again:

```
!  ... continued from above ...

R1#

*Nov  7 16:26:36.911: Auto-RP(0): Received RP-announce, from 10.100.3.3, RP_cnt 1, ht
181

*Nov  7 16:26:36.911: Auto-RP(0): Added with (226.26.26.26/32, RP:10.100.3.3), PIMv2
v1

*Nov  7 16:26:36.915: Auto-RP(0): Build RP-Discovery packet

*Nov  7 16:26:36.915: Auto-RP:  Build mapping (225.25.25.25/32, RP:10.100.1.1), PIMv2
v1,

*Nov  7 16:26:36.915: Auto-RP:  Build mapping (226.26.26.26/32, RP:10.100.3.3), PIMv2
v1.

*Nov  7 16:26:36.915: Auto-RP(0): Send RP-discovery packet on FastEthernet0/0 (2 RP
entries)

*Nov  7 16:26:36.915: Auto-RP(0): Send RP-discovery packet on Serial0/0/0 (2 RP
entries)

R1#

*Nov  7 16:26:36.915: Auto-RP(0): Send RP-discovery packet on Serial0/0/1 (2 RP
entries)

*Nov  7 16:26:36.915: Auto-RP: Send RP-discovery packet on Loopback1 (2 RP entries)
```

Within a short amount of time, R3 sends its candidacy announcement for the 226.26.26.26 multicast group. R1 receives this packet and, acting as the RP mapping agent, evaluates it against the existing RP. Since the IP address of 10.100.3.3 is higher than 10.100.1.1, the mapping agent elects R3 as the RP for 226.26.26.26. R1 remains the RP for the 225.25.25.25 group.

R1 sends notification of the winners of the group-to-RP elections to the 224.0.1.40 RP Discovery group. All multicast routers running PIM-SM or sparse-dense mode have been implicitly subscribed to this group and install this information in their multicast routing tables.

During this time, the PIM protocol running on R3 has logged the following output. Analyze the Auto-RP election from R3's perspective:

```
R3#
*Nov  7 16:26:48.763: Auto-RP(0): Received RP-discovery, from 10.100.1.1, RP_cnt 1,
ht 181
*Nov  7 16:26:48.763: Auto-RP(0): Added with (225.25.25.25/32, RP:10.100.1.1), PIMv2
v1
*Nov  7 16:26:48.763: Auto-RP(0): Added with (226.26.26.26/32, RP:10.100.1.1), PIMv2
v1
R3#
*Nov  7 16:27:16.863: Auto-RP(0): Build RP-Announce for 10.100.3.3, PIMv2/v1, ttl 3,
ht 181
*Nov  7 16:27:16.863: Auto-RP(0):  Build announce entry for (226.26.26.26/32)
*Nov  7 16:27:16.863: Auto-RP(0): Send RP-Announce packet on FastEthernet0/0
*Nov  7 16:27:16.863: Auto-RP(0): Send RP-Announce packet on Serial0/0/0
*Nov  7 16:27:16.863: Auto-RP(0): Send RP-Announce packet on Serial0/0/1
*Nov  7 16:27:16.863: Auto-RP: Send RP-Announce packet on Loopback3
*Nov  7 16:27:16.871: Auto-RP(0): Received RP-discovery, from 10.100.1.1, RP_cnt 2,
ht 181
*Nov  7 16:27:16.871: Auto-RP(0): Update (225.25.25.25/32, RP:10.100.1.1), PIMv2 v1
*Nov  7 16:27:16.871: Auto-RP(0): Added with (226.26.26.26/32, RP:10.100.3.3), PIMv2
v1
```

Notice that when R1 floods the first RP discovery packet, the mapping agent has not yet received an Auto-RP announcement packet from R3. After R3 sends the announcement, the mapping agent compares the IP addresses of the two candidates for the 226.26.26.26 network and elects R3 as the RP. R1 then floods the new group-to-RP mappings to all routers within its scope via multicast.

Issue the **undebug all** command on R1 and R3 to stop debugging PIM Auto-RP events:

```
R1# undebug all
```

```
R3# undebug all
```

Step 5: Verify the RP Mappings

Use the **show ip pim rp** command on the Auto-RP routers to view group-to-RP mappings:

```
R1# show ip pim rp
Group: 226.26.26.26, RP: 10.100.3.3, v2, v1, uptime 00:53:51, expires 00:02:03
Group: 225.25.25.25, RP: 10.100.1.1, v2, v1, next RP-reachable in 00:01:10
```

```
R3# show ip pim rp
Group: 226.26.26.26, RP: 10.100.3.3, v2, v1, next RP-reachable in 00:01:17
Group: 225.25.25.25, RP: 10.100.1.1, v2, v1, uptime 00:54:40, expires 00:02:23
```

For a full view of the group-to-RP mappings, issue the **show ip pim rp mapping** command on all routers. This command discloses how the RP was elected and which router performed the mapping. It is extremely useful in debugging Auto-RP elections:

```
R1# show ip pim rp mapping
```

```
PIM Group-to-RP Mappings
This system is an RP (Auto-RP)
This system is an RP-mapping agent (Loopback1)

Group(s) 225.25.25.25/32
  RP 10.100.1.1 (?), v2v1
    Info source: 10.100.1.1 (?), elected via Auto-RP
      Uptime: 00:54:25, expires: 00:02:34
Group(s) 226.26.26.26/32
  RP 10.100.3.3 (?), v2v1
    Info source: 10.100.3.3 (?), elected via Auto-RP
      Uptime: 00:53:57, expires: 00:01:58
  RP 10.100.1.1 (?), v2v1
    Info source: 10.100.1.1 (?), via Auto-RP
      Uptime: 00:54:25, expires: 00:02:32
```

R2# **show ip pim rp mapping**

```
PIM Group-to-RP Mappings

Group(s) 225.25.25.25/32
  RP 10.100.1.1 (?), v2v1
    Info source: 10.100.1.1 (?), elected via Auto-RP
      Uptime: 00:58:36, expires: 00:02:24
Group(s) 226.26.26.26/32
  RP 10.100.3.3 (?), v2v1
    Info source: 10.100.1.1 (?), elected via Auto-RP
      Uptime: 00:54:06, expires: 00:02:27
```

R3# **show ip pim rp mapping**

```
PIM Group-to-RP Mappings
This system is an RP (Auto-RP)

Group(s) 225.25.25.25/32
  RP 10.100.1.1 (?), v2v1
    Info source: 10.100.1.1 (?), elected via Auto-RP
      Uptime: 00:54:44, expires: 00:02:20
Group(s) 226.26.26.26/32
  RP 10.100.3.3 (?), v2v1
    Info source: 10.100.1.1 (?), elected via Auto-RP
      Uptime: 00:54:16, expires: 00:02:15
```

How did each router learn these mappings?

_____

_____

Because you configured R1 as a mapping agent, PIM routers that are not elected as the Auto-RP track the number of RP discovery messages received. Verify this with the **show ip pim autorp** command on R2.

```
R2# show ip pim autorp
AutoRP Information:
  AutoRP is enabled.


PIM AutoRP Statistics: Sent/Received
  RP Announce: 0/0, RP Discovery: 0/96
```

Step 6: Verify Multicast Operation

Issue multicast pings to generate the (S, G) state in the multicast network. Use a repeat count of 100 to generate a stream of multicast packets flowing through the network:

```
SW1# ping
Protocol [ip]:
Target IP address: 225.25.25.25
Repeat count [1]: 100
Datagram size [100]:
Timeout in seconds [2]:
Extended commands [n]:
Sweep range of sizes [n]:
Type escape sequence to abort.
Sending 100, 100-byte ICMP Echos to 225.25.25.25, timeout is 2 seconds:

Reply to request 0 from 172.16.20.2, 8 ms
Reply to request 0 from 172.16.13.1, 36 ms
Reply to request 0 from 172.16.203.3, 36 ms
Reply to request 1 from 172.16.20.2, 4 ms
Reply to request 1 from 172.16.13.1, 28 ms
Reply to request 1 from 172.16.203.3, 28 ms
Reply to request 2 from 172.16.20.2, 8 ms
Reply to request 2 from 172.16.13.1, 32 ms
Reply to request 2 from 172.16.203.3, 32 ms
  ...
```

Display the multicast routing entry for 225.25.25.25 on each router with the **show ip mroute** *group-address* command:

```
R1# show ip mroute 225.25.25.25
IP Multicast Routing Table
Flags: D - Dense, S - Sparse, B - Bidir Group, s - SSM Group, C - Connected,
       L - Local, P - Pruned, R - RP-bit set, F - Register flag,
       T - SPT-bit set, J - Join SPT, M - MSDP created entry,
```

```
              X - Proxy Join Timer Running, A - Candidate for MSDP Advertisement,
              U - URD, I - Received Source Specific Host Report,
              Z - Multicast Tunnel, z - MDT-data group sender,
              Y - Joined MDT-data group, y - Sending to MDT-data group
Outgoing interface flags: H - Hardware switched, A - Assert winner
 Timers: Uptime/Expires
 Interface state: Interface, Next-Hop or VCD, State/Mode

 (*, 225.25.25.25), 02:39:52/00:03:20, RP 10.100.1.1, flags: SJCL
   Incoming interface: Null, RPF nbr 0.0.0.0
   Outgoing interface list:
     FastEthernet0/0, Forward/Sparse-Dense, 00:18:52/00:03:20
     Loopback1, Forward/Sparse-Dense, 02:39:52/00:02:15

 (10.100.20.4, 225.25.25.25), 00:03:14/00:02:59, flags: LT
   Incoming interface: FastEthernet0/0, RPF nbr 10.100.13.3
   Outgoing interface list:
     Loopback1, Forward/Sparse-Dense, 00:03:15/00:02:14
```

```
R2# show ip mroute 225.25.25.25
<output omitted>

 (*, 225.25.25.25), 00:02:36/stopped, RP 10.100.1.1, flags: SJPLF
   Incoming interface: Serial0/0/1, RPF nbr 10.100.203.3
   Outgoing interface list: Null

 (10.100.20.4, 225.25.25.25), 00:02:36/00:03:28, flags: LFT
   Incoming interface: FastEthernet0/0, RPF nbr 0.0.0.0
   Outgoing interface list:
     Serial0/0/1, Forward/Sparse-Dense, 00:02:36/00:02:52
```

```
R3# show ip mroute 225.25.25.25
<output omitted>

(*, 225.25.25.25), 00:19:07/00:02:59, RP 10.100.1.1, flags: SJCL
   Incoming interface: FastEthernet0/0, RPF nbr 10.100.13.1
   Outgoing interface list:
     Serial0/0/1, Forward/Sparse-Dense, 00:02:29/00:02:59
     Loopback3, Forward/Sparse-Dense, 00:19:05/00:02:02

 (10.100.20.4, 225.25.25.25), 00:03:27/00:03:27, flags: LT
   Incoming interface: Serial0/0/1, RPF nbr 10.100.203.2
   Outgoing interface list:
     FastEthernet0/0, Forward/Sparse-Dense, 00:03:28/00:03:11
     Loopback3, Forward/Sparse-Dense, 00:03:28/00:02:01
```

Which PIM mode is the 225.25.25.25 group using on the routers based on the flags in the output shown above and why?

_____

To which router will R2 send PIMv2 Register messages for the 225.25.25.25 group?

_____

To which router will R2 send PIMv2 Register messages for the 226.26.26.26 group?

_____

_____

Step 7: Explore Auto-RP Operation with Sparse-Dense Mode

Enable Auto-RP debugging on R1 with the **debug ip pim auto-rp** command. Shut down the Loopback3 interface on R3:

```
R1# debug ip pim auto-rp
```

```
R3(config)# interface loopback 3
R3(config-if)# shutdown
```

How will this affect the Auto-RP election?

_____

_____

_____

_____

Issue the repeated multicast ping to generate (S, G) state on your routers before R1 takes over as the RP for the 226.26.26.26 group:

```
SW1# ping
Protocol [ip]:
Target IP address: 226.26.26.26
Repeat count [1]: 100
Datagram size [100]:
Timeout in seconds [2]:
Extended commands [n]:
Sweep range of sizes [n]:
Type escape sequence to abort.
Sending 100, 100-byte ICMP Echos to 226.26.26.26, timeout is 2 seconds:
.........................................................
Reply to request 60 from 10.100.13.1, 48 ms
Reply to request 61 from 10.100.13.1, 48 ms
Reply to request 62 from 10.100.13.1, 28 ms
Reply to request 63 from 10.100.13.1, 28 ms
```

```
Reply to request 64 from 10.100.13.1, 28 ms
Reply to request 65 from 10.100.13.1, 32 ms
Reply to request 66 from 10.100.13.1, 28 ms
Reply to request 67 from 10.100.13.1, 28 ms
Reply to request 68 from 10.100.13.1, 28 ms
Reply to request 69 from 10.100.13.1, 28 ms
   ... continues through request 99 ...
```

Why were so many pings dropped before reaching the IGMP-subscribed loopback interfaces on R1 and R3?

_____

_____

_____

_____

How does this affect multicast routing?

_____

_____

_____

If Auto-RP debugging were enabled, you would see the following output on the mapping agent after 3 minutes:

```
*Nov  7 18:35:34.839: Auto-RP(0): Mapping (226.26.26.26/32, RP:10.100.3.3) expired,

*Nov  7 18:35:34.843: Auto-RP(0): Build RP-Discovery packet

*Nov  7 18:35:34.843: Auto-RP:  Build mapping (225.25.25.25/32, RP:10.100.1.1), PIMv2
v1,

*Nov  7 18:35:34.843: Auto-RP:  Build mapping (226.26.26.26/32, RP:10.100.1.1),
PIMv2 v1.

*Nov  7 18:35:34.843: Auto-RP(0): Send RP-discovery packet on FastEthernet0/0 (1 RP
entries)

*Nov  7 18:35:34.843: Auto-RP(0): Send RP-discovery packet on Serial0/0/0 (1 RP
entries)

*Nov  7 18:35:34.843: Auto-RP(0): Send RP-discovery packet on Serial0/0/1 (1 RP
entries)

*Nov  7 18:35:34.843: Auto-RP: Send RP-discovery packet on Loopback1 (1 RP entries)
```

Explain the preceding output.

_____

_____

_____

_____

You can check the resulting group-to-RP mappings by using the **show ip pim rp mapping** command:

```
R1# show ip pim rp mapping
PIM Group-to-RP Mappings
```

```
This system is an RP (Auto-RP)
This system is an RP-mapping agent (Loopback1)

Group(s) 225.25.25.25/32
  RP 10.100.1.1 (?), v2v1
    Info source: 10.100.1.1 (?), elected via Auto-RP
        Uptime: 02:53:45, expires: 00:02:12
Group(s) 226.26.26.26/32
  RP 10.100.1.1 (?), v2v1
    Info source: 10.100.1.1 (?), elected via Auto-RP
        Uptime: 02:53:45, expires: 00:02:12
```

Auto-RP allows you to configure backup RPs in a sparse mode or sparse-dense mode network. If you configured a static RP and later it became unreachable, receivers would no longer be able to use the shared tree to receive data. Auto-RP provides a layer of redundancy in sparse mode networks by using mapping agents to delegate RP roles to RP candidates.

Step 8: Verify the Operation of Dense-Mode Fallback

How will the status of the RPs in the network change if you shut down the Loopback1 interface on R1?

_____

_____

Will the PIM mappings in the network change their behavior immediately or after a short time? Which mode is PIM now operating in for the active groups?

_____

_____

Verify your answers with the **show ip pim rp mapping** and **show ip mroute summary** commands on R2 after the mappings expire:

```
R1# configure terminal
R1(config)# interface loopback 1
R1(config-if)# shutdown
R2# show ip pim rp mapping
PIM Group-to-RP Mappings

Group(s) 225.25.25.25/32
  RP 10.100.1.1 (?), v2v1
    Info source: 10.100.1.1 (?), elected via Auto-RP
        Uptime: 03:06:13, expires: 00:00:18
Group(s) 226.26.26.26/32
  RP 10.100.1.1 (?), v2v1
    Info source: 10.100.1.1 (?), elected via Auto-RP
        Uptime: 00:08:38, expires: 00:00:18
SW1# ping
```

```
Protocol [ip]:

Target IP address: 225.25.25.25

Repeat count [1]: 100

Datagram size [100]:

Timeout in seconds [2]:

Extended commands [n]:

Sweep range of sizes [n]:

Type escape sequence to abort.

Sending 100, 100-byte ICMP Echos to 225.25.25.25, timeout is 2 seconds:

.........................................................

Reply to request 61 from 10.100.20.2, 8 ms

Reply to request 62 from 10.100.20.2, 4 ms

Reply to request 63 from 10.100.20.2, 4 ms

Reply to request 64 from 10.100.20.2, 4 ms

Reply to request 65 from 10.100.20.2, 4 ms

Reply to request 66 from 10.100.20.2, 4 ms

Reply to request 67 from 10.100.20.2, 4 ms

    ... continues through request 99 ...
```

```
R2# show ip pim rp mapping
PIM Group-to-RP Mappings


R2# show ip mroute
IP Multicast Routing Table
Flags: D - Dense, S - Sparse, B - Bidir Group, s - SSM Group, C - Connected,
       L - Local, P - Pruned, R - RP-bit set, F - Register flag,
       T - SPT-bit set, J - Join SPT, M - MSDP created entry,
       X - Proxy Join Timer Running, A - Candidate for MSDP Advertisement,
       U - URD, I - Received Source Specific Host Report,
       Z - Multicast Tunnel, z - MDT-data group sender,
       Y - Joined MDT-data group, y - Sending to MDT-data group
Outgoing interface flags: H - Hardware switched, A - Assert winner
 Timers: Uptime/Expires
 Interface state: Interface, Next-Hop or VCD, State/Mode


(*, 225.25.25.25), 00:05:09/stopped, RP 0.0.0.0, flags: DL
  Incoming interface: Null, RPF nbr 0.0.0.0
  Outgoing interface list:
    Serial0/0/1, Forward/Sparse-Dense, 00:05:09/00:00:00
    Serial0/0/0, Forward/Sparse-Dense, 00:05:09/00:00:00


(10.100.20.4, 225.25.25.25), 00:00:06/00:02:57, flags: PLT
  Incoming interface: FastEthernet0/0, RPF nbr 0.0.0.0
```

```
  Outgoing interface list:
    Serial0/0/0, Prune/Sparse-Dense, 00:00:07/00:02:55, A
    Serial0/0/1, Prune/Sparse-Dense, 00:00:06/00:02:53

(*, 224.0.1.40), 00:16:56/00:02:38, RP 0.0.0.0, flags: DCL
  Incoming interface: Null, RPF nbr 0.0.0.0
  Outgoing interface list:
    Serial0/0/1, Forward/Sparse-Dense, 00:16:56/00:00:00
    Serial0/0/0, Forward/Sparse-Dense, 00:16:56/00:00:00
    FastEthernet0/0, Forward/Sparse-Dense, 00:16:56/00:00:00
```

When the group-to-RP mappings expire on R2, PIM realizes that there is no longer an RP for the 225.25.25.25 and 226.26.26.26 groups and converts those groups to use dense mode operation. When this occurs, PIM floods multicast data out all interfaces and then prunes back to R2 because there are no other receivers of the 225.25.25.25 group.

Ping from SW1 again and then enable the loopback interfaces you shut down on R1 and R3:

```
SW1# ping
Protocol [ip]:
Target IP address: 225.25.25.25
Repeat count [1]: 100
Datagram size [100]:
Timeout in seconds [2]:
Extended commands [n]:
Sweep range of sizes [n]:
Type escape sequence to abort.
Sending 100, 100-byte ICMP Echos to 225.25.25.25, timeout is 2 seconds:

Reply to request 0 from 10.100.20.2, 8 ms
Reply to request 1 from 10.100.20.2, 4 ms
Reply to request 2 from 10.100.20.2, 4 ms
Reply to request 3 from 10.100.20.2, 8 ms
Reply to request 4 from 10.100.20.2, 8 ms
Reply to request 5 from 10.100.20.2, 4 ms
Reply to request 6 from 10.100.20.2, 4 ms
Reply to request 7 from 10.100.20.2, 4 ms
Reply to request 8 from 10.100.20.2, 4 ms
Reply to request 9 from 10.100.20.2, 4 ms
Reply to request 10 from 10.100.20.2, 4 ms
Reply to request 11 from 10.100.20.2, 4 ms
Reply to request 12 from 10.100.20.2, 8 ms
Reply to request 12 from 10.100.13.1, 32 ms
Reply to request 13 from 10.100.20.2, 12 ms
Reply to request 13 from 10.100.13.1, 28 ms
Reply to request 14 from 10.100.20.2, 4 ms
```

```
Reply to request 14 from 10.100.13.1, 28 ms
Reply to request 15 from 10.100.20.2, 4 ms
Reply to request 15 from 10.100.13.1, 28 ms
Reply to request 16 from 10.100.20.2, 4 ms
Reply to request 16 from 10.100.13.1, 44 ms
Reply to request 16 from 10.100.203.3, 28 ms
! ... continued below ...
```

Over the period highlighted, both loopback interfaces were opened, and PIM-DM flooded traffic to them. No RPs for these groups were sent to R2 by the mapping agent, so it continues to employ PIM-DM flood-and-prune behavior.

```
! ... continued from above ...
Reply to request 17 from 10.100.20.2, 4 ms
Reply to request 17 from 10.100.13.1, 44 ms
Reply to request 17 from 10.100.203.3, 28 ms
Reply to request 18 from 10.100.20.2, 8 ms
Reply to request 18 from 10.100.13.1, 44 ms
Reply to request 18 from 10.100.203.3, 28 ms
Reply to request 19 from 10.100.20.2, 8 ms
Reply to request 19 from 10.100.13.1, 44 ms
Reply to request 19 from 10.100.203.3, 32 ms
Reply to request 20 from 10.100.20.2, 8 ms
Reply to request 20 from 10.100.13.1, 44 ms
Reply to request 20 from 10.100.203.3, 32 ms
Reply to request 21 from 10.100.20.2, 8 ms
Reply to request 21 from 10.100.13.1, 44 ms
Reply to request 21 from 10.100.203.3, 32 ms
Reply to request 22 from 10.100.20.2, 8 ms
Reply to request 22 from 10.100.13.1, 44 ms
Reply to request 22 from 10.100.203.3, 28 ms
Reply to request 23 from 10.100.20.2, 8 ms
Reply to request 23 from 10.100.13.1, 48 ms
Reply to request 23 from 10.100.203.3, 32 ms
Reply to request 24 from 10.100.20.2, 4 ms
Reply to request 24 from 10.100.13.1, 44 ms
Reply to request 24 from 10.100.203.3, 28 ms
Reply to request 25 from 10.100.20.2, 4 ms
Reply to request 25 from 10.100.13.1, 44 ms
Reply to request 25 from 10.100.203.3, 28 ms
Reply to request 26 from 10.100.20.2, 8 ms
Reply to request 26 from 10.100.13.1, 44 ms
Reply to request 26 from 10.100.203.3, 28 ms
Reply to request 27 from 10.100.20.2, 4 ms
Reply to request 27 from 10.100.13.1, 44 ms
```

```
Reply to request 27 from 10.100.203.3, 28 ms
Reply to request 28 from 10.100.20.2, 4 ms
Reply to request 28 from 10.100.13.1, 44 ms
Reply to request 28 from 10.100.203.3, 28 ms
Reply to request 29 from 10.100.20.2, 4 ms
Reply to request 29 from 10.100.13.1, 44 ms
Reply to request 29 from 10.100.203.3, 32 ms
Reply to request 30 from 10.100.20.2, 4 ms
Reply to request 31 from 10.100.20.2, 8 ms
Reply to request 32 from 10.100.20.2, 4 ms
Reply to request 33 from 10.100.20.2, 4 ms
Reply to request 34 from 10.100.20.2, 4 ms
! ... continued below ...
```

R2 hears R1's Auto-RP announcement to the 224.0.1.240 group. Because there are now RPs in the network, R2 converts the 225.25.25.25 and 226.26.26.26 state to use PIM-SM. R2 does not begin forwarding data to the RP because the mapping agent has not yet elected an RP for the 225.25.25.25 group. R2 waits to receive the RP address from the mapping agent before it begins encapsulating multicast data as unicasts to R1, the RP:

```
! ... continued from above ...
Reply to request 35 from 10.100.20.2, 4 ms
Reply to request 36 from 10.100.20.2, 8 ms
Reply to request 37 from 10.100.20.2, 4 ms
Reply to request 38 from 10.100.20.2, 4 ms
Reply to request 39 from 10.100.20.2, 4 ms
Reply to request 40 from 10.100.20.2, 4 ms
Reply to request 41 from 10.100.20.2, 8 ms
Reply to request 42 from 10.100.20.2, 4 ms
Reply to request 43 from 10.100.20.2, 4 ms
Reply to request 44 from 10.100.20.2, 8 ms
Reply to request 45 from 10.100.20.2, 8 ms
Reply to request 46 from 10.100.20.2, 8 ms
Reply to request 47 from 10.100.20.2, 8 ms
Reply to request 48 from 10.100.20.2, 4 ms
Reply to request 49 from 10.100.20.2, 4 ms
Reply to request 50 from 10.100.20.2, 4 ms
Reply to request 51 from 10.100.20.2, 8 ms
Reply to request 52 from 10.100.20.2, 4 ms
Reply to request 53 from 10.100.20.2, 4 ms
Reply to request 54 from 10.100.20.2, 4 ms
Reply to request 55 from 10.100.20.2, 4 ms
Reply to request 56 from 10.100.20.2, 8 ms
Reply to request 57 from 10.100.20.2, 4 ms
Reply to request 58 from 10.100.20.2, 4 ms
Reply to request 59 from 10.100.20.2, 8 ms
```

```
Reply to request 59 from 10.100.13.1, 44 ms
Reply to request 59 from 10.100.203.3, 32 ms
Reply to request 60 from 10.100.20.2, 8 ms
Reply to request 60 from 10.100.13.1, 44 ms
Reply to request 60 from 10.100.203.3, 32 ms
```

Request 59 is the first packet that R2 encapsulates in a unicast packet and sends to the RP. R1, the RP, forwards the multicast traffic down the shared tree to any subscribers of the 225.25.25.25 group.

When R2 converts a group to a different mode, multicast packets are inevitably dropped before reaching receivers. Although sparse-dense mode brings a high level of resiliency compared to sparse mode, packets are still lost during the transition to and recovery from dense-mode fallback.

This lab demonstrates two basic features of resiliency available on Cisco routers; however, there are more advanced ways to deploy high-availability solutions in a multicast network.

The first three labs on multicast provided the foundation to understand sparse-dense mode. Explain how the concepts in those first three labs lead to an in-depth understanding of PIM sparse-dense mode.

_____

_____

_____

_____

_____

_____

_____

_____

_____

_____

TCL Script Output

```
R1# tclsh
R1(tcl)# foreach address {
+>(tcl)# 10.100.1.1
+>(tcl)# 10.100.13.1
+>(tcl)# 10.100.102.1
+>(tcl)# 10.100.103.1
+>(tcl)# 10.100.2.2
+>(tcl)# 10.100.20.2
+>(tcl)# 10.100.102.2
+>(tcl)# 10.100.203.2
+>(tcl)# 10.100.3.3
+>(tcl)# 10.100.13.3
```

```
+>(tcl)# 10.100.103.3
+>(tcl)# 10.100.203.3
+>(tcl)# 10.100.20.4
+>(tcl)# } { ping $address }


Type escape sequence to abort.
Sending 5, 100-byte ICMP Echos to 10.100.1.1, timeout is 2 seconds:
!!!!!
Success rate is 100 percent (5/5), round-trip min/avg/max = 1/1/4 ms
Type escape sequence to abort.
Sending 5, 100-byte ICMP Echos to 10.100.13.1, timeout is 2 seconds:
!!!!!
Success rate is 100 percent (5/5), round-trip min/avg/max = 1/1/4 ms
Type escape sequence to abort.
Sending 5, 100-byte ICMP Echos to 10.100.102.1, timeout is 2 seconds:
!!!!!
Success rate is 100 percent (5/5), round-trip min/avg/max = 56/56/60 ms
Type escape sequence to abort.
Sending 5, 100-byte ICMP Echos to 10.100.103.1, timeout is 2 seconds:
!!!!!
Success rate is 100 percent (5/5), round-trip min/avg/max = 56/56/60 ms
Type escape sequence to abort.
Sending 5, 100-byte ICMP Echos to 10.100.2.2, timeout is 2 seconds:
!!!!!
Success rate is 100 percent (5/5), round-trip min/avg/max = 12/15/16 ms
Type escape sequence to abort.
Sending 5, 100-byte ICMP Echos to 10.100.20.2, timeout is 2 seconds:
!!!!!
Success rate is 100 percent (5/5), round-trip min/avg/max = 12/15/16 ms
Type escape sequence to abort.
Sending 5, 100-byte ICMP Echos to 10.100.102.2, timeout is 2 seconds:
!!!!!
Success rate is 100 percent (5/5), round-trip min/avg/max = 28/28/32 ms
Type escape sequence to abort.
Sending 5, 100-byte ICMP Echos to 10.100.203.2, timeout is 2 seconds:
!!!!!
Success rate is 100 percent (5/5), round-trip min/avg/max = 12/14/16 ms
Type escape sequence to abort.
Sending 5, 100-byte ICMP Echos to 10.100.3.3, timeout is 2 seconds:
!!!!!
Success rate is 100 percent (5/5), round-trip min/avg/max = 1/2/4 ms
Type escape sequence to abort.
Sending 5, 100-byte ICMP Echos to 10.100.13.3, timeout is 2 seconds:
!!!!!
```

```
Success rate is 100 percent (5/5), round-trip min/avg/max = 1/1/1 ms
Type escape sequence to abort.
Sending 5, 100-byte ICMP Echos to 10.100.103.3, timeout is 2 seconds:
!!!!!
Success rate is 100 percent (5/5), round-trip min/avg/max = 28/28/32 ms
Type escape sequence to abort.
Sending 5, 100-byte ICMP Echos to 10.100.203.3, timeout is 2 seconds:
!!!!!
Success rate is 100 percent (5/5), round-trip min/avg/max = 1/2/4 ms
Type escape sequence to abort.
Sending 5, 100-byte ICMP Echos to 10.100.20.4, timeout is 2 seconds:
!!!!!
Success rate is 100 percent (5/5), round-trip min/avg/max = 16/16/20 ms
R1(tcl)#  tclquit
```

```
R2# tclsh
R2(tcl)# foreach address {
+>(tcl)# 10.100.1.1
+>(tcl)# 10.100.13.1
+>(tcl)# 10.100.102.1
+>(tcl)# 10.100.103.1
+>(tcl)# 10.100.2.2
+>(tcl)# 10.100.20.2
+>(tcl)# 10.100.102.2
+>(tcl)# 10.100.203.2
+>(tcl)# 10.100.3.3
+>(tcl)# 10.100.13.3
+>(tcl)# 10.100.103.3
+>(tcl)# 10.100.203.3
+>(tcl)# 10.100.20.4
+>(tcl)# } { ping $address }

Type escape sequence to abort.
Sending 5, 100-byte ICMP Echos to 10.100.1.1, timeout is 2 seconds:
!!!!!
Success rate is 100 percent (5/5), round-trip min/avg/max = 12/15/16 ms
Type escape sequence to abort.
Sending 5, 100-byte ICMP Echos to 10.100.13.1, timeout is 2 seconds:
!!!!!
Success rate is 100 percent (5/5), round-trip min/avg/max = 12/15/16 ms
Type escape sequence to abort.
Sending 5, 100-byte ICMP Echos to 10.100.102.1, timeout is 2 seconds:
!!!!!
Success rate is 100 percent (5/5), round-trip min/avg/max = 28/28/28 ms
Type escape sequence to abort.
```

```
Sending 5, 100-byte ICMP Echos to 10.100.103.1, timeout is 2 seconds:
!!!!!
Success rate is 100 percent (5/5), round-trip min/avg/max = 28/29/32 ms
Type escape sequence to abort.
Sending 5, 100-byte ICMP Echos to 10.100.2.2, timeout is 2 seconds:
!!!!!
Success rate is 100 percent (5/5), round-trip min/avg/max = 1/1/4 ms
Type escape sequence to abort.
Sending 5, 100-byte ICMP Echos to 10.100.20.2, timeout is 2 seconds:
!!!!!
Success rate is 100 percent (5/5), round-trip min/avg/max = 1/1/4 ms
Type escape sequence to abort.
Sending 5, 100-byte ICMP Echos to 10.100.102.2, timeout is 2 seconds:
!!!!!
Success rate is 100 percent (5/5), round-trip min/avg/max = 56/57/64 ms
Type escape sequence to abort.
Sending 5, 100-byte ICMP Echos to 10.100.203.2, timeout is 2 seconds:
!!!!!
Success rate is 100 percent (5/5), round-trip min/avg/max = 28/29/36 ms
Type escape sequence to abort.
Sending 5, 100-byte ICMP Echos to 10.100.3.3, timeout is 2 seconds:
!!!!!
Success rate is 100 percent (5/5), round-trip min/avg/max = 12/14/16 ms
Type escape sequence to abort.
Sending 5, 100-byte ICMP Echos to 10.100.13.3, timeout is 2 seconds:
!!!!!
Success rate is 100 percent (5/5), round-trip min/avg/max = 12/14/16 ms
Type escape sequence to abort.
Sending 5, 100-byte ICMP Echos to 10.100.103.3, timeout is 2 seconds:
!!!!!
Success rate is 100 percent (5/5), round-trip min/avg/max = 12/15/16 ms
Type escape sequence to abort.
Sending 5, 100-byte ICMP Echos to 10.100.203.3, timeout is 2 seconds:
!!!!!
Success rate is 100 percent (5/5), round-trip min/avg/max = 12/15/16 ms
Type escape sequence to abort.
Sending 5, 100-byte ICMP Echos to 10.100.20.4, timeout is 2 seconds:
!!!!!
Success rate is 100 percent (5/5), round-trip min/avg/max = 1/2/4 ms
R2(tcl)#  tclquit
```

```
R3# tclsh
R3(tcl)# foreach address {
+>(tcl)# 10.100.1.1
+>(tcl)# 10.100.13.1
```

```
+>(tcl)# 10.100.102.1
+>(tcl)# 10.100.103.1
+>(tcl)# 10.100.2.2
+>(tcl)# 10.100.20.2
+>(tcl)# 10.100.102.2
+>(tcl)# 10.100.203.2
+>(tcl)# 10.100.3.3
+>(tcl)# 10.100.13.3
+>(tcl)# 10.100.103.3
+>(tcl)# 10.100.203.3
+>(tcl)# 10.100.20.4
+>(tcl)# } { ping $address }


Type escape sequence to abort.
Sending 5, 100-byte ICMP Echos to 10.100.1.1, timeout is 2 seconds:
!!!!!
Success rate is 100 percent (5/5), round-trip min/avg/max = 1/2/4 ms
Type escape sequence to abort.
Sending 5, 100-byte ICMP Echos to 10.100.13.1, timeout is 2 seconds:
!!!!!
Success rate is 100 percent (5/5), round-trip min/avg/max = 1/2/4 ms
Type escape sequence to abort.
Sending 5, 100-byte ICMP Echos to 10.100.102.1, timeout is 2 seconds:
!!!!!
Success rate is 100 percent (5/5), round-trip min/avg/max = 1/2/4 ms
Type escape sequence to abort.
Sending 5, 100-byte ICMP Echos to 10.100.103.1, timeout is 2 seconds:
!!!!!
Success rate is 100 percent (5/5), round-trip min/avg/max = 28/28/32 ms
Type escape sequence to abort.
Sending 5, 100-byte ICMP Echos to 10.100.2.2, timeout is 2 seconds:
!!!!!
Success rate is 100 percent (5/5), round-trip min/avg/max = 12/15/16 ms
Type escape sequence to abort.
Sending 5, 100-byte ICMP Echos to 10.100.20.2, timeout is 2 seconds:
!!!!!
Success rate is 100 percent (5/5), round-trip min/avg/max = 12/15/16 ms
Type escape sequence to abort.
Sending 5, 100-byte ICMP Echos to 10.100.102.2, timeout is 2 seconds:
!!!!!
Success rate is 100 percent (5/5), round-trip min/avg/max = 20/20/24 ms
Type escape sequence to abort.
Sending 5, 100-byte ICMP Echos to 10.100.203.2, timeout is 2 seconds:
!!!!!
```

```
Success rate is 100 percent (5/5), round-trip min/avg/max = 12/13/16 ms
Type escape sequence to abort.
Sending 5, 100-byte ICMP Echos to 10.100.3.3, timeout is 2 seconds:
!!!!!
Success rate is 100 percent (5/5), round-trip min/avg/max = 1/1/4 ms
Type escape sequence to abort.
Sending 5, 100-byte ICMP Echos to 10.100.13.3, timeout is 2 seconds:
!!!!!
Success rate is 100 percent (5/5), round-trip min/avg/max = 1/1/4 ms
Type escape sequence to abort.
Sending 5, 100-byte ICMP Echos to 10.100.103.3, timeout is 2 seconds:
!!!!!
Success rate is 100 percent (5/5), round-trip min/avg/max = 56/57/64 ms
Type escape sequence to abort.
Sending 5, 100-byte ICMP Echos to 10.100.203.3, timeout is 2 seconds:
!!!!!
Success rate is 100 percent (5/5), round-trip min/avg/max = 28/29/36 ms
Type escape sequence to abort.
Sending 5, 100-byte ICMP Echos to 10.100.20.4, timeout is 2 seconds:
!!!!!
Success rate is 100 percent (5/5), round-trip min/avg/max = 16/16/16 ms
R3(tcl)# tclquit
```

Lab 8-1: Configuring OSPF for IPv6 (8.7.1)

The objectives of this lab are as follows:

- Configure a static IPv6 address on an interface

- Change the default-link local address on an interface

- Configure an EUI-64 IPv6 address on an interface

- Enable IPv6 routing and Cisco Express Forwarding (CEF)

- Configure and verify single-area OSPFv3 operation

Figure 8-1 illustrates the topology that will be used for this lab.

Figure 8-1   Topology Diagram for Lab 8-1

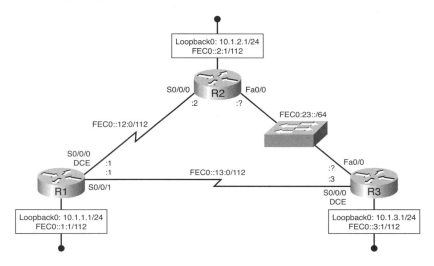

Scenario

For this lab, you will configure IPv6 addresses on interfaces, both static addresses and EUI-64 addresses. Then, you will configure OSPFv3 to route between the IPv6 networks.

Step 1: Configuring the Loopback Interfaces

Configure the loopback interface on each router with both the IPv4 address and IPv6 address given in the diagram. The IPv4 address is configured the traditional way with the **ip address** *address mask* command. The IPv6 address configuration is similar, using the **ipv6 address** *address/mask* command. IPv6 addresses let you put in the mask length with a /mask, rather than typing the whole mask out in hexadecimal (imagine typing up to 128 bits worth of 1s).

You also can put in the abbreviated form of an IPv6 address. IPv6 addresses normally are 8 groups of 16 bit groups of hexadecimal, separated by colons. You can abbreviate any continuous group of 0s with "::". You can only use this abbreviation once per address. For example, FEC0:0:0:0:0:0:12:1 /112 can be shortened to FEC0::12:1 /112:

```
R1(config)# interface loopback 0
R1(config-if)# ip address 10.1.1.1 255.255.255.0
R1(config-if)# ipv6 address FEC0::1:1/112
R2(config)# interface loopback 0
R2(config-if)# ip address 10.1.2.1 255.255.255.0
R2(config-if)# ipv6 address FEC0::2:1/112
R3(config)# interface loopback 0
R3(config-if)# ip address 10.1.3.1 255.255.255.0
R3(config-if)# ipv6 address FEC0::3:1/112
```

If you accidentally put the wrong IPv6 address on an interface, make sure you take it off with the **no** version of the command you entered. Unlike IPv4 addresses, where the **ip address** command over-writes the existing address, multiple IPv6 addresses can exist on an interface. Applying in the **ipv6 address** command multiple times to a single interface will add more addresses, not replace them.

Also, notice that we put both an IPv4 and IPv6 address on the same interface, and neither conflict with each other. This is because they are different Layer 3 protocols, and they run independently.

Step 2: Configuring Static IPv6 Addresses

Now, configure the two serial links with IPv6 addresses. Use the **ipv6 address** *address/mask* command again to configure the interfaces with the addresses given in the diagram. Remember to set the clockrates where appropriate and issue the **no shutdown** command on the interfaces. Use the **ping** command to verify local subnet connectivity:

```
R1(config)# interface serial 0/0/0
R1(config-if)# ipv6 address FEC0::12:1/112
R1(config-if)# clockrate 64000
R1(config-if)# no shutdown
R1(config-if)# interface serial 0/0/1
R1(config-if)# ipv6 address FEC0::13:1/112
R1(config-if)# clockrate 64000
R1(config-if)# no shutdown
R2(config)# interface serial 0/0/0
R2(config-if)# ipv6 address FEC0::12:2/112
R2(config-if)# no shutdown
R3(config)# interface serial 0/0/0
R3(config-if)# ipv6 address FEC0::13:3/112
R3(config-if)# clockrate 64000
R3(config-if)# no shutdown
R1# ping FEC0::12:2
```

```
Type escape sequence to abort.
Sending 5, 100-byte ICMP Echos to FEC0::12:2, timeout is 2 seconds:
!!!!!
Success rate is 100 percent (5/5), round-trip min/avg/max = 28/28/28 ms
R1# ping FEC0::13:3

Type escape sequence to abort.
Sending 5, 100-byte ICMP Echos to FEC0::13:3, timeout is 2 seconds:
!!!!!
Success rate is 100 percent (5/5), round-trip min/avg/max = 28/28/28 ms
R2# ping FEC0::12:1

Type escape sequence to abort.
Sending 5, 100-byte ICMP Echos to FEC0::12:1, timeout is 2 seconds:
!!!!!
Success rate is 100 percent (5/5), round-trip min/avg/max = 28/28/28 ms
R3# ping FEC0::13:1

Type escape sequence to abort.
Sending 5, 100-byte ICMP Echos to FEC0::13:1, timeout is 2 seconds:
!!!!!
Success rate is 100 percent (5/5), round-trip min/avg/max = 28/28/28 ms
```

Step 3: Changing the Link-Local Address on an Interface

Use the **show ipv6 interface** command to look at IPv6 related properties of the router interfaces. You can also specify a specific type/number of an interface with this command to see the output for only that interface:

```
R1# show ipv6 interface serial 0/0/0
Serial0/0/0 is up, line protocol is up
  IPv6 is enabled, link-local address is FE80::219:6FF:FE23:4380
  No Virtual link-local address(es):
  Global unicast address(es):
    FEC0::12:1, subnet is FEC0::12:0/112
  Joined group address(es):
    FF02::1
    FF02::2
    FF02::1:FF12:1
    FF02::1:FF23:4380
  MTU is 1500 bytes
  ICMP error messages limited to one every 100 milliseconds
  ICMP redirects are enabled
  ICMP unreachables are sent
```

```
    ND DAD is enabled, number of DAD attempts: 1

    ND reachable time is 30000 milliseconds
```

```
R2# show ipv6 interface serial 0/0/0

Serial0/0/0 is up, line protocol is up

  IPv6 is enabled, link-local address is FE80::218:B9FF:FE92:28D8

  Global unicast address(es):

    FEC0::12:2, subnet is FEC0::12:0/112

  Joined group address(es):

    FF02::1

    FF02::2

    FF02::1:FF12:2

    FF02::1:FF92:28D8

  MTU is 1500 bytes

  ICMP error messages limited to one every 100 milliseconds

  ICMP redirects are enabled

  ND DAD is enabled, number of DAD attempts: 1

  ND reachable time is 30000 milliseconds
```

Notice that in addition to the address you already configured, there is a link local address starting with FE80. Your actual address may vary. You can change this on the link between R1 and R2 by putting the link-local address FE80::1 on R1 and FE80::2 on R2. There is no subnet mask on link-local addresses because they are not routed; hence the term "link-local." To configure this, use the command **ipv6 address** *address* **link-local**. Verify that you can ping the link local address on the other side. When pinging link local addresses, you must specify an outgoing interface because the addresses are not routed and not in the routing table:

```
R1(config)# interface serial 0/0/0

R1(config-if)# ipv6 address FE80::1 link-local
```

```
R2(config)# interface serial 0/0/0

R2(config-if)# ipv6 address FE80::2 link-local
```

```
R1# ping FE80::2

Output Interface: Serial0/0/0

Type escape sequence to abort.

Sending 5, 100-byte ICMP Echos to FE80::2, timeout is 2 seconds:

Packet sent with a source address of FE80::1

!!!!!

Success rate is 100 percent (5/5), round-trip min/avg/max = 28/28/28 ms
```

```
R2# ping FE80::1

Output Interface: Serial0/0/0

Type escape sequence to abort.

Sending 5, 100-byte ICMP Echos to FE80::1, timeout is 2 seconds:

Packet sent with a source address of FE80::2

!!!!!

Success rate is 100 percent (5/5), round-trip min/avg/max = 28/28/28 ms
```

Verify the link local addresses with the command **show ipv6 interface**:

```
R1# show ipv6 interface serial 0/0/0
Serial0/0/0 is up, line protocol is up
  IPv6 is enabled, link-local address is FE80::1
  No Virtual link-local address(es):
  Global unicast address(es):
    FEC0::12:1, subnet is FEC0::12:0/112
  Joined group address(es):
    FF02::1
    FF02::2
    FF02::1:FF00:1
    FF02::1:FF12:1
  MTU is 1500 bytes
  ICMP error messages limited to one every 100 milliseconds
  ICMP redirects are enabled
  ICMP unreachables are sent
  ND DAD is enabled, number of DAD attempts: 1
  ND reachable time is 30000 milliseconds
```

```
R2# show ipv6 interface serial 0/0/0
Serial0/0/0 is up, line protocol is up
  IPv6 is enabled, link-local address is FE80::2
  Global unicast address(es):
    FEC0::12:2, subnet is FEC0::12:0/112
  Joined group address(es):
    FF02::1
    FF02::2
    FF02::1:FF00:2
    FF02::1:FF12:2
  MTU is 1500 bytes
  ICMP error messages limited to one every 100 milliseconds
  ICMP redirects are enabled
  ND DAD is enabled, number of DAD attempts: 1
  ND reachable time is 30000 milliseconds
```

Step 4: Configuring EUI-64 Addresses

EUI-64 IPv6 addresses are addresses where the first 64 bits are the network portion of the address and specified, and the second 64 bits are the host portion of the address and automatically generated by the device. To configure IPv6 EUI-64 addresses on an interface, use **ipv6 address** *address/mask* **eui-64**. Configure this on the FastEthernet interfaces of R2 and R3 with the subnet given in the diagram. Also, make sure you put a **no shutdown** on the interfaces. Find out the IPv6 addresses of the interfaces with **show ipv6 interface** or **show ipv6 interface brief**, and then ping the other side of the link:

```
R2(config)# interface fastethernet 0/0
R2(config-if)# ipv6 address FEC0:23::/64 eui-64
```

```
R2(config-if)# no shutdown
```

```
R3(config)# interface fastethernet 0/0
R3(config-if)# ipv6 address FEC0:23::/64 eui-64
R3(config-if)# no shutdown
```

```
R2# show ipv6 interface brief
FastEthernet0/0             [up/up]
    FE80::218:B9FF:FE92:28D8
    FEC0:23::218:B9FF:FE92:28D8
FastEthernet0/1             [administratively down/down]
Serial0/0/0                 [up/up]
    FE80::2
    FEC0::12:2
Serial0/0/1                 [administratively down/down]
Serial0/1/0                 [administratively down/down]
Serial0/1/1                 [administratively down/down]
Loopback0                   [up/up]
    FE80::218:B9FF:FE92:28D8
    FEC0::2:1
```

```
R3# show ipv6 interface brief
FastEthernet0/0             [up/up]
    FE80::218:B9FF:FECD:BEF0
    FEC0:23::218:B9FF:FECD:BEF0
FastEthernet0/1             [administratively down/down]
Serial0/0/0                 [up/up]
    FE80::218:B9FF:FECD:BEF0
    FEC0::13:3
Serial0/0/1                 [administratively down/down]
Serial0/1/0                 [administratively down/down]
Serial0/1/1                 [administratively down/down]
Loopback0                   [up/up]
    FE80::218:B9FF:FECD:BEF0
    FEC0::3:1
```

Note Your addresses *will* be different from the addresses displayed in the example because EUI-64 addresses include the MAC address of the interface in them, which will be unique per interface.

```
R2# ping FEC0:23::218:B9FF:FECD:BEF0

Type escape sequence to abort.
Sending 5, 100-byte ICMP Echos to FEC0:23::218:B9FF:FECD:BEF0, timeout is 2 seconds:
!!!!!
Success rate is 100 percent (5/5), round-trip min/avg/max = 0/0/4 ms
```

```
R3# ping FEC0:23::218:B9FF:FE92:28D8
```

```
Type escape sequence to abort.
Sending 5, 100-byte ICMP Echos to FEC0:23::218:B9FF:FE92:28D8, timeout is 2 seconds:
!!!!!
Success rate is 100 percent (5/5), round-trip min/avg/max = 0/0/0 ms
```

At this point in the lab you should have local subnet connectivity.

Step 5: Enabling IPv6 Routing and CEF

As of the time of this writing, the current IOS version has IPv6 routing and CEF disabled by default. To enable IPv6 routing, use the **ipv6 unicast-routing** command in global configuration mode. To enable IPv6 CEF, use the **ipv6 cef** command. Use these commands on all three routers:

```
R1(config)# ipv6 unicast-routing
R1(config)# ipv6 cef
R2(config)# ipv6 unicast-routing
R2(config)# ipv6 cef
R3(config)# ipv6 unicast-routing
R3(config)# ipv6 cef
```

Step 6: Setting Up OSPFv3

Unlike IPv4 OSPF, where networks are added to the OSPF process with **network** statements under the routing protocol configuration prompt, IPv6 OSPF uses the **ipv6 ospf** *process* **area** *area* command in interface configuration mode to add an interface to an area. This method has both its advantages and disadvantages compared to the old method. Add all interfaces shown on the diagram into OSPF process 1, area 0. Once you add the interfaces to the OSPF process with this command, the OSPF process will start automatically. If the adjacencies don't come up after a reasonable period of time, troubleshoot using the **debug ipv6 ospf adjacency** and **debug ipv6 packet** commands. Make sure that the packets are being sent to their destinations and that adjacencies are forming correctly:

```
R1(config)# interface loopback0
R1(config-if)# ipv6 ospf 1 area 0
R1(config-if)# interface serial0/0/0
R1(config-if)# ipv6 ospf 1 area 0
R1(config-if)# interface serial0/0/1
R1(config-if)# ipv6 ospf 1 area 0
R2(config)# interface loopback0
R2(config-if)# ipv6 ospf 1 area 0
R2(config-if)# interface serial0/0/0
R2(config-if)# ipv6 ospf 1 area 0
R2(config-if)# interface fastethernet0/0
R2(config-if)# ipv6 ospf 1 area 0
R3(config)# interface loopback0
R3(config-if)# ipv6 ospf 1 area 0
R3(config-if)# interface serial0/0/0
R3(config-if)# ipv6 ospf 1 area 0
```

```
R3(config-if)# interface fastethernet0/0
R3(config-if)# ipv6 ospf 1 area 0
```

Verify that you have OSPFv3 neighbors with the **show ipv6 ospf neighbor** command.

```
R1# show ipv6 ospf neighbor
```

Neighbor ID	Pri	State	Dead Time	Interface ID	Interface
10.1.3.1	1	FULL/ -	00:00:39	6	Serial0/0/1
10.1.2.1	1	FULL/ -	00:00:34	6	Serial0/0/0

```
R2#show ipv6 ospf neighbor
```

Neighbor ID	Pri	State	Dead Time	Interface ID	Interface
10.1.3.1	1	FULL/DR	00:00:39	4	FastEthernet0/0
10.1.1.1	1	FULL/ -	00:00:32	6	Serial0/0/0

```
R3#show ipv6 ospf neighbor
```

Neighbor ID	Pri	State	Dead Time	Interface ID	Interface
10.1.2.1	1	FULL/BDR	00:00:39	4	FastEthernet0/0
10.1.1.1	1	FULL/ -	00:00:39	7	Serial0/0/0

The router IDs for each router are created the same way that they are in OSPFv2 or BGP. Without any IPv4 addresses on the router, the OSPFv3 process will not start unless you manually set the router IDs. This is why the loopback interfaces have both IPv4 and IPv6 addresses.

Display the routing table on all three routers with the **show ipv6 route** command:

```
R1# show ipv6 route
IPv6 Routing Table - 11 entries
Codes: C - Connected, L - Local, S - Static, R - RIP, B - BGP
       U - Per-user Static route
       I1 - ISIS L1, I2 - ISIS L2, IA - ISIS interarea, IS - ISIS summary
       O - OSPF intra, OI - OSPF inter, OE1 - OSPF ext 1, OE2 - OSPF ext 2
       ON1 - OSPF NSSA ext 1, ON2 - OSPF NSSA ext 2
       D - EIGRP, EX - EIGRP external
L   FE80::/10 [0/0]
     via ::, Null0
C   FEC0::1:0/112 [0/0]
     via ::, Loopback0
L   FEC0::1:1/128 [0/0]
     via ::, Loopback0
O   FEC0::2:1/128 [110/64]
     via FE80::2, Serial0/0/0
O   FEC0::3:1/128 [110/64]
     via FE80::218:B9FF:FECD:BEF0, Serial0/0/1
C   FEC0::12:0/112 [0/0]
```

```
         via ::, Serial0/0/0
L    FEC0::12:1/128 [0/0]
         via ::, Serial0/0/0
C    FEC0::13:0/112 [0/0]
         via ::, Serial0/0/1
L    FEC0::13:1/128 [0/0]
         via ::, Serial0/0/1
O    FEC0:23::/64 [110/65]
         via FE80::2, Serial0/0/0
         via FE80::218:B9FF:FECD:BEF0, Serial0/0/1
L    FF00::/8 [0/0]
         via ::, Null0
```

R2# **show ipv6 route**

```
IPv6 Routing Table - 11 entries
Codes: C - Connected, L - Local, S - Static, R - RIP, B - BGP
        U - Per-user Static route
        I1 - ISIS L1, I2 - ISIS L2, IA - ISIS interarea, IS - ISIS summary
        O - OSPF intra, OI - OSPF inter, OE1 - OSPF ext 1, OE2 - OSPF ext 2
        ON1 - OSPF NSSA ext 1, ON2 - OSPF NSSA ext 2
L    FE80::/10 [0/0]
         via ::, Null0
O    FEC0::1:1/128 [110/64]
         via FE80::1, Serial0/0/0
C    FEC0::2:0/112 [0/0]
         via ::, Loopback0
L    FEC0::2:1/128 [0/0]
         via ::, Loopback0
O    FEC0::3:1/128 [110/1]
         via FE80::218:B9FF:FECD:BEF0, FastEthernet0/0
C    FEC0::12:0/112 [0/0]
         via ::, Serial0/0/0
L    FEC0::12:2/128 [0/0]
         via ::, Serial0/0/0
O    FEC0::13:0/112 [110/65]
         via FE80::218:B9FF:FECD:BEF0, FastEthernet0/0
C    FEC0:23::/64 [0/0]
         via ::, FastEthernet0/0
L    FEC0:23::218:B9FF:FE92:28D8/128 [0/0]
         via ::, FastEthernet0/0
L    FF00::/8 [0/0]
         via ::, Null0
```

R3# **show ipv6 route**

```
IPv6 Routing Table - 11 entries
```

```
Codes: C - Connected, L - Local, S - Static, R - RIP, B - BGP
       U - Per-user Static route
       I1 - ISIS L1, I2 - ISIS L2, IA - ISIS interarea, IS - ISIS summary
       O - OSPF intra, OI - OSPF inter, OE1 - OSPF ext 1, OE2 - OSPF ext 2
       ON1 - OSPF NSSA ext 1, ON2 - OSPF NSSA ext 2
L    FE80::/10 [0/0]
      via ::, Null0
O    FEC0::1:1/128 [110/64]
      via FE80::219:6FF:FE23:4380, Serial0/0/0
O    FEC0::2:1/128 [110/1]
      via FE80::218:B9FF:FE92:28D8, FastEthernet0/0
C    FEC0::3:0/112 [0/0]
      via ::, Loopback0
L    FEC0::3:1/128 [0/0]
      via ::, Loopback0
O    FEC0::12:0/112 [110/65]
      via FE80::218:B9FF:FE92:28D8, FastEthernet0/0
C    FEC0::13:0/112 [0/0]
      via ::, Serial0/0/0
L    FEC0::13:3/128 [0/0]
      via ::, Serial0/0/0
C    FEC0:23::/64 [0/0]
      via ::, FastEthernet0/0
L    FEC0:23::218:B9FF:FECD:BEF0/128 [0/0]
      via ::, FastEthernet0/0
L    FF00::/8 [0/0]
      via ::, Null0
```

You can also look at per-interface OSPF behavior with **show ipv6 ospf interface**:

```
R1# show ipv6 ospf interface
Serial0/0/1 is up, line protocol is up
  Link Local Address FE80::219:6FF:FE23:4380, Interface ID 7
  Area 0, Process ID 1, Instance ID 0, Router ID 10.1.1.1
  Network Type POINT_TO_POINT, Cost: 64
  Transmit Delay is 1 sec, State POINT_TO_POINT,
  Timer intervals configured, Hello 10, Dead 40, Wait 40, Retransmit 5
    Hello due in 00:00:06
  Index 1/3/3, flood queue length 0
  Next 0x0(0)/0x0(0)/0x0(0)
  Last flood scan length is 2, maximum is 2
  Last flood scan time is 0 msec, maximum is 0 msec
  Neighbor Count is 1, Adjacent neighbor count is 1
    Adjacent with neighbor 10.1.3.1
```

```
    Suppress hello for 0 neighbor(s)
Serial0/0/0 is up, line protocol is up
    Link Local Address FE80::1, Interface ID 6
    Area 0, Process ID 1, Instance ID 0, Router ID 10.1.1.1
    Network Type POINT_TO_POINT, Cost: 64
    Transmit Delay is 1 sec, State POINT_TO_POINT,
    Timer intervals configured, Hello 10, Dead 40, Wait 40, Retransmit 5
      Hello due in 00:00:00
    Index 1/2/2, flood queue length 0
    Next 0x0(0)/0x0(0)/0x0(0)
    Last flood scan length is 1, maximum is 4
    Last flood scan time is 0 msec, maximum is 0 msec
    Neighbor Count is 1, Adjacent neighbor count is 1
      Adjacent with neighbor 10.1.2.1
    Suppress hello for 0 neighbor(s)
Loopback0 is up, line protocol is up
    Link Local Address FE80::219:6FF:FE23:4380, Interface ID 20
    Area 0, Process ID 1, Instance ID 0, Router ID 10.1.1.1
    Network Type LOOPBACK, Cost: 1
    Loopback interface is treated as a stub Host
```
```
R2# show ipv6 ospf interface
FastEthernet0/0 is up, line protocol is up
    Link Local Address FE80::218:B9FF:FE92:28D8, Interface ID 4
    Area 0, Process ID 1, Instance ID 0, Router ID 10.1.2.1
    Network Type BROADCAST, Cost: 1
    Transmit Delay is 1 sec, State BDR, Priority 1
    Designated Router (ID) 10.1.3.1, local address FE80::218:B9FF:FECD:BEF0
    Backup Designated router (ID) 10.1.2.1, local address FE80::218:B9FF:FE92:28D8
    Timer intervals configured, Hello 10, Dead 40, Wait 40, Retransmit 5
      Hello due in 00:00:04
    Index 1/3/3, flood queue length 0
    Next 0x0(0)/0x0(0)/0x0(0)
    Last flood scan length is 2, maximum is 2
    Last flood scan time is 0 msec, maximum is 0 msec
    Neighbor Count is 1, Adjacent neighbor count is 1
      Adjacent with neighbor 10.1.3.1   (Designated Router)
    Suppress hello for 0 neighbor(s)
Serial0/0/0 is up, line protocol is up
    Link Local Address FE80::2, Interface ID 6
    Area 0, Process ID 1, Instance ID 0, Router ID 10.1.2.1
    Network Type POINT_TO_POINT, Cost: 64
    Transmit Delay is 1 sec, State POINT_TO_POINT,
```

```
       Timer intervals configured, Hello 10, Dead 40, Wait 40, Retransmit 5
         Hello due in 00:00:07
       Index 1/2/2, flood queue length 0
       Next 0x0(0)/0x0(0)/0x0(0)
       Last flood scan length is 1, maximum is 4
       Last flood scan time is 0 msec, maximum is 0 msec
       Neighbor Count is 1, Adjacent neighbor count is 1
         Adjacent with neighbor 10.1.1.1
       Suppress hello for 0 neighbor(s)
    Loopback0 is up, line protocol is up
       Link Local Address FE80::218:B9FF:FE92:28D8, Interface ID 17
       Area 0, Process ID 1, Instance ID 0, Router ID 10.1.2.1
       Network Type LOOPBACK, Cost: 1
       Loopback interface is treated as a stub Host
```

```
R3# show ipv6 ospf interface
```
```
FastEthernet0/0 is up, line protocol is up
    Link Local Address FE80::218:B9FF:FECD:BEF0, Interface ID 4
    Area 0, Process ID 1, Instance ID 0, Router ID 10.1.3.1
    Network Type BROADCAST, Cost: 1
    Transmit Delay is 1 sec, State DR, Priority 1
    Designated Router (ID) 10.1.3.1, local address FE80::218:B9FF:FECD:BEF0
    Backup Designated router (ID) 10.1.2.1, local address FE80::218:B9FF:FE92:28D8
    Timer intervals configured, Hello 10, Dead 40, Wait 40, Retransmit 5
      Hello due in 00:00:09
    Index 1/3/3, flood queue length 0
    Next 0x0(0)/0x0(0)/0x0(0)
    Last flood scan length is 1, maximum is 4
    Last flood scan time is 0 msec, maximum is 0 msec
    Neighbor Count is 1, Adjacent neighbor count is 1
      Adjacent with neighbor 10.1.2.1   (Backup Designated Router)
    Suppress hello for 0 neighbor(s)
  Serial0/0/0 is up, line protocol is up
    Link Local Address FE80::218:B9FF:FECD:BEF0, Interface ID 6
    Area 0, Process ID 1, Instance ID 0, Router ID 10.1.3.1
    Network Type POINT_TO_POINT, Cost: 64
    Transmit Delay is 1 sec, State POINT_TO_POINT,
    Timer intervals configured, Hello 10, Dead 40, Wait 40, Retransmit 5
      Hello due in 00:00:07
    Index 1/2/2, flood queue length 0
    Next 0x0(0)/0x0(0)/0x0(0)
    Last flood scan length is 1, maximum is 4
    Last flood scan time is 0 msec, maximum is 0 msec
    Neighbor Count is 1, Adjacent neighbor count is 1
```

```
      Adjacent with neighbor 10.1.1.1
   Suppress hello for 0 neighbor(s)
Loopback0 is up, line protocol is up
   Link Local Address FE80::218:B9FF:FECD:BEF0, Interface ID 17
   Area 0, Process ID 1, Instance ID 0, Router ID 10.1.3.1
   Network Type LOOPBACK, Cost: 1
   Loopback interface is treated as a stub Host
```

Challenge: Summarizing OSPFv3 Areas

The commands available for OSPFv3 are very close to the commands available for OSPFv2. On R2, add in two loopback interfaces, with the addresses FEC0:500::100:1 /112 and FEC0:500::200:1 /112. Add both of these interfaces to the OSPF process in area 500. Summarize area 500 to FEC0:500:: /64. To enter the OSPF configuration mode, use the **ipv6 router ospf** *process* command. Then apply the **area range** command to summarize the address. Use the question mark if you need help.

_____

_____

_____

_____

_____

_____

_____

_____

TCL Script Output

Modify the script for the correct addresses on the FEC0:23:: /64 subnet. You can download this TCL script at www.ciscopress.com/title/1587132133 under the More Information section on the page.

```
tclsh

foreach address {
FEC0::1:1
FEC0::2:1
FEC0::3:1
FEC0::12:1
FEC0::12:2
FEC0::13:1
FEC0::13:3
FEC0:23::
FEC0:23::
```

```
} {
ping $address }
```

```
R1# tclsh
R1(tcl)#
R1(tcl)# foreach address {
+>(tcl)# FEC0::1:1
+>(tcl)# FEC0::2:1
+>(tcl)# FEC0::3:1
+>(tcl)# FEC0::12:1
+>(tcl)# FEC0::12:2
+>(tcl)# FEC0::13:1
+>(tcl)# FEC0::13:3
+>(tcl)# FEC0:23::218:B9FF:FE92:28D8
+>(tcl)# FEC0:23::218:B9FF:FECD:BEF0
+>(tcl)# } {
+>(tcl)# ping $address }

Type escape sequence to abort.
Sending 5, 100-byte ICMP Echos to FEC0::1:1, timeout is 2 seconds:
!!!!!
Success rate is 100 percent (5/5), round-trip min/avg/max = 0/0/0 ms
Type escape sequence to abort.
Sending 5, 100-byte ICMP Echos to FEC0::2:1, timeout is 2 seconds:
!!!!!
Success rate is 100 percent (5/5), round-trip min/avg/max = 28/28/28 ms
Type escape sequence to abort.
Sending 5, 100-byte ICMP Echos to FEC0::3:1, timeout is 2 seconds:
!!!!!
Success rate is 100 percent (5/5), round-trip min/avg/max = 28/28/28 ms
Type escape sequence to abort.
Sending 5, 100-byte ICMP Echos to FEC0::12:1, timeout is 2 seconds:
!!!!!
Success rate is 100 percent (5/5), round-trip min/avg/max = 0/0/0 ms
Type escape sequence to abort.
Sending 5, 100-byte ICMP Echos to FEC0::12:2, timeout is 2 seconds:
!!!!!
Success rate is 100 percent (5/5), round-trip min/avg/max = 28/28/28 ms
Type escape sequence to abort.
Sending 5, 100-byte ICMP Echos to FEC0::13:1, timeout is 2 seconds:
!!!!!
Success rate is 100 percent (5/5), round-trip min/avg/max = 0/0/4 ms
Type escape sequence to abort.
Sending 5, 100-byte ICMP Echos to FEC0::13:3, timeout is 2 seconds:
!!!!!
```

```
Success rate is 100 percent (5/5), round-trip min/avg/max = 28/28/28 ms
Type escape sequence to abort.
Sending 5, 100-byte ICMP Echos to FEC0:23::218:B9FF:FE92:28D8, timeout is 2 seconds:
!!!!!
Success rate is 100 percent (5/5), round-trip min/avg/max = 28/28/32 ms
Type escape sequence to abort.
Sending 5, 100-byte ICMP Echos to FEC0:23::218:B9FF:FECD:BEF0, timeout is 2 seconds:
!!!!!
Success rate is 100 percent (5/5), round-trip min/avg/max = 28/28/32 ms
R1(tcl)# tclquit
```

```
R2# tclsh
R2(tcl)#
R2(tcl)# foreach address {
+>(tcl)# FEC0::1:1
+>(tcl)# FEC0::2:1
+>(tcl)# FEC0::3:1
+>(tcl)# FEC0::12:1
+>(tcl)# FEC0::12:2
+>(tcl)# FEC0::13:1
+>(tcl)# FEC0::13:3
+>(tcl)# FEC0:23::218:B9FF:FE92:28D8
+>(tcl)# FEC0:23::218:B9FF:FECD:BEF0
+>(tcl)# } {
+>(tcl)# ping $address }

Type escape sequence to abort.
Sending 5, 100-byte ICMP Echos to FEC0::1:1, timeout is 2 seconds:
!!!!!
Success rate is 100 percent (5/5), round-trip min/avg/max = 28/28/28 ms
Type escape sequence to abort.
Sending 5, 100-byte ICMP Echos to FEC0::2:1, timeout is 2 seconds:
!!!!!
Success rate is 100 percent (5/5), round-trip min/avg/max = 0/0/0 ms
Type escape sequence to abort.
Sending 5, 100-byte ICMP Echos to FEC0::3:1, timeout is 2 seconds:
!!!!!
Success rate is 100 percent (5/5), round-trip min/avg/max = 0/0/0 ms
Type escape sequence to abort.
Sending 5, 100-byte ICMP Echos to FEC0::12:1, timeout is 2 seconds:
!!!!!
Success rate is 100 percent (5/5), round-trip min/avg/max = 28/28/32 ms
Type escape sequence to abort.
Sending 5, 100-byte ICMP Echos to FEC0::12:2, timeout is 2 seconds:
!!!!!
```

```
Success rate is 100 percent (5/5), round-trip min/avg/max = 0/0/0 ms
Type escape sequence to abort.
Sending 5, 100-byte ICMP Echos to FEC0::13:1, timeout is 2 seconds:
!!!!!
Success rate is 100 percent (5/5), round-trip min/avg/max = 28/28/32 ms
Type escape sequence to abort.
Sending 5, 100-byte ICMP Echos to FEC0::13:3, timeout is 2 seconds:
!!!!!
Success rate is 100 percent (5/5), round-trip min/avg/max = 0/0/4 ms
Type escape sequence to abort.
Sending 5, 100-byte ICMP Echos to FEC0:23::218:B9FF:FE92:28D8, timeout is 2 seconds:
!!!!!
Success rate is 100 percent (5/5), round-trip min/avg/max = 0/0/0 ms
Type escape sequence to abort.
Sending 5, 100-byte ICMP Echos to FEC0:23::218:B9FF:FECD:BEF0, timeout is 2 seconds:
!!!!!
Success rate is 100 percent (5/5), round-trip min/avg/max = 0/0/4 ms
R2(tcl)# tclquit
```
```
R3# tclsh
R3(tcl)#
R3(tcl)# foreach address {
+>(tcl)# FEC0::1:1
+>(tcl)# FEC0::2:1
+>(tcl)# FEC0::3:1
+>(tcl)# FEC0::12:1
+>(tcl)# FEC0::12:2
+>(tcl)# FEC0::13:1
+>(tcl)# FEC0::13:3
+>(tcl)# FEC0:23::218:B9FF:FE92:28D8
+>(tcl)# FEC0:23::218:B9FF:FECD:BEF0
+>(tcl)# } {
+>(tcl)# ping $address }

Type escape sequence to abort.
Sending 5, 100-byte ICMP Echos to FEC0::1:1, timeout is 2 seconds:
!!!!!
Success rate is 100 percent (5/5), round-trip min/avg/max = 28/28/32 ms
Type escape sequence to abort.
Sending 5, 100-byte ICMP Echos to FEC0::2:1, timeout is 2 seconds:
!!!!!
Success rate is 100 percent (5/5), round-trip min/avg/max = 0/1/4 ms
Type escape sequence to abort.
Sending 5, 100-byte ICMP Echos to FEC0::3:1, timeout is 2 seconds:
!!!!!
```

```
Success rate is 100 percent (5/5), round-trip min/avg/max = 0/0/4 ms
Type escape sequence to abort.
Sending 5, 100-byte ICMP Echos to FEC0::12:1, timeout is 2 seconds:
!!!!!
Success rate is 100 percent (5/5), round-trip min/avg/max = 28/28/32 ms
Type escape sequence to abort.
Sending 5, 100-byte ICMP Echos to FEC0::12:2, timeout is 2 seconds:
!!!!!
Success rate is 100 percent (5/5), round-trip min/avg/max = 0/0/4 ms
Type escape sequence to abort.
Sending 5, 100-byte ICMP Echos to FEC0::13:1, timeout is 2 seconds:
!!!!!
Success rate is 100 percent (5/5), round-trip min/avg/max = 28/28/32 ms
Type escape sequence to abort.
Sending 5, 100-byte ICMP Echos to FEC0::13:3, timeout is 2 seconds:
!!!!!
Success rate is 100 percent (5/5), round-trip min/avg/max = 0/0/0 ms
Type escape sequence to abort.
Sending 5, 100-byte ICMP Echos to FEC0:23::218:B9FF:FE92:28D8, timeout is 2 seconds:
!!!!!
Success rate is 100 percent (5/5), round-trip min/avg/max = 0/0/0 ms
Type escape sequence to abort.
Sending 5, 100-byte ICMP Echos to FEC0:23::218:B9FF:FECD:BEF0, timeout is 2 seconds:
!!!!!
Success rate is 100 percent (5/5), round-trip min/avg/max = 0/0/0 ms
R3(tcl)# tclquit
```

Lab 8-2: Using Manual IPv6 Tunnels (8.7.2)

The objectives of this lab are as follows:

- Configure Enhanced Interior Gateway Routing Protocol (EIGRP) for IPv4

- Create a manual IPv6 tunnel

- Configure OSPFv3

Figure 8-2 illustrates the topology that will be used for this lab.

Figure 8-2   Topology Diagram for Lab 8-2

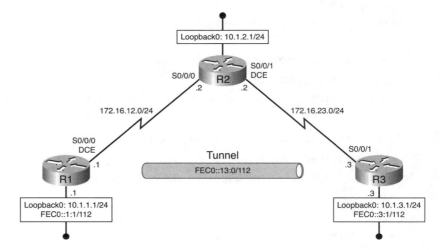

Scenario

For this lab, you will configure EIGRP for full connectivity between all IPv4 subnets. Then you will create a manual IPv6 tunnel and run OSPFv3 over it.

Step 1: Configure Loopbacks and Physical Interfaces

Configure the loopback interfaces with IPv4 addresses and IPv6 addresses where appropriate. Also configure the serial interfaces with the IPv4 addresses shown in Figure 8-2. Set the clockrates on the appropriate interfaces and issue **no shutdown** on all serial connections. Verify that you have local subnet connectivity with **ping**:

```
R1(config)# interface loopback 0
R1(config-if)# ip address 10.1.1.1 255.255.255.0
R1(config-if)# ipv6 address FEC0::1:1/112
R1(config-if)# interface serial 0/0/0
R1(config-if)# ip address 172.16.12.1 255.255.255.0
R1(config-if)# clockrate 64000
R1(config-if)# no shutdown
```

```
R2(config)# interface loopback 0
R2(config-if)# ip address 10.1.2.1 255.255.255.0
```

```
R2(config-if)# interface serial 0/0/0
R2(config-if)# ip address 172.16.12.2 255.255.255.0
R2(config-if)# no shutdown
R2(config-if)# interface serial 0/0/1
R2(config-if)# ip address 172.16.23.2 255.255.255.0
R2(config-if)# clockrate 64000
R2(config-if)# no shutdown
R3(config)# interface loopback 0
R3(config-if)# ip address 10.1.3.1 255.255.255.0
R3(config-if)# ipv6 address FEC0::3:1/112
R3(config-if)# interface serial 0/0/1
R3(config-if)# ip address 172.16.23.3 255.255.255.0
R3(config-if)# no shutdown
```

Step 2: Configure EIGRP

Configure EIGRP for AS 1 for the major networks 172.16.0.0 and 10.0.0.0 on all three routers. Make sure you disable auto-summarization. You should have full IPv4 connectivity after this:

```
R1(config)# router eigrp 1
R1(config-router)# no auto-summary
R1(config-router)# network 10.0.0.0
R1(config-router)# network 172.16.0.0
R2(config)# router eigrp 1
R2(config-router)# no auto-summary
R2(config-router)# network 10.0.0.0
R2(config-router)# network 172.16.0.0
R3(config)# router eigrp 1
R3(config-router)# no auto-summary
R3(config-router)# network 10.0.0.0
R3(config-router)# network 172.16.0.0
```

Step 3: Configure a Manual IPv6 Tunnel

A tunnel is a logical interface that acts as a logical connection between two endpoints. It is similar to a loopback interface in that there is no corresponding physical interface, but it is different in that there is more than one router involved. An IPv6 manual tunnel is a type of tunnel that has hard-coded source and destination addresses, with an IPv6 address on the tunnel itself. To configure a manual IPv6 tunnel, first issue the **interface tunnel** *number* command. For simplicity, use tunnel number 0 on both routers.

Next configure the tunnel mode for a manual tunnel with the **tunnel mode ipv6ip** command. Then configure an IPv6 address with the **ipv6 address** *address/mask* command. Finally, assign source and destination addresses for the tunnel using the **tunnel source** *address* and **tunnel destination** *address* commands. You can also specify the source by interface:

```
R1(config)# interface tunnel 0
R1(config-if)# tunnel mode ipv6ip
```

```
R1(config-if)# tunnel source serial 0/0/0
R1(config-if)# tunnel destination 172.16.23.3
R1(config-if)# ipv6 address FEC0::13:1/112
```
```
R3(config)# interface tunnel 0
R3(config-if)# tunnel mode ipv6ip
R3(config-if)# tunnel source serial 0/0/1
R3(config-if)# tunnel destination 172.16.12.1
R3(config-if)# ipv6 address FEC0::13:3/112
```

Verify that you can ping across the tunnel to the other side:

```
R1# ping FEC0::13:3


Type escape sequence to abort.
Sending 5, 100-byte ICMP Echos to FEC0::13:3, timeout is 2 seconds:
!!!!!
Success rate is 100 percent (5/5), round-trip min/avg/max = 64/66/68 ms
```
```
R3# ping FEC0::13:1


Type escape sequence to abort.
Sending 5, 100-byte ICMP Echos to FEC0::13:1, timeout is 2 seconds:
!!!!!
Success rate is 100 percent (5/5), round-trip min/avg/max = 64/66/68 ms
```

Step 4: Configure OSPFv3 Over a Tunnel

Enable IPv6 routing with the **ipv6 unicast-routing** command on R1 and R3. Configure OSPFv3 on those routers to run over the tunnel and advertise the loopback interfaces into OSPFv3. Verify the configuration using the **show ipv6 ospf neighbor** command and verifying that you can ping the remote loopback interfaces:

```
R1(config)# ipv6 unicast-routing
R1(config)# interface loopback0
R1(config-if)# ipv6 ospf 1 area 0
R1(config-if)# interface tunnel0
R1(config-if)# ipv6 ospf 1 area 0
```
```
R3(config)# ipv6 unicast-routing
R3(config)# interface loopback0
R3(config-if)# ipv6 ospf 1 area 0
R3(config-if)# interface tunnel0
R3(config-if)# ipv6 ospf 1 area 0
```
```
R1# show ipv6 ospf neighbor


Neighbor ID     Pri   State         Dead Time   Interface ID   Interface
10.1.3.1          1   FULL/  -      00:00:37    18             Tunnel0
```
```
R3# show ipv6 ospf neighbor
```

```
Neighbor ID      Pri   State        Dead Time   Interface ID   Interface
10.1.1.1           1   FULL/   -    00:00:39    21             Tunnel0
```

```
R1# ping FEC0::3:1

Type escape sequence to abort.
Sending 5, 100-byte ICMP Echos to FEC0::3:1, timeout is 2 seconds:
!!!!!
Success rate is 100 percent (5/5), round-trip min/avg/max = 64/64/68 ms
```

```
R3# ping FEC0::1:1

Type escape sequence to abort.
Sending 5, 100-byte ICMP Echos to FEC0::1:1, timeout is 2 seconds:
!!!!!
Success rate is 100 percent (5/5), round-trip min/avg/max = 64/66/68 ms
```

TCL Script Output

You can download this TCL script at www.ciscopress.com/title/1587132133 under the More Information section on the page.

```
tclsh

foreach address {
10.1.1.1
10.1.2.1
10.1.3.1
172.16.12.1
172.16.12.2
172.16.23.2
172.16.23.3
FEC0::1:1
FEC0::3:1
FEC0::13:1
FEC0::13:3
} {
ping $address }

R1# tclsh

R1(tcl)#
R1(tcl)# foreach address {
+>(tcl)# 10.1.1.1
+>(tcl)# 10.1.2.1
+>(tcl)# 10.1.3.1
+>(tcl)# 172.16.12.1
```

```
+>(tcl)# 172.16.12.2
+>(tcl)# 172.16.23.2
+>(tcl)# 172.16.23.3
+>(tcl)# FEC0::1:1
+>(tcl)# FEC0::3:1
+>(tcl)# FEC0::13:1
+>(tcl)# FEC0::13:3
+>(tcl)# } {
+>(tcl)# ping $address }

Type escape sequence to abort.
Sending 5, 100-byte ICMP Echos to 10.1.1.1, timeout is 2 seconds:
!!!!!
Success rate is 100 percent (5/5), round-trip min/avg/max = 1/1/4 ms
Type escape sequence to abort.
Sending 5, 100-byte ICMP Echos to 10.1.2.1, timeout is 2 seconds:
!!!!!
Success rate is 100 percent (5/5), round-trip min/avg/max = 28/28/32 ms
Type escape sequence to abort.
Sending 5, 100-byte ICMP Echos to 10.1.3.1, timeout is 2 seconds:
!!!!!
Success rate is 100 percent (5/5), round-trip min/avg/max = 56/56/56 ms
Type escape sequence to abort.
Sending 5, 100-byte ICMP Echos to 172.16.12.1, timeout is 2 seconds:
!!!!!
Success rate is 100 percent (5/5), round-trip min/avg/max = 56/57/64 ms
Type escape sequence to abort.
Sending 5, 100-byte ICMP Echos to 172.16.12.2, timeout is 2 seconds:
!!!!!
Success rate is 100 percent (5/5), round-trip min/avg/max = 28/28/32 ms
Type escape sequence to abort.
Sending 5, 100-byte ICMP Echos to 172.16.23.2, timeout is 2 seconds:
!!!!!
Success rate is 100 percent (5/5), round-trip min/avg/max = 28/28/32 ms
Type escape sequence to abort.
Sending 5, 100-byte ICMP Echos to 172.16.23.3, timeout is 2 seconds:
!!!!!
Success rate is 100 percent (5/5), round-trip min/avg/max = 56/56/60 ms
Type escape sequence to abort.
Sending 5, 100-byte ICMP Echos to FEC0::1:1, timeout is 2 seconds:
!!!!!
Success rate is 100 percent (5/5), round-trip min/avg/max = 0/0/4 ms
Type escape sequence to abort.
Sending 5, 100-byte ICMP Echos to FEC0::3:1, timeout is 2 seconds:
```

```
!!!!!
Success rate is 100 percent (5/5), round-trip min/avg/max = 64/66/68 ms
Type escape sequence to abort.
Sending 5, 100-byte ICMP Echos to FEC0::13:1, timeout is 2 seconds:
!!!!!
Success rate is 100 percent (5/5), round-trip min/avg/max = 0/0/0 ms
Type escape sequence to abort.
Sending 5, 100-byte ICMP Echos to FEC0::13:3, timeout is 2 seconds:
!!!!!
Success rate is 100 percent (5/5), round-trip min/avg/max = 64/68/80 ms
R1(tcl)#tclquit
```

```
R2# tclsh
R2(tcl)#
R2(tcl)# foreach address {
+>(tcl)# 10.1.1.1
+>(tcl)# 10.1.2.1
+>(tcl)# 10.1.3.1
+>(tcl)# 172.16.12.1
+>(tcl)# 172.16.12.2
+>(tcl)# 172.16.23.2
+>(tcl)# 172.16.23.3
+>(tcl)# FEC0::1:1
+>(tcl)# FEC0::3:1
+>(tcl)# FEC0::13:1
+>(tcl)# FEC0::13:3
+>(tcl)# } {
+>(tcl)# ping $address }

Type escape sequence to abort.
Sending 5, 100-byte ICMP Echos to 10.1.1.1, timeout is 2 seconds:
!!!!!
Success rate is 100 percent (5/5), round-trip min/avg/max = 28/28/32 ms
Type escape sequence to abort.
Sending 5, 100-byte ICMP Echos to 10.1.2.1, timeout is 2 seconds:
!!!!!
Success rate is 100 percent (5/5), round-trip min/avg/max = 1/1/4 ms
Type escape sequence to abort.
Sending 5, 100-byte ICMP Echos to 10.1.3.1, timeout is 2 seconds:
!!!!!
Success rate is 100 percent (5/5), round-trip min/avg/max = 28/28/32 ms
Type escape sequence to abort.
Sending 5, 100-byte ICMP Echos to 172.16.12.1, timeout is 2 seconds:
!!!!!
Success rate is 100 percent (5/5), round-trip min/avg/max = 28/28/32 ms
```

```
Type escape sequence to abort.
Sending 5, 100-byte ICMP Echos to 172.16.12.2, timeout is 2 seconds:
!!!!!
Success rate is 100 percent (5/5), round-trip min/avg/max = 56/58/68 ms
Type escape sequence to abort.
Sending 5, 100-byte ICMP Echos to 172.16.23.2, timeout is 2 seconds:
!!!!!
Success rate is 100 percent (5/5), round-trip min/avg/max = 56/57/64 ms
Type escape sequence to abort.
Sending 5, 100-byte ICMP Echos to 172.16.23.3, timeout is 2 seconds:
!!!!!
Success rate is 100 percent (5/5), round-trip min/avg/max = 28/28/28 ms% Unrecognized
host or address, or protocol not running.
% Unrecognized host or address, or protocol not running.
% Unrecognized host or address, or protocol not running.
% Unrecognized host or address, or protocol not running.
R2(tcl)# tclquit
```

```
R3# tclsh
R3(tcl)#
R3(tcl)# foreach address {
+>(tcl)# 10.1.1.1
+>(tcl)# 10.1.2.1
+>(tcl)# 10.1.3.1
+>(tcl)# 172.16.12.1
+>(tcl)# 172.16.12.2
+>(tcl)# 172.16.23.2
+>(tcl)# 172.16.23.3
+>(tcl)# FEC0::1:1
+>(tcl)# FEC0::3:1
+>(tcl)# FEC0::13:1
+>(tcl)# FEC0::13:3
+>(tcl)# } {
+>(tcl)# ping $address }

Type escape sequence to abort.
Sending 5, 100-byte ICMP Echos to 10.1.1.1, timeout is 2 seconds:
!!!!!
Success rate is 100 percent (5/5), round-trip min/avg/max = 56/56/60 ms
Type escape sequence to abort.
Sending 5, 100-byte ICMP Echos to 10.1.2.1, timeout is 2 seconds:
!!!!!
Success rate is 100 percent (5/5), round-trip min/avg/max = 28/28/32 ms
Type escape sequence to abort.
Sending 5, 100-byte ICMP Echos to 10.1.3.1, timeout is 2 seconds:
```

```
!!!!!
Success rate is 100 percent (5/5), round-trip min/avg/max = 1/1/1 ms
Type escape sequence to abort.
Sending 5, 100-byte ICMP Echos to 172.16.12.1, timeout is 2 seconds:
!!!!!
Success rate is 100 percent (5/5), round-trip min/avg/max = 56/56/56 ms
Type escape sequence to abort.
Sending 5, 100-byte ICMP Echos to 172.16.12.2, timeout is 2 seconds:
!!!!!
Success rate is 100 percent (5/5), round-trip min/avg/max = 28/32/52 ms
Type escape sequence to abort.
Sending 5, 100-byte ICMP Echos to 172.16.23.2, timeout is 2 seconds:
!!!!!
Success rate is 100 percent (5/5), round-trip min/avg/max = 28/28/28 ms
Type escape sequence to abort.
Sending 5, 100-byte ICMP Echos to 172.16.23.3, timeout is 2 seconds:
!!!!!
Success rate is 100 percent (5/5), round-trip min/avg/max = 56/57/64 ms
Type escape sequence to abort.
Sending 5, 100-byte ICMP Echos to FEC0::1:1, timeout is 2 seconds:
!!!!!
Success rate is 100 percent (5/5), round-trip min/avg/max = 64/67/68 ms
Type escape sequence to abort.
Sending 5, 100-byte ICMP Echos to FEC0::3:1, timeout is 2 seconds:
!!!!!
Success rate is 100 percent (5/5), round-trip min/avg/max = 0/0/0 ms
Type escape sequence to abort.
Sending 5, 100-byte ICMP Echos to FEC0::13:1, timeout is 2 seconds:
!!!!!
Success rate is 100 percent (5/5), round-trip min/avg/max = 64/67/68 ms
Type escape sequence to abort.
Sending 5, 100-byte ICMP Echos to FEC0::13:3, timeout is 2 seconds:
!!!!!
Success rate is 100 percent (5/5), round-trip min/avg/max = 0/0/0 ms
R3(tcl)# tclquit
```

Lab 8-3: Configuring 6to4 Tunnels (8.7.3)

The objectives of this lab are as follows:

- Configure EIGRP for IPv4

- Create a 6to4 tunnel

- Configure static IPv6 routes

Figure 8-3 illustrates the topology that will be used for this lab.

Figure 8-3   Topology Diagram for Lab 8-3

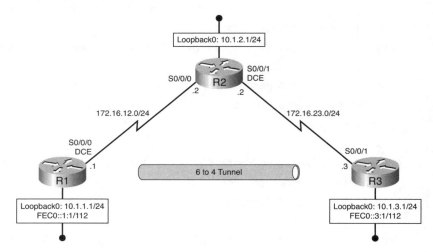

Scenario

For this lab, you will configure EIGRP for full connectivity between all IPv4 subnets. Then you will create a 6to4 tunnel and create static routes to go over it.

Step 1: Configure Loopbacks and Physical Interfaces

Configure the loopback interfaces with IPv4 addresses and IPv6 addresses where appropriate. Also configure the serial interfaces with the IPv4 addresses shown in the diagram. Set the clockrates on the appropriate interfaces and issue **no shutdown** on all serial connections. Verify that you have local subnet connectivity with **ping**:

```
R1(config)# interface loopback0
R1(config-if)# ip address 10.1.1.1 255.255.255.0
R1(config-if)# ipv6 address FEC0::1:1/112
R1(config-if)# interface serial0/0/0
R1(config-if)# ip address 172.16.12.1 255.255.255.0
R1(config-if)# clockrate 64000
R1(config-if)# no shutdown
```
```
R2(config)# interface loopback0
R2(config-if)# ip address 10.1.2.1 255.255.255.0
R2(config-if)# interface serial0/0/0
```

```
R2(config-if)# ip address 172.16.12.2 255.255.255.0
R2(config-if)# no shutdown
R2(config-if)# interface serial0/0/1
R2(config-if)# ip address 172.16.23.2 255.255.255.0
R2(config-if)# clockrate 64000
R2(config-if)# no shutdown
```

```
R3(config)# interface loopback0
R3(config-if)# ip address 10.1.3.1 255.255.255.0
R3(config-if)# ipv6 address FEC0::3:1/112
R3(config-if)# interface serial0/0/1
R3(config-if)# ip address 172.16.23.3 255.255.255.0
R3(config-if)# no shutdown
```

Step 2: Configure EIGRP

Configure EIGRP for AS 1 for the major networks 172.16.0.0 and 10.0.0.0 on all three routers. Make sure you disable auto-summarization. You should have full IPv4 connectivity after this:

```
R1(config)# router eigrp 1
R1(config-router)# no auto-summary
R1(config-router)# network 10.0.0.0
R1(config-router)# network 172.16.0.0
```

```
R2(config)# router eigrp 1
R2(config-router)# no auto-summary
R2(config-router)# network 10.0.0.0
R2(config-router)# network 172.16.0.0
```

```
R3(config)# router eigrp 1
R3(config-router)# no auto-summary
R3(config-router)# network 10.0.0.0
R3(config-router)# network 172.16.0.0
```

Step 3: Configure a Manual IPv6 Tunnel

A tunnel is a logical interface that acts as a logical connection between two endpoints. It is similar to a loopback interface in that there is no corresponding physical interface, but it is different in that there is more than one router involved. A 6to4 tunnel uses special IPv6 addresses in the 2002::/16 address space. The first 16 bits are the hexadecimal number 2002, and the next 32 bits are the original source IPv4 address in hexadecimal form. A 6to4 tunnel does not require a destination address because it is not a point-to-point link.

In this lab, you will configure routers R1 and R3 for a 6to4 tunnel to provide IPv6 connectivity between their loopback interfaces. To configure a 6to4 tunnel, get the tunnel interface configuration prompt using the **interface tunnel** *number* command. For simplicity, use interface number 0.

Next, set the tunnel mode with the **tunnel mode ipv6ip 6to4** command. Then set up the IPv6 address with the **ipv6 address** *address/mask* command. The address for R1 is 2002:AC10:0C01:1::1/64 because AC10:0C01 corresponds to 172.16.12.1, with 172 being AC, 16 being 10, 12 being C, and 1 being 1. The 1 after this address is just a more specific subnet, and the 1 at the end is the host address. R3's address is 2002:AC10:1703:1::3/64. Notice that the two addresses are not in the same /64 subnet.

After setting the IPv6 addresses, set the source interface for the tunnel with the **tunnel source** *type/number* command. Now that all the tunnel settings are set, set up an IPv6 static route for the whole 2002::/16 with the global command **ipv6 route** *address/mask interface*, with the interface being the tunnel you just created. Verify that you can ping the other side of the tunnel once all the commands have been entered:

```
R1(config)# interface tunnel 0
R1(config-if)# tunnel mode ipv6ip 6to4
R1(config-if)# ipv6 address 2002:AC10:0C01:1::1/64
R1(config-if)# tunnel source serial 0/0/0
R1(config-if)# exit
R1(config)# ipv6 route 2002::/16 tunnel0
R3(config)# interface tunnel 0
R3(config-if)# tunnel mode ipv6ip 6to4
R3(config-if)# ipv6 address 2002:AC10:1703:1::3/64
R3(config-if)# tunnel source serial 0/0/1
R3(config-if)# exit
R3(config)# ipv6 route 2002::/16 tunnel0
```

```
R1# ping 2002:AC10:1703:1::3

Type escape sequence to abort.
Sending 5, 100-byte ICMP Echos to 2002:AC10:1703:1::3, timeout is 2 seconds:
!!!!!
Success rate is 100 percent (5/5), round-trip min/avg/max = 64/67/68 ms
```

```
R3# ping 2002:AC10:C01:1::1

Type escape sequence to abort.
Sending 5, 100-byte ICMP Echos to 2002:AC10:C01:1::1, timeout is 2 seconds:
!!!!!
Success rate is 100 percent (5/5), round-trip min/avg/max = 64/66/68 ms
```

Step 4: Configure Static IPv6 Routes

Just like IPv4, IPv6 can have static routes entered into its routing table. You already created one for the 2002::/16 network in Step 4. For this section of the lab, you will put a static route on R1 telling it how to get to R3's loopback address. On R3, you will put a static default route pointing to R1. Just like in IPv4, static routes with a next-hop IPv6 address are created with the **ipv6 route** *address/mask next-hop* command. The next hop for both routers is the IPv6 address of the other end of the tunnel. Before entering these commands, enable IPv6 routing with the **ipv6 unicast-routing** command. You can verify by using the **show ipv6 route** command or by pinging the remote loopback address from each router:

```
R1(config)# ipv6 unicast-routing
R1(config)# ipv6 route FEC0::3:0/112 2002:AC10:1703:1::3
```

```
R3(config)# ipv6 unicast-routing
R3(config)# ipv6 route FEC0::1:0/112 2002:AC10:C01:1::1
```

```
R1# show ipv6 route
IPv6 Routing Table - 8 entries
Codes: C - Connected, L - Local, S - Static, R - RIP, B - BGP
       U - Per-user Static route
       I1 - ISIS L1, I2 - ISIS L2, IA - ISIS interarea, IS - ISIS summary
       O - OSPF intra, OI - OSPF inter, OE1 - OSPF ext 1, OE2 - OSPF ext 2
       ON1 - OSPF NSSA ext 1, ON2 - OSPF NSSA ext 2
       D - EIGRP, EX - EIGRP external
S    2002::/16 [1/0]
      via ::, Tunnel0
C    2002:AC10:C01:1::/64 [0/0]
      via ::, Tunnel0
L    2002:AC10:C01:1::1/128 [0/0]
      via ::, Tunnel0
L    FE80::/10 [0/0]
      via ::, Null0
C    FEC0::1:0/112 [0/0]
      via ::, Loopback0
L    FEC0::1:1/128 [0/0]
      via ::, Loopback0
S    FEC0::3:0/112 [1/0]
      via 2002:AC10:1703:1::3
L    FF00::/8 [0/0]
      via ::, Null0
```

```
R3# show ipv6 route
IPv6 Routing Table - 8 entries
Codes: C - Connected, L - Local, S - Static, R - RIP, B - BGP
       U - Per-user Static route
       I1 - ISIS L1, I2 - ISIS L2, IA - ISIS interarea, IS - ISIS summary
       O - OSPF intra, OI - OSPF inter, OE1 - OSPF ext 1, OE2 - OSPF ext 2
       ON1 - OSPF NSSA ext 1, ON2 - OSPF NSSA ext 2
S    2002::/16 [1/0]
      via ::, Tunnel0
C    2002:AC10:1703:1::/64 [0/0]
      via ::, Tunnel0
L    2002:AC10:1703:1::3/128 [0/0]
      via ::, Tunnel0
L    FE80::/10 [0/0]
      via ::, Null0
S    FEC0::1:0/112 [1/0]
```

```
          via 2002:AC10:C01:1::1
C   FEC0::3:0/112 [0/0]
      via ::, Loopback0
L   FEC0::3:1/128 [0/0]
      via ::, Loopback0
L   FF00::/8 [0/0]
      via ::, Null0
```

```
R1# ping FEC0::3:1

Type escape sequence to abort.
Sending 5, 100-byte ICMP Echos to FEC0::3:1, timeout is 2 seconds:
!!!!!
Success rate is 100 percent (5/5), round-trip min/avg/max = 64/67/68 ms
```

```
R3# ping FEC0::1:1

Type escape sequence to abort.
Sending 5, 100-byte ICMP Echos to FEC0::1:1, timeout is 2 seconds:
!!!!!
Success rate is 100 percent (5/5), round-trip min/avg/max = 64/66/68 ms
```

TCL Script Output

You can download this TCL script at www.ciscopress.com/title/1587132133 under the More Information section on the page.

```
tclsh

foreach address {
10.1.1.1
10.1.2.1
10.1.3.1
172.16.12.1
172.16.12.2
172.16.23.2
172.16.23.3
FEC0::1:1
FEC0::3:1
2002:AC10:C01:1::1
2002:AC10:1703:1::3
} {
ping $address }

R1# tclsh
R1(tcl)#
R1(tcl)# foreach address {
+>(tcl)# 10.1.1.1
```

```
+>(tcl)# 10.1.2.1
+>(tcl)# 10.1.3.1
+>(tcl)# 172.16.12.1
+>(tcl)# 172.16.12.2
+>(tcl)# 172.16.23.2
+>(tcl)# 172.16.23.3
+>(tcl)# FEC0::1:1
+>(tcl)# FEC0::3:1
+>(tcl)# 2002:AC10:C01:1::1
+>(tcl)# 2002:AC10:1703:1::3
+>(tcl)# } {
+>(tcl)# ping $address }

Type escape sequence to abort.
Sending 5, 100-byte ICMP Echos to 10.1.1.1, timeout is 2 seconds:
!!!!!
Success rate is 100 percent (5/5), round-trip min/avg/max = 1/1/4 ms
Type escape sequence to abort.
Sending 5, 100-byte ICMP Echos to 10.1.2.1, timeout is 2 seconds:
!!!!!
Success rate is 100 percent (5/5), round-trip min/avg/max = 28/28/32 ms
Type escape sequence to abort.
Sending 5, 100-byte ICMP Echos to 10.1.3.1, timeout is 2 seconds:
!!!!!
Success rate is 100 percent (5/5), round-trip min/avg/max = 56/56/56 ms
Type escape sequence to abort.
Sending 5, 100-byte ICMP Echos to 172.16.12.1, timeout is 2 seconds:
!!!!!
Success rate is 100 percent (5/5), round-trip min/avg/max = 56/58/64 ms
Type escape sequence to abort.
Sending 5, 100-byte ICMP Echos to 172.16.12.2, timeout is 2 seconds:
!!!!!
Success rate is 100 percent (5/5), round-trip min/avg/max = 28/28/32 ms
Type escape sequence to abort.
Sending 5, 100-byte ICMP Echos to 172.16.23.2, timeout is 2 seconds:
!!!!!
Success rate is 100 percent (5/5), round-trip min/avg/max = 28/29/32 ms
Type escape sequence to abort.
Sending 5, 100-byte ICMP Echos to 172.16.23.3, timeout is 2 seconds:
!!!!!
Success rate is 100 percent (5/5), round-trip min/avg/max = 56/56/56 ms
Type escape sequence to abort.
Sending 5, 100-byte ICMP Echos to FEC0::1:1, timeout is 2 seconds:
!!!!!
```

```
Success rate is 100 percent (5/5), round-trip min/avg/max = 0/0/0 ms
Type escape sequence to abort.
Sending 5, 100-byte ICMP Echos to FEC0::3:1, timeout is 2 seconds:
!!!!!
Success rate is 100 percent (5/5), round-trip min/avg/max = 64/67/68 ms
Type escape sequence to abort.
Sending 5, 100-byte ICMP Echos to 2002:AC10:C01:1::1, timeout is 2 seconds:
!!!!!
Success rate is 100 percent (5/5), round-trip min/avg/max = 0/0/0 ms
Type escape sequence to abort.
Sending 5, 100-byte ICMP Echos to 2002:AC10:1703:1::3, timeout is 2 seconds:
!!!!!
Success rate is 100 percent (5/5), round-trip min/avg/max = 64/66/68 ms
R1(tcl)# tclquit
```

```
R2# tclsh
R2(tcl)#
R2(tcl)# foreach address {
+>(tcl)# 10.1.1.1
+>(tcl)# 10.1.2.1
+>(tcl)# 10.1.3.1
+>(tcl)# 172.16.12.1
+>(tcl)# 172.16.12.2
+>(tcl)# 172.16.23.2
+>(tcl)# 172.16.23.3
+>(tcl)# FEC0::1:1
+>(tcl)# FEC0::3:1
+>(tcl)# 2002:AC10:C01:1::1
+>(tcl)# 2002:AC10:1703:1::3
+>(tcl)# } {
+>(tcl)# ping $address }

Type escape sequence to abort.
Sending 5, 100-byte ICMP Echos to 10.1.1.1, timeout is 2 seconds:
!!!!!
Success rate is 100 percent (5/5), round-trip min/avg/max = 28/28/28 ms
Type escape sequence to abort.
Sending 5, 100-byte ICMP Echos to 10.1.2.1, timeout is 2 seconds:
!!!!!
Success rate is 100 percent (5/5), round-trip min/avg/max = 1/1/4 ms
Type escape sequence to abort.
Sending 5, 100-byte ICMP Echos to 10.1.3.1, timeout is 2 seconds:
!!!!!
Success rate is 100 percent (5/5), round-trip min/avg/max = 28/28/28 ms
Type escape sequence to abort.
```

```
Sending 5, 100-byte ICMP Echos to 172.16.12.1, timeout is 2 seconds:
!!!!!
Success rate is 100 percent (5/5), round-trip min/avg/max = 28/28/32 ms
Type escape sequence to abort.
Sending 5, 100-byte ICMP Echos to 172.16.12.2, timeout is 2 seconds:
!!!!!
Success rate is 100 percent (5/5), round-trip min/avg/max = 56/63/84 ms
Type escape sequence to abort.
Sending 5, 100-byte ICMP Echos to 172.16.23.2, timeout is 2 seconds:
!!!!!
Success rate is 100 percent (5/5), round-trip min/avg/max = 56/57/64 ms
Type escape sequence to abort.
Sending 5, 100-byte ICMP Echos to 172.16.23.3, timeout is 2 seconds:
!!!!!
Success rate is 100 percent (5/5), round-trip min/avg/max = 28/28/32 ms% Unrecognized
host or address, or protocol not running.
% Unrecognized host or address, or protocol not running.
% Unrecognized host or address, or protocol not running.
% Unrecognized host or address, or protocol not running.

R2(tcl)# tclquit
```

```
R3# tclsh
R3(tcl)#
R3(tcl)# foreach address {
+>(tcl)# 10.1.1.1
+>(tcl)# 10.1.2.1
+>(tcl)# 10.1.3.1
+>(tcl)# 172.16.12.1
+>(tcl)# 172.16.12.2
+>(tcl)# 172.16.23.2
+>(tcl)# 172.16.23.3
+>(tcl)# FEC0::1:1
+>(tcl)# FEC0::3:1
+>(tcl)# 2002:AC10:C01:1::1
+>(tcl)# 2002:AC10:1703:1::3
+>(tcl)# } {
+>(tcl)# ping $address }

Type escape sequence to abort.
Sending 5, 100-byte ICMP Echos to 10.1.1.1, timeout is 2 seconds:
!!!!!
Success rate is 100 percent (5/5), round-trip min/avg/max = 56/56/56 ms
Type escape sequence to abort.
Sending 5, 100-byte ICMP Echos to 10.1.2.1, timeout is 2 seconds:
```

```
!!!!!
Success rate is 100 percent (5/5), round-trip min/avg/max = 28/28/32 ms
Type escape sequence to abort.
Sending 5, 100-byte ICMP Echos to 10.1.3.1, timeout is 2 seconds:
!!!!!
Success rate is 100 percent (5/5), round-trip min/avg/max = 1/1/4 ms
Type escape sequence to abort.
Sending 5, 100-byte ICMP Echos to 172.16.12.1, timeout is 2 seconds:
!!!!!
Success rate is 100 percent (5/5), round-trip min/avg/max = 56/56/56 ms
Type escape sequence to abort.
Sending 5, 100-byte ICMP Echos to 172.16.12.2, timeout is 2 seconds:
!!!!!
Success rate is 100 percent (5/5), round-trip min/avg/max = 28/28/28 ms
Type escape sequence to abort.
Sending 5, 100-byte ICMP Echos to 172.16.23.2, timeout is 2 seconds:
!!!!!
Success rate is 100 percent (5/5), round-trip min/avg/max = 28/28/28 ms
Type escape sequence to abort.
Sending 5, 100-byte ICMP Echos to 172.16.23.3, timeout is 2 seconds:
!!!!!
Success rate is 100 percent (5/5), round-trip min/avg/max = 56/57/64 ms
Type escape sequence to abort.
Sending 5, 100-byte ICMP Echos to FEC0::1:1, timeout is 2 seconds:
!!!!!
Success rate is 100 percent (5/5), round-trip min/avg/max = 64/65/68 ms
Type escape sequence to abort.
Sending 5, 100-byte ICMP Echos to FEC0::3:1, timeout is 2 seconds:
!!!!!
Success rate is 100 percent (5/5), round-trip min/avg/max = 0/0/4 ms
Type escape sequence to abort.
Sending 5, 100-byte ICMP Echos to 2002:AC10:C01:1::1, timeout is 2 seconds:
!!!!!
Success rate is 100 percent (5/5), round-trip min/avg/max = 64/66/68 ms
Type escape sequence to abort.
Sending 5, 100-byte ICMP Echos to 2002:AC10:1703:1::3, timeout is 2 seconds:
!!!!!
Success rate is 100 percent (5/5), round-trip min/avg/max = 0/0/4 ms
R3(tcl)# tclquit
```

Lab 8-4: IPv6 Challenge Lab

Implement the topology diagram shown in Figure 8-4, according to the following requirements:

- Configure all interfaces shown in the diagram with the IPv4 or IPv6 addresses shown.

- Use EUI-64 addresses on the link between R3 and R4.

- Configure EIGRP AS 1 on R1, R2, and R3 to route all IPv4 networks.

- Disable automatic summarization.

- Configure a manual IPv6 tunnel between R1 and R3.

- All IPv6 networks should be included in OSPF area 0 on R1, R3, and R4.

- Manually configure a router ID of 172.16.4.1 on R4 (this address does not need to be reachable).

Figure 8-4   Topology Diagram for Lab 8-4

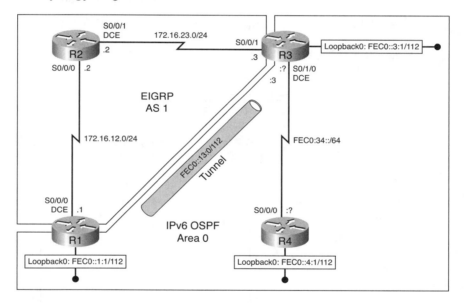

Lab 8-5: IPv6 Troubleshooting Lab

In this lab, you will troubleshoot existing configurations to get a working topology. Cut and paste the Initial Configurations from this lab into your four routers. Some of these configurations are correct. Some of these configurations are intentionally wrong. Your goal is to use troubleshooting techniques to fix anything in the scenario that prevents full IPv6 connectivity. Full IPv6 connectivity means every address in the scenario should be reachable from every router. If you don't know where to start, try pinging remote addresses and see which ones are reachable (either manually performing pings or using a TCL script).

Implement the topology diagram shown in Figure 8-5, according to the following requirements:

- Use the IPv6 addressing scheme shown in the diagram.

- All interfaces must be in OSPFv3 area 0.

- The router IDs will be manually configured.

- Do not use static routes, default routes, or other routing protocols.

- All IPv6 addresses in the topology must be reachable from all routers.

Figure 8-5   Topology Diagram

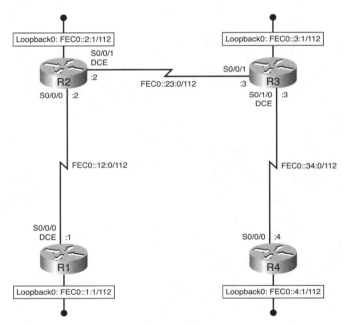

Initial Configurations

You can download these router configurations at www.ciscopress.com/title/1587132133 under the More Information section on the page.

```
R1# show run
!
hostname R1
!
ipv6 unicast-routing
!
```

```
interface Loopback0
 ipv6 address FEC0::1:1/112
!
interface Serial0/0/0
 ipv6 address FEC0::12:1/112
 ipv6 ospf 1 area 0
 clock rate 64000
 no shutdown
!
ipv6 router ospf 1
 router-id 172.16.1.1
!
end
```

R2# **show run**
```
!
hostname R2
!
ipv6 unicast-routing
!
interface Loopback0
 ipv6 address FEC0::2:1/112
 ipv6 ospf 1 area 0
!
interface Serial0/0/0
 ipv6 address FEC0::12:2/112
 ipv6 ospf 1 area 0
 no shutdown
!
interface Serial0/0/1
 ipv6 address FEC0::23:2/112
 ipv6 ospf 1 area 0
 clock rate 64000
 no shutdown
!
ipv6 router ospf 1
 router-id 172.16.2.1
!
end
```

R3# **show run**
```
!
hostname R3
!
ipv6 unicast-routing
!
```

```
interface Loopback0
 ipv6 address FEC0::3:1/112
 ipv6 ospf 1 area 0
!
interface Serial0/0/1
 ipv6 address FEC0::23:3/112
 ipv6 ospf 1 area 0
 no shutdown
!
interface Serial0/1/0
 ipv6 address FEC0::34:3/112
 ipv6 ospf 1 area 0
 clock rate 64000
 no shutdown
!
ipv6 router ospf 1
 router-id 172.16.3.1
!
end
```

```
R4# show run
!
hostname R4
!
ipv6 unicast-routing
!
interface Loopback0
 ipv6 address FEC0::4:1/112
 ipv6 ospf 1 area 0
!
interface Serial0/0/0
 ipv6 address FEC0::34:4/112
 ipv6 ospf 100 area 0
 no shutdown
!
ipv6 router ospf 1
 router-id 172.16.4.1
!
end
```

CHAPTER 9

Case Studies

Case Study 1: EIGRP

The International Travel Agency (ITA) needs its core network set up with Enhanced Interior Gateway Routing Protocol (EIGRP) with the specifications in the list that follows. It has also recently acquired Local Travel Agency, which was running the Open Shortest Path First (OSPF) Protocol.

Plan, design, and implement the complex ITA EIGRP network based on the topology diagram and addressing scheme in Figure 9-1 and the following specifications:

- The ITA core network is running EIGRP in AS 1.

- Summarize the loopback interfaces on R2 with the best possible summary to the other EIGRP routers.

- Loopback 192 on R3 represents a connection to the Internet. Originate a default route into EIGRP from R3.

- The Local Travel Agency router, R4, needs to communicate with the ITA core via OSPF area 0.

- Redistribute OSPF into EIGRP.

- Originate a default route into the OSPF process from R3.

- Configure R2 to act as a DHCP server on the Ethernet subnet between R2 and R3.

Implement the design on the lab set of routers. Verify that all configurations are operational and functioning according to the guidelines.

Figure 9-1   Topology Diagram for Case Study 1

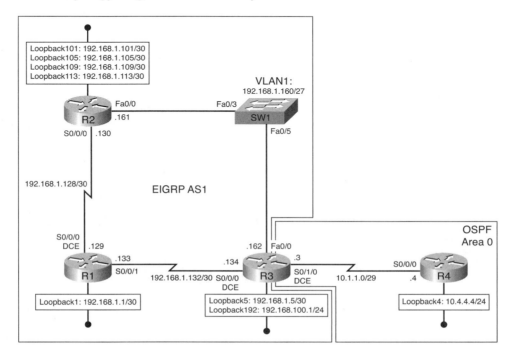

Case Study 2: OSPF: Four Routers

The International Travel Agency (ITA) needs its core network set up for OSPF with the specifications in the list that follows and the addressing scheme shown in the topology diagram.

Plan, design, and implement the ITA network shown in Figure 9-2 (if you are using a Cisco router as the Frame Relay switch) or Figure 9-3 (if you are using an Adtran Atlas 550 as the Frame Relay switch), according to the following set of requirements:

- Use the addressing scheme shown in the diagram.

- Use OSPF with various networks shown in the diagram.

- Configure the OSPF backbone area to be on Loopback 0 on Headquarters.

- Configure the Frame Relay subnets as point-to-point subinterfaces. The link between Headquarters and East should be in area 100, and the link between Headquarters and West should be in area 300.

- Area 300 should be configured as a not-so-stubby area (NSSA).

- Configure East's loopback interfaces to be in area 200. Summarize this area with the most efficient summary.

- Redistribute the loopback network on West into OSPF.

- Create virtual links as necessary for full connectivity.

- Make sure that all loopback interfaces get advertised with the correct subnet mask.

Verify that all configurations are operational and functioning according to the guidelines.

Figure 9-2   Topology Diagram for Case Study 2, Using a Cisco Router as the Frame Relay Switch

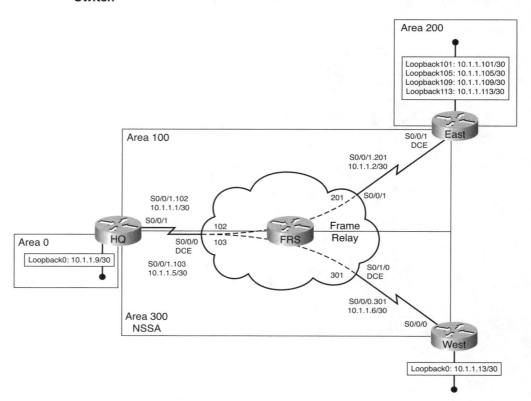

Figure 9-3   Topology Diagram for Case Study 2, Using an Adtran Atlas 550 as the Frame Relay Switch

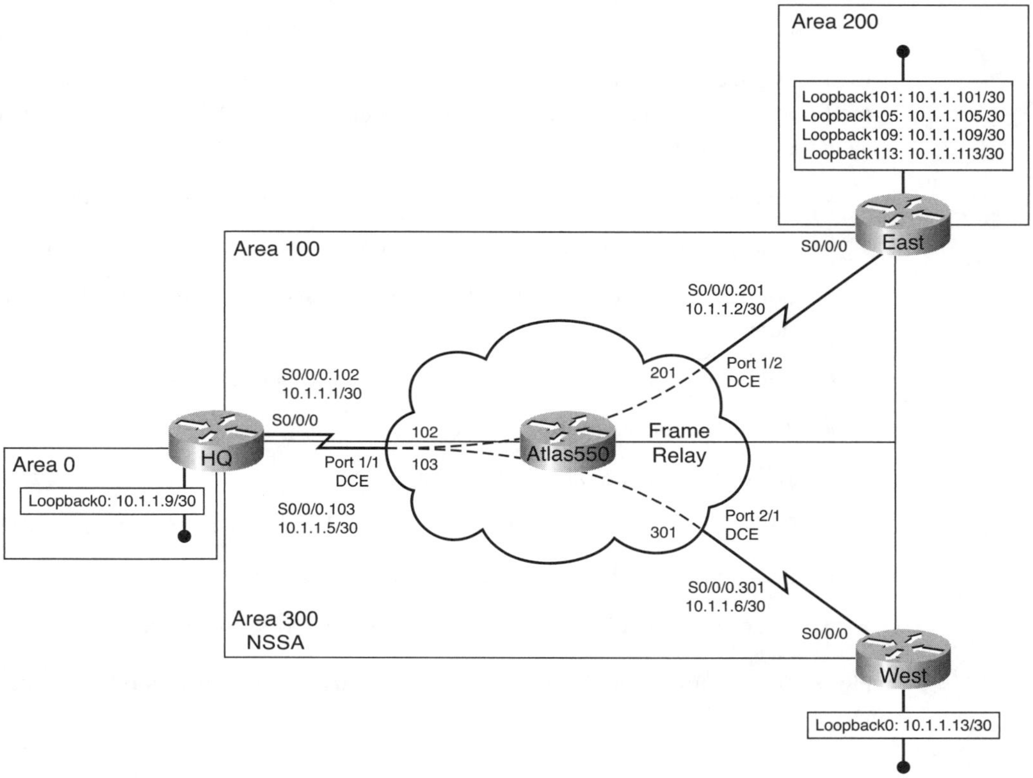

Case Study 3: OSPF: Five Routers

The International Travel Agency (ITA) needs its core network set up for OSPF with the specifications in the list that follows and the addressing scheme shown in the topology diagram.

Plan, design, and implement the ITA network shown in Figure 9-4 (if you are using a Cisco router as the Frame Relay switch) or Figure 9-5 (if you are using an Adtran Atlas 550 as the Frame Relay switch), according to the following set of requirements:

- Configure the OSPF backbone area on the Ethernet connection between R1 and R5.
- Configure the Frame Relay subnet as a point-to-multipoint network in area 100.
- Configure R2's loopback interfaces to be in area 200. Summarize this area with the most efficient summary.
- Configure the Ethernet connection between R3 and R4 to be in area 300.
- Add the loopback on R3 to area 300.
- Make area 300 a totally NSSA area.
- Redistribute the loopback networks on R4 that do not belong in any OSPF area.
- Create virtual links as necessary for full connectivity.
- Make sure that all loopback interfaces get advertised with the correct subnet mask.

Figure 9-4   Topology Diagram for Case Study 3, Using a Cisco Router as the Frame Relay Switch

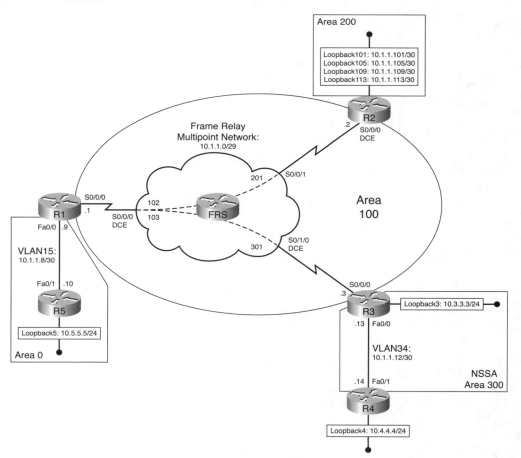

Figure 9-5   Topology Diagram for Case Study 3, Using an Adtran Atlas 550 as the Frame Relay Switch

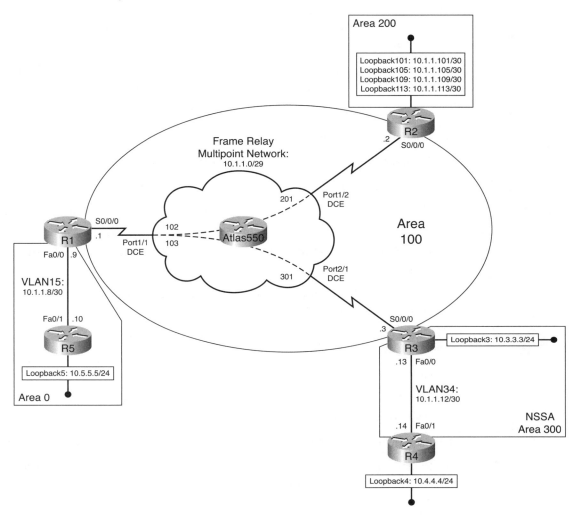

Verify that all configurations are operational and functioning according to the guidelines.

Case Study 4: BGP

The International Travel Agency (ITA) needs both its core network and its Travel Data Providers (TDP) network set up with EIGRP. Configure Border Gateway Protocol (BGP) to advertise routes between the two networks.

Plan, design, and implement the ITA core network and the TDP network shown in Figure 9-6 according to the following set of requirements, and allow the networks to communicate via BGP:

- Use the addressing scheme shown in Figure 9-6.

- Configure the ITA network to be in EIGRP AS 65001.

- Configure the TDP network to be in EIGRP AS 65002.

- Disable automatic-summarization in both EIGRP domains.

- Configure the ITA network to be in BGP AS 65001, and the TDP network to be in BGP AS 65002.

- Advertise the 192.168.14.0/30 and 192.168.34.0/30 networks in both EIGRP autonomous systems.

- All routers will be participating in BGP. Configure all routers for a full mesh of Interior Border Gateway Protocol (IBGP) peers in each system.

- Peer R1 and R2 are using loopback addresses, not their directly connected interfaces.

- Advertise all loopback interfaces into the BGP process, except on R2, where the only loopback advertised is Loopback 2.

- On R2, create a static summary route for the rest of its loopback interfaces and advertise this static route in BGP.

- R4 should send a summary route to ITA representing all of R5's loopback interfaces.

- Routers in the TDP AS should prefer the path to ITA networks via the Ethernet link between R1 and R4. Accomplish this by modifying the multi-exit discriminator (MED) advertised to TDP.

- Routers in the ITA AS should prefer the path to TDP networks via the Ethernet link between R1 and R4. Accomplish this by modifying the local preference of routes being advertised in from TDP.

Verify that all implementations are operational and functional according to the guidelines.

Figure 9-6   Topology Diagram for Case Study 4

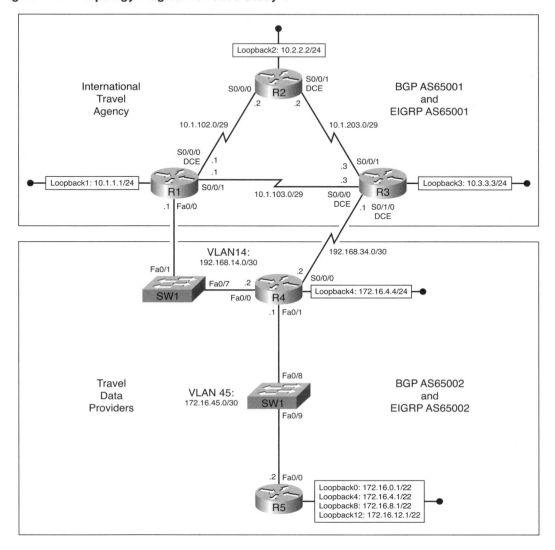

Notes

Notes

Notes

Notes

Notes

Notes

Notes